The Caspian

Touted as the world's next Arabia and a region of unbridled opportunity following the Soviet collapse in 1991, the Caspian Sea and the turbulent oil rush that characterised the ensuing decade captured the world's attention in what at first sight appeared to be a triumph of capitalism over communism. Yet rather than engendering immediate wealth and prosperity for foreign multinationals, regional powers and local populations, successive years have seen problems both historical and contemporary erect significant hurdles in the path of development.

The Caspian reshapes a Caspian debate long defined by one-sided and politically motivated analyses and, at times, fantastic reporting. Bringing together a whole range of influential voices from academia, the media, the oil industry, civil service, the military and diplomatic corps, this book rewrites the region's recent history from the perspective of the players themselves, ferreting out the nuances that characterise contemporary Caspian energy and security politics.

Shirin Akiner is Lecturer in Central Asian Studies at the School of Oriental and African Studies, University of London, UK.

CENTRAL ASIA RESEARCH FORUM

Series Editor: Shirin Akiner, School of Oriental and African Studies,
University of London

Other titles in the series:

SUSTAINABLE DEVELOPMENT IN
CENTRAL ASIA
*Edited by Shirin Akiner, Sander Tideman,
and John Hay*

QAIDU AND THE RISE OF THE
INDEPENDENT MONGOL STATE
IN CENTRAL ASIA
Michal Biran

TAJIKISTAN
*Edited by Mohammad-Reza Djalili,
Frederic Gare, and Shirin Akiner*

UZBEKISTAN ON THE
THRESHOLD OF THE
TWENTY-FIRST CENTURY
Tradition and survival
Islam Karimov

TRADITION AND SOCIETY IN
TURKMENISTAN
Gender, oral culture, and song
Carole Blackwell

LIFE OF ALIMQUL
A native chronicle of nineteenth-century
Central Asia
Edited and translated by Timur Beisembiev

CENTRAL ASIA
Aspects of transition
Edited by Tom Everett-Heath

THE HEART OF ASIA
A history of Russia, Turkestan
and the Central Asian Khanates from
the earliest times
Frances Henry Skrine and Edward Denison Ross

THE CASPIAN
Politics, energy and security
Edited by Shirin Akiner

ISLAM AND COLONIALISM
Western perspectives on Soviet Asia
Will Myer

AZERI WOMEN IN TRANSITION
Women in Soviet and post-Soviet
Azerbaijan
Farideh Heyat

THE POST-SOVIET DECLINE OF
CENTRAL ASIA
Sustainable development and
comprehensive capital
Eric Sievers

PROSPECTS FOR PASTORALISM
IN KAZAKSTAN AND
TURKMENISTAN
From state farms to private flocks
Edited by Carol Kerven

MUSLIM REFORMIST POLITICAL
THOUGHT
Revivalists, modernists, and
free will
Sarfraz Khan

ECONOMIC DEVELOPMENT IN
KAZAKHSTAN
The role of large enterprises and
foreign investment
Anne E. Peck

The Caspian

Politics, energy and security

Edited by
Shirin Akiner

RoutledgeCurzon
Taylor & Francis Group

LONDON AND NEW YORK

First published 2004 by RoutledgeCurzon
2 Park Square, Milton Park, Abingdon, Oxon, OX14 4RN

Simultaneously published in the USA and Canada
By RoutledgeCurzon
270 Madison Ave, New York NY 10016

RoutledgeCurzon is an imprint of the Taylor & Francis Group

Transferred to Digital Printing 2006

© 2004 Shirin Akiner editorial matter and
selection; individual chapters © the individual contributors

Typeset in Baskerville by
Florence Production Ltd, Stoodleigh, Devon

All rights reserved. No part of this book may be reprinted or
reproduced or utilised in any form or by any electronic,
mechanical, or other means, now known or hereafter
invented, including photocopying and recording, or in any
information storage or retrieval system, without permission in
writing from the publishers.

The publisher makes no representation, express or implied,
with regard to the accuracy of the information contained in
this book and cannot accept any legal responsibility or liability
for any errors or omissions that may be made.

British Library Cataloguing in Publication Data
A catalogue record of this book is available
from the British Library

Library of Congress Cataloging in Publication Data
The Caspian: politics, energy and security/edited by
  Shirin Akiner.
     p. cm.–(Central Asia research forum series)
   Includes bibliographical references and index.
   1. Petroleum industry and trade—Caspian Sea Region.
   2. Gas industry—Caspian Sea Region. 3. Caspian Sea Region—
   Politics and government. 4. Geopolitics—Caspian Sea Region.
   I. Akiner, Shirin. III. Series.
   HD9576.C372 C372 2004
   338.2′728′09475—dc22   2003027445

ISBN10: 0–700–70501–5 (hbk)
ISBN10: 0–415–40574–2 (pbk)

ISBN13: 978–0–700–70501–6 (hbk)
ISBN13: 978–0–415–40574–4 (pbk)

Contents

Illustrations

Figures

Maps

Tables

Contributors

Terence (Terry) Adams holds a doctorate in Earth Sciences from the University of Wales. Founding President of the Azerbaijan International Oil Company (AIOC); held this post from 1994 to 1998. Senior Associate, Cambridge Energy Research Programme, and Director of Caspian Energy Programme at the Centre for Energy and Mineral Law and Policy, University of Dundee.

Shirin Akiner is Lecturer in Central Asian Studies at the School of Oriental and African Studies, University of London, and Associate Fellow of the Royal Institute of International Affairs, London. Publications include: *Central Asia: New Arc of Conflict?* (Royal United Services Institute, 1993); *Formation of Kazakh Identity* (Royal Institute of International Affairs, 1995); *Tajikistan: Disintegration or Reconciliation?* (Royal Institute of International Affairs, 2001).

Oksana Antonenko holds advanced degrees from Moscow State University in Political Economy, and Harvard University (Kennedy School of Government) in International Affairs and Security. Senior Fellow and Programme Director for Russia and Eurasia at the International Institute for Strategic Studies. Has implemented numerous research projects on security issues in the Caucasus and Central Asia.

Richard Auty is Professor of Economic Geography, University of Lancaster. Research and publications focus on natural resources and economic development; transition to market economy in Asia; industrial policy in developing countries. Senior Research Fellow and Director of Project 'Environmental, export and human development problems in natural resource-based growth models', based at the World Institute for Development Economics Research of the United Nations University (UNU/WIDER) in Helsinki.

Charles Blandy served in the British Army for 28 years, retired in April 1986 with the rank of Lieutenant Colonel. Currently a Research Fellow at the Conflict Studies Research Centre (CSRC), Camberley (UK), where his geographical area of responsibility embraces North and South Caucasus, and the Caspian basin. Visited Chechnya and Daghestan during the first conflict in December 1995; has returned to the region on numerous occasions since then.

Suha Bolukbaşi holds a doctorate in International Relations from the University of Virginia; Professor of International Relations, Middle East Technical University, Ankara. Scholarly publications include *Türkiye'nin Dış Politika Gündemi: Kimlik, Demokrasi, Güvenlik* (Turkey's Foreign Policy Agenda: Identity, Democracy, and Security) (Ankara, Liberte Yayınları, 2001); 'Nation-Building in Azerbaijan: the Soviet Legacy and the Impact of the Karabakh Conflict', in E. Zürcher, ed., *Identity Politics in Central Asia and the Muslim World* (I. B. Tauris, London/New York, 2000); 'The Growth of Nationalism in Azerbaijan', in S. M. Yurukel, ed., *Contrasts and Solutions in the Caucasus* (Aarhus University Press, Aarhus, 1998).

Germana Canzi received a masters degree in Russian and Post-Soviet Studies from the London School of Economics and Political Science, where she specialised in Caspian issues. Holds a *Laurea* in Political Science from Milan State University. Has authored several papers on energy issues. Currently works as energy and climate expert at the European Policy Office of Environmental Organisation WWF (Worldwide Fund for Nature).

Reinhard Drifte is Emeritus Professor of Japanese Politics, University of Newcastle. Has published extensively on Japanese foreign and security policy, security issues in North East Asia, and on EU–Asian relations.

Anoushiravan Ehteshami is Director of the Institute for Middle Eastern and Islamic Studies and Professor of International Relations at the University of Durham. Numerous publications include *The Foreign Policies of Middle East States* (co-editor) (Lynne Rienner, 2002); *Iran's Security Policy in the Post-Revolutionary Era* (co-author) (RAND, 2001); *The Changing Balance of Power in Asia* (ECSSR, 1998).

Farshid Farzin is a consultant with Atieh Bahar Consulting, based in Tehran, specialising in Iranian Constitutional Law. Holds an LLM from Azad University (Tehran). Author of a number of legal texts and a frequent contributor to the UK-based publication *Iran Focus*.

Urs Gerber read modern history and constitutional law at the University of Bern. Joined the Swiss General Staff in 1984 as a civil servant; worked in planning, security policy and strategic intelligence directorates. Headed Swiss Verification Unit. Has a professional interest in South Caucasus, which he toured several times.

Vyacheslav Gizzatov is a graduate of the Higher Diplomatic Academy of the Soviet Union. Served in the Soviet diplomatic service, then, post-1991, in the diplomatic service of Kazakhstan. Deputy Minister of Foreign Affairs, with special responsibility for Caspian negotiations in 1993–1996; subsequently ambassador of Kazakhstan to Iran, then Germany.

Ali Granmayeh is a former Iranian diplomat. He received his doctoral degree from the University of London, and is currently a consultant on international relations and a Research Associate at the Centre of Near and Middle Eastern Studies, School of Oriental and African Studies, University of London.

Majid Jafar holds masters degrees from the universities of Cambridge (Engineering) and London (International Relations); worked for several years in Europe and the Middle East in the oil and gas industry with Shell International and other energy companies. Currently at the Harvard Business School.

Marika Karayianni holds degrees in Law from the University of Athens and in European Political and Administrative Studies from the College of Europe, Bruges; and is writing a doctoral dissertation on *Legal Aspects of Caspian Oil and Gas Development* at the National and Kapodistrian University of Athens. Member of the International Center for Black Sea Studies.

Mevlut Katik is a London-based journalist and analyst; has extensive experience covering developments in the Caucasus and Central Asia. Holds masters degrees from the University of Ankara and from Bilkent University, Ankara. Currently completing a doctoral thesis at the London School of Economics on *The Political Economy of Caspian Oil and Gas*.

Siamak Namazi is Managing Director of Atieh Bahar Consulting, based in Tehran. Holds degrees in International Relations from Tufts University and in Urban Planning from Rutgers University. Editor of *Iran Energy Focus* (a UK-based publication) and a frequent contributor to journals dealing with Iran and the Caspian area, including (co-author) 'Decentralization and Sustainable Human Development: The Case of Iran's Councils', in the *Encyclopedia of Life Support Systems*, S. Sassen *et al.*, eds (UNESCO, 2003); 'The Caspian's Environmental Woes', in *The Caspian Region at a Crossroad: Challenges of a New Frontier of Energy and Development*, H. Amirahmadi, ed. (St Martin's Press, 2000); 'Islamic Republic of Iran', (co-author) in *The World Encyclopedia of Political Systems and Parties*, D. Kaple, ed. (Facts on Files, 1999).

Nasib Nassibli is Professor and Chair of the Department of International Relations at Khazar University, Baku. Also President of the Foundation of Azerbaijani Studies. Served from 1992 to 1994 as ambassador of Azerbaijan to Iran. Has published five books and nearly a hundred articles on the Republic of Azerbaijan and Iranian Azerbaijan, also on oil and geopolitics of the Caucasus.

Willy Olsen trained in Oslo as an economist. Has held a number of senior positions in Statoil and was responsible for Statoil's negotiations in Azerbaijan in 1991–1994; he was a member of the foreign oil company team that negotiated the Production Sharing Agreement for Azeri–Chirag–Guneshli.

Carter Page is Vice-President in Merrill Lynch's Global Equity Capital Markets group; Business Manager for the Europe, Middle East and Africa region. Previously, an International Affairs Fellow at the Council on Foreign Relations where his research focused on the economic development of the former Soviet Union and the Middle East, with an emphasis on Caspian Sea energy resource issues.

John Roberts is the principal specialist with Platts Energy Group focusing on the geopolitics of energy; also a senior partner in Methinks Ltd., an Edinburgh-based consultancy specialising in Central Asian, Middle Eastern and development issues. He has written and lectured extensively on energy development. Publications include *Caspian Pipelines* (Royal Institute of International Affairs, 1996) and *Visions and Mirages: The Middle East in a New Era* (Mainstream, 1995).

Preface

In the early 1990s, outside the oil industry, little was known in the West about the Caspian Sea other than the fact that it was the source of delectable caviar. Since then, however, it has attracted massive international interest. Innumerable newspaper and magazine articles, as well as an increasing number of books and academic dissertations, have been devoted to this region. There has been much speculation over the size of the hydrocarbon reserves, the prospects for developing this 'black gold' and the likely effect of this process on regional prosperity and security. Today, the Caspian Sea has become, in popular imagination at least, a metaphor for a 'rags to riches' – or 'camels to cars' – transformation.

Some of the material that has appeared in print owes more to fantasy than to the situation on the ground. Yet, the more serious studies have been well researched and have undoubtedly contributed to a better understanding of the complexities of the Caspian region. Much of the commentary has focused on the struggle for political influence, particularly as reflected in debates over the legal status of the Caspian Sea and projected routes for export pipelines. The main contenders in this power play are Iran, Russia, the United States and, with strong US backing, Turkey. More recently, Japan, China and India have signalled an interest in Caspian hydrocarbons and have begun to make substantial investments in this sector, backed up by high-level diplomatic and governmental initiatives. Thus, from the perspective of geopolitics, the Caspian basin reflects interlocking sets of global rivalries, tensions and hegemonic ambitions.

Most analysts, consciously or not, have tended to represent a particular political stance. Consequently, even when purporting to be objective, they start from the premise that the policies of a given country, whichever it may be, are 'best' for the region as a whole. The concerns and objections of other states are often brushed aside as opportunistic posturing. Similarly, oil companies, too, are sometimes represented as little more than adjuncts of bigger political projects.

Studies such as these, despite their bias, are important and must be given due weight, if only because they represent a certain political reality. However, it is equally important to balance such approaches by considering other interpretations. The aim of this book is not to retrace well-trodden paths by repeating, merely for the sake of repetition, arguments concerning the legal status of the Caspian Sea and other such issues. Rather, by juxtaposing the views of authors from different backgrounds, it demonstrates implicitly how the same 'facts' – the same narratives – can be perceived in different ways. For example, Iranian anxiety over the potential security threats posed by the policies of Russia and the United States in the Caspian region are matched by similar Turkish concerns over Russian and Iranian policies; for Azerbaijan, the Karabagh conflict is the prism through which foreign relations are viewed. It is important to understand the assumptions that underlie these different perceptions because they inform the decision-making environment. This in turn influences policy planning and, in some cases, provides the basis for the political, legal and diplomatic briefs that will be pursued in international negotiations.

The contributors to this book are drawn from extra-regional states – the United States, the United Kingdom, Germany, Greece, Italy, Norway, Switzerland and the United Arab Emirates – as well as from Turkey, which may be considered a part of the wider Caspian region, and from four of the Caspian littoral states – Azerbaijan, Iran, Kazakhstan and Russia. Turkmenistan is not formally represented, although the views of Turkmen officials and specialists have been incorporated (without attribution, owing to political sensitivities) into some of the chapters. This geographic spread is in part deliberate, in part random. The intention is to provide a variety of regional views, from countries that are in one way or another directly involved in Caspian developments, as well as from some that have more peripheral interests in the region. The professional backgrounds of the authors are also diverse: they include academics, civil servants, diplomats, journalists, representatives of the oil industry and the military.

The chapters are written in different styles. Some, for example, are heavily footnoted, while others have no references at all. Rather than impose editorial uniformity, these different modes of expression have, wherever possible, been preserved. In a sense, 'the medium is the message' – or at least, a part of the message, as the stylistic variation reflects the diversity of views that this book seeks to encapsulate. There is, inevitably, some repetition as several chapters discuss similar topics, although from different perspectives. In such cases, cross-references are indicated in the text (in brackets, in bold print). Some authors advance a highly subjective interpretation of events. Such views are not necessarily shared by the editor, but they have been left to stand without comment, since they are part of the fabric of the debate.

Shirin Akiner, London, 2004

Acknowledgements

The idea for this volume developed out of an international conference on *The New Security Architecture in the Caspian Region*, held at the Conflict Studies Research Centre, Royal Military Academy, Sandhurst, in 1996. This pioneering event brought together speakers from a wide range of backgrounds, drawn from Central Asia, Europe, Iran, Turkey and the US. It provoked a lively debate, leading to a fruitful exchange of ideas. The original intention was to publish the contributions to this conference. However, there were a number of factors that prevented the implementation of this project, not least the rapidly changing situation in the Caspian Sea. It seemed preferable to wait until more time had elapsed after the collapse of the Soviet Union before attempting to draw some conclusions (though even now, more than a decade after the emergence of three independent states around the Caspian littoral, any assessment must of necessity be tentative and provisional). The same idea of bringing together different perspectives has been followed in this present work, although with different contributors. Thus, in a very direct way the 1996 conference provided the inspiration as well as the impetus for this volume. Special thanks, therefore, must be given to Charles Dick, Director of the Conflict Studies Research Centre, without whose support the 1996 conference would not have taken place. Anne Aldis, likewise of the Conflict Studies Research Centre, also provided valuable help and I am very grateful to her for her input.

Many other friends and colleagues were generous with their help and advice, among them Fumitaki Okubo, to whom I am particularly grateful for his careful reading of several of the papers in this book. I am also much indebted to Chris Boucek, Tom Dimitroff, Hamid Ghaffarzadeh, Emil Majidov, Carter Page, John Roberts, Fergus Robertson, David Skeels, Zachary Thomas, Dauren Toleukhanov and Douglas Townsend. Special thanks are owed to Laurent Ruseckas of Cambridge Energy Research Associates (CERA) and Andrew McAuslan of the Baku–Tbilisi–Ceyhan Pipeline Company for granting permission to reproduce maps of the region.

Finally, I would like to thank the editorial staff at Curzon, later RoutledgeCurzon, and Florence Production for their patience and professionalism.

Shirin Akiner, London, 2004

Abbreviations

ACG	. Azeri–Chirag–Guneshli
ADB	Asian Development Bank
AFP	Agence France Presse
Agip KCO	*see* KCO
AIOC	Azerbaijan International Operating Company
ANS	Azerbaijan News Agency
AP	Associated Press
API	American Petroleum Institute
b/d	barrels per day
bcm	billion cubic metres
BG	British Gas
bl	barrel(s)
BlackSeaFor	Black Sea Naval Co-operation Task Group
bnbls	billion barrels
BP	British Petroleum
BR	Baltic Republics
BSEC	Black Sea Economic Co-operation Organisation
BTC	Baku–Tbilisi–Ceyhan (pipeline, company, consortium)
c/mcf	US cents per thousand cubic feet
CACR	Central Asia and the Caucasus Review
CEE	Central and Eastern Europe
CEP	Caspian Environmental Programme
CERA	Cambridge Energy Research Associates
CIS	Commonwealth of Independent States
CITES	Convention of International Trade in Endangered Species of Wild Fauna and Flora
CNOOC	China National Offshore Oil Corporation
CNPC	Chinese National Petroleum Company
CPC	Caspian Pipeline Consortium
CSCE	Conference for Security and Co-operation in Europe
CSRC	Conflict Studies Research Centre
EAPC	Euro-Atlantic Partnership Council
EBRD	European Bank of Reconstruction and Development
ECO	Economic Co-operation Organisation

EIA	Energy Information Administration
Eni	Ente Nazionale Idrocarburi
EU	European Union
FBIS-CEU	Foreign Broadcast Information Service, Central Eurasia
FDI	foreign direct investment
FSU	former Soviet Union
GUUAM	Georgia, Ukraine, Uzbekistan, Azerbaijan and Moldova
ICJ	International Court of Justice
IEA	International Energy Agency
IMF	International Monetary Fund
IMO	International Maritime Organisation
INOGATE	Interstate Oil and Gas Transport to Europe
IRNA	Iranian state news agency
JETRO	Japanese Export Trade Organisation
JICA	Japan International Co-operation Agency
KCO	Kazakhstan North Caspian Operating Company
LDP	Liberal Democratic Party (Japan)
LNG	liquified natural gas
LPG	liquefied petroleum gas
m	million(s)
mcf	thousand cubic feet
mcm	thousand cubic metres
MEED	Middle East Economic Digest
MEES	Middle East Economic Survey
MEP	Main Export Pipeline
mt/y	million tonnes per year
MVD	Ministry of Interior (Russian acronym)
NBS	National Bureau of Asian Research
NGO	non-governmental organisation
NKR	Nagorno Karabagh Republic
o.e.	oil equivalent
ODA	overseas development aid
OGJ	Oil and Gas Journal
OIC	Organisation of Islamic Conference
OIES	Oxford Institute for Energy Studies
OKIOC	Offshore Kazakhstan International Operating Company
OPEC	Organisation of the Petroleum Exporting Countries
OSCE	Organisation for Security and Co-operation in Europe
PEDCO	PetroIran Development Company
PfP	Partnership for Peace (NATO)
PKK	Kurdish Workers' Party
PSA	Production Sharing Agreement
PSG	Consortium of Bechtel Corporation and General Electric Capital Structural Finance Group
PSO	peace support operations
RFE/RL	Radio Free Europe/Radio Liberty

RLS	Radio-Location Station (Gabala, Azerbaijan)
RSFSR	Russian Soviet Federative Socialist Republic
SBPF	State Border Protection Forces
SINOPEC	China Petroleum and Chemical Corporation
SOCAR	State Oil Company of the Azerbaijan Republic
SOFAZ	State Oil Fund of Azerbaijan
SRC	Silk Road country
SSR	Soviet Socialist Republic (Union Republic of the Soviet Union)
SWG	Special Working Group
TACIS	Technical Assistance to the Commonwealth of Independent States
TAP	Turkmenistan–Afghanistan–Pakistan (pipeline)
tcf	trillion cubic feet
TCGP	Trans-Caspian Gas Pipeline
tcm	trillion cubic metres
TCO	Tengiz Chevroil
TFE	TotalFinaElf
TI	Transparency International
TPAO	Turkish State Petroleum Company
TRACECA	Transport Corridor Europe–Caucasus–Asia
UNCLOS	United Nations Conference on the Law of the Sea
UNDP	United Nations Development Programme
VTS	vessel tracking system
WTI	West Texas Intermediary Crude
WWF	Worldwide Fund for Nature
WPS	What the Papers Say (independent Russian media monitoring agency)
ytf	yet-to-find (reserves)

Personal names and place names

Personal names and place names have been transliterated in accordance with common usage; where different forms are current (e.g. 'Nazarbaev' and 'Nazarbayev'), one of these has been adhered to throughout this work. However, with reference to the 'Treaty of Golestan/Gulistan', for historical reasons both forms have been retained. For the sake of consistency rather than political bias, the term 'Karabagh' has been used in all the chapters that refer to this area, although some authors originally preferred 'Karabakh', or 'Nagorno-Karabakh'. The terms 'Azeri' and 'Azerbaijani' are used synonymously. Also, 'Azerbaijan' denotes both 'Azerbaijan SSR' and (post-Soviet) 'Azerbaijan Republic'; Kazakhstan is used for both 'Kazakh SSR' and (post-Soviet) 'Republic of Kazakhstan'; 'Turkmenistan' denotes 'Turkmen SSR' and the post-Soviet state 'Turkmenistan'.

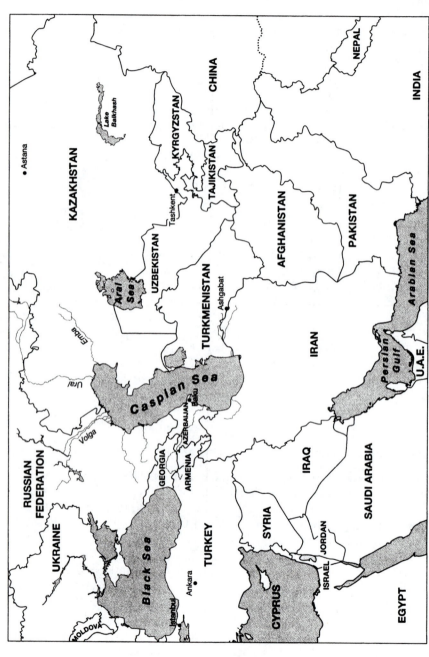

Map 1 The Eurasian region

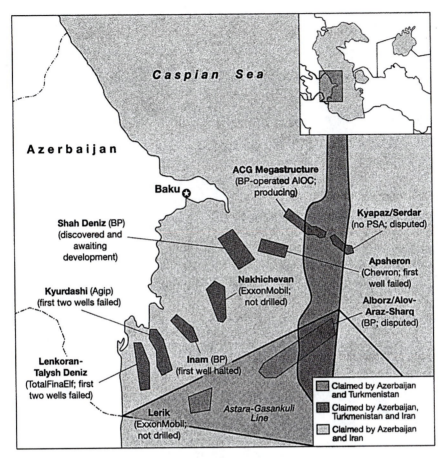

Map 2 Disputed areas of the South Caspian (as of 2003)

Source: Cambridge Energy Research Associates.

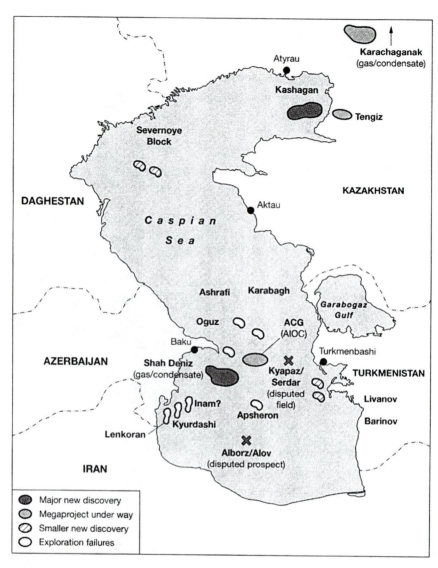

Map 3 Exploration results in the Caspian region

Source: Cambridge Energy Research Associates.

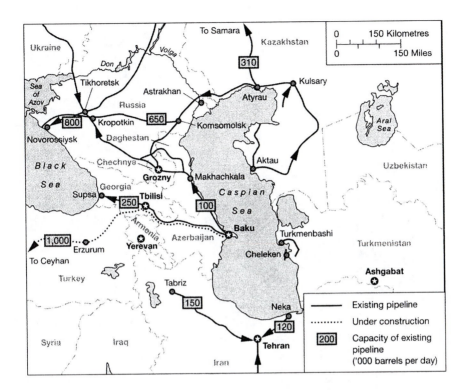

Map 4 Oil pipelines in the Caspian

    Source: Cambridge Energy Research Associates, updated by Shirin Akiner 2004.

Map 5 Armenian-occupied territory in Azerbaijan

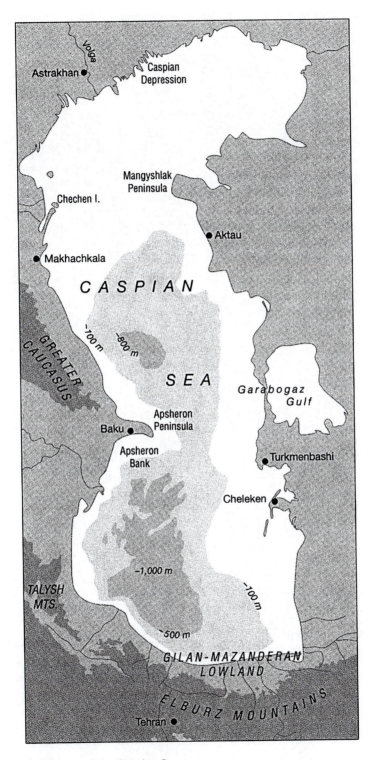

Map 6 Hydrogeology of the Caspian Sea

  Note: All depths shown are approximate.

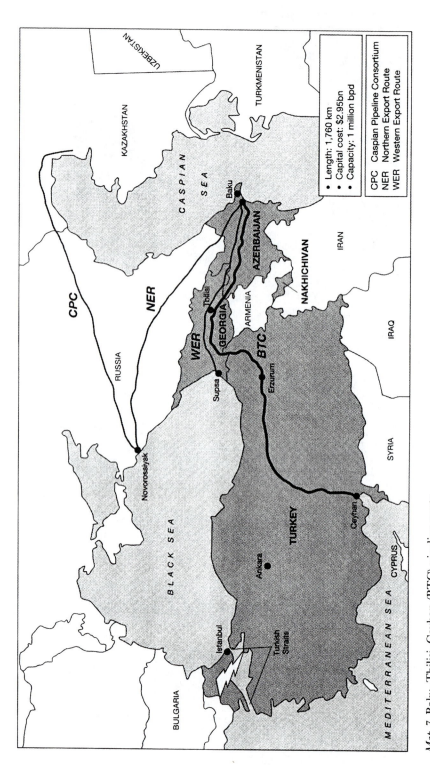

Map 7 Baku–Tbilisi–Ceyhan (BTC) pipeline route

Source: Baku–Tbilisi–Ceyhan Pipeline Company

Part I
Background

1 Caspian intersections: contextual introduction

Shirin Akiner

The region

The Caspian Sea is the largest inland sea in the world. A long, sinuous stretch of water, it spans the imaginary divide between Asia and Europe. Landlocked, its sole links to an open sea are via river and canal. The sea is today bordered by five independent states: along the north west, by the Russian Federation (including the constituent republics of Daghestan and Kalmykia), the north east by Kazakhstan, the south east by Turkmenistan, the south by Iran and the south west by Azerbaijan.

Around the rim of the Caspian Sea different peoples and cultures have for centuries converged, overlapped and intermingled. Archaeological evidence reveals traces of human settlements in the south west that date back to prehistoric times. Some 3,000 years ago, the southern littoral was colonised by Iranians (ancestors of the modern Iranians, also of the Talysh who live in the lowlands between Lenkoran and Astara). Further north, the mountains of Daghestan that stretch along the western coast were home to indigenous peoples of the Caucasus. Today, there are over a dozen distinct Caucasian groups; in the coastal region, the most numerous groups are the Avars, Lezghins and Darghins; further inland, there are Chechens and Ingush. In the seventh century AD, Arab armies conquered, and for a while occupied, Iran and the Caucasus. This was the start of the Islamisation of the region. At approximately the same period, there was heavy Turkic immigration into the Caspian basin. Over the next 500-odd years, consecutive waves of Turkic groups (among them the forebears of the modern Azerbaijanis, Kazakhs, Tatars and Turkmen) settled around the sea, with a strong concentration in the south west (present-day Azerbaijan).[1] The Slav presence dates from the mid-sixteenth century. It followed Ivan the Terrible's conquest of the Tatar Khanate of Astrakhan (on the lower reaches of the Volga River) in 1556, which established a Russian foothold on the Caspian rim. In the mid-seventeenth century another ethnic element was added when Kalmyk Mongols from Central Asia settled in the coastal steppe to the south of the Volga estuary. In the twentieth century, especially during the Soviet period, there was further immigration into the region, introducing yet more cultural and ethnic variety.

The Caspian Sea has always had great economic significance. Since time immemorial, the rich fish stocks have been exploited by coastal communities as a source of nutrition, but also as an important commodity to be traded with inland regions. Advances in navigation and shipbuilding technology led to the development of maritime routes linking the main ports. Cargoes could be transported across the sea more quickly and efficiently than by the long overland routes. This boosted north–south, east–west commercial ties by allowing for an increase not only of volume, but of diversity of trade turnover. Better transport also facilitated the movement of people. Coastal cities became cosmopolitan centres, with a lively exchange of goods, as well as ideas.

The strategic importance of the sea became apparent in the early eighteenth century, during the Russo-Iranian struggle for control of the Caucasus. In 1723, under Peter the Great, Russia established the first naval base on the Caspian coast at Astrakhan, in the Volga delta. Some 20 years later, the first Iranian warship set sail on the Caspian Sea. It was an uneven contest, however, and Russia soon established military and naval supremacy on and around the Caspian Sea. This position of dominance was eventually inherited by the Soviet Union and, only slightly modified by bilateral treaties with Iran, remained in force until the last years of the twentieth century.

First oil boom

For Western Europe, the Caspian region was little known territory. This changed in the late nineteenth century, when a commercial oil industry developed in and around Baku. From antiquity, the area had been famous for its oil and gas deposits. In the early nineteenth century, soon after the Baku Khanate had passed under Russian control, there was some attempt to increase crude oil production. Nevertheless, it was still a very small-scale operation.[2] It was only in the 1870s that more intensive exploitation of these reserves became possible. By this time the necessary technology was in place and global demand for oil products was increasing by leaps and bounds. The decision of the Russian government to open the area to private investment was the trigger for what was to become a massive oil boom. Entrepreneurs from abroad as well as from within the Russian empire converged on Baku in 'wild competition', outbidding one another as they scrambled to carve out fortunes in this new El Dorado.[3] From this point onwards, the future of the region was inextricably tied to the exploitation of its oil: this became its primary link with the external world (see **Adams**, p. 90).

The Nobel brothers Robert and Ludwig[4] played a crucial role in the development of Caspian oil. They took their first steps in 1875, when Robert, who had recently acquired a few oil properties near Baku, purchased a small refinery. He was soon joined by Ludwig, and together they proceeded to lay the foundations of a modern oil industry. They brought in drilling specialists from Pennsylvania and, when necessary, invented their own machinery.

Their refinery was furnished with the most advanced equipment of the time. In terms of organisation and business practice, too, they were unique among their competitors. They drew on the best available scientific and academic resources in order to improve performance. Moreover, in an otherwise cut-throat environment, they succeeded in maintaining a reputation for the highest integrity. They soon became the premier producers in the region and thereafter went on to establish a huge commercial empire.

One of the most significant contributions of the Nobel brothers to the Baku oil industry was the modernisation of export facilities. Until the 1870s, crude oil and its products were mostly transported in goat or ram skin bags, loaded on to camels or horses, and carried by caravan to distant destinations. Some oil was later shipped in wooden barrels across the Caspian Sea from Baku to Astrakhan, where it was transferred to barges and transported up the Volga. This was somewhat safer than the overland route but, nevertheless, it was still a long, arduous and expensive undertaking. Ludwig Nobel had the brilliant idea of shipping oil in bulk. He commissioned a large, purpose-built tanker and launched it on the Caspian in 1878. It proved to be highly successful and revolutionised oil transport not only here, but throughout the world.[5]

It was not long before competition over transport routes emerged. Another company, backed by the French branch of the Rothschild banking family, financed the building of the Baku–Batumi railroad. Completed in 1883, this opened an alternative route to the West for Caspian oil. In 1892, a new player, Samuel & Co. (later renamed the Shell Transport and Trading Company) entered the scene with a spectacular new venture. This was the transportation of Caspian oil, in purpose-built tankers, from Batumi via the Suez Canal to Singapore, then on to the Far East. This opened up a voracious new market for Caspian oil.[6] Yet another route was mooted at the turn of the century, when the Russian government proposed the construction of a pipeline from Baku to the Persian Gulf. However, this project was fiercely opposed by the British, who considered this region to form part of their sphere of influence. They regarded the Russian plan as a challenge to their own strategic interests. In the event, this pipeline was not built as the Iranian authorities failed to approve the project. However, the lobbying and manoeuvring that surrounded these negotiations prefigured with uncanny similarity the 'pipeline politics' of the late twentieth century, when 'spheres of influence' and political calculations again dominated the choice of pipeline routes.

Throughout this period the Baku oilfields continued to expand. By 1895, Russian output, almost entirely from the Caspian, accounted for nearly half the daily global production.[7] Oil wealth transformed Baku. In the mid-nineteenth century the city covered some 60 hectares and had a population of around 13,000. By 1907/8, it encompassed an area of 1,100 hectares and had a population of 248,300.[8] It was an extraordinary fusion of the old and the new, of East and West. This was reflected in the thriving intellectual life of the city where, in 1873, the first national theatre was opened and, in 1894, the first public library. The first Azerbaijani opera was performed in 1908. Educational establishments offered different types of instruction and a variety of fields of study (traditional, European, secular, religious and various combinations of these spheres), while learned societies debated philosophical, social and political topics. Civil institutions were developed, including trade and professional organisations, such as the Producers' Association for the oil industry.[9] A contemporary visitor described Baku as:

> commercially and ethnographically the Johannesburg of Russia ... The modern, stone-built palaces of the oil kings, the new technical school, erected on the best European model, and hundreds of fine public buildings, are not more conspicuous than the ancient land marks of the city ... and the thousands of small shops in which sad-eyed Asiatic sell the famous Caucasian carpets, hammered and filigree silver goods, 'slop' clothing, and all kinds of ancient weapons.[10]

By the end of the nineteenth century Baku had become one of the largest industrial centres in the Russian empire. The millionaire oil magnates (of whom the ten most powerful were said to be 'eight Mohammedans, one Armenian and one Swede') formed a caste apart, living in luxurious palaces and frequenting exclusive establishments in the part of Baku that was known as the 'White Town'.[11] There was also a multi-ethnic proletariat, most of whom lived in dire poverty in the 'Black Town'.[12] The Black Town proved to be fertile ground for revolutionary ideas. Several leading Bolsheviks were clandestinely based here, including Stalin. They organised demonstrations and strikes, at first on a local level, later throughout Transcaucasus. One of the chief targets was the oil industry. At the same time, there was also an upsurge of ethnic violence. The roots of this conflict were unclear; it seemed to draw upon historic grievances as well as current economic inequalities. There may well have been an element of political manipulation. The outcome was a horrendous series of inter-communal clashes between Armenians and Azerbaijanis in 1905.[13] This caused a general breakdown of law and order. The oilfields were set on fire and almost all the derricks were razed to the ground. The foreign personnel of the oil companies found themselves in grave danger, threatened by marauding gangs of robbers and murderers; the chief representative of the Nobel enterprise was among those who were assassinated. All of this had a disastrous effect on the oil industry. Investment in new technology dried up as confidence in the stability of the region was shaken. Production stagnated; by 1915, Russian oil (still almost entirely from Baku) accounted for around one sixth of world output.[14]

Towards the end of the First World War, the Caspian oilfields acquired new importance as Allied and Central Powers vied for mastery of this potentially valuable source of energy supplies. A third camp, that of the Bolsheviks, was also trying to win control of the region. In 1918 Baku changed hands several times. In August, a small British force took the city, but soon withdrew. Ottoman–German troops then occupied Baku. In November, Allied units returned and an independent republic was proclaimed. It was overthrown by the Bolsheviks in April 1920. By this time, Soviet power had been established in the northern Caucasus and Central Asia, thus almost the entire Caspian littoral region, save only a stretch of Iranian coastline in the south, was now under Soviet rule. Foreign businesses were nationalised and the region was isolated from the world beyond the Soviet frontiers.

Across the Caspian Sea, the oil industry in Kazakhstan began somewhat later than in Azerbaijan, and, initially, was much less significant. Oil was first struck in 1899, in a remote area of western Kazakhstan. It was not, however, commercially viable at that time. The Dossor oilfield, to the east of Atyrau, was discovered in 1911. This, with reserves of 7 million tonnes, was more promising. Later, while the region was still under Tsarist colonial administration, other oilfields were developed, but the impact of the industry on the life of the local population, largely nomadic, was negligible. In the early twentieth century, there were also attempts to extract oil in Turkmenistan. The area had only been incorporated into the Russian empire in the 1880s, and the infrastructure for any form of industrial development was almost entirely lacking. However, the Nobels began developing a number of properties in Cheleken and Krasnovodsk (modern Turkmenbashi) on the Caspian coast.

Soviet era

Almost all the territory that had formerly belonged to the Russian empire was incorporated into the Soviet Union in the early 1920s. Shortly after, a national delimitation was carried out, as a result of which four Union Republics were created around the Caspian Sea – the Azerbaijan, Kazakh and Turkmen Soviet Socialist Republics (SSRs) and the Russian Soviet Federative Socialist Republic (RSFSR). The part of the RSFSR that bordered the Caspian Sea included the territory of the Kalmyk and Daghestan Autonomous Soviet Socialist Republics.

In the following decades an intensive campaign of social engineering was implemented throughout the country. The aim was to modernise and Sovietise society. An important aspect of this programme was the emphasis on raising literacy standards. To this end, compulsory schooling, free and universal, was introduced. Tertiary education was also expanded. Each Union Republic (SSR) was endowed with at least one university, several vocational and polytechnical colleges, and a national Academy of Sciences comprising numerous institutes of advanced research. Other social goals included the provision of universal health care, the emancipation of women and the secularisation of society. They were achieved by using all the means of coercion and persuasion that could be exercised by a totalitarian regime. Consequently, within a decade or two a significant degree of societal change had been accomplished. Some traditions and cultural predilections survived, but overall there was a deep rupture with the past.

The imposition of a centrally planned economy meant that there were strong regional specialisations. Thus, Azerbaijan continued to be one of the leading centres of oil production in the Soviet Union (although rivalled, and later surpassed, by production from the Volga–Ural region and Siberia). After the Second World War, open-sea oil exploration and extraction in the Caspian, off the coast of Azerbaijan, was developed on a large scale.[15] Moreover, Azerbaijan was the chief manufacturer of equipment for the entire Soviet oil industry, furnishing 70 per cent of its requirements. Its higher educational establishments, too, were geared to providing specialised technical and scientific training for this sector. In Kazakhstan, there was a wider range of industrial development. This included the extracting and processing of ferrous and non-ferrous metals, coal mining and heavy engineering. Oil production was also expanded, though less intensively than in Azerbaijan. Much of the Kazakh output was destined for use in the Soviet military–industrial complex, a significant part of which was located in this republic, including the nuclear test site at Semipalatinsk and the space centre at Baikonur. Agriculture, too, was a priority sector. The nomads were sedentarised and collective farming introduced in the early 1930s. Kazakhstan was developed to become one of the chief producers of meat and grain for the Soviet Union. Turkmenistan experienced a similar type of development to the other two republics, but of a less intensive nature. Here, too, the nomads were sedentarised and intensive methods of agriculture were introduced. The principal specialisation was cotton cultivation, as a result of which Turkmenistan became one of the main cotton-producing areas of the USSR. There was also some industrialisation; this included the exploitation of oil and gas resources,[16] mostly located in the west of the country, in the vicinity of the Caspian Sea.

From the 1920s onwards, very few foreigners visited the Soviet part of the Caspian basin. It was rarely mentioned in academic writings, let alone in press reports. During the Second World War, the region briefly regained international significance when in 1942 German forces mounted 'Operation Edelweiss' in an attempt to seize control of the Caucasian oilfields. However, they were stopped at Stalingrad by the Red Army. In the mid-1940s, the Cold War began and once again there was little further foreign access to this region. The Caspian Sea might almost be said to have become the 'Invisible Sea'. In so far as it was remembered at all, it was regarded as a Soviet–Iranian preserve.

Second oil boom: the first phase

Throughout much of the Cold War the Caspian region experienced a period of relative geopolitical and economic stability. However, it remained difficult for Westerners to visit the Soviet littoral zone. The situation began to change in the late 1980s. When Mikhail Gorbachev came to power in 1985, he attempted to liberalise the Soviet system and, in particular, to reform the stagnant economy. Joint ventures with Western firms were cautiously welcomed. Some oil executives, daringly as it seemed at the time, began to consider seriously opportunities for re-engagement in the Caspian region. The Soviet oil industry had failed to keep pace with technological advances in the West and by this time was outmoded and inefficient, with a decaying infrastructure. It was against this background that, at the end of the 1980s, the US oil company Chevron entered into discussions with the Soviet authorities to explore possibilities for developing the giant Tengiz field. This had been discovered in western Kazakhstan, on the northern littoral of the Caspian, in 1979. It was estimated to hold some 6–9 billion barrels of recoverable oil. Although the field had been developed in the 1980s (with Hungarian involvement, under the auspices of the Communist-bloc Council for Mutual Economic Aid), its full potential had not been realised.

In December 1991 the Soviet Union was dissolved. Chevron then continued its negotiations with the government of the now independent state of Kazakhstan. In 1993, the TengizChevroil partnership was formed, to implement a US$20 billion, 40-year joint venture. Several other agreements were concluded with the Kazakh authorities over the next few years, including two more for the development of world-class deposits. One of these was Karachaganak, a huge oil and gas condensate field in western Kazakhstan. Like Tengiz, it had been discovered in 1979, but not fully developed during the Soviet period. In 1992, BG (British Gas) and Eni (Italy) were awarded exclusive rights to negotiate a contract for the rehabilitation and development of this field. Five years later, in November 1997, BG and Eni, in partnership with Texaco (US) and LUKoil (Russia), concluded a Production Sharing Agreement (PSA) for this field. That same year, a PSA was signed with the North Caspian Consortium and activities commenced with the operator, Kazakhstan CaspiShelf Consortium – a multinational consortium comprising European, US and Kazakh partners – undertaking seismic exploration of the north Caspian shelf. In July 2000, the Offshore Kazakhstan International Operating Company (OKIOC), the operator at that time, discovered the massive Kashagan deposit. Located in the northern part of the Caspian Sea, some 75 km south of Atyrau, this is proving to be one of the largest oilfields in the world.

In Azerbaijan, too, there was growing foreign involvement. In 1994, the Azerbaijan International Operating Company (AIOC), comprising the State Oil Company of the Azerbaijan Republic (SOCAR) together with European, US, Russian, Turkish, Japanese and Saudi Arabian partners, signed a PSA to develop Azeri, Chirag and deepwater Guneshli, an offshore megastructure – a deal that was popularly dubbed the 'Contract of the Century'. In 1995, a Production Sharing Agreement was signed with the Caspian International Petroleum Company (SOCAR, LUKoil, Agip and Pennzoil), to drill in another contract area, the Karabagh Prospect (though this later turned out to be unsuccessful). A third major deal was concluded in June 1996 for prospecting and developing the Shah Deniz field. Located offshore in the Caspian some 70 km south of Baku, potential recoverable reserves here were estimated at 250–500 billion barrels of oil, and 2–4 trillion cubic feet of gas. The contracting parties this time included SOCAR, BP, Statoil, LUKoil, Elf and the Turkish State Petroleum Company, as well as Naftiran Intertrade Company of Iran. Several more deals were concluded over the following years; by 2000, over 20 PSAs were in place.[17]

Turkmenistan attracted less attention, owing to its relatively limited oil resources and the logistical constraints associated with its more isolated geography. However, in 1993 the Argentine company Bridas secured a concession to explore for gas in an onshore field. Later, agreements were signed with other companies, notably the Cheleken Production Sharing Agreement with Lamarg Energy Group for the development of two offshore fields. In 1996 an agreement covering the development of three large offshore petroleum and gas deposits (Barinov, Livonov and Shafag) was concluded with Petronas, the Malaysian state energy company. In 1998, following President Niyazov's visit to the United States, Mobil and its partner, the UK-based Monument Oil and Gas, signed a strategic agreement with the Turkmen authorities for exploration and development in the Garashsyzlyk area, onshore in western Turkmenistan (the Garashsyzlyk oilfield, however, was not included in the contract).

The deals of the early post-Soviet era fired popular imagination in the region and abroad. By the mid-1990s, fabulous estimates of the hydrocarbon wealth of the Caspian Sea were being bandied about by the media, as well as by government officials and academics. Turkmenistan alone was often spoken of as a 'second Kuwait'. The region as a whole was compared to the Middle East. As during the first oil boom, a century earlier, the 'black gold' of the Caspian was again a magnet for foreign investment. This time, however, it benefited not only Baku, but also towns and cities in Kazakhstan and even some in Turkmenistan. Senior executives of major oil companies visited the region with increasing frequency. Teams of foreign consultants, technical specialists, lawyers, financial advisers and many other professionals began to open offices in their main centres of operation and thus to establish a permanent presence. The tastes, needs and expectations of the growing expatriate communities created demands for hitherto unheard of services and skills. As in the nineteenth century, there was a rapid and dramatic change in the physical appearance of the capital cities, also of the towns and settlements near the oilfields where large, American-style suburbs began to appear. The tenor of life was transformed, becoming, at least superficially, more Western.[18]

Gradually, the initial excitement about the region's prospects was tempered by more sober assessments. It became clear that, whatever the size of the reserves, they would be difficult to exploit and, consequently, production costs would be very much higher than in the Middle East or other large oil provinces round the world. This was partly owing to the technical difficulties of extraction. Many of the hydrocarbon reservoirs were deep and high pressure, and presented serious corrosion problems. Fields such as Tengiz were 'the oil-industry equivalent of alligator wrestling ... a geologist's dream, but a petroleum engineer's nightmare'.[19] There were also many logistical problems. Several of the deposits, especially in western Kazakhstan, were located in remote areas, with extreme ranges of temperature and fierce winds.[20] Transporting personnel to such places, let alone machinery, was expensive and difficult. Elsewhere conditions were less harsh, but the infrastructure throughout the region was old, inefficient and in urgent need of repair. Consequently, major engineering work was required. Moreover, modern rigs and other vital equipment had to be shipped in. This caused costly delays, resulting in budget overruns.

There were other factors that impinged on the competitiveness of the Caspian region. Some of these were similar to those encountered by oil companies a century before, while others were new, products of the post-Soviet era. One of the most important new issues was the legal status of the Caspian Sea. Prior to the disintegration of the Soviet Union, there had been only two littoral entities, Iran in the south and Russia, subsequently the Soviet Union, in the north. For some two hundred years, the activities of these states had conformed to a condominium-type model of joint use and joint sovereignty. This arrangement was not acceptable either to the newly independent states of Azerbaijan, Kazakhstan and Turkmenistan, or to the oil companies who were eager to exploit offshore resources. Iran, and initially Russia, however, wanted the sea to be treated as an 'indivisible reservoir', the object of common use by all the littoral states. As discussed elsewhere in this volume, particularly by Ali Granmayeh and Vyacheslav Gizzatov, this question is still the subject of debate and negotiation.

Another, equally pressing problem, was a new version of an old issue, namely, the need to diversify export routes to carry Caspian oil to world markets. In the early 1990s, existing oil and gas pipelines from the region formed part of what had been the internal Soviet network, much of which was now under Russian control. This situation was highly unsatisfactory not only for the newly independent states, but also for foreign investors, who wanted to export hydrocarbons from the Caspian without the potential threat of Russian interference. Several competing routes were proposed, all with unique advantages and disadvantages. Matters were complicated by the fact that political calculations played as great a role as economic, technical and environmental concerns. The key players were not only the littoral states and the oil companies, but extra-regional states such as Turkey and, most powerful of all, the United States (see chapters by Suha Bolukbaşi and Carter Page). Moreover, as highlighted by Anoushiravan Ehteshami, John Roberts and Terry Adams, global energy requirements played a part in determining the choice of pipeline routes from the Caspian region. An awareness of the wider significance of Caspian oil was reflected in the growing engagement of Asian powers such as Japan in the region (see chapter by Reinhard Drifte).

A third concern that emerged during the 1990s was the question of regional stability. This was not only a question of security, but of risk perception, and hence of the attractiveness of the Caspian region to investors. Different types of threats to security are discussed in this volume. One is ethnic conflict. This is a recurring problem, defined by historic wrongs and grievances. At the beginning of the twentieth century, it took the form of violent communal clashes. Today, it is linked to territorial and separatist struggles. The conflicts that represent the most immediate danger for the western Caspian littoral are the Karabagh conflict, involving Armenians and Azerbaijanis (discussed by Nasib Nassibli), and the Chechen separatist struggle (see Chapter 19 by Charles Blandy). However, as Urs Gerber demonstrates, there are several other 'hot spots' in the Caucasus. All of these are highly volatile and could rapidly escalate into larger conflicts. Moreover, they provide ready bases for terrorist activities. Another possible threat to security is discussed by Mevlut Katik, who examines the build-up of armed forces around the Caspian rim and discusses the potential for inter-state maritime conflict. Environmental security and the dangers of long-term damage to the fragile ecology of the sea are discussed by Shirin Akiner (Chapter 21).

To understand the development of Caspian oil it is important to take account not only of the international aspects of this process, but also of the national contexts and the national perspectives of the littoral states. In this volume, there are case studies of each of the Caspian states. However, the strategic priorities and capabilities of these individual nations are diverse. The focus of these chapters is similarly disparate. Iran and Russia are major regional powers. They have long histories of independent statehood, and are familiar with the process of international negotiations. Moreover, although in the 1990s both states had serious internal political and economic problems, nevertheless they were relatively stable, with experienced administrations in place. Caspian developments are important to these states, but they represent only a small part of their economic and foreign policies. Thus, the chapters by Oksana Antonenko and Siamak Namazi/Farshid Farzin, which respectively examine the evolution of Russian and Iranian positions with regard to Caspian issues, focus on one segment of broad and complex national agendas.

Azerbaijan, Kazakhstan and Turkmenistan, by contrast, are highly dependent on Caspian oil and gas. In their modern form, these are young states. Prior to the collapse of the Soviet Union in 1991 they had had no exposure to the international arena. Consequently, during the past decade they have had to construct foreign policies from scratch. All three states have world-class hydrocarbon reserves which they must exploit in order to sustain socio-economic development. However, in their initial dealings with multinational corporations they found themselves at a considerable disadvantage. The decision makers in these states had a limited understanding of how a market economy works. Moreover, they were under great pressure from foreign governments who lobbied aggressively in support of companies that were based on their territories (even if these companies were, in fact, international entities). Indeed, the symbiotic relationship was so close that at times, some energy companies appeared to act as extensions of their government's foreign policy – a phenomenon that is not unknown elsewhere in the developing world.[21] This coalition of national and commercial interests was to be observed in the struggle to secure promising exploration and development contracts, as well as in the disputes over the legal status of the Caspian Sea and over proposed pipeline routes.

At the same time, the new states faced massive domestic problems. The sudden and unexpected collapse of the Soviet Union brought severe economic dislocation. Trade and transport links were disrupted, manufacturing industries ground to a halt and the agricultural sector was devastated. Hyperinflation soon took hold. There was widespread unemployment, poverty and social deprivation.[22] In Azerbaijan, the cost of the war with Karabagh and the influx of nearly a million refugees and displaced persons imposed additional burdens. In all three states (as indeed in Russia, too) the political order was in transition. A different style of statecraft was now required. The Soviet-era institutions for regulating state–society relations were no longer acceptable: a new framework would have to be constructed, including new systems of public administration and law. The same was true of the business environment: Western-style commercial and financial institutions did not exist. A new outlook, as well as new skills, would have to be inculcated, not least in order to secure a flow of Western investments. All of this would take time and, in the meanwhile, the situation was chaotic and largely unregulated.[23]

The Caspian policies of these newly independent states can be understood only by taking into account the challenges that they faced following the sudden demise of the Soviet Union. Consequently, the chapters on Azerbaijan, Kazakhstan and Turkmenistan take a broader approach than those on Iran and Russia. Nasib Nassibli, Majid Jafar and Germana Canzi examine social and political issues, while Richard Auty, Willy Olsen and Marika Karayianni focus more specifically on problems of governance and resource management.

The final chapter summarises the achievements of the first decade since the collapse of the Soviet Union, and tentatively looks ahead to prospects for the development of Caspian oil in the next ten years.

Notes

1 For brief histories of some of the Turkic and Islamic peoples, see S. Akiner, *Islamic Peoples of the Soviet Union*, Kegan Paul International, London, 1986, 2nd edn, relevant sections.

2 J. D. Henry, *Baku: An Eventful History*, Archibald Constable & Co., London, no date on title page (but Author's Preface is dated 1905), p. 30, notes that in 1829 there were 82 petroleum pits in use.

3 See Henry, *op. cit.*, pp. 51–81, for an exhilarating account of the 'wealth of romance in the finance of oil', as played out in the early years of the oil industry in Baku.

4 Emmanuel Nobel was born in Sweden in 1801. A prolific inventor of military equipment, he went to Russia in 1837, at the invitation of the government, to produce submarine mines. He had great technical success, but his career ended in financial disaster. His son Alfred (who was educated in St Petersburg) acquired international fame for his work in applied chemistry, particularly on the industrial application of explosives; two other sons, Robert and Ludwig, had business interests in St Petersburg and it was from there that they expanded their activities to Baku.

5 An erudite and readable account of the development of the oil industry in Baku is given by D. Yergin, *The Prize: The Quest for Oil, Money and Power*, Simon & Schuster, London, 1991/1993; see particularly pp. 59–70.

6 Yergin, *op. cit.*, pp. 60–68.

7 For a chart of world crude oil production at this period, see Yergin, *op. cit.*, p. 830; also Henry, *op. cit.*, p. 5.

8 Sh. S. Fatullaev, *Gradostroitel'stvo Baku – nachala XX vekov*, Stroiizdat, Leningrad, 1978, p. 75. The population of Baku at the turn of the century comprised 44

nationalities, including 74,254 Russians, 53,827 Tartars (i.e. Azerbaijanis – SA), 34,259 Armenians, 18,572 Persians; also several thousand Jews, Germans, Kazakhs, Lezghins, Georgians, Poles and Greeks (Henry, *op. cit.*, p. 11).

9 This developed out of a series of conferences, the first of which was held in 1884. Its members included representatives of firms of oil producers, refiners and transporters. Its aims were internal self-regulation, and joint representation of the views of the industry to government. By the early twentieth century it had a large annual income and was 'maintaining a huge hospital, several ambulances and technical and statistical staffs, and publishing records of the world's oil trade' (Henry, *op. cit.*, pp. 120–130).

10 Henry, *op. cit.*, p. 12.

11 Essad-Bey, *Blood and Oil in the Orient* (transl. from the German by Elsa Talmey), Nash & Grayson, London, 1930, pp. 34–46.

12 Essad-Bey, himself the son of an oil magnate, recalled in his memoirs that 'thousands and thousands of workmen lived in damp, unlighted, dark, dirty barracks, where three slept together on a small uncovered wooden cot. There was no other furniture . . . Water was very scarce and solely for drinking; all washing – without soap – had to be done in the oil-dregs . . . The working day lasted for sixteen hours without interruption; even that seemed too short to some of the owners' (Essad-Bey, *op. cit.*, pp. 18–19).

13 Henry, *op. cit.*, p. 150, gives graphic descriptions of the massacres in 1905, when the Azerbaijanis (then known as Tartars) were largely victorious. Essad-Bey, *op. cit.*, pp. 84–95, gives an account of the equally barbaric revenge taken by Armenians in 1918. See also Yergin, *op. cit.*, p. 131.

14 Yergin, *op. cit.*, p. 830.

15 Construction of the massive Oil Rocks platform was commenced in 1947; located some 45 km offshore, to the east of Baku, it was a city on piles, with high-rise buildings and over 200 km of streets. In 1949, the first oil in the world to be extracted from an offshore field was produced here.

16 Gas was discovered in 1951. Soviet-era Turkmen production peaked in 1989, at just less than 90 bcm (O. Skagen, *Caspian Gas*, Royal Institute of International Affairs, London, 1997, p. 13).

17 Energy Information Administration, US Department of Energy (www.eia.doe. gov), *Azerbaijan Country Analysis*.

18 By 2001, construction of an American-style luxury complex for Chevron employees was close to completion in Atyrau. An enclosed compound, fenced off from the dusty, decaying 'native' town, it comprised 86 large houses, a school and leisure amenities such as swimming pools and tennis courts (S. LeVine, 'Look out Houston; Oil's Latest Boomtown is Rising in Kazakhstan', *Wall Street Journal*, 25 July 2001).

19 Speech by E. P. Price, Vice-President Chevron Overseas Petroleum Inc., to the World Affairs Council of Orange City County, Irvine, California, 9 August 1994.

20 At Tengiz, for example, when a large computer was installed, a triple-walled enclosure had to be built to protect it from dust storms (*ibid.*).

21 See, for example, S. Strange, 'States, Firms and Diplomacy', in *International Political Economy: Perspectives on Global Power and Wealth*, eds D. A. Lake and J. A. Frieden, 3rd edn, Routledge, London, 1995, pp. 65–67.

22 The economic problems of Kazakhstan are well documented in Ye. Kalyuzhnova, *The Kazakstani Economy: Independence and Transition*, Macmillan, London, 1998. For an overview of economic trends in all three countries see European Bank for Reconstruction and Development, *Transition Report 1998*, EBRD, London, 1998.

23 See further S. Akiner, 'Emerging Political Order in the New Caspian States: Azerbaijan, Kazakstan and Turkmenistan', in *Crossroads and Conflict: Security and Foreign Policy in the Caucasus and Central Asia*, eds Gary K. Bertsch, Cassady Craft, Scott A. Jones and Michael D. Beck, Routledge, New York, 2000, pp. 90–128.

Part II
Legal Issues

2 Legal history of the Caspian Sea

Ali Granmayeh

Historical background

From the early seventeenth century, the Caspian Sea was divided between Russian and Iranian spheres of influence. Iran was never a naval power in the Caspian Sea, and its activities were for the most part restricted to commercial navigation and to inshore fishing. The only exception was when Nader Shah (1736–1747) succeeded, despite Russian attempts at sabotage, to construct a shipyard on the Caspian coast in 1742 and to launch the first Iranian gunship in the Caspian Sea.[1] For Russia, the Caspian Sea was the route to the south, giving easy access to Iran's northern territories. Peter the Great established the first Russian naval base on the Caspian at Astrakhan in 1723 and occupied five Persian provinces on the south and east banks of the Caspian Sea. Even after the evacuation of northern Iran, under the Treaty of Rasht in 1729 Russia retained control over navigation and trade in the Caspian Sea. The Caspian route also enabled the Russian army to occupy the Iranian territories of Derbent and Baku in 1796, and to send troops to the Russo-Iranian war fronts during the Caucasian wars of 1804–1812 and 1826–1828.[2]

In April 1920, the Soviet Socialist Republic of Azerbaijan was proclaimed. The flotilla of the new Bolshevik regime continued to dominate the Caspian Sea.[3] In August 1941 the Red Army occupied northern Iran; from then on, until the end of the Second World War, the Caspian Sea was used as a supply route to carry Allied aid to the Soviet Union.[4] At the end of 1991, the Soviet Union ceased to exist and four independent successor states emerged around the rim of the Caspian Sea – Azerbaijan, Kazakhstan, the Russian Federation and Turkmenistan. Thus, virtually overnight, the number of littoral states was augmented from two to five.

Russian/Soviet–Iranian agreements on the status of the Caspian Sea

1. Peace Treaty of Golestan (Gulistan), 12 October 1813

This treaty, which ended the Russo-Iranian wars of the nineteenth century, records the first agreement between the Russian and Iranian governments over the Caspian Sea. Article 5 granted equal privileges to Russian and Persian merchant vessels to navigate the sea and enter each other's harbours. However, the Russian navy was given the exclusive right to sail the Caspian Sea: 'The Russian flag shall fly over Russian warships, which are permitted to sail in the Caspian as before; no other nation whatever shall be allowed warships in the Caspian.'[5]

2. Peace Treaty of Turkmanchai, 22 February 1828

Article 8 of this treaty gave the same privileges as the Treaty of Golestan to Russian and Persian vessels. In addition, Persian vessels sailing the Caspian Sea were permitted, in the event of shipwreck, to enter Russian rivers to receive aid and assistance. However, Article 8 reaffirmed Russian naval superiority and denied Iran the right to maintain gunboats in the Caspian Sea: 'As for war vessels, those which bear the Russian military flag, being *ab antiquo* the only ones which have had the right to navigate on the Caspian Sea, this same exclusive privilege is, for this reason, equally reserved and assured today; so that, with the exception of Russia, no other power shall be able to have war vessels on the Caspian sea.'[6]

3. Treaty of Friendship between Persia and Russia, 26 February 1921

In this first treaty between Iran and the new Soviet regime, the latter renounced Tsarist concessions held in Iran (Article 1), returned the Russian base on the Iranian island of Ashuradeh in the Caspian Sea (Article 3), and ceded the Russian installation at the port of Bandar-e Anzali to Iran. However, the most significant change to Iran's rights in the Caspian Sea was made in Article 11, which denounced Article 8 of the Turkmanchai Treaty, which had forbidden Iran to have armed vessels in the Caspian Sea, and added: 'The two high contracting parties shall enjoy equal rights of free navigation on the sea, under their own flags, as from the date of signing of the present treaty.'[7]

4. Agreement on Trade and Navigation between Iran and the USSR, 25 March 1940

This agreement, which was concluded after long talks and arguments between the two countries at the beginning of the Second World War, was precipitated by the Nazi–Soviet pact of August 1939. Germany had become Iran's number one trading partner and there was a pressing need for Soviet territory to be used as a transit route between these two countries.[8] Article 12 of this agreement describes the privileges of merchant vessels of each country in crossing the Caspian Sea and enjoying the assistance of the other party where necessary. It also asserted that coastal trade was reserved for the national vessels of each of the contracting parties.[9]

This article also defined, for the first time in Caspian-related agreements, a 10-mile exclusion zone in the coastal waters of each country: 'Regardless of the preceding stipulations each of the contracting parties retains for the vessels under its own flag the fishing rights in its own offshore waters up to ten nautical miles, as well as the right to enjoy the facilities and premiums in regard to the import of fish caught by the crews of vessels sailing under its flag.'[10] Nonetheless, the tense atmosphere of wartime, and Soviet anxiety over possible infiltration of the Caspian Sea by the hostile powers through Iran, were implicitly reflected in Article 13, which stated that only vessels belonging to the citizens and commercial and transport organisations of either of the contracting parties, 'sailing under the Soviet or Iranian flag respectively, should be found over the entire Caspian Sea'.[11] The same Soviet anxiety is demonstrated in the notes exchanged between the signatories at the conclusion of the agreement:

> Since the Caspian Sea, regarded by both contracting parties as a Soviet–Iranian Sea, is of exceptional interest to the contracting parties, it is agreed that the two governments will take the steps necessary to ensure that citizens of third countries employed on vessels belonging to the contracting parties, or on their ports on the Caspian Sea, shall not use their employment or presence in these vessels and ports for purposes outside the duties of their employment.[12]

Thus, the Caspian Sea was defined as a Soviet and Iranian sea, whose entirety was open to navigation by Soviet and Iranian vessels as in a condominium, while the exclusive fishing zone of each part was limited to 10 nautical miles in its respective coastal waters.[13]

In search of a new legal regime: early approaches 1992–1994

After the collapse of the Soviet Union, a new set of littoral states was created, each of which had different attitudes and ambitions regarding this shared stretch of water. Russia and Iran had been reassured by the Alma-Ata Declaration (21 December 1991), which confirmed that the other littoral states would observe the international agreements of the Soviet Union, thus including the Soviet–Iranian treaties of 1921 and 1940 on the Caspian Sea.[14] Consequently, Tehran and Moscow stressed that the joint utilisation of the Caspian Sea, as defined in these treaties, should serve as the legal basis for the rights and obligations of all littoral states in the Caspian Sea.[15] However, under the new circumstances, the joint utilisation system would not be feasible without a supervisory mechanism. Iran, therefore, proposed the formation of a regional organisation of littoral states to co-ordinate all activities relating to fisheries, oil and gas exploration, transport, and the prevention of pollution in the Caspian Sea.[16] This initiative was discussed at a meeting of experts from the five states in Tehran in October 1992. It was decided that a body of experts would study the responsibilities of the projected organisation, then report back to their respective governments. In 1994, when representatives of the Caspian states met in Moscow, the formation of a regulatory regional organisation was mentioned favourably, but no agreement was signed on this issue.[17]

In the meantime, three out of five countries around the Caspian Sea unilaterally claimed a national sector and entered into negotiations over energy operations in their sectors with foreign contractors. These three states claimed that the division of the northern part of the Caspian Sea made in the 1970s – an internal Soviet agreement whereby the respective Soviet republics were allocated economic zones – should now be considered as the basis for international boundaries.[18]

During 1992–1993, Turkmenistan adopted a law on its international frontiers, terrestrial and maritime, according to which coastal waters, territorial sea and an exclusive economic zone was established.[19] That same year it signed a contract with foreign companies for the development of the Cheleken offshore field in the eastern Caspian. Kazakhstan, basing its case on the rules laid down at the United Nations Conference on the Law of the sea (UNCLOS 1982), called for a full division of the Caspian Sea into national sectors. Subsequently, it claimed a sovereign right in its territorial waters, as well as an exclusive economic zone in the Caspian Sea. The Kazakh draft asserted that 'the inner borders of territorial waters of each zone of the Caspian Sea are regarded as the state borders of the littoral states and are guaranteed by respective demarcation schemes and elements of reconnaissance'.[20] The document also described the exclusive zone as 'a bordering zone up to 200 miles, with regard to which the littoral state is entitled to enact laws regarding the rights to disclosure, processing and preservation of natural resources'.[21] Given that the entire width of the Caspian Sea is, in some places, around 200 miles, allocation of such an expanse to each littoral state was impossible. Kazakhstan later amended this position to combine the principles of 200 miles and equidistance from opposite shores.[22]

Azerbaijan adopted a more ambitious agenda. In 1992, the government (then headed by President Elchibey) declared its opposition to the Russian–Iranian concept that the new legal status of the Caspian Sea should be decided on the basis of the 1940 Soviet–Iranian Agreement.[23] President Aliev (who succeeded Elchibey as head of state in 1993) maintained the same attitude. In 1994, a landmark agreement was signed with an international consortium (dubbed 'Contract of the Century', see below), which included some areas that extended 120 miles east of Baku and far beyond the median line. Since then, Azerbaijan has continued to claim a superior right in the Caspian Sea, on the grounds that the Soviet oil authority based in Baku played a pre-eminent role in developing the Caspian oilfields. As President Aliev commented: 'In drafting the division principle, we should recognize the degree to which every littoral country has developed the shelf and the value of the sea for each country.'[24]

Second phase: 1995–1997

In 1995, there was a noticeable change in Russia's position. There were two main reasons for this. First, although Russia had condemned Azerbaijan for taking unilateral action in concluding the 1994 'Contract of the Century' (see below), Russia itself was now a participating party in this project. Second, there was the question of the benefit which could accrue to Russia if the export pipeline passed through Russian territory. Consequently, in August 1995 the Russian ambassador to Turkey, Vadim Kuznetsev, stated that Russia was ready to modify its position on the legal status of the Caspian Sea, if Azerbaijan agreed to export its oil through the Russian pipeline.[25]

Iran, the only country which had wholeheartedly supported Russia's early stance on the Caspian Sea, had to be persuaded to accept the new Russian initiatives. In October 1995, Russian Deputy Foreign Minister Alexander Bolshakov discussed with Iranian officials in Tehran a draft proposal on the legal status of the Caspian Sea. This stipulated that each Caspian littoral state should be allocated 10 miles of marine territory exclusively for the seabed mineral exploration, and another 20 miles territory for fishing. Concerning the exploration of the free sea beyond these territories, it was proposed that a Board comprised of representatives of the five littoral states of the Caspian Sea should issue the necessary permits for fishery, mineral exploration and oil drilling. Iran neither approved nor rejected this proposal, but Foreign Minister Velayati suggested that the five littoral states should sit together at the negotiating table to discuss it, since each might have specific viewpoints that should be taken into consideration.[26]

On 22 October 1996, the Russian news agency Interfax quoted an unnamed source in the Russian government as having said that to unlock the current deadlock and achieve mutual understanding with Kazakhstan and Azerbaijan, Russia was ready to drop its tough opposition to dividing the Caspian Sea into national sectors.[27] A complete division of the sea into national sectors, as proposed by Azerbaijan, was ruled out. However, a compromise solution, whereby each coastal state would be allocated a band 35–40 miles wide along the coastline as national sector, was considered feasible; areas outside these sectors should be considered as the common asset of all five states, open to their joint use.[28]

Iran was still adamantly opposed to any division of the Caspian Sea. In the 'Joint Declaration on Caspian Sea Issues', signed by Iranian President Rafsanjani and Kazakh President Nazarbaev on 11 May 1996 in Tehran (see p. 56), no decision was made about the status of the Caspian Sea. The first article of the Declaration stated: 'The parties consider that the drawing up and conclusion of the convention on the legal status of the Caspian Sea, on the basis of a consensus between the five coastal states, is a task of the utmost importance which must not be delayed.'[29]

President Nazarbaev signed a similar joint statement with President Aliev on 16 September 1996 in Baku. However, in it, unlike the previous statement, both these parties recognised the rights of littoral states to 'develop the mineral and biological resources in their sectors' of the sea. Thus, Azerbaijan and Kazakhstan confirmed that their positions on the status of the Caspian Sea were close, and asserted their intention to proceed with plans to extract the sea's oil and gas reserves.[30]

The foreign ministers of the Caspian states met in Ashgabat on 12 November 1996. They failed to achieve rapprochement on the sea's legal status. However, Russia used the opportunity to announce that it would accept a coastal zone 45 miles in width for each Caspian state. Russian Foreign Minister Primakov acknowledged that 'many Caspian states are pinning their hopes for economic growth on oil production. Russia is ready to recognize their jurisdiction over sites outside the zone, providing they are being or about to be developed.' He added that the criteria for such sites would be defined by experts. As for other sites, the Caspian states should 'develop them jointly'.[31] Primakov also said that Russia could agree to widening the fishing zone from 10 miles (as defined in the Soviet–Iranian Treaty of 1940) to 20 miles.[32] This new proposal, particularly the 'site jurisdiction' principle, was intended to satisfy Azerbaijan and Kazakhstan. On the margin of the Ashgabat meeting, the Russian foreign minister signed a Memorandum of Understanding with his Iranian and Turkmen counterparts to set up a joint company to develop oil and gas resources. Primakov said that the other Caspian littoral states, likewise foreign investors, were welcome to join the company.[33]

On 27 February 1997, the presidents of Turkmenistan and Kazakhstan signed a joint statement in Almaty (formerly Alma-Ata), emphasising the rights of their respective countries within their 'national sectors' in the Caspian Sea. President Niyazov stressed that the Caspian Sea had been divided legally into territorial economic zones during the Soviet period, and that each of the littoral Soviet republics, likewise Iran, had its own maritime borders. This principle should continue to be respected now, but at the same time, he added, work to determine the legal status of the Caspian Sea should continue.[34] Iran took exception to the Kazakh–Turkmen statement. In a letter to the UN Secretary-General, Iran's representative to the United Nations pointed out that the accord of 27 February between Kazakhstan and Turkmenistan was against the principles of international law.[35] It was stressed that Iran did not accept the concept of a dividing line as the administrative and national boundary between the littoral states.[36]

By the end of 1997, it was clear that Russia was making a determined bid for domination of the Caspian Sea. The first shipment of early oil produced by the Azerbaijan International Operating Company (AIOC) was transported on 12 November 1997 by the Russian (Transneft) pipeline to the port of Novorossiysk (Russian Federation) on the Black Sea. On his return from the inauguration ceremony in Baku, First Deputy Prime Minister Boris Nemtsev triumphantly commented: 'We won when it became clear that the oil pipeline would go through Russia ... the twenty-first century will really be Russia's century'.[37] Iran and Turkmenistan maintained an isolationist policy towards this development. Iran condemned Azerbaijan's commencement of the commercial exploitation of a Caspian oilfield; Turkmenistan expressed the view that the interests of all Caspian states should be taken into consideration.[38]

Disputes arising from lack of legal regime

Russia and Iran versus Azerbaijan: fallout from the 'Contract of the Century'

The first post-Soviet conflict over the unilateral exploitation of the Caspian Sea stemmed from Azerbaijan's agreement with an international consortium, signed on 20 September 1994, for the exploration and production of oil and gas. The subject of this US$8 billion agreement, known popularly as the 'Contract of the Century', was a 30-year project for the development of three offshore fields: Azeri, Chirag and deepwater Guneshli.[39] Russia and Iran harmonised their objection to this agreement, stressing that Azerbaijan had no right to sign such an agreement.[40] Thereafter, Russia's reaction changed from complaint and accusation to warning.[41] Russian Deputy Foreign Minister Albert Chernishev described Azerbaijan's exploitation of Caspian oil without the permission of other littoral states as 'robbery'.[42] On 27 October 1994 a Russian newspaper reported that President Yeltsin had issued instructions to his government for the imposition of financial, commercial and naval sanctions against Azerbaijan if the latter continued to implement the oil agreement.[43] Semi-official comments were made to the effect that Russia might advance its oil operations into the territory which Azerbaijan claimed as its national sector.[44] Russia's criticism of this contract was paradoxical, since it was in fact in partnership with the same consortium (with a 10 per cent share). Minister of Energy and Fuel Yuri Shafranik justified the involvement of LUKoil, Russia's major oil company, in this project on the grounds that Russia's general policy was to 'encourage Russian companies to join profitable projects in the CIS'.[45] He also emphasised that Russians had contributed to the creation of these resources by virtue of their 'labour, mind and energy'.[46] Yet, Russian officials did not speak with a unified voice, indicating domestic rifts in policy making. The stance of the Ministry of Foreign Affairs was clearly at variance with Russian commercial interests.

The Iranian reaction to Azerbaijan's oil deal was negative.[47] On 12 October, Iranian Deputy Foreign Minister Mahmoud Vaezi met with Russian Foreign Minister Kozyrev in Moscow, where the latter praised Iran's standpoint on Caspian Sea problems and reiterated that the resources of the sea should be divided between the littoral countries on an equitable basis. A spokesman for the Russian Foreign Ministry went further, saying that the (non-existent) Organisation of Caspian States was the 'most important outcome of President Rafsanjani's initiative'.[48] Responding to complaints about the Azeri–Chirag–Guneshli project, Azerbaijani President Aliev commented that the division of the Caspian Sea had been fixed as early as 1970 by the Soviet authorities and that Russia had registered no objection to Azerbaijan's oil deal following the conclusion of the agreement with the consortium. Furthermore, in an interview with Baku TV on 22 October, on his return from a CIS summit in Moscow, Aliev stated that Russia was not only in favour of Azerbaijan's oil operation in the Caspian Sea but had agreed to reschedule Azerbaijan's debts to Russia until 1996. Aliev could also rely on a comment by Russian Prime Minister Viktor Chernomyrdin who, according to Itar-Tass, had told him that the Russian government saw 'no problem with the signing of Azerbaijan's oil contract'.[49]

The argument of Iran's Deputy Foreign Minister Vaezi that the legal status of the Caspian Sea should be resolved on the basis of the 1940 Soviet–Iranian agreement was also rejected. Azerbaijan's Foreign Minister stated that the Soviet–Iranian agreement did not extend to the sea-floor and that the mineral resources in Azerbaijan's section of the Caspian shelf belonged 'exclusively to Azerbaijan'.[50] However, political statements and legal debates apart, Azerbaijan tried to placate Iran with the offer of shares in the international consortium. On 2 November 1994, Natiq Aliev, the head of Azerbaijan's State Oil Company (SOCAR), disclosed at a press conference that Azerbaijan had faced financial problems to fulfil its commitments in the oil consortium. He explained that 'the minimum work required by the contract obliged Azerbaijan to carry out a 680-million dollar plan to construct offshore rigs, develop the project infrastructure and drill at least three test wells'. He added that if Azerbaijan failed to find the necessary finance, it might transfer a part of its share in the project to foreign companies.[51] On 10 November, Iranian Oil Minister Gholamreza Aqazadeh arrived in Baku at the invitation of President Aliev. The next day, at a meeting with Aqazadeh, Aliev claimed that Azerbaijan was interested in forging closer relations with Iran, including co-operation on the issue of oil production and export. He further explained that 'some foreign powers were attempting to create obstacles in the way of Tehran–Baku bilateral co-operation in the Caspian Sea', but that he had assured them that the Republic of Azerbaijan would resist such attempts.[52]

On 12 November, Iran and Azerbaijan signed an agreement on the transfer of a quarter of Azerbaijan's shares in the international oil consortium to Iran. This gave Iran 5 per cent of the total shares of the Western-led consortium. Upon his return from Baku, the Iranian oil minister stated that the deal required Iran to invest US$300–350 million as its share in the consortium.[53] Russia posed no official reaction to Iran's partnership in Azerbaijan's oil consortium. However, comments in the Russian media suggested that Azerbaijan was trying to 'buy' Iran's support. They warned Iran that Moscow would recognise neither the original agreement of Azerbaijan with the consortium nor Iran's partnership in it.[53]

On 15 November, the parliament of Azerbaijan unanimously ratified the agreement which had been signed between SOCAR and the consortium on 20 September. However, the Speaker of Parliament, Rasul Guliev, stated that the documents which gave Iran 25 per cent of Azerbaijan's share in the consortium, would take effect only after it had been endorsed by other members of the consortium. International oil journals expressed pessimism over the issue and commented that all members of the consortium, except Azerbaijan, were against Iran's partnership. On the other hand, Azerbaijan's ambassador to Iran insisted that his country, as an independent state, had made a decision to transfer part of its shares to Iran and all objections of outsiders were 'nonsense'.[54]

The moment of truth came in March 1995, when Iran's participation in the consortium encountered the disapproval and opposition of the Western partners. Iranian Foreign Minister Velayati commented that the unilateral cancellation of the oil agreement between Iran and Azerbaijan was not in the long term in the latter's best interest. He cautioned: 'Before the legal regime of the Caspian Sea has been determined, such agreements are not valid; and the implementation of such agreements can be completed only when the legal basis of the Caspian Sea is determined.'[55]

Politicians in Baku tried to reduce the damage to their ties with Iran while taking advantage of the situation to please the Americans. They insisted that it was the consortium's decision not to admit Iran and that 'Azerbaijan had to go along with it'. President Aliev sent the Parliamentary Deputy Speaker, Yashar Aliev, to Iran with an explanatory letter to President Rafsanjani. In a press interview, Yashar Aliev admitted that pressure from the US had been behind the exclusion of Iran.[56] On the other hand, an Azerbaijani government spokesman dismissed reports of US pressure as 'absolutely groundless'.[57] Furthermore, President Aliev himself welcomed the replacement of Iran in the consortium with an American company (Exxon) and told the US Under-Secretary of Energy, William White, that the long-term presence of American companies would guarantee the strategic interests of the US in the region. He also told US Senator Richard Shelby that Baku had 'created the right conditions for promoting US investment in the republic by meeting Washington's request to exclude Iran from the international consortium'.[58]

After this episode, however, Azerbaijan's policy again became more conciliatory towards Iran. In October 1995, the head of SOCAR, Natiq Aliev, arrived in Tehran with a proposal that Iran should participate in another of Azerbaijan's oil projects, namely, the consortium which was assigned to develop the Shah Deniz field in the Caspian Sea. He assured Iran that the other members of the consortium (all European firms) had also agreed to Iran's partnership.[59] Consequently, in 1996 Iran's semi-state oil company OIEC (Oil Industries Engineering and Construction) acquired a 10 per cent share in the Shah Deniz project and, in 1997, a 10 per cent share in the Lenkoran Deniz and Talysh Deniz projects.[60] Exploration in Shah Deniz failed to reach oil but discovered a promising source of natural gas.

Nonetheless, Iran maintained its negative attitude towards Azerbaijan's oil operations in general and the US-dominated consortium in particular. The official ceremony marking the first shipment of oil produced by AIOC on 12 November 1997 was attended by representatives of Russia and Kazakhstan, but boycotted by Iran and Turkmenistan. Instead, Iran lodged a petition at the United Nations and called for the suspension of offshore operations and the sale of Caspian oil by Azerbaijan as long as the status of the Caspian Sea was not legally clarified.[61]

Turkmenistan versus Azerbaijan: Kyapaz/Serdar and other disputed oilfields

In January 1997 Russian and Western media reported that Turkmenistan had claimed sovereignty over an area of the Caspian Sea where two of the oilfields developed by Azerbaijan, Azeri and Chirag, were located. These two fields are known in Turkmenistan as Khazar and Osman respectively. The Foreign Ministry of Azerbaijan rejected Turkmen claims over these fields, again justifying its position by reference to the 1970 Soviet division of the Caspian Sea that had allocated 'national sectors' (i.e. economic zones) to the respective Union republics; maps of this period were said to indicate clearly that the ownership of these oilfields had been assigned to Azerbaijan. Furthermore, it was stated, the companies (mainly Western) which had in 1994 signed the multibillion dollar deal with Azerbaijan to develop the said oilfields, had 'studied this issue in detail and would never have signed the contract if there had been any doubt'.[62]

The conflict over Azeri–Chirag/Khazar–Osman was still fresh, when a third oilfield, known as Kyapaz in Azerbaijan, and Serdar in Turkmenistan, emerged as a matter of dispute between the two countries. In July 1997, when President Aliev paid a visit to Russia, SOCAR and the Russian oil majors LUKoil and Rosneft signed an agreement in Moscow for the development of the Kyapaz resources.[63] This field is located in the middle of the Caspian Sea, 145 km off the coast of Azerbaijan (see Map 2, p. xxi). According to Azeri sources, Kyapaz field was discovered by Azerbaijani experts in 1959; the first oil well was dug in 1986; in 1988, the first year of production, the yield was over 300 million tons.[64]

The government of Turkmenistan blamed both Azerbaijan and Russia for the deals over its claimed territory (i.e. Serdar). This put the Russian government in a difficult position. Russia had earlier condemned Azerbaijan for taking unilateral action without regard for the rights of other littoral states. It now stood accused of the same behaviour. At a meeting with President Niyazov in Ashgabat, Russian Deputy Foreign Minister Boris Pastukhov insisted that his ministry would not have given a green light to the agreement if it had been informed of the true situation. In addition, Russian Deputy Minister of Fuel and Energy Sergey Kiriyenko explained that the agreement did not affect anyone's interest because it did not deal with the extraction of oil, but only with costly prospecting operations.[65] Nevertheless, President Niyazov's representation to the Russian leadership resulted in Rosneft withdrawing from the project on 1 August. That same day, Russian Deputy Prime Minister Valery Serov informed President Niyazov that the Russian government had decided to annul the agreement over Kyapaz/Serdar.[66]

Turkmenistan issued an international tender in September 1997 for the development of the same field but did not receive a favourable result. The government of Azerbaijan warned that it would impose sanctions against companies operating in Azerbaijan 'if they take part in any non-Azerbaijani tender to explore or develop a disputed oil and gas field to which Azerbaijan lays claim'.[67] In June 1998, the US oil company Mobil was awarded the contract to develop the Serdar deposit but failed to go ahead with the job. A statement dated 26 June said that the company had received a warning from Azeri officials not to work on the disputed oilfield.[68] Consequently, the project was suspended.

While Azerbaijan regarded the case of Azeri–Chirag as non-negotiable, it was prepared to reach a compromise, along the lines of a joint venture, over the Kyapaz/Serdar field. On 23 August 1999, President Aliev stated that he had proposed founding a joint Azerbaijani–Turkmen company which would choose an investor for the exploitation of Kyapaz, so that the project would be equally favourable for both parties; however, he claimed, Turkmenistan had not responded to the Azerbaijani proposal.[69]

Meanwhile, a dispute was averted between Iran and Turkmenistan over oil operations in the south eastern part of the Caspian. In summer 1997, Turkmenistan had invited tenders for 11 blocks in its 'national sector' in the Caspian Sea. However, this was an area which was located in the 'border waters' of the two countries. Iran voiced its objection and following bilateral negotiations, Turkmenistan withdrew three of the 11 blocks from the tender in October 1997. Thereafter, the two countries decided to operate jointly in the 'non-clarified' areas until such time as the legal status of the Caspian Sea should be decided.

Kazakhstan versus Russia

Oil exploration in the north Caspian by LUKoil caused conflict between Russia and Kazakhstan in late 1997. The latter claimed that the Russians were operating within its 'national sector' in the Caspian Sea. Yet, both countries decided to resolve the matter before it escalated. Following bilateral negotiations, it was agreed that the oil companies of the two countries work together to develop the disputed oilfields. After two days of high-level talks behind closed doors, a memorandum on joint drilling was signed on 10 February 1998 between Kazakhoil and LUKoil.[70] This was a prelude to the agreement concluded between President Yeltsin and President Nazarbaev in July 1998 over the division of the seabed in the north Caspian (discussed below). The final steps to resolve the disputed fields were made in May 2002, when Russia and Kazakhstan signed an additional protocol on joint production arrangements for three disputed gas fields, Kurmangazy, Tsentralnoe and Khvalynskoe, in the north Caspian Sea.[71]

Russia, Iran and the Trans-Caspian Gas Pipeline (TCGP)

Turkmenistan owns the third largest natural gas reserves in the world. However, the dependence of Turkmenistan on Russia for the export of gas has never pleased Ashgabat (see **Canzi**). Moreover, transporting Turkmen gas to Turkey via Iran raised the issue of US sanctions barring US companies from investing in an Iran-related energy project. The alternative route, discussed during the visit of Turkmen President Saparmurat Niyazov to the US in April 1998, was the laying of a pipeline on the Caspian seabed linking the port city of Turkmenbashi on the east of the Caspian Sea to Baku; this could eventually be extended via Azerbaijan and Georgia to Turkey. As explained by the US special envoy to the Caspian region, Washington envisaged the sub-sea pipeline as part of a 'trans-Caspian oil and gas corridor which would join the resource-rich Central Asian states of Turkmenistan and Kazakhstan to the west, with Baku as the hub'.[72]

News of the Trans-Caspian Gas Pipeline (TCGP) project was received in Tehran and Moscow with dismay. Iran and Russia expressed their opposition to such a pipeline 'due to environmental considerations', adding that they would 'not allow others to make one-sided decisions'. Iranian Foreign Minister Kharrazi reiterated the point that 'because no consensus has been reached so far among the Caspian Sea littoral states over a new legal regime for the sea, no party, especially foreign companies, can take a measure which will violate the rights of the others'.[73]

In June that year US petroleum giant Amoco confirmed its plans to proceed with the TCGP. However, Ashgabat insisted that the pipeline issue be linked to the dispute over ownership of the three offshore oilfields.[74] In 1999, a contract was concluded between Turkmenistan and a new investor, namely the Trans-Caspian Gas Pipeline consortium. This consortium was formed by PSG International (a joint venture between US firms Bechtel and GE Capital Structured Finance Group) and Shell. At a meeting in Istanbul on 18 November 1999, representatives of the countries concerned – Azerbaijan, Georgia, Turkmenistan and Turkey – signed an agreement supporting the TCGP project.[75] Iran and Russia once again expressed their objections. On 28 November, a joint statement was issued in Tehran by Iranian Foreign Minister Kharrazi and Russian Foreign Minster Ivanov, which expressed their 'categorical disagreement with a sub-sea project before the final achievement, by all Caspian littoral states, of a general agreement on the legal status of the Caspian Sea, and a guarantee on its ecological safety'. Moreover, the two sides 'openly express their unhappiness with the realisation of any project for a Trans-Caspian underwater pipeline which is ecologically dangerous in view of the extremely active geodynamics' of the seabed.[76]

In January 2000, delegates of Azerbaijan, Georgia, Turkey and Turkmenistan, and US special envoy on Caspian energy issues John Wolf, met in Ashgabat to discuss a framework document on the planned 1,700-kilometre Trans-Caspian Gas Pipeline. The next step was the signing of separate agreements between each country and the contractors, PSG and Shell. Russia was also invited to participate in the project. The total cost was estimated at $2.5 billion; US Ex–Im Bank was expected to support the venture.[77] However, the project failed to materialise, not because of

Russian–Iranian objections, but owing to other serious problems. The main issue was the disagreement between Turkmenistan and Azerbaijan over their quota for the export of gas through TCGP;[78] but there was also disagreement between Turkmenistan and the consortium over the pricing of gas, and President Niyazov's insistence on several hundred million dollars of pre-financing for the project.[79] It has also to be mentioned that in the first half of 2000, Turkmenistan signed a 30-year agreement with Russia's Gazprom for the export of up to 50 billion cubic metres of gas per year (bcm/y), and Azerbaijan concluded an agreement with Turkey for the export of gas, starting at 5 bcm/y, from its newly discovered resources at the Shah Deniz field.[80] The visit of Turkish President Demirel to Turkmenistan and his offer of a 22-year agreement to buy 16 bcm/y of Turkmen gas could not save the project.

Iran versus Azerbaijan: Alborz/Alov dispute

The most serious confrontation in the Caspian Sea occurred in July 2001 between Iran and Azerbaijan in a disputed zone. The offshore field, called 'Alborz' in Iran and 'Alov–Araz–Sharq' (hereafter shortened to 'Alov') in Azerbaijan, is located about 90 miles south east of Azerbaijani capital Baku and would be within Iranian waters if Iran acquired a 20 per cent share of the Caspian Sea (see Map 2, p. xxi). Iran resorted to military means to stop oil operations by Azerbaijan's contractors in this area.

In July 1998, when the Azerbaijani President was visiting London, an agreement between SOCAR and British Petroleum (BP) was signed over the exploration and development of the Alov field.[81] On 14 December 1998, Iran announced that a 'South Caspian Study Project' had been awarded to Anglo-Dutch Shell and UK independent Lasmo. The two companies were assigned to carry out a two-part study of the unexplored waters in the southern part of the sea.[82] According to Iranian reports, the project covered an area of 'a minimum of 10,000 square kilometres'; a preliminary study had been implemented by a subsidiary of the National Iranian Oil Company named Khazar Exploration and Production Company. In order to safeguard the deal against obstructions, the Shell–Lasmo consortium estimated the value of the project as US$19.8 million, a figure just below the threshold placed by the US extraterritorial sanctions against Iran. This project signalled Iran's major strategic entry into the Caspian Sea. Nothing was mentioned in the contract about specific locations, but it became clear in a separate contract, signed in 1999 with the semi-state PetroIran Development Company (PEDCO), that the Alborz block was included in the Iranian project.[83]

On 10 December, the Azerbaijani Foreign Ministry lodged a protest at the deal between Iran and the Shell–Lasmo consortium – two days before the signing of the agreement was officially announced.[84] On 16 December, Ilham Aliev, vice-president of SOCAR (and President Aliev's son), condemned the Iranian agreement and threatened Iranian companies with expulsion from Azerbaijan. Saying that Iran had previously expressed an interest in the Alov project, Ilham Aliev added: 'Iran's signing of the contract with the British companies Shell and Lasmo for a seismic study in the Caspian will complicate Iranian companies' activities in Azerbaijan. This will influence the possibility of them getting a project in Azerbaijan in future.'[85] In response, the Iranian Foreign Ministry referred to the Soviet–Iranian treaties of 1921 and 1940, pointing out that there was no document on the division or restriction of the limits of the Caspian Sea and, consequently, the issue of the Azeri sector of the sea lacked legal basis. The Iranian press were more outspoken. As one paper expressed it: 'If Baku feels that it is justified in exploiting what it considers to be its property, then it should be prepared for others to do the same.'[86]

Concurrently, the creation of an international consortium to explore and develop the deposits of Alov was announced by Azerbaijan, turning the dispute into a potential confrontation. Predictably, the Iranian Foreign Ministry rejected the validity of this agreement.[87] When Iranian PEDCO embarked upon seismological operations in 1999 in designated blocks, including Alborz, it faced indirect obstruction by Azerbaijan. According to an Iranian source, the Dutch–Norwegian company Fugro-Geotem which had been invited by the Iranian firm for co-operation in seismic research, was threatened by the vice-president of SOCAR, Ilham Aliev, who stated that its assets in Azerbaijan would be seized if it did not suspend working in the Iranian project.[88] This was the prelude to Iran's subsequent retaliatory action when information was received on the SOCAR/BP Amoco intention to carry out exploration studies in the Alborz/Alov field.

On 21 July 2001, Iran's Deputy Foreign Minister Ali Ahani summoned the Azerbaijani Chargé d'Affaires and handed him a strong protest at the violation of the 'Alborz oil region' by Azerbaijan. The note stressed Iran's firm resolve not to permit foreign countries or companies to engage in any activity which was against its national interest. 'Otherwise, Iran will hold Azerbaijan responsible for any such acts', it added.[89] Two days later, an Iranian gunship entered the disputed waters and demanded that two Azerbaijani survey vessels, operated by BP–Amoco, leave the region. An Iranian warplane also flew over the location in a warning manner. The survey vessels had no choice but to return to Baku 'in the interests of safety', a BP official said. The spokesman for BP in Azerbaijan added: 'In the light of what has happened, we have decided to put our marine operations in the contract area on hold and we will be evaluating our options for the future.'[90] On the same day as this incident, British ambassador to Iran Nicholas Brown met with Secretary of the Supreme Council of National Security Hassan Rowhani, to assure him that British companies would not operate in areas which were subject to Iranian objection.[91]

The reaction of Azerbaijan was sharp, yet conciliatory. On the evening of 23 July, Prime Minister Artur Rasizade summoned the Iranian ambassador, to hand him a note of protest and demand an explanation. Rasizade called Iran's move a 'gross violation of international norms' that could cause 'serious damage' to relations.[92] The following day, the Azerbaijani foreign minister commented: 'We will not get into a war but we will stand up for our rights.' However, on 26 July, President Aliev received the Iranian ambassador to express his wishes for the promotion of 'friendly and good neighbourly' ties with Iran, on the basis of mutual and constructive co-operation. 'The differences between Iran and Azerbaijan should be settled through negotiations between the two countries', Aliev said.[93] On 1 August, Aliev warned that Iran must not use force to get its way in a tense territorial dispute, but also appealed to anti-Iranian radicals in his own country not to 'create any incident'.[94] Aliev's conciliatory gesture encouraged the Iranian media to downgrade the tension. A Tehran daily commented that the Azerbaijani president had 'very wisely' decided to order a stop to all exploratory operations in the disputed area.[95] It was also reported that the dispute was 'only over a single field known in Azerbaijan as Alov, which consists of 1,400 square kilometres, rather than the entire Alov–Araz–Sharq contract with BP'.[96]

Russia and Kazakhstan urged Iran and Azerbaijan to settle their conflict by peaceful means. Turkmenistan blamed Azerbaijan for the crisis.[97] However, on 3 August, at the informal summit of CIS heads of state in Sochi, Russian President Putin voiced implicit criticism of Iran.[98] The US government also announced that it was 'particularly concerned' by Iran's threat to use force in the Caspian Sea. A State Department spokesman slammed Iran for violating Azerbaijan's airspace, describing the incidents as 'provocative and counterproductive to efforts to achieve a peaceful resolution of Caspian boundary dispute'.[99]

The July confrontation incident, likewise, caused tension between Iran and Turkey, as the latter decided to intervene in support of Azerbaijan. In a statement issued on 8 August, Turkey called on both Iran and Azerbaijan to 'abstain from using force and threats of force'. However, on 13 August, the Iranian ambassador was called to the Turkish Foreign Ministry in Ankara and told that Turkey was prepared to send in troops if Iran took military action against Azerbaijan. On 23 August, a squadron of Turkish F-16s arrived in Baku to stage an air-show and flypast over the Azerbaijani capital. Simultaneously, the Turkish army chief of staff General Hussein Kivrikoglu paid an official visit to Azerbaijan. This time, it was Iran's turn to summon the Turkish ambassador to the Foreign Ministry in Tehran and hand him a note of protest against 'the adventurous interference of Turkey in Iran–Azerbaijan relations'.[100]

Nonetheless, President Aliev's management of the rising tension was praised by the Iranian government. On 28 August, Iran's Deputy Foreign Minister Ali Ahani met President Aliev in Baku and extended Iran's 'gratitude' to him for the latter's 'initiative in disenchanting the opportunists' in the dispute. Aliev replied that there was no need for the deployment of military forces in the sea and that there was no prospect of war among the littoral states. Meantime, he urged that the issue of the legal status of the Caspian Sea should be resolved in the shortest possible time as, he said, 'Baku is to sign agreements worth 10 to 15 billion dollars with foreign firms'.[101]

After the confrontation between Iran and Azerbaijan in July 2001, work was suspended in the Alov–Araz–Sharq field by BP, the operating company, which had special interests in both countries. Originally, the first appraisal drilling had been scheduled for 2002. According to some reports, the field is the second-biggest in Azerbaijani waters, with reserves estimated at US$9 billion worth of oil and gas. BP would not say how long the suspension would last, adding that it was up to the Caspian countries to resolve the issue of delineation.[102]

Momentum for a Russian-tailored legal regime: 1998–2003

The year 1998 was a turning point for the division of the Caspian Sea. In February, Russian President Yeltsin commented that the resources of the Caspian Sea must be developed on the basis of a legal status that would be accepted by all five littoral states; Russia, he said, was making a great effort to achieve that goal.[103] This statement coincided with the preliminary accord between Russia and Kazakhstan over the division of the northern part of the Caspian Sea. Concurrently, an official at the Russia Foreign Ministry announced that his country wanted to 'abandon its earlier insistence on establishing a 45-mile coastal zone for each of the Caspian states'. It was also disclosed that Russia was about to propose a division of the seabed without regard to the surface and depth of the water.[104]

In the meantime, Russia and Azerbaijan were reaching agreement over the principle of dividing the Caspian seabed among the coastal states. A protocol signed in Baku on 27 March stated: 'The sides agreed that the division of the bed of the Caspian Sea into sectoral zones be carried out in line with an agreement between the relevant contiguous and opposite states on the basis of the principle of equidistant points (the median line) and other universally recognized principles of international law.' In the concluding part of the document, the Azerbaijani side welcomed the 'constructive position of the Russian side', characterising it as 'a landmark in resolving the problem of the legal status of the Caspian Sea'.[105]

Prior to this, accord had been reached between Kazakhstan and Turkmenistan in April 1997 over their 'national sectors'; in October that year, Turkmenistan and Iran had also reached an understanding over the oilfields located in 'border waters' between the two countries. In early 1998, the border dispute between Azerbaijan and Turkmenistan in the Caspian Sea also seemed to be nearly resolved. Following consultations between the two countries, a joint communiqué was signed on 31 March in Baku, stating that the two sides reaffirmed that the Caspian Sea, in the sector between the Azerbaijan Republic and Turkmenistan, should be divided up along the median line in accordance with the universally recognised principles and norms of international law.[106] However, the sticking point was the definition of the median line: the two parties could not reach agreement on this and the matter remained unresolved.[107]

Iran had already expressed approval of the anticipated 'bilateral' agreement between Azerbaijan and Turkmenistan.[108] In mid-April, Kazakh Foreign Minster Tokaev claimed that most of the littoral states had reached consensus on the need for a division according to national territorial waters' jurisdiction. He was optimistic that Iran would accept this view.[109] On 29 May, Foreign Minister Kharrazi announced that although Tehran still favoured common ownership, it was prepared to consider division on certain conditions.[110] Meanwhile, Turkmen President Niyazov announced that Turkmenistan shared Iran's support for the principle of each of the Caspian states having sovereignty over a 45-mile coastal area, while the rest of the sea would be used jointly by all five littoral countries.[111]

However, the milestone in the post-Soviet legal history of the Caspian Sea was the agreement which Russian President Yeltsin and Kazakh President Nazarbaev signed on 6 July 1998 in Moscow: 'The northern part of the Caspian Sea and its subsoil minerals – while preserving the joint use of the surface water, including freedom of navigation, agreed norms for fishing and environmental protection – shall be divided between the parties along the modified median line.' There followed a definition of the modified median line, and how it should be determined; management of seabed resources within the boundaries of each sector; and ownership of newly discovered deposits of hydrocarbons around the modified median line before the conclusion of agreement. Finally, the document stipulated that 'it shall not impede the efforts of the Caspian-rim states for reaching a common accord, and shall be regarded by the parties as part of the common accord'.[112]

Iran immediately criticised the Russian–Kazakh accord, protesting against references to a 'Kazakh sector' and a 'Russian sector'. Such expressions, in the Iranian view, were a violation of the existing legal regime of the Caspian Sea.[113] Likewise, on 8 July, Turkmen President Niyazov criticised the agreement.[114] Meanwhile, on 19 July, Russian Deputy Foreign Minister Pastukhov and his Iranian counterpart Sarmadi signed in Tehran a joint statement on the Caspian Sea, whereby both parties agreed that the Soviet–Iranian treaties of 1921 and 1940 were legally valid; that the Caspian Sea should be demilitarised; that a general agreement should be signed by the Caspian states on the protection of natural and biological resources of the sea; and that running pipelines through the Caspian Sea for transit of oil and gas would lead to a major environmental disaster in the world's biggest lake. However, they agreed in principle that the Caspian seabed should be equally and equitably divided among the Caspian littoral states; and that there should be multilateral consultations to decide an acceptable principle for the delimitation.[115]

By this time, Russia and Iran had emerged as the focal points for two different views on the status of the Caspian Sea. Russia was actively persuading other Caspian states to negotiate bilateral agreements on the division of the seabed. The Russian formula for division, based on the size of the shoreline, would give Iran some 12–13 per cent of the Caspian Sea. Iran, however, was now advocating a division, if such there had to be, based on the principle of equality sharing among the littoral states; this would give Iran, like the other littoral states, a 20 per cent share of the Caspian Sea.

In May 2000, the Iranian *Majles* (parliament) approved a bill which authorised the National Iranian Oil Company to explore, develop and exploit oil and gas resources in the Caspian Sea.[116] This was a signal that Iran would not remain idle in the face of unilateral operations by the other littoral states; also, it strengthened the position of Iran's oil establishment and enabled it to make deals with foreign companies over the exploitation of resources in the 'Iranian sector' of the Caspian Sea.[117] It was noteworthy that, prior to this bill, Iran had already signed contracts with three European companies for exploration in the south Caspian in 1998; also, in 1999, PetroIran had been charged with setting up exploration and development joint ventures in the Caspian Sea with international firms.[118] However, reasserting the validity of the treaties of 1921 and 1940, Foreign Minister Kharrazi said in February 2001 that the Caspian Sea was not without a legal regime and that the only legal bases for the operations of the littoral states were the aforesaid treaties; 'common ownership' was the only lawful option within the framework of these treaties.[119]

In January 2001, Azerbaijan joined the Russian camp. During President Putin's visit to Azerbaijan, he and President Aliev agreed to sign a joint statement allowing for the delimitation of the Caspian seabed (not the surface waters), between the two countries. A modified median line was to be drawn from an agreed point in the sea's centre to the Azeri–Russian border on the shoreline.[120] Iran reacted angrily, reminding Russia and the other Caspian states that it wanted to be consulted on the sharing of the sea's resources; any agreement on the legal status of the Caspian Sea must be reached with the consent of all the countries bordering the sea.[121] A draft agreement, based on the Putin–Aliev statement, was prepared for signature by the two heads of state the following summer. It specified the geographical co-ordinates of the modified median line. However, it was emphasised that this would not prevent the conclusion of a general agreement by all the littoral states on the status of the Caspian Sea; moreover, the parties were said to 'regard this bilateral agreement as part of their general understanding'.[122] The agreement was finally signed by Presidents Aliev and Putin in Moscow on 23 September 2002.

In March 2001, President Khatami visited Moscow and negotiated with President Putin over a wide range of Russian–Iranian issues. It was their first meeting. Neither was able to persuade the other to change position on the division of the Caspian Sea.[123] Yet, they did identify other points of mutual agreement. In a joint statement, issued on 14 March 2001, they agreed that Iran and Russia would not recognise any national borders in the Caspian Sea, nor would they approve any underwater pipeline to be laid on the Caspian seabed.[124]

The confrontation between Iran and Azerbaijan in July 2001 provided Russia with a golden opportunity to strengthen its position in the Caspian Sea. At the informal August summit of CIS heads of state in Sochi, the presidents of Azerbaijan and Kazakhstan sought Russia's support in the face of Iran's demands. Reportedly, Putin stated that there had been a border between Soviet and Iranian territories in the Caspian Sea and that the Soviet successor states – Russia, Azerbaijan, Kazakhstan and Turkmenistan – had inherited that border with Iran.[125] Putin also apparently suggested that a four-party commission could be created to work out a united CIS front on this issue.[126] Turkmenistan's response was to confirm that it planned to convene a five-party summit in Ashgabat.[127] Kalyuzhny told a parliamentary commission at the State Duma in November of a new Russian formula for a partition along a median line in disputed waters, to be based on 'resource-sharing', and the 'calculation of the historical costs made by different countries'.[128] Russia had in fact proposed this principle as a means of resolving the Turkmen–Azerbaijani disputed zone, but had failed to persuade Turkmenistan to accept it. Nor was it likely that this formula would satisfy Iran, which had not previously undertaken operations in any part of the Caspian Sea.[129]

In December 2001, Azerbaijan took another step forward in reaching accord with its Caspian neighbours, when it signed a joint statement with Kazakhstan on dividing their sections in the Caspian Sea. In addition, Baku had offered a share of the disputed oilfield Alov to Russia's LUKoil, in an attempt to strengthen its position against Iran.[130] An attempt to bridge the gap between the two camps – namely, the proponents of 'proportional' division and those of 'equal' division – was made at a conference held in Moscow on 26–27 February (2002). Turkmenistan refused to attend and, as expected, the event was dominated by representatives of Azerbaijan, Kazakhstan and Russia. The presence of US special envoy on Caspian affairs, Steven Mann, at this meeting was meaningful, as the Russian foreign minister called in his opening address for broader co-operation between the Caspian nations, and also interaction with states located outside the Caspian region.[131] Iran again stressed that it would not accept less than 20 per cent of the Caspian Sea as its 'lawful' share.[132] Nevertheless, the representative of the host country, Viktor Kalyuzhny, claimed that Iran was engaged in the search for a compromise.[133] The Iranian delegation made conciliatory statements and exercised maximum diplomatic restraint on this occasion, attempting, on the one hand, to adhere to its declared policy and, on the other hand, to avoid antagonising Russia. Yet, despite this good will, no progress was achieved.

Meanwhile, the rift between Tehran and Moscow over the Caspian Sea was widening. Iran's oil minister was quoted as saying: 'Our stand is clear; we will not wait for a resolution of the legal regime in the Caspian Sea; we have begun operations there based on our own legal perception, and we will not permit any country's operation in the part of the sea which we regard as our sector.'[134] Statements such as these aroused Russian resentment. Nevertheless, beneath the surface, a degree of moderation was discernible in the Iranian stance and Kalyuzhny expressed the hope that Tehran would eventually change its demands.[135] Washington's concerns were expressed by Steven Mann. He complained of the corruption which had hindered growth in the Caspian states and the lack of legal guarantees which scared away the foreign investors. 'Successful development of the Caspian basin is not something we can consider inevitable', said Steven Mann.[136]

The Moscow conference was supposed to have prepared the ground for the Ashgabat summit, but the absence of Turkmen representatives in Moscow had had a negative impact on the entire process. This was possibly the reason for the increased urgency that Kazakhstan and Azerbaijan placed on an alliance with Russia, regarding this as a safeguard for their energy operations in the Caspian Sea. Kazakhstan joined the criticism of Iran's delaying tactics, accusing the latter of creating a situation in which prospecting and extracting Caspian oil was impossible; it was claimed that Iran was deliberately blocking the Caspian projects in order to keep oil prices high.[137] Meanwhile, a parliamentary debate over the Caspian Sea in Tehran had elicited views from some of the deputies that, on the basis of the Soviet–Iranian treaties, Iran was entitled to 50 per cent – and not 20 per cent – of the Caspian Sea. This caused further outrage in Almaty; the Kazakh media suggested that Iran was planning to claim parts of Kazakhstan's oil deposits in the Caspian Sea.[138]

The Moscow conference was the culmination of a series of meetings of deputy foreign ministers, 'experts' and 'special envoys on Caspian affairs'. It had become clear that this level of participation was not of sufficient weight to activate a policy that would be acceptable to the heads of the Caspian states. Only a summit meeting could carry matters forward.[139] This important (and much postponed) event was convened on 23–24 April 2002 in Ashgabat. From the outset, it was doomed to failure. On the first day, each of the five presidents – Putin, Aliev, Nazarbaev, Niyazov and Khatami – stubbornly stressed their positions, with no hint of flexibility or mutual understanding.[140] Before the end of the first session, President Khatami had walked out of the meeting, supposedly in protest against the tense atmosphere and the powerful coalition formed by Russia, Kazakhstan and Azerbaijan. Yet, despite conflicting attitudes, no animosity was observed between the Iranian and Russian delegations. The main confrontation occurred between Azerbaijan and Turkmenistan. President Aliev stated that the Caspian seabed had been divided under Soviet rule, thus Azerbaijan was operating within its own national sector.[141] The Turkmen president responded by saying that Soviet rule had passed; he condemned the implementation of unilateral operations in disputed areas which would cause problems to other littoral countries. He then raised a question: 'There is a field 84 kms from the Turkmen shore, and 180 kms from the Azeri shore; whose territory is it?' He warned: 'One can smell blood behind the Caspian Sea issue, and everyone of us must understand that it is not an easy problem to solve.'[142]

On the first day of the summit conference, a declaration of general principles had been prepared for the signature of the heads of state. All five leaders declined to sign it. It was announced that, at the suggestion of the Russian president, the next summit of Caspian states would be held in

April 2003 in Tehran.[143] The host of the conference, President Niyazov, disclosed at a press conference on the last day of conference that he himself had prevented the signing of the joint declaration. 'It is an empty document that cannot be adopted', he said.

Some of the leaders who attended the summit described it as 'fruitful'.[144] In reality, despite months of diplomatic preparation, it did not even yield a joint statement to affirm that the Caspian Sea should remain a sea of peace and friendship. Neither was agreement reached on principles for drawing a median line.[145] Yet, despite the debacle of the actual event, it did trigger progress on some issues. After the conference, President Niyazov announced at a meeting of the Turkmen Cabinet that a bilateral agreement over the division of national sectors between his country and Kazakhstan had been prepared for signature. He also confirmed that Turkmenistan would accept the republican boundaries which had been defined by the Soviet Union in the 1970s.[146] Subsequently, it was announced in Baku, that a delegation headed by the vice-president of SOCAR was to visit Ashgabat to negotiate with Turkmen officials over the disputed fields in the Caspian Sea.[147]

Another encouraging development was the visit of President Aliev to Iran. This long-awaited event took place on 19 May, less than a month after the summit. SOCAR officials who accompanied him on this trip were satisfied that Iran appeared more flexible than ever on the issue of dividing the Caspian Sea. Natiq Aliev, the president of SOCAR, hinted that a compromise on the territorial question was now possible.[148] Also, to Iran's satisfaction and pleasure, President Aliev announced that Baku would stop exploration in the disputed Alborz/Alov field until the border issue had been settled.[149] He commented at a press conference in Tehran that 'extensive understanding' had been achieved by Azeri and Iranian experts over the legal regime of the Caspian Sea; it was anticipated that further negotiations by the two sides in Baku would deepen this process. Iranian President Khatami likewise expressed assurance that Iran and Azerbaijan would reach an accord on the Caspian Sea very soon.[150]

Thus, it was beginning to seem as though there was a genuine desire among the littoral states to find acceptable common solutions to Caspian issues. It was in this context of relative optimism that Russia suddenly announced plans for a naval exercise in the Caspian Sea, to be carried out in mid-2002.[151] This show of force came at a sensitive moment and was bound to cause concern to the countries that did not support Russia's views on the Caspian. President Putin stated that the fleet was the main source of protection for the economic and political interests of the Russian Federation in the Caspian Sea; therefore, the fleet should consolidate its presence in the region. Given that the bilateral agreements that had been signed to date on the division of the Caspian had referred only to the seabed and not the surface waters, the Russian navy's area of operation was unlimited. Inevitably, this was a source of anxiety for its Caspian neighbours.[152]

A few months later, however, the situation began to look more promising. On 26–27 February 2003, the eighth session of the Special Working Group on the Caspian Sea, comprising deputy foreign ministers and senior officials of the littoral states, convened in Baku to consider a draft convention on a proposed legal regime. The document included such principles as the demilitarisation of the Caspian; free merchant shipping for littoral states; the peaceful movement of military vessels of the littoral states; the protection of the Caspian ecosystem. Unlike the meeting in Ashgabat in April 2002, the discussions on this occasion were amicable and constructive. Major points of contention remained, particularly regarding articles on the division of the sea, yet some solid progress was made.[153] It seemed likely that at long last a process was under way that would eventually lead to a final resolution of the legal regime of the Caspian Sea.

Ten years on

A decade after the disintegration of the Soviet Union, fundamental issues regarding the Caspian remained unresolved. Nevertheless, more progress had been made behind the scenes than was sometimes evident in public pronouncements. Initially, Russia's preferred option had been the joint utilisation of the Caspian Sea – both the seabed and the surface waters – in a condominium arrangement. However, faced with the resistance of its maritime neighbours, Kazakhstan and Azerbaijan, Russia had abandoned some elements of its ideal solution and accepted bilateral divisions of the seabed. Yet, it had succeeded in retaining the condominium status of the surface waters, thereby allowing the Russian navy and merchant fleet to enjoy freedom of navigation across the entire Caspian Sea, likewise Russian citizens the freedom of fishing rights. Azerbaijan and Kazakhstan had also accepted the need to sacrifice part of their declared principles (i.e. the division of both the seabed and of the surface waters). By late 2002, Russia had finalised an agreement on the seabed border with Kazakhstan and concluded a similar agreement with Azerbaijan. Kazakhstan and Azerbaijan had also reached agreement and had no outstanding problems. These three states concluded a trilateral agreement based on the previous bilateral agreements in May 2003.[154]

Thus, in the northern part of the Caspian Sea, a *de facto* legal regime had been created by the division of the seabed along a modified median line, with joint utilisation of the surface waters for navigation and fishery. However, it was still not clear whether such an arrangement could be extended to the south. This would depend upon the willingness of Turkmenistan and Iran to compromise. Both had, in fact, already shifted from their initial positions. Turkmenistan had been a pioneering advocate of the division of the Caspian Sea, passing a law to define its national sector in 1993. It had often criticised bilateral agreements, yet reached an accord with Kazakhstan in April 1997 over respective 'national sectors' and, similarly, an understanding with Iran in October 1997 over oilfields in 'border waters'. Even with Azerbaijan, outstanding disagreements were over the methodology of delimitation (definition of the median line) rather than the principle.

Iran's position also revealed policy changes. Thus, in negotiations with Turkmenistan, Iran had raised objections to operations in the 'border waters', but had not opposed Turkmenistan's other offshore projects, though these amounted to a violation of the condominium principle. The Iranian–Turkmen compromise of October 1997 implicitly signalled that Iran had accepted the principle of division even before it shifted from advocacy of the condominium doctrine to a dual option solution in late 1998. Thus, Iran had moved from calling for joint ownership of all the sea's resources by all the littoral states to a division based on equal shares. This was later modified to a claim for 20 per cent of the sea, not the resources, for each littoral state. In 2000, the Iranian Oil Ministry asserted that it would not wait any longer for clarification of the legal status of the Caspian Sea and would drill within Iran's claimed 20 per cent share. Iran continued to insist on a 20 per cent share of the sea at the session of the Special Working Group on the Legal Status of the Caspian Sea, held in Baku on 26–27 February 2003,[155] and in subsequent meetings held later that year in Almaty in May and in Moscow in July.[156]

The Iranian position, as held at this time, ran contrary to the interests of Azerbaijan and Turkmenistan. However, a compromise between Azerbaijan and Turkmenistan would leave Iran with a difficult situation. If (or when) Turkmenistan consented to a modified median line division, Iran's resistance would be a challenge to the common interests of the Caspian states and, by extension, to the security of international investments. Such a challenge would surely fail. If Iran did not consent to a median line division, it is unlikely that it would be able to attract international partnership for its operations within disputed territories. The cases of Kyapaz/Serdar and Alborz/Alov indicated that international investment would not be forthcoming for such projects. In an attempt to resolve this dilemma, in March 2003 Iran and Turkmenistan agreed to start work on demarcating their common maritime border.[157]

Legal options

Whatever terms are used to describe the Caspian Sea – 'sea', 'border sea', 'enclosed sea' or 'semi-enclosed sea' – the reality is that this giant natural basin is a lake, and thus falls outside the application of the 1982 United Nations Convention on the Law of the sea. However, the Caspian Sea cannot be 'readily qualified as an international lake' due to its exceptional characteristics (*sui generis*). Experts in international law have commented that 'coastal states might elect to employ rules applicable to international watercourses, including lakes, in the settlement of the legal regime of the Caspian Sea'.[158] As such, everything is in the hands of the Caspian states.

As a precedent and pattern to determine a new legal regime for the Caspian Sea, two models are cited: one, the prevalent regime of the partition of international lakes, as applies in the cases of Lake Geneva and Lake Chad; the other, the regime whereby adjacent waters are partitioned and the rest of the lake remains under the joint ownership of coastal states, as applies in the case of Lake Constance (Bodensee). In each of these cases, agreement was reached between the respective littoral states. For the Caspian Sea, efforts to reach consensus on a new legal regime have been hampered by the fact that the sub-soil resources of the sea are unevenly distributed. Consequently, a division of the sea would not benefit all countries equally. This has greatly complicated negotiations.

After a decade of disputes and arguments, the only common expression by the five Caspian states has been that the legal status of the Caspian Sea should be decided by all these states through a multilateral agreement. In reality, the only progress towards the formation of a new legal status of the Caspian Sea has been achieved through a series (as yet not comprehensive) of bilateral agreements. Nevertheless, it is generally agreed that at least a mutual understanding between the coastal states is necessary whether or not the sea is divided. Some international lawyers, seeking precedents for maritime territories passed from a single sovereign state to numerous successor states, have made reference to the case of the Gulf of Fonseca.[159] Here, no attempt was made to divide the joint waters, and in 1992 the International Court of Justice advised that, even in absence of a treaty over condominium status, the Gulf of Fonseca could remain under joint ownership of the three sovereign states.[160] Such a regime would ensure that the economic benefits arising from exploitation of the Caspian would be shared among the Caspian states.[161] This approach to the common ownership of mineral resources (e.g. oil and gas) was favoured by Iran.

The current dual system in the Caspian Sea is functioning and projects, supported by international investment, are being implemented. However, this remains a temporary solution. Tensions between, on the one hand, the proponents of equality in division and, on the other, the proponents of division along a modified median line, could lead to serious confrontation if one side refused to give in to the other. Yet, the situation is not quite as black as it may sometimes appear: many of the outstanding problems could be overcome by careful and sensitive drafting of agreements, as indeed has already occurred in some of the border disputes among neighbouring Caspian states. The driving force for reaching an agreement is that Russia and Iran, like the other three littoral states, are in need of a settlement in the Caspian Sea so as to develop their own energy resources without obstruction. All these states are trying to attract foreign investment, but investment needs security. As one Western analyst commented: 'The stakes involved in oil and gas development are very high, and they extend well behind the region. But the incentives to resolve the legal and political disputes peacefully are also very high. We must hope that they are high enough.'[162] At the end of the first post-Soviet decade, the outlook was still unclear, but positive developments were beginning to outweigh negative factors.

Notes

(I) denotes books and journals in Persian.

1 Laurence Lockhart, *Nadir Shah: A Critical Study Based Mainly upon Contemporary Sources*, Luzac & Co., London, 1938, p. 289.

2 See further Jonas Hanway, *An Historical Account of the British Trade over the Caspian Sea*, 4 vols, London, 1753.

3 In May 1920, while pursuing the White army, Soviet troops invaded the Iranian port of Anzali on the Caspian coast. For the history of Azerbaijan during this period, see T. Swietochowski, *Russian Azerbaijan 1905–1920: The Shaping of National Identity in a Muslim Community*, Cambridge University Press, New York, 1985.

4 *Great Soviet Encyclopaedia* (English edition), vol. 11, Macmillan, New York, 1976, p. 169.

5 Quoted in J. C. Hurewitz (ed.), *The Middle East and North Africa in World Politics: A Documentary Record*, vol. 1: *European Expansion 1535–1914*, Yale University Press, New Haven/London, 1975, p. 198.

6 *Ibid.*, p. 233.

7 Quoted in J. C. Hurewitz (ed.), *Diplomacy in the Near and Middle East*, Van Nostard, Princeton, 1956, p. 92.

8 L. Woodward, *British Foreign Policy in the Second World War*, vol. 2, HMSO, London, 1971, p. 26.

9 Quoted in J. Degras (ed.), *Soviet Documents on Foreign Policy*, vol. 3, 1933–1941, Octagon, London, 1978, p. 433.

10 *Ibid.*

11 Since 1935, 'Iran' has been used in official documents in place of 'Persia'.

12 Degras, *ibid.*, p. 434.

13 Other Soviet–Iranian treaties were signed between 1921 and 1940: on 1 October 1927, 27 October 1931, 27 August 1935; these agreements regulated the commerce, navigation and fishing rights of the two countries, and of their nationals, in the Caspian Sea. However, the two major treaties of 26 February 1921 and 25 March 1940 are generally regarded as the basic legal documents which set out the status of the Caspian Sea during the Soviet era. For an Iranian legal interpretation of the Soviet–Iranian treaties of 1921 and 1940, and their application to the current status of the Caspian Sea, see Jamshid Momtaz, 'The Legal Regime of the Caspian Sea', *Iran News* (Tehran), 29 January–1 February 1998.

14 The Alma-Ata Declaration of 21 December 1991 stated: 'Members of the Commonwealth guarantee, in accordance with their constitutional procedures, the fulfilment of international obligations, stemming from the treaties and agreements of the former USSR.' *Summary of World Broadcast* (hereafter *SWB*), *SU (Soviet Union)*, 23 December 1991.

15 For an Iranian perception of the condominium status of the Caspian Sea, see M. Dabiri, 'The Legal Regime of the Caspian Sea: A Basis for Peace and Development', *Journal of Central Asia and Caucasia Research* (Tehran), Summer 1994, pp. 1–20.

16 *Commonwealth of Independent States and the Middle East* (hereafter *Commonwealth*), Mayrock Centre for Soviet and East European Studies, Hebrew University, no. 10, 1992.

17 See S. Vinogradov, and P. Wouters, 'The Caspian Sea: Quest for a New Legal Regime', *Leiden Journal of International Law*, vol. 9, 1996, pp. 87–98; A. Khodakov, 'The Legal Framework for Regional Co-operation in the Caspian Sea Region', *Labyrinth* (Central Asia Quarterly), London, Summer 1995, pp. 30–33.

18 The heads of the four Caspian states of the Commonwealth of Independent States (CIS) – Russia, Azerbaijan, Kazakhstan and Turkmenistan – asserted at a meeting in Astrakhan in October 1993 that 'the comprehensive solution of

the problem of rational utilization of the Caspian Sea requires the participation of all Caspian states'. See further S. Bolukbaşi, 'The Controversy over the Caspian Sea Mineral Resources: Clashing Interests', *Europe–Asia Studies*, vol. 50, no. 3, Glasgow, May 1998.

19 Khodakov, *ibid.*

20 Henn-Juri Uibopuu, 'The Caspian Sea: a Tangle of Legal Problems', *World Today*, London, Royal Institute of International Affairs, vol. 51, no. 6, June 1995, pp. 119–123.

21 *Ibid.*

22 As a senior Kazakh official commented: 'Since the width of the sea nowhere exceeds 200 nautical miles, one side of each country's exclusive economic zones will follow the line of equidistance from the two coasts: the middle of the sea' (V. Gizzatov, 'The Legal Status of the Caspian Sea', *Labyrinth*, London, Summer 1995, pp. 33–36).

23 *Radio Free Europe/Radio Liberty, Daily Report* (hereafter *RFE/RL*), 17 November 1994.

24 *SWB*, 23 December 1991.

25 *SWB*, 31 August 1995.

26 In October 1996, Foreign Minister Velayati disclosed that new proposals had been put forward on the status of the Caspian Sea; he welcomed them as a sign of 'flexibility' on the part of all the coastal states and the 'first step to resolving the matter' (*Tehran Times*, 16 October 1996). The options were as follows: a) that the subsoil and its resources should be shared equally by the five littoral states; b) that the coastal margins should be allocated to the coastal states, the rest of the sea to be shared in common by the five states; c) that each coastal state should be allowed to extend its margin from the traditional 12-mile limit to 40 miles, the rest of the sea be shared in common among the littoral states. *Iran News*, 23 October; 30 October 1995.

27 *SWB*, 24 October 1996.

28 *Ibid.*

29 The last article reiterated the point: 'The parties want to intensify and raise the status of the negotiation process among the Caspian states on the legal status of the Caspian Sea. This is why they support the organisation, in the near future, of a meeting of the foreign ministers of the Caspian states' (*Ettela'at* (I), 11 June 1996). One of the chief reasons for Iran's objection to any sort of division of the Caspian Sea was the stance of the US on this issue. President Clinton had expressed his support for this solution in his message of 20 May 1995 to President Aliev: 'We will support the Caspian states' efforts to sign an agreement on the division of the Caspian' (*SWB*, 27 May 1995). Iranian Foreign Minister Velayati described such messages as 'meddling' and 'clear interference by the US in the regional affairs of the Caspian Sea' (*Tehran Times*, 13 June 1995).

30 *SWB*, 20 September 1996.

31 *SWB*, 14 November 1996.

32 *Ibid.*

33 *Ettela'at* (international edition), 13, 14, 15 November 1996.

34 *SWB*, 30 February 1997.

35 Communication dated 12 September 1997 (*Tehran Times*, 14 September 1997).

36 *Ibid.*

37 *SWB*, 18 November 1997.

38 *SWB*, 13 November 1997; *SWB, SU*, 12 November 1997.

39 *SWB*, 23 September 1994.

40 In his statement of 27 September 1994, Russian Foreign Minister Kozyrev warned that any operations for the development of Caspian Sea resources should 'meet the interests of all the countries in the Caspian Sea region including Russia, Azerbaijan and Iran' (*SWB*, 27 September 1994).

41 Kozyrev approached President Aliev with a complaint that the northern part of the Caspian Sea had not been divided between Russia and the three other former Soviet republics, and, moreover, Russia had not been consulted over the Azerbaijan oil deal (*SWB*, 18 October 1994).

42 *Ettela'at* (I), 7 October 1994.

43 *Nezavisimaya gazeta*, cited in *Salam* (I), 29 October 1994.

44 'Russia may legally prospect for, and explore Caspian offshore oil fields 10 mile away from Baku', it was stressed (*SWB*, 9 November 1996).

45 *SWB*, 27 September 1994.

46 *SWB*, 8 November 1994.

47 On 4 October 1994, an 'expert' told IRNA that unilateral actions by littoral states in the Caspian Sea were 'illegal'. He stressed that under the laws governing the Caspian Sea, the resources of the sea should be exploited jointly by all littoral states (*Ettela'at* (I), 4 October 1994).

48 *Tehran Times*, 15 October 1994; *Ettela'at* (I), 13 October 1994. On 21 October, an official of the Russian Foreign Ministry, Mikhail Demurin, explained that Iran and Russia shared a very close view on issues related to the Caspian Sea, and that after adopting a new convention on the legal regime of the Caspian Sea 'Azerbaijan would have to revise its agreement with the consortium of Western oil companies' (*Ettela'at* (I), 24 October 1994).

49 *SWB*, 18 October 1994; *Salam* (I), 24 October 1994; *SWB, SU*, 13 October 1994.

50 *RFE/RL*, 17 November 1994.

51 *SWB*, Weekly Economic Report, 11 November 1994.

52 *SWB*, 12 November 1994; *SWB*, 14 November 1994; *Tehran Times*, 13 November 1994.

53 *Commonwealth*, No. 11–12, 1994; *Ettela'at* (I), 14 November 1994.

54 *RFE/RL*, Daily Report, 17 November 1994; *Kayhan Hav'ai* (I), 30 November 1994.

55 *Kayhan Hava'i* (I), 19 April 1995; *SWB, SU*, 21 April 1995. In the midst of the Tehran–Baku row over the exclusion of Iran from the consortium, a Tehran newspaper raised the question: 'Why was nothing mentioned about the legal status of the Caspian Sea last November when Iranian Minister of Petroleum Aqazadeh was negotiating Iran's partnership in the multi-national consortium in Baku?' See *Salam* (I), 20 April 1995.

56 *Tehran Times*, 16 May 1995; *Iran News*, 13 July 1995; *Iran News*, 13 July 1995.

57 *SWB*, 21 April 1995.

58 *Ettela'at* (I), 7 June 1995; *SWB*, 25 August 1995.

59 *Tehran Times*, 12 October 1995; *Ettela'at* (I), 27 October 1995.

60 *SWB*, 1 November 1996; 17 May 1997.

61 *SWB*, 14 November 1997; *Ettela'at* (I), 12 December 1998.

62 Likewise, SOCAR issued a statement to the effect that 'the Azeri and Chirag oil fields were in the Azerbaijani sector, the borders of which were defined by the Ministry of Oil and Gas of the former Soviet Union' (*SWB*, 30 January 1997).

63 *SWB*, 6 July 1997.

64 Turan News Agency (AZ), quoted by *Salam* (I), 14 September 1997.

65 *SWB*, 14 July 1997; SWB, 30 July 1997.

66 *SWB*, 3 August 1997.

67 *SWB*, 28 June 1997.

68 *SWB*, 26 June 1997.

69 *SWB*, 3 September 1999.

70 *SWB*, 20 February 1998.

71 *RFE/RL*, 13 March 2002.

72 Agence France-Presse (AFP), 30 July 1998.

73 *Ettela'at* (I), 23 April 1998.
74 AFP, 30 July 1998.
75 *Middle East Economic Survey* (*MEES*), 6 December 1999.
76 *Ibid.*
77 *RFE/RL*, 20 January 2000.
78 Azerbaijan had wanted to share the TCGP capacity (between 16 bcm and 30 bcm a year) on a 50–50 per cent basis with Turkmenistan; however, the Turkmen president announced that he would let Azerbaijan have access only to one-sixth of the pipeline, or 5 bcm/y of the pipeline's ultimate 30 bcm/y capacity (*MEES*, 6 March 2000).
79 *MEES*, 27 March; 3 April; 19 June 2000.
80 *Hart's Middle East Oil and Gas*, 7 March 2000; *MEES*, 3 April 2000; Reuters, 2 June 2000.
81 Partners of this consortium and the ratio of their shares as of 2003 were: BP Amoco (UK) 15 per cent; TPAO (Turkey) 10 per cent; Statoil (Norway) 15 per cent; ExxonMobil (US) 15 per cent; Alberta Energy (Canada) 5 per cent; SOCAR 40 per cent. The operator of the project was BP Amoco.
82 German firm Veba joined the project in 2000. Later, Lasmo and Veba were purchased by Italian Eni and BP Amoco respectively.
83 *Kayhan Hava'i* (I), 21 December 1998.
84 *Tehran Times*, 29 July 1999; *SWB*, 14 December 1998.
85 *SWB*, Economic Weekly, 1 January 1999.
86 *Kayhan Hava'i* (I), 21 December 1998; *Iran News*, 12 December 1998.
87 'It is devoid of legal grounds. In the case of the division of the sea, some of the oil fields in the areas specified in the recent contract will belong to Iran; the oil companies have already been cautioned and given warning on the issue' (*SWB*, 14 December 1998).
88 Abbas Maleki, 'A New Look at South Caspian', *Tehran Times*, 29 July 2001.
89 *Ettela'at* (I), 22 July 2001.
90 *Financial Times*, 24 July 2001; AFP, quoted by *Tehran Times*, 25 July 2001.
91 *Ettela'at* (I), 24 July 2001.
92 *Financial Times*, 24 July; *ibid.*, 25 July 2001.
93 *Iran* (I), 28 July 2001.
94 AFP, 1 August 2001. There were also inflammatory statements made in Baku and Tehran by hardliners on both sides.
95 *Iran* (I), 2 August 2001.
96 IRNA in *Tehran Times*, 28 July 2001.
97 On 30 July, following a meeting between the Azeri ambassador to Moscow and Russia's Deputy Foreign Minister and Special Envoy for the Caspian Sea Viktor Kalyuzhny, a statement was issued by the Russian Foreign Ministry to the effect that: 'The Russian side has called on Azerbaijan and Iran to act in the spirit of good neighbours, to show wisdom and to conduct a direct dialogue to reduce these tensions and find a mutually acceptable just solution' (*Financial Times*, 3 August 2001).
98 'The Caspian Sea must be a sea of peace and tranquillity. Everything must be done to have all disputes resolved through peaceful means by direct dialogue. Russia is ready to assist in any way possible to negotiate disagreements in the spirit of neighbourly relations and mutual understanding, in line with principles of international law. It is impermissible to resort to military means.' However, a Russian commentator reported that at the summit, which was attended by 10 CIS heads of state, including the three Caspian states, 'Azerbaijan was given unconditional support' (A. Dubnov, 'Tehran Guns for Caspian Oil', *Institute of War and Peace Reporting*, 24 August 2001).
99 AFP, 14 August 2001.

100 AFP, 8 August 2001; Dubnov, *ibid.*; M. Lelyveld, 'Iran: Hurdles Remain in Improving Ties with Azerbaijan' (*RFE/RL*, 21 August 2001); *Tehran Times*, 26 August 2001.

101 *Ettela'at* (international edition), 30 July 2001.

102 A. Sultanova, 'Tensions Flare over Oil, Caspian Sea', Associated Press (AP), 24 July 2001; D. Stern, 'Russia Urges Resolution to Caspian Oil Dispute', *Financial Times*, 3 August 2001.

103 The delimitation line on the Caspian Sea as a continuation of the terrestrial border between Astara (Azerbaijan) and Gasankuli (Turkmenistan) was established unilaterally by order No. 3 of the NKVD (Soviet Ministry of Internal Affairs) in 1935 but was never recognised by Iran as the Soviet–Iranian border (S. Vinogradov, and P. Wouters, 'The Caspian Sea: Current Legal Problems', *Zeitschrift für Auslandisches Öffentliches Recht und Volkerrecht*, 55/2, 1995, p. 609); *SWB*, 2 April 1998.

104 *SWB*, 14 February 1998.

105 *SWB*, 2 April 1998.

106 *SWB*, 3 April 1998.

107 The chairman of the Azerbaijani State Committee for Geodesy and Geography was quoted as saying that 'in determining the median line, Ashgabat has proposed using the rule of equal latitudes, as envisaged in article 15 of the 1982 Convention on the Law of the sea. This method stipulates a simple arithmetical division of the Caspian (drawing a line connecting the two shores and dividing it in halves) without taking into account shoreline contours, the existence of banks, islands and so on. International principles of division would be infringed if the Turkmen condition were applied in this case.' Azerbaijan, however, was insisting that the principle of equidistance between the closest shore points should be applied in determining the median line; Baku's position coincided with the Russian and Kazakh points of view, he added. *SWB*, 1 April 1998.

108 In mid-February, the Iranian media reported that, according to Turkmen sources, President Khatami had, in a letter to president Niyazov, announced Tehran's support for the agreement between Turkmenistan and Azerbaijan over establishing a border between their respective sectors in the Caspian Sea. Turkmen Foreign Minister Shikhmuradov had described the agreement, approved by Iran, as a 'purely practical deal to divide parts of the Caspian shelf, that also took into account the relevant interests of other littoral states' (*Iran News*, 14 February 1998).

109 *Ettela'at* (international edition), 17 April 1998.

110 'If all the littoral states decide to divide the Caspian Sea, this division should be based on equal shares and fair exploitation rights for each country; a single regime should prevail for the seabed and the surface of the Caspian Sea', Kharrazi said in Ashgabat (*SWB*, 2 June 1998).

111 Statement of 16 May (*SWB*, 21 May 1998).

112 *SWB*, 12 July 1998.

113 *Tehran Times*, 30 May 1998.

114 *SWB*, 11 July 1998.

115 After Tehran, Pastukhov went to Baku for consultations. However, according to Russian reports, he failed to reach agreement with Azerbaijani officials (*Ettela'at* (international edition), 21 July 1998; *SWB*, 31 July 1998).

116 AFP, 11 July 2001.

117 *Interfax*, 22 May 2002.

118 The Iranian Oil Ministry consulted the legislature for bypassing the 'buy-back' formula to let Iran's Caspian projects be more competitive with similar projects in other Caspian countries. Due to constitutional restrictions, and limitations in the law on Attraction and Protection of Foreign Investment, the 'buy-back'

formula had been the sole option open to foreign investors. If the Caspian oil and gas projects were approved by the *Majles*, foreign investment in Iran's hydrocarbon sector, in the form of Production Sharing Agreements, would take place for the first time since 1979 (*Iran* (I), 11 January 2001).

119 *Iran* (I), 11 January 2001.
120 AFP, 11 January 2001
121 *Iran* (I), 11 January 2001.
122 *Interfax*, 22 May 2002.
123 Prior to this summit, Kalyuzhny, Russian special envoy on Caspian affairs, had noted that Iran's call for 20 per cent-based division would not be placed on the agenda for consultation (*Hayat-e No* (I), 17 January 2001).
124 *Moscow Times*, 15 March 2001; *Iran News*, 27 February 2001.
125 *Hayat-e No* (I), 5 August 2001.
126 However, Kalyuzhny did not confirm that the '4+1' option had ever been suggested by Putin (*ibid.*).
127 The planned summit was postponed several times over – twice in April 2001 and again in October 2001; it was finally convened in April 2002 in Ashgabat.
128 M. Lelyveld, 'Russia: Will a New Formula for Sharing Caspian Riches Work?', *RFE/RL, Features*, 28 November 2001.
129 *Ibid.*
130 M. Lelyveld, 'Russia: Caspian Meeting Ends with Few Clues on Progress', *RFE/RL, Features*, 28 January 2002.
131 *Moscow Times*, 27 February 2002.
132 *Ettela'at* (I), 27 February 2002.
133 *Moscow Times*, 27 February 2002; *Ettela'at* (international edition), 1 March 2002.
134 *Iran* (I), 20 February 2002.
135 M. Lelyveld, 'Iran: Another Caspian Row in the Making', *RFE/RL, Features*, 26 February 2002.
136 *Moscow Times*, 27 February 2002.
137 M. Lelyveld, 'Iran: Tehran Seems to Be Blocking Caspian Summit', *RFE/RL, Features*, 12 March 2002.
138 *Ibid.*
139 Kalyuzhny quoted in M. Lelyveld, 'Conflicts Likely at Presidents Summit', *RFE/RL, Features*, 19 April 2002.
140 This meeting was widely reported in the media; see, for example: *RFE/RL, Daily Report*, 23 April 2002; *ibid.*, 24 April 2002; *Aftab-e Yazd* (I), 25 April 2002; *Iran* (I), 16 April 2002.
141 He argued that the absence of a legal regime in the Caspian Sea was no obstacle to the exploitation of the sea resources. Aliev ruled out the use of force in Caspian disputes and advised all Caspian states to solve their conflicts through negotiations. He made a special reference, in this context, to the experience of Russia and Azerbaijan and the bilateral agreements which they concluded with their neighbouring coastal states (*Iran* (I), 26 April 2002).
142 *RFE/RL*, 24 April 2002.
143 AP, 24 April 02.
144 *Norouz* (I), 27 April 2002.
145 *Interfax*, 24 April 2002; M. Lelyveld, 'Caspian: Summit Failure Generates Further Concerns for Future Division of the sea', *RFE/RL*, 26 April 2002.
146 *Norouz* (I), 27 April 2002.
147 www.eurasianet.org/departments/insight/articles/22.05.2002.
148 *Ibid.*
149 *Ettela'at* (international edition), 21 May 2002.
150 *Ibid.*
151 This military exercise was announced by President Putin during his visit to Astrakhan on 25 April, immediately after the Ashgabat conference.

152 Putin insisted that Russia would continue to resolve problems in the Caspian Sea through bilateral agreements with neighbouring states. In the case of issues such as the protection of the marine environment, he agreed that a different type of agreement should be concluded (*Bonyan* (I), 27 April 2002; *Norouz* (I), 30 April 2002).

153 H. Peimani, 'Baku Caspian Meeting Created Hopes but not Concrete Results', *Central Asia–Caucasus Analyst*, 12 March 2003.

154 *RFE/RL Newsline*, 15 May 2003.

155 AFP, 27 February 2003.

156 Some slight shift was perhaps to be observed in the statement by Mehdi Safari, the presidential envoy on the Caspian Sea, when, while attending the tenth meeting of the SWG, he indicated that Iran had 'proposed a technical formula, based on international principles and laws', which would give it between 19.7 per cent and 20.3 per cent of the sea (IRNA, 20 July 2003). However, in March 2004 Iranian Foreign Ministry spokesman Hamid-Reza Asefi 'dismissed as unfounded' reports on Iran's change of position regarding the Caspian Sea (10 March 2004, IRNA).

157 AFP, 28 March 2003, reporting an announcement in Turkmenistan's leading state-run newspaper.

158 S. Vinogradov and P. Wouters, *Zeitschrift für Auslandisches Öffentliches Recht und Volkerrecht*, 55/2, pp. 604–623.

159 R. Rodman Bundy, 'The Caspian – Sea or Lake: Consequences in International Law', *Labyrinth* (Central Asia Quarterly), London, Summer 1995, pp. 26–29; M. Movahed, 'A Brief Look at the Legal Order of the Caspian Sea and its Related Matters', *Journal of the Bar Association* (I), Tehran, April 2001.

160 Spanish colonial rule in the region surrounding the Gulf of Fonseca came to an end in 1821; thereafter, the Central American Federation was created. When this, too, disintegrated, three independent countries emerged on the coast of the Gulf of Fonseca: Honduras, El Salvador and Nicaragua. See *International Court of Justice (IC) Reports 1992*, The Gulf of Fonseca Case, p. 351.

161 S. Vinogradov and P. Wouters, 'The Caspian Sea: Quest for a New Legal Regime', *Leiden Journal of International Law*, 1996, vol. 9, pp. 87–98.

162 E. Fersht, 'Oil and the Demarcation of the Caspian Sea', in M. Nordquist and J. Norton Moore, *Security Flashpoints: Oil, Islands, Sea Access and Military Confrontation*, Martinus Nijhoff, The Hague, 1998, p. 290.

3 Negotiations on the legal status of the Caspian Sea 1992–1996: view from Kazakhstan

Vyacheslav Gizzatov

From 1992 onwards the littoral states have been carrying on negotiations on the question of the legal status of the Caspian Sea. As a whole they have been useful from the point of view of familiarisation with the approaches of the countries concerned, as well as for understanding the complexity of the problem itself, discovering a possible basis for convergence in pursuit of achieving agreement.

However, we must note with regret the existence of serious differences in the Caspian states' positions. Over twelve years after the disintegration of the Soviet Union, no final agreement has yet been reached on the legal status of the Caspian. A number of disagreements and differences of opinion still remain. At the same time, a high level of mutual understanding has been achieved, likewise a basis for consensus in questions of a legal regime for navigation, fishery, overseas air traffic, environmental protection and the rational use of bio-resources. There is also agreement that the exploitation of the Caspian Sea should be conducted exclusively for peaceful purposes.

This chapter looks at the first phase of the quest to reach a joint agreement on these issues. It was a learning period for all concerned. Each of the five littoral states began by setting out its ideal claims; gradually, however, the states started to negotiate these claims, realising the need to make concessions and build alliances. By early 1996, it seemed as though a final agreement was within reach. National agendas had been modified to the extent that between four of the states there seemed to be a relatively high degree of co-ordination of positions. The chief obstacle at this stage seemed to be Turkmenistan, which remained intent on pursuing a unilateral policy. In 1992, it had adopted the Law on the State Frontiers of Turkmenistan, whereby it laid claim to a 12-mile sector of the Caspian. Nevertheless, there was still widespread optimism that a mutually acceptable solution might be found in the near future. Such hopes proved to be premature. Subsequently, new areas of dissent emerged between the Caspian states; external actors also became more active in the region and helped to influence the policies of the individual states. By the end of the 1990s, there were signs of an incipient trend towards the militarisation of the Caspian. These developments are discussed elsewhere in this volume. The aim here is to outline the arguments that shaped Kazakh thinking on the legal status of the Caspian Sea, and that formed the basis for the negotiations that resulted in the signing of two Joint Declarations in 1996 (see Annexes to this chapter).

Two approaches

Analyses of the first post-Soviet draft documents on the legal status of the Caspian Sea, and official declarations and statements by representatives of the Caspian states, reveal the existence of two conceptually diverse approaches. One was based on the premise that the Caspian Sea had been a sea of common use up until the collapse of the Soviet Union, i.e. that there had existed a Soviet–Iranian Caspian condominium. Consequently, it was argued, this condominium should be maintained, albeit in a new form that incorporated all five independent littoral states. The other approach held that a new regime was now required, whereby the Caspian Sea should be delimited among littoral states in one form or another.

The essence of the issue lay in the fact that the supporters of the 'condominium' concept considered that the Caspian Sea was not, and should not be, subdivided. Consequently, they insisted, all the coastal states had an equal right to participate in its use and none of them had any grounds to obtain exclusive rights to any part of its resources except by agreement with all other states. They regarded unilateral attempts by some of the littoral states to explore the mineral resources of the sea as illegitimate, as they were carried out without the consent of the other Caspian states, thus violating the existing regime of a condominium. Proponents of the other view, among them Kazakhstan, wanted national interests to be defined and protected by a full delimitation of the sea. Both these approaches hinged on the question of whether or not the claim that the Caspian Sea had been an object of common use could be substantiated by historical and legal documents. Below I shall outline the main arguments. First, however, there is a need for clarification of terminology. As international legislation makes no difference between the establishment of a condominium and objects of common use, I shall use the term condominium here.

History

Proponents of the condominium concept substantiated their position by reference to international treaties on the Caspian Sea. There were three strands in the treaty argument. Firstly, it was suggested that at one stage the Caspian was, *de facto* and *de jure* (as evidenced by relevant treaties), to be wholly under Russian sovereignty; the implication was that any rights of other states in the Caspian resulted from Russian concessions. Secondly, it was suggested that the statement which occurs in a number of twentieth-century treaties that the Caspian 'is a Soviet and Iranian sea' indicated that the Caspian was regarded by the two littoral states of the time as subject to their joint ownership and control. Thirdly, it was claimed that the absence of any provision in boundary treaties for a frontier in the Caspian indicated that the Caspian was owned in common by the littoral states. I shall deal with each suggestion in turn.

Historical documents testify that at the beginning of the eighteenth century Russia regarded Persia and the Persian shore of the Caspian as foreign territory. Some time around 1701 Peter the Great sent one Artemiy Volynskiy to Persia with instructions to report in detail on the harbours, settlements and rivers around the Caspian. At the same time a Russian expedition under Prince Berkovich-Cherkasskiy landed on the eastern shore of the Caspian. There was concluded a commercial treaty permitting Russian merchants to trade in Persia. At that time Russia clearly accepted the existence of Persian rights over part of the Caspian shores and the need to conclude treaties with Persia in order to establish any Russian rights there.

In 1721–1722 Russian troops moved into Persia's Caspian provinces, ostensibly to assist Persia in subduing Afghan rebels. Semyon Avraamov, the Russian consul in Persia, was instructed to offer Russian help on condition that Persia ceded to Russia certain provinces along the Caspian Sea. It is evident that Russia was in no doubt at that time that the Caspian provinces were under Persian sovereignty.

On 23 September 1723 the Persian shah's ambassador in St Petersburg, Ismail Bek, signed a treaty with Russia under which Persia was to cede to Russia the towns of Derbent and Baku, with all the territories belonging to them, as well as the provinces of Gilan, Mazandaran and Astarabad. However, this treaty was not ratified by Persia. In accordance with a peace treaty concluded between Russia and Persia on 21 January 1732 Russia agreed to withdraw from the Caspian provinces and to give them back to Persia. So treaties between the Russian Empire and Persia signed at the beginning of the eighteenth century clearly testify to recognition of Persian sovereignty over the south Caspian shore.

In the nineteenth century Russia resumed its attempts to re-establish its power over the Persian Caspian shore. Under Article 5 of the Treaty of Gulistan (Golestan) of October 1813, Russia was permitted to exercise exclusive rights to navigate warships along the coasts of the Caspian Sea. The Treaty of Turkmanchai (see **Granmayeh**, p. 18) reiterated Russia's exclusive right to deploy warships on the Caspian Sea. The Treaties of Gulistan and Turkmanchai are crucial to understanding the subsequent events in the evolution of the regime of the Caspian Sea. An Anglo-Russian Convention on Afghanistan, Persia and Tibet dated 18/31 August 1907 divided Persia, without its consent, into a northern zone, passed to Russian influence, and a southern zone, passed to British influence. That Convention reinforced Russia's hegemony in the Caspian as established in the Treaty of Gulistan and the Treaty of Turkmanchai.

Early in the twentieth century the situation changed radically. In 1921 the new Soviet Government of Russia concluded a Treaty of Friendship with Persia, the main mission of which was to counteract British attempts to gain navigation control over the Caspian Sea. In accordance with that treaty, Russia renounced 'the tyrannical policy carried out by the Colonising

Governments of Russia' and declared the whole body of treaties and conventions concluded with Persia by the Tsarist Government, which crushed the rights of the Persian people, to be null and void. The Treaty of Turkmanchai was abrogated: the two parties agreed to enjoy equal rights to free navigation under their own flags. Other states were deprived of the right to sail in the Caspian Sea: only the Soviet and Iranian flags could fly there.

That provision of the Treaty of 1921 is the background to the often-quoted statement that the Caspian Sea is a Soviet and Iranian sea. However, this phrase appears not in the main body of the Treaty, but in Note N13 attached to the Convention on Establishment, Commerce and Navigation (1931). Its purpose was to remind contracting parties of their obligation not to permit foreign workers to be engaged in subversive activities while in Caspian ports. The phrase 'the Soviet and Iranian Sea', as it appeared in the legislative documents of that time, signifies no more than restoration of justice with respect to Iran, which obtained the right to navigate. There is no evidence whatever suggesting that the phrase was intended or understood at the time to make a statement concerning the juridical status of the Caspian. Thus no treaty practice with respect to the Caspian Sea gives any reason to assert the existence of a condominium in the Caspian or any other regime of joint ownership or jurisdiction.

Regarding general provisions under international law that might be relevant to the condominium concept, there is no presumption that land or frontier inland water between two or more states constitutes a condominium. International legislation has no provisions according to which such a status can be obtained automatically. A condominium or 'an object of common utilisation' should be established either by treaty or through the unequivocal practice of the states concerned, as a matter of customary international law. The treaty practice, as discussed above, does not bear out claims that the Caspian was treated by the littoral states as a condominium. On the contrary, there is some evidence in the implementation of the treaties that plainly indicate that it was not.

Fisheries

One indication that the sea was not treated as a condominium was the unilateral grant of fishery rights in the Caspian Sea by Persia. This was clearly incompatible with the existence of a condominium. The first documented grant of rights over Caspian resources was the Persian grant of a concession to the Lianozov Brothers for the monopoly of the sturgeon fisheries in the south Caspian Sea. The concession was renewed in 1879, 1886, 1893 and 1896; in 1906 the term of the concession was extended to 1925. Later, those concessional rights were transferred to the Soviet Government, which was evidenced in Protocol N3 to the Persia–USSR Fisheries Agreement of 1927. The 1927 fisheries concession expired in 1953 and the USSR acknowledged in the Note dated 2 February 1953 that Iran had 'exercised its legal right' to terminate the concession and that in consequence Iran obtained the right to exploit the fisheries itself. The conclusion that can be drawn from this is that Persia acted unilaterally, granting exclusive rights to exploit resources in a part of the Caspian that was regarded as under exclusive Persian ownership. Persia's competence to grant such rights was recognised by both the Tsarist Government of Russia and the Soviet Government. Those facts are not compatible with the existence of a condominium regime for the waters in question during that period.

Mineral rights

Let us examine the practice of the littoral states in respect to Caspian mineral resources. The USSR started oil explorations in the Caspian in 1949. Had a condominium been in existence, one would have expected consultations with the co-owner, Iran. However, such consultations did not take place. Iran started oil operations in the continental shelf later and also without any consultations with the Soviet Union. That practice unequivocally indicates that both the Soviet Union and Iran did not consider Caspian mineral resources as an object of co-ownership, which was evidenced not only by their activities, but also by juridical sources. Thus, in the Soviet naval international–juridical reference book published in 1966, it was stated in respect of the Caspian that 'the resources of the continental shelf also belong to each party (USSR and Iran) within the limits of its respective area of the sea'. This statement undoubtedly reflected the official Soviet position of the time. Incidentally, this was supported by the 1968 USSR Decree on Measures Relating to the Prevention of Pollution of the Caspian Sea, which regulated Soviet oilfield activities. Although the Decree did not specify territorial extent, it is evident that it purported to impose obligations only on Soviet ministries, enterprises and vessels. There is no indication that the Decree had any application to Iranian activities in the Caspian or that there was any consultation with Iran concerning the Decree.

Regarding Iranian practice, the Act of 18 June 1955 on the Exploration and Exploitation of the Natural Resources of the Continental Shelf contains a Note to Article 2 concerning the Caspian, which is as follows:

> The submarine areas as well as natural resources of the seabed and the subsoil thereof, up to the limit of the continental shelf adjacent to the Iranian coast have belonged and shall continue to belong to Iran and shall remain under its sovereignty. Note: in respect to the Caspian Sea, the principles of international law relating to enclosed seas shall remain applicable.

Treaty implementation

The practice of the littoral states testifies to an accepted division of the Caspian Sea between the USSR and Iran, despite the fact that agreements signed by the two states did not contain any indications of this. In reality,

Soviet frontier guards ensured protection of the borders along the line Astara (Azerbaijan)–Gasankuli (Turkmenistan) in compliance with the Soviet NKVD Decree of 1935 and Iranian vessels could not cross this line to the north without permission. There was also a clear delimitation of the airspace over the Caspian along this line; on the Soviet side, this was heavily guarded. Those who wished to over-fly the area had to obtain permission from the Soviet authorities. All these cases serve as additional proof of the fact that there was no condominium regime in the Caspian at the time, and that this was recognised both by the USSR and Iran. I cannot find any evidence in the national legislation of the Soviet Union and its constituent republics to support the condominium claim. Article 4 of the Law of the USSR on Waters of 1970 states:

> All waters (or water objects) in the USSR shall constitute the unified water fund. The unified water fund shall include: (1) rivers, lakes, water reservoirs, other surface waters and water resources . . . (3) internal seas and other internal sea waters of the USSR.

No mention is made of any exception for the Caspian, in order to accommodate its alleged status as a condominium. Similarly the 1982 Law on the State Boundary of the USSR states:

> There shall be relegated to internal waters of the USSR: . . . (5) waters of rivers, lakes and other waters whose shores belong to the USSR.

Again no mention is made of any exception for the Caspian.

Regarding the exploitation of the Caspian underwater mineral resources I would like to demonstrate how this matter was treated by Soviet legislation. Under Article 76 of the Soviet Constitution, the Union Republics were sovereign soviet socialist states. Each republic exercised state power independently on its territory. The Union bodies managed the determination of 'general measures for the rational use and protection of natural resources'. According to the Constitution of the Kazakh Soviet Socialist Republic, the Republic exercised the exclusive right to its own land, mineral resources, waters and forests. Thus, according to Soviet legislation, ownership of minerals of the Caspian Sea was vested in each republic in the environs of the coastline.

In 1970 the Ministry of the Oil Industry of the USSR divided the Soviet part of the Caspian Sea into sectors belonging to Azerbaijan, Kazakhstan, Russia and Turkmenistan. As a basis for division into sectors, the median line was taken, as is generally adopted in international practice. Some experts have argued that this division was made on the basis of an administrative decision and cannot be regarded as a basis for international legal rulings. I cannot agree with this; in the former Soviet Union there did not exist state frontiers between the Union republics as understood from the point of view of international law. The borders were of an administrative–territorial character and, after the dissolution of the USSR, they were acknowledged by the newly independent states as interstate boundaries. There is no reason to make an exception for the Caspian region, which was also divided into national sectors allocated to the constituent republics of the Soviet Union.

Post-Soviet practice

The practice of the littoral states after the collapse of the Soviet Union also speaks to the effect of the absence of any joint utilisation of Caspian mineral resources. In point 2 of the Agreement between Azerbaijan and Russia, dated 20 November 1993, it is stated that the oilfields Azeri and Chirag belong to 'the Azerbaijan sector of the Caspian Sea'. The intergovernmental Agreement on Azerbaijan Oil Transportation through Russian Territory, signed in January 1996 by President Aliev and Prime Minister Chernomyrdin, also speaks of 'Azerbaijan oil extracted out of the Caspian Sea'. In Article 2 of this Agreement the Russian part admits that it 'does not own Azerbaijan oil'; i.e. at the highest governmental level it is acknowledged that Azerbaijan owns oil, extracted in the Azerbaijan sector of the Caspian Sea. Moreover, in both cases negotiations were held without the involvement of the other Caspian states; further, the agreements were signed without their participation. This means that both Russia and Azerbaijan did not regard the Caspian as a condominium or 'an object of common use', and did not consider the other Caspian states as having any legal interest in this matter.

Thus, a study of the whole body of treaty practice concerning the Caspian suggests that there is no support whatsoever for the argument that the Caspian was, historically speaking, a condominium. On the contrary, there are clear indications that the Caspian Sea was never considered to be a condominium.

Ecosystem

I would like to dwell on one more argument that was also often adduced in support of the condominium concept. This is the unity of an ecosystem which, allegedly, cannot be divided. This argument is utterly unpersuasive. Every land and maritime boundary in the world divides a unified ecosystem. Assertions that ecosystems should not be divided have in the past failed to convince international tribunals. (Thus, for example, the attempt to substantiate claims for a particular boundary line in the Gulf of Maine on the basis of the alleged ecological unity of certain areas was unsuccessful in the International Court.)

The ecological unity of the Caspian may make the co-operation of the littoral states in its management desirable, but it does not necessarily make a condominium, as opposed to any other form of co-operation, desirable. Much less does it entail the proposition that a condominium automatically exists in the Caspian.

Kazakhstan's position

Kazakhstan's position on the legal status of the Caspian Sea is clear and constructive. It proceeds from the concept of an enclosed sea and is an attempt to apply the main principles and provisions of the UN Convention on the Law of the sea to the Caspian. Nevertheless it does not mean a mechanical incorporation of the UN Convention provisions into a Convention on the Legal Status of the Caspian Sea. When we speak about applying the principles and some provisions of the UN Convention to the Caspian, we mean the adaptation of world practice to the peculiarities of the Caspian Sea. As applied to the Caspian, these provisions, if agreed upon by the parties concerned, could be transformed into norms. These might differ in legal status and terminological definition from the UN Convention. We have tried to take into account the peculiarities of the Caspian Sea, giving due consideration to the legal interests of all the littoral states, their shared interests in the utilisation of the Caspian and maintenance of its ecosystem, and the common desire for co-operation to secure development, peace and stability in the region.

Without going into a detailed consideration of Kazakhstan's position and its constituent elements, I shall set out here the main principles. Kazakhstan considers that the Caspian seabed and subsoil assets should be delimited among the littoral states, which should enjoy national jurisdiction and exclusive rights to explore and develop mineral resources in their parts of the seabed. We have taken into account international regulations and practice concerning mineral resources deposited beneath frontier waters. Likewise, we have given consideration to the long-standing practice of the USSR and Iran in the Caspian, which provides evidence that for many decades they prospected for oil independently and without mutual consultation. Thus we follow customary law, which actually served as a legal basis for Soviet and Iranian activities in exploiting Caspian oil. We are sure that such an approach meets the legitimate rights of all the Caspian states to the greatest extent possible.

Firstly, this enhances the responsibility of each littoral state for a correct and secure utilisation of the Caspian seabed resources in its corresponding part of the sea, and promotes efficient legal regulation of such an activity on the basis of the national legislation. Secondly, this decision opens a way for each littoral state to attract foreign direct investment, as well as to apply the most modern and safe technologies. This is crucial for the development of Caspian resources today, and in the foreseeable future. Thirdly, it creates a reliable and long-term legal basis for the activities of the Caspian states in the development of the seabed resources, avoiding the disputes in regard to definite deposits in the Caspian, which are inevitable if the other approach is applied. Thus we are talking about the establishment of a strong legal basis for the sake of peace and stability in the region.

I would like to stress that the government of Kazakhstan would allow other Caspian states to participate in the development of oil and gas deposits in Kazakhstan's sector of the seabed of the Caspian. There may be diverse forms of participation. Such participation would allow the Caspian states to implement their economic interests, to gain profit from the exploitation of the seabed. Kazakhstan is ready to negotiate on this issue both on a bilateral and multilateral basis. In this connection I would commend to your attention the Joint Declarations on Caspian Sea issues signed by Kazakhstan with both Russia and Iran, texts of which can be found in the Annexes below.

Annex 1

JOINT DECLARATION ON CASPIAN SEA ISSUES

During the talks which took place in Tehran on 11 May 1996, which corresponds to 22nd ovdibehesht of 1375 a.h., the President of the Republic of Kazakhstan and the President of the Islamic Republic of Iran discussed issues concerning the legal status of the Caspian Sea, also co-operation between the coastal states, exploitation and use of the mineral and biological resources of the sea, and protection of the natural environment. Taking into consideration the specific nature of the ecosystem of the Caspian Sea they came to the following mutual understanding:

1.   The parties consider that the drawing up and conclusion of the Convention on the legal status of the Caspian Sea, on the basis of a consensus between the five coastal states, is a task of the utmost importance which must not be delayed. The legal status of the Caspian Sea will encompass such issues as maritime traffic, the use of biological and mineral resources, protection of the environment, including raising the sea level, defining the limits of the sovereign laws and jurisdiction of the coastal states.

   Agreements will be concluded on various types of activity in the Caspian on the basis of the Convention on the legal status.

2.   The parties stress that the Caspian Sea and its mineral and biological resources belong to the coastal states and only these states have the right to take decisions on the issues concerning various activities in the Caspian.

3.   The parties agree that the activities of the coastal states in the Caspian region should be conducted on the basis of the following principles:

   •   adherence to the principles of the UN Charter stipulating respect for territorial integrity, political independence, sovereign equality of states, non-use, or threat of use, of force;

   •   use of the Caspian Sea exclusively for peaceful purposes;

- preservation of the Caspian Sea as a zone of peace, good neighbourliness, friendship and co-operation and solving of all problems related to the Caspian Sea by peaceful means;
- protection of the environment and the prevention of pollution of the Caspian Sea;
- preservation, reproduction and rational use of the biological resources of the Caspian Sea;
- responsibility of the Caspian states, physical and legal persons, for damage to the environment as well as to each other as a result of exploitation of the Caspian Sea and its resources;
- freedom and guarantee of safe commercial navigation in the Caspian Sea;
- compliance with other principles which will be agreed upon by them;
- the parties support the creation of an organisation for co-operation of the Caspian countries in accordance with the Communiqué of the Conference of the Heads of the Caspian states on 17 February 1992, which corresponds to 29th bahman of 1370 a.h., which would become a permanent mechanism for the realisation of the above listed principles and would promote the co-ordination of activities of the coastal states within the Caspian Sea.

4. The parties agree that only vessels sailing under the flags of the coastal states may navigate in the Caspian Sea.
5. The parties recognise each other's rights to exploitation and use of the mineral and biological resources of the Caspian Sea and if necessary will co-operate when using the natural resources within the Caspian Sea, help and consult each other in this field.
6. The parties want to intensify and raise the status of the negotiation process among the Caspian states on the legal status of the Caspian Sea. This is why they support a proposal to organise, in the near future, a meeting of the foreign ministers of the five Caspian states.

Signed two copies each in Kazakh, Persian and Russian with all texts being equally authentic.

President of the
Republic of Kazakhstan

President of the
Islamic Republic of Iran

Nursultan Nazarbaev

Akbar Khashemi Rafsanjani

(Translated by H. Plater-Zyberk)

Annex 2

JOINT DECLARATION ON CO-OPERATION IN THE USE OF THE CASPIAN SEA

Following discussions held in the city of Almaty on 27 April 1996 regarding the legal status of the Caspian Sea and the development of co-operation between the Caspian states, the President of the Republic of Kazakhstan N. A. Nazarbaev and the President of the Russian Federation B. N. Yeltsin came to the following mutual understanding:

1. The parties consider that the conclusion of the Convention on the Legal Status of the Caspian Sea is a task of utmost importance, which must not be delayed. The new legal status of the Caspian Sea should be determined by the Caspian states, based on consensus. No one has the right to decide the legal status of the Caspian Sea unilaterally. As a complex issue, the legal status should include problems of navigation, the use of biological and mineral resources, ecology, including the raising of the level of the sea and determining the limits of jurisdiction of the coastal states. The preparation of the convention of the legal status of the Caspian Sea will facilitate the conclusion of agreements on individual aspects of Caspian activities.

2. The parties agree that the activities of the littoral states in the Caspian Sea should be conducted on the basis of the following principles:
    *   the Caspian states will in their relations respect the principles of the UN Charter stipulating respect for sovereignty, territorial integrity, political independence, sovereign equality of states, non-use of force, or the threat of force;
    *   use of the Caspian Sea for peaceful purposes only;
    *   preservation of the Caspian Sea as a zone of peace, good neighbourliness, friendship and co-operation, resolving all questions linked with the Caspian Sea by peaceful means;
    *   protection of the environment and prevention of pollution of the Caspian Sea;
    *   preservation, reproduction and rational use of the biological resources of the Caspian Sea;
    *   responsibility of the Caspian states for damage to the environment as well as to each other as a result of exploitation of the Caspian Sea and its resources;
    *   freedom and guarantee of safe commercial navigation of the Caspian Sea states;
    *   and also compliance with other principles which will be agreed by them.

3. The parties agree that only vessels sailing under the flags of the coastal states may navigate in the Caspian Sea. The order and conditions of navigation in the Caspian Sea will be determined by separate agreements.

4. The parties are convinced that joint co-operation in harnessing the natural resources of the Caspian Sea is in their mutual interest. They accept each other's rights to conduct work to exploit the mineral and biological resources of the Caspian Sea and will exchange specific proposals on development of mutually beneficial co-operation, in accordance with an agreed programme, including geophysical and geological exploration work as well as exploitation of hydrocarbons, taking into consideration the experience and capabilities of the parties.

5. The parties wish to strengthen and raise the status of the negotiations among the Caspian states, on the legal status of the Caspian Sea. This is why they support a proposal to organise, in the near future, a meeting of the foreign ministers of the five Caspian states to consider the issues concerning the legal status and other problems of the Caspian Sea.

President of the
Republic of Kazakhstan

President of the
Russian Federation

(Signed)

(Signed)

Almaty,
27 April 1996

(Translated by H. Plater-Zyberk)

Part III

Geopolitics and Pipelines

4 Geopolitics of hydrocarbons in Central and Western Asia

Anoushiravan Ehteshami

Introduction

One of the unexpected by-products of the political chaos that followed the implosion of the Soviet superpower in 1991 was the emergence of the Caspian region as a potentially significant energy zone for the twenty-first century. In tandem with Central Asia's growing importance as a new sub-region of west Asia and the vast Eurasian landmass, the Caspian region developed in the course of the last decade of the twentieth century into an important security and strategic arena with an apparent potential to provide additional energy for the world economy. Such important strategic and geopolitical factors as hydrocarbon deposits and supply routes, and fears of Central Asian and Caucasian political instabilities affecting the neighbouring regions, combined to give these new countries and territories of the post-Cold War international system particular importance.

So extensive did regional and international interest in the Caspian region become in the 1990s that at times these post-Soviet territories resembled the battlefields of the Cold War era, where often rivalries between several Western powers, Western oil companies and Asian regional powers – such as Iran, Turkey, Pakistan, India, China, South Korea and of course Russia – were played out on the canvass of the new international order. In the post-Cold War environment, however, it was the remaining superpower, the United States, which displayed its force and flexed its considerable military and economic muscles most vigorously in pursuit of its emerging and evolving interests in the post-Soviet Caspian region. From the mid-1990s, the US began applying considerable pressure on its regional allies and adversaries alike to accept its presence and policies in west Asia.[1] Much of the backdrop to the exploration of the Caspian's hydrocarbon deposits, therefore, has been provided by the rivalries between regional and external powers for access and for development of the deposits.

Geopolitics of hydrocarbons on the eve of the twenty-first century

The erosion of the European continent's ideological and concrete walls, which began with their rapid fall in the late 1980s, coincided with the Soviet super-state's own overhaul strategy. The de-escalation in the Cold War and the dawn of a post-Cold War order was presaged by the 'downsizing' of the Soviet Union. The Caucasus was at the heart of the nationality crisis facing the Soviet state. Indeed, the first stitches of the Soviet fabric were undone in the Caucasus, towards the end of the 1980s, that is to say well before the European walls had begun to crumble. It was evident then that the Caspian region was to become of vital strategic importance to regional and international players, but the reason for its future importance – oil – was not yet apparent.[2] Baku, suffering from Moscow's neglect, was anxious to disguise the extent of its oil wealth until such time as it would be able to take control of this resource in the name of the Azeri state itself. The Baku leadership got its chance far sooner than anyone had expected, however, when a major armed conflict broke out between Azerbaijan and Armenia, causing a degree of panic in the Caucasus and the neighbouring regions (see **Nassibli**, p. 161). Thus, the regional states accelerated their pace of adjustment to the 'new realities' with remarkable ease when it finally became clear that the Soviet empire was not to survive the twentieth century and that Moscow's grip had been loosened forever.

The break-up of the Soviet Union provided the backdrop for the new geopolitical dynamics of hydrocarbons in the post-Cold War international order, but in addition to this development there were two other forces at play. First, the strategic changes in the Persian Gulf sub-region in the 1990s, where two of its key oil states, Iran and Iraq, found themselves in conflict with the world's biggest importer and consumer of oil, the US. The tussle between these three states left a clear mark on the political economy of oil, in which the US market was closed off to Iranian oil exports and Iraq was taken out of the international oil market, more or less completely for the next decade. Due to these circumstances, the US began the process of developing a parallel energy strategy in which Persian Gulf oil would play a minor role and other, preferably non-OPEC producers, would be targeted as the future suppliers of hydrocarbons for the American market. The arrival of Caspian oil on the map merely encouraged the US, and Western energy companies, actively to develop this energy strategy.

The other factor affecting the politics of oil in the 1990s was the impact of the relatively low oil prices during much of that decade on the established oil states. Low oil prices not only threatened the rentier economies of the Gulf region with a serious fiscal crisis, but actually left the world's main oil exporters severely short of the necessary investment capital for the modernisation and development of their oil industries. Oil income was badly needed not only for the financing of current expenditure in these states, but also for investment in future growth. Indeed, the oil price crisis had become so grave that in the late 1990s the oil exporters of the Middle East co-operated with their non-Middle Eastern counterparts in an effort to curtail production and boost prices. That this strategy worked was evident from rapid oil price increases: at the start of the twenty-first century prices had shot up from around US$12 a barrel in January 1999 to over US$30, hovering above the US$25 mark for much of the time. That proved to be the high-water mark as prices began their inevitable slide towards US$15 per barrel as we entered the twenty-first century.

To summarise, on the eve of the new millennium international interest in unexplored sources of hydrocarbons increased dramatically, even though low oil prices had dampened initial enthusiasm for the exploration of the Caspian's underdeveloped oil reserves. Nonetheless, as oil was again on the international agenda at the precise moment that the post-Soviet Caspian states were discovering the advantages of having a strategic resource under their soil, it was inevitable that the international spotlight should again fall on these new republics. The return of oil to the centre stage at the international level suited these new republics as much as it did the oil companies, which by the mid-1990s were in active search of new energy-related investment opportunities.[3] Thus, if not for immediate exploration, then such factors as concerns over supplier reliability and the need to develop potential strategic reserves drove international interest in Caspian oil.

Geopolitics of the Caspian

The Caspian Sea and its hinterland fall within the strategic orbit of several powers of different size, capability and ambition. Some of these powers had already exploited the Caspian's (non-oil) resources for economic gain. Others, in particular the new republics (Azerbaijan, Kazakhstan and Turkmenistan), regarded the Caspian as their only waterway and an important source of food and related products. For these states, unhindered access to the sea was a vital national objective. But in reality, just as in the twentieth century, only two powers finally determined the fate of the Caspian, so there could again be the same two powers which would have the resources to shape, if not determine, the Caspian's new geopolitics in the new century. The two powers in question were of course Iran and Russia, which dominated the southern and northern shores of the Caspian Sea respectively. But whereas at the beginning of the twentieth century Iran and the Soviet Union were left to their own devices to deal with their shared maritime border in the Caspian, in the twenty-first century, for strategic as much as for economic and political reasons, there was an increase in the efforts of several external powers to counterbalance Iranian and Russian power. More specifically, there was an attempt to check the entrenchment of Iranian and Russian influence in the Caspian basin.[4]

But, despite their indisputable reach, neither Tehran nor Moscow was able to stamp its own authority on the post-Soviet Caspian basin. The Caucasus, a region which had suffered severely from the tremors of the Soviet collapse, remained volatile. It had already suffered as a result of the inter-state conflict between Armenia and Azerbaijan, and felt the impact of Iranian–Azeri animosities, secessionist movements in Abkhazia and South Ossetia, and Russia's bloody military campaigns against separatist Chechen forces. Yet the evidence suggested that internal problems were unlikely to deter Iran or

Russia from active involvement in the Caspian region. On the contrary, the two states were likely to use every resource at their disposal to defend their interests in this increasingly strategic region. Indeed, in Russia's case, the Chechen wars of 1994–1996 and 1999 to the present, far from being a foreign-policy adventure, was part of a concerted effort to keep the Caspian's northbound supply routes within the Russian Federation (see **Blandy**).

In broader terms, the other actor which invested economic and security–political capital in the Caspian was the US. Despite the administration's ban on aid to the republic, the US had weighed in behind Azerbaijan, and also supported the other new Caspian states – Kazakhstan and Turkmenistan – in their efforts to consolidate their independence. In response to this strategy of the US, Armenia and Georgia began to form a closer economic relationship. At the same time, Armenia moved closer to Iran and Russia, signing a military co-operation treaty with the latter and entering into the pipeline politics of the Caspian by agreeing to the construction of a pipeline to take Iranian natural gas across its territory. In the event, this was one of the many pipeline projects that remained unrealised, but the close relationship between Iran and Armenia remained (see **Nassibli**, p. 176).

These 'alliances' and complex interrelationships revealed the weaving of the new cloth of Caspian strategic interdependencies. It was clear that a greater and more targeted involvement of the US was emerging in this isolated corner of west Asia. By the same token, there was engagement at a more direct level between the US (as the 'intrusive power' in the region), its local allies and the Caspian's resident heavyweights. In this sense, it could be argued that the post-Soviet scramble for Caspian oil cast the dye for future (oil-related) tensions in this region. These tensions might well take the shape of confrontations between the US-led West and a combination of regional powers – as had already happened in the oil-rich Persian Gulf.

The desire for control, which had perhaps been one of the defining features of the global oil business since the early 1900s, soon surfaced as a variable in Caspian interrelations. Following the collapse of the Soviet Union, the outside world's interest in 'free access' to the hydrocarbon resources of the Caspian increased. But in the West, especially in Washington, these interests were matched by fears that, in the medium term, regional powers such as Iran and Russia might, for their own selfish reasons, choose to block outside influence in the Caspian, thereby maintaining control of this increasingly strategic area.

Would the development of Caspian oil be accompanied by armed conflict for control of these resources? This would depend on several key developments. The most important of which were likely to be the following:

- the impact on the international oil market of growing interest from Asian hydrocarbon consumers (China, India, Japan, South Korea) in the deposits of the Caspian states;
- new hydrocarbon finds in the Caspian basin;
- fluctuations in the flow of oil from the Persian Gulf;

- massive increases in Caspian output to challenge the dominance of the Persian Gulf states;
- tensions between OPEC and the Caspian states if the Caspian states were to attempt to undermine OPEC's controlled output strategy;
- the full return of Iraqi oil to the market.

There were also regional factors which could affect the geopolitics of Caspian energy resources. These included the risk of political and ethnic upheavals in the Caucasus (see **Gerber**), which might threaten the security of Caspian hydrocarbon supply routes. The possibility of hegemonic rivalry among the Caspian states themselves could also not be discounted.

Geopolitics and geoeconomics of Caspian oil

To find and develop the Caspian's hydrocarbon resources was a big enough task in itself, requiring considerable technical skill and experience. But in the Caspian this problem was overshadowed by the difficulties associated with establishing viable (both structurally and economically) transport routes for these resources to reach the market. Most of the main hydrocarbon deposits were located offshore. Advanced Western know-how and technology were required in order to exploit them. Moreover, the skills and expertise of corporate leaders in the oil industry were needed to bring the oil and gas to international markets and consumers. And, above all, an adequate pipeline infrastructure had to be constructed. However, this issue was, from the outset, highly politicised.[5] On the one hand, the US wanted to by-pass Iranian and Russian territories by the construction of the Caspian and the Baku–Ceyhan pipelines. On the other, Iran and Russia tried to make the business case for the building and strengthening of existing north–south transportation routes. The fact that the Baku–Ceyhan pipeline – a project with an estimated price tag of US$3.5 billion – was even discussed was testimony to the power of the US and its ability to convince local actors in the Caucasus that political and security considerations should override financial calculations. It was an even greater triumph that the project proceeded to the point of formal sanction, enabling construction to begin in 2002 (see **Roberts**).

However, neither Iran nor Russia was prepared to abandon the Caspian's strategic prizes without a struggle; both continued to be engaged in their diplomatic battles for alternative transport routes out of the Caspian. The pivotal element in Iran's involvement in Caspian oil transportation was Neka, a port on the southern shore of the Caspian Sea that was already wholly devoted to oil storage and transportation. Existing facilities included eight oil bunkers outside the port zone as well as considerable capacity within this zone. There were five berths, with a phased development plan for extending this to nine berths in the future.[6] In 1996, despite US opposition to Iranian participation in the transport of Caspian oil, Tehran and Almaty signed a swap agreement whereby Kazakhstan would deliver 2 million tonnes of crude oil to Neka, and in exchange Iran would allocate an equivalent amount of its own oil on world markets to Kazakhstan. The deal foundered in 1997, when the refineries in northern Iran refused to accept Kazakh oil on account of its high sulphur content. However, the arrangement was revived in 2002 and, by the beginning of 2003, Iran was importing about 50,000 barrels per day (b/d) from Kazakhstan.[7] Volumes would be substantially increased when the Canadian company PetroKazakhstan (formerly known as Hurricane Hydrocarbons), operating the Kumkol field in southern Kazakhstan, began implementing an agreed swap deal at the end of that year. In March 2000 Tehran had taken a further step to enhance the viability of the Iranian option by pushing ahead with the construction of a 350-kilometre oil pipeline from Neka to Rey (near Tehran), one of the principle refineries in northern Iran. An upgrade was completed in September 2003 and a further upgrade was scheduled for 2004, which would enable Iran to shift up to 200,000 b/d of Caspian oil to its refining network. Future plans included the construction of a pipeline from Kazakhstan via Turkmenistan to Iran; TotalFinaElf undertook a feasibility study, due for completion in 2005, for this project.

Russia also sought to realise its pipeline ambitions. After some hesitation (see **Antonenko**) it joined the Caspian Pipeline Consortium (the Russian Federation acquired 24 per cent of the shareholding and Russian companies LUKoil and Rosneft, in partnership with Western companies, held a further 20 per cent stake).[8] This was formed to build a pipeline from the Tengiz field in western Kazakhstan to the Russian port of Novorossiysk on the Black Sea. The project was delayed by numerous financial and management problems, but was finally inaugurated in 2001. Meanwhile, other pipelines linking the region to Russia remained operational. The pipeline from Atyrau (Kazakhstan) to Samara (Volga region) had, after upgrading, a capacity of 310,000 b/d. Further south, the Baku–Novorossiysk pipeline via Chechnya had a capacity of 120,000 b/d. 'Early oil' exports from the offshore Azeri–Chirag–Guneshli field through this pipeline began in 1997 and, in 2001, averaged 50,000 b/d. A short spur was added in 2000, to bypass Chechnya and to connect direct to the Russian Caspian port of Makhachkala. An upgrade was planned for completion in 2005 which would expand capacity to 360,000 b/d.[9]

Apart from the hype that surrounded the potential of Caspian oil and natural gas reserves, the key attraction of the Caspian reserves to international oil companies was that, at least in the early years, the new states were prepared to offer fairly generous concessions to the oil majors. This was particularly welcome at a time when the oil business itself was consolidating and very few new business opportunities in upstream investment were forthcoming. Here was a potential bonanza situation with few political strings attached. Few questions were raised, at least in public debates, concerning such issues as the substantial problem of security. Few commentators even questioned the authenticity of the data on Caspian reserves.[10] It was at this critical juncture that Western states entered into co-operative arrangements with the Caspian states, which in turn provided the conditions for closer political and diplomatic relations. In short, there was an unexpected and untested convergence of interests between very different groups of states.

By and large, the relationship between these states on the one hand, and the West, and in particular the US, on the other hand, was at this stage governed by two simple calculations. For the former, 'Oil and gas reserves are just about the only effective symbol of the new republics' independence, a unique tool to execute their development projects and also their only means to possibly distance themselves from Russia'.[11] On the part of the US, the expectation was that 'the Caspian region will hopefully save [the US and its allies] from total dependence on Middle East oil'.[12] The chief US concern was that 'stable and assured energy supplied from the Caspian [would reduce American] vulnerability to disruption in world energy supplies'.[13] From the perspective of the US, having invested in the exploration of the Caspian's oil, it was vital that this oil should not flow southwards via the Straits of Hormuz since this would defeat the object of diversification of supplies by giving countries like Iran an even greater lever in relation to the Caspian–Persian Gulf energy zone and effective control over both Persian Gulf and Caspian oil flows. There were similar objections to westward routes, since this would reinforce Russia's position in the Caspian. Thus, the only acceptable routes were those that ran westwards and eastwards.

It was based on such a confluence of interests that the US began the process of developing a Caspian strategy. Although the US had made its presence felt in this region as early as 1993, it was in 1997 that it declared a new commitment to what had thus far been seen as Russia's domain – its so-called 'near abroad'. The US not only actively encouraged the development of the Caspian's hydrocarbon deposits and sought to secure a 'safe passage' for Caspian oil and gas, but also assembled a security regime which offered protection for the states of the Caspian basin. Furthermore, it tried to encourage the development of democracy and the market system in these countries.

The US had accepted that it could not realise these ambitious programmes without the support of local actors and allies, and, in the classic manner of Cold War diplomacy, it set about creating the conditions for the expansion of its influence in this region. Thus, between 1997 and 2000, Israeli involvement in the region was increased, while Turkey became the main pillar of US oil strategy in the Caspian. Moreover, the Pentagon revised its existing areas of responsibility for its commands by reassigning the Caucasus and Central Asia to specific and different US military commands.[14]

In a word, encouraged by the mineral wealth of the Caspian states and now no longer hampered by the pressures of the Cold War, the US set about creating new levers of influence in the heart of Asia. Thus, it tried to nestle the Caspian countries into a pro-Western orbit. In this context, US actions – which could be interpreted as displaying neo-hegemonic tendencies – signalled what appeared to be a long-term commitment to the Caspian, in which 'NATO and American involvement [would have to be] sustained and open-ended'.[15] Regional powers in the shape of Iran, India, China, Pakistan and Russia began to take stock of this reality. While some of these states started looking for ways of accommodating the US, others were actively seeking ways of rendering the American presence limited and ineffective in the long run.

Caspian energy reserves

Proven Caspian oil reserves were, as the estimates in Table 4.1 indicate, not too impressive. However, the region's potential oil reserves were massive and could, if found, turn the Caspian into a leading source of energy for future decades. It was based on these estimates that some analysts calculated the Caspian's locked hydrocarbons to be worth somewhere in the region of US$4 trillion in total. And it was this kind of sum that drove the oil majors' interest in the strategic reserves of the Caspian, despite the fact that the cost of extracting a barrel of oil there was many times higher than in the Persian Gulf (in the Persian Gulf extraction costs were generally below US$1 per barrel, while in the Caspian the cost was likely to be around or above US$5 per barrel, thus on a par with the North Sea costs).

It was estimated that by 2015 the Caspian would be producing up to 4 million barrels of oil per day, more than Iran's output in 2000. Such a level of output, if sustained, would bring significant riches to the producer countries, generating in excess of US$10 billion in annual income for these countries. But, as the Caspian's reserves were much smaller than those of the Persian Gulf, the Caspian oil states and the oil majors would be seeking to optimise the return on their huge investments by maximising output. Such a strategy was not only likely to fall foul of the Gulf states, but also of other non-OPEC exporting countries with equally limited reserves (such as Mexico, Yemen and Indonesia) who were also looking for revenue maximisation through exports. The estimates of the Caspian's natural gas reserves, by contrast with the oil, were more encouraging. These statistics shown in Table 4.1, therefore, provided support for the contention that this region

Table 4.1 Oil and gas resources of the Caspian region

Country	Oil proven resources (low/high range) (bbl)	Oil potential resources (bbl)	Gas proven resources (Tcf)	Gas potential resources (Tcf)
Azerbaijan	7/12.5	32	30	35
Iran*	0.1	15	0	10.6
Kazakhstan	9/17.6	92	65	88.3
Russia*	0.3	7	n/a	n/a
Turkmenistan	0.5/1.7	38	71	158.9

Source: Energy Information Administration of the USA, August 2003.

Notes
*Only regions near the Caspian included.
bbl = billion barrels, Tcf = trillion cubic feet.

would probably emerge as a key player in the international energy market of the twenty-first century.

Domestic and regional problems

Assuming that the hydrocarbon projects would proceed smoothly, the Caspian states were set to develop into fully fledged oil states in the first quarter of the twenty-first century. They would then encounter a wide and diverse range of problems which would have to be managed. One such negative effect would be a growing disparity between the rich and the poor across the region as a whole, as well as within the countries themselves. A two-speed Caspian basin, divided between a small group of haves and many havenots, would impose tremendous tensions on the region's already fragile socio-economic, ethnic and state structures. The consequences would probably lead to more interstate tensions and prolonged crises between groups within countries as well as between the states of the region. Also, the Caspian states would probably discover that their oil wealth would more than likely bring them into direct competition with their OPEC counterparts. Such rivalries, if allowed to fester, could have serious consequences for the international oil market and, ultimately, for the economic stability of the new oil states themselves.

Some of these problems might be avoided, however, if these states were prepared to revisit history and not to repeat the mistakes of the Persian Gulf's oil-based socio-economic systems. Thus, they could with profit draw some useful lessons from the actions and experiences of their southern neighbours. Certainly, oil wealth transformed societies and economies in the Gulf states; the huge injection of capital enabled them to create new and sophisticated economies virtually from scratch in less than a generation. However, such rapid transformation was not cost free.[16] Firstly, the Gulf experience shows that rapid injection of capital and hard currency into developing economies is likely to be highly destabilising and inflationary. Therefore, in the Caspian's fragile economic situation, capital should be allowed to enter the local economy only slowly, and then solely for realisable and well-thought out investment projects. Secondly, governments should refrain from raising the population's expectations in relation to the application of oil income. They should not be given to believe that oil will be a panacea for all their ills: it has not been a limitless blessing in the Persian Gulf, and is not likely to be in the Caspian either. Thirdly, these states should not underestimate the impact of the inevitable disparities in wealth, income and opportunity that sustained and substantial oil wealth will bring. Fourthly, oil wealth impacts on relations with neighbouring countries. Therefore, just as the oil income will have to be carefully managed, so too will relations with the 'havenot' neighbours in a volatile and potentially unstable region.

Lastly, these states need to understand the volatile nature of the oil business as well as the sorts of interdependencies that oil exports can generate between an economy based on oil production and an international economic system still dependent on it. With regard to the former factor, careful planning, not only of output but also of consumption, will be required. No new oil state can afford to let itself become totally hostage to the volatile international oil market, and certainly not those who find themselves outside of the OPEC cartel. The oil states of the Caspian will need to develop their economies along several tracks consecutively. They could take a lead from countries such as Bahrain, Qatar, Saudi Arabia and the United Arab Emirates that have pursued the goal of creating a diversified economic base, while maintaining the oil sector as their chief source of revenue and hard currency.

On the question of interdependencies, the economic fortunes of the Gulf states are fully tied to the prosperity of Western consumer societies, whose economies and consumption patterns ultimately determine the international price of oil. So, too, are their economic development strategies, in terms of access to know-how, planning and execution. This pattern is likely to be repeated in the Caspian region: oil is likely to be their link to the outside world. However, these new states should be aware that, while oil prices are not as elastic as those for most other commodities, nevertheless, oil is the one commodity which is super-sensitive to such factors as international political changes (major security crises, global environmental debates, political upheavals, etc.), the weather (in terms of warm winters dampening demand in the West) and international economic developments (note the impact of the Asian economic and financial crisis of the late 1990s on the price of oil). Thus, oil will inevitably internationalise the producer's economy: 'Oil availability and cost are an integral part of international comparative advantages in many product lines. And Western lifestyle, if not lifeblood – from fertilisers for food, gasoline for transport, and plastics and chemicals as the building blocks of modern life – is vitally dependent on oil.'[17]

Consequently, if oil wealth is allowed to dictate the producing country's diplomacy, it can give birth to, and drive, new types of tensions. By extension, the new oil states must consider their national security. Their hydrocarbon deposits and related facilities will need to be protected from the risk of attack or any other form of hazard. On the other hand, oil and oil income can provide the means as well as the rationale for militarisation of the producer state. This in turn can encourage an expensive and futile arms race, deepen sub-regional rivalries and encourage regional powers to intervene. The recent history of the Persian Gulf provides ample evidence of the ways in which oil states can lose control. These include a fear of internal change (even if sought through peaceful and democratic means), leading in turn to the entrenchment of authoritarian regimes. There is also the possibility of predatory tendencies emerging in the larger states; smaller countries risk ending up as potential prey for their more powerful neighbours. Massive imports of arms make interference in the internal affairs of others more likely, increasing the potential for conflict. Worst of all, a pervasive sense of distrust and suspicion enters interstate relations. This catalogue of the problems that the Persian Gulf has experienced can almost all be linked to the regional dynamics that oil has created.

It is therefore imperative that the Caspian's new states pay attention to the dynamics that oil production and oil wealth create and from the outset control this tendency by establishing mechanisms and structures that minimise regional instability. It is ironic that the West is already feeding into Caspian rivalries, heightening tensions over the oil transportation routes out of the region, and straining relations between the new Caspian states and their Iranian and Russian neighbours – the very two countries which have the means at their disposal to undermine or reinforce the prosperity of the new oil states.

Conclusions

It could be claimed that the demise of the Soviet empire provided the primary impulse for the changing dynamics of the Caspian region. An equally important catalyst for future change in this region, however, is oil and the relationship between this resource and the geopolitics of the Caspian basin. Indeed, it could be argued that within less than a decade the Caspian's hydrocarbon resources emerged as one of the main determining factors in intraregional relationships in the Caucasus and Central Asia. Oil defined the geopolitics of the Persian Gulf and it is doing so again to the north of Iran. In other words, in the twenty-first century the spatial recognition of the Caspian states as post-Soviet political and economic appendages has been superseded by a perspective driven by oil. We now see these countries through a new prism, based on a 'geo-economic and geo-strategic model, characterised by the importance of oil, gas, and pipelines'.[18]

Despite the increasing 'hydrocarbonisation' of their economies, the size of the region's hydrocarbon deposits means that the Caspian states must prepare for life after oil much sooner than the established oil states. Indeed, if we were to adopt a more accurate point of reference for the conditions of the Caspian's oil wealth then we should compare the oil potential of the Caspian states not with the Persian Gulf, but rather with that of the North Sea states.[19] It has been suggested that the Caspian states will need to hope for the same coincidence of events in the twenty-first century which enhanced the potential of the North Sea's oil producers in the third quarter of the twentieth century (namely, the need for relatively high prices after the 1974 oil price rises to justify expenditure on expensive offshore technologies, high demand, political uncertainty in the Gulf, and application of technologies which could secure high margins despite high extraction and transportation costs).

But, as things stand, there is every chance that history may not be as generous to the Caspian states as it was to the North Sea's oil producers. First, prices are likely to fall in the first quarter of this century, which will lower commercial interest in producing oil from such high-cost locations as the Caspian. Secondly, high taxation in the Western economies will probably begin to check the growth in demand for fossil fuels, precisely at the juncture that Caspian producers will be going online. Furthermore, as the high cost of fossil fuel in the West is encouraging the search for 'clean' energy so there will come a time in the mid-twenty-first century when every oil state will be looking at low demand from their traditional markets. In this scenario, it will be the high-cost producers who will sink first. Thirdly, as OPEC's oil producers open their upstream operations to foreign investment (as Kuwaiti, Qatari, Iraqi and Iranian oil sectors are already doing), so the majors are likely to reduce their exposure in the Caspian and refocus on the oil-rich regions. Fourthly, major investment in the hydrocarbon industries of the Gulf states will inevitably lead to more output of oil and natural gas, hence a cheaper barrel of oil at the well-head. This will increase competition against the Caspian producers.

Finally, other non-OPEC producers in Africa, the Middle East, Latin America and Asia are already supplying oil to their own regions as well as for the international market. Indeed, as the market becomes more region-alised (Venezuela and Mexico supply the American market, Indonesia, Brunei and Malaysia supply the Asian countries, the Gulf states feed both the European and Asian markets, Libya and Algeria concentrate on Europe), it is hard to see how the Caspian's new producers can capture a significant share of the market in any of these high-demand zones. Geography becomes a key factor: lack of access to the high seas conditions the options of the Caspian states, which means that the direction of pipelines and transport routes is likely to determine the direction of hydrocarbon exports as well, irrespective of the market conditions at the consumer end. In a highly competitive market place, limiting one's options will result in high premiums having to be offered to lure carriers and consumers alike, which will inevitably eat into anticipated profit margins.

It is not all doom and gloom, however. Other indicators may provide a more encouraging outlook for the Caspian oil producers. One of the key positive indicators has to be the changing nature of demand. Most observers expect an explosion in Asian demand, sustained by average annual economic growth rates of over 5.5 per cent in the next two decades. By 2015, China alone will probably be importing some 4 million barrels of oil a day – equivalent to the Caspian basin's projected output figure – and India a further 1 million barrels per day. Furthermore, in a world where demand for oil could reach 100 million b/d by 2020, and for oil equivalents 150 million b/d, the Caspian states will be well placed to reap benefits through their hydrocarbons exports. Moreover, if the prediction that some 60 per cent of the world's total energy demand in 2020 will be met from oil and natural gas proves to be accurate, then the Caspian exporters are unlikely to be suffering from lack of customers.[20]

In the medium term, the Caspian oil states could also benefit from other factors, such as the decline in non-OPEC output from 2005, and the rapid increases in domestic demand in some of the established oil exporting countries (Algeria, Indonesia, Iran, Iraq, Nigeria). They would consequently decrease their oil exports, which would open a window of opportunity for the Caspian producers.

If the Caspian basin's geopolitical situation is to work to the advantage of the region as a whole, it is important to enable not only the littoral states, but also their neighbours to share in the benefits of wealth generation. This would require certain fundamentals to be put in place. The end of the Cold War has opened up a limitless range of possibilities in the Caspian region and elsewhere in the world, yet it is still Cold War politics which seems to be dictating the thinking of the key actors. Therefore, if oil is to reach its full potential, a new web of prosperity must be woven around the Caspian. The actors in this development must learn to treat this mineral less as a strategic resource to be controlled, but more as a commodity whose benefits should be shared. In other words, development without security is today an impossibility. However, if oil is to provide the catalyst for the development of the Caspian region, then its security must be defined much more broadly than merely assuring the safety of its fixed assets. For the Caspian region to avoid the political and security traumas of the Persian Gulf, the five littoral states will need to incorporate into their definition of security not only the interests of the few haves but also the needs of the many havenots.

Notes

1 For details, see A. Ehteshami, 'The Geopolitics of Hydrocarbons in West Asia', *Iranian Journal of International Affairs*, vol. XI, no. 3, Fall 1999, pp. 435–454; A. Myers Jaffe and R. A. Manning, 'The Myth of the Caspian "Great Game": The Real Geopolitics of Energy', *Survival*, vol. XXXX, no. 4, Winter 1998–1999, pp. 112–129.

2 See J. Hemming, *The Implications of the Revival of the Oil Industry in Azerbaijan*, Durham Middle East Papers 58, Durham (UK), 1998.

3 To put the problem facing the oil companies at that time in perspective, let us note that for various reasons (sanctions, war, etc.), for much of the 1990s Libya, Algeria, Iraq and Iran were almost completely off their investment lists. North Sea oil was reaching the end of its natural production cycle and the Gulf Arab states were unprepared to allow foreign investment into their core oil businesses. To the frustration of the oil companies, these problems were occurring just as demand was taking off in the Far East, Europe and Latin America.

4 E. Herzig, *The New Caucasus: Armenia, Azerbaijan and Georgia*, Pinter/Royal Institute for International Affairs, London, 1999.

5 For an excellent discussion of the related issues see R. H. Dekmejian and H. H. Simonian, *Troubled Waters: The Geopolitics of the Caspian Region*, I. B. Tauris, London, 2001.

6 M. R. Farzanegan, 'Iranian Options Most Economically Viable for Exporting Caspian Oil', *Oil and Gas Journal*, 17 March 2003.

7 *Dow Jones Newswires*, 6 February 2003.

8 *Kazakhstan: Investment Profile 2001*, EBRD, London, 2001.

9 Website of Energy Information Administration, US Department of Energy, Caspian region, information as of mid-2003 (http://eia.doe.gov).

10 For a useful discussion of the reserves issue, see *The Changing Face of Energy Politics*, OECD, Paris, 2000.

11 M. Mozaffari, 'The Oil and Gas of the Caspian Sea: Regional Co-operation and Competition', in M. Mozaffari (ed.), *Security Politics in the Commonwealth of Independent States: The Southern Belt*, Macmillan, London, 1997, p. 200.

12 The US Secretary for Energy, quoted in Jaffe and Manning, *op. cit.*, p. 112.
13 Statement of Counsellor Jan Kalicki, chief government CIS energy strategist based in the US Department of Commerce. Press release, February 1998.
14 In 1998 the Caucasus became an area of responsibility for the European Command of the United States, while Central Asia was brought under the responsibility of the US Central Command. These US security moves were underlined by several gestures, such as joint military exercises with Uzbekistan, Kazakhstan and Kyrgystan on the one hand, and the very public material and political support that Washington gave to the leaders of these countries on the other. See M. Shimizu (ed.), *The Caspian Basin and Its Impact on Eurasian Power Games*, Institute of Developing Economies, Tokyo, 1998.
15 B. McGuinn, 'NATO's Prize: The Euro-Atlantic Security System and the Caspian Sea Region', *Silk Road*, vol. 1, no. 2, December 1997, p. 16.
16 See J. Amuzegar, *Managing the Oil Wealth: OPEC's Windfalls and Pitfalls*, I. B. Tauris, London, 1999; K. A. Chaudhry, *The Price of Wealth: Economies and Institutions in the Middle East*, Cornell University Press, Ithaca, New York, 1997.
17 Amuzegar, *op. cit.*, p. 12.
18 M. Mohamadi, quoted in Shimizu, *op. cit.*, p. 8.
19 T. Waelde, S. Vinogradov and A. Zamora, 'The Caspian Dilemma: Prosperity or Conflict?', *OPEC Bulletin*, vol. XXX, no. 10, October 1999, pp. 12–15 and p. 54; J. Lee, 'Oil Price Trends and Investment Prospects in the Caspian Sea', *Caspian Oil and Gas Resources: Transport Routes Security and Economic Development*, Institute for International Energy Studies, Tehran, 1999, pp. 142–153.
20 In 1999, Exxon was predicting that 75 per cent of the world's oil and natural gas would be produced from fields not yet onstream. See *OPEC Bulletin*, vol. XXX, no. 10, October 1999, p. 21. The *World Energy Outlook 2002*, International Energy Agency, OECD, Paris, gives more recent, but nevertheless similar, estimates.

5   Pipeline politics

John Roberts

The fall of the Soviet Union coincided with two key developments in the development of Caspian energy: negotiations with a leading US oil company on development of the Tengiz oilfield in Kazakhstan and a rundown of the oil industry in Azerbaijan just as Soviet oilmen were struggling to develop substantial proven reserves in relatively complex deepwater formations. This made it extremely important for the new governments of Kazakhstan and Azerbaijan, now deprived of Moscow's largesse, to secure quick and effective development of these major resources in order to boost the limited stream of government revenues. At the same time they had to cope with a change of pipeline policy in Moscow. The old Soviet system had served all the republics of the Soviet Union on an integrated basis, but now the natural preference of the Russian energy companies would be to use the system for Russian energy first and, only secondarily, to carry oil and gas produced by fellow Soviet producers that could now be regarded as commercial rivals. For the next ten years, Azerbaijan and Kazakhstan would work assiduously to develop new export routes that were either independent of Russia or at least less susceptible to Russian control whilst still having to remain on good terms with Moscow to ensure that their existing oil and gas export systems were not jeopardised. So, too, would Turkmenistan, though in a somewhat more erratic fashion. A decade of effort would eventually lead to the development of two major oil export pipeline systems and the construction or upgrading of a number of lesser oil and gas lines. The two major lines, both of which were to prove complex and contentious, were the Caspian Pipeline Consortium's 1,510-km line connecting Kazakhstan's giant Tengiz oilfield with the Russian Black Sea port of Novorossiysk, and the 1,760-km line from Baku through Georgia to the Turkish Mediterranean port of Ceyhan. The CPC line opened for business in 2001 while the first contracts for actual physical construction of the Baku–Tbilisi–Ceyhan line were awarded in August 2002, with completion scheduled for early 2005.

A major theme of the first decade of independence was, naturally, the development of indigenous energy resources. In particular, this meant the development of two giant energy fields in Kazakhstan: Tengiz and the gas-and-condensate field at Karachaganak. It also meant the development of two giant offshore projects in Azerbaijan: the Azeri–Chirag–Guneshli

(ACG) oil megastructure and the virtually adjacent Shah Deniz gas field. Finally, it entailed the continued carriage to market of considerable volumes of previously developed Turkmen gas. These five elements remained constant throughout the decade and, even in 2002, they are only just beginning to be challenged by the emergence of a sixth major element, Kazakhstan's giant offshore oil discovery at Kashagan. A combination of commercial, geographical and political factors – combined with ownership and operating structures at Tengiz, Karachaganak and ACG – ensured that the main focus would be on the development of new routes to the west, in essence to reach the European and Mediterranean markets and, beyond that, the US. Development of routes to the east or south – with the notable exception of a limited opening for Turkmen gas sales to Iran – would generally remain an issue for a new generation of field development and energy strategy. Overall, the main issue in this first decade of independence was how to secure the required export capacity for the expected production from these leading fields. Kazakhstan needed facilities to serve a proposed plateau production level of 700,000 barrels per day (b/d) – i.e. 35 million tonnes per year (mt/y) – from Tengiz, and some 200,000 b/d of condensate from Karachaganak (whilst also looking at the longer-term development of a gas export system for Karachaganak). Azerbaijan would require export facilities for a proposed plateau production level at ACG of 800,000 b/d (40 mt/y), a target raised in 2001/2002 to 1.0 mb/d (50 mt/y). Against this was the reality that, as of 1992, Kazakhstan had agreements with Russia to carry barely 10 mt/y of crude to international markets, whilst Azerbaijan's sole oil pipeline to the rest of the world was a run-down line through the rebellious Russian republic of Chechnya, which possessed a nominal capacity at its Azerbaijani end of just 9 mt/y. One result of the imbalance between pipeline capacity and export potential was, until the opening of CPC, a heavy reliance by Kazakhstan on alternative methods for oil transportation. By 2001, it was estimated that oil companies in Kazakhstan were exporting as much as 350,000 b/d (17.5 mt/y) by various alternative methods, of which some 240,000 b/d was exported by rail; much of the rest was sent by ship across the Caspian to Baku or through the Volga–Don canal system to the Black Sea.

The immediate years in the wake of the Soviet collapse and the unexpected attainment of political independence by the new Caspian republics were tough for both the governments and peoples of the newly independent states, with old industries collapsing and both national and personal incomes contracting. In the case of Azerbaijan, oil revenues – often in the form of upfront payments for production sharing contracts – came to form virtually the sole source of hard cash for a country which had to cope not only with independence, but also with the aftermath of civil strife. The Karabagh conflict (see **Nassibli**, p. 161) had resulted in the loss of around one-fifth of its territory and the displacement of up to 1 million of its 7 million people. Kazakhstan enjoyed both a more diverse economy and a considerably less troubled transition from Soviet rule to independence. Even so, oil revenues were what gave the government its ability to weather the economic storms that accompanied the collapse of its Soviet-era economy.

At independence, the pipeline issue immediately came to the fore. In the Soviet era there was no problem: any oil or gas discoveries in any Soviet republic that were considered worth developing would be plugged in to the national network. If they could not be plugged in, they were regarded as not worth developing. But the priorities for Kazakhstan and Azerbaijan were different. They had to consider not only how to develop their resources – and, in the case of Kazakhstan in particular, how to maintain development of existing resources – but also how their exports should be taken to market. As early as 1993, Kazakh officials were openly complaining that the new post-Soviet regime in Russia was taking advantage of its pipeline monopoly to make Kazakhstan pay a heavy price for its reliance on Russia's gasline system. For, while Kazakhstan is a gas producer, its production is concentrated in the northwest of the country and its principal outlet and transit route – including such gas as may eventually be shipped to Kazakhstan's industrial centres in the east of the country – is via Russia. And not only did Russia use its position as a monopsony purchaser to force Kazakhstan to accept only a fraction of the world price for gas entering Russia from western Kazakhstan, it also used its position as monopoly shipper to force the Kazakhs to pay much higher prices for gas exported from Russia to eastern Kazakhstan. During its first decade of independence, lack of funds and lack of a sufficiently large internal market meant that Kazakhstan could not pursue a prime strategic goal of its long-term energy policy: development of an internal west-to-east gas pipeline that would enable gas produced at Karachaganak and elsewhere in northwestern Kazakhstan to move directly to the former capital at Almaty and other industrial cities in the east without having to transit Russia. The Karachaganak developers said in mid-2002 that they expected a new pipeline to carry condensate from the field to an intersection with the CPC line to be completed in early 2003. This target was achieved and pipeline operations commenced in July 2003 (though interrupted shortly afterwards, owing to technical problems, and not resumed until April 2004). However, it was not clear when they expected to be able to export large volumes of Karachaganak gas, which depends on the ability of Eni, BG and their partners to tap into the Gazprom system at Orenburg.

The issue of new external pipelines was not immediately of crucial importance to the newly independent states, although its long-term importance was never denied. Throughout the first decade of independence, much of Kazakhstan's oil output was able to secure access to a mixture of soft and hard cash markets by reason of its continued input into the Russian export system. In the early years, some 9–10 mt/y (180,000–200,000 b/d) of oil was transferred into Russia's giant east–west Druzhba pipeline system via the existing pipeline from Atyrau at the northern end of the Caspian Sea to the Russian refining centre at Samara. In recent years this has gradually been increased so that, as of July 2002, Kazakhstan now has rights to ship some 15mt/y through this route, plus a further 2.5 mt/y via a new Russian line from the Caspian coastal port of Makhachkala that connects with the southern Russian pipeline system and its Black Sea export terminal at Novorossiysk. But while such levels are adequate to handle most of Kazakhstan's Soviet-era export capabilities, the development of new sources of oil prompted the need for new export systems. At the same time, fresh thought had to be given to development of new systems for gas exports, or for increased gas exports via the existing Russian network.

To a large extent, the issue of pipelines as a key theme in what some have termed a new Great Game for control of the Eurasian heartland arose because of the accident of timing. Under Mikhail Gorbachev, the Soviet Union had recognised the need to secure Western expertise in developing problematic energy reserves. Despite intensive efforts at Tengiz, a field known to contain several billions of barrels of recoverable oil, the Soviets themselves were only able to produce the merest trickle of actual production. So, in the late 1980s and early 1990s, Moscow negotiated with a US company Chevron for the investment of Western capital and provision of Western expertise in developing the field. But, because these negotiations were not completed when Kazakhstan secured independence in late 1991, no firm agreement had been made concerning actual delivery of Tengiz oil to international markets – although the general route had been agreed: it would be via a new major oil pipeline to Novorossiysk, which the Russians began building in the 1980s. In fact, it was not until April 1993 that a final agreement was signed between Chevron and the state authorities of newly independent Kazakhstan, whereby the US company would secure a half share in the field – and become its operator.

In Azerbaijan, a roughly similar case situation obtained. Soviet geologists had discovered a cluster of major oilfields off Azerbaijan's Caspian coast, but with relatively little actual production at the time of independence. Yet the scale of the reserves meant vast amounts of cash would be required to develop the new resources. It was not until 1993 that the Azerbaijani government first reached agreement on a major offshore development, and it did so by getting a cluster of international companies who were interested in securing access to this new resource to pool their involvement in a single concession, which was given rights to develop three fields – Azeri, Chirag and (deepwater) Guneshli. Internal instability meant that a final agreement on developing the ACG megastructure was only concluded in September 1994, with the developers' consortium becoming known as the Azerbaijan International Operating Company (AIOC). Initially, the new company acted as its own operator but, in time, British Petroleum (BP) became first the dominant member of the group, then later the formal operator of the concession. This had important ramifications for the development of pipeline policy, leading to the development in 1998–1999 of a policy to construct a direct oil export pipeline from Baku to Ceyhan.

In the months immediately following independence, the most notable proposals for new pipeline systems came from two sources: a buccaneering oil entrepreneur called John Deuss and Botaş, the Turkish state pipeline monopoly. Deuss, who had secured international notoriety as an oil trader by selling oil from the Persian Gulf to apartheid-era South Africa, in defiance of recommended (but non-mandatory) UN sanctions, clearly saw the emergence of new opportunities for oil trading. The interest of Botaş reflected Turkey's triple roles as owner of Ceyhan, the nearest open-water oil terminal to the Caspian; as a major oil consumer in its own right; and as a country with historic – but previously underdeveloped – ethnic, linguistic and religious ties to the newly independent Caspian states. In October 1992, Deuss hosted a private conclave in Bermuda to which leading oil companies were invited. At this meeting, his associates put forward a range of options for the carrying of oil by pipeline from the Caspian to Western markets. The initial studies undertaken by his specially formed Caspian Pipeline Consortium (CPC) included possible systems that would take in Azerbaijani oil as well, but Deuss and his group were primarily concerned with the transport of oil from Tengiz to Western markets.

In time, CPC was to focus on only one route: the completion of the system begun in the Soviet era intended to link Tengiz with the Kazakh refining centre at Atyrau and thence to the Russian pipeline interconnection at Tikhoretsk and on to the Black Sea port of Novorossiysk. Roughly half of this proposed 1,500-km line would have to be brand new; the rest would consist of pipe laid down by the Soviets (though this would need to be upgraded to Western standards). Although Botaş kept producing proposals for Azerbaijani exports, no real progress could be made in this regard until September 1994, when AIOC signed the deal that was popularly dubbed the 'Contract of the Century' for the development of the ACG complex (see **Olsen**, p. 130). The problem confronting CPC was a complex one. The authority of the then still new Russian President Boris Yeltsin was uncertain. Oil transport through Russia was monopolised by state-owned Transneft, which had no wish to open its lines to foreign competitors to Russia's state-dominated oil companies. Deuss's own history told against him. He believed the venture could be put together as a tripartite deal between the governments of Russia, Kazakhstan and Oman. The Omanis were involved because Deuss had become president of the Oman Oil Company, which acted as the international arm – in energy matters – of the Omani state authorities, although mainstream Omani oil and gas operations continued to be under the control of the well-established Petroleum Development Oman. Deuss failed to get the project off the ground, despite conducting some extremely useful and detailed feasibility studies along CPC's chosen route. Ultimately, it took a restructuring of the company in 1996, in which Deuss was ousted and 50 per cent of the company was assigned to a consortium of private companies developing energy resources in Kazakhstan. There followed two years of wrangling before the first contracts for actual construction and pipeline delivery were signed in late 1998 and early 1999. The line itself was physically completed in March 2001, formally opened in November 2001 and by July 2002, following months of elaborate testing, was operating with reasonable efficiency. Actual costs for developing the first phase of the project were put at \$2.6 billion. In mid-2002 the line possessed a capacity of 32 mt/y of which 28 mt/y was allocated to Kazakhstan and 4 mt/y to Russia. The project was officially classified as having four phases, with Phase IV taking capacity to 67 mt/y. Despite constant press references to intended capacity increases, as of July 2002, neither CPC nor its partners had committed themselves to investing any further funds in expansion activities.

The CPC line essentially took the best part of a decade to develop because it had to resolve a basic conundrum: how to develop an oil pipeline that would transit Russia, but would possess both the management structure and operational rights that would ensure it remained effectively independent of both local and national Russian bodies that might seek to curb its use. After all, to a Russian energy industry that tended to adopt classic Soviet zero-sum conflict methodology, any line that was primarily intended to serve Kazakh exporters would effectively be helping to deprive Russian exporters of potential markets. Convincing enough Russians that there might be a win-win scenario was not easy, even after the giant Russian oil company, LUKoil, secured a stake in the project as a result of the 1996 restructuring. Indeed, to this day the local authorities in southern Russia remain highly suspicious of the CPC line and are still seeking ways to extract more cash from the passage of Kazakh oil across their territory.

For Azerbaijan, the issue of how to get its oil to market fell into two parts. The first was the delivery of what was termed 'early oil', initial production of upwards of 100,000 b/d from ACG. Subsequently, as output was expanded, a Main Export Pipeline (MEP) would be required. Development of the ACG complex and development of the export pipeline system naturally went hand in hand, and, as with Kazakhstan, it would take much longer than expected to get an assured MEP project on track. In the years before the signing of the 1994 ACG contract, and, indeed, for some time thereafter, much of the focus was on how to reach the Turkish market by the most direct means possible – namely, a link with the existing Iraq–Turkey oil pipeline at Midyat in southeastern Turkey. There were several problems in this regard. Getting a pipeline through the southern Caucasus would not be easy. The most direct route would be along the Araks valley, which extends all the way from Azerbaijan to Turkey. But this would also mean transiting Armenia or Iran. And Azerbaijan could not countenance a route that transited Armenia (and also Armenian-controlled terrain in Azerbaijan itself) until there was a resolution of the 13-year-old Karabagh conflict. At the same time, a route through Iran would run up against objections from the US, which had sanctions against Iran. In addition, the US Amoco oil company was one of the biggest partners in AIOC. To the north, the options were via Georgia and via Russia. In 1994, Georgia was still in a state of severe instability. So, much of the initial focus was, naturally, on reviving the oil pipeline between Baku and Novorossiysk (which had originally been built to carry oil to Azerbaijan, rather than export oil from Azerbaijan).

By October 1995, however, developments in Georgia had improved sufficiently for AIOC to propose an initial two-pipe solution: renovation of the Baku–Novorossiysk line and development of a second line through Georgia. AIOC restored the Azerbaijani section of the line and pumping to Novorossiysk began in 1997. But the condition of the Russian sector of the line remained uncertain; although the system's capacity was supposed to be 9 mt/y (180,000 b/d) in Azerbaijan and 15 mt/y (300,000 b/d) in southern Russia, in practice, AIOC reckoned the system could carry no more than 2.5 mt/y (50,000 b/d). Moreover, with the various Chechen crises, transit was often interrupted and, in Chechnya itself, there was much illegal tapping into the line (although this did not, in theory, affect AIOC, since the transit arrangement simply provided for AIOC to receive at Novorossiysk as much oil as it put in at the Azeri–Russian border). As for the Georgian line, initial hopes that a working line could be developed largely by adaptation of existing gas and product lines proved unfounded, and in the end a brand new 926-km line to a new terminal at Supsa on the Black Sea was constructed at a cost of $590 million. This was a lot of money for a line with an initial capacity of just 100,000 b/d. But since its opening in December 1998 it has proved to be the backbone of AIOC's export system and has subsequently been expanded to 145,000 b/d, and later, by stages, to some 250,000 b/d (see Map 4, p. xxiv). Indeed, from 1997 to 1999, the only question was whether the planned MEP would simply be an enlargement of the Baku–Supsa system or whether, after following the same route as Baku–Supsa into Georgia, it would then branch off to head southeast to the Turkish port of Ceyhan.

In the end, the route to Ceyhan via Tbilisi (Georgia) was chosen as a result of several factors. Above all it offered the possibility of a large-scale system that would go direct to an open-water port, without any need for tankers to transit the Turkish straits. Throughout the 1990s, Turkish concerns at the impact of increasing tanker traffic in the congested straits of the Bosporus and Dardanelles had promoted the government to adopt an increasingly aggressive attitude in favour of the Baku–Ceyhan project, to the extent that, in defiance of some more moderate voices within the Turkish energy industry, it would oppose what seemed to be the logical compromise: a limited expansion of capacity to Supsa and then, when this proved that Azerbaijani reserves could be successfully developed in volume, either an extension from Supsa to Ceyhan or a spur off the Baku–Supsa line to Ceyhan.

The US government enthusiastically bought into the direct Baku–Tbilisi–Ceyhan scenario, viewing the project as a way of ensuring direct exports of oil from not only Azerbaijan but also Kazakhstan to the west in a way that would completely bypass both Russia and Iran. But in pushing so hard for a direct connection to Ceyhan, rather than intermediate development at Supsa, Turkey and the US also were adopting a high-risk strategy. BP, by now the operator at AIOC and therefore taking the lead in developing the MEP project, wanted to be sure that such a line would prove commercial. So did its partners in AIOC. Botaş helped the project along by agreeing to build the Turkish section, roughly 60 per cent of what was planned as a 1,760-km system, for a flat $1.4 billion. It was duly awarded a lump sum turnkey contract for this amount in October 2000, when the governments of Azerbaijan, Turkey and Georgia agreed to go ahead with the project. But the Botaş contract would only take effect as and when a series of formal host government agreements and engineering studies had been concluded, and when a formal company to build and operate the pipeline had been formed and was in a position to award contracts for the Azerbaijani and Georgian sections of the line. In the event, it was not until 1 August 2002 that the Baku–Tbilisi–Ceyhan (BTC) Pipeline Company was officially inaugurated, although it did accompany its formation with the award of contracts to build the 442-km section in Azerbaijan and the 248-km section in Georgia at the same time. Shortly afterwards, it formally gave Botaş notice to proceed with construction of what had become the 1,071-km Turkish sections of the system.

A generally higher level of oil prices in the late 1990s and early 2000s clearly contributed to improving the line's commercial viability. Even after the first contracts for physical construction were awarded, there were still doubts concerning the ability of the BTC Pipeline Company to secure sufficient oil required to fill the 1 million barrels per day (mb/d) line. This was a big project and it only made sense if it were a big pipeline. In effect, it needed to have a capacity of 1 mb/d (50 mt/y) to yield the kind of revenues that would justify its actual construction. It was originally assumed that there would have to be considerable input of Kazakh crude into the system, since ACG alone would not be able to come up with enough oil. This assumption was underpinned by the failure of international oil companies to make any subsequent oil discoveries off Azerbaijan to rival those of ACG. What is more, while oil produced by the State Oil Company of Azerbaijan (SOCAR) would continue to prove sufficient to fill the Baku–Novorossiysk line, it would be up to AIOC – and the ACG field complex – to continue to fill the Baku–Supsa line, which by 2002 was routinely carrying 130,000 b/d.

While Kazakh leaders throughout the 1990s voiced interest in exporting their county's crude via a Baku–Ceyhan line, they were not prepared to commit specific volumes to such a project. For them, quite naturally, CPC was the immediate concern. But BP and SOCAR came to the conclusion that the ACG reserve base was larger than they first thought – 5.3 billion barrels against 4.6 billion barrels – and that ACG output could, as early as 2008, be raised to 1 mb/d. In effect, the AIOC partners came to the conclusion they could fill almost all the line with oil produced at ACG output and condensate from Shah Deniz, leaving only some modest capacity spare for other prospective Azerbaijani developments, or, possibly, for oil from some of Kazakhstan's smaller fields that were not tied in to the Tengiz network. Thus, the basis on which, in mid-2002, the line was being developed, was the estimate that ACG would be pumping at around 1 mb/d for five or six years from around 2008 to 2014 and then, as its output fell off, the way would be opened for new oil from Kashagan to take its place. In late June 2002, Italy's Eni, the operator at Kashagan, formally announced that its analyses of the first three drilling wells had led it to conclude that the giant Kazakh field contained some 38 billion barrels of reserves-in-place and that recoverable reserves total some 7–9 billion barrels. Earlier in the year, Eni had announced that it was taking a 5 per cent stake in the Baku–Tbilisi–Ceyhan project, thus giving it an automatic right to ship up to 50,000 b/d through the system. This placed it in a strong position to conclude a subsequent agreement whereby Kashagan crude would start substituting for ACG oil in the system. The interconnections between Kashagan and the BTC project grew substantially in August 2002 when it was disclosed that three Kashagan partners, Eni, TotalFinaElf (TFE) and Itochu, had between them accumulated 12.5 per cent of the shares in BTC.

At the same time as BP was seeking to develop the twin projects of a major oilfield complex and a major oil export pipeline, it was also trying to achieve the same combination of field and line development with respect to the giant Shah Deniz gas field. Azerbaijan and Turkey reached agreement on 12 March 2001 on the supply of gas from 2005 onwards. In June 2002, BP officials said that formal sanction – approval – for a pipeline from Baku to a junction with Turkey's main east–west trunkline at Erzurum, together with the award of actual construction contracts, would be forthcoming in the third quarter of 2002. In the event, the formal decision on construction was announced in February 2003. It was confirmed that the first deliveries of Azerbaijani gas were expected to reach Turkey in early 2006. Physical construction of the pipeline would start in the second quarter of 2004 with first delivery of gas to Turkey due to start in the third quarter of 2005. The gas supply agreement called for initial deliveries to peak at 6.6 billion cubic metres per year (bcm/y), but the project's design provided for its capacity to be capable of increase to 30 bcm/y. Azerbaijan wanted to sell gas not only to Turkey but via Turkey to southern Europe; in 2002 it held talks with Greece on possible sales. Shah Deniz alone could easily support sustained output of 16 bcm/y, so the main problem at this point was developing capacity between Turkey and Greece, a problem that was being addressed by all three countries, with active support from the European Union. The ability of the line eventually to carry much more than 16 bcm/y left open the possibility, however remote, that one day some Turkmen gas might also flow west through the system.

For Turkmenistan, the main question in the wake of the collapse of the Soviet Union was how its gas might reach hard cash markets. As of 2003, this was still an unanswered question, not least because of the contradictory approaches taken by Turkmenistan's idiosyncratic dictator Saparmurat Niyazov in his handling of relations with the guardians of his country's three most obvious export potential routes: Russia, Iran and Azerbaijan (see **Canzi**).

In the final years of the Soviet Union, Turkmenistan was producing considerable volumes of gas, and much of this found its way to European markets via the integrated Soviet gas pipeline network. Independence prompted Turkmen leader Saparmurat Niyazov to declare that Turkmenistan (which he believed contained the world's fourth largest gas reserves) would soon enjoy a standard of living to rival that of the richest Gulf Arab oil producers. Thus, his government stated in 1993 that within eight years Turkmenistan would be producing 320,000 b/d of oil and 130 bcm/y of gas. By comparison, 1992 production levels were 109,000 b/d for oil and 56.1 bcm/y for gas.

It did not turn out that way. Initially, Russia quite naturally chose to focus on retaining its own share of the European gas import market and, with Russian domestic gas consumption falling, there was simply no reason for it to allow Turkmenistan significant access to what was now Russia's gas distribution and export network. With gas export outlets curtailed, gas production fell. As for oil, Niyazov's failure to achieve the necessary conditions for stable foreign investment ensured that only a handful of foreign companies were prepared to enter the Turkmen market. So, in 2000, Turkmenistan hydrocarbon production totalled just 144,000 b/d and a mere 16.7 bcm, far short of the wonderful prospects unveiled in the early days of independence. What is more, the main customer for the country's limited gas exports was Ukraine, which could not afford to pay hard cash for the bulk of its imports. Consequently, Turkmenistan became engaged in a series of on-off sales agreements and debt rescheduling arrangements with Ukraine.

Niyazov, in the early 1990s, considered that the ideal solution would be the creation of a massive purpose-built line from the gas fields of south-central Turkmenistan – including three major fields close to the tri-border point with Iran and Afghanistan – through northern Iran and Turkey to southern and Central Europe. This was the Grand Trunkline project. In late 1994 Niyazov even laid a foundation plaque to mark the start of the venture. But there was no cash and no real organisation, although there was the gas in place to fill the projected 30-bcm/y line.

In 1995, Niyazov began supporting the concept of a Trans-Caspian line that would carry 30 bcm/y of gas under the Caspian and across Azerbaijan and Georgia to Turkey, with Turkey itself purchasing 16 bcm/y and acting as a transit route for a further 14 bcm/y of Turkmen gas sales to southern Europe. But Niyazov could not reach agreement with the project's main developers, the PSG group and Shell, and, once it became clear that Azerbaijan had itself made a major gas discovery at Shah Deniz – and that Niyazov was not prepared to compromise on the volume of gas that Azerbaijan might supply to the system – the project collapsed. At the end of 2002 the project was not officially dead – there is still a formal 16-bcm/y sale-and-purchase agreement in place with Turkey – but it was so moribund as to be virtually beyond resuscitation (see **Canzi**, p. 187).

Turkmenistan did make some progress in the mid-1990s with regard to Iran. A 200-km 10–12 bcm/y capacity line was opened in 1997 between the Turkmen gas fields around Korpeje, on the eastern shore of the Caspian, and the Iranian gas distribution system at Kurtkui. But actual deliveries only ran at around 2 bcm/y although there were signs of modest growth in 2001. The existence of this line did not serve the main Turkmen gas fields, which were located farther east. However, somewhat paradoxically, it ensured that the first deliveries of so-called Iranian gas to Turkey in December 2001 via the new 574-km line from Tabriz in Iran to the Erzurum line in Turkey did in fact consist of Turkmen gas that had previously been inserted into the Iranian system. As of mid-2002, Turkmenistan continued to rely on export routes via Uzbekistan, Kazakhstan and, above all, Russia, with Ukraine as its principal customer. Development of almost any non-Russian gas system would enable Turkmenistan to reach hard cash markets, whereas the Ukrainian gas deals were conducted on a basis of both cash and barter, and were also subject to repeated arguments concerning non-payment. An explanation for the Turkmen leader's inability to conclude successful alternative export arrangements may simply have been that he felt more comfortable negotiating with former Soviet apparatchiks than with officials from other cultures. In the case of his negotiations with Shell and PSG, corporate sources told this writer that one reason for the failure of this project was that Niyazov demanded as much as $500 million in up-front payments.

With the emergence of Hamid Karzai as the head of government in a US-backed administration in neighbouring Afghanistan, Niyazov once again voiced enthusiastic support for a project he had backed in the mid-1990s, namely the development of a major gasline through Afghanistan to Pakistan. Two projects, both entailing a pipeline to export Turkmen gas, as well as a second pipeline to carry oil from a variety of Caspian countries to a terminal on Pakistan's Indian Ocean coast, were developed by rival companies in the mid-1990s: Argentina's Bridas and US Unocal. The Bridas project foundered when it lost favour with Niyazov, even though it had the rights to develop the giant Yashlar gas field that it had discovered close to the projected starting point of the gasline. The Unocal project foundered in the face of US political opposition to the then Taleban administration in Kabul. By the time Afghanistan became a politically acceptable route under Karzai, however, other circumstances had changed. Since the mid-1990s, Pakistan has itself made some gas discoveries, so that while it stands in need of gas imports, these may no longer be on the scale envisaged a few years ago. The main potential market for gas in the region is India, but two things stand in the way of getting Central Asian gas to that potentially huge market. One is the dire state of Indo-Pakistan relations which makes a cross-border pipeline an impossibility until a real political rapprochement is first achieved; the second is the need for major reform of the internal Indian market, including a complex combination of price liberalisation, fairer negotiation of initial gas supply agreements and tougher regulation to ensure that such agreements are then honoured. In the meantime, gas supplies to India are more likely to be delivered in the form of liquefied natural gas (LNG) from the Gulf, or piped gas from Iran, rather than piped gas from the Caspian (see **Canzi**, p. 187, **Adams**, p. 103).

Over the decade, a host of other pipeline proposals have been made. Some are still under consideration and may indeed prove useful at some later date. Plans for pipelines from Kazakhstan to China and from Kazakhstan to Iran fall into this category. They are both being discussed seriously and both could yield significant dividends. A line to China would also, in all probability, include the effective construction of an internal Kazakh west-to-east oil pipeline that would enable oil from its Caspian regions to be supplied to Almaty and other eastern cities (see **Akiner**, p. 391). A line to Iran would open up new markets in the Far East, where there is still a premium on oil deliveries by comparison with oil shipped westwards. The China National Oil Corporation has for five years been considering the former project and France's TotalFinaElf has for just as long been considering the latter. But the China project suffers because of the immense distances required to take Kazakh oil to major centres of demand within China, thus making a 20 mt/y line – and that is the capacity the Chinese agreed to study – difficult to justify on purely commercial grounds. A 50 mt/y line would be easier to justify, but Kazakhstan probably could not commit enough oil to fill such a line on its own (particularly with its principal international operators firmly looking westwards in the search for oil markets), so a degree of input from Russia might also be required.

As for the Iran line, this makes eminently good sense in terms of ensuring a new direction for Kazakh exports, but suffers from the fact that much of the thinking behind such a project has been predicated on its ability to be implemented in phases. Thus, northern Iran would itself be the market for much of these exports with, initially at least, Caspian producers receiving Iranian oil in the Gulf in place of their own oil deliveries to Tehran and nearby industrial cities. This project may yet be achieved. TotalFinaElf is a major shareholder in the Kashagan venture, and in the long run there are some great advantages to be gained from an Iranian route. But, as of 2003, Kazakhstan's prime concern was still to get the maximum use possible out of CPC and thus test the reliability of this export route. Also, it was watching and waiting while the Baku–Tbilisi–Ceyhan project advanced. Finally, it was working out just how to deal with the complexities of developing the Kashagan field. If new lines were to be built from Kazakhstan that would almost certainly be a function of a decision by the Kashagan partners, based on their conclusion that alternative export systems were required.

Numerous pipelines to bypass the Bosporous have been discussed from time to time, but there seemed little likelihood that any of them would be built in the near future. However, in April 2004 one such project seemed to be gaining momentum. Thrace Development Ltd, with partners from the US, UK, Turkey and Kazakhstan, claimed it had secured some 500,000 b/d in committed throughput for a pipeline to run through Turkish Thrace from Kiyikoy on the Black Sea to the Gulf of Saros on the Agean. This would make the line commercially viable.

The case for alternative systems is that they promote competition and, particularly in the case of non-Russian export routes, they provide the kind of competition that makes it increasingly likely that existing routes that transit Russia will also operate on essentially commercial lines. The common plea of the oil producers during the Caspian producers' first decade of independence was for multiple pipelines. With the launching of the BTC line, that is what they will have. BTC, since it will essentially be owned by international oil companies, will operate on a strictly commercial basis. And that in turn should mean that not only the existing lines through Russia will likewise start to work on a commercial basis as Russia's monopoly on Kazakh export routes wanes, but that future lines through Iran and perhaps even China will also have to operate on a competitive basis. By the end of 2003, there was still a long way to go in developing a real pipeline infrastructure to bring Caspian oil and gas to market – not least in terms of internal pipeline construction – but just over a decade after the disintegration of the Soviet Union, the Caspian was finally entering the pipeline era (see Maps 2 and 7).

As for how many lines will eventually be built, where they will go and how big they will be, that will depend on the triangular relationship between the success of existing pipelines, the speed of Caspian field development and the eventual peak of Caspian oil production. At present, there is a common view – though not yet, perhaps, a real consensus – that Caspian oil production should reach some 4.0 mb/d in or around 2014, and that subsequent increases thereafter may prove to be relatively small. In this case, with roughly 1 mb/d of Caspian oil production required for domestic use, that would leave 3 mb/d available for exports. It is reasonable to presume that BTC will take 1 mb/d, that CPC will eventually be expanded so that it takes at least 1 mb/d of Caspian oil and that existing smaller lines will continue to take a further 0.4–0.5 mb/d. This means there is room for a further line of 0.5 mb/d capacity, or, if one is optimistic about the eventual plateau production for Caspian crude, of perhaps 1.0 mb/d. But the figures do seem to suggest that, once BTC is under way, there will only be room for one further major oil pipeline, or maybe for two lesser lines. What is clear is that no decision on such a line, or lines, needs to be taken for several years.

6   Caspian energy development

Terence Adams

Historical context

Since its origins in 1875, oil and gas development in the Caspian has had a long and chequered history, and Baku oil has not always lived up to investor expectations. Nevertheless the early development of oil at Baku with its international oil terminal at Batumi on the Black Sea laid down the technical and commercial foundations of global oil. In 1900 Baku oil production led the world. But it was also a time of serious exploitation of the oil workers that led to socialist revolution in the Caucasus. Yet Baku oilmen were amongst the first to demonstrate the competitive advantage of applied technology. The commissioning of the Baku–Batumi pipeline in 1905 saw the construction of the world's first long distance trans-national pipeline for oil exports to international markets. Also from pioneering investments at Batumi, the Rothschild family set new parameters for risk financing in international oil and gas. But from its earliest days Baku oil was sensitive to the global oil price. Before the First World War this involved international price wars between oil producers in Europe and the United States.

The Shell Oil Company owes its origins to Baku oil and the Rothschild company at Batumi. This was the first company to exploit new tanker technology through the Suez Canal, to deliver cheap Russian oil to emerging markets in East Asia. By 1910 the complexity of risk management at Baku was such that it drove Shell and others towards a process of global mergers and acquisitions. This was an industry trend not too different to what we see today. For global oil, size has always mattered, and for Baku oil, access to the Black Sea for international oil export to global markets has always been commercially critical.

Baku oil became a military target for Germany and Turkey in the First World War (to be repeated by Hitler in the Second). In 1919 it was also a military target for the Bolsheviks, who desperately needed Baku oil to fuel their ongoing Russian Revolution. The British and their Western Allies returned to Baku and the Caucasus in 1918, and for a brief period promoted the creation of three newly independent republics (Armenia, Georgia and Azerbaijan). In support of this political initiative, the badly damaged oil facilities in Baku were substantially refurbished by the British military. But despite renewed investment in Baku oil, the economic cost of maintaining regional security in the Caucasus against a Bolshevik takeover was not seen to be in the commercial or political interests of either Britain or the US. In 1919 the region with its new Republics were abandoned to their fate. This is perhaps a geopolitical message as fresh today as it was then. In 1921 the Caucasus became an integral part of the Soviet Union. Foreign investments in Baku oil were nationalised by the Soviets, and for the next 70 years external energy investments in the Caspian were closed to the West.

But with the collapse of the former Soviet Union (FSU) in 1991, the Caspian and the Caucasus once more opened to Western energy investment. By then Soviet experts had already built up a substantial database on Caspian oil and gas that had confirmed the presence of many new giant oil and gas fields. But constraints imposed by the inadequacies of Soviet offshore oil technology, and the redirection of Soviet energy investment in the 1970s from the Caspian to Siberia, meant that by 1992 there were several undeveloped giant oil and gas fields in the Caspian available for foreign licensing. There were two in Kazakhstan and one in Azerbaijan that became the focus of intense and extended negotiation by the multinationals. It was equally believed that there were many untested low-risk giant oil prospects in the Caspian shallow waters off Kazakhstan, and in the deeper waters offshore Azerbaijan, Turkmenistan and Iran. It was therefore access to low technical risk and high-volume oil reserves that drove Western energy investment back into the Caspian. For the multinational energy investors, access to Black Sea oil terminals once more became a critical priority. But the Caspian track record for new energy investment has been uneven. There have been excessive bouts of investor optimism, followed by equally dramatic periods of great pessimism. So what are the realities, what are the current challenges, and how will the future export of Caspian oil impact on the global oil market?

Caspian oil

Since the collapse of the Soviet Union renewed Western energy investment in the Caspian has progressed through three distinct phases. Phase One covered the period 1992 to 1996. It was a time of difficult access and general pessimism. There was much hostility and misunderstanding. The Western investor faced an opaque Soviet business culture that displayed both resentment and suspicion to outside interference. The Western media were consistently highlighting the problems; in particular, the geographical isolation of the Caspian would present massive difficulties for regional export and support logistics. In addition there were serious concerns over regional security arising from active ethnic conflicts in the Caucasus. Business risk was high. But access through new Production Sharing and Joint Venture Contracts to the undeveloped giant fields of Tengiz and Karachaganak in Kazakhstan, and Azeri–Chirag–Guneshli in Azerbaijan, drove the process forward. These three fields still dominate Caspian energy development today.

Phase Two covered the period 1996 to 1998; it was a time of unbridled optimism. The Caspian became a global exploration 'hot spot'. Major projects were working, Caspian oil was getting to market, and excessive hyperbole raised investor and national expectations to unreal levels. But the collapse in 1998 of the global oil price extinguished this euphoria, and the latest Caspian oil boom withered on the vine. Phase Three extends from 1999 until today, during which time a greater sense of business reality has set in. Hardnosed economic screening placed Caspian oil and gas investment into a more realistic and global context. Existing mega-giant projects continued to develop but at a slower pace than was originally predicted. Two new super-giant discoveries were made (Kashagan in Kazakhstan, and Shah Deniz in Azerbaijan); but there were also a significant number of failed Caspian exploration wells.

Twelve years of investor experience has shown that Caspian exploration and development is a high-cost exercise. To remain commercially competitive the Caspian requires a global oil price that is consistently above US$18–20/bl (per barrel) real. Caspian exploration failure costs are high (US$300–500m per project), but in the success case with the discovery of giant fields and large reserves, finding costs are low (30–50 cents/bl). With both deficient infrastructure and geographical isolation Caspian development costs are high. But there is a realistic expectation that applied technology will drive these costs down. Similarly with the successful development of existing Caspian export systems and with two new regional main export pipelines (the one from Tengiz to Novorossiysk already operational, the one from Baku to Ceyhan still under construction), a fall in oil transportation cost is confidently predicted. In 2003, a fully built-up cost for Caspian oil was roughly US$12–15/bl. This compares to the high-cost end in the North Sea, and is some two to three times more expensive than an equivalent OPEC barrel in the Persian Gulf. Nevertheless with new technology and lower transportation tariffs Caspian built up costs will fall. In future a cost band of US$8–10/bl should keep Caspian oil globally competitive. Nevertheless upstream oil and gas investment in the Caspian is not for the faint hearted. It only suits those multinational energy companies that have large and diversified global risk portfolios, with the critical ability to self-finance large-scale Caspian investment off strong company balance sheets.

Caspian energy development has suffered from both media hyperbole and politicisation of the investment process by the US and Turkey. In the 1990s CIA energy analysts helped fuel expectations for Middle East reserve equivalents in the Caspian, with predictions of 200 billon barrels (bnbls) yet-to-find. This would have placed Caspian oil potential on par with Kuwait and the United Arab Emirates combined. Some even saw for the Caspian the possible emergence of a new Saudi Arabia! What was being ignored was that this huge reserve prediction had sat at the extreme end of a CIA risk projection curve. It was therefore never realistically expected to occur. For their most likely case the CIA had proposed a more modest yet-to-find estimate of 50–70 bnbls that matched much of what the industry perceives today. However, recent exploration drilling failures suggest that there is now an even stronger bias towards the lower end (50 bnbls yet-to-find). The Caspian is therefore more comparable to a new North Sea. It is not a Middle East. This carries strong strategic overtones particularly for Europe and the Black Sea.

This more conservative view of Caspian oil has been confirmed by substantial exploration drilling in both the oil basins of the North and South Caspian. These two basins have very different hydrocarbon systems. In the North Caspian play (characteristics specific to an oil/gas field) types are dominated by super-giant Palaeozoic reef traps, as seen at Tengiz and now at Kashagan. Subordinate Mesozoic sandstone reservoirs contain more modest oil volumes onshore. LUKoil has also found a new Mesozoic sandstone oil play straddling the offshore boundary between Russia and Kazakhstan. Conventional estimates place Kazakh proven remaining oil reserves at 8–10 bnbls recoverable. Speculative yet-to-find recoverable oil is seen to fall within a 30–50 bnbls range that is entirely dependent on the discovery of new super-giant fields comparable to Tengiz and Kashagan. The commercial viability of the deeply buried carbonate reservoirs at Kashagan has now been confirmed. However, the costs of deep drilling in what is a technically complex drilling environment are very high (see **Akiner**, p. 382). Application of novel technologies will be needed to monetise the project. The commercial disposal of high volumes of associated gas cap gas that is required for simultaneous oil production has also not been fully resolved. Oilfield development in what are the most environmentally sensitive shallow waters of the Caspian – these are the main breeding grounds for Caspian sturgeon and caviar production, – also the severe climatic conditions that render inshore waters ice bound in the winter, all increase Kashagan oil development cost to very significant levels. There are in fact many technical challenges to be resolved before substantial oil reserves in Kazakhstan can be developed with confidence (see **Akiner**, p. 382). Therefore current offshore yet-to-find reserve forecasts are based on a limited number of appraisal wells and can be subject to dramatic change in either direction.

In the South Caspian basin failed exploration drilling has significantly reduced estimates of future oil potential. Again the industry consensus placed Azerbaijan–West Turkmen proven remaining recoverable oil reserves at 6–8 bnbls, with a projected recoverable of 20 bnbls yet-to-find. However, the latter figure must now be seriously challenged. Until recently the South Caspian basin was thought to possess a significant number of large untested and prospective deepwater traps. The bulk of oil discoveries in the South Caspian basin are all confined to the sandstone reservoirs of three Plio-Pleistocene palaeo-delta systems within the Azeri–Turkmen offshore areas. There are some smaller but coeval untested palaeo-deltas in the Iranian offshore but these are generally considered to be relatively non-prospective. Recent drilling has effectively confirmed that only the clean sandstone reservoirs of the north-central palaeo-Volga delta south of the Apsheron ridge (which geologically connects Baku to Turkmenbashi in the east) can support high well productivities that are both sustainable and commercially viable. Equivalent deeply buried reservoir sandstones in the Kura palaeo-delta to the west and the Uzboi palaeo-delta to the east are of very poor quality. The presence of clay minerals and volcanic detritus disrupts reservoir performance, and well productivities are generally low and not sustainable.

Thirteen dry holes drilled in offshore Azerbaijan since 1996 have also more precisely defined the limits of the main South Caspian oil and gas fairway. This is narrower than was originally perceived. Specialist sedimentological studies in the South Caspian have confirmed the high-performance nature of the sandstone reservoirs of the palaeo-Volga south of the Apsheron Ridge. The new geological model suggests that good reservoir development is unlikely to extend to the large untested deepwater prospects of the South Caspian which makes them a high-risk play. These prospects had previously accounted for the bulk of South Caspian ytf (15–17 bnbls recoverable). Together with high-risk development costs in very deep water, and with an increased risk of finding non-commercial gas rather than oil, the expectation for substantial new oil potential in the South Caspian has been materially downgraded.

From this analysis one can now predict with confidence that, if there are no serious dislocations in the development process, by 2010 the Caspian should be producing around 3 million barrels a day (b/d) or 150 million tonnes a year (mt/y). Two-thirds of this oil production will be from the North Caspian basin with one-third from the South Caspian basin. But to achieve these production levels it will require a substantial investment of incremental capital that depends on three essential factors: a sustainable global oil price that remains above US$18–20/bl real, the absence of regional political conflict, and clear signs that serious deficiencies in Caspian infrastructure and the business environment are being addressed as a matter of urgency. Caspian production could eventually peak by 2020 at 5 million b/d (50 mt/y), primarily from the North Caspian. But even at this level the Caspian would only contribute some 3 per cent to future global oil supply. The Caspian will therefore never be a strategic supply alternative to the OPEC oil producers in the Gulf. But it is strategically important to Europe, and to a lesser extent the east coast refineries of the US.

There is now a ten-year track record for project management in the Caspian. Space prevents a comprehensive overview but the basic messages are simple. Caspian Soviet hydrocarbon infrastructure is seriously deficient through under investment and long-term neglect. Also much of it is not where it is most needed. There are Caspian construction facilities but all are in considerable need of new investment and expansion. Critical path items such as offshore drilling rigs, heavy lift equipment, marine fleets and pipe laying barges are available but more are needed. Those that already exist need substantial upgrade and capital injection to bring them up to Western insurable operating standards. The unpredictability of costs involved in the upgrade of Caspian Soviet infrastructure is a serious commercial risk, as shown by the common experience of Caspian operators so far. Skilled manpower and local management cadres are both in short supply, especially in the North Caspian. Contractual obligations in Caspian energy agreements that impose high levels of front-end local content for both materials and manpower exacerbate the problem. None can be resolved within a shortened time frame, and the idea that multiple Caspian mega-projects can proceed simultaneously without inherent delays is certainly flawed. Caspian oil and gas development will almost certainly proceed more slowly in the future than many currently predict, and this will impact directly on levels of future Caspian oil movement across the Black Sea.

But of equal concern to the Caspian energy investor is the ability to finance long-term energy investment from conventional sources of international project financing. It is important to note that of the US$13 billion foreign capital invested in Caspian energy projects so far only US$400 million was obtained through conventional third-party financing. The rest was all self-financed off company balance sheets. Can or will investors continue to do this in the future? Caspian energy investment must compete for capital in a global market. Therefore for most investors capital rationing in the Caspian seems inevitable. To access some US$15–30 billion of new long-term Caspian borrowing over the next ten to 15 years will be difficult. It would require private sector banks to have considerably greater confidence in Caspian track record than they currently hold. Even then these banks would still expect the multinational lending agencies to cover political risk financing, as well as requiring up to 60 per cent or more of equity financing from the energy investors themselves.

But what in the end will prove to be the greatest challenge is the absence of general reform and 'good governance' within the governments of the Caspian states themselves. Business risk arising from generally corrupt ex-Soviet bureaucracies is well recognised. It requires no further elaboration here. But developments in Kazakhstan have alarmed Caspian energy investors (see **Akiner**, p. 380). Kazakh foreign operators have been subject to spurious and continued harassment from local tax authorities and environmental interest groups. Fundamental legal rights within Production Sharing Agreements (PSAs) are also being challenged by the Kazakh government. In general Caspian governments and politicians do not particularly like international PSAs, although they are the most successful form of international long-term petroleum contracts developed so far. For Caspian governments there is a fundamental downside. For multibillion-dollar oil projects within a PSA the contractual cost recovery mechanism is applied in such a way that material cash flows to the State are significantly delayed (generally seven to nine years from start up). This reflects the early cost recovery of capital and operating costs through 'Cost Oil' by the foreign investor, who in all fairness has taken all the front-end financial risk. Both government and investor reach 'Profit Oil' at the same time, which is then shared in proportions negotiated under original contracts.

However, once high levels of front-end investment have been made by the foreign operator, governments are then tempted to renegotiate contract terms to the disadvantage of the investor. This is now happening in Kazakhstan. The government is attacking 'transfer pricing' under Kazakh oil contracts, which is seriously eroding investor confidence in the long-term sanctity and security of the contractual arrangements. Likewise the increasing monopoly that is developing over Kazakh oil transport under the state company KazTransOil (first established in 1997, now a daughter company of KazMunaiGaz, the state oil and gas company and regulator that was created in 2002) is causing considerable concern, with fears that this monopoly will create a negative environment comparable to that which exists in Russia – a result of the conduct of Transneft, the Russian state oil transport company. If such hostility continues to grow within the Caspian business environment, the pace of Caspian oil and gas development will inevitably slow and materially reduce levels of projected oil production.

Add to this the additional risks in regional security arising from both frozen and active ethnic conflicts in the Caucasus, together with the political uncertainties that surround the future of the ruling elites in these states, and the fragility of the Caspian business environment is truly demonstrated. The Western-led campaign against al-Qaeda and Taleban forces in Afghanistan in autumn 2001 and subsequent sporadic hostilities can perhaps only increase instability in the region, especially in the north Caucasus. Nevertheless, after some ten years of foreign oil investment in the Caspian a positive track record has emerged. In general Caspian PSAs are working well compared to those of Russia in the north. Development pace, cash flow and protection of long-term returns are the genuine uncertainties. But for the larger multinationals with global risk portfolios, their presence in the Caspian is assured. Access to giant oil and gas reserves in the Caspian is too attractive an opportunity for them to miss.

Caspian oil transportation

Over the past five years there has been considerable success in the development of Caspian regional oil transportation. Some 800,000 b/d (40 mt/y) of export capacity was already available before an additional 600,000 b/d (28 mt/y) came on line with the successful commissioning of phase one of the Caspian Pipeline Consortium (CPC) pipeline from Tengiz to Novorossiysk (October 2001). Multiple oil export routes by pipeline, railway and river barge, all with competitive tariffs, are working well. Attractive commercial netbacks and regional markets thirsty for environmentally friendly Caspian oil have both dictated a predominantly westward movement of Caspian oil into the Black Sea and to the Mediterranean. Within a ten-year time frame it is predicted that these markets will absorb up to 2.5–3 million b/d (125–150 mt/y) of Caspian crude. Significant volumes of Caspian oil will also move south to Iran (up to 500,000 b/d or 25 mt/y) for oil swaps from the Persian Gulf. However, Iran is a market for Caspian crude (to be supplied primarily from Kazakhstan and Turkmenistan), rather than a transit country to take Caspian oil into the Persian Gulf. It is difficult to conceive that Iran would allow the transit of material volumes of Caspian crude which would then move to and undermine their own Iranian oil markets in East Asia. Therefore the bulk of north Caspian and Russian export oil must transit the Black Sea en route to international markets.

Competitive tariffs and operational security will ensure that the multiple export options we see functioning today will continue to operate in the future; together with two new regional pipelines (one pending) to supply oil markets in the West. The Caspian Pipeline Consortium exiting the North Caspian will feed some 1.2 million b/d (60 mt/y) into the Black Sea. Baku–Tbilisi–Ceyhan (BTC) will bypass the Black Sea and will feed 1 million b/d (50 mt/y) into the Mediterranean. With the declaration in 2001 by BP of significant reserves growth at Azerbaijan International Operating Company (AIOC) – from 3.7 bnbls to 5.2 bnbls – the commerciality of the BTC pipeline was secured. The BTC pipeline has now been fully sanctioned by its sponsor group and construction is already under way; the pipeline is expected to be operational in 2005. However, it should be noted that surplus Kazakh crude from the new discovery at Kashagan will not be available for early BTC operations. By the time that field goes on stream, AIOC will require the full BTC design capacity for its own field production. There will also be no surplus Azeri crude for shipment to Iran, as all Azeri crude will be needed to service BTC. Some Kazakh onshore (North Buzachi) oil could move to Baku to fill the empty Baku–Supsa pipeline, if this spare capacity becomes available once BTC is commissioned. Only when the AIOC production goes off peak at around 2015 could substantial export capacity be made available in BTC for others, unless of course the system's capacity were expanded. Nevertheless, multiple export routes will continue to service the Caspian energy investor with perhaps the additional construction of a new land pipeline from Kazakhstan to Iran sometime early in the next decade (see **Roberts**).

Caspian export and Bosporus transit

Preferential markets for these Caspian oil flows have developed in both the Black Sea region itself and more importantly within the Mediterranean. Following the collapse of the FSU, crude markets in the Black Sea are once again developing but at a slower rate than was originally expected. It is predicted that Black Sea demand will increase from 10.8 mt/y in 2000 to 18 mt/y in 2010. However, Black Sea refineries are primarily configured to run on sour crude for residual fuel oil production, for which there is a strong demand. For this the Russian export blend (32 degree API and 2.9 per cent sulphur) has a competitive advantage. Therefore for the foreseeable future the bulk of Caspian lighter crude (32 to 48 degrees API with low or no sulphur) will of necessity move to the Mediterranean, through the heavily congested Turkish Bosporus Straits. The eastern Mediterranean market is fairly large (Turkey, Greece and Israel), but refineries here prefer supplies of cheap sour crude from the Middle East. Such crude is readily available, from Iran, Syria and Saudi Arabia through the Suez Canal and Sumed pipeline. There is no commercial incentive for the east Mediterranean refineries to pay a premium for Caspian light crude which will need to search for premium market share elsewhere.

The eastern coastal markets of Europe are large with a market focus on Italy. Here refineries run at around 50 per cent on sweet crude, with an increasing demand for low sulphur fuels; Caspian supplies will be in direct market competition with North African producers. Exceptionally keen Caspian pricing will be needed to displace established Libyan crude supply. Therefore the most important coastal markets for Caspian crude will be in the western Mediterranean, which has the largest demand for sweet crude imports in the Mediterranean region. Refineries in Spain and France and pipeline links to refineries in Germany and Switzerland must be the primary target for Caspian crude supply into the Mediterranean. Here Caspian crude will need to displace, on a highly competitive basis, North and West African supplies. The remaining markets of Central Europe are not large, and are already almost entirely supplied by Russia through their Druzhba export system. Some media profile has been given to the fact that Poland, Hungary and Slovenia are searching for new supplies as alternatives to the North Sea. But their demand volumes are still modest. Therefore to a large extent Caspian oil export must focus on Mediterranean markets to the west, where there is a refinery demand for 'just in time' supplies. This would give preference to smaller tanker sizes that are also suitable for continued Bosporus transits. This may well colour current Russian thinking on continued oil transits through the Bosporus.

However, there are alternative trading views. It is believed that resistance from Middle East and North African producers against infiltration of Caspian crude into their established Mediterranean markets will be so intense, that it would of necessity drive Caspian oil to more distant markets in both north-west Europe (where the North Sea supply is potentially in terminal decline), and to markets on the eastern seaboard of the US. In this event large tankers would be the most commercially viable transportation option. This would automatically require deepwater export facilities for Caspian exports, such as the existing terminal at Ceyhan (or Vlore on the Adriatic, if the port is ever built). The passage of such large tankers through the Bosporus would be prohibited and the need for a Bosporus pipeline bypass for Black Sea export would then be critical. But, if the use of smaller tanker transport were to continue to expand from the Black Sea, then either a more highly controlled and improved maritime oil transit through the Bosporus must be adopted, or a bypass pipeline built.

For Turkey, oil transit and the transit of other hazardous cargoes through the congested Turkish Straits is an international bottleneck of immense historical, social and economic importance. It presents a difficult challenge involving legal status and multinational rights of passage (under the now outdated Montreux Convention of 1936), technical marine management, cost sharing, and important elements of potential regional conflict. For mariners, the Bosporus is one of the most hazardous, crowded and difficult waterways in the world. The channel currently handles over 50,000 vessel transits a year (up from 25,000 in 1988). With the projected economic growth expected for the littoral states of the Black Sea, these levels of transit are expected to grow exponentially. Oil tankers (including not only crude oil and refined product but also LPG) account for less than 15 per cent of the total shipping, and their share is expected to decline as non-oil traffic, such as dry-bulk and container vessels, continue to grow even faster than oil. But none of this takes into account the number of daily ferry and other shuttle boats that transport 2 million people from one side to the other. These currently exceed more than 1,000 crossings per day. All this adds to the complexity and risk. For Turkey it is the multibillion-dollar loss exposure that would arise from a single catastrophic marine disaster at the heart of Istanbul that is now the pressing issue. But Russian and Caspian oil investors are polarised over their conflicting views on transit risk, between those who believe a Bosporus bypass should be built as soon as practicable, and those who believe a Bosporus oil transit can continue to be safely managed using upgraded marine technology.

Comparisons are made with hazardous cargo transits through the Houston Shipping Canal, the Mississippi River, the Malacca and Singapore Straits, and the Suez Canal. However, the incidence of marine accidents in the Bosporus are significantly higher than in these channels (6 Bosporus marine accidents per million transit miles, versus 3 in the Suez Canal, and 0.2 in the Mississippi River). These statistics are quite startling but do in fact reflect the incremental benefits that arise from high-level marine and traffic management systems, especially vessel tracking systems (VTS) that have been adopted elsewhere. Undoubtedly the Bosporus will benefit materially from the installation of their new US$30 million VTS system. But it would be in the interests of all if all Bosporus transit vessels (especially for hazardous cargoes) took on a Bosporus pilot. This is not yet mandatory. Similarly Bosporus transit risk would be materially reduced if standards of vessel quality and reliability were raised to European Union (EU) and US requirements. But this would present an enormous commercial and political challenge for Russia and the other Black Sea states. However, Russia will be obliged in 2005 to meet EU tanker standards at its receiving terminals for future oil deliveries, so if Russia wishes to retain its European market share perhaps the new tanker requirement is not an issue.

Total oil flows through the Bosporus have grown significantly in recent years but not hugely. Between 1998 and 2000 growth was 7 per cent per year, reflecting both the commissioning of the Supsa terminal in Georgia and the impact of high oil prices on increased Russian production. But it should be noted that the 74 mt/y Bosporus oil transit of 2000 is still significantly lower than the 91 mt/y transit peak of 1989 (which it should be pointed out was a time when non-oil traffic was also much lighter).

It could be argued that improved marine management in the Straits would obviate the requirement for a new Bosporus bypass. Most Caspian multinationals see a 50 mt/y increase in crude transit through the Bosporus as requiring no more than one modern double-hulled Suezmax tanker daily.

But herein lies the rub. The current terms of the governing international Montreux Convention prevent Turkey from either imposing new transit rules and operating standards to lower transit risk, or retrieving the costs involved in upgrading Bosporus marine management systems. Current transit through the Straits is, in economic jargon, a 'free good'. As long as shippers believe they can continue to move their oil freely through the Bosporus there are few incentives for them to undertake increased costs from either the building of a bypass pipeline or to contribute financially to improved control systems in the Bosporus. Turkey is therefore left on the horns of a political and environmental dilemma.

BP and the BTC Sponsor Group have declared their firm opposition to the Bosporus route. They regard the transit risks as unacceptable, both from the point of view of international reputation and environmental economic prudence. They recognise the magnitude of the multibillion-dollar 'negative opportunity costs' that could arise from a catastrophic oil disaster at the heart of Istanbul. This would be far greater than, say, the *Exxon Valdez* incident in Alaska (with a reputed retrieval cost of US$10 billion). For BP's South Caspian export, BTC is already its most expedient Bosporus bypass. For the past three years the focus of Turkey's political attention on BTC largely removed the transit crisis in the Bosporus from the regional debate. Turkey's environmental arguments were seen by many to reflect its support for BTC rather than the realities of a catastrophic threat to Istanbul. But with the commissioning of CPC and the associated growth in oil transit volumes, the Bosporus transit issue is once more centre stage. It needs to be addressed with urgency. A multilateral initiative between the Caspian and Russian oil exporters and the Black Sea littoral states is now urgently required to progress this critical debate.

Russia currently believes that it already has Turkish agreement for short-to-medium-term free transit of its oil through the Bosporus, and has repeatedly stated so in public. In addition, both Russia and the North Caspian oil exporters believe they too have the support of the US government on this issue, arising from the intense diplomatic pressure imposed on Russia by the US State Department to facilitate a final resolution of the CPC trunk pipeline (and thus protect US investment in Kazakhstan). Consequently, early agreement to a new Bosporus bypass may not be high on the Russian agenda today. Recent statements from Russia suggest that it believes that a Bosporus bypass is not required until such time as oil transits through the Bosporus exceed 120 mt/y, probably early in the next decade. Veiled threats have been made within the media that Turkish gas supply from Russia would be at risk if Russian Bosporus transits were blocked.

In fact, Turkey has no existing international legal redress to impose a new solution. In 1994, following a major tanker accident in the Straits, the Turkish government did unilaterally impose a new set of regulations governing the passage of oil tankers through the Bosporus. These regulations were presented to the International Maritime Organisation (IMO) for review and comment. Subsequently, the IMO approved the more important parts of the new Turkish regulatory regime but, due to the constraints of the Montreux Convention, they could not be made mandatory, and many shippers still do not respect them. At the same time the European Union too has been moving aggressively to strengthen regulations concerning tanker movements in EU waters. A draft EU Directive has moved forward from 2012 to 2005 the date by which EU oil terminals will handle only double-hulled tankers. Given Turkey's own initiative to prepare for EU membership, it is unrealistic to expect that such maritime standards should not equally apply to the Bosporus. Environmental activism has also arrived at the Bosporus that imposes further pressure on the oil shippers to respond to increased international reputation risk.

The case for a market-led solution is now compelling. A commercial risk assessment for improved shipping standards through the Straits in comparison to a new pipeline bypass is now the only practical basis on which to progress. If, for example, a five-year deadline is envisaged for such a bypass to be put in place, then the final decision on any route selection must be made within the next two years, to allow sufficient lead time for design, financing, construction and commissioning. Time for Turkey is clearly of the essence and Bosporus transit is certainly a Caspian energy issue that requires the attention of both Russian and Caspian energy investors as a matter of urgent priority.

Caspian and Central Asian gas

Oil, once it is on board a tanker, is an internationally tradable commodity. Gas export on the other hand (excluding LNG) is generally tied to regional markets through dedicated pipelines under long-term sales and purchase agreements. The Caspian region, including Central Asia together with Russia, Iran and Iraq, incorporates a surfeit of proven remaining recoverable gas reserves of 82 trillion cubic metres (tcm). This represents more than half of the world total (151 tcm). But there is a corresponding dearth of regional gas markets. For the South Caspian, including Iran, up to 2010/2015 this gas market will be Turkey, with possible onward transits to the European Union. For the North Caspian and Central Asia the gas market will be Russia. Remote geography, complex geopolitics, and high development and transportation costs will combine to frustrate export of Central Asian gas to alternative international markets. Current conflicts in Afghanistan, if successfully resolved, could perhaps at some time in the distant future resurrect visions of a Central Asian gas line through Afghanistan to Pakistan and India. Until last year the trans-national gas pipeline from Central Asia across the Caspian and through the Caucasus to Turkey and beyond received intense geopolitical support from the US government (see **Canzi**, p. 187). But with the discovery of a super-giant gas condensate field at Shah Deniz (offshore Azerbaijan) long-term commercial competition and unrealistic commercial demands from the Turkmen government removed this politically fraught option from the Caspian gas agenda.

So what are the critical issues surrounding future domestic gas demand in Turkey? Until its recent economic crisis Turkey was forecasting rises in demand for imported gas (primarily power sector driven) of some 42 billion cubic metres (bcm) per year in 2005, 55 bcm per year in 2010, and 83 bcm per year by 2015. Turkey consumed 14.5 bcm in 2000. But new economic realities suggest that for the coming decade it would be prudent to revise downwards Turkey's optimistic gas demand projections, to a 23–28 bcm per year low/high case in 2005, and 38–45 bcm per year in 2010. There will inevitably be a market bias towards the lower case. But Turkey has been particularly vigilant in securing future gas supplies. It already has supply and purchase agreements (SPAs) in place for the contractual supply of 52 bcm per year. For at least the coming decade the Turkish domestic gas market is oversupplied. Therefore new opportunities for market growth in Turkey for South Caspian gas including Iran ('eastern gas') are effectively closed.

But could Turkey then become a transit hub for 'eastern gas' supplies to markets in the EU? For this a Balkans transit must hold the key. An alternative solution could emerge for a direct gas pipeline from Turkey to Greece and onwards into Italy. Intergovernmental discussions are currently taking place. But in both scenarios Russian interests in these markets are likely to dictate the outcome. Russia is highly protective of its lucrative gas position in Europe. For 'eastern gas' to access an EU market the first step required should be the negotiation of a commercially driven gas swap arrangement with Russia, to back out its current 14 bcm per year supply to the Turkish market through the Balkans. This would not only accommodate an increased market share for 'eastern gas' in Turkey, but would also allow 'eastern gas' access to existing Balkan gas infrastructure, for more direct gas transits into Europe.

But this would only happen if it were clearly in the national interest of Russia so to do. It would require that it be commercially more beneficial for Russia to redirect its Balkan supplies away from Turkey into its own domestic gas market, where there is a current supply shortfall and where domestic gas prices are expected to rise to commercial levels. Alternatively, Russia could redirect its Balkan gas supplies into more lucrative gas markets in Western Europe where higher gas prices generally prevail. It is impossible to envisage that 'eastern gas' could also back out Russian 'Blue Stream' gas from the Turkish market. 'Blue Stream' is a Russian prestige project that directly links with Turkey across their common offshore Black Sea border. It enjoys exceptional levels of political commitment and investment. The project involves the application of leading-edge technology in an aggressively corrosive physical environment, where long-term maintenance will be difficult. Environmental risk for this novel Black Sea project is high. (This is reflected in the simultaneous laying of two gas lines, to ensure continuity of gas supply.) But it would be an equally brave political decision by Europe, if it were to unilaterally select a Turkey–Greece solution for the direct export of 'eastern gas' to Italy and Europe. The Greek gas market is very small (4 bcm per year). Russia is protective of its Italian gas market and would want to ensure that it would not be undermined. Any Turkey–Greece gas transit would need an early Russian 'buy in' commitment to protect Europe's broader interests, to secure its long-term dependence on other Russian gas supplies. Consequently, in all scenarios Russia can to a large extent dictate the pace of how and when a Turkish–European transit hub may form. It is unlikely to be soon.

The regional context for Caspian–Central Asian gas is different. Despite current geopolitical events in Central Asia it is difficult to envisage that in the short to medium term (2010) gas from this region will ever cross Afghanistan to markets in Pakistan and India (see **Roberts**, p. 87). Likewise an alternative land route through Iran to these same markets is also most unlikely. Iran will wish to control access to these markets for its own gas supplies. North Iran will absorb some small amounts of Turkmen gas (+/–7 bcm per year) for domestic use. But for the same competitive reasons Iran will never be a transit country for Turkmen gas to Turkey. The gas markets of China and East Asia are potentially very large, but in the short to medium term remote geography, politics and built-up delivery costs will combine to undermine a Central Asian gas supply. China and East Asia already have more commercially attractive options, such as east Siberian Russian gas for which a new project is already in progress. The gas market in China will become increasingly more important to Russia in the coming decade, and will continue to undermine the competitiveness of Caspian–Central Asian gas for many years to come.

Therefore for Kazakhstan, Turkmenistan and Uzbekistan, supplying gas ('southern gas') to the Russian domestic gas market is now the only real option. Russia needs this Caspian–Central Asian 'southern gas'. For various reasons Russian domestic gas supplies are in decline. Despite operating their west Siberian gas fields at full capacity, Russian gas production fell from 545.6 bcm in 1999 to 523.2 bcm in 2000. Over the same period Russian domestic consumption increased by 31 bcm per year, from 533.1 bcm in 1999 to 564.1 in 2000. Therefore the current squeeze for Russian domestic gas is real. For Russia to preserve its lucrative supply of gas to Europe, which is critical to central government for generating hard currency reserves, then current shortfalls of gas into the Russian domestic sector must be acquired from elsewhere. This Russia can do through the purchase of southern Caspian–Central Asian gas where there is an existing gas surplus. However, it is difficult to envisage that Russia would then go one step further, to allow commercial transit of Central Asian gas to Europe to compete with Russian gas in the markets of the EU. The same constraints may not of course apply for the delivery of 'southern' gas to the high-risk markets of the Caucasus, Ukraine and the Balkans, where debt repayments are uncertain and where Russia needs security of transit for its own export of gas to Europe.

Likewise, despite the hopes of many, it is most unlikely that Russia will in the short-to-medium term engage in a major structural reform of Gazprom. This semi-state monopoly is serving Russian interests well and sees no urgency in the need to expand external investment within its domestic gas sector. But, even with Russia as a semi-monopolistic buyer, this need not necessarily be bad news for the southern states. The current evolution of a two-tier

domestic gas market in Russia (regulated and unregulated) is already producing commercially attractive net-back pricing in the unregulated gas sector.
Russia will make every effort to drive down the price it pays for 'southern gas'
through barter deals, political pressures and market competition between the
main suppliers. But Russia is still dependent on security of supply from 'southern gas', which means it cannot drive down prices to unrealistic levels without strategic risk to itself. Southern gas tariffs of between US$25 and US$40
mcm (thousand cubic metres) should be realistically achievable.

Within this context the urgency with which the Kazakh foreign oil companies will need to dispose of their associated gas cap gas for future oil and
condensate production will weigh heavily into this market equation. But the
increasing dependence of Russia on southern gas supplies will itself reinforce
and bring discipline to the market. It would seem unlikely that Russia could
or would even wish to attract sufficient global capital for major new investments in its own gas upstream to meet its domestic shortfall in gas supply.
Time is not on its side. Thus Russia and 'southern gas' are already in a commercially symbiotic relationship, that has directly attracted private sector gas
investment from Russian oil and gas companies, both in Russia and in the
southern states. By 2005 Russia should be importing between 43 and 56 bcm
per year of Caspian–Central Asian gas. These amounts could double by 2010,
but this will need substantial sums of capital investment in both field and infrastructure upgrades that will reinforce the need for competitive gas tariffs being
paid by Russia to support this new investment.

It would therefore seem that Caspian–Central Asian gas may have a
brighter future in the short to medium term than many currently perceive.
This is particularly true when all factors are placed within a Caspian–Central
Asian demographic context. Likewise, if co-operation between Russia, the US
and Europe develops from current geopolitical events in Central Asia, then
one could perhaps envisage the development of a coherent and integrated
Russian–EU energy supply strategy. This would have material benefits in
terms of improved regional security for Central Asia, the Caspian and the
countries of the Black Sea region.

Conclusions

The post-Soviet history of Caspian energy investment has generated a decade
of unprecedented misinformation and misunderstanding. Extreme views have
been forcefully expressed, with some considerable interference in the private
sector investment process by various political powers. Some saw the province
emerging as an alternative global oil supplier to the Middle East. Others
saw the geographical isolation of the Caspian as an insurmountable obstacle
that together with the many frozen conflicts seen within the region would pro-
hibit any large-scale oil developments that could benefit the West. A fictional
James Bond film, *The World is not Enough*, was based on much of the attendant
intrigue, and correctly identified the Bosporus as the critical bottleneck
through which Caspian oil must pass to reach its primary market.

Three proven but undeveloped Soviet oil and gas fields (Tengiz, Karachaganak and Azeri–Chirag–Guneshli) drove original Western energy investment into the Caspian, and the same three fields dominate Caspian energy development today. To a large extent Western exploration activity has confirmed earlier Soviet resource predictions. Two new super-giant fields have been discovered (Kashagan and Shah Deniz), but thirteen dry holes so far in the South Caspian offshore have materially downgraded future expectations for new oil. Exploration failure costs have been exceptionally high but, when successful, exploration finding costs have been correspondingly low. Development costs are also high but, with the application of new technology and falling transportation costs, the fully built-up cost of the Caspian barrel should soon fall within an US$8–10 per barrel band. Caspian oil is globally competitive, but still needs a sustainable oil price in excess of US$18–20 per barrel to maintain commerciality and investor confidence. However, once phased financial commitments have been made for mega-projects, the multinationals will continue to invest even against cyclical downturns in international oil price. Therefore Caspian exploration and production suits those multinationals with international portfolios that allow for risk investment over the longer term.

To summarise present thinking, Caspian proven remaining recoverable oil reserves fall within the range of 8–10 bnbls for the North Caspian basin, and 6–8 bnbls in the South Caspian. Caspian yet-to-find potential is currently predicted to reach 50 bnbls, the bulk of which will be confined to the North Caspian basin. By 2010, Caspian production should reach some 3 million b/d, two-thirds from the North and one-third from the South. Caspian production could peak at 5 million b/d by 2020, which conventional industry wisdom would suggest would provide a 3 per cent contribution to future global oil supply. Caspian energy supplies will never be a strategic alternative to the OPEC producers of the Persian Gulf, but are certainly strategically important to consumers in Europe and the Black Sea.

The development of Caspian export capacity continues to improve. Multiple export options already exist that can accommodate up to 1.4 million b/d through pipelines, rail systems and barges through the Volga–Don. The northern regional CPC pipeline from Tengiz to Novorossiysk has come on stream with an incremental export capacity of 560,000 b/d. In the South Caspian, it is expected that the Baku–Tbilisi–Ceyhan pipeline will become operational in 2005. Up to 500,000 b/d of Caspian crude will move to north Iran. Iran provides a market for Caspian crude but is not a transit country. The bulk of Caspian sweet crude will move to markets in the west Mediterranean where it must displace alternative supplies from North Africa, West Africa and the Middle East. Resistance to market penetration may provoke the need for Caspian sweet crude to access more distant markets in north-west Europe and the US eastern seaboard. In this event economies of scale will dictate the use of large tankers (ultra large and very large crude carriers) from an appropriate deepwater port such as only currently exists at Ceyhan.

Yet the Caspian business environment is characterised by a high degree of risk. There are several factors that contribute to this risk. One is that the pace of Caspian oil development is heavily dependent on the timely construction of new support infrastructure and the training of critical manpower. Another is that new Caspian energy investment will require freely available conventional global financing; this is by no means certain to materialise – a necessary self-imposed capital rationing by Caspian multinationals will result in development constraints. A third and very important factor is that the absence of 'good governance' in the Caspian states will erode investor confidence and slow down the investment process. Finally, the resolution of Caspian legal title is essential, especially if the demand for conventional project financing is increased.

Nevertheless the realities and fundamentals of Caspian oil development are now more clearly understood. The nature of Caspian business risk although demanding, is also clearly manageable. As a potential global oil producer the Caspian has been materially downsized, but for the coming decades the Caspian will be strategically important to Europe for future energy supplies, at a time when North Sea oil production is already in terminal decline.

Note

This paper draws on publications prepared for the Centre for European Policy Studies, Brussels, and the Royal Institute for International Affairs, London. The considerable contribution of Laurent Ruseckas, the Caspian Regional Director for CERA, is fully acknowledged.

Selected bibliography

Historical and political background on Caspian oil development

T. Swietochowski, *Russia and Azerbaijan: A Borderland in Transition*, Colombia University Press, New York, 1995.

R. W. Toft, *The Russian Rockerfellers: The Saga of the Nobel Family and the Russian Oil Industry*, Hoover Institute Press, Stanford, 1976.

D. Yergin, *The Prize: The Epic Quest for Oil, Money and Power*, Simon & Schuster, New York, 1991.

Caspian energy in a geopolitical context

R. Ebel and R. Menon, *Energy and Conflict in Central Asia and the Caucasus*, Rowan & Littlefield, National Bureau of Asian Research, Lanham, MD, 2001.

Caspian energy issues

W. Ascher and N. Mirovitskaya, *The Caspian Sea: A Quest for Environmental Security*, NATO Science Series 2, Environment vol. 67, Kluwer Academic Press, Dordrecht, The Netherlands, 2000.

H. Dekmeijan and H. Simonian, *Troubled Waters: The Geopolitics of the Caspian Area*, I. B. Tauris, London, 2002.

Caspian oil in a global context

J. Mitchell, K. Morita, N. Selley and J. Stern, *The New Economy of Oil: Impacts on Business, Geopolitics and Society*, Royal Institute of International Affairs, Energy and Environment Programme, London, 2001.

Part IV
Socio-economic Issues

7 Natural resources, governance and transition in Azerbaijan, Kazakhstan and Turkmenistan

Richard Auty

This chapter applies models of economic development and governance to assess the development prospects of the energy-rich Caspian basin countries in transition to a market economy. Natural resource abundance should facilitate economic development because the rents (the residual revenue after deducting all costs of production including a normal risk-related return on capital) can be used to boost the levels of investment and taxation, while the foreign exchange from resource exports can enhance import capacity. However, research on the developing market economies shows that the resource-rich countries have often squandered these advantages in recent decades (Auty 2001a). For example, World Bank data on natural resource rents, available for the year 1994 only, show an inverse relationship between natural resource rents and per capita GDP growth (see Table 7.1).

The adverse effects of resource abundance are potentially stronger for mineral economies than for crop-driven economies (Auty 2001a). This is because mining is capital-intensive so that tax revenues dominate the domestic economic impact and thereby concentrate the rents on the government. This increases the risk that rents will not be effectively deployed because governments are less likely to treat windfall revenues as temporary than private agents such as farmers are, so they tend to spend revenues too quickly and in doing so distort the economy. In contrast, the export of peasant cash crops is more conducive to economic development because the rents are diffused across a wider set of domestic economic agents (Baldwin 1956; Bevan *et al.* 1987). Table 7.1 shows that, among six classes of natural resource endowment, the small mineral economies whether oil exporters or hard mineral exporters have the highest rents in relation to GDP but the slowest per capita GDP growth since the mid-1980s.

Consistent with these findings from the developing market economies, models of resource-driven economic growth suggest that natural resource abundance may hamper the transition towards a market economy (Auty 2001a). More specifically, the models suggest that compared with resource-poor countries, the mineral-rich countries in transition will experience:

- slower implementation of reform;
- higher levels of rent-seeking and corruption;

Table 7.1 Share of rents in GDP 1994 and per capita GDP growth, six natural resource endowment categories

Resource endowment	Pasture and cropland rent (per cent GDP)	Mineral rent (per cent GDP)	Total rent (per cent GDP)	Per capita GDP growth 1985–1997 (per cent/yr)
Resource-poor[1,2]				
Large	7.34	3.22	10.56	4.7
Small	5.41	4.45	9.86	2.4
Resource-rich				
Large	5.83	6.86	12.65	1.9
Small, non-mineral	12.89	2.53	15.42	0.9
Small, hard mineral	9.62	7.89	17.51	−0.4
Small, oil exporter	2.18	19.04	21.22	−0.7

Source: Derived from World Bank (2000).

Notes
1 Resource-poor = 1970 cropland/head < 0.3 hectares.
2 Large = 1970 GDP > US$7 billion.

- faster rebound of the real exchange rate and therefore slower economic restructuring;
- steeper falls in GDP and tax revenues, and lagged resumption of economic growth.

However, the economic models on which these hypotheses are based are not deterministic in their outcome because governance plays a critical role in determining development. A handful of resource-rich countries including Malaysia, Botswana and Chile engendered developmental political states, which combine the high autonomy required to pursue a coherent economic policy with the aim of raising welfare throughout society. A fundamental task of the enabling governments that are associated with the developmental political state is to provide the institutions and public goods that are required to lower transaction costs and stimulate economic growth. Micro-institutions like civic associations engender trust and thereby facilitate exchange at low incomes when most transactions are local and the prime consideration is risk-reduction in a relatively isolated environment. However, development entails economic specialisation and expanding trading horizons that demand the formation of formal institutions at the macro level, notably the rule of law and property rights.

A model of enabling governance (Auty 2001b) elaborates Olson's (2000) theory that the provision of public goods will be more effective, the wider the encompassing interest of the political state (i.e. the more it tends towards a consensual democracy rather than an oligarchy or an autonomous preda-tory state). It takes account of differences in the natural resource endowment because lower-income countries still depend heavily on the primary sector for economic growth so that the scale of the natural resource rents is significant. Resource-poor countries are more likely to spawn a developmental political state because, with lower natural resource rents, their governments have a greater incentive to boost output in order to advance their interests. In addition, sanctions against rapacious government behaviour are likely to be stronger in resource-poor countries because of a lower tolerance by the majority poor of inequitable asset distribution and rent-seeking behaviour. Rent-seeking behaviour diverts effort from raising productivity towards lobbying politicians for rent, creating significant scope for corruption. Hence governments in resource-poor countries are likely to align their interests with those of the majority poor. In contrast, rent-seeking in resource-rich countries drives a wedge between the interests of the government and those whom the government favours, and the majority of the population.

Stated more formally, assuming there are two sources of income available to governments, resource rents and returns to investment, then high-rent and low-rent countries yield contrasting outcomes. The government in the high-rent country will find it easier to satisfy its financial needs by capturing the rents than by investing to generate wealth so that the latter will be neglected in favour of the former. Effort will be diverted into the political process by which rents are extracted and away from measures to raise productivity, like improving institutions. Indeed, effective institutions may be regarded as an impediment to rent-seeking behaviour because they increase government accountability and promote competition that eliminates rents. In contrast, governments of resource-poor countries have an interest in maximising production and so in improving institutions. For example, if the remuneration of political leaders is 1 per cent of total output, the leadership maximises its remuneration by maximising national output.

The model of enabling governance focuses upon the degree to which the expenditure on the provision of public goods is traded off against the accommodation of rent-seeking behaviour. However, in addition to the interaction between natural resources and the political state, two other conditions affect the outcome in the transition economies. They are the institutional legacy from central planning and the inherited gap between the demand for public services under central planning and the government revenue available to meet that demand. Each of these is briefly elaborated below.

The institutional endowment may be conceived as the sanctions against anti-social behaviour. For the reasons given above, such sanctions are likely to be weaker in resource-rich countries but not inevitably so. For example, the balance of racial groups restrained rent seeking in Malaysia while tribal homogeneity and shared experience of drought produced a similar outcome in diamond-rich Botswana. However, more commonly such sanctions are absent and government leaders in resource-rich countries feel free not only to capture the rents but also to invest them overseas. The gain to the domestic economy is therefore further diminished by capital flight.

Turning to the compression of government expenditure, central planners were able to repress consumer demand in order to divert a larger fraction of output to public goods provision than a market economy at a comparable stage of development. The collapse of central planning brought a sharp compression in the productive capacity of the economy, and thereby in public revenue, due to disruption of trading links and withdrawal of Soviet subsidies. Among the economies in transition, gradual reformers like China postponed the gap while the faster reformers of Central and East Europe (CEE) lost productive capacity equivalent to one-fifth of GDP and the associated ability to provide public goods. Elsewhere, the countries of the Commonwealth of Independent States (CIS) lost on average almost half their output, and in some cases more than three-fifths of GDP, while government revenue shrank by still more thereby exerting massive compression on the provision of public goods (EBRD 1999, 58). Although the resulting sharp rise in poverty might be expected to strengthen sanctions against predatory government behaviour, this was not the case, especially in the energy-rich countries.

Summarising, the enabling governance model suggests that institutional capital accumulates faster the lower the natural resource rents, the stronger the sanctions against anti-social behaviour (i.e. the broader the encompassing interest of the state), the smaller the post-communist compression of GDP and the greater the extent of competitive markets, which reduce rent-seeking opportunities (Aslund 1999). This chapter tests the hypotheses generated by the resource-driven economic model and the enabling governance model in three energy-rich Caspian region countries in transition, Azerbaijan, Kazakhstan and Turkmenistan. The next section estimates the economic growth potential of the natural resource rents under the assumption of a developmental political state. The third section then tests the hypotheses from the economic model by comparing the progress of transition reform in the energy-rich economies with other sub-groups of transition economy. The fourth section tests the hypotheses generated by the governance model. The conclusion summarises the findings and assesses the implications.

Prospects for economic growth under developmental political states

The estimates of energy reserves in Azerbaijan, Kazakhstan and Turkmenistan vary greatly. In the 1990s some sources suggested that together these three states may contain up to 200 billion barrels of oil, sufficient to make this the second largest oil province after the Persian Gulf. By the end of the decade more modest predictions were being made (see **Ehteshami**, p. 70, **Adams**, p. 92 and **Olsen**, p. 132). However, the rents available to governments within the region depend not only upon volatile oil prices, but also upon the costs of extraction, which tend to be relatively high. This is due not only to distance from markets but also the heavy capital investment required in a relatively high-risk area in order to revitalise production from existing fields and to develop new fields. Based on the experience of the Azerbaijan International Oil Corporation (AIOC), PlanEcon (1997) estimates production costs at US$10.96 per barrel (/bl), including a hefty US$4.44/bl for shipment via pipeline or tanker, but excluding the corporate share of gross profit. However, the estimated production costs for the Tengiz field in Kazakhstan suggest both capital costs and operating costs of around US$2/bl, while transportation costs fall from US$6/bl to US$3.50/bl with the opening of the CPC (Caspian Pipeline Consortium) pipeline, making the delivered cost of oil US$7.50/bl (see also **Adams**, p. 92).

The rent comprises any surplus revenue that is not required by a competitive producer in order to remain in production. The rent can be taxed away by the government as compensation for the once-for-all depletion of the country's natural capital and invested in alternative wealth-generating assets to ensure sustainable development. In order to estimate the rents, both the return on capital and taxation must be added to the basic cost of production and the sum must then be subtracted from the realised price of oil. PlanEcon adds a further US$1.88/bl, and this lifts the cost range per barrel of oil to between US$9.40 and US$12.80. The rents on Caspian basin oil are likely to be low through the medium term for two reasons in addition to the relatively high delivered cost. First, some of the oil reserves have a high sulphur content, which lowers prices by up to 25 per cent compared with North Sea oil. Second, oil prices have been projected to fall from US$28/bl in 2001 to US$18/bl by 2005, though admittedly the war in Iraq in 2003 and subsequent unrest there may alter this trajectory. The projected price decline reflects a substantial expansion in global oil reserves to over 1 trillion barrels in the late 1990s, some 50 per cent higher than in 1975 (BP 1998).

In the case of Azerbaijan the oil sector was neglected towards the close of Soviet rule and requires substantial investment. Oil reserves are currently conservatively estimated at 7 billion barrels and gas around 850 bcm, around 0.65 per cent of world reserves in each case (*Financial Times* 2000a). An optimistic scenario assumes production reaches 1.6 million barrels per day (b/d) by 2003, which even with oil at US$17 per barrel lifts the share of hydrocarbons to 30 per cent of GDP and 85 per cent of exports (Rosenberg and Saavalainen 1998).

The International Energy Agency (IEA) projects Azerbaijani oil production will only quintuple to around 1.2 million b/d by 2007 (Fueg 2000) but the World Bank (1999) is even more cautious and assumes oil production reaches 569,000 by 2006 and 908,000 by 2010. This would push oil exports to US$1.98 billion by 2006 and generate government revenue reaching 10.6 per cent of GDP in 2006, some three-fifths of total government revenue. Under this scenario the potential impact of the oil sector on the Azerbaijani economy is modest until mid-decade. This reflects the long lead-time on investment and front-loading of capital recovery. (The contracts give operating costs and capital recovery first claim on revenues, subject to them not exceeding 60 per cent of the total. Of the remainder, one-eighth of the total revenue accrues to the Azerbaijani government.) However, the oil agreements include contract bonuses that bring forward revenues to the government. In addition, in the absence of a price collapse like that of 1998, oil investment will drive the economy until the rents expand.

Estimates of Kazakh oil production by 2010 range from a 'cautious' three-fold increase to 1.8 million barrels per day as the massive Kashagan field comes on stream (Fueg 2000) to 2.4 million barrels per day (EIA 2003). The cautious estimate suggests a potential rent stream from oil of US$3.5 billion per annum by 2005, rising above US$5.3 billion by 2010. This gives a range of 25–35 per cent of non-mining GDP, larger than the windfalls experienced by Nigeria during the 1974–1978 and 1979–1981 oil booms.

Turning to Turkmenistan, the country's oil reserves are modest, but it has the third largest natural gas reserves in the world. However, transportation costs for gas are much higher per unit of heat value than those for oil and this combines with the country's isolated location to shrink the potential rents. The World Bank estimates the cost of gas extraction in Turkmenistan at 50–55 US cents per thousand cubic feet (c/mcf); this is the equivalent of US$17.65–19.42 per thousand cubic metres (see **Adams**, p. 104). These figures imply that, in order to generate even a modest rent, the transport costs must not exceed US$1.75/mcf on CIS sales and US$2.50/mcf on EU sales. This implies rents from 45c/mcf to 20c/mcf. (A rule-of-thumb transport cost through the existing CIS network is 40c/mcf per 1,000 km so gas exports into Russia incur total costs of US$1.80/mcf using the existing network, and US$2.05/mcf for a new pipeline.)

The alignment of domestic gas prices with world prices would generate around US$800 million in rents, while recovery of pre-reform CIS markets would generate rents around US$1.6 billion. Finally, a relatively modest build-up of exports to 30 billion cubic metres in new markets south and west of Turkmenistan could add almost US$300 million more in rent. Unfortunately, the break-up of the Soviet Union precipitated a steep decline in gas production, which fell from 80 billion cubic metres per year in 1990 to barely one-quarter of that level by 1998. A slow recovery is forecast by the IEA, to only 50 billion cubic metres by 2010, well below pre-reform levels. This might generate US$0.9 billion in rent, perhaps one-fifth of a recovering GDP.

The scale of projected energy rents in all three countries suggests that, carefully managed, they could boost economic growth to a level that would double per capita GDP each decade. In order to do this, however, governments must create a capital development fund to sterilise the rents and prevent them from strengthening the real exchange rate and triggering Dutch disease effects (the shrinkage of tradeable sectors, notably agriculture and manufacturing). In addition, a mineral revenue stabilisation fund is required in order to smooth the flow of revenues to the government in the face of volatile prices and prevent public expenditure from amplifying the boom–bust cycle. Both these funds should be transparent to reduce opportunities for corruption and promote informed debate about the most effective use of the rents. Finally, a project evaluation unit is required to compare the alternative investment options open to the government in allocating the rents. These three institutions will function most effectively under a developmental state. Unfortunately, as the next two sections show, all three countries are drifting towards authoritarian states and economic performance is weak.

Adverse economic impacts of mineral wealth to date

A comparison between the energy-rich and resource-poor countries in the Caspian basin region (Auty 2001c) suggests that natural resource abundance slowed reform in the 1990s (see Table 7.2). Moreover, the faster progress of the resource-poor countries occurred despite the fact that reforms were delayed by civil strife in three out of four of them, whereas civil strife affected only one energy-rich country, Azerbaijan. It is possible that in the absence of civil strife the resource-poor countries would have progressed still further with reform, as Kyrgyzstan may show.

The resource-poor countries also experienced a greater compression of government revenue than the energy-rich countries, due to the greater fall in their output as a whole. The mean figure for 1998 of the share of government revenue in GDP is 14.2 per cent in the resource-poor Caspian countries compared with 15.7 per cent of GDP for the energy economies (IMF 2000, 19). However, contrary to the predictions of the resource-driven economic model, the higher share of government revenue and natural resource rents in the GDP of energy-rich countries is not associated with higher levels of corruption and rent-seeking behaviour. Although state intervention is indeed higher in the energy-rich countries than in the resource-poor ones, according to the EBRD, other indices of corruption, including the bribe tax and share of the black economy in GDP, do not support the hypothesis that the mineral-rich countries experience more corruption than the resource-poor countries (Table 7.2). This outcome is also contrary to the findings of Leite and Weidmann (1999). It seems that corruption is strongly related to institutional capital. For example, the CEE transition countries, including the Baltic republics (BR), exhibit significantly lower corruption than those in the Caspian region. However, the fact remains that corruption is very high in the energy-rich Caspian countries and this trend seems likely to continue.

The economic model also predicts that energy-rich countries will experience slower progress in the competitive restructuring of their economies than the resource-poor countries. This is due to the combination of slower reform and the Dutch disease effects. Consistent with this hypothesis, the

Table 7.2 Transition reform indices, by country group and countries

Country group	Reform index	Private firms (per cent GDP)	Black economy (per cent GDP)	Continued growth (years)	1998 GDP as per cent 1989 GDP
CEE + BR	3.3	68.0	18.2	5.11	87.0
Caspian region	2.3	50.6	41.3	2.11	51.9
Resource-poor	2.5	55.0	63.0	3.00	44.0
Energy-rich	2.1	41.7	47.5	1.33	50.0
Azerbaijan	2.2	45.0	61.0	3.00	44.0
Kazakhstan	2.7	55.0	34.0	0.00	61.0
Turkmenistan	1.4	25.0	n.a.	1.00	44.0

Source: EBRD (1999), Johnson *et al.* (1997), Freedom House (2000).

post-transition rebound of the real exchange rate since 1994 has been stronger in Kazakhstan, but less so in Turkmenistan and Azerbaijan. Data on the monthly dollar wage provide an index of the exchange rate rebound. They show a rate of US$120 in Kazakhstan in 1998 (Gurgen *et al.* 1999, 15), which received by far the largest foreign investment per capita in the Caspian region, compared with US$50–55 in Turkmenistan. The average dollar wage for Azerbaijan was lower than expected, given its large oil-related investment, at US$40, on a par with resource-poor Kyrgyzstan (Valdevieso 1998, 9). However, the dollar wage in the three other resource-poor countries ranged downwards from US$30 in Georgia to US$22 in Armenia and US$12 in Tajikistan. Data covering the years 1995–1999 show real exchange rate appreciation in excess of 200 per cent for Azerbaijan and Turkmenistan, and 100 per cent for resource-rich Uzbekistan, whereas the rates rose very little or actually declined for other countries surveyed (Pastor and van Rooden 2000, 7).

Table 7.3 uses employment shares to measure the changing structure of the economy in response to the transition. It shows that the successful reformers of CEE experienced a slight contraction in industry and non-market services that was offset by a sizeable expansion in market services. The energy-rich Caspian countries exhibit a much larger fall in industry that is offset by a slight rise in agriculture and a larger rise in market services. The resource-poor Caspian countries had the most dramatic restructuring with a sharp rise in agricultural employment offsetting the halving of industrial employment and a fall in non-market services. Restructuring in the energy-rich economies therefore lags behind that in the resource-poor countries. This carries implications for income distribution because, although the capital-intensive mining export sector is dynamic, it employs relatively few workers compared with investment-starved agriculture and manufacturing.

Further evidence of Dutch disease effects emerge from Table 7.4, which compares the actual structure of employment in the principal tradeable sectors, agriculture and industry, with the expected structure for market economies of a similar size and level of development. Both oil-rich economies (Azerbaijan and Kazakhstan) exhibit trends that are consistent with Dutch

Table 7.3 Change in employment composition, by sector 1990–1997 (per cent total)

	Agriculture	Industry	Non-market services	Market services
Central + East Europe	14 → 13	41 → 35	24 → 20	22 → 31
Caspian region	31 → 44	37 → 15	17 → 25	14 → 16
Resource-poor	30 → 52	31 → 14	26 → 21	12 → 13
Energy-rich	32 → 34	26 → 17	24 → 23	16 → 23
Azerbaijan[1]	32 → 29	25 → 14	25 → 26	17 → 27
Kazakhstan	22 → 25	31 → 18	25 → 20	17 → 32
Turkmenistan	42 → 49	21 → 18	23 → 22	13 → 11

Source: Derived from **EBRD** (2000).

Note: 1 Data are for 1990–1996.

Table 7.4 Dutch disease effects 1990–1997 (actual + expected employment share)

	Index	1990	1997	Departure from norm in 1997
Energy-rich				
Azerbaijan[1]	Agriculture	0.31	0.29	−0.13
	Industry	0.25	0.14	−0.05
	Distortion	+0.03	−0.18	
Kazakhstan	Agriculture	0.22	0.25	−0.03
	Industry	0.31	0.18	−0.05
	Distortion	+0.05	−0.08	
Turkmenistan	Agriculture	0.42	0.49	+0.06
	Industry	0.21	0.18	−0.02
	Distortion	+0.13	+0.04	
Resource-poor				
Armenia	Agriculture	0.18	0.41	+0.08
	Industry	0.42	0.21	−0.01
	Distortion	+0.14	+0.07	
Georgia[1]	Agriculture	0.26	0.53	+0.13
	Industry	0.20	0.10	−0.10
	Distortion	+0.08	+0.03	
Kyrgyzstan	Agriculture	0.33	0.48	+0.14
	Industry	0.28	0.14	−0.08
	Distortion	+0.10	+0.06	
Tajikistan	Agriculture	0.43	0.64	+0.14
	Industry	0.22	0.12	−0.05
	Distortion	+0.10	+0.09	

Source: Derived from EBRD (2000).

Notes
For example, Azerbaijani employment in agriculture and manufacturing in 1990 was 5 per cent higher than the norms for a market economy at a similar level of income whereas by 1997 it was 18 per cent lower. The final column shows that in 1997 agricultural employment in Azerbaijan was two-thirds of the size expected and manufacturing three-quarters.

1 Data are for 1990–1996.

disease effects: employment in the tradeable sector (agriculture and manufacturing) in 1997 is below the level expected in these two energy-rich countries, whereas it is significantly larger than expected in all four resource-poor countries. This reflects a sharp expansion of agricultural employment within the resource-poor countries (by around one-half or more), whereas in the energy-rich economies, agriculture either contracted, or if it expanded it did so only modestly (Table 7.4).

Finally, turning to the hypothesis about economic growth, Table 7.5 shows that the faster reformers of CEE experienced a shallower downturn in GDP compared to the Caspian region countries as a whole. More specifically, the transition trajectory of the faster-reforming CEE countries is one of a relatively modest decline in output, an early revival of growth and a steady recovery to seven-eighths of the pre-transition output within six years of reform. Compared with the faster reformers, output fell by twice as much

Table 7.5 Transition growth trajectories, by country and regional groups

Country group	Reform index	Cumulative GDP decline to low (per cent)	Year of lowest GDP	Cumulative GDP growth from low (per cent)	Annual GDP growth from low (per cent)	Ratio of GDP low to six-year transition GDP
CEE + BR	3.3	28.9	1993	24.8	3.8	0.87
Caspian region	2.3	55.1	1995	14.6	4.1	0.58
Resource-poor	2.5	66.0	1995	21.9	5.1	0.53
Energy-rich	2.1	54.2	1996	7.4	3.3	0.55
Azerbaijan	2.2	63.1	1995	17.8	5.4	0.50
Kazakhstan	2.7	40.0	1998	0.0	0.0	0.69
Turkmenistan	1.4	59.5	1997	4.5	4.5	0.45

Source: Derived from Fischer and Sahay (2000), 34.

in the Caspian region and bottomed out two years later, but GDP growth was subsequently more vigorous. The relative dynamism of the Azerbaijani economy may be attributed to its small size relative to foreign investment upon which that growth strongly depends. However, the energy-rich countries experienced a more modest output collapse than the strife-ridden resource-poor countries and also a later and less robust economic recovery. In summary, the transition trajectory of the fast-reforming CEE countries traces a shallow U-shape compared with a V-shape for the resource-poor countries and the reverse-J of the energy-rich economies. Overall, resource abundance does appear to be hampering reform in the energy-rich Caspian basin countries. This points to deficiencies in the provision of public goods to which attention now turns.

Governance and institutions in the energy-rich Caspian countries

In contrast to the CEE countries, the post-Soviet political states in the Caspian region countries have converged on a centrist autonomous political state, with varying degrees of predation. The inherited institutions remain deficient (see Table 7.6). Social cohesion helps to strengthen social sanctions against government predation. An index of social cohesion is provided by the EBRD (1999, 108), based on the ratio of seats won in the first post-reform election by the successor to the communist parties compared with seats won by the largest non-communist party. Social cohesion is highest where the seats won by the non-communist party significantly exceed those won by the communist party. High scores are recorded for the CEE countries and low scores for the Central Asian countries.

Resource-poor Armenia and Georgia exhibit relatively high social cohesion, while resource-poor Kyrgyzstan strengthened its democratic institutions until the late 1990s. However, the energy-rich countries significantly weak-

Table 7.6 Indices of social capital, by natural resource endowment and country

Country group	Macro-distortion index[1]	Social cohesion index[2]	Index of corruption	Political freedom
CEE + BR[3]	−0.70	2.7 [4]	2.3	3.7
Resource-poor Caspian	*0.92*	*1.80*	*7.6*	*9.3*
Energy-rich Caspian	*1.11*	*0.08*	*7.2*	*11.7*
Azerbaijan	1.00	0.17	7.5	10.0
Kazakhstan	1.07	0.06	7.0	11.0
Turkmenistan	1.27	0.01	7.0	14.0

Source: Derived from EBRD (1999), except 1.

Notes
1 Distortion increases moving from negative to positive (de Melo *et al.* 1996).
2 Ratio seats of communist party to seats of largest non-communist party (per cent) Central and Eastern Europe (Croatia, Czech Republic, Estonia, Hungary, Latvia, Lithuania, Poland, Slovenia, Slovak Republic).
3 Central and Eastern Europe and the Baltic Republics (Croatia, Czech Republic, Estonia, Hungary, Latvia, Lithuania, Poland, Slovak Republic and Slovenia).
4 Excluding Estonia whose index dwarfs all others because communists won no seats.

ened nascent democratic institutions. The repression of political parties reduces the extent to which power is contested and renders the nature of public finances opaque, fostering corruption by both the elite and the bureaucracy, inflicting high transaction costs that depress economic incentives. Aslund (1999) argues that stalled reform may be the optimum goal for such regimes because it secures stabilisation via Western financial assistance without completing the competitive markets that curb rent-seeking opportunities.

The leaders of the energy-rich states have not used the revenues from contract bonuses to strengthen institutions, cushion the poor or enhance the effectiveness of their oil rent deployment strategy. Rather, they have shown few qualms about siphoning away the energy rents for personal use, leaving the populace at large to shoulder the burden of adjustment to the compression of government revenues. One consequence is that the salaries of civil servants are commonly one-fifth or less of the sum required to cover basic needs so that, like the political leadership, civil servants abuse their positions to augment their incomes by levying illicit imposts. The required rents are created by multiplying bureaucratic obstacles, thereby further delaying progress towards the establishment of an enabling environment.

Figure 7.1 shows how a pair of interlocked vicious circles of corruption represses the economy under these conditions. The starting point is low remuneration in the over-staffed public sector that obliges public employees to seek ways to make up the extra income that they need to meet their basic needs. This leads to abuse of the state monopoly in the provision of key services by levying illegal imposts on the private sector. The payment of these imposts diverts effort into rent-seeking behaviour, away from both the efficient provision of public services by government employees and from efforts to improve efficiency by private firms. This raises the cost of production and depresses investment while encouraging firms to seek exemptions from legitimate taxation in order to offset the costs imposed by rent-seeking (the Government Revenue circuit in Figure 7.1). This in turn reduces the flow of legitimate revenue into the public sector and, when combined with retarded private sector employment creation due to low investment, leaves workers trapped in low-paid public sector jobs (the Government Employment circuit in Figure 7.1). In this way the corruption of the public sector represses the economy and becomes self-perpetuating.

Deficient post-Soviet macro-institutions led the new political states of the CIS to draw upon local variants of micro (bonding) institutions based on social ties within a local region (Azerbaijan) or a family (Kazakhstan and Turkmenistan) or a clan (Uzbekistan). Of the three energy-rich states, Turkmenistan is most deficient in macro-institutional capital and most extreme in repressing civil society. It is an autonomous predatory state with a cult of personality built around the president, Niyazov (Lubin 2000). The president retains the right to enact laws and has the power to appoint within the judiciary and the executive, and to dissolve the parliament. Opposition parties are considered 'unnecessary' and what little open dissent has surfaced has been quickly quashed (see **Canzi**, p. 186).

The strategy of the Turkmen government after the Soviet collapse has been to encourage foreign investment while avoiding social dislocation by subsidising water, gas and electricity until the hydrocarbon rents flow to the rescue. Accordingly, the legal system was revised but this failed to have the desired effect on inward investment. This is partly because of the capriciousness of the changes and the fact that the president scrutinises all

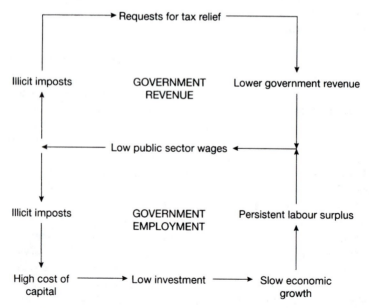

Figure 7.1 Vicious circles of rent-seeking behaviour

contracts and retains the power to control employment, including that by foreign investors (Lubin 2000). Turkmenistan, the slowest Caspian basin reformer, is reported to have advised the International Monetary Fund (IMF) that it requires no assistance provided that the IMF revives neighbouring economies so that their demand for natural gas increases along with their capacity to pay for it other than by bartering shoddy goods.

Civil society is stronger in Azerbaijan than in either of the energy-rich Central Asian countries but macro-institutions of accountability have been systematically repressed and they are weaker than those in Kazakhstan. Although after independence government revenue collapsed to less than one-fifth of GDP and the poverty rate ballooned to embrace more than half the population, the Azerbaijani government did not align its interests with the populace but used the oil revenues to enhance the autonomy of the president, enriching his family and the family's associates. The Production Sharing Agreements provided a direct route to personal enrichment. Half of the estimated US$3.75 billion potential revenue (i.e. at world prices) generated by oil between 1996 and 2000 found its way onto domestic markets at low prices. However, US$1.5 billion of the estimated production was exported and this may have contributed several US$100 million to the presidential assets, but not the billions claimed by some opponents. The presidential fortune was also augmented by cuts on business deals. President Heidar Aliev was reported by one seasoned observer to receive a cut from every business ranging from construction through trade. Meanwhile,although cabinet officials in Azerbaijan are poorly paid according to the public accounts, they are believed to receive payments in excess of US$100,000 (*Economist* 1998). Elsewhere, an aspirant to the post of tax inspector would-expect to make a payment of US$50,000 to secure the post. Another estimate suggests that 5–6 per cent of GDP is paid to access state-owned health services, whereas official health expenditure is 1.6 per cent of GDP. The State Oil Fund of Azerbaijan (SOFAZ), established by presidential decree in December 1999, is intended to ensure that oil revenues will be used for the benefit of 'future generations' of citizens (Tsalik 2003, 108). SOFAZ is an independent legal entity. Nevertheless, the president exercises a high degree of control over this body. Some opposition leaders, as well as non-governmental organisations (NGOs) and other representatives of civil society, are concerned that the existence of an off-budget fund might heighten the possibility of corruption (see **Karayianni**).

Outside the oil sector, the 1995 Constitution rendered Azerbaijan's three high courts (Constitutional, Supreme and Economic) subservient to the president while the parliament's power to scrutinise the budget and impeach the president became nominal when Aliev supporters 'won' all but eight of the 125 seats in the 1995 parliamentary election. Aliev further consolidated his power by 'winning' re-election to a further term as president in 1998. Originally, he had planned to stand again in October 2003. However, his health was already failing and, as an 'insurance policy', his son Ilham was also registered as a presidential candidate. On the eve of the election

Heidar Aliev withdrew his candidacy and Ilham was duly elected president (see **Nassibli**, p. 176). Heidar Aliev died on 12 December 2003. Yet systems that he created remain in place. In the absence of an impartial judiciary and civil service, ministries form lines of patronage whose ability to deliver rewards (such as tax relief, relaxed regulation and preferential contracts) seems set to depend upon proximity to the Aliev family and their cronies.

Azerbaijani growth has been driven largely by the oil sector, which the government allows to function relatively unscathed by illicit imposts. However, the multiplier from such investment appears to be as little as 0.65 compared for example, with a figure of 1.8 for Aberdeen, so that there is considerable leakage. Meanwhile, illicit imposts and the relative strength of the real exchange rate repress investment in the non-mining tradeables so that businesses find it more profitable to import than to invest in local production. The agricultural sector has acted as a reservoir for surplus labour (see Table 7.3), but deficient markets for finance, farm inputs and farm products have caused commercial production to give way to subsistence farming. Some 2 million Azerbaijanis, one-quarter of the workforce, are estimated to have sought employment abroad. However, this regression into an inadequate subsistence base led to spontaneous disturbances in four different parts of the country in late 2000, including Nakhichevan, the homeland of the president. In this way, a freer civil society may counter-balance the consequences of repressed political institutions by pressuring the leadership to restart reform.

In terms of preconditions, Kazakhstan shares features with Azerbaijan. However, Kazakhstan is richer in natural resources, and not only in energy but also in land and other minerals. This has reinforced the complacency of the leadership towards the majority poor. Since 1995, the government has sought to sideline the parliament and in the 1999 elections the president banned his main opponent and 'won' with more than 80 per cent of the vote. More than half the parliamentary deputies would have lost their seats without manipulation of the votes (*Financial Times* 2000b). Yet the parliament has managed to retain greater capacity to scrutinise public spending than its counterparts in other energy-rich countries within the region. Nevertheless, civic society is weaker than in the Caucasus. Leading dissenters are at first ignored, then harassed by the state bureaucracy and finally bought off (and effectively muzzled) with a 'position' within the government. The result is a 'submerging democracy' in which power has been consolidated on the Nazerbaev family, key ministers (who may be disgraced if they become too powerful, like the former Prime Minister Kazhegeldin) and an elite of several thousand Moscow-educated officials (see **Jafar**, p. 206).

The privatisation of natural resource assets in Kazakhstan is seen by the government as a way of bringing forward receipts and the oil sector alone was estimated to have yielded US$2 billion in net revenue (bonuses, privatisation and asset sales, profit oil and taxes) by 2000 (Fueg 2000). However, large sums did not appear in the government budget, including the US$800 million and US$450 million, respectively, that Mobil and Chevron expended to enter the Tengiz partnership. In addition, export prices are recorded at well below world prices, even after allowing for a price discount due to the lower quality of Kazakh oil, so that in excess of US$5/bl may find its way into offshore accounts. The ruling family may well have amassed assets in excess of US$1 billion. The creation of the National Oil Fund in 2000 is supposed to ensure that oil revenues are used for the benefit of the people, but the low level of oversight and the fact that the president enjoys wide-ranging, exclusive powers over the Fund raises concerns that there will be a lack of public accountability (Tsalik 2003, 151).

Meanwhile, natural resources also provide sizeable opportunities for regional officials to enrich themselves while contributing far less than they might in a more transparent society to closing the social expenditure gap. Responsibility for the latter falls on foreign investors who must take over the social services of the former state enterprises in ways that hinder corporate restructuring while diminishing government responsibility for the outcome. This also causes social spending to vary widely between regions, depending upon the extent of foreign investment. The lagging regions depend on neglect-ed economic sectors that include not only manufacturing and agriculture but also non-hydrocarbon mining. In the latter, the conglomorates (combinaty) skim profits at the expense of maintaining long-term productive capacity.

The widening income differential is reflected in mounting unofficial un-employment and it risks exacerbating the ethnic divide between a more prosperous north and east, dominated by Russians, and a lagging south and west where Kazakhs are dominant. The government has responded to fears of a regional divide by channelling rents from the state oil company into the construction of the new capital city at Astana, rather than into measures to improve social welfare in lagging regions. In the absence of institutional reform to boost public accountability, higher oil rents are likely to distort the economy and exacerbate social tensions still further.

Conclusions

Economic data for the first decade of independence suggest that the devel-opment trajectory of the energy-rich Caspian basin countries has indeed been less favourable than that of the resource-poor countries, despite the severity of civil strife in three out of the four resource-poor countries (com-pared with one of the three energy-rich countries). Both economic reform and the restructuring of the economy have proceeded faster in the resource-poor countries and although the loss of GDP was greater (due in large part to civil strife) recovery has been faster and more robust. Nevertheless, the evidence does not support the expectation of the resource-driven economic models that corruption will necessarily be more extreme in the energy-rich countries; Botswana, Chile and Malaysia, for example, exhibit relatively low levels of corruption.

The governance model suggests that movement towards an enabling government is most likely with low natural resource rent, strong sanctions against anti-social behaviour, less GDP compression and the emergence of competitive markets. These hypotheses suggest less favourable political prospects for the energy-rich countries than the resource-poor countries. Certainly, the energy-rich countries, with Turkmenistan the most extreme, are converging on the predatory autocratic model of political state. Unfortunately, the resource-poor countries may follow, albeit at a slower pace, due to regional pressures to conform (Kopstein and Reilly 2000).

A rent-fuelled oil boom may initially postpone an economic downturn but, without appropriate institutions, the rent stream is likely to be mismanaged. In the absence of institutional reform, an expansion in mineral rents is likely to propel the energy-rich countries into increasing dependence on a single commodity whose own competitiveness is eventually sapped by predation that outstrips the rents and depresses investment incentives (Auty 2001a). Worse, pressures within the region for political convergence may cause the energy-rich Caspian countries to drag the resource-poor countries down with them. However, the synergy between the energy-rich and resource-poor Caspian basin countries may also hold the key to improvement. This is because the economic and governance models suggest that resource-poor countries afford more favourable conditions for economic and political reform. Consequently, external agencies can bolster these trends to foster a more promising norm for the countries in the region to converge upon.

References

Aslund, A., *Why has Russia's Economic Transformation been so Arduous?*, Paper to the World Bank Annual Conference on Development Economics, Washington DC, 1999.

Auty, R. M. (ed.) (2001a), *Resource Abundance and Economic Development*, Oxford University Press, Oxford, 2001.

Auty, R. M., *A Model of Enabling Governance and its Application to Low-income Transition Economies* (2001b), Working Paper 0101, Lancaster University: Department of Geography, 2001.

Auty, R. M. (2001c), 'Transition Reform in the Mineral-rich Caspian Region Countries', *Resource Policy*, 27 (1), 2001, pp. 25–32.

Baldwin, Robert E., 'Patterns of Development in Newly Settled Regions', *Manchester School of Social and Economic Studies*, 24, 1956, pp. 161–179.

Bevan, D. L., Collier, P. and Gunning, J. W., 'Consequences of a Commodity Boom in a Controlled Economy: Accumulation and Redistribution in Kenya', *World Bank Economic Review*, 1, 1997, pp. 489–513.

British Petroleum (BP), *BP Statistical Review of World Energy 1997*, BP, London, 1998.

De Melo, M., Denizer, C., Gelb, A. H. and Tenev, S. working paper, later published as 'Circumstance and choice: the role of initial conditions and policies in transition economies', *The World Bank Economic Review*, 15 (1), 1–31, 2001.

Economist, 'Central Asia Survey', *The Economist*, 7 February 1998.

Energy Information Administration (EIA), US Department of Energy (http://eia.doe.gov/emeu/cabs/caspgrdh.html), August 2003.

European Bank of Reconstruction and Development (EBRD), *Transition Report 1999: Ten Years of Transition*, EBRD, London, 1999.

European Bank of Reconstruction and Development (EBRD), *Changing composition of employment in transition economies*, (data base, mimeo), EBRD, London, 2000.

Financial Times (2000a), 'Azerbaijan: A Survey', *Financial Times*, 22 November 2000.

Financial Times (2000b), 'Kazakhhstan: A Survey', *Financial Times*, 11 December 2000.

Fischer, S. and Sahay, R., 'The Economies in Transition: Taking Stock', *Finance and Development*, 37 (3), 2000, pp. 2–6.

Freedom House, *Political Freedom Indicators*, Freedom House, London, 2000.

Fueg, J.-C., *Caspian States Oil and Gas Production and Revenue Projection*, Paper presented to Royal Institute of International Affairs Conference, 6 October 2000, London.

Gurgen, E., Snoek, H., Craig, J., McHigh, J., Izvorski, I. and van Rooden, R., 'Economic Reforms in Kazakhstan, Kyrgyz Republic, Tajikistan, Turkmenistan and Uzbekistan', *IMF Occasional Paper 183*, International Monetary Fund, Washington DC, 1999.

Hoffman, D., 'Azerbaijan: The Politicization of Oil', in Ebel, R. and Menon, R. (eds), *Energy and Conflict in Central Asia and the Caucasus*, Rowman & Littlefield, Lanham MD, 2000, pp. 55–77.

International Energy Agency, *World Energy Outlook 2002*, OECD/IEA, 2002.

International Monetary Fund, 'Republic of Tajikistan: Recent Economic Developments', *IMF Staff Country Report 00/27*, IMF, Washington DC, 2000.

Johnson, S., Kaufman, D. and Shleifer, A., 'The Unofficial Economy in Transition', *Brookings Papers on Economic Activity*, 2, 1997, pp. 159–239.

Kopstein, J. S. and Reilly, D. A., 'Geographic Diffusion and the Transformation of the Post-communist World', *World Politics*, 53, 2000, pp. 1–37.

Leite, C. and Weidmann, J., 'Does Mother Nature Corrupt – Natural Resources, Corruption and Economic Growth', *IMF Working Paper 99/85*, IMF, Washington DC, 1999.

Lubin, N., 'Turkmenistan's Energy: A Source of Wealth or Instability?' in Ebel, R. and Menon, R., *op. cit.*, pp. 107–121.

Luong, P. J. 'Kazakhstan: The Long-term Cost of Short-term Gains', in Ebel, R. and Menon, R., *op. cit.*, pp. 79–106.

Olson, M., *Power and Prosperity: Outgrowing Communist and Capitalist Dictatorships*, Basic Books, New York, 2000.

Pastor, G. and van Rooden, R., 'Turkmenistan: The Burden of Current Agricultural Policies, *IMF Working Paper 00/98*, IMF, Washington DC, 2000.

PlanEcon, *The Sophisticated Way to Model Earnings* (mimeo), Meridian International Conference Centre, Washington DC, 1997.

Rosenberg, C. B. and Saavalainen, T. O., 'How to Deal with Azerbaijan's Oil Boom? Policy Strategies in a Resource-rich Transition Economy', *IMF Working Paper 98/6*, IMF, Washington DC, 1998.

State Department, *Caspian Region Energy Development Report* (mimeo), Meridian International Conference Centre, Washington DC, 1997.

Tsalik, S., *Caspian Oil Windfalls: Who Will Benefit?*, Caspian Revenue Watch, Open Society Institute, New York, 2003.

Valdevieso, L. M., 'Macroeconomic Developments in the Baltics, Russia and Other Countries of the Former Soviet Union, 1992–97', *IMF Occasional Paper 175*, IMF, Washington DC, 1998.

World Bank, *Country Economic Memorandum: Azerbaijan*, World Bank, Washington DC, 1999.

World Bank, *World Development Indicators 2000*, World Bank, Washington DC, 2000.

8 The role of oil in the development of Azerbaijan

Willy Olsen

Introduction

In the late 1980s foreign oil company executives travelled to Azerbaijan to look for business opportunities. They were welcomed by Soviet and Azeri oil officials. The Soviet objective was to sustain the high Soviet oil production into the future, but they needed Western technology and Western financing to succeed. The Azeri hope was to rebuild Azerbaijan as a major oil nation. They knew that there were large discoveries to be made, but lacked the money and technology for such projects.

In September 1994, the Production Sharing Agreement for the Azeri–Chirag–deepwater Guneshli prospects was finally signed in Baku after a complex negotiation process. AIOC – the Azerbaijan International Operating Company – was now a reality.[1] Azerbaijan's ambition was then – and still is – that future foreign investments for exploiting its oil and gas resources should:

- help protect independence;
- ensure international recognition;
- attract international investment to all sectors, including the non-oil sector;
- create the potential for a brighter economic future, democracy and market economy.

A new world has undoubtedly taken shape in the last decade, but the expectation widely held of a fast track to democracy and market reforms has not been fulfilled. The transition process has been difficult and slow. Will the petroleum revenues be a blessing or a curse for Azerbaijan? That question has come far more to the forefront in recent years – also for the oil companies – than it was when negotiations began in the early 1990s. The aim of this chapter is to discuss some of the challenges ahead for the oil industry, and for Azerbaijan as it becomes a republic increasingly dominated by petroleum revenues.

The historical perspective

The history of oil in Azerbaijan is an obligatory part of any briefing given to international oil industry executives visiting – or working in – Azerbaijan.

The Azerbaijani leadership knows its oil history and is proud of its many achievements. A few key points to remember:

- Commercial oil output began in Baku in the mid-nineteenth century, making Transcaucasia one of the world's first oil provinces.
- Azerbaijan was the world's largest oil producer at the beginning of the twentieth century.
- Azeri oil was of crucial importance to the Soviet army during the Second World War.
- Neft Dashlari – or Oily Rocks – was a triumph of engineering and planning in the late 1940s. One of the first offshore oil developments in the world, it was a massive oil industrial complex located in the middle of the sea.
- The Azeri oil industry supplied a significant share of the oil equipment required for the exploitation of oil and gas in western Siberia.

When the Nobel brothers travelled to Baku in 1873, they were looking for walnut trees, and wood for making rifle stocks.[2] Instead they found themselves attracted to oil. The Nobels built up the region's first leading international oil company. The idea of establishing commercial oil operations in the Azerbaijan capital came from Robert Nobel, who persuaded his brother Ludwig to join the venture. The Nobel brothers were responsible for crucial innovations in the oil industry such as the world's first oil tanker, which operated in the Caspian Sea.

The result of foreign involvement in the development of oil was a spectacular boom – its visible monument became the city of Baku, the fastest growing metropolitan centre in the Russian empire. Very soon the key question became the issue of markets for the oil. World markets were clearly the most rewarding. The result was first the building of railroads, then a pipeline to Batumi on the Black Sea (see **Akiner**, p. 4). A century ago, Baku dominated the world oil scene. Today, there is a major difference: Baku is just one of many oil cities.

Azerbaijan remained Europe's leading oil producer well into the twentieth century. By this time, the region had been incorporated into the Soviet Union. Some of the known deposits in Azerbaijan were, however, in difficult locations, or in geological formations that required advanced extraction technologies. These were unavailable to the Soviet oil industry. Discovery of oil in the Volga–Ural region, and later in western Siberia, led to a switch in Soviet investment priorities; as a result, investments in the Caspian region decreased. In 1940, Baku accounted for about 70 per cent of Soviet oil production. When Azerbaijan became independent, the figure was only 2 per cent. During 70 years of Soviet rule, some 1.5 billion tonnes of oil were produced in Azerbaijan, but the country had almost been forgotten by the Western world, and by Western oil companies. In the early 1990s, when the first foreign oil companies started travelling to Baku again, it was producing just above 200,000 barrels of oil per day and importing oil from Russia to run the refineries.

Foreign companies renewed their interest in Azerbaijan, Turkmenistan and Kazakhstan as a consequence of the political and economic liberalisation of the Soviet Union in the mid-1980s. The break-up of the Soviet Union in 1991 opened new opportunities to foreign investors who could start negotiations directly with the leadership in the new independent states. In the early years of Azerbaijan, oil was seen as a tool to help the republic consolidate its political position, both in the region as well as in the world-wide arena by bringing economic independence and international recognition to the country. When the BP/Statoil alliance brought the former British Prime Minister Margaret Thatcher to Baku in September 1992, she was received like royalty. Jubilant people lined the streets. She had by then retired from politics, but in Azerbaijan she was still the best known Western politician. She was the first senior Western politician to visit Azerbaijan. She met President Abulfaz Elchibey and expressed her strong support for the market reforms he was attempting to introduce. She also emphasised the benefits of engaging foreign oil companies to participate in the development of Azerbaijan. When she left, the BP/Statoil alliance was able to sign two agreements: an exclusive right to negotiate a contract for the Chirag field, and an exclusive right to negotiate a contract for the Shah Deniz prospect.

These negotiations took place in a country that was experiencing more difficulties – more political and economic turmoil – than any other former Soviet republic. After the collapse of the USSR, the country had four leaders in less than 18 months. The human costs and the economic and political implications of the on-going war in Karabagh (see **Nassibli**, p. 161) were enormous. The economy collapsed. Seventy years of Soviet hegemony had resulted in serious structural imbalances in the country's economy. For decades the emphasis had been on the production of raw materials, notably oil, cotton and grapes. Industry was concentrated in the Baku–Sumgait region and heavily dependent on exports to, and imports from, Russia. Thus, for example, Azerbaijan imported 70 per cent of its grain and 50 per cent of its meat and dairy products from Russia. The national income declined by 31 per cent in 1992. And the downward trend continued in 1993. The situation was desperate for a large portion of the population. Food was scarce. Inflation grew out of control.

The government had to deal with a wide range of very complex issues. The Karabagh conflict had the highest priority. But Azerbaijan also implemented a radical shift in foreign policy orientation by turning away from Russia. The record of Azerbaijan's foreign policy since 1991 demonstrates a firm resistance to Russian efforts to establish influence over the country.[3] Oil negotiations were a key issue, but only one of many difficult matters that preoccupied the minds of the president and his government. The leadership lacked people with experience in running a new country and experience in international negotiations. They were afraid of making the wrong decisions, and worried about the consequences. The key questions that they asked themselves were, would the terms offered by the companies benefit the host nation or only the foreign oil companies? How could they be sure that they had been able to get a good deal?

The foreign oil companies also had a major communication challenge. They had to convince the government, the state oil company officials, and the public at large that they were not trying to 'steal' the oil, but that an agreement had to be mutually beneficial in order to survive in the long term. Many Azeri oilmen, who in the past had had to struggle to get funds from Moscow for investments, had high hopes of foreign companies funding their many plans. The foreign oil companies had to make it clear that they would not make new investments without controlling the activities all the way. The negotiations were difficult. First, the group of international oil companies had to agree on a joint negotiating strategy. They started with different views on the required return on the investment, also on the best way to proceed. It took many – and long – meetings to hammer out a joint position.

Secondly, Azerbaijan brought in Western advisers who had strong views on what would be of benefit to Azerbaijan. Thirdly, Azerbaijan had to understand fully the consequences of signing a Production Sharing Agreement (PSA). The negotiators from the State Oil Company of the Azerbaijan Republic (SOCAR) came up to speed quickly, but they had to bring the political leadership on board. And then, there were different views within the Azeri oil sector itself on what the contract should contain. In the end, the existing and producing part of the Guneshli field was kept outside the contract, whilst the deeper portion of the Guneshli field was included.

In August 1993, the companies tried to break the deadlock by drawing up a draft Production Sharing Agreement for the combined Azeri–Chirag–Guneshli fields. The advantages were outlined in a presentation to the government and the State Oil Company as follows:

- potential US$80 billion profit to Azerbaijan;
- US$10 billion of foreign investments;
- meeting urgent domestic gas and oil supply priorities;
- strategic export pipeline to world markets;
- improvements to infrastructure.

The foreign oil companies emphasised that a rapid resolution of the negotiations would accelerate the development of the Azerbaijan economy, re-establish Azerbaijan as a strategic regional energy centre and make the country into a significant player in world oil export markets.[4] Azerbaijan, however, was still uncertain. Professor Kemp, of the University of Aberdeen, was invited by the companies to write a 'fairness opinion' in October 1993, in order to reassure the negotiators from Azerbaijan that the terms offered in the PSA were fair. He wrote in his conclusions that

> the scope of the proposed agreement is fully in conformity with modern practice in the design of PSAs. The economic terms provide for returns to Azerbaijan which are fully consistent with those available internationally in the petroleum industry today. Seen as a package, the terms generally represent a very fair deal for Azerbaijan.[5]

Yet it took almost another year, two sets of different Azeri negotiators, and a change of political leadership to bring negotiations to a close.

'Contract of the Century'

When the first contract was finally signed in September 1994, it became a milestone for Azerbaijan, as well as for the foreign oil companies. In popular parlance it was dubbed the 'Contract of the Century'. The description under-lined the importance of the contract, and reminded people of the past. One of the local newspapers wrote that the agreement had 'no analogue in the history of the world oil industry'. Azerbaijan had forged closer ties to the West by using its only available asset. The Azeri leadership carefully structured the AIOC consortium, and involved Russia as well. The Russian oil and energy minister was present at the signing ceremony. Political balance was of crucial importance. A balance was also maintained between American and European interests, with a slightly higher US share than European. Moscow's interests were represented through the Russian company LUKoil. Turkey was represented through the Turkish State Petroleum Company (TPAO). British Petroleum (BP) was the largest shareholder, but not in a dominating position versus Amoco. The companies could not agree on who should be the operator. A compromise was reached whereby a joint consor-tium with representatives from all the companies should operate the project. (Five years later, however, BP acquired Amoco and became the operator.) SOCAR became an equal partner with significant influence.

Azerbaijan made an attempt a few months later to get Iranian involvement in AIOC, but the US companies, who had the right to prevent any new company from joining the consortium, blocked this. Behind the US compa-nies' position was the US government's policy of isolating Iran. The Iranians did, however, get a share in the next large Production Sharing Agreement, the Shah Deniz prospect, signed in 1996, where the American companies had no participation. Other deals quickly followed. Some twenty PSAs were signed by the end of the decade, placing Azerbaijan well ahead in the race for investments.

The Azeri–Chirag–Guneshli project looked very attractive commercially. It was a large multi-billion barrel field, and with known reserves. New partners wanted to join the consortium. Exxon acquired an interest, as did Japanese companies. The Japanese involvement was important for the polit-ical leadership in Baku, because it opened the door to Japanese financing. AIOC made steady progress after the PSA was signed. First an old drilling rig was upgraded, and then an early production scheme was developed, including export solutions, as specified in the contract. Three primary export options were evaluated: a northern route to international market sales via Russia by pipeline; a western route to international market sales via Georgia by rail and/or pipeline; a southern route for crude oil swaps with Iran by ves-sel. All three options presented the partners with a host of political, logistical and financial challenges due to unresolved territorial conflicts and competing strategic and commercial interests of regional and external powers.

The northern early route was essentially a reversal of the crude line from Grozny, the Chechen capital, with some limited upgrading, and a short section of new pipe to be constructed near Baku. This route was initially favoured by Azerbaijan's own leadership. The western route required considerable construction of both a new pipeline and the repair of existing pipelines. This route was given diplomatic support by the US and Turkish governments (see Map 7). The third option, via Iran, was not pursued as a consequence of the US embargo of Iran in mid-1995. In the end, the partnership decided – endorsed by the leadership in Baku – to develop a dual pipeline system. The decision was driven both by politics and by solid commercial factors. It gave the consortium operational flexibility, maximum export capacity and a stronger negotiating position. With hindsight, the decision to use both the northern and western options paid off, and secured a continuous export of oil throughout the Chechen conflict.

First oil was produced three years after signing of the contract. Transportation was initially only available through Russia. Production start-up was a cause for great celebration and 12 November was declared a national holiday. The US Energy Secretary Federico Pena hailed the occasion as the beginning of a 'new era for the region'. Russian Deputy Prime Minister Boris Nemtsov described the event as a great success for both Azerbaijan and Russia, since many had doubted whether Russia would manage to meet its commitment for the early oil to flow via the northern Baku–Grozny–Novorossiysk pipeline route.

President Heidar Aliev called for the main pipeline to export Azerbaijani oil to world markets to run to the Turkish port of Ceyhan. He expressed his 'regret' that the question of the pipeline route had given rise to disputes amongst the international community. The start-up of early oil production and the expected future activity level created a surge of optimism. AIOC's ambitions were higher than the early oil scheme. The plan was to reach a production level of 700,000 barrels per day by 2003.

Azerbaijan – or more correctly, Baku – began to attract foreign investment. New hotels, office blocks and apartment blocks were built. The service sector expanded with restaurants and shops. Private houses, many of them grand houses built by Azerbaijan's first 'oil barons' in the late nineteenth–early twentieth century, were refurbished. More than 50 oil firms were established in Baku within a short period of time. Baku was once more in fashion, home to a new generation of 'oil barons'. In 1995, signature bonus payments amounted to US$122 million. Table 8.1 shows foreign direct investments and the payment of signature bonuses in the latter part of the 1990s (all figures in US$ millions).[6]

Table 8.1 FDI and government bonus receipts, Azerbaijan 1996–1999

	1996	*1997*	*1998*	*1999*
Foreign direct oil investments	487	845	832	350
Government oil bonus receipts	37	64	75	155

Then the oil price collapsed in 1998, with almost immediate consequences. Projects had to be reassessed with the aim of making them more robust against periods of low oil prices. In addition, geopolitical discussions on pipeline routes and capacity dominated discussions, slowing down new investments in the Azeri–Chirag field by at least two to three years. A step-by-step approach to increase export capacity through Georgia, to allow for building up production, would have been desirable, but this was not politically acceptable. The Azeri government, Turkey and the US administration favoured moving ahead rapidly with the construction of a major export pipeline for oil to Ceyhan. Yet the sobering experience of the late 1990s may, nevertheless, prove to be to the long-term benefit of Azerbaijan. The low oil prices showed the country that Caspian oil was not insulated from global oil price fluctuations. The importance of cost-efficient developments and operations was emphasised and accepted. The need for the government to avoid becoming totally dependent on the oil sector became obvious to everyone.

The Caspian reserve base

Since 1994, many analysts have focused on the potential for a new 'Great Game' in which Russia, Iran, Turkey, the US and even China could fight for hegemony in Central Asia and the Caucasus. Geopolitical issues have dominated the debate since the US developed a more coherent Caspian policy in 1997. Washington's approach was to influence the pipeline routes chosen for future flows of Caspian oil and gas. Support for the 'east–west corridor' became official US policy. For many analysts one overriding question was still the size of the oil and gas reserves in the Caspian region. Was it worth fighting for? Could the reserve base support 'multiple export pipelines'? Was the Caspian another Middle East? Or just another North Sea? How important would Caspian oil be in the global energy market? A figure of 200 billion barrels of potential oil equivalent reserves came out of the US in the spring of 1997. This estimate created a 'Caspian hype'. The oil companies did little to dampen expectations. They were keen to see US and European involvement – and engagement – in the Caspian in order to reduce the political risks involved in investing in the region. High US attention would ensure that the companies had an open channel to the local leadership and also to Russia. Charles Curtis, the Deputy Secretary in the US Department of Energy, said in early 1996[7] that 'the investments in the Caspian and Central Asia served US national security interests, and that the partnerships formed in the area between US and foreign business and government interests strengthened and reinforced the important bilateral relationship with the host states'. He emphasised the point that the development of the Caspian was critical to stabilising the region, likewise to its relationship with Russia. The oil companies welcomed his views.

The US had clearly based their reserve assessments on extensive work carried out earlier by the CIA. Thus, in 1989 the CIA had made an assessment of the North Caspian basin and presented its findings in a report entitled 'The North Caspian Basin: Salvation for Soviet Oil Production'.[8] The report's conclusion was that only one new oil region had the potential to stabilise Soviet oil production at the high level of the late 1980s – the North Caspian basin. The CIA estimate was 30–50 billion barrels of recoverable oil in the North Caspian, but noted that the region presented greater challenges to Soviet oilmen than any other region. Two to four years had been needed to drill and complete wells at deep fields in the North Caspian. Pressure in the reservoirs was three to four times higher than pressure found in west Siberia. High concentrations of extremely toxic and corrosive gas posed a significant danger to life and environment.

The CIA report stated that the Soviets regarded the development of this basin as a priority, but that in order to achieve this they would need extensive help from Western technology and equipment. Thus foreign involvement in the North Caspian area was already on the agenda before the collapse of the USSR. Discussions on the Tengiz field were in place when, in December 1991, Kazakhstan became independent. The gigantic fields – Tengiz and Karachaganak – were offered to foreign companies. The Tengiz agreement was signed in the 1993 with Chevron as an operator, whilst British Gas/Eni won the tender for Karachaganak in competition with BP/Statoil.

The Kazakh government had initially planned to keep the offshore acreage 'for future generations', to quote a senior Kazakh representative who met with Statoil officials in the summer of 1992.[9] However, Kazakhstan quickly changed its mind when it realised that the unexplored acreage in the North Caspian Sea could have considerable economic value. Companies were invited to tender for offshore acreage. In the mid-1990s, an international consortium signed the PSA. The participants were Agip, British Gas, BP, Mobil, Shell, Statoil and Total. KazakhstanCaspishelf held the Kazakh interest. The first well drilled by OKIOC revealed the gigantic Kashagan field in 2000.

So how large, in fact, are the Caspian reserves? In its Caspian Review in 1998–1999 the International Energy Agency (IEA) considered a reasonable range of proven oil reserves to be 15–40 billion barrels, with about 70–150 billion barrels of additional oil reserves a possibility. At a Caspian conference in Paris in December 1999, a paper by the IEA estimated that the Caspian reserves represented between 1.5 per cent and 4 per cent of the world's proven oil reserves, and 6 per cent of the gas reserves. By way of comparison, the Middle East holds some 65 per cent of the world's oil reserves.

To date, far too few wells have been drilled to predict with any degree of certainty the Caspian oil and gas potential. It will take many more years to establish the true scale. The Caspian contains some 250 undrilled prospects. Some will yield commercial discoveries of hydrocarbons. Others will not. We have already experienced that. Exploration drilling over the past few years has downsized predictions regarding expected oil reserves in the South Caspian basin, but strengthened projections for the North Caspian basin. But the Caspian still has some very significant fields, large enough to support the development of export solutions.

The Tengiz and Karachaganak fields in Kazakhstan and Azeri–Chirag–Guneshli in Azerbaijan were found in the Soviet period. The Kashagan discovery in Kazakhstan and the Shah Deniz find in Azerbaijan are among the largest world-wide discoveries in recent years. They are all world-class fields, and will be the mainstay of the development of the Caspian hydrocarbon potential. Large fields such as these are required to build up the early infrastructure that is necessary for smaller fields to become commercially viable.

Caspian offshore resources discovered to date total some 40–50 billion barrels of oil equivalents (o.e.). Statoil's estimate is that the total offshore oil and gas resources could be in the range of 65 billion barrels of o.e. The Caspian region may supply local and global markets with more than 6 million barrels of o.e. around 2015. As a comparison, the combined oil and gas production of Norway and the UK was some 8–9 billion barrels o.e. in 2000. The Caspian oil contribution will be important at the margin, and will add to diversity and security of supply for importers. Its role will, however, not be pivotal.

Key challenges facing the oil industry

Developing the Caspian potential will not be a simple task. The oil companies have experienced a slower build-up than hoped when the Production Sharing Agreements were signed, and are still facing considerable challenges. These could delay future projects. Progress will continue to be influenced by a number of different issues such as the following:

- export solutions;
- local industrial capabilities;
- environmental issues;
- delimitation of the Caspian Sea.

Export pipelines

Development of the oil and gas potential of the Caspian Sea has been hostage to pipeline politics since it has been impossible to isolate oil and natural gas pipelines in the Caspian region from geopolitics. The US has supported the Baku–Tbilisi–Ceyhan (BTC) pipeline since 1997, and was also arguing for a Trans-Caspian pipeline to carry natural gas from Turkmenistan to Turkey. Two reasons for the unswerving US support of BTC were the denial of Iran as a pipeline transit country and the minimisation of Russia in the movement of oil out of the region.[10] During the past couple of years there has been a growing awareness that transiting the Bosporus with large volumes of oil constitutes a major hazard. As **Adams** and **Bolukbaşi** argue (see pp. 98, 223), it is now accepted that this is a real obstacle, and not merely an argument put forward by Turkey to force through the decision to build an export pipeline to Ceyhan in the Mediterranean. The oil industry has come to realise the risk of a serious accident in the Turkish Straits is too high. Thus, this cannot be the sole route for oil exports. Additional pipeline solutions will be required.

The first major export pipeline system – the Caspian Pipeline Consortium (CPC) – is already transporting crude oil from Tengiz to the Black Sea. Most of the CPC oil will have to transit the Bosporus to reach world markets. Kazakhstan will, however, require further transportation capacity to handle additional volumes when the gigantic Kashagan field starts production. Should the Kazakh volumes go across the Caspian Sea, making Baku a 'transportation hub', or should a new pipeline go south, or east, or north? Pipeline issues will no doubt continue to be hotly debated, but the CPC has demonstrated that export pipelines can actually be built.

Azerbaijan is currently linked to world markets through two oil pipelines, through Russia and Georgia (see Map 7). The capacity is limited and will not allow for full-scale development of the Azeri–Chirag–Guneshli fields. Construction of BTC was commenced in September 2002. The anticipated date for it to become operational is early 2005. This pipeline alone involves an investment of about US$3 billion. Many have questioned the economic viability of the export pipeline, seeing it as a 'political pipeline'. The leading partners are, however, confident that the pipeline will be economic on the basis of the volumes that will be available from the fields currently being developed in Azerbaijan. As regards gas, Shah Deniz is the first major gas discovery in the Caspian Sea. The field holds some 15 tcf (trillion cubic feet) of proven resources. That gas is ready for development. Azerbaijan has entered into its first gas contract with Turkey, allowing the first stage of the Shah Deniz field to be developed. The companies involved intend to construct an export line for the gas, in parallel with the BTC oil line. They believe that this, too, is a commercially viable project. The target is to supply first gas to Georgia and to Turkey by 2006, constructing a 1,000-km pipeline from Azerbaijan through Georgia to Erzurum in Turkey, where it will connect to an existing gas transmission system. Shah Deniz is the backbone of Azerbaijan's gas future, and could open the door to markets beyond Turkey (see **Roberts**, p. 85). However, Caspian gas development will depend on access to markets that currently have limited ability to absorb large volumes of new gas. Investments in field developments will not be made unless the companies have firm gas sales contracts in place.

Local content

Another issue, rapidly growing in importance, is the use of local resources. Local content is as high on the agenda in the Caspian region as it is in Venezuela, Iran, Angola and Nigeria. The objective is to develop a competent local oil and gas industry. Transfer of technology will therefore be a high priority. For almost 30 years that discussion has been familiar in Norway. However, Caspian countries have limited access to the global resources that are required for developing the oil and gas sector, such as, for example, marine drilling and construction fleets, or modern fabrication facilities. Lack of drilling rigs has already slowed down exploration, and will continue to be a limiting factor delaying exploration on some of the PSAs that have been signed. The old Soviet industrial infrastructure suffered tremendously from lack of investment and maintenance. Thus, Azerbaijan does not have an industry able to meet today's requirements. The domestic service industry has not yet been converted to the international standards required by foreign oil companies.

A report on revitalising the Azeri oil industry sector, developed jointly by Norwegian and Azeri experts, is premised on the underlying assumption that a new and modernised local oil service industry will develop 'automatically', in response to the demands of the oil companies when they start to award large field development contracts. However, the tempo and depth of this development will to a large extent depend on steps taken by the Azerbaijani industry itself, by foreign oil companies and contractors, and by the Azerbaijani authorities.[11]

Azerbaijani authorities can help in this process by establishing improved framework conditions for long-term investments and the use of existing industrial infrastructure and labour by foreign companies through tax policy, administrative practices and by encouraging local/international industry alliances. For Azerbaijan to reap maximum benefits of its hydrocarbon resources it is not enough only to export oil and gas. National production of oil equipment and services should also actively be developed, but the domestic industry needs to become competitive to maintain the attractiveness of the Azeri offshore developments.

Some US$100 billion may be invested in developing the Caspian oil and gas discoveries over the next 20 years. A significant share of the investments will be in Azerbaijan for developing Azeri–Chirag and Shah Deniz, for building export pipelines and for rebuilding local infrastructure. Every US dollar spent in the oil and gas sector has a multiplier effect on the total economy that might be three times as large as the investments themselves. This will create jobs. It will mean the development of high-quality local competence. It will mean income for employees and for the government. Yet the absence of critical support infrastructure and skilled manpower may substantially slow down developments. There is, too, a risk that Azerbaijan will become a two-speed economy. This would be characterised by a dynamic oil sector, but non-oil related sectors would lag behind, showing little sign of recovery and requiring massive investments to bring them up to modern international standards.

Legal and environmental challenges

Another significant challenge facing the Caspian region is the environment. The problem arises from both man-made and natural causes. The countries that emerged from the former Soviet Union are confronting difficult economic and administrative adjustments that complicate environmental management and natural resource protection efforts. The Caspian Sea is a fragile ecosystem because its closed nature causes the self-cleaning process to be slow. The environmental challenges will only grow in importance. The challenges differ between the northern and southern regions of the Caspian. While prospective structures in Kazakhstan are in 2–8 metres of water depth, covered by ice for 4–5 months of the year, the resources in the south may be in 500–800 metres of water depth and with the risk of eruptions from mud volcanoes. Also, the Caspian contains a number of species that are particularly sensitive to increased water pollution. These include the caviar-bearing sturgeon, which is the cornerstone of the region's fishing industry (see **Akiner**, chapter 21). As an oil industry, we need to ensure that we protect the environment by using the best environmental practices.

Another challenge is the delimitation of the Caspian Sea. This remains an unsolved issue and may become an obstacle to efficient co-operation and development of the oil and gas resources in the region. Despite bouts of intensive diplomacy, it has been difficult to break the deadlock on a formula for a legal division of the seabed and the waters. To date, the lack of an agreed legal regime has had limited impact on progress in the relevant projects. Nevertheless, tensions could rise if exploration resulted in discoveries in disputed areas. Without a proper resolution of this matter, oil and gas developments will not be able to make a full contribution to the regional economy.

Will oil be a blessing?

In 1998, journalists visiting Baku brought back stories that reflected the optimism that was felt in the region. They wrote of expectations in Azerbaijan of a 'wall of money' coming their way. One could read in American newspapers that 'the region's wealth will shower unimaginable wealth on people whose annual per capita GDP today hovers between US$400 to US$600 building a new El Dorado in nations where camels still outnumber automobiles'.[12]

However, a Central Asia specialist at the Carnegie Endowment for International Peace, Martha Brill Olcott, understood better the realities of the situation when she wrote that 'the most grandiose oil and gas projects are still in their early stages, with their viability and pace of development uncertain. The reality of post-communist development has instead been an increase in corruption and sharp drop in living standards once protected by a comprehensive welfare net.'[13] The experience of the 1990s has shown that the transition will be a complex, demanding and lengthy . process, and that the new nations were poorly equipped to take advantage of the new opportunities in the early 1990s. It was also noted that 'neither political institutions and elites, nor economic infrastructure were ready for the challenge of independence'.[14]

Azerbaijan has only experienced twelve years of independence since the demise of the Soviet Union. It is therefore far too early to speak authoritatively of the long-term influence that hydrocarbon-derived revenues will have on state and society. We have, however, already seen some of the challenges ahead. Oil-related revenues accounted for nearly half (47 per cent) of the consolidated budget in 1997. Major revenues from the oil sector will not materialise for several years at the earliest, but the first signs of the so-called 'Dutch disease' are already in evidence. In 1997–1998 the inflow of foreign direct investments into Azerbaijan reached 30 per cent of GDP. Of this, 80 per cent were directed to the oil sector. The substantial influx of hard currency resulted in a significant exchange rate appreciation of the national currency, also in a loss of competitiveness. The monetary authorities were forced to devalue the national currency in 1999. During 1996–1998 the share of import in trade turnover increased by 50 per cent, and the government foreign debt doubled between 1997 and 2000.

The projected high growth rates in the Azeri oil and gas sector from 2005 onwards will depend crucially on the successful implementation of a few large projects:

- full field development of the Azeri–Chirag–Guneshli field;
- development of the Shah Deniz gas field and transportation system;
- construction of the Baku–Tbilisi–Ceyhan pipeline.

The current plan for the AIOC development envisages production start-up in 2004–2005, reaching a production plateau of almost 1 million barrels per day in 2008–2010. This is at least five years behind the early calculations. Shah Deniz could be developed in parallel with Azeri–Chirag, with the aim of delivering first gas in 2006. However, adverse developments in oil and gas prices – or delays in the completion of one or more of these projects – could significantly impact the future economic development of Azerbaijan. Large capital inflows could also easily cause the exchange rate to drift upwards and domestic inflation to rise, subjecting the rest of the economy to Dutch disease. This would complicate efforts to increase the competitiveness of non-oil sectors.

Oil wealth has often been a mixed blessing for developing countries. While it floods a state with revenues, it can also promote the formation of state-dominated institutions that are antithetical to both economic and political liberalisation. Empirical findings suggest (see **Auty**) a positive correlation between resource abundance on the one hand, and long-term economic and political deterioration on the other. Many nations blessed with rich revenues have been irresistibly tempted to spend the revenues in an unproductive manner. Dutch disease, moral hazard incentives and economic rent seeking have impaired the long-term growth potential of several economies that suddenly benefited from valuable new resources.

The oil fund

In an attempt to avoid the mistakes of the past, several countries have set up oil stabilisation funds. The intention of such funds has been to separate the extraction of petroleum from the use of revenues. By setting aside a large share of revenues when the cash flow from the extraction of

non-renewable resources is high, the countries have tried to meet future policy challenges. The aim of the oil funds has basically been to protect the
domestic economy from the negative impact of sharp and unpredictable variations in the oil price and revenues; to prevent wasteful use of the revenues;
to distribute the wealth fairly among generations; and to establish a simple
and transparent mechanism for managing the flow of oil revenues.[15]

In December 1999 President Aliev issued a decree to establish an
Azerbaijan Oil Fund to accumulate oil and gas revenues, and to manage
them efficiently. The chief reason for the establishment of the Oil Fund was
the fact that the government had set itself a vast agenda of social and
economic reform. It also wanted to counteract macroeconomic distortions
and excessive spending in an oil booming economy. The high oil prices
from late 1999 to 2001, coupled with substantial signature bonuses from
the oil companies, gave a massive boost to the Fund. As of 1 October 2002,
it held assets amounting to US$627 million. The creation of this Fund has
been a key element in raising Azerbaijan's long-term foreign currency rating.

Yet many questions remain. It is not at all clear that the Oil Fund will
in fact ensure transparency. Will the Oil Fund help managing the high
expectations of the 'wall of money' that many Azerbaijanis are anticipating?
Setting up a fund is no guarantee that the resources will not be misused. It
is a tool for making the use of oil revenues transparent. It is not, however,
a substitute for sound fiscal management. Ultimately, the success of the Oil
Fund will depend on the political will to manage the oil revenues wisely.
The message from the Azeri Oil Fund management is that it will make
every effort to be transparent, undergoing regular audits, publishing regular
reports and auditing findings (see **Karayianni**). These are necessary
measures. Azerbaijan expects to channel more than US$52 billion to the
Oil Fund in the period 2008–2015. The International Monetary Fund (IMF)
has emphasised that the Oil Fund can play an important role in the financing
of policies to improve the living standards of the population and the country's
infrastructure. But the potential for Dutch disease means that the authorities in Azerbaijan will have to move cautiously with regard to the expenditure
of these funds.[16] There are also persistent concerns about the nature of state
governance (see **Auty**).

International financial institutions, likewise the Azeri government, are
fully aware of the historic evidence from other petro-states, and the need
to avoid a similar fate. But will they be able to? A generation from now,
will the resource-rich Caspian states look more like Norway or more like
Nigeria? Will the revenues be spent wisely on such measures as improving
infrastructure, health, education and agriculture, and creating new job
opportunities? Will they be used to consolidate political and economic independence? Or will the oil wealth be wasted through corruption, frittered
away on the construction of mega-projects for public show, on heavy subsidies for consumer goods and services, on programmes to keep the incumbents
in power, even on an arms race? These are the unanswered questions that
preoccupy all who have an interest in the future of Azerbaijan.

In the West, to date, most of the interest in the Caspian region has been focused on such issues as the geopolitical situation, pipeline routes and the oil and gas potential. The many conflicts in the Caucasus, especially in Karabagh, have also attracted international attention. However, the huge economic and social problems in the region are rarely mentioned. Yet the ability of petro-states to handle oil revenues effectively – the 'paradox of plenty', as it has been called – is beginning to be acknowledged as a potentially dangerous phenomenon in the resource-rich countries of the developing world. In Azerbaijan the situation is all the more desperate since, in addition to a host of social and economic problems, it also has to cope with the many refugees and internally displaced people whose lives were shattered by regional conflicts.

Since 1995, Azerbaijan has been largely successful in eliminating its macroeconomic imbalances. The authorities, actively supported by the IMF and other international financial institutions, have managed to stabilise the situation and to restore economic growth. The development in GDP is a good indicator of a turbulent decade. As illustrated in Table 8.2, it took eight years to regain the same level of GDP as in 1990.

Strong growth in the oil sector has contributed to strong growth in the GDP since 1995, but has not led to a reduction in income inequality. Non-oil industrial output, which played an important role in the economy in the 1980s, has continued to decline. Moreover, more than half of the 1 million internally displaced persons do not have jobs and live on pitifully small government allowances.[17] The socio-economic challenges in Azerbaijan will undoubtedly gain in importance in the years to come. Social tension will rise further if the government fails to convert oil revenues into economic growth throughout the republic. Despite strong economic growth alluded to above, poverty and inequality remain major concerns. There has been an increase in the unemployment rate, while health and education indicators show worrying downward trends. Poverty and inequality influence the rate and quality of economic growth. They influence the societies where foreign oil companies will be engaged for a very long period.

The challenges facing Azerbaijan are immense. In terms of UN classification Azerbaijan is among the medium-level developing countries. It was ranked no. 89 out of the 175 countries listed in the UNDP's *Human Development Report 2003*. Drawing on data for 2001, this document assessed the GDP per capita in Azerbaijan at slightly above US$650 (US$3,090, PPP). However,

Table 8.2 GDP changes in Azerbaijan 1991–2000

Year	1991	1992	1993	1994	1995	1996	1997	1998	1999	2000
Change in real GDP	99.3	76.8	59.1	47.4	88.2	89.3	94.5	104.00	111.8	124.5

Note: 1990 = 100.

official statistics are often misleading. The World Bank made a poverty assessment in 1995 and concluded that some 61.5 per cent of the households were poor.[18] The situation was especially difficult among the households of refugees and displaced persons. In the enclave of Nakhichevan almost 85 per cent of the households were categorised as 'poor'. See Table 8.3.

Poverty reduction has assumed a position of growing importance in Azerbaijan's reform agenda. An interim report was recently produced that contained a candid discussion of poverty in the republic.[19] The report outlines the poverty reduction strategy that the government hopes to implement in the years to come.

The poverty problem has its roots in the historic legacy from the Soviet period. Azerbaijan was ranked as no. 10 among the 15 Soviet republics in terms of the population's material well-being. After regaining independence, Azerbaijan ran up against political, military, economic and social problems. The Karabagh conflict turned close to 1 million people into internally displaced persons. Azerbaijan's industrial sector lost its markets in the other Soviet republics resulting in a downward slide. A large number of enterprises ceased operations. In addition Azerbaijan has suffered from a number of other unanticipated setbacks in recent years – earthquakes, landslides and drought. The health care and educational sectors have not escaped the negative developments. In 2000, according to the *Human Development Report 2003* (pp. 255, 267), government spending on health stood at 0.9 per cent and on education at 4.2 per cent of GDP – this is comparable with countries such as Cameroon, Haiti and Guinea. Most of this was expended on wages and salaries and not on basic, and much needed, improvements to infrastructure. The system of universal and free medical care has been gradually dropped. Funds allocated for medicine have been cut to a fraction of their previous level; immunisation efforts have practically stopped. This has led to a sharp increase in epidemics of infectious diseases. Municipal services are falling short of meeting even the minimum needs of the population. The funding of education is far below a satisfactory level.

An additional challenge for Azerbaijan is the high incidence of corruption. This is recognised within the country itself. In a poll conducted on behalf of Statoil in Azerbaijan in the summer of 2000, corruption was ranked even higher than the Karabagh conflict as an obstacle to the positive development of the country's potential. It has been argued that endemic corruption is not new to Azerbaijan. Corruption is comprised of a long-standing set of practices that were engendered and institutionalised throughout the Soviet

Table 8.3 Poverty assessment in Azerbaijan 1995

	Poor	*Very poor*	*Not poor*
In Azerbaijan as a whole (%)	61.5	20.4	38.5
In Baku (%)	59.6	19.6	40.4
Refugees and displaced persons (%)	74.5	37.5	25.5

period. Such practices have persisted right through the present day, despite the collapse of the USSR and the rejection of communism, as current bureaucracies and organisational practices have remained essentially unchanged.[20]

However, not only is corruption a legacy of Azerbaijan's past, there is evidence to show that corruption is more prevalent in resource-rich countries than in resource-poor ones. Looking at Corruption Perceptions Index of Transparency International (TI) for the year 2000, we find that the ten most corrupt countries in the world control 15 per cent of total oil reserves and 48 per cent of total gas reserves. And of those ten countries, eight are in the bottom half of UNDP's Human Development Index ranking health, wealth and educational achievement. The TI rankings for 2001 and 2002 did not alter this picture. If unchecked, corruption, particularly administrative corruption, will be a major constraint to Azerbaijan's economic growth and poverty alleviation programmes.

The oil industry encounters corruption both directly and indirectly. We, the foreign oil companies, can be exposed directly, in our own operations and through the actions of our employees or subcontractors. We are also exposed indirectly, since corruption is an obstacle to stability and progress in local communities and host countries. So far corruption has not had a major impact on the oil developments in Azerbaijan, but it represents a major risk to the successful implementation of future projects. Suppliers – of whom there are many – are more at risk than the oil companies, since the latter can get access to the highest level of government with their complaints. It is small businesses that tend to be most affected by corruption.

The PSAs and the projects are so crucial to the political leadership that they become almost 'protected' from corrupt practices. Therefore, corruption has not, so far, had any significant impact on the large oil companies' activities in Azerbaijan. The early oil project was implemented on schedule without corruption being a problem. Signature bonuses are often described as corruption, but these bonuses are one of the elements in a Production Sharing Agreement, and must be seen as part of the fiscal regime. Bonuses are frequently used in many oil-producing countries, and are clearly documented in the oil companies' accounts. Most of the countries using signature bonus as a system are often in acute need of revenues. They cannot afford to wait many years for the revenues to come.

A study of elite perceptions in Azerbaijan shows that the political opposition views international oil companies as largely free of corruption. At the same time, however, the influence of 'Big Oil' on Azerbaijani society is seen as corrupting. In other words, while the companies themselves may adhere to high ethical standards, the effect of their interaction with host governments may not always be benign. This has led some stakeholders to conclude that international oil companies should assume greater responsibility for the way in which national authorities use or abuse the revenue streams generated by the industry.[21] Corruption is therefore a serious issue for the oil companies and will require transparency in all operations to ensure that we maintain the licence to operate under changing governments.

Wherever corruption exists in the world economy, market forces are distorted, national reputation suffers and investors hesitate. The oil industry will therefore have to work actively to discourage all such practices. Statoil's position on corruption is similar to the policies of a growing number of companies world-wide. Statoil's president outlined his views to a world gathering of oil executives in Calgary in June 2000 when he emphasised that the company believes in practising full openness towards all stakeholders, including agents and subcontractors. This complements the training that we give our own staff to explain the principles and advantages of promoting business ethics, transparency and accountability, including the adoption of strict methods of accounting and audit.[22]

The recent high-level initiatives supported by the World Bank and IMF are important to improve governance in Azerbaijan. A clearer separation of regulatory and commercial functions could also contribute to improved governance. The reforms currently under way in the government structure are clearly aimed at achieving that goal. Bureaucratic red tape, too, is a serious problem. Various licensing requirements and excessive official procedures are a hindrance to conducting business in Azerbaijan. Largely as a result of this adverse business climate, foreign investments in non-oil related sectors have remained very low. If there is one clear lesson from the experience of oil exporters, it is that developmental outcomes depend on the character of state institutions.[23] In other words, governance matters. Therein lies much of the difference between the experience of petro-states like Nigeria and Norway.

The oil industry in Azerbaijan is prepared to invest millions of US dollars over the next ten years to develop two large oil and gas projects, Azeri–Chirag–Guneshli and Shah Deniz, also the pipeline systems required to bring oil and gas to markets. Governance will be crucial to ensure successful implementation of the projects. Can foreign oil companies play a constructive role? There was a time when international companies were reluctant to engage in problems related to politics, or to have an opinion on basic values. The view was that business should stick to business. That view is no longer valid – if it ever was. During the last decade a large number of companies have established corporate social responsibility policies. Several have also joined the UN initiative called Global Compact; launched by Kofi Annan's address at the World Economics Forum in Davos in 1999, this aims to promote shared values and principles, and to give a human face to the global market. In many oil companies the basic corporate values include the responsibility to promote human rights, argue against corruption and safeguard the environment.

The industry's primary contribution is measured in terms of value creation. This is the impact that large investments will have on employment, procurement of goods and services, transfer of technology and expertise, as well as tax revenues. These spin-offs could help to generate local growth and development. The industry also stresses that its presence has a less tangible effect – a result of the example set by conducting business in a manner that is ethical, sustainable and socially responsible. The argument is that creating value and conveying values go together, much as financial, environmental and social performance are inextricably linked.

A poll conducted on behalf of Statoil in 2000 showed that 70 per cent of the political leaders in Azerbaijan believed that investments by foreign oil companies would be beneficial and contribute to the development of the country. Among local non-governmental organisations (NGOs) 73 per cent of representatives were of the same opinion. They were not only enthusiastic about the prospects for economic growth, but saw the oil companies as important partners in the development of civil society. Can the industry meet their expectations? Many oil companies have during the last few years expanded and intensified their dialogue with stakeholders on corporate social responsibility. A stakeholder dialogue is about revealing complexities, so that alliances and co-operation can be built on realities rather than rhetoric. It is also about managing expectations as to roles, responsibilities, opportunities and constraints, in order to facilitate partnerships for growth and development. At the very least, the aim is to avoid a situation in which business, government and civil society work at cross-purposes.[24] This marks a radical departure from the recent past, when corporations and NGOs largely refused to listen to each other.

Oil companies can never assume the responsibility of political institutions, or become substitutes for such institutions. But the industry can take part in the dialogue. And can, too, apply its values and standards wherever it operates. Can the Norwegian experience be of value? For the first time in its history, Azerbaijan has indigenous control of its natural riches, and the revenues linked to the development of the energy sector. Will the energy revenues bring a better life to the citizens of Azerbaijan? Will the country be able to translate its windfall profits into self-sustaining and stable development paths? Or will Azerbaijan follow other petro-states that have not had the state institutions capable of handling the large petroleum revenues? Will the revenues trickle down or trickle away? Will the oil and gas revenues be a blessing or a curse? These are still open questions.

An effective oil strategy *can* change the nation. When I look at my own country, Norway, I see how the country has been transformed since oil and gas was discovered some 30 years ago. We have built a domestic oil and gas industry that is internationally competitive. We have used the Norwegian Continental Shelf as a 'greenhouse' for the development of new and effective offshore technologies with international market potential. The petroleum revenues have improved Norway's financial position and made it possible to develop further our welfare society. The revenues have allowed us to send a greater number of students to university, transforming Norway into more of a knowledge-based society than previously.

Norway was ranked first in the *UN Human Development Report 2003*. Today we find ourselves living in one of the richest societies in the world. Still, we are a society faced with social and economic challenges. The petroleum fund is growing fast. However, we must resist the temptation to use too much money from the fund to meet current needs. One Norwegian analyst believes that the main challenge for Norway is to make sure that the oil revenues and the oil fund do not create a false sense of security. 'Norway may need to immunise the oil fund from political interference. A false sense of security leads people to underrate or overlook the need for good policies and institutions, good education and good investments. Awash in cash, they may find that hard choices can be avoided', is the message.[25]

When I first visited Baku in the early 1990s, I heard time and time again from the Azeri oil veterans – the 'heroes' – that 'Our strategy is to develop our oil resources to the benefit of future generations as much as it has benefited past generations.' Or to quote Namik Nasrullayev, the then economy minister, 'The oil is a temporary resource. Our aim is to use it to create an active economy and generate jobs.'[26] Today I still hear the message that Azerbaijan would like to go down the path of Norway, but I also hear many people, especially the young, expressing doubt as to the extent to which the country will succeed in following this path, or are committed to this strategy.

A comparative study of Angola and Azerbaijan, carried out in 2000, revealed that the jury is still out on what direction the two countries will take. On the one hand, there is a danger that oil resources in both places will continue to trickle away instead of trickling down to the population at large. On the other hand, concerted action by international oil companies and the Bretton Woods institutions are believed to provide the best hope of moving the present political leadership in Angola and Azerbaijan into a sound developmental direction.[27] The Norwegian researchers regard Azerbaijan as having the best potential for succeeding: 'Some rays of hope exist, and the situation looks somewhat better in Azerbaijan than Angola. The positive elements in the Azerbaijani picture are, first of all, a literate population. Although reduced spending on education threatens to spoil some of the achievements of the past.'

An ongoing public debate around the use of the petroleum revenues is essential if Azerbaijan is to succeed. Willingness to seek advice and learn from experience gained in other countries is important. The frank report on the poverty situation shows a willingness to address critical questions. The path to success will be far from straightforward. It will require considerable Western engagement, contributing to a development where oil revenues become the lubricant and not the irritant. The decision to establish the Oil Fund in 1999 was clearly made to please the IMF, but the experience of the last five years has shown the government how important it is to avoid dependency on revenues from the petroleum sector. A successful development of oil and gas alone is not enough to ensure the harmonious development of the country's economy. In the early years of the oil era in Norway, Prime Minister Trygve Bratteli told Parliament: 'We cannot live only on the oil revenues.'[28] He gave very sound advice to Norway then. It is still very sound advice for Norway. Maybe also for the Caspian petro-states?

Notes

1 The following foreign companies were involved in 1993–1994: BP 24.467 per cent, Amoco 24.3 per cent, Unocal 16 per cent, Pennzoil 15.3 per cent, Statoil 12.233 per cent, McDermott 3.5 per cent, Turkish Petroleum Company

(TPAO) 2.5 per cent, Ramco 1.7 per cent. LUKoil entered the consortium in May 1994.

2 D. Yergin and T. Gustafson, 'Evolution of an Oil Rush', *New York Times*, 6 August 1997.

3 L. Le Cornu, 'A Small State's Struggle for Independence in the Post Soviet Period', PhD thesis, Oxford University, January 2001.

4 Unpublished joint presentation by foreign oil companies.

5 A. G. Kemp, unpublished paper, 1993.

6 Source: Azerbaijan authorities and IMF staff estimates.

7 Deputy Secretary Charles Curtis at the CERA conference, Houston, February 1996.

8 A confidential research paper produced by the CIA, based on 'information available as of 15 February 1989'. It was 'sanitized' in 1999 and released for circulation on 30 January 2001.

9 Author's meeting in Almaty with Kazakh officials.

10 *CSIS – The Strategic Energy Initiative*, November 2000.

11 *Revitalisation of the Azeri Industrial Capabilities*, report from INTSOK, the Norwegian Oil and Gas Partners, Spring 2001.

12 F. Viviano, 'Caspian Basin Boom Transforms Entire Area', *San Francisco Chronicle*, 10 August; *Washington Times*, 15 August 1998.

13 M. Brill Olcott, 'The Caspian False Promise', *Foreign Policy*, Summer 1998.

14 E. Herzig, *The New Caucasus*, Royal Institute of International Affairs, London, 1999.

15 Shamir Sharifov, chairman of the Azeri Oil Fund, Statoil seminar, Oslo, March 2001.

16 International Monetary Fund's assessment of Azerbaijan's Interim Poverty Reduction Strategy Paper, June 2001.

17 World Bank, *Azerbaijan: Poverty Reduction Strategy Paper* (Interim Report), May 2001.

18 World Bank, *Report No. 15601-AZ: Azerbaijan – Poverty Assessment*.

19 World Bank, *Azerbaijan: Poverty Reduction Strategy Paper* (Interim Report), May 2001.

20 A. Cooley, paper presented at Columbia University, 'Caspian Meeting', Baku, May 1999.

21 D. Heradstveit, 'Elite Perceptions of Ethical Problems facing the Western Oil Industry in Azerbaijan', paper presented at Norwegian Institute of Foreign Relations, Autumn 1999.

22 Olav Fjell, president of Statoil, speech at World Petroleum Congress, Calgary, 14 June 2000.

23 T. L. Karl, *The Paradox of Plenty: Oil Booms and Petro-states*, University of California Press, London, 1997.

24 Let me illustrate the industry's approach by using Statoil as an example. Over the last six months, Statoil has entered into co-operation agreements with the United Nations High Commissioner for Refugees as well as the Norwegian Refugee Council and the Norwegian Red Cross. The main objective of these agreements is to raise the awareness and improve the knowledge and understanding of human rights and humanitarian issues throughout the organisation.

25 Professor T. Gylfason, 'Lessons from the Dutch Disease', paper presented to a conference organised by Statoil on the Paradox of Wealth, Oslo, March 2001.

26 *Financial Times*, 22 November 2000.

27 H. O. Bergesen, T. Haugland and L. Lunde, 'Petro-States – Predatory or Developmental', Fridtjof Nansen Institute and ECON Centre for Economic Analysis, Oslo, 2000.

28 Debate in Parliament 1974 based on White Paper no. 25 (1973–1974) on the use of oil revenues.

9 Production Sharing Agreements and National Oil Funds

Marika Karayianni

Introduction

The Caspian Sea has been characterised as the next Persian Gulf. This is a wildly exaggerated evaluation of the region's potential. It holds 10 billion barrels of proven oil reserves, and an estimated additional 50–70 billion barrels of recoverable oil. This amounts to 4–6 per cent of the world's proven oil reserves, currently estimated at 1,034 billion barrels.[1] With respect to natural gas, the Caspian contains around 10–18 trillion cubic metres of proven reserves, i.e. 7–10 per cent of the world's proven gas reserves. Oil is easier to extract and transport, which is why oil is set to lead Caspian energy development in the following decade.

The experience of investments in the Caspian Sea region over the past ten years has shown that exploration costs are very high, around US$12–15 per barrel, thus two to three times more expensive than equivalent exploration costs in the Persian Gulf. Exploration failure costs are high too, estimated at around US$300–500 million per project. Offshore location of the fields, underdeveloped infrastructure and geographical isolation are the main reasons for these high costs. However, the introduction of new technology and lower transit tariffs are expected to diminish the exploration cost to US$8–10/bl in the future.[2]

These assessments indicate that the Caspian reservoir does not match the Middle East, rather it should be considered as a second North Sea. This conclusion is of particular importance to the European Union (EU), where demand for external energy supplies will increase up to 90 per cent for oil and 70 per cent for natural gas within 20 to 30 years. The eastern enlargement of the EU, which has widened EU boundaries to the Black Sea and the Caucasus, is likely to strengthen these trends. Consequently, diversification of supply must become a strategic priority. The North Sea currently provides 4.4 per cent of world oil production; however, according to current prognoses, it will be worked out within 25 years.[3] Russia and the Caspian emerge as the most competitive alternatives to the North Sea, though they will not necessarily replace energy supplies from the Middle East.

There are substantial differences between the North and South Caspian basin, both with regard to the volume of hydrocarbons and the geology of the subsoil. Kazakhstan leads Caspian oil production with proven reserves of 5.4 billion barrels and estimated reserves up to 50 billion barrels. Oil exploration in Azerbaijan suffered a number of setbacks in 2001–2003. Foreign companies operating in Azerbaijan encountered geological obstacles, which in turn added to the technical difficulties of drilling. Several fields were closed owing to failure to discover recoverable oil reserves; these included the Kyurdashi and Lenkoran Deniz–Talysh Deniz fields.[4] Serious shortcomings in infrastructure, as well as the lack of sufficient local expertise further exacerbated these problems. The extent of gas reserves in Turkmenistan remains a matter of speculation, owing to insufficient exploration, in large part the result of an unfavourable investment climate (see **Canzi**).

The investment process

Negotiations on the delimitation of the Caspian Sea have been in progress for over a decade. As of 2003, bilateral agreements had been concluded between the littoral states of the North Caspian – Azerbaijan, Kazakhstan and Russia. In the South Caspian, too, progress was being made towards resolving outstanding disputes. Without waiting for a full multilateral agreement on the legal status of the sea, the littoral states have been actively engaging in exploration projects. In particular, Azerbaijan and Kazakhstan have made substantial progress in developing their offshore oil reserves. Azerbaijan has signed over 20 Production Sharing Agreements (PSAs), both onshore and offshore. Kazakhstan also has opened its resources to development by foreign companies. International oil projects in Kazakhstan have taken the form of Joint Ventures, PSAs and exploration/field concessions. Overall, the two countries have received considerable sums of foreign direct investment in their oil and natural gas sectors. The decade of 1992–2002 witnessed total investment of over US$13 billion in upstream development in Azerbaijan, Kazakhstan and Turkmenistan. This comprised US$8.2 billion allocated to Kazakhstan, US$4.3 billion to Azerbaijan and US$600 million to Turkmenistan. Most of these investments were directed to five giant fields: Tengiz, Karachaganak and Kashagan in Kazakhstan and Azeri–Chirag–Guneshli and Shah Deniz in Azerbaijan.[5] It was anticipated that investment would reach US$21 billion in the following five years.

During this period, the oil industry in Azerbaijan received 70–80 per cent of total foreign investment. As a result of this large influx of capital into the oil sector, the decline in Azerbaijan's oil production was halted. From 1998 onwards the trend was towards growth. In 2001, Azerbaijan witnessed its fourth consecutive annual increase in average oil production, with output rising to 311,200 barrels per day.[6] Kazakhstan was equally important to world energy markets. With sufficient export options, it was expected that Kazakhstan could become one of the world's largest oil producers and exporters. As in Azerbaijan, the main driver behind Kazakhstan's economic growth was foreign investment in the oil and natural gas sector. By 2002, the oil industry accounted for approximately 30 per cent of the Kazakh government's budget revenue; oil accounted for half of Kazakhstan's exports.[7]

It is questionable whether the transition economies of the Caspian countries will be able to absorb this huge amount of capital investment, given the fact that they lack the necessary institutional framework, infrastructure and experience. As indicated above, economic growth in Azerbaijan and Kazakhstan is almost entirely dependent on the development of the oil and gas industries. In the early 1990s, following the collapse of the Soviet Union, these new states suffered severe economic decline. There were, however, high hopes that all such problems would be resolved by the development of the oil and gas fields. This proved to be an illusion. After a decade of massive foreign investment, the local economies are still underdeveloped. There are few signs of structural change in other sectors of their economies, such as agriculture, trade and tourism, which might have facilitated a balanced transition to a free market economy. These countries remain vulnerable to external shocks due to the lack of diversification of economic growth. Moreover, corruption and poverty are rampant.

Production Sharing Agreements

The granting of Production Sharing Agreements (PSAs) by the governments of Azerbaijan and Kazakhstan to foreign oil and gas companies for exploration of the fields was, and remains, the main way of attracting foreign direct investment. A PSA is defined as follows:

> A PSA is a contractual agreement under which the State awards an investor the exclusive right to search, prospect and extract mineral resources from a specific natural resource for a certain period of time. The investor undertakes the obligation to carry out these works for the said period of time, at its own expense and bearing all risks. As a consequence, the foreign oil and gas company acts as a contractor for the host country in developing its oil and gas resources and receives a share of the production at rates specified in a contract to recoup its costs and make a profit.[8]

Azerbaijan, Kazakhstan and Turkmenistan have all signed PSAs. Iran has abstained from this contracting practice on the grounds that there must be a consensus on the legal status of the Caspian before the signature of contracts for exploration. No Production Sharing Agreements have yet been signed to develop oilfields in the 'Russian sector' of the Caspian. Foreign companies operating in the region favour the contractual mechanism provided by PSAs because they ensure a solid legal basis for oil exploration. The regional governments, however, did not share this attitude as they blamed the PSAs for the delay in delivering revenues to the state budget, though in fact this was due in large part to the slow extraction process in the Caspian (around seven to nine years from the commencement of field development).[9]

Among the Caspian littoral states, Azerbaijan has had the longest experience of the operation of Production Sharing Agreements with multinational oil consortia. The PSA establishes the contractual relations between the foreign company and the State Oil Company of the Azerbaijan Republic (SOCAR). SOCAR acts in a dual capacity as representative of the government of Azerbaijan and as a full member of the contract. Each PSA, once agreed and finalised, is passed to the Azerbaijani parliament for ratification. After ratification, it takes the form of a separate law. The government of Azerbaijan granted the first such PSA, known as the 'Contract of the Century', to the Azerbaijan International Operating Company (AIOC) in 1994 to develop the offshore Azeri–Chirag–Guneshli (ACG) field. Since then, the Azerbaijan parliament has ratified a total of 22 PSAs for the exploration of oil and gas fields in Azerbaijan. By 2002, 32 companies from 14 countries were working on projects based on PSAs.

Azerbaijan's policy regarding disclosure of oil revenues emphasises the need for transparency. The texts of the PSAs for the ACG and Shah Deniz projects have been published on the BP website, likewise the environmental and social impact assessments. However, few people in Azerbaijan have access to the Internet and, consequently, the vast majority of the population, including many opposition activists, are not aware that such information is available in the public domain.[10] Consequently, there are widespread suspicions that the oil revenues are being misappropriated by those in power. Such concerns are exacerbated by the low level of oversight (see below), which leaves the oil revenues open to political manipulation.[11] This in turn perpetuates corruption in public administration and prevents the proper distribution of oil wealth. On the positive side, the PSAs have to date provided a stable legal and tax framework for international oil companies; they take priority over prevailing and future legislation in cases where PSAs would be adversely affected by legislation. The parties to the PSA are subject only to negotiable profit taxes and bonuses, and social charges for local employees. Parties are exempt from all other taxes, including royalties.[12]

State Oil Funds in Azerbaijan and Kazakhstan

As mentioned above, the local economies of Azerbaijan and Kazakhstan rely almost entirely on the oil and gas sector. Oil revenues account for up to 50 per cent of the income in the Azerbaijani state budget. At the same time, according to some estimates, almost half the households in Azerbaijan live below the poverty line.[13] Despite massive foreign investments, reforms to encourage institutional renewal and good governance in these countries have not been sufficiently supported by the Western community. The Partnership and Co-operation Agreements, which the EU has signed with all the countries of the former Soviet Union, have not produced the desired effects, mainly due to the absence of efficient implementation mechanisms. As a result, these countries have not yet developed a sound legal and tax framework, which will protect their economies and will provide a solid basis for an equitable distribution of the wealth emanating from the oil development.

In order to avoid the dependence of the economies of the Caspian states on the oil sector and to ensure that the oil revenues from the PSAs flow into the state budgets, the World Bank and the IMF have for many years supported the creation of National Oil Funds in these states. The aim is to secure the transparent management and allocation of the revenues from the oil exploration. It was envisaged that such Oil Funds should have four major sources of revenue:

- sales of government shares under the PSAs;
- surplus and performance bonuses, paid to the governments by the companies under the PSAs;
- rent of sale assets belonging to the governments under the PSAs;
- income from investing and managing the assets of the Oil Fund.

Azerbaijan and Kazakhstan have already created such funds. Turkmenistan, however, has, to date, not followed suit.

Azerbaijan was the first to initiate such a scheme. On 29 December 1999 President Aliev issued a decree announcing his intention to establish a State Oil Fund of Azerbaijan (SOFAZ). Samir Rauf oglu Sharifov was appointed executive director of SOFAZ in January 2001. By 1 October 2001, SOFAZ's assets totalled US$627 million.[14] Following an open tender, held in February 2002, the accountants Ernst and Young were appointed by President Aliev to audit SOFAZ financial statements for the year 2001. A Supervisory Board was created in accordance with the presidential decree of 27 December 2001; it consisted of ten members, including Prime Minister Artur Rasizade, Minister of Finance Avaz Alekberov, Minister for Economic Development Farhad Aliev, First Vice-President of SOCAR Ilham Aliev (son of President Aliev) and Chairman of the Board of the National Bank Elman Rustamov. The first meeting of the Supervisory Board was held on 16 July 2002, chaired by President Aliev.

The Oil Fund is accountable and responsible to the President of Azerbaijan, who has the power to appoint or dismiss the Fund's director. Likewise, the president must approve the appointment of members to its Supervisory Board. Information on the legal framework and management structure of SOFAZ, also reports and statistics on performance, are published on an official website.[15] The current management no longer permits the use of income from production sharing revenues, bonuses and other oil revenues to cover the state budget deficit. However, concerns remain over how the money will be used and whether or not SOFAZ's activities will be effectively monitored. In particular, there is unease that the high degree of personal control wielded by the president could lead to abuses of power and misuse of funds. Some believe that this undermines the efforts of the IMF and the World Bank to establish an independent mechanism to use the oil revenues responsibly.[16]

In Kazakhstan, the situation regarding the National Oil Fund is even more opaque. It appears to have been established initially as a secret fund, details of which only came to light as the result of a series of major scandals that erupted in 2001, involving senior figures in the government as well as President Nazarbaev's own family. The immediate causes of these incidents were, on the surface, somewhat varied. The underlying problem, however, was the perception that there was massive abuse of power and misappropriation of public funds by the political elite. Such issues had surfaced previously when a former Kazakh Prime Minister, Akezhan Kazhegeldin, had called for the creation of a People's Oil Fund. Kazhegeldin subsequently fell from power and was himself accused of corruption and other abuses of power. He was disqualified from running in the presidential elections of January 1999 on a minor legal technicality. The opposition party that he had founded, the Republican People's Party of Kazakhstan, suffered constant harassment. In these circumstances, Kazhegeldin felt he had no option but to leave his country and to live abroad in self-imposed exile (mainly in Europe and the US). In August 2001, he was tried *in absentia* by the Supreme Court of Kazakhstan. He was found guilty and sentenced to ten years in prison.[17]

It was against this background that, on 4 April 2002, the then Prime Minister, Imangali Tasmagambetov, admitted to parliament that the Kazakh authorities had created a Fund, in which to deposit the revenue, amounting to US$660 million, which it had received from the US oil major Chevron (now ChevronTexaco) in exchange for Kazakhstan's 5 per cent stake in the joint venture at the Tengiz oilfield. This entity was, in effect, a National Oil Fund.[18] It was disclosed that the Fund would be replenished with extra-budgetary revenues, taxes from oil companies, and signature bonuses and royalties paid by foreign partners in joint ventures. By 2002 the Fund held US$1.3 billion.[19]

The degree of secrecy that had surrounded the creation of the Fund fuelled rumours of corruption in high circles.[20] In order to dispel such suspicions, President Nazarbaev called for the creation of a Board of Trustees in order to ensure accountability. An Oversight Council has indeed been created, but it lacks independence and is therefore unable to function effectively. Almost all its members are presidential appointees. Moreover, it is chaired by the president, who also holds the tie-breaking vote. The Fund operates with a relative degree of transparency, but key documents are often not disclosed. For example, Production Sharing Agreements and Joint Venture Agreements have not as yet been published. Reports are produced at regular intervals for the Ministry of Finance, but are not available for public scrutiny. Only summaries of the annual report and audit are published. An official website has been created that provides some information relating to such issues as the legal framework and management structure of the Fund,[21] but it is less transparent than the corresponding website in Azerbaijan.[22]

Conclusions

During the Soviet period corruption was endemic in the republics of the Caucasus and Central Asia. This trend has unfortunately continued up to the present. According to the corruption index of Transparency International 1999, Kazakhstan ranked 84 out of 99 of the most corrupt countries. Its neighbours Armenia and Russia ranked 80 and 82 respectively, while Georgia tied with Kazakhstan, Kyrgyzstan and Uzbekistan at 87, and Azerbaijan ranked at 96. In 2002, the situation had not changed greatly: on the same index of corruption, out of the 102 countries listed, Kazakhstan ranked 88, Azerbaijan 95. Interestingly, Azerbaijan came only slightly ahead of energy-rich Indonesia and Nigeria on the index, thus illustrating that economic development and improved standards of living do not necessarily stem from oil revenues (see **Auty**).

The Report of the European Bank of Reconstruction and Development (EBRD) on Central Asia and the Caucasus of November 2001 called for greater transparency in business practices in order to promote foreign direct investment and economic growth. The report, which concentrated primarily on the energy sector, suggested that corruption was a far more serious threat to economic stability than many potential investors realise: 'Natural resource wealth tends to be associated with corruption, as productive entrepreneurship may offer fewer rewards than the pursuit of political influence.'[23]

Unless new legislation on the contracting terms and the monitoring of the management of the oil revenues is created, there is a strong possibility that billions of dollars will continue to be directed to the pockets of the 'elites' of the Caspian states, rather than to projects to alleviate the real needs of these struggling economies and societies. The ongoing problems of pollution, poverty, human rights abuses and corruption clearly indicate the failure of regional governments to protect their citizens. The reluctance of these governments to recognise the social and institutional problems of oil development will only lead to a further impasse. Thus, the enormous sums of money that are flowing into the region may well add to the sad experience of oil exploitation during the Soviet era. It is to be hoped that international financial institutions, especially the World Bank and the EBRD, will seek to assist and promote institutional renewal, openness and transparency and good governance as policy targets for the governing elites. The external powers that have strategic interests in the Caspian, such as the US and the EU, likewise have a major role to play in this field.

Notes

1 J. Roberts, 'Caspian Oil and Gas: How Far have We Come and Where are We Going?', *Platts Energy Group Report*, 20 March 2002.

2 T. Adams, 'Europe's Black Sea Dimension', *Caspian Oil and Gas Development and the Black Sea Region: An Overview*, Center for European Policy Studies and International Center for Black Sea Studies (CEPS–ICBSS), Brussels, 2002.

3 European Commission, Green Paper, *Towards a European Strategy for the Security of Energy Supply*, Brussels, 29 November 2000.

4 *Alexander's Oil and Gas Connections*, www.gasandoil.com, 9 April 2002.
5 *Caspian Energy Watch*, 'Will the Caspian Stay on Track as Investment Accelerates?', Cambridge Energy Research Associates (CERA), Spring 2002.
6 EIA, *Country Analysis: Azerbaijan*, 2002.
7 EIA, *Country Analysis: Kazakhstan*, 2002.
8 *FSU Oil and Gas Monitor*, 10 April 2002, 'Foreign Investment in the Russian Oil Industry: Part II, PSAs', by A. Heinrich and H. Pleines.
9 Adams, *op. cit.*
10 In 2001, according to official sources, there were only 3.2 per 1,000 people in Azerbaijan who were Internet users (UNDP, *Human Development Report 2003*, Oxford University Press, Oxford/New York, p. 275).
11 'Will a "Resource Curse" Befall Azerbaijan and Kazakhstan?', *Eurasianet*, 27 June 2003. See also S. Tsalik, *Caspian Oil Windfalls: Who Will Benefit?*, Caspian Revenue Watch, Open Society Institute, New York, 2003, esp. pp. 117–119.
12 *How to Deal with Azerbaijan's Oil Boom? Policy Strategies in Resource-rich Transition Economies*, IMF Working Paper, 98/6, European II Department.
13 There is great discrepancy in estimates of the scale of poverty in Azerbaijan. Informal sources suggest that in 2000, 80 per cent of the population were living below the poverty line; *Pocketing Caspian Black Gold: Who are the Real Beneficiaries of Oil Infrastructure in Georgia and Azerbaijan?*, Central and Eastern Europe (CEE) Bankwatch Network (www.bankwatch.org), April 2002, p. 9.
14 Information Office of the State Oil Fund of the Republic of Azerbaijan, press release, 10 October 2002.
15 http://www.oilfund.az/html.
16 See CEE Bankwatch, *op. cit.* For a more positive assessment of Azerbaijan's performance in managing oil revenues, see Tsalik, *op. cit.*, esp. pp. 117–125.
17 A substantial fine was also imposed on him and his property was confiscated.
18 For a description of the history, structure and workings of the Kazakh National Oil Fund, see Tsalik, *op. cit.*, pp. 145–160.
19 Statement by G. Marchenko, Governor of the National Bank of Kazakhstan, at the Eurasia Economic Summit, held in Almaty in April 2002.
20 www.tol.cz, 'Kazakh scandals throw spotlight on Democracy', 16–22 April 2002.
21 http://www.nationalfund.kz/
22 For a comparison of the two websites, see Tsalik, *op. cit.*, p. 189.
23 EBRD Report on Central Asia and the Caucasus, November 2001.

Part V
Regional Perspectives

10 Azerbaijan: policy priorities towards the Caspian Sea

Nasib Nassibli

The geopolitical situation in the Caspian region changed drastically after the collapse of the Soviet Union in 1991. All the newly independent states of the region have embarked on the process of consolidating their independence. Neither the Caucasus nor Central Asia (which together form the Caspian region) can any longer be regarded as being within Russia's backyard. The development of the Caspian Sea's abundant hydrocarbon reserves has played a catalytic role in this process. The world's major oil companies have already invested over US$8 billion in exploration and development operations in the Azerbaijan and Kazakh sectors of the Caspian, while more than US$100 billion are expected to be invested over the next 25–30 years.[1] Progress has been made on the construction of new export pipelines.

These developments have turned Baku into the centre of the booming Caspian oil industry. Yet the Azerbaijan Republic also faces serious problems. In addition to the difficulties of transition that are shared by all the regional states, Azerbaijan must contend with a number of specific issues. One is that it would like to leave the Russian sphere of influence, but has complicated historical and contemporary links to the former centre of empire. Another problem is that Azerbaijan has a far from simple relationship with another close neighbour, the Islamic Republic of Iran. A large part of Azerbaijan's historic territory, as well as some three-quarters of the world community of Azerbaijanis, lie within the borders of Iran. Moreover, many Azerbaijanis share a common faith with their Iranian neighbours; indeed, within the Muslim world, Azerbaijan ranks second only to Iran in the size of its Shia Muslim community (or at least nominally so; many Azerbaijanis do not regard themselves as 'Shia' or 'Sunni' but simply as 'Muslims'). Finally, Azerbaijan is suffering the consequences of the 15-year-long Karabagh conflict. Approximately one-fifth of Azerbaijan's land is currently under Armenian occupation. It is encircled and blockaded by hostile neighbours – the Russian Federation, Armenia and Iran.

Attempts to break the geopolitical blockade

Azerbaijan's political orientation has been largely determined by its geography. It lacks natural defences. Moreover, in the north, the Derbent pass provides easy entry to foreign marauders (and nowadays possibly to criminals and terrorists). History has further contributed to Azerbaijan's current predicament. One crucial event was the forcible conversion of the population to Shiism. This happened in the early sixteenth century, when the Safavid dynasty of Iran held sway over the territory of Azerbaijan. As a result, Azerbaijan became estranged from the rest of the Turkic world, which remained Sunni Muslim. Gradually, the Azerbaijanis (sometimes known as Azerbaijani Turks) ideologically and culturally merged with the Persians. Furthermore, as a result of a century and a half of war between the Safavids and Ottoman Turks, Azerbaijan's links with the wider world to the west and the east were severed. In the nineteenth century, as a consequence of the Iranian–Russian wars of 1804–1813 and 1826–1828 the independent Azerbaijan Khanates were divided between these two empires. Thus, Azerbaijan became yet more firmly embedded in a north–south axis.[2]

After the collapse of the Soviet Union, a new geopolitical triangle emerged, encompassing Moscow, Yerevan and Tehran. Moscow–Yerevan relations have long assumed the proportions of a strategic alliance and close economic, political and strategic co-operation between them is flourishing. The fact that Russia supplied Armenia with more than US$1 billion worth of weaponry between 1994 and 1996 is irrefutable evidence of this.[3] Also, the Russian Federation has put pressure on Azerbaijan and supported Armenia in every possible way. The active role of the West, and the growing involvement and authority of its closest ally, Turkey, in the Caspian basin, has also brought the positions of the region's historical rivals, Russia and Iran, closer together. Iran's aspiration to build its own nuclear weapon and the speedy armament of the country is easily explained by Tehran's close co-operation with Moscow.[4] Another reason for the formation of the Moscow–Yerevan–Tehran triangle is the desire of these countries to thwart the process of revitalisation of the Azerbaijan Republic.[5]

Resistance to Russia's revanchism

Russia has had to retreat from the region for the first time in 500 years. This has created tensions in Russia's political elite between those who favour a pro-Atlantic orientation and those who favour a pro-Eurasian orientation. This debate was high on the agenda in 1992. The pro-Atlantic forces wanted integration with the West, while the pro-Eurasian camp believed that the future of the two-headed eagle was bound up with the restoration of the empire.[6] Andrei Kozyrev, Russia's then foreign minister, an outright pro-Atlantic politician, was the first to use the term 'near abroad' in an interview with *Izvestiya* newspaper in early 1992.[7] Later that year, speaking in Stockholm at a meeting of the Conference for Security and Co-operation in Europe (CSCE), Kozyrev spoke of the necessity to establish a military and economic federation, or confederation, of former Soviet republics. Of course, it is possible to find differences of emphasis within these two groupings. In general, however, all shades of opinion within the Russian political elite with regard to the preservation of the Russian Federation's geopolitical authority have been unanimously supportive. The fact that various Russian ministries (e.g. Foreign Affairs and Defence on the one hand, and Fuel and Energy on the other) pursue differing tactics does not alter the general strategic course.[8] In other words, despite the frequent changes of governments and foreign ministers, Moscow's intention to bring back its previous satellites under the same umbrella has not subsided.

The main thrust of Russian foreign policy on the territory of the former USSR has been the thesis that Russia is historically 'responsible' for stability in the region. Accordingly, the international community should vest the task of safeguarding peace and stability in the region in Russia.[9] Consequently, in February 1993 President Yeltsin urged the United Nations to give Russian armed forces the status of peacekeeping troops in order for them to be able to intervene in conflicts on the territories of former Union member-states.[10] In fact, the document, entitled 'Recommendations', prepared by the Russian State Duma Committee for International Relations (chaired by ethnic Armenian Yevgeni Ambartsumov) and forwarded to the government, stated that:

> The Russian Federation, which is internationally considered to be the legal successor of the USSR, must be governed by a doctrine (like the US Monroe doctrine in Latin America) envisioning protection of its vital interests on the entire geographical and political territory of the former USSR. Russia must also achieve the recognition of its interests by the international community. The Russian Federation must obtain the international community's consent for playing the role of a guarantor of political and military stability in ex-USSR. It is necessary to urge the seven super-powers of the West to assist Russia in this function and provide hard currency aid for the formation of prompt operation forces (blue berets).[11]

Moscow's objective of bringing the 'near abroad' back within its sphere of influence is focused on Azerbaijan for the following reasons:

- Control over Azerbaijan would provide the Russian Federation with the opportunity of strengthening its strategic interests in the Caspian region and extending them to the Middle East; the strategically important Gabala Radio-Location Station (RLS), a Soviet-era installation situated on the territory of Azerbaijan, has made this country even more important for Russia, since it could serve as an outpost for Russia to keep the Middle East under control with aviation and ballistic missiles.
- Moscow could prevent the expansion of Western influence in the Caspian region.
- Russia could set an insurmountable obstruction in the way of Turkic integration; it could also thwart the spread of Turkey's authority in Central Asia, North Caucasus and along the Volga.

• Russia could ensure its economic interests in the Caspian region, exerting control over the region's abundant hydrocarbon reserves, as well as overland, air, information and sea arteries.

Lacking the necessary material, technological and ideological capabilities to bring pressure on Azerbaijan, Moscow has resorted to military and political pressure. This entails support for Armenia and ethnic Armenians in Karabagh. Moscow is deliberately retarding the resolution of this conflict in order to turn Azerbaijan into a hostage of this stand-off (see more about this topic in the next section). Moscow has also attempted to sow the seeds of separatist strife among the ethnic minorities in Azerbaijan (for example, the Lezghins and the Talysh) and thus to federalise the Azerbaijan Republic. Moscow has also attempted to undermine internal stability in Azerbaijan by providing support for the disruptive activities of the military opposition. Further, it has resorted to various provocative actions, including assassination attempts on the life of the head of state. There have been attempts to station Russian military units on the territory of Azerbaijan and frontier guard troops on the republic's southern frontiers. Moreover, Russia has tried to hamper the transfer of the Gabala RLS to Azerbaijan's jurisdiction, despite having signed an agreement to this effect. Finally, Moscow tries to use other tools as a means of exerting pressure and blackmail on Azerbaijan, e.g. by manipulation of the fate of the hundreds of thousands of Azerbaijanis who still live in Russia.

Since 1991, there have been three phases in the relationship between Azerbaijan and Russia. Azerbaijan's first president, Ayaz Mutalibov (1991–1992), tried to make concessions to Russia in an effort to win Moscow's neutrality in resolving the Armenian–Azerbaijan conflict. For this, he regarded it necessary to sign the document on establishing the Commonwealth of Independent States (CIS). However, after Russian troops perpetrated a brutal massacre in the Azerbaijani town of Khojali on 26 February 1992, President Mutalibov's authority evaporated and he stepped down. He was succeeded by Abulfaz Elchibey, Azerbaijan's first democratically elected president.

The priority for Elchibey was to safeguard and strengthen Azerbaijan independence. During his term of office, Azerbaijan's national currency unit, the *manat*, was introduced. On 7 October 1992 the Azerbaijan parliament rejected the CIS agreement. The framework subsequent agreement on friendship and co-operation, signed with the Russian Federation on 12 October, envisaged a bilateral relationship between the two states. Russian troops were withdrawn from Azerbaijan. At the same time, negotiations with foreign petroleum companies were accelerated. President Elchibey proposed the Azerbaijan–Georgia–Ukraine economic co-operation triangle as an alternative to CIS integration.

In 1993, however, Moscow redoubled efforts to implement its 'near abroad' concept. In unofficial talks with the Elchibey government, high-ranking Russian officials conveyed the message that the time of 'disobedience' was over and called on Azerbaijan to join the move to 'integration' within the CIS. When this effort came to nothing, Moscow stepped up pressure on Azerbaijan in various ways. For example, Russia's 1993 trade tariffs with Azerbaijan were higher than with any other CIS member state. In late March–early April, Azerbaijan's Kalbajar province was seized by Armenian troops with the direct participation of Russian military units. Elchibey rejected the proposal of a return of the Russian army to Azerbaijan in the capacity of a peacekeeping force. Moscow then supported an armed uprising in Ganja (led by colonel Surat Husseinov), in an attempt to get rid of Azerbaijan's national democratic government. As Elchibey said later, 'in order to prevent a civil war' and 'to upset Russia's plot' (i.e. to prevent Moscow from bringing Mutalibov to power), he stepped down.

Azerbaijan's new leader, Heidar Aliev, was an experienced politician. He realised that he had first to appease the instigator of the Ganja rebellion, or at least to neutralise him. Then, in a bid to satisfy Russia, he immediately suspended talks with Western oil companies. In his meetings with President Yeltsin and other leading Russian politicians, Aliev vowed to pursue a different foreign policy from that of his predecessor. He agreed that Azerbaijan should join the CIS. He also signed up to the treaty on Collective Security and Economic Co-operation. Nevertheless, Aliev, still only acting president, was in no hurry to implement these undertakings. In accordance with the agreement on collective security, Russian military units were to have been stationed on the Azerbaijan–Iranian border, but Aliev insisted that they be placed on the Azerbaijan–Armenian frontier. He also deferred a decision on stationing Russian peacekeeping forces in Karabagh and on a resolution of the issue of the Gabala RLS.

By making some concessions to Moscow in the oil sector (for instance, by giving Russia's LUKoil a 10 per cent stake in the oil consortium that was being established), Azerbaijan's new government counted on the creation of a pro-Azerbaijan lobby in Moscow. In fact, influential members of the Russian energy lobby (e.g. Prime Minister Chernomyrdin, Energy Minister Shafrannik and head of LUKoil Alakbarov) did contribute to relaxing pressure on Azerbaijan. This, however, could not alter Moscow's traditional policy in the Caucasus. Russia did not change its pro-Armenian position in the Karabagh conflict. Furthermore, Moscow continued to insist that its troops be placed on the Azerbaijan–Iranian border and that a CIS anti-aircraft defence system be established in South Caucasus. Under such circumstances, it was clear that further compromises with Moscow would be useless. In December 1993, President Aliev, with the mediation of Turkey, turned westwards. Thus, an irrational anti-Azerbaijan policy, coupled with unequivocal support for Armenian aggression and ethnic separatism, led to a significant reduction of Russian influence and prestige in Azerbaijan.[12]

Armenian aggression/Karabagh problem

Ever since Azerbaijan regained its independence in 1991, the Karabagh problem has paralysed the country. It has deprived the nation of the joyous expectations that for decades the people have associated with independence.

The current troubles started in the late 1980s, when Armenia renewed its claims on Karabagh (an autonomous region located within Azerbaijan but having a majority Armenian population). Rumours were spread that Armenians living in the Karabagh region were subject to 'discrimination'. It was claimed that Karabagh was economically and culturally underdeveloped and that Azerbaijan was obstructing links between Armenia and Karabagh. Moscow and Baku refuted these accusations in official statements. The Armenian lobby then insisted that 'Karabagh has always been a part of Armenia', and that this region was 'presented to Azerbaijan' by Stalin. Particular importance was attached to the fact that the choice of self-determination of ethnic Armenians from Karabagh (78 per cent of the total population of 185,000 of Karabagh) 'gives them the right to join with Armenia'.

In August 1987, a group of senior Armenian academics sent a petition to Moscow demanding that both Karabagh and Nakhichevan be separated from Azerbaijan and annexed to Armenia. (Nakhichevan, located within Armenia, was administratively subordinated to Azerbaijan, with Azerbaijanis constituting over 90 per cent of the population.) The local administrative council of Karabagh passed a decision on joining Soviet Armenia. This provoked widespread anger among the Azerbaijanis. During armed clashes on 27–29 February, 1988 in Sumgait city, not far from Baku, 26 Armenians and six Azerbaijanis were slain.[13] The Armenian Supreme Soviet called on Moscow and Baku in June to unite Karabagh with Armenia. In January 1989, Moscow withdrew Karabagh from Azerbaijan's jurisdiction, subordinating it directly to Moscow. Thereupon the Azerbaijan Supreme Soviet, in response to popular demand, adopted the law 'On sovereignty', stating that the laws of the Azerbaijan Republic must be enforced throughout its territory. In retaliation, the Armenian Supreme Soviet adopted a law on 1 December 1989 uniting Karabagh with Armenia. The KGB then masterminded the killing of several Armenians on 13–17 January. Large numbers of Soviet troops were sent to Baku on 20 January; there ensued a brutal slaughter of peaceful residents of the city. A state of emergency was announced throughout Azerbaijan. This lasted until the collapse of the USSR in December 1991.

With the aid of Soviet military units stationed there, Karabagh separatists tried to forcefully drive the Azerbaijanis out of Karabagh. In February 1992, while the presidents of Azerbaijan and Armenia were meeting in Tehran, Armenians, aided by Russia's 366th regiment, obliterated Azerbaijan's Khojali settlement from the face of the earth. In May that year, during further negotiations in Tehran, Armenian separatists took the city of Shusha, the most strategic centre of the Azerbaijanis of Karabagh. In late March 1993, with the direct participation of Russian military units, Azerbaijan's strategic province of Kalbajar, located outside Karabagh, was occupied following simultaneous attacks launched from Armenia and Karabagh. Later, Armenians seized six more provinces beyond the boundaries of Karabagh. Thus, on the eve of the signing of the Russian-sponsored cease-fire treaty in Bishkek in May 1994, the Azerbaijan Republic lost one-fifth of its territory and had about 1 million refugees and displaced persons; more than 20,000 people had been killed in action (see Map 5).

Azerbaijan and Armenia both became members of the Conference for Security and Co-operation in Europe (CSCE) in January 1992 and of the United Nations in March 1992. After the Khojali carnage, the CSCE decided to convene a conference on Karabagh in Minsk, to be attended by nine countries. The objectives of the conference were to normalise relations between Azerbaijan and Armenia, and to agree on the status of the Azerbaijani and Armenian populations of Karabagh. Azerbaijan and Armenia were full-fledged participants of the conference, whereas representatives of the Armenian and Azerbaijani communities of Karabagh had to take part in the capacity of interested parties. The United Nations Security Council, by resolution 822, required Armenian forces to withdraw immediately from Kalbajar province, which was beyond the administrative boundaries of Karabagh. In addition, this and subsequent resolutions recognised Azerbaijan's territorial integrity. In May 1993, as plans for the withdrawal of occupying troops from Kalbajar province were being finalised (Yerevan had given its consent to that), there were new acts of aggression by Armenian armed forces. Since then, the Karabagh conflict has been a recurring item of the conference later renamed Organisation for Security and Co-operation in Europe (OSCE). As of 2003, however, it was still unresolved.

This brief overview of developments in the past 15 years in Karabagh shows that it is this problem that has largely dominated the relationship between Azerbaijan and Armenia. The two republics remain in a state of hostility, without diplomatic relations. The only explanation for this continuing state of 'frozen conflict' is Armenia's aggression – backed by Moscow – against Azerbaijan.

Struggling against pressure from Iran

As mentioned above, in the early nineteenth century northern Azerbaijan was absorbed into the Russian empire, southern Azerbaijan into Iran. A large part of this southern part of ethnically Azerbaijan territory still lies within Iran. This has influenced relations between the two countries. In the 1980s, in Soviet Azerbaijan calls for reunification with the south (i.e. Iranian Azerbaijan) were at times even more powerful than those calling for independence.[14] The largest political organisation of the early 1990s, the Azerbaijan Popular Front, attached particular importance to this issue, stressing the need 'to eliminate all obstacles in the way of cultural and economic co-operation with South Azerbaijan'.[15]

The declaration of independence proclaimed by the Azerbaijan Republic in October 1991 caused concern in Tehran. It is indicative that Iranian Foreign Minister Velayati suggested the establishment of a powerful Soviet confederation, which he believed would prevent the West from gaining control over the independent republics.[16] Some Iranian officials put forward the idea of annexing what used to be 'Iran's ancient land' of the Azerbaijan Republic (i.e. northern Azerbaijan). Governing circles in Iran did not back the idea. Yet Persian chauvinism was perturbed by the growing role of the Turkic element in independent Azerbaijan and the potential threat to Iran that this so-called Turkisation might pose. Therefore, Iran's theocratic regime attempted to lure the Azerbaijan Republic into its political orbit in order to minimise Azerbaijan's influence on the Turkic population of Iran.

Islamic revolution and Islamic governance occupied a particular place in Iranian propaganda. Groups of Iranian clergymen came to Azerbaijan to preach Islamic values. The idea of exporting Islamic revolution was advocated in periodicals, books and other publications that were sent to newly independent Azerbaijan. A number of Iranian-owned newspapers and magazines were produced in Baku. Some analysts in Azerbaijan believed that Iran had the following geopolitical objectives:

- to prevent the formation of an independent, democratic Azerbaijan Republic and to combat the spread of its influence over southern Azerbaijan, thus safeguarding Iran's territorial integrity and internal stability;
- to prevent the growing authority of the US and Turkey in Azerbaijan and in Central Asia;
- to prevent solidarity and closer integration within the Turkic world;
- to establish an outpost for pressure on Muslims in the North Caucasus, Central Asia and along the Volga;
- to use the territory of Azerbaijan as an export market for Iranian goods;
- to create an Islamic regime in the Azerbaijan Republic, in accordance with the 'Export of Islamic Revolution' doctrine.

The first foreign visit of Azerbaijan's first president, A. Mutalibov, made in late 1991, was to Iran. Official circles in Baku hoped that the visit would improve relations with Iran. An agreement was reached in Tehran to use the territory of Iran for contacts with Nakhichevan, under blockade by the Armenians. Documents were also signed on setting up a Free Economic Zone in Nakhichevan and expanding relations between the two countries. By going to Iran with a large delegation on the occasion of the anniversary of the Iranian revolution, Mutalibov made a significant gesture of rapprochement with Iran. A spokesman for the Azerbaijan government announced that Azerbaijan had no intention of interfering in the internal affairs of Iran and 'ruled out the idea of establishing a united Azerbaijan'.[17]

In 1992, Iran assumed the role of mediator in the Karabagh conflict. In late February of that year, Armenian and Azerbaijani presidents signed a ceasefire accord in Tehran. Yet hardly had the ink on the document dried, when Armenians surrounded Khojali, and, as described above, slaughtered most of its inhabitants. Armenians then took over Azerbaijan's strategic fore-post in Karabagh – the city of Shusha. Iran was held responsible for making serious concessions to the Armenian party. This caused public outrage in Azerbaijan. Media publications described the overlapping positions of Armenia and Iran.

Some Azerbaijanis believed that Tehran was not interested in a comprehensive settlement of the dispute, but rather that through the dispute it was trying to promote its authority in the region by brokering its own solution.

One of the key objectives of independent Azerbaijan's Iranian policy was to create a favourable environment for the reunion of families and relatives that had for many years been separated from each other. It also aimed to facilitate the process of migration. However, the proposal of Azerbaijan to sign a framework agreement on mutual recognition of the two countries' independence, state borders and non-interference with the internal affairs of each other (a similar agreement had been signed with Russia) received a lukewarm response from Iran. Neither did Tehran react to such proposals as a mutual exchange of television broadcasts.

Discontented with Elchibey's policy with respect to Iran, which strove to broaden bilateral relations on terms of parity, Tehran started supporting the opposition in Azerbaijan, encouraging it to take unlawful action against the legitimate government. This resulted in the June 1993 *coup d'état* against the Elchibey government. When Heidar Aliev came to power, relations between Iran and Azerbaijan improved somewhat. Iran built a refugee camp at its own expense to assist Azerbaijani refugees, and provided other kinds of humanitarian aid. Iranian dignitaries began paying frequent visits to Azerbaijan; many new agreements were signed. Representatives of Iran's spiritual leader were sent to all parts of Azerbaijan.

Then, in late 1993, Azerbaijani–Iranian relations entered a new stage. Heidar Aliev's foreign policy priorities switched from Russo-Iranian to Turkish–Western. In September 1994, Azerbaijan signed the so-called 'Contract of the Century' for oil production from its national sector in the Caspian Sea. Iran's attitude to Heidar Aliev and to the Azerbaijan government changed drastically. The Iranian media started calling him the 'servant of America and Zionism', a label that they had invented for Elchibey. Iran's demand that Azerbaijan stop all official contacts with the US and Israel became a key issue for Iranian officials.[18] The Iranian press published a series of stories advocating the return of 'fourteen ancient Iranian cities' to Iran, claiming that such requests were being sent to them by citizens of the Azerbaijan Republic.[19] Leaders of the so-called Azerbaijan Islamic Party were put on trial in Azerbaijan in April 1997 on charges of espionage in favour of Iran. This further incensed the Iranians. The Islamists were found guilty and convicted; during the proceedings the court also heard evidence of the extensive hostile activities that Iran was engaged in on the territory of the Azerbaijan Republic.[20] On the question of the utilisation of Caspian energy resources, Tehran began supporting the position of Russia. The Iranian government also expanded relations with Armenia, a country at war with Azerbaijan.[21] Thus was formed the Moscow–Yerevan–Tehran alliance.

Rapprochement with Turkey, the US and Georgia

In order to preserve its national independence, restore territorial integrity and resist Iran's pressure, the Azerbaijan Republic has had to break the blockade imposed on it by the Moscow–Yerevan–Tehran alliance. To carry out this task, Azerbaijan has had to take an alternative course. In other words, it has had to choose an alliance based around Turkey, the US and Georgia in order to safeguard its security and to ensure the future.

After coming to power, President Aliev maintained extensive communication with Russian officials, but also resuscitated contacts with the West. Moreover, he actively sought to improve relations with Turkey, in particular with President Suleiman Demirel. Turkey was the first country to recognise Azerbaijan's independence. During this period, four other new Turkic states were established in Central Asia; several Turkish statesmen claimed that the new century would be the century of the Turkic world. Having become NATO's co-ordinator in the region, Turkey was trying to contribute to the Organisation's enlargement in the direction of the Caspian region. The richness of the Caspian littoral states in hydrocarbon reserves was of great significance for Turkey. Thus, political, economic and strategic interests, as well as ethnic and cultural factors, encouraged Turkey to join the struggle for influence in the Caspian basin.

On the political front, Turkey, as a member of the OSCE Minsk Group, tried to achieve a fair and impartial solution to the Karabagh problem. However, Turkey's traditional foreign policy in favour of maintaining the status quo could not make it influential in this area.[22] A particular focus of Turkish policy was to gain access to the abundant oil reserves of the Caspian basin.[23] In the coming decade Turkey's needs for energy are expected to double. Thus, the country's needs of 20.8 billion cubic metres of gas in the year 2000 are expected to amount to 53.6 billion cubic metres by 2010. One of the most important steps that Turkey took to assist Azerbaijan was Ankara's support for Heidar Aliev in opening contacts with the West. With the mediation of Suleiman Demirel, Heidar Aliev paid his first visit to France in December 1993, followed by a series of visits to other European capitals.

In early 1994, negotiations with foreign companies were resumed. While in London on an official visit in February, President Aliev signed an intergovernmental agreement whereby the Azerbaijan and British governments agreed to act as co-guarantors of the commitments assumed by BP and the State Oil Company of the Azerbaijan Republic (SOCAR). The positive change in the international environment accelerated the signing of the so-called 'Contract of the Century' on 20 September 1994. The contract led to the growing interest of Western countries, the US in particular, in establishing stability in the region. In other words, Baku had now resumed the pro-Western track in its foreign policy that the Elchibey government had tried unsuccessfully to promote. It was as a result of this policy that the Azerbaijan Republic managed to endure the constant pressure on the part of Russia (including attempts on the life of the head of state, support for the armed opposition, an economic embargo and economic ultimatums). In November 1997 Azerbaijan was able to export its first contract oil to foreign markets. In this period (September 1994 to late 1997), issues relating to oil pipelines were resolved and numerous agreements signed on the establishment of new consortia. President Aliev announced that he was firmly inclined towards the Baku–Ceyhan alternative of the main export pipeline and that Azerbaijan would not change its position on the legal status of the Caspian Sea. The new Constitution of the Azerbaijan Republic adopted in November 1995 confirmed that the Azerbaijan sector of the Caspian Sea is an inseparable part of the Azerbaijan Republic. While these negotiations were under way, the US started taking an interest in developments in the Caucasus. The US representative in the United Nations, Madeleine Albright, stated that the US did not recognise a 'special role' for the Russian Federation in the Caucasus and could only agree to the stationing of Russian military units in Karabagh as part of a larger contingent supervised by the OSCE.[24]

The US thus turned into the main author and advocate for the processes unfolding in the Caucasus and Central Asia. Henceforth, the Caspian basin was to be part of the strategic interests of the US.[25] The US State Department's report *Energy Development in the Caspian Basin* (1997) outlined four key directions in US policy. These were as follows:

- 'Solution of regional conflicts': This dwelt upon the resolution of the Armenian–Azerbaijan conflict, other sources of ethnic tension in the Caucasus, as well as the civil war in Tajikistan. According to the authors of the document, these conflicts make it possible for foreign forces like Iran to become involved. In addition, delaying solution of the disputes created a favourable environment for destructive Islamic movements to emerge.
- 'Increasing and expanding the world's energy-supply': This stipulated the need for the exploitation of Caspian energy resources in addition to those of the Persian Gulf, thereby insuring Western energy interests.
- 'Sovereignty and independence of Caspian basin countries': This envisaged eliminating dependence on the oil pipeline crossing the territory of Russia. It was felt that this dependence would enable Russia to raise the fee for the use of the pipeline to an extremely high level, as well as to exert political pressure.
- 'Iran's isolation': This was needed to limit this country's revenues, which, it was claimed, were spent on building weapons of mass destruction, augmenting its arsenal of conventional weapons and supporting terrorism. The authors of the report considered that the best way to attain this goal was to prevent Iran from having any involvement in Caspian energy developments.

The document also outlined US policies with regard to Russia and Turkey. It was indicated that there was no need to irritate Russia without reason, because Washington was 'sharing a number of [important] interests with Russia pertaining to control over nuclear weapons and NATO enlargement'. It suggested that political pressure should not be applied to Russian companies operating in the Caspian region, because this market 'has historically been managed by Russia'. As far as Turkey was concerned, the authors proposed providing assistance to Turkey, a NATO fellow ally, to take control over security in the region – a region surrounded by hostile states. It was also felt that Turkey could promote economic revitalisation. For this, it was necessary to support the construction of the main export pipeline through the territory of Turkey and to assist Turkey in addressing its growing need for energy.[26]

Between 1995 and 1998, the US government became noticeably more active and coherent in its policy in the Caspian region. Thus, in January 1995, the US embassy in Azerbaijan announced that its government would not agree to the Baku–Iran–Nakhichevan–Ceyhan oil pipeline; shortly after, the US embassy in Turkey proposed the Baku–Armenia–Ceyhan route. It was highlighted that this pipeline would positively affect settlement of the Armenian–Azerbaijan conflict.[27] In November 1997, the US Energy Secretary Federico Pena visited the Caucasus and Central Asian republics on behalf of the US president and urged leaders of the regional states to clarify their attitude to the Trans-Caspian gas pipeline and the Baku–Ceyhan oil pipeline projects before October 1998. A little later, the First Lady of the US paid a courtesy visit to Central Asia.

In February 1998, following an appeal by the US government, foreign ministers of Azerbaijan and Turkmenistan embarked on negotiations concerning the disputed Caspian oilfield Kyapaz/Serdar (for a discussion of this dispute see below). The US government allocated US$750,000 to Ashgabat to finance a feasibility study for a gas pipeline to be built along the Caspian seabed from Turkmenbashi to Baku. At the same time, the White House urged the Turkish government to make the Baku–Ceyhan project commercially viable. In the summer of 1998, the US administration established the position of special counsellor for Caspian energy diplomacy and appointed an experienced diplomat, Richard Morningstar, to the post. The US Congress embarked on active discussions of the 'Silk Road Strategy' draft law.

In September 1998, 235 American troops took part in joint exercises with the military forces of Uzbekistan, Kyrgyzstan, Russia, Turkey, Georgia and Azerbaijan in the vicinity of Tashkent. This was the first joint military training session to be attended by US military on the territory of the CIS. In this period, Washington announced that the CIS territory was the area of America's 'military responsibility'.[28] In October 1998, the new US Energy Secretary Bill Richardson, together with representatives from the five regional countries, signed the Ankara Declaration calling for the construction of a pipeline to run from Baku via Tbilisi to Ceyhan. In the same month, the White House administration met with America's 15 largest oil companies in order to convince the latter that the Baku–Tbilisi–Ceyhan (BTC) line was preferable to others from the geo-strategic and geopolitical standpoints. Washington was clearly determined to push through this pipeline, regarding it as a nucleus for geopolitical developments in the region.[29]

The US attached particular importance to Georgia in its Caspian strategy. Georgia's determination to consolidate its independence (and its clear intention to leave Russia's sphere of influence), as well as the fact that it is a transit country for Caspian oil and gas has turned this country into the West's strongest ally in the region. Turkey, too, has displayed keenness on enhancing contacts with Georgia. Consequently, Georgia has received substantial financial, military and technical assistance from the West and won strong political backing.[30] Mutual economic and political interests have also brought Georgia and Azerbaijan closer over recent years. Bilateral relations assumed the proportions of a strategic alliance after President Aliev's visit to Tbilisi in March 1996. On this occasion, Azerbaijan and Georgia signed a declaration 'On peace, stability and security in the Caucasus', based on the concept of a 'Common Caucasian House'. Azerbaijan was one of the co-founders of the regional organisation GUUAM.[31]

Georgia is currently integrating with political and economic entities of NATO and the West. Regarding Georgia as Azerbaijan's only access to Europe under present conditions, Baku has given preference to this country in its oil and gas exports to world markets. The Baku–Supsa and BTC oil routes not only increase Georgia's geopolitical significance, but promise vast revenues to the country. According to the president of the Georgian International Oil Corporation, the country will earn US$200–250 million per year for running the BTC pipeline through its territory.[32] As a result of such developments, the union Azerbaijan–Georgia–Turkey has become ever more prominent in the region.

After 1998, some commentators noted a weakening of interest on the part of the US (and Western Europe) in the Caspian basin. The reason for this lay in contradictory US policy vectors, particularly regarding Azerbaijan.[33] Several mutually contradictory issues needed to be resolved simultaneously: establishing normal relations with Russia; ending Russian influence in Armenia and taking the South Caucasus into an undivided US sphere of influence; and connecting Central Asia to the West by means of Azerbaijan's hydrocarbon and geopolitical resources. Washington's policy of containment of Iran further complicated the situation. Therefore, despite Azerbaijan's whole-hearted efforts to develop strategic, economic and political contacts with the US, the latter failed to display active involvement in the resolution of the Karabagh problem and likewise in other issues relating to stability and security in the South Caucasus. As noted by a number of influential speakers at a 1999 Harvard conference on the Caspian basin, 'one should recognise that while local powers often want and demand a strong American role that does not necessarily mean it is in the US interest to provide it'.[34]

Co-operation with Europe

West European countries were among the first to recognise the state independence of the Republic of Azerbaijan: Germany on 12 December 1991, United Kingdom on 31 December 1991 and France on 3 January 1992. The European Union (EU) recognised Azerbaijan as an independent state on 31 December 1991. Shortly afterwards, diplomatic relations were established.

Several European countries opened embassies in Baku. Azerbaijan, with some delay, also appointed diplomatic missions to European capitals. An Azerbaijani mission was established in Brussels in December 1995. A Partnership and Co-operation Agreement between Azerbaijan and the EU was signed in Luxembourg on 22 April 1996.

The Elchibey government followed a pro-Western course, hoping for an expansion of ties with West European countries. However, the negative stereotyping of Azerbaijan that arose as a consequence of the Karabagh conflict had enormous effect in Europe. Nevertheless, European officials firmly expressed support for a peaceful solution to the Karabagh problem and recognised the territorial integrity of Azerbaijan.[35] In May 1993, the European Commission announced the launching of the TRACECA (Transport Corridor Europe–Caucasus–Asia) programme. The purpose of this programme was to establish direct contacts between the Black Sea and Caspian Sea regions, Caucasus and Central Asia via the east–west transport corridor. This, it was believed, would contribute to the political and economic independence of the newly independent republics in the region by providing access to Europe and world markets. Azerbaijan's geographical position made it pivotal to the project. Azerbaijan was also included in other EU interstate projects, such as INOGATE (construction of pipelines) and RARP (Regional Agricultural Reform Project). In September 1998, Baku hosted a 'Restoration of the Ancient Silk Road' conference attended by representatives of 32 states (including several presidents) and 12 international organisations. During the Baku Summit, the agreement on TRACECA and documents on co-operation in the fields of maritime, overland and railway transport, as well as customs regulations were signed. The conference decided to set up a permanent TRACECA secretariat in Baku.[36] By 1999, 25 technical assistance projects (totalling €35 million) and 11 infrastructure projects (totalling €47 million) had been funded as part of the programme.

During the 1990s much progress was made in the field of political and military integration with the Euro-Atlantic union. In May 2000, the Council of Europe began the admission process of Azerbaijan to this organisation and opened its office in Baku. However, this process has not always been smooth. The insistence of European Union member-states on including the aggressor Armenia into the TRACECA programme aroused discontent in Azerbaijan. Also, despite setting up the Minsk Group to resolve the Karabagh conflict, EU member-states have not displayed due perseverance in reaching a negotiated settlement.

Restoration of relations with Central Asia

As mentioned above, the course of history separated Azerbaijan from the East for decades. In particular, the excessive centralisation in the Soviet period meant that, despite being part of the same empire, Azerbaijan's ties with Central Asia were limited. The demise of the Soviet empire prompted a restoration of relations between Azerbaijan and this enormous region. However, President Elchibey took a peculiar approach in forging relations with what he believed were the 'fraternal' republics of Central Asia. He lambasted the Central Asian presidents, calling them 'feudal communist leaders'. This could not but lead to a strain in relations with these republics. Eventually, Uzbek President Islam Karimov went so far as to order the suspension of Baku–Tashkent flights.

Yet Azerbaijan's geopolitical and geo-economic interests required the establishment of good relations with the region. One by one, the Central Asian states opened embassies in Baku. Kazakhstan's growing oil exports and search for a reliable route compelled the country to co-ordinate its policies with Baku. Kazakhstan began to export a portion of its oil along the Baku–Batumi railway to world markets. In 1998, 2.2 million tonnes of Chevron oil were transported via this route, while in 1999 the figure amounted to some 5 million tonnes.[37] The then Kazakh prime minister envisaged that 10 million tonnes of crude would be delivered to Batumi via Azerbaijani and Georgian railways.[38] In June 1997, the presidents of Azerbaijan and Kazakhstan signed a letter of intent on co-operation in transporting oil to foreign markets.[39]

Kazakh President Nazarbaev was among those who signed the Ankara Declaration on the Baku–Tbilisi–Ceyhan pipeline in October 1998. In December of the same year, Mobil, Chevron and Shell, in conjunction with the State Oil Company of Kazakhstan, signed an agreement in Washington on the construction of a Caspian sub-sea oil and gas pipeline, to be linked to the Baku–Ceyhan pipeline; US$20 million was allocated for the work.[40] While on an official visit to Baku in April 2000, President Nazarbaev said, 'We support the Baku–Tbilisi–Ceyhan (BTC) route and we will immediately join this project as soon as we discover more oil reserves.'[41] The discovery of world-class reserves in Kazakhstan's Kashagan field further boosted the chances of the implementation of the BTC route. Shortly after the discovery, President Nazarbaev said in a televised address that Kazakhstan 'must actively integrate with the Baku–Ceyhan pipeline project'.[42]

Azerbaijan's relations with another Caspian nation, Turkmenistan, did not, however, develop so smoothly. Differences and disagreements between Azerbaijan and Turkmenistan are based on three mutually intertwined issues. Firstly, there is disagreement over the issue of the legal status of the Caspian Sea. Despite initial support for the principle of dividing the Caspian into national sectors in the first post-Soviet years, from mid-1995 Ashgabat started to back the condominium principle proposed by Russia and Iran.[43] It was in this period that Turkmenistan declared itself an 'eternally neutral country'. In 1997, Turkmenistan put forward the idea of dividing the Caspian into five 'independent seas',[44] which was not exactly what Baku (and partly Astana) was advocating but was definitely different from the Moscow–Tehran position.

The second point of disagreement between Azerbaijan and Turkmenistan is related to jurisdiction over some of the Caspian oilfields. Turkmenistan lays claim to the fields Chirag, Azeri and Kyapaz (known as 'Serdar' in

Turkmenistan), regarding the first as being partially located in the Turkmen sector of the Caspian Sea, and the last two as fully within the Turkmen sector.[45] The third bone of contention between the two countries concerns the Trans-Caspian gas pipeline. Baku maintained that, in the light of the discovery of immense gas reserves in the Shah Deniz field, Azerbaijan should have a 15 billion cubic metre quota in the pipeline. However, Ashgabat turned down the demand, preferring to see the failure of the project rather than to make concessions (see **Canzi**, p. 187).

Azerbaijan's relations with Uzbekistan are not directly determined by the oil factor. Geopolitical interests led to the establishment of amicable relations with this country, the only republic of Central Asia to have declared Armenia an aggressor state. Of all the Central Asian countries, only Uzbekistan joined the GUUAM organisation (see above). Until December 2002, when it opened an embassy in Ashgabat, Azerbaijan had its only embassy in Central Asia in Tashkent.

Azerbaijan's oil diplomacy: pros and cons

In 1991, when independence had just been regained, Azerbaijanis were optimistic about the country's future. There was hope for an early resolution of the Karabagh conflict and confidence that the economic potential of the country would be realised. These hopes were largely connected with oil. By then, Ramco had opened its representation in Baku (May 1989). Amoco chose the Azerbaijan sector of the Caspian for operations (June 1991) and agreed to develop it jointly with BP, Statoil, Ramco, Unocal and McDermott (September 1991). In February 1992, Pennzoil and Ramco launched talks on the Guneshli field. In June 1993, the State Oil Company of the Azerbaijan Republic (SOCAR) and Amoco, BP, Statoil, Pennzoil, McDermott, Ramco, TPAO (Turkish State Petroleum Company) and Unocal signed the Declaration of Utilisation on the joint development of Chirag, Azeri and deepwater Guneshli fields; in September 1994, the so-called 'Contract of the Century', a 30-year contract, worth US$7.5 billion, was signed for developing these fields.[46]

Since then, Azerbaijan has achieved significant progress in the oil sector. Twenty-one international contracts have been signed with 33 oil giants, representing 15 countries; by 2000, a total of US$3.2 billion had been invested in Azerbaijan's oil sector.[47] By 2003, this figure had risen to some $5 billion. Early oil from the 'Contract of the Century' was produced in November 1997; by 2005, production is expected to amount to 30 million tonnes of oil; by 2010 to 70 million tonnes; and in 2020, 120 million tonnes (even pessimists estimate that a production level of 90 million tonnes will be reached by this period).[48] One trillion cubic metres of gas and 300 million tonnes of oil condensate were discovered in the Shah Deniz field, giving Azerbaijan the opportunity to transform from a country importing gas into a gas exporter. In 2000, the Azerbaijan International Operating Company (AIOC) announced its intention to construct a pipeline to export gas to

Turkey.[49] The 'early oil' pipelines are in operation (Baku–Novorossiysk since 1997 and Baku–Supsa since 1999) with combined capacity of 220,000 barrels per day. The construction of the BTC pipeline is progressing.

However, hopes that oil would play a crucial role in resolving the country's economic problems have not been justified as yet. In some spheres, Azerbaijan's situation has gone from bad to worse. Conflicting interests in Caspian oil on the part of Russia and Iran, on the one hand, and the US and Europe on the other, have jeopardised Azerbaijan's independence and security. If not adequately backed by the US and European countries, Azerbaijan, though clearly pro-Western, will be unable to withstand the pressure imposed by the Moscow–Tehran–Yerevan triangle. As one US commentator observed, 'US deeds fall short of its rhetorical support for the new countries of the region. Particularly in the crucial energy sector, US actions are having the effect of undermining these countries' sovereignty.'[50] Azerbaijan's oil diplomacy has also not proved effective in countering Armenia's aggression. Hopes that transnational oil companies and countries that have stakes in Azerbaijan's oil industry would help to achieve a fair solution to the conflict turned out to be mistaken. Worse, there is a danger that Baku might be compelled to sign an unfair and disgraceful accord on 'Prosperity instead of Karabagh', thus playing into the hands of certain political and business circles (including oil giants).

The oil interests of Western companies and countries (including geopolitical interests of the latter) have brought about some political stability in the republic. Yet economic interest should not be transformed into a factor retarding democratisation. If this were to happen, the latent contempt for the ruling regime may turn into overt animosity towards the West, and towards Western values, including democracy and democratic forces within the country. Public opinion surveys show symptoms of the deteriorating reputation of Western countries in the wake of their ambiguous policy in the region.[51] One such poll revealed that 21 per cent of respondents believed that foreign oil companies actually represented a threat to the country's sovereignty.[52]

Azerbaijan has already contracted 'the oil-dollar disease' that is so widespread in many oil exporting countries. Symptoms of the so-called 'Dutch disease' are already surfacing. By 1999, some 30–40 per cent of the state budget was made up of oil revenues.[53] Oil products constituted 55–70 per cent of exports.[54] Foreign investment is overwhelmingly directed to the oil industry.[55] Meanwhile, there is continuing decline in non-oil sectors of the economy.[56] Privatisation and structural changes are stalling.[57] Living standards of most of the population have reached a catastrophically low level. The minimum wage is a mere US$5 per month. An average wage (if paid at all) amounts to US$75.[58] However, the minimum subsistence income is estimated to be approximately US$80. Problems are intensified by the presence of over 1 million refugees, most of whom lack access to basic amenities. On the other hand, those in government are getting richer by the day, thereby further alienating themselves from rank-and-file people. Expensive hotels, luxurious foreign cars and spectacular villas are a dazzling contrast to a deplorable urban infrastructure, roads in particular. Sharp social stratification is evident, as there is no middle class. Heider Aliev's rule may have benefited foreign investors, but it brought misery to the majority of the population, large numbers of whom live below the poverty margin. One frequent visitor to the region gave a stark assessment of the situation in 2003:

> Corruption and bribery are rampant in Azerbaijan, from police officers on the beat to the government's top offices. The number of police per capita far exceeds internationally accepted standards, making the country a police state in the truest sense of those words. The police do the president's bidding, including kidnapping political opponents . . . Worst of all, the country's economy is firmly under governmental control. To do business there, one must either pay bribes or become part of the regime's support structure.[59]

International institutions have similarly stressed the high level of corruption.[60] Progress towards democratisation has been painfully slow. The ruling pro-presidential party New Azerbaijan gained an overwhelming victory in the parliamentary elections of November 2000, but there were so many gross cases of fraud that the authorities themselves were forced to cancel the results in some constituencies. Re-elections were held in January 2001, but monitors noted that serious electoral violations still occurred.[61]

In late 1999, Azerbaijan earned its first US$25 million from the sale of oil. Since then, there have been conflicting figures as to the speed and volumes of the country's oil revenues.[62] One thing remains certain, however: the role of oil revenues in the future will only rise. Therefore, the proper use of these revenues has become a crucial issue. In December 1999, under pressure from the World Bank, President Aliev decreed the establishment of the Oil Fund (see **Karayianni**). According to the decree, from 2001 onwards, the Oil Fund was to accumulate revenues from such sources as the sale of Azerbaijan crude oil and gas, per acre payments, starting payments for the lease of state property under agreements concluded with foreign companies, revenues from the sale of assets under the contracts, etc.

Expenditures from the Oil Fund were to be endorsed by the president.[63] In order to ensure transparency and to prevent misuse of oil revenues, the Fund was regulated by a special law and made accountable to him, also to the *Milli Majlis* parliament and to the public through regular disclosure of accounts. Some advocated the use of oil revenues to target such issues as the social needs of the population, the elimination of the budget deficit and the development of small businesses.[64] Others, however, believed that more attention should be paid to studying the lessons provided by international experience. In other words, they feared that the revenues, instead of turning into a positive factor for the country's future, would be spent on populist gestures by the incumbent regime. This would further complicate Azerbaijan's already precarious status, by spending oil revenues ineffectively.[65]

Conclusions and outlook

The Caspian basin has not turned into a region of peace and co-operation. The struggle for Caspian oil is not yet over. On the one hand, the alliance of Baku–Tbilisi–Ankara (and by extension, Washington and Tel-Aviv) is strengthening in parallel with the implementation of economic projects. Realisation of the first stage of the 'Contract of the Century', which requires an investment of US$10–12 billion in the next several years, has already been started. The construction of the BTC pipeline was inaugurated in September 2002, at a ceremony attended by the presidents of Azerbaijan, Georgia and Turkey, and by US Energy Secretary Spencer Abraham. By this time, the legal and financial aspects of the Baku–Tbilisi–Erzurum gas pipeline project were close to being resolved and construction was scheduled to start in 2004.

The events of 11 September 2001 contributed to the geopolitical importance of the South Caucasus, including Azerbaijan. It was after that event that Section 907 of the Freedom Support Act was suspended for one year (and the suspension extended again in 2003). This infamous act, imposed as a result of the Karabagh conflict, banned the US government's direct humanitarian assistance to Azerbaijan. Once it was lifted, the way was opened to the provision of US$54 million-worth of assistance to Azerbaijan. Azerbaijan's military co-operation with the US and Turkey was also considerably stepped up. Relations with Moscow improved somewhat after Vladimir Putin was elected president. He initiated a relatively pragmatic approach to determining the legal status of the Caspian (see **Antonenko**). As a result, when Putin visited Baku in January 2001, Russia and Azerbaijan were able to sign a bilateral declaration on co-operation in the Caspian Sea region. The following year, in April 2002, a protocol was signed which determined the points of demarcation of the Caspian Sea shelf along the border between the two countries, based on the principle of 'sectoral division of seabed – common water use', as set out in the declaration of January 2001. In early 2002 Russian LUKoil seemed set to join the BTC pipeline consortium – a signal that closer regional co-operation was on the agenda. The fact that it did not pursue this project most probably had more to do with internal company priorities than a political realignment in Moscow.

Relations with Iran remained difficult. This was clearly demonstrated in the summer of 2001, when Tehran displayed its military capabilities in the Caspian by sending its gunboats and military aircraft to disputed areas, thus reiterating its protest at the division of the Caspian water reserves into national sectors along a median line. The demonstrative manoeuvring of Turkish fighter jets in the sky above Baku that followed shortly after this incident was a symbolic response to Iran's hostile action. As the Chief-of-Staff of the Turkish Armed Forces stated during his visit to Baku, his country would not be a passive onlooker in the event of armed aggression against Azerbaijan (see **Katik**). Heidar Aliev succeeded in defusing the situation by adopting a conciliatory approach towards Tehran. Relations with Iran received a further boost when President Aliev visited Tehran in May 2002. There he confirmed that the Azeri side would cease exploration in the disputed area until the border issue had been settled. Legal experts on both sides seemed satisfied that it would be possible to find a compromise solution to the territorial question in the near future.

However, despite these improvements, it would be naive to expect that the Moscow–Tehran–Yerevan triangle would so easily change its policy. Jointly and singly, they constitute an ongoing source of concern for Azerbaijan. Moreover, the rapprochement between Russia and Turkmenistan, culminating in the massive gas deal that the two countries concluded in April 2003, is potentially detrimental to Azerbaijan's interests. It could give additional backing to Ashgabat over the Kyapaz/Serdar issue. Russia's invitation to Iran, in early 2003, to join a Russo-Turkmen consortium to develop fields located in the Turkmen sector of the Caspian was clearly intended to lay the foundation for a strategic relationship between these three countries. This emerging alliance means that Azerbaijan could eventually be almost entirely surrounded by a bloc of hostile states. This would have serious consequences for the unresolved ethnic conflicts in the region, particularly the Karabagh issue. This is a matter of paramount importance. Until it is resolved, it will continue to be used as a bargaining card by the regional powers and this will undoubtedly have a negative effect on the peace process.

In this highly complex environment Azerbaijan was handicapped by intense uncertainties in the domestic arena. Concern over the health of President Aliev mounted after he collapsed twice while delivering a television address in April 2003. Despite his age (he turned 80 in May that year) he seemed determined to stand again in the elections scheduled for October. However, his obvious frailty made it increasingly unlikely that he would continue to play an active part in politics. This triggered a wave of speculation as to who might succeed him. A covert power struggle emerged as prospective candidates sought to bolster their positions. The administration was riven by factional infighting. Independent political activists, as well as the press, were likewise absorbed by this drama. Aliev's preferred 'heir' was his son Ilham (born 1961). On 4 August, Ilham was made prime minister of Azerbaijan, thus ensuring that he would be first in line of succession if his father should step down or die.

Ilham Aliev was in fact a sound candidate for the post of president. In 1994, he had been appointed first vice-president of SOCAR, with responsibility for external relations, including all foreign oil contracts. In 1995, he was elected to the Azerbaijani parliament and later led Azerbaijan's delegation to the Parliamentary Assembly of the Council of Europe. Yet he showed little evidence of the political acumen that was so characteristic of his father. Many feared that if he did come to power, he would be unable to govern the country for long. Moreover, there were strong presidential rivals within the ruling elite, including former parliamentary speaker Rasul Guliev, head of the state custom committee Kamaladdin Heidarov and head of the presidential administration Ramiz Mehtiev. The main opposition candidate in the presidential elections was Isa Gamber, chairman of the Musavat party and sole nominee of the Democratic Congress (an alliance of independent parties). Speculation over the leadership issue seriously distracted attention from internal as well as external problems throughout that summer. Heidar Aliev withdrew his candidacy just before the election and his son Ilham was duly elected president on 15 October 2003, gaining, according to official estimates, 77 per cent of the vote. There were many irregularities in the conduct of the poll and national and international observers reported scenes of police brutality.[66] So the new presidential term was inaugurated in an atmosphere of fear and repression. This heightened uncertainties about the future. Heidar Aliev died on 12 December 2003. At the time of writing, President Ilham Aliev had only been in office a few months and it was difficult to predict what course he would follow. Most people expected that the political repression and corruption that characterised the previous regime would continue. Optimists hoped that Washington would press for free and fair elections to be held in November 2005, but they were in the minority.

Notes

1 Seventh International Oil and Gas Conference (Caspian Oil and Gas 2000), 6–9 June 2000, Baku, Azerbaijan; speeches of representatives from Azerbaijan and Kazakhstan.

2 N. Nassibli, 'Azerbaijan's Geopolitics an Oil Pipeline Issue', *Perceptions*, December 1999–February 2000, pp. 97–98.

3 M. Sieff, 'Armenia Armed by Russia for Battles with Azerbaijan', *Washington Times*, 10 April 1997, p. A11.

4 See, for example, R. Herrmann, 'Russian Policy in the Middle East: Strategic Change and Tactical Contradictions', *Middle East Journal*, vol. 48, no. 3, Summer 1994, pp. 455–456; P. Tyler, 'Russia's Links to Iran Offer a Case Study in Arms Leaks', *New York Times*, 10 May 2000, p. A6.

5 S. Cornell, 'Iran and the Caucasus', *Middle East Policy*, vol. 5, no. 4, January 1998, pp. 59–64.

6 See F. Thom, 'Eurasianism: A New Russian Foreign Policy?' *Uncaptive Minds*, Summer, 1994, pp. 65–77; J. Valdez, 'The Near Abroad, the West, and National Identity in Russian Foreign Policy', in A. Dawisha and K. Dawisha (eds), *The Making of Foreign Policy in Russia and the New States of Eurasia*, M. E. Sharpe, Armonk, New York, 1995, pp. 84–109.

7 *Izvestiya*, 2 January 1992.

8 On the different camps within the Russian government, see, for example, T. Timothy and S. John, 'Russian National Interests and the Caspian Sea', *Perceptions*, December 1999–February 2000, p. 83.

9 Much has been written on this issue. See A. Shoumikhin, 'Developing Caspian Oil: Between Conflict and Co-operation', *Co-operative Strategy: An International Journal*, vol. 16, no. 4, 1997, pp. 342–343; D. Trenin, 'Russia's Security Interests and Policies in the Caucasus Region', in B. Coppieters (ed.), *Contested Borders in the Caucasus*, Amsterdam, VUB University Press, 1996, chapter 3.

10 U. Ozdag, 'S.S.C.B.' den Rusiya Federasiyonuna (1985–1993)', *Avrasiya Dosyasi*, vol. 3, no. 4, 1996, p.174.

11 *Izvestiya*, 8 August 1992.

12 According to a survey conducted in late 1999, 15.7 per cent of respondents regarded Russia as a friendly country, 28.4 per cent as an unfriendly country,

18 per cent as a neutral country, 2 per cent as a hostile country, while 25.9 per cent had difficulty in answering (*Azadlig*, 28 December 1999).

13 Armenians and pro-Armenian Western authors claim that the developments were exacerbated by the Sumgait tragedy and maintain that it is Azerbaijan that is to blame for the escalation. However, there had already been bloody inter-ethnic strife in Armenia and Karabagh and the flow of people ousted from Armenia to Azerbaijan had started.

14 G. Winrow, 'Azerbaijan and Iran', in A. Rubinshtein and O. Smolanski (eds), *Regional Rivalries in the New Eurasia: Russia, Turkey, and Iran*, M. E. Sharp, Armonk, New York/London, 1995, p. 96.

15 T. Swietochowski, 'Azerbaijan: Between Ethnic Conflict and Irredentism', *Armenian Review*, vol. 43, no. 2–3, 1990, p. 45.

16 Winrow, *op. cit.*, p. 96.

17 *Avrasiya Dosyasi*, cilt 2, sayi 1, 1995, p. 128.

18 *Millet*, 10 July 1995; *Ayna/Zerkalo*, 7 October 1995; *Azerbaycan*, 5 March 1996.

19 *Jomhuriye Eslami*, 20 Dey 1374.

20 See, for example, *Ayna/Zerkalo*, 18 April 1997, 17 May 1997; *Azadlig*, 11 January 1997, 1 February 1997.

21 *Nezavisimaya Gazeta*, 25 November 1998.

22 M. Budak, 'Azerbaycan–Ermenistan Ilişkilerinde Daglik Karabag Meselesi ve Turkiyenin Politikasi', *Kafkasya Arastirmalari*, 2, Istanbul, 1996, pp. 132–137.

23 A. N. Pamir, 'Turkiye'nin Enerji Gereksinimi, Uluslararasi Boruhatlari ve Jeostratejisi', *Stratejik Analiz*, cilt 1, sayi 1, 2000, p. 49; O. Demirag, 'Energy Demand of Turkey, Provisions for Oil and Gas Supply and TPAO's Role and Strategy in this Context', Address at the Seventh International Caspian Oil and Gas Exhibition and Conference, 6–9 June 2000, Baku.

24 *Caucasus Regional Researches*, no. 1, 1996, p. 46.

25 For statements and speeches made by US officials on the matter, see, for example, *USIS Washington File*, 14–15 December 1998; *Los Angeles Times*, 1 December 1998, p. 9; A. Cohen, 'Ethnic Conflicts Threaten U. S. Interests in the Caucasus', *The Heritage Foundation Backgrounder*, no. 1222, 25 September 1998.

26 P. Clawson, 'Iran and Caspian Basin Oil and Gas', *Perceptions*, December 1997–February 1998, pp. 19–20.

27 J. Mareska, 'A "Peace Pipeline" to End the Nagorno-Karabakh Conflict', *Caspian Crossroads*, no. 1 (1995), pp. 17–18.

28 *Current Digest of the Post-Soviet Press*, 21 October 1998.

29 *USIS Washington File*, 29 October 1998; *Los Angeles Times*, 29 October 1998.

30 R. Synovits, 'Georgia: Most Important Transit Country Upgrades Infrastructure', RFE/RL, 29 June 1998; *Turkish Daily News*, 17 April 1998; *Nezavisimoye Voennoe Obozreniye*, no. 42, 6–12 November 1998.

31 GUUAM was established in 1996 to further regional co-operation, particularly the development of the Eurasian Trans-Caucasus transportation corridor (TRACECA). The founder members were Georgia, Ukraine, Azerbaijan and Moldova. Uzbekistan acceded to the organsiation in 1999, at a meeting of the five heads of state in Washington DC, on the occasion of the NATO Golden Jubilee celebrations. GUUAM received very considerable Western (more specifically, US) support and encouragement and was clearly intended to counterbalance Russian influence. By June 2000, Uzbek President Karimov was expressing open dissatisfaction with GUUAM and later suspended membership. In 2003, however, the Uzbeks were indicating that they wished to resume active participation.

32 Azer-Press, 7 December 1999.

33 *Succession and Long-term Stability in the Caspian Region: Caspian Studies Program, Experts Conference Report*, Harvard University, John F. Kennedy School of Government, October 1999, pp. 5–8.

34 *Ibid.*, p. 8.
35 *Azerbaijan*, 14 October 1993, 18 December 1993.
36 For information on TRACECA see: http://www.traceca.org/whatis.htm.
37 *Interfax* (Russian edn), 27 January 1999.
38 S. Liesman, 'Three Oil Giants and Kazakhstan will Push Plan for Caspian Sea Pipeline to Turkey', *Wall Street Journal*, 10 December 1998, p. 4; *Azadlig*, 27 October 1998, p. 8.
39 *Oil and Gas Journal*, 9 March 1998, p. 32.
40 *Interfax* (English edn), 27 January 1999; *Agence France Presse*, 10 December 1998.
41 *Turkistan-Newsletter*, vol. 101:036, 21 April 2000.
42 *Turkistan-Newsletter*, vol. 4:135, 10 July 2000.
43 R. Menon, 'Treacherous Terrain: The Political and Security Dimensions of Energy Development in the Caspian Sea Zone', *NBR Analysis*, vol. 9, no. 1, p. 20.
44 *Azadlig*, 24 December 1998.
45 *Commonwealth of Independent States and the Middle East*, vol. 22, no. 1–2, 1997, pp. 9–10; Y. Kerbanov, 'The New Legal Status of the Caspian Sea is the Basis of Regional Co-operation and Stability', *Perceptions*, December 1997–February 1998, pp. 14–15; V. Mesamed, 'Turkmenistan: Oil, Gas, and Caspian Politics', in M. Croissant and B. Aras (eds), *Oil and Geopolitics in the Caspian Sea Region*, Praeger, Westport/London, 1997, pp. 214–215.
46 *Azerbaijan International*, Autumn 1994 (2.4), p. 29; S. Bagirov, 'Azerbaijani Oil: Glimpses of a Long History', *Perceptions*, vol. 1, no. 2, June–August 1996, pp. 31–51.
47 The Seventh International Caspian Oil and Gas Exhibition and Conference (Caspian Oil and Gas, 2000), June 6–9, Baku, Azerbaijan, speeches of Natik Aliev, president of SOCAR and K. Yusifzadeh, vice-president of SOCAR.
48 A. N. Pamir, *Baku–Ceyhan Boru Hatti. Ortaasya ve Kafkasya'da Bitmeyen Oyun*, Asam, Ankara, 1999, pp. 96–97.
49 *Caspian Investor*, August 1999, vol. 2, no. 10, pp. 3, 11–13; RFE/RL, 31 May 2000.
50 S. F. Starr, 'Power Failure: American Policy in the Caspian', *The National Interest*, no. 47, Spring 1997, p. 20.
51 *Yeni Musavat*, 24–26 October 1998; *Azadlig*, 2 June 2000.
52 *Zerkalo*, 20 April 2000.
53 D. Hoffman, 'Oil and Development in Post-Soviet Azerbaijan', *NBR Analysis*, vol. 10, no. 3, August 1999, p. 23.
54 *Country Report: Azerbaijan*, Economist Intelligence Unit, first quarter 2000, p. 35.
55 By 2001, it was estimated at 80 per cent of total foreign investment (S. Tsalik, *Caspian Oil Windfalls: Who Will Benefit?*, Caspian Revenue Watch, Open Society, New York, 2003, p. 92).
56 For example, in 1996 production in the engineering sector decreased by 18 per cent compared to 1995, and by a further 3 per cent in 1997. *Country Report: Azerbaijan*, Economist Intelligence Unit, first quarter 1998, p. 16.
57 See further *EBRD Transition Report 2002: Agriculture and Rural Transition*, EBRD, London, 2002, pp. 118–119.
58 These estimates are open to debate and some Azerbaijani opposition figures would set them at a considerably lower level. The UNDP *Human Development Report 2003: Millennium Goals: A Compact to End Human Poverty*, Oxford University Press, Oxford/New York, 2003, p. 249, ranks Azerbaijan, as well as Turkmenistan and Kazakhstan in the 'medium human development category', but does not rank them on the human poverty index regarding the percentage of the population living below the income poverty level.
59 Letter by C. J. Tripp, Professor of Political Science, Westminster College, Salt Lake City, published in *Washington Times*, 6 March 2003.
60 Transparency International (TI) placed Azerbaijan 96 out of 99 governments in its corruption perception index for 1997, and 95 out of 102 in 2002. This

put it in the same league as Uganda and Indonesia (http://www.transparency. org). A joint survey by the European Bank for Reconstruction and Development and the World Bank showed that Azerbaijan was the most corrupt country of Eastern Europe (*Zerkalo*, 2 June 2000).

61 The Freedom House Survey for 2002 gave Azerbaijan a democratisation score of 5.75 on a scale of 1–7, with 1 representing the best score (http://www. freedomhouse.org/ratings/index/htm).

62 The Azerbaijan government announced that net oil profits in the year 2005 will constitute US$1 billion (*Country Report: Azerbaijan*, Economist Intelligence Unit, first quarter 2000, p. 18). According to a statement by the Azerbaijan prime minister, the country's oil revenues in 25 years were expected to amount to US$210 billion (A. Rasizade, 'Azerbaijan and the Oil Trade: Prospects and Pitfalls', *Brown Journal of World Affairs*, vol. 4, no. 2, 1997, p. 283).

63 *Azadlig*, 2 February 2000, 12 July 2000; *Zerkalo*, 12 August 2000.

64 *Azadlig*, 1–3 April 2000; *Zerkalo*, 11 December 2000.

65 See further N. Nassibli, 'Azerbaijan: Oil and Politics in the Country's Future', in Croissant and Aras, *op. cit.*, pp. 122–125.

66 *RFE/RL Newsline*, vol. 7, no. 200, 21 October 2003; *Turkistan-Newsletter*, 21 October 2003; P. Bouckaert, 'A Stolen Election and Oil Stability', *International Herald Tribune*, 20 October 2003.

11 Turkmenistan's Caspian resources and its international political economy

Germana Canzi

When the Soviet Union collapsed in 1991, Turkmenistan began life as an actor in the international arena with no experience of foreign policy and with no precise concept of its national interest. It was unclear whether the 70-odd years of Soviet social engineering had incorporated some sense of national identity.[1] Thus, one of the main concerns of the newly independent state was the search for 'status',[2] a confirmation of its existence as an independent actor. This entailed, amongst other things, the creation of an independent foreign policy through treaties and membership of international organisations. In the complex process of post-Soviet nation building, and not unlike other newly independent states, it has been subject to multiple sources of influence in its foreign policy decision making. Therefore, it has been looking to some international actors for ideological support, to others for financial aid and to yet others for military protection. Moreover, Turkmenistan is so much in need of foreign investment that the government has been trying to shape its foreign relations accordingly, at least in the first few years of independence.

Historical background

Before the establishment of Soviet rule, Turkmenistan never existed as an independent state. The Turkmen nation was for long periods divided among different regional powers such as the Persian empire, the Khanate of Khiva and the Emirate of Bukhara. The territory of present-day Turkmenistan was brought under the control of the Tsarist empire in 1884–1885.

The geopolitical orientation of what is now Turkmenistan was for centuries determined by the Karakum desert, which covers some 90 per cent of the country, rather than by the Caspian Sea. Historic cities such as Konya Urgench and Nisa Merv were situated on the edge of the desert, close to the overland trade routes to Persia, China, India and Russia. Turkmen maritime activity around the Caspian Sea was limited to that of the local tribes of the bay of Balkhan, who gradually abandoned nomadism in favour of a sedentary way of life supported primarily by fishing.[3] It was only towards the end of the seventeenth century that the Caspian Sea became strategically important. The first indication of this was Peter the Great's conquest of the western littoral areas. The Russian conquest of the region continued during the nineteenth century, culminating in the absorption of Turkmen lands into the Tsarist empire in the 1880s.

The Bolsheviks attempted to gain power in 1917, but were ousted by nationalist elements, aided by a British expeditionary mission, which set up an independent government. However, this government was soon overthrown and, by early 1920, the region was fully in the hands of the Red Army. The Turkmen Soviet Socialist Republic of Turkmenistan (also known as Turkmenia) was created in October 1924, as a constituent entity within the Soviet Union; the borders that were drawn at that time have remained unaltered up to the present.

Independence

The Turkmen Soviet Socialist Republic declared independence in October 1991, on the eve of the disintegration of the Soviet Union. In December 1991 the newly independent Turkmenistan joined the newly established Commonwealth of Independent States (CIS). A new Constitution, adopted in May 1992, provided for an executive president as head of state and government. The following month, Saparmurad Niyazov, the former first party secretary of the Communist Party of Turkmenistan, stood as sole candidate in the presidential election; virtually all the votes cast were in his favour. In January 1994 his term of office was extended by referendum until 2002; according to official estimates, 99 per cent of the population supported this motion. In January 2000 the Turkmen National Forum (an annual meeting of some 2,700 leading public figures) confirmed him in office for life.

In theory, legislative authority is vested in the Assembly (*Majlis*). In practice, however, the president exercises absolute control over the organs of state. There are two supposedly advisory bodies, but their function in actual fact is to rubber stamp presidential decrees. One is the People's Council, comprised of elected members as well as official appointees; the other is the Council of Elders (*Yashulylar Maslakhaty*), a body of senior citizens personally selected by the president to provide 'wise guidance'. There is only one registered political party in Turkmenistan. This is the Democratic Party of Turkmenistan, formerly the Communist Party of Turkmenistan (renamed shortly before the collapse of the Soviet Union). In early 1992 there was an abortive attempt to create a Peasants' Party; it was never allowed to develop into an active organisation and soon disappeared from sight. Unregistered groups are banned. The only active opposition to the present leadership comes from organisations based abroad.

Turkmenistan acceded to the United Nations on 2 March 1992 and subsequently joined the main UN funds, programmes and special agencies, including UNESCO, UNCTAD, the World Health Organisation, the International Monetary Fund and the World Bank; it acquired observer status in the World Trade Organisation. Turkmenistan also joined several regional organisations. These included the Economic Co-operation Organisation, the NATO Partnership for Peace programme, and the Organisation for Security and Co-operation in Europe (OSCE). It became a member of the Organisation for Islamic Conference in 1992 and the Non-Aligned Movement in 1995. Like other Central Asian states, it has joined the Asian Development Bank, the European Bank for Reconstruction, and the Islamic Development Bank. The country is, too, a signatory of the Final Act of the Helsinki Convention.

In the early twentieth century, Turkmen identity was still primarily shaped by local and tribal stratification. Under Soviet rule, however, some degree of national consolidation did take place. The Turkmen language was standardised and unified, and it became the vehicle for a modern literature. Universal education was introduced and national cultural and academic institutions were developed. Today, compared with other states of the region, Turkmenistan is one of the most ethnically homogeneous. Since independence, President Niyazov has skilfully exploited and favoured nationalism as a state ideology. The complexity of Turkmen national identity was one of the chief factors that appears to have convinced Niyazov of the need for a highly centralised state. The title of *Turkmenbashi* ('Leader of the Turkmen'), which was bestowed on him in 1993, can be seen as a move towards the reinforcement of Turkmen cohesion.

Yet despite these attempts, Soviet and post-Soviet, at nation building, Turkmenistan's national identity remains ambiguous: in some ways, it is more of a confederation of tribes than a nation.[4] These sub-ethnic identities seldom rise to the surface, but they could one day become a potentially complicating factor in domestic politics. Furthermore, the existence of Turkmen diasporas in Turkey, Xinjiang, Iraq and especially Iran and Afghanistan, constitutes a potential influence of ethnicity on foreign policy. To date, foreign policy initiatives towards these groups have been mainly addressed towards cultural and linguistic co-operation. Nevertheless, one might speculate that the issue of diaspora relations could well influence relations with countries that are involved in the proposed pipeline routes.

The 'Open Door' policy: 1992–1998

During the Soviet period, industrial development in Turkmenistan was chiefly concentrated in the oil and gas sectors. In agriculture, the cultivation of cotton predominated, making this one of the main cotton-producing areas in the Soviet Union. After independence, Turkmenistan favoured a gradualist approach to economic reform. In 1993 a programme called 'Ten years of stability' was initiated, aimed at guaranteeing the provision of free utilities to the population, to be funded by the anticipated revenues from oil and gas exportation.[5] In November that year Turkmenistan launched its own currency, the *manat*. One of the main targets of the economic policy was a diversification of production, with the objective of reaching self-sufficiency in food production. Reforms did not, however, emphasise the necessity for market oriented reforms; rather, they maintained the principal features of centralised economies of the Soviet era. A new wave of reforms started at the end of 1995, with an ambitious plan for macroeconomic stabilisation. Yet the document outlining the package of reforms, prepared on behalf of the Turkmen government by the European Bank of Reconstruction and Development (EBRD), pointed to a continuing insistence on the need for a gradualist approach to reforms.[6] In the years after that, the EBRD became increasingly critical, in particular towards the lack of political reform in the country. In addition, in the 2001 Transition Report, the organisation highlighted that Turkmenistan had actually been the only country in Central Asia to move backwards with economic reform.

Turkmen natural gas was the country's main source of income for growth, its known gas resources estimated at around 13 trillion cubic metres.[7] However, the idea of relying on gas exports was – and remains – limited by the characteristics of post-Soviet markets. Turkmenistan was forced to use existing pipelines and to export mainly to insolvent buyers. Gas arrears owed to Turkmenistan by Ukraine, Georgia, Azerbaijan, Uzbekistan and Tajikistan were estimated to be around 10 per cent of GDP, and often the repayments tended to be in barter. Thus, Turkmenistan urgently needed the construction of new pipelines to connect it to non-CIS markets. Turkmenistan also hoped to benefit from the development of its considerable oil reserves. Crude oil production in Turkmenistan had peaked in 1975, then entered a slow decline. Oil production in the last few years of the Soviet era was around 16 million tonnes per year.

After independence, exploration concessions were granted to foreign companies. These included the Cheleken offshore project, operated by Larmag Energy of the Netherlands, and a joint venture with the Argentine company Bridas to develop the Keimir and Ak-Patlauk oilfields and, likewise, to prospect in south-eastern Turkmenistan. In 1996 an agreement covering the development of Barinov, Livonov and Shafag, three offshore petroleum and gas deposits, was signed with the Malaysian state energy company Petronas; an Exploration and Production Sharing Agreement for oilfields in the Nebitdag region (western Turkmenistan) was also reached with Monument Oil and Gas of the UK (now part of Eni of Italy). In the same year, contracts for the upgrading and reconstruction of the Turkmenbashi oil refinery on the Caspian Sea were awarded to foreign consortia. The first was to a Japanese–Turkish consortium for the installation of a plant to produce high octane gasoline; the second to an Iranian–French consortium for a catalytic cracking plant; and the third to a German company for production of lubricants and other oils. A groundbreaking deal was concluded in January 1997, when Mobil Exploration and Producing Turkmenistan (Mobil later merged with Exxon), and its partner, Monument Oil and Gas, signed a strategic agreement with the Republic of Turkmenistan; in July 1998, a further agreement for the exploration and development of the Garashsyzlyk area, located onshore in western Turkmenistan was signed.

Initially, investor confidence in Turkmenistan was low. Yet gradually, despite its conservative approach to reform, the country began to attract

more favourable attention. The presence of major international oil companies played a crucial role in this upbeat assessment. In January 1998,
London-based credit rating agency Fitch Ibca gave Turkmenistan a B credit
rating for hard currency loans.[8] The rating was important for the development of the country's resources because it paved the way to loans from
multilateral and development banks. Later that year, a series of multilateral
loans were provided to Turkmenistan by the EBRD and the Japan Overseas
Economic Co-operation Fund. Turkmenistan also attracted increasing attention from export-credit agencies, through which governments of industrial
nations sponsor trade or projects. They usually included forms of insurance
against commercial and political risk, ranging from currency inconvertibility
to war or revolution. Thus, for example, Japan's export credit agency Jexim
provided a loan of ¥9.8 billion to the Turkmenistan State Bank of Foreign
Economic Affairs to build a cotton textile plant.[9] Other loans provided by
Japanese and supra-national institutions were geared towards the development of the transport and technical infrastructure, with the aim of improving
the country's connection to outside markets.

The most important development at this time was the first US Export–
Import Bank loan for the country, a direct consequence of President Niyazov's
visit to the US in April 1998. The purpose of the loan was to finance the
export of pipeline equipment from the US to Turkmenistan, and the upgrade
of an internal pipeline system. In an official statement, James H. Harmon,
chairman of the US agency stated: 'This is the first time Ex–Im Bank has
financed an oil transaction in Turkmenistan. Turkmenistan's vast oil and gas
sector represent a huge potential export market for US goods and services.
Ex–Im Bank believes this is the first of many more infrastructure projects in
Turkmenistan that we will finance in the future.'[10] Declarations of mutual
US–Turkmen co-operation and friendship were issued before, during and
after the visit.

Several other sources of funding and technical assistance for Turkmenistan
were initiated during this period. The EU–Tacis programme, active in the
country since 1992, had by 1997 allocated €10 million to various projects (e.g.
the development of a new petroleum law, bank restructuring and tax reform).
A further tranche of €10 million was announced for 1998–1999. Programmes
in strengthening public services were being implemented by UN agencies
(UNDP, WHO, UNICEF, etc.). Bilateral assistance was provided by, among
others, Japan, Turkey, Israel, the Netherlands, the UK and the US.

Isolationism and repression

In March 1998 Turkmenistan hosted an international oil and gas exhibition.
The Deputy Energy Minister Khoshgeldy Babayev presented an impressive
list of projects which, it was hoped, would attract foreign participation.
However, the new investor-friendly approach seemed largely rhetorical, as
legal frameworks, especially in the field of energy, were still unclear. Most
observers agreed that even the Energy Law adopted on 7 March 1997 did

not provide sufficient guarantees for investors. Moreover, the political environment was fraught with uncertainties. Several companies that had initially shown interest in Turkmenistan had seen their relationships with the government steadily deteriorating; consequently, they had withdrawn from agreements. These included the International Petroleum Corporation (Canadian) and Lamarg (Netherlands). Petronas was one of the few companies that remained active. Other projects that continued to be developed were the Cheleken Production Sharing Agreement, operated by Dubai-based Dragon Oil,[11] and the Nebitdag Production Sharing Agreement, operated by UK-based Burren Energy.[12]

From this point onwards, the international standing of Turkmenistan declined sharply. It became evident that attempts at economic reform had ground to a halt. In the late 1990s, the government still retained extensive control over resources. The transfer of medium and large scale enterprise to private ownership had petered out altogether. Strategic assets continued to be owned by the state, and the state also held a stake of 50 per cent or more in all major commercial investments. Corruption was rampant. Problems were compounded by the lack of transparency in official procedures, the endless bureaucratic red tape, the high turnover of personnel at levels of the system and the increasingly idiosyncratic behaviour of President Niyazov. Added to this, there was the volatility experienced on debt capital emerging markets after October 1997. Inevitably, foreign companies were wary of making large-scale investments in the country.[13] Over the next few years, several companies closed their offices or put their operations on hold. International organisations such as the IMF and EBRD likewise began to scale down their operations, unable to function efficiently in this rigid, restrictive environment. Foreign-funded assistance programmes, governmental and non-governmental, were curtailed for similar reasons.

Meanwhile, political repression heightened. By this time most of the leading dissidents were abroad. The majority had settled in Moscow where, by 1998, they were beginning to establish a co-ordinated opposition in exile. In 2001 Boris Shikhmuradov, one of Niyazov's closest associates (and a former Foreign Minister), also defected to Moscow. He formed his own party and was outspoken in his condemnation of President Niyazov, and the Turkmen authorities tried unsuccessfully to extradite him. Shikhmuradov later moved to the West; in May 2002, the Turkmen government demanded his extradition from the US but, again, without success.[14]

Within Turkmenistan itself, there were outbreaks of civil unrest and anti-government demonstrations. This triggered a wide-scale purge of the security services; also, several senior government figures were arrested for alleged offences ranging from corruption to murder, torture, embezzlement and drug-trafficking.[15] On 25 November 2002 there was an assassination attempt against President Niyazov. Mass arrests soon followed. Turkmen Special Forces raided the Uzbek embassy in Ashgabat, claiming that embassy staff had aided and abetted the plotters. No incriminating evidence was found, but a week later, at a separate location in Turkmenistan, they captured

Shikhmuradov. He was put on trial within weeks, along with several alleged accomplices. He was rapidly found guilty of treason and sentenced to life imprisonment. The trial proceedings brought back disturbing memories of Stalinist show trials in the 1930s.

Thus, after a relatively promising beginning in the early years of independence, by the end of the first decade of independence the economic as well as the political outlook for Turkmenistan seemed bleak. International credit ratings were revised downwards, reflecting concerns over the country's political and economic stability. This in turn made it yet more difficult to secure the necessary funding for the construction of vital export pipelines.

Pipeline projects

When Turkmenistan acquired independence, it was entirely dependent on the Russian pipeline system. The main projects under consideration during the 1990s involved the export of gas or oil in three directions: westwards to Europe, eastwards to Asia, and southwards to Afghanistan and Pakistan. Most of these projects, however, have been hampered by political constraints as well as technical problems. Nevertheless, Turkmen officials remained (at least in public) optimistic about the prospects for the implementation of the many pipeline projects that were mooted over these years. Indeed, from time to time there were encouraging signs of international support for some of these projects. Numerous Memoranda of Intent were signed and some feasibility studies were executed. Generally, however, interest waned before serious progress had been made. As of the end of 2002, only one export gas pipeline from Turkmenistan had been constructed. This was the Korpeje–Kurtkui pipeline, inaugurated in December 1997, connecting Turkmenistan with Iran. There was an announcement that a second pipeline to Iran, the Artik–Loftabad pipeline, had been inaugurated in 2000, but this was not mentioned again and does not seem to have materialised. Three other routes remained under discussion (see below), although prospects for construction seemed distant.

Trans-Caspian pipeline

One project that initially attracted much support was the plan to transport Turkmen natural gas to the West by means of an underwater pipeline from Turkmenistan to Turkey, via Azerbaijan, ultimately to connect with the EU grid near Vienna. It was estimated that the 2,000-kilometre pipeline (715 km in Turkmenistan, 300 km along the seabed, 408 km in Azerbaijan, 200 km in Georgia and 320 km in Turkey) would cost over US$3 billion. This project received high-level backing from the US administration, which saw it as a way of detaching Turkmenistan from both Russian and Iranian spheres of influence.

In 1999, the now-defunct US energy concern Enron announced the results of a feasibility study for this pipeline. In February that year an agreement was concluded with the Turkmen government appointing the PSG Corporation (a US partnership between Bechtel and General Electric Capital), as operator for the Trans-Caspian project. President Niyazov expressed his satisfaction, noting that this was a 'crucial event for Turkmenistan'. He went on to state: 'We are not concealing the fact that behind the event stand the efforts of our friends, primarily US President Bill Clinton and Vice President Al Gore.'[16] In July 1999, ambassador John Wolf, special adviser to the US president and US secretary of state for Caspian basin energy diplomacy, had a meeting with President Niyazov during which he presented a personal message from Vice-President Gore reiterating the US administration's support for this pipeline, and stressing that it would be of great importance for the consolidation of Turkmen independence.

The proposed pipeline would enable Turkmenistan to fully realise its energy potential and become integrated into both global and regional energy systems. This would enhance co-operation across the breadth of Eurasia. The US envoy updated President Niyazov on recent developments, including the outcome of his meetings with the presidents of Turkey, Georgia and Azerbaijan, all of whom were eager to accelerate the implementation of the project. A few days previously, successful discussions had been held between the PSG consortium (that was to carry out the project), and the Turkmen government.[17] United States' government financing had been arranged for most of the route. It was anticipated that the 2,000-km pipeline would be built in 28 months. In August 1999 the project received a new boost when Royal Dutch/Shell became a 'strategic partner' of Turkmenistan in developing the various gas deposits that were to be the main source of supply for the pipeline. This gave it a lead role in the project. It seemed very probable, at this stage, that it would be possible to finalise outstanding organisational issues and to begin construction in the near future.

Within a few months, however, problems began to surface. Azerbaijan began to insist that the envisaged pipeline make provision for the eventual export of Azerbaijani gas via the route. This move was prompted by the discovery of substantial gas reserves in Shah Deniz off the coast of Azerbaijan, which gave rise to hopes that Baku itself would become a major exporter in its own right within a few years. For Azerbaijan, an alternative project for the export of its gas to Turkey, entailing the construction of a pipeline across Georgia, without the participation of Turkmenistan, began to seem increasingly attractive. Meanwhile, President Niyazov himself had apparently changed his mind about the project. In part, this might have been a reaction to the Azerbaijani position, but it was also likely to have been influenced by the prospect of concluding a major Turkmen–Russian gas deal.

Niyazov did not reject the Trans-Caspian project, but made increasingly critical statements about it and delayed implementation of agreements. Moreover, he imposed exorbitant financial conditions on potential investors. Yet in August 2000 he assured the new Turkish ambassador to Turkmenistan that it would 'be good for both countries to move forward on the trans-Caspian pipeline'.[18] By this time US support for the project began to appear less enthusiastic than previously. Ambassador Wolf denied this, but stressed the need for the project to be financed commercially:

> We have always made it clear that . . . we would be prepared to help with US government-backed Export–Import Bank credits and Overseas Private Investment Corporation project insurance to support the project. OPIC insurance would be very important because it would reassure commercial investors that they would have a government guarantee for the project. And we have been very consistent in the position for two years.[19]

The project, for the foreseeable future, was shelved in March 2003, when Royal Dutch/Shell decided to reduce its activities in Turkmenistan.

Trans-Afghan pipeline

The construction of oil and gas pipelines from Turkmenistan to Pakistan has periodically attracted attention over the past ten years. The initial proposal for this project came from Bridas, an Argentine company, in the early 1990s. However, the relationship between Bridas and the Turkmen government soon soured, leading to complicated legal disputes. In October 1995 the project was revived when Turkmenistan signed an agreement with the Delta Oil Company (Saudi Arabia) and US oil giant Unocal, giving the two companies permission to buy natural gas from Turkmenistan close to the border with Afghanistan. The agreement was then developed into a project for the construction of a gas pipeline, 1,464 km in length, from the Dauletabad gas field in southern Turkmenistan via Afghanistan to Multan in Pakistan. The estimated cost was US$2 billion. The project included a proposal for eventually lengthening the pipeline to India. Indian energy authorities also signed an agreement with Unocal in January 1997 for a trans-Indian pipeline from Turkmenistan to Bangladesh and Myanmar.[20]

A consortium was created that included, apart from Saudi Delta Oil and Unocal, Japan's Itochu Corporation, Korea's Hyundai and Pakistan's Crescent Group. A certain amount of progress was made in winning the support of the various warring factions in Afghanistan. Turkmenistan, alone among the states of the region, maintained diplomatic relations with all the factions involved in the Afghan conflict. It refused to sign a joint declaration of CIS members condemning the Taleban in the autumn of 1996. Turkmenistan also continued to cultivate good relations with Pakistan and India. President Niyazov visited New Delhi in February 1997 to discuss agreements on trade and co-operation in various fields between the two countries. A Turkmen–Pakistani agreement was signed in 1998, including, among other provisions, co-operation in military training.

In December 1997 an official Taleban delegation visited the US at the invitation of Unocal.[21] The outlook for the construction of the pipeline was beginning to look promising. In February 1998, a team from Unocal went on a three-day visit to Kabul, where it held talks with Taleban government authorities on oil and gas exploration and pipeline projects. However, a little later in the year, a Unocal official declared that the project was to be put on hold indefinitely.[22] Increasing instability in the region as well as poor prospects for financing this project no doubt influenced this decision. Multilateral lending agencies, among them the World Bank, had been approached, but had declined to participate in the structuring of a project-financing facility.

In late 2001, after the international intervention in Afghanistan, and the overthrow of the Taleban, this project began to attract renewed international interest. The presidents of Afghanistan, Pakistan and Turkmenistan were scheduled to meet on 26 October 2001 to sign a framework agreement on building a Turkmenistan–Afghanistan–Pakistan (TAP) export pipeline. In the event, the meeting was postponed at Pakistan's request, owing chiefly to domestic problems in Islamabad. However, officials from the three countries had already initialled the agreement.[23] Two months later, on 27 December 2002, the three leaders finally met in Ashgabat to sign the document that set the legal framework for the TAP project pipeline. This envisaged the construction of a 1,500-km-long pipeline, capable of transporting some 30 billion cubic metres of natural gas annually. It was anticipated that there would be substantial benefits for the participating states. These would include the creation of new employment opportunities in Afghanistan, as well as large transit fees and the development of the infrastructure. For Turkmenistan, the principal benefit would be a diversification of routes to carry its huge gas resources to international markets, thereby reducing its dependence on the Russian pipeline system. Pakistan would receive a stable source of energy for its domestic market. According to current estimates, it would cost over US$3 billion to build. It was anticipated that the Asian Development Bank (ADB) and World Bank would provide most of the finance. The US Agency for International Development (USAID) was also expected to play a significant role in the project.

On paper the project undoubtedly had merit. However, the practical obstacles were enormous. Not only were there technical problems (which would certainly have been costly to overcome), but the political risk in all the TAP states was high. Moreover, India, probably the pipeline's main long-term customer for the future, was still wary of participating in the project. Without dramatic improvement in its relationship with Pakistan, it was highly unlikely to favour any policy that would make it dependent on Islamabad for energy supplies. Revealingly, India was not present at the signing of the TAP agreement meeting in Ashgabat. Factors such as these would certainly complicate efforts to put together a financial package for the project. Thus, although a major feasibility study was carried out in 2003 (supported by the ADB), it seems unlikely that this pipeline will be constructed in the near future (see further **Roberts**, p. 87, **Adams**, p. 103).

Trans-Asian pipeline

Another even more long-term project is the construction of a trans-Asian gas pipeline running from Turkmenistan via Uzbekistan and Kazakhstan to

China and eventually to Japan. The length would be some 6,000 km, and the estimated cost would exceed US$12 billion (and more than US$22 billion if extended to Japan). This would make it one of the most costly and ambitious infrastructure projects planned anywhere in the world. The project was elaborated in a memorandum of understanding between China, Japan and Turkmenistan, signed in early 1995. Formal agreement and feasibility studies were carried out by Mitsubishi Corporation, Exxon Corporation and the China National Petroleum Corporation, later joined by Esso China, a unit of Exxon Corporation of the US (currently ExxonMobil). For China this pipeline would be extremely important, because it would bring energy to the coast, while stimulating the industrial development of the western and central regions. Japan also has a great need for energy, considering that it accounts for over 30 per cent of natural gas consumption in the Asia-Pacific region.[24] However, under present conditions this project is not viable.

Caspian negotiations

From the outset, Turkmenistan's approach was that issues relating to the Caspian Sea, including the legal status, should be resolved jointly by all Caspian states. President Niyazov pointed out that 'the riches of the Caspian were not for one side only'. He called for all sides to work together to produce a document or 'convention', on the basis of which internationally accepted legal norms could be established, aimed at regulating navigation, exploiting biological and mineral resources and protecting the ecosystem.[25] Turkmen legal experts held that the Caspian Sea is unique and that, consequently, a non-traditional resolution was required, to be decided by the Caspian states themselves. Specifically, Turkmenistan proposed that each littoral state should have its own border and fishing zone, a defined section of the shelf to exploit the mineral resources, the width of this zone to be determined by consultation with all Caspian states. The remaining part of the Caspian – the 'Caspian centre' – was to be determined by the condominium principle of joint exploitation.

The Turkmen approach was broadly in line with that of Iran and Russia, although there were some points of difference. In particular, Turkmenistan took a firm position on the concept of a coastal or littoral zone, regarding this as a territorial question and thus a matter of national security. It supported free navigation based on international legal agreement by all littoral states, but was against naval activity in the Caspian. Initially, Azerbaijan and Kazakhstan adopted somewhat different positions (see **Granmayeh**, **Gizzatov**). However, by 1995, some measure of convergence had been reached between the five littoral states. Yet hopes of an early final resolution to the legal status of the Caspian Sea soon evaporated.

In 1997 Azerbaijan and Turkmenistan became embroiled in a dispute over the Kyapaz/Serdar offshore oilfield (see Map 2). This was located in an area that Turkmenistan regarded as being within its territorial waters but which was being developed on Azerbaijan's behalf by an international consortium (see **Granmayeh**). In November 1997 Turkmenistan appealed, unsuccessfully, to the UN for assistance in settling the dispute. Russia offered to mediate, as did the US.[26] The matter remained unresolved, however, and in mid-2001 Turkmenistan closed its embassy in Baku. The excuse for this action was 'temporary financial difficulties', but it was clearly intended to convey Turkmenistan's indignation at Azerbaijan's intransigence. Both countries took steps to defend their territorial waters, purchasing patrol boats from the US. Turkmenistan ordered an additional 20 such vessels from Ukraine, half of which were capable of carrying large calibre machine guns.

It was in this tense atmosphere that President Niyazov invited the heads of state of the littoral states to assemble in Ashgabat for a summit meeting to decide on the legal regime for the sea. Azerbaijan, Kazakhstan and Russia had, by this time, reached a common standpoint, based on the principle that the surface of the sea should be used in common, but the seabed be divided into national sectors. Iran and Turkmenistan shared largely similar positions, advocating a division of the seabed and the surface of the sea into equal national sectors. The meeting was postponed several times. When it finally took place on 23–24 April 2002 the results were inconclusive. No agreements were signed; there was not even a joint declaration. In February 2003, discussions were resumed at a session of the Special Working Group on the legal status of the Caspian, attended by deputy foreign ministers and senior officials of the littoral states. Again, no final agreement was reached, but Turkmenistan appeared to have modified its position slightly, bringing it a little closer to Russia, Kazakhstan and Azerbaijan. Turkmen–Azerbaijani relations, however, were still strained. Azerbaijan opened an embassy in Ashgabat in December 2002, but the Turkmen embassy in Baku remained closed. By early 2004 no significant changes had taken place in Turkmenistan's stance. However, it was continuing to engage in bilateral talks with its neighbours.

Geopolitical orientation of the Caspian region

The most distinctive feature of Turkmenistan's post-Soviet foreign policy is the so-called 'positive neutrality', recognised by a UN General Assembly resolution of 12 December 1995. This status is defined as a 'means for creating positive and constructive state positions on issues of protecting peace and stability, developing friendly relations and co-operation between states'. The full implications of this policy are not clear but, in practical terms, Turkmenistan has increasingly shied away from involvement in active multilateral associations. In the early years of independence it joined several regional organisations. Since then, however, it has concentrated on developing bilateral relations. It remains a member of the CIS, but has refused to participate in the CIS Collective Security Treaty. It continues to look sceptically towards Central Asian economic integration. It declined to become a member of the Central Asian Union (formed in 1994 between Uzbekistan, Kazakhstan and Kyrgyzstan, later joined by Tajikistan), though in 2002 it acquired observer status in the relaunched Central Asian Co-operation Organisation.

Over the past decade, the driving force behind Turkmenistan's foreign policy has been the need to exploit its energy resources. Two issues have been dominant: pipeline politics and the resolution of the legal status of the Caspian Sea. Consequently, the crucial relationships for Turkmenistan have been those that directly impact on its interests in these areas. Thus, Russia and Iran, the main regional powers, have occupied an important place in Turkmenistan's foreign policy. Since independence, the relationship with Iran has followed a relatively smooth course. With Russia, however, there has been less consistency.

In the early 1990s, Turkmenistan seemed inclined to distance itself from Moscow. Instead, it gave priority to its relationship with the US. The US established diplomatic relations with Turkmenistan soon after the demise of the Soviet Union. It signalled its friendly intentions by opening an embassy in Ashgabat and conceding the status of Most-Favoured-Nation to Turkmenistan. Turkmenistan welcomed US interest and became one of the first countries of Central Asia to sign the Partnership for Peace agreement with NATO (1994). Relations between the two states reached a new degree of intensity with the prospect of constructing the Trans-Caspian pipeline (see above). In April 1998 President Niyazov visited Washington and on his return spoke warmly of 'our friends' President Clinton and Vice-President Gore. However, the relationship cooled rapidly when it became clear that there was no possibility of implementing this project in the near future. By late 1999, Turkmenistan was moving back into the Russian orbit. In autumn 2001, following the US-led operation 'Enduring Freedom' against the Taleban and al-Qaeda in Afghanistan, Turkmenistan offered limited access to its facilities, but stipulated that they were to be used only for humanitarian assistance.

Turkmenistan's relationship with the European Union has been mainly restricted to Tacis programmes. These have focused primarily on the food sector, enterprise restructuring and the development of human resources. A Partnership and Co-operation Agreement was signed in 1998, but not ratified. Bilateral relations with individual European countries, as with countries in other parts of the world, have remained at a relatively low level. Apart from the US and European Union, the largest providers of aid to date have been Israel, Turkey and Japan. Turkmenistan's main trading partners are Russia and Ukraine, and outside the CIS, Iran and Turkey.

Turkmen–Russian relations

Even before the formal disintegration of the Soviet Union, Turkmenistan declared its independence. However, relations with Russia remained extremely important. There were several reasons for this. Firstly, Russia was Turkmenistan's main trading partner. Secondly, Turkmenistan was still firmly tied to Russia's 'steel umbilical chord' (i.e. the Soviet-era system of oil and gas pipelines).[27] Thirdly, Turkmenistan was dependent on Russia for the security of its external borders. These three issues had to be addressed simultaneously. Geography, if nothing else, meant that Turkmenistan could not sever its links with Russia. Rather, the relationship had to be managed in such a way as to serve Turkmenistan's interests.

The first steps towards reducing dependency on Russia for defence and security were taken in early 1992, when Turkmenistan took the decision to create its own armed forces. An interim Russo-Turkmen agreement was concluded in March 1992, establishing joint jurisdiction over former Soviet military formations and installations located on the territory of Turkmenistan (with the exception of air force and air defence installations, which remained under the control of the Russian Defence Ministry). Later that year, a Treaty of Friendship and Co-operation was signed between the two countries. This set out the framework for bilateral relations in a number of fields including political, economic, trade, diplomatic and cultural ties. The Russian Ministry of Defence undertook to provide assistance in setting up a national army in Turkmenistan, providing equipment, training and funding. Some 50 Russian officers were seconded to the fledgling Turkmen Ministry of Defence on contract.

Initially, President Niyazov spoke in glowing terms of the 'unique and productive' military co-operation with Russia. By early 1993, however, there was dissatisfaction on both sides. Russian air-force exercises over Turkmen territory, scheduled to be held in April 1993, were vetoed, apparently on the orders of President Niyazov himself. Relations further deteriorated with allegations of discrimination against Russian military personnel on contract to the Turkmen government. The crisis was eventually defused and further agreements were signed covering the training of Turkmen military personnel at Russian military academies, joint border control, exchange of intelligence and other such issues. The agreement on dual nationality gave a further boost to bilateral relations.

Energy issues were – and remain – a priority in Russian–Turkmen relations. After the Soviet Union disintegrated, Turkmenistan's natural gas output continued to be exported through the existing pipeline system, running across Kazakhstan and Uzbekistan to Russia, and thence to Ukraine and other CIS customers. From 1991 to 1993, Russia's main gas company, Gazprom, which now had control of this network, allowed Turkmenistan to export its gas to Western markets. In October 1993, however, it restricted Turkmenistan's access to the pipeline to deliveries to CIS markets. As described above, a number of pipeline projects were under discussion in the 1990s. In November 1995, Russia and Turkmenistan formed a joint-stock company, Turkmenrosgaz; a stake of 51 per cent was owned by the Turkmen government, 44 per cent by Gazprom and the remaining 5 per cent by ITERA, a US-registered company. The joint venture thereafter controlled all gas exports from Turkmenistan to the CIS. Ukraine was the main destination, taking some 80 per cent of Turkmenistan's gas exports. However, Ukraine repeatedly failed to pay in full. Consequently, in March 1997 Turkmenistan suspended deliveries. Turkmenrosgaz was disbanded.

Economic relations between Russia and Turkmenistan were adversely affected by these developments. The situation was exacerbated by the dispute between Azerbaijan and Turkmenistan over the Kyapaz/Serdar field, which at this time was leading to growing tension in the Caspian Sea. Russia offered to mediate. However, its credibility as an 'honest broker' was undermined by the fact that it was the Russian companies Rosneft and LUKoil that had signed the deal with the State Oil Company of the Azerbaijan Republic (SOCAR) to develop the oilfield. Moreover, Russian First Deputy Prime Minister and Fuel and Energy Minister Boris Nemtsov had presided over the signing of this deal. Moscow insisted that the agreement had been concluded with independent commercial entities. However, after a meeting between the Russian and Turkmen leaders, President Yeltsin announced that the deal had been a mistake and was to be cancelled. Baku, too, adopted a more conciliatory tone towards the Turkmen authorities and the project was shelved, at least for the foreseeable future.

Moscow appeared to have lost influence in Ashgabat. The Trans-Caspian pipeline project was gathering momentum and President Niyazov seemed increasingly to favour a pro-Western orientation. Yet a year later, he had again shifted his stance and a new closeness was apparent in Turkmen–Russian relations. In late 1999 Ashgabat signed an agreement with Moscow for the sale of 20 billion cubic metres of natural gas, to be increased to 50 billion cubic metres by 2004. In April 2003 the presidents of Turkmenistan and Russia signed a milestone 25-year agreement on co-operation in the gas sector. At the same time, the Turkmen national oil company Turkmenneftegaz and Russian Gazexport also signed a long-term contract for gas purchases. Until 2006, Turkmen gas would be bought at US$44 per 1,000 cubic metres; half of the cost would be covered by supplies of Russian goods and technology. From 2007, payment for Turkmen gas would be at world prices.

On his return from Moscow, President Niyazov had a meeting with Ukrainian President Kuchma. In 2001, Turkmenistan had concluded a five-year deal with Ukraine for the supply of 250 billion cubic metres of gas. Prior to this, agreement had been reached on the restructuring of Ukraine's debt to Turkmenistan (which included arrears and penalties dating back to 1993–1994). President Niyazov assured his Ukrainian counterpart that the April 2003 agreement with Russia did not contravene Turkmenistan's previous contract with Ukraine, which was valid until 2006. Further, President Niyazov proposed a tripartite political and economic agreement between Ukraine, Russia and Turkmenistan. Among other issues on the agenda, the two leaders discussed the construction of a northern pipeline, to run from Turkmenistan via Kazakhstan to Ukraine. President Niyazov emphasised that this, along with the existing pipeline that runs via Uzbekistan, would meet the gas needs of both Russia and Ukraine. These new developments effectively replaced the plan to export Turkmen gas via the proposed Western-backed Trans-Caspian pipeline discussed above.

Yet even while pursuing rapprochement in the energy sector, Turkmenistan remained suspicious of Russian political intentions. Thus, following the attempted assassination of President Niyazov in November 2002,

Turkmen officials openly accused Moscow of masterminding the attack.[28] However, further investigations implicated many other suspects, including Georgians, Azerbaijanis, Chechens, Uzbeks and a US citizen of Moldovan Russian origin. No permanent damage appeared to have been done to Turkmen–Russian relations, but resentment of Russia's refusal to extradite Turkmen opposition leaders clearly festered. In April 2003, the Turkmen government suddenly and unilaterally revoked the right of citizens to hold dual Russian–Turkmen citizenship. This caused panic among the Russian population in Turkmenistan. If they chose to keep their Russian passports they would lose the right of residence and right to own property in Turkmenistan; if they opted for Turkmen citizenship, they would lose the freedom to travel to and from Russia. Thus, they were faced with the choice of abandoning their possessions and emigrating in haste, or of being trapped in a country where their future seemed increasingly unsafe.[29] The Russian government found itself powerless to mitigate the decision of the Turkmen authorities, lacking effective levers of influence.

Iran

After independence, developing good relations with Iran was one of Turkmenistan's first foreign-policy priorities. The two countries share a land border of almost 1,000 km and have a long history of economic and cultural ties. Moreover, there is a large Turkmen diaspora in Iran (generally estimated to number some 500,000). During the Soviet period there was very little cross-border contact. Since independence, however, both governments have supported the rebuilding of links. In August 1992 President Niyazov made his first official visit abroad to Iran. This was followed by high-level Iranian delegations to Ashgabat, including a visit by Foreign Minister Ali Akbar Velayati in January 1993, and by President Hashemi Rafsanjani in October of that year. In January 1994, the Turkmen president again went to Tehran. Several important agreements were signed, including one on military co-operation. The Mashhad–Sarakhs–Tejen railroad was inaugurated in May 1996. This gave Turkmenistan access, through the Iranian rail network, to the port of Bandar-e Abbas on the Persian Gulf. Turkmenistan also joined the Economic Co-operation Organisation and the Caspian Sea Co-operation Council; both were organisations in which Iran played a pivotal role.

In January 1995 Turkmenistan, Iran and Turkey established the Turkmenistan Transcontinental Pipeline Company, a joint venture for the construction of a gas pipeline from Turkmenistan to Turkey via Iran. However, the project did not secure the necessary funding and was shelved. Meanwhile, work continued on a less ambitious project to link Turkmen and Iranian gas pipeline networks. The Korpeje–Kurtkui pipeline, which linked the Korpeje gas field in south-western Turkmenistan to the village of Kurtkui in northern Iran, was inaugurated on 29 December 1998. This relatively small project carried wider implications, being truly the first export of Turkmen gas outside the former Soviet Union. There were high hopes that it might in the future be extended to Turkey and thence to Western Europe. The ceremony was marked by the presence of President Khatami, making his first visit abroad since taking power in August 1997. He commented that 'the event marks another step towards bolstering Tehran–Ashgabat relations'.[30] For his part, Niyazov referred to 'the record of warm and sincere ties between the two countries ... determined to strengthen their good and fraternal ties'.[31] The previous day, Turkmen and Iranian energy ministers had signed a memorandum of understanding with Royal Dutch/Shell for the extension of the pipeline. US opposition to a pipeline through Iran remained strong.[32] However, in March 1998, a senior US government official had indicated that the US was perhaps rethinking its attitude to sanctions against European and Asian countries investing in Iran's energy sector.[33] This would undoubtedly have made it easier to raise finance for the proposed Turkmenistan–Turkey–Europe pipeline. In the event, however, there was no change in the US position and, despite some European support for the project, as of 2004 there seemed little prospect of securing funding in the near future.

Turkmen and Iranian approaches to the division of the Caspian Sea were initially close. Later, there was some divergence of opinion regarding the conceptual basis of the legal regime but, overall, the two countries remained broadly in agreement. In particular, they were united in their opposition to external intervention in Caspian affairs. There were incipient disagreements over territorial waters but these were rapidly defused through bilateral negotiations. This was highlighted in mid-1997, when Turkmenistan invited tenders for 11 blocks in what it regarded as its 'national sector'. Iran objected, since the area was located in the 'border waters' of the two countries. The matter was resolved when Turkmenistan withdrew three of the 11 blocks from the tender. For the remainder, the two countries agreed to operate jointly in disputed areas until full clarification of the legal status of the sea had been established (see **Granmayeh**).

The two countries continued to maintain close diplomatic contact and to co-ordinate their positions on the Caspian and other regional issues. This was highlighted in March 2003 when, following the session of the Special Working Group on the Caspian, held in Baku in February to discuss a draft convention on the Caspian Sea, President Niyazov went to Tehran for follow-up talks with President Khatami. By this time, Moscow, too, was again courting Iran. Having reached agreement on the division of the North Caspian with Kazakhstan and Azerbaijan, it began seeking a similar resolution in the South Caspian. In 2003, the possibility of Iran joining Russia and Turkmenistan to exploit jointly structures located on the borders of the proposed national sectors was under discussion.

Conclusions

President Niyazov, like other leaders in the newly independent states of Central Asia, has tried to establish a position in the international arena.

However, he has a limited understanding of how the international community operates. He has placed excessive hope in the potential wealth to be provided by oil and gas revenues. His social policies, such as the provision of free goods and services to the citizens, have been based on expectations that Turkmenistan is a 'second Kuwait'. Personification of power has meant that there are no decision-makers in Turkmenistan other than the president. For a while it seemed that international corporations were at ease with the political stability that Niyazov's authoritarian rule seemed able to provide. During the second half of the 1990s, however, President Niyazov's eccentric behaviour began to cause alarm among the international community. There was a sharp loss of confidence, and foreign organisations, commercial and intergovernmental, began to reduce their activities in the region. Increasing domestic instability, coupled with a dire record on human rights, made foreign companies reluctant to engage in enterprises in Turkmenistan. Most of the pipeline projects that had earlier attracted enthusiastic support had been postponed indefinitely. Foreign investment continued to flow into the country, but it was mainly linked to relatively small-scale projects.

Thus, at the beginning of its second decade of independence, the outlook for Turkmenistan was considerably less optimistic than had been the case ten years before. Yet it would be wrong to assume that this is a country with no prospects. It possesses vast reserves of natural gas and has enormous potential for growth. This is because natural gas is the fossil fuel with the highest demand growth projections in many parts of the world, owing to its lower greenhouse gas emissions, compared to coal and crude oil. Whatever its current problems, Turkmenistan is therefore likely to become a major regional energy supplier at some stage and eventually to play a crucial role in the emerging regional alignments.

Notes

The author wishes to thank Dr Shirin Akiner for help in the preparation of this article for publication.

1 See M. Ochs, 'Turkmenistan: the quest for stability and control', in *Conflict, Cleavage and Change in Central Asia and the Caucasus*, in K. Dawisha and B. Parrot (eds), Cambridge University Press, Cambridge, 1997, pp. 312–318.
2 Holsti, in an important analysis of international politics, calls 'status' one of the goals of foreign policy. Other, interconnected, categories in this framework are 'security', 'autonomy' and 'economic welfare'. K. J. Holsti, *International Politics: A Framework for Analysis*, Prentice-Hall, London, 1992, ch. 4.
3 W. Raczka, 'Le Turkmenistan, futur Koweit de la Caspienne?', *Cahiers d'études sur la Méditerranée orientale et le monde turco-iranien*, no. 23, janvier–juin, 1997.
4 A. Bohr, 'Turkmenistan and the Turkmen', in *The Nationalities Question in the Post-Soviet States*, ed. G. Smith, Longman, London and New York, 1996, p. 348.
5 M. Orazov and G. Khalova, 'Programma reformirovaniya ekonomiki Turkmenistana 10 let stabil'nosti', *Voprosy Ekonomiki*, no. 10, pp. 95–99 (1995/10).
6 European Bank for Reconstruction and Development, *Transition Report 1997: Enterprise and Growth*, 1997, pp. 205–207.
7 M. McCauley (ed.), *Investing in the Caspian Sea Region: Opportunity and Risk*, Cartermill Publishing, London, 1996, p. 70.

8 'Turkmenistan Receives Credit-rating', RFE/RL, 9 January 1998.

9 'Agencies Show Faith in Turkmenistan', *Project Finance*, February 1998, p. 12.

10 Ex–Im Bank news release, 10 March 1998.

11 Dragon Oil was originally based in Dublin and London; in 1999 the Emirates National Oil Company became the major shareholder and the headquarters of the company were subsequently moved to Dubai.

12 Burren Energy, founded in 1994, went into Turkmenistan in 1997 as a partner of Monument Oil and Gas. It took over Monument's interests in 2000. It currently operates 90 wells in Turkmenistan ('Burren Gearing Up to Accelerate Exploration', D. Blackwell, 16 June 2003, www.ft.com).

13 'Turkmens Upbeat about Energy Projects, Others Wary', *Reuters*, 12 March 1998.

14 *RFE/RL Central Asia Report*, vol. 2, no. 19, 16 May 2002.

15 Among the accused were the former head of the National Security Committee, Muhammad Nazarov, and members of his staff; also the former Minister of Defence, the Chairman of the National Bank and the head of the main television channel (*RFE/RL Central Asia Report*, vol. 2, no. 18, 9 May 2002).

16 *Interfax*, 19 February 1999.

17 Turkmen Television first channel, Ashgabat, 19 July 1999.

18 'Turkmenistan: US Official Discusses Trans-Caspian Pipeline', Naz Nazar, *RFE/RL*, 14 August 2000.

19 *Ibid.*

20 *Oil and Gas Journal*, 20 January 1997.

21 'Afghanistan: Afghan Taleban say Ready for Gas Pipeline Accord', *Reuters Business Briefing*, 4 January 1998.

22 *BBC Summary of World Broadcasts*, 22 August 1998.

23 *RFE/RL Newsline*, 21 October 2002.

24 The National Pipeline Research Society of Japan (NPRSJ) has predicted a growing energy deficit for the next century, as its natural gas demand will more than double by 2010 (*Pipe Line and Gas Industry*, 1/97, p. 4).

25 Personal communication, London 1995, Yagmur Kochumov, senior legal adviser, Turkmen Ministry of Foreign Affairs.

26 'Who will Mediate the Kyapaz Dispute?', *RFE/RL*, 20 November 1997.

27 J. Roberts, *Caspian Pipelines*, Royal Institute of International Affairs, London, 1996.

28 United Press International, 26 November 2002.

29 10 April 2003, during President Niyazov's state visit to Moscow. (*RFE/RL Newsline*, 18 April 2003).

30 *BBC Summary of World Broadcasts*, 30 December 1997.

31 *Ibid.*

32 'Albright Cautious on Pipeline Decision Meaning', *Reuters*, 29 July 1997.

33 *Financial Times*, 26 March 1998.

12 Kazakhstan: oil, politics and the new 'Great Game'

Majid Jafar

Introduction

Since the collapse of the Soviet Union and the end of the Cold War in the early 1990s, the newly independent republics of Central Asia around the Caspian Sea have drawn the world's attention, primarily for the reasons of their expected abundance of energy reserves, and their strategic location between Europe and Asia. These factors became all the more important in the aftermath of the attacks of 11 September 2001 on the World Trade Center and the Pentagon in the US. The 'War on Terror' that was subsequently unleashed made global dependence on Arabian Gulf oil reserves seem more problematic, and the new resources in the Caspian region and in Russia that much more attractive. In addition, the geographic position of the newly independent republics of the Caspian basin – bordering as they do Afghanistan, Iran, Russia, China and the Middle East – became even more relevant. The increased sense of the risks arising from militant Islamic fundamentalism and 'failed states' brought the focus on these countries for security reasons that could not have been foreseen prior to 11 September. Thus, their importance at a political as well as an economic level seems assured for some years to come.

Of these countries, Kazakhstan is the largest and is also likely to prove the most significant in terms of oil and gas reserves. Approximately two-thirds the size of the United States, Kazakhstan is expected to hold enormous fossil fuel reserves as well as plentiful supplies of other minerals and metals. It is therefore of importance to the future world supply of energy. As foreign investment pours into the country's oil and gas sectors, this landlocked Central Asian state is beginning to realise its enormous production potential. With sufficient export options, it is thought Kazakhstan could become one of the world's key oil producers and exporters in the next decade. This perception has caused a frenzy among foreign oil companies and their governments, particularly with the Middle East largely closed to foreign investment, a world of high oil prices, and few alternatives to declining production in more traditional regions of the world.

This vast potential wealth is coupled with a unique geopolitical position – Kazakhstan has long borders with both Russia and China, as well as with three of the other Central Asian states, and of course the inland Caspian

Sea. It has also been courting the US, and other nations in the Islamic world. Kazakhstan styles itself as a force for stability and balance in its region, as well as the best engine for economic growth. As has often been pointed out, with a geopolitical position on the cross-roads of Asia and Europe and huge hydrocarbon potential, Kazakhstan must surely rank within the system of international relations as a centre-most regional power. The processes of nation building in this modern fledgling state, and the benefits and harmful effects of its oil wealth, will therefore be crucial. This chapter considers the interlinked themes of oil wealth, political stability and international relations.

Brief overview of modern history

The modern Republic of Kazakhstan is the ninth largest country in the world. It lies at the very heart of the great Eurasian steppe, that great band of grassland stretching from Mongolia to Hungary, which served for millennia as the highway and grazing ground of nomadic horseback peoples. The Kazakhs emerged in the late fifteenth century as a distinct ethnic group, under the leadership of their own khans (chiefs or princes). By origin, they were descended from Mongols and Turkic peoples. They established one of the world's last great nomadic empires, stretching across the steppe and desert north, east and west of the Syr-Darya, and stretching north into what is now southern Siberia. Over time they came to be divided into three 'hordes' (tribal confederations) – the Great Horde (*Ulu Juz*) in the south, the Middle Horde (*Orta Juz*) in the centre and north east, and the Lesser Horde (*Kishi Juz*) in the west of the country. Kazakhs today still identify to a large extent with these groupings.

The Kazakhs sought help from the Russians against external enemies from the east in the mid-eighteenth century. This eventually led to Russian annexation of Kazakh lands, followed by formal incorporation into the Russian Empire. In the twentieth century, in the chaos that followed the Russian revolution, a Kazakh nationalist movement known as the Alash Orda emerged as the party of power. As a matter of expediency, they united with the Bolsheviks and signed an accord to safeguard the interests of the fledgling 'Kazakh nation'. Thus, Kazakhstan was incorporated into the Soviet Union, first as a subordinate entity within the Russian Soviet Federal Socialist Republic (RSFSR), and then, in 1936, as a full Soviet Socialist Republic, with the national borders it has today and Almaty as its capital.

The Soviet era had a huge sociological impact on the people of Kazakhstan. Key events included the policy of 'denomadisation', accompanied by the introduction of collectivised agriculture. There was also large-scale industrialisation and a massive influx of other ethnic groups, both voluntary immigrants (mainly Slavs) and deported 'punished peoples' (Germans, Koreans, Chechens and others). This accentuated the republic's multi-ethnic nature. Such developments reduced the Kazakh population to the status of a minority within their own territorial unit and suppressed any religious or national identity.

It also tied the Kazakh economy closely to that of Russia. Yet the Soviet era also brought some positive benefits – many of them crucial for the modern establishment of a modern state. These included a rapid rise in literacy, industrial productivity and urbanisation, as well as the development of a political bureaucracy and state institutions. Kazakhstan also became a regional and nuclear power, with a considerable number of nuclear warheads on its territory and the major Soviet space-launch centre at Baikonur. Thus, when the Soviet Union collapsed in December 1991, Kazakhstan was well able to take its place in the international community.

Kazakhstan's hydrocarbon reserves in perspective

Kazakhstan is the second largest oil producer among former Soviet republics (after Russia), by 2002 producing almost 1 million barrels per day (b/d). It has significant petroleum reserves, with proven oil reserve estimates ranging from 9 billion to 17.6 billion barrels.[1] In addition, it is believed by many that Kazakhstan's possible hydrocarbon reserves, both onshore and offshore, could dwarf its proven reserves – with optimistic estimates falling between 30 billion and 50 billion barrels. Most of this is projected to come from the Kazakh sector of the Caspian Sea.

In the first decade of independence, Kazakhstan received approximately US$13 billion in foreign investment in its oil and gas industries – more than any other former Soviet country. This level of investment enabled a production rise from 530,000 b/d in 1992 to 939,000 b/d in 2002. Output has been increasing by almost 15 per cent a year since 1998. If all the fields which are planned are brought online, it is anticipated that oil production could reach 1.2 million b/d by 2005, 2 million b/d by 2010, and as much as 2.5 million b/d by 2015 (i.e. the same level as the UK in 2001).

A large proportion of Kazakh current production comes from two fields – Tengiz and Karachaganak. The Tengiz development is led by Chevron-Texaco, which signed a US$20 billion agreement in 1993 and has since increased production ten-fold. The US$8 billion Karachaganak project is conducted by the Karachaganak Petroleum Operating partnership, led by the British Gas (BG) Group and Agip/Eni of Italy; it is focused on condensate production. In addition, the offshore Kashagan block is being operated by Eni, as part of another international consortium. This project, with estimated possible oil reserves of up to 40 billion barrels, is seen as an indicator of the whole Caspian region's oil supply potential.

Kazakhstan also has proven reserves of 65 trillion cubic feet of natural gas, with over 40 per cent of this situated in the giant Karachaganak field, an extension of Russia's Orenburg field. Other significant gas producing areas include the Tengiz, Zhanazhol and Uritau fields. In addition, rising associated gas production at the Tengiz field will result in Tengiz becoming the second largest producing field for natural gas in Kazakhstan. The gas development has definitely come second to oil, however, partly caused by a poor pipeline infrastructure, and partly because the reserves are generally far from markets and population centres. As a result, a lot of gas (35 per cent of consumption) is actually imported from Uzbekistan, though in 1999 the government passed a law requiring companies to include gas utilisation projects in their development plans.

Buoyed by increasing oil exports, the country has experienced impressive economic growth – from 2.7 per cent in 1999, the real gross domestic product rose by 9.8 per cent in 2000 and by 13.2 per cent in 2001 – easily the best result since independence.[2] According to Minister of Economy and Trade Zhaksibek Kulekeyev, the oil industry accounted for approximately 30 per cent of the government's budget revenue, and half the country's exports. However, in March 2002 the government approved a three-year plan that aimed at a more modest annual GDP growth of 5–7 per cent. Under present conditions this goal seems well within reach.

Despite the extreme optimism shown by some politicians, it is important to look beyond projections at the current reality of Kazakhstan's oil production, and to put the figures in perspective. Production today is barely 1 per cent of global production (with exports even less than this).[3] And, despite being granted observer status by OPEC in 2001, this figure puts it on a par with relatively minor players in the oil-exporting club such as Syria and Brazil. Thus, the entire Caspian basin's proven reserves today make it comparable to the North Sea, and several orders of magnitude smaller than the Middle East.

Despite attempts to compare Caspian oil and gas reserves with those of the Middle East, they differ in one crucial aspect, aside from debates over quantity and quality, and that is the cost of production. This important fact is often missed – the cost of producing and delivering a barrel of Caspian oil is expected to be around US$12 per barrel on average (with half of this going on transportation costs), again comparable to the North Sea and significantly more expensive than in the Middle East, where the costs can be as low as US$2 per barrel. As such, the oil business in the Caspian becomes considerably less lucrative in a low oil price scenario. In addition, a lot of the production is expected to be 'sour' – with a high sulphur content. This further reduces its value in international oil markets.

There is also the issue of the environmental impact, where some major challenges remain to be addressed. The Caspian Sea is after all an important natural resource for all concerned, as well as being the location for the world's caviar industry. There is the issue of passage through the Bosporus, which is a very tight water channel with already a lot of traffic, and over 30 million people living on its 30-km coastline. Any oil spill or other environmental damage could have disastrous effects and severely impede future hydrocarbon development in the region.

The challenges ahead

In addition to the issues outlined above, there are several key hurdles, some unique to the region, which need to be overcome. One of the challenges facing Kazakhstan's oil development is that of export routes to the markets.

The region itself is completely landlocked and at least 1,000 km to an open sea in any direction. The pipelines in the Caspian Sea region that were completed prior to 1997 were designed to link the Soviet Union internally, and were routed through Russia. Most of the existing Russian oil export pipelines terminate at the Russian Black Sea port of Novorossiysk, requiring tankers to transit the crowded and ecologically and politically sensitive Bosporus in order to gain access to the Mediterranean and Western markets (see Map 4). There is also considerable debate as to whether this is the best market, with the higher forecasted growth of the East Asian market suggesting a potentially more attractive alternative.

Up until 2001, most Kazakh oil was exported through Russia, via the Atyrau–Samara pipeline which, after upgrading, had a crude capacity of 310,000 barrels per day. Additional supplies were sent by rail or by barge across the Caspian. A key development in increasing Kazakhstan's oil exporting potential was the launch of the Caspian Pipeline Consortium (CPC) project. Construction began in 1999. The first oil through this pipeline was scheduled for the middle of 2001, but customs issues and technical difficulties led to delays. After Russia agreed on transit tariffs, the pipeline was officially opened on 27 November 2001 and by mid-2002 was fully operational. This allows Kazakhstan to pipe oil directly from the Tengiz field to Novorossiysk on the Russian Black Sea coast. The current capacity is 565,000 b/d; when the second phase is completed (scheduled for 2015), this will be increased to 1.34 million b/d.

Russia is still the main focus for Kazakh oil exports. This was reaffirmed in June 2002, when a bilateral 15-year oil transit agreement was signed under which Kazakhstan would export at least 350,000 b/d of oil annually via the Russian pipeline network.[4] Meanwhile, in the South Caspian Sea, construction of the Baku–Tbilisi–Ceyhan pipeline was inaugurated in September 2002. President Nazarbaev expressed general support for this project on several occasions, but procrastinated over making a formal commitment to use the pipeline. However, in March 2003, Azerbaijan and Kazakhstan were said to have reached 'an unexpected degree of consensus' on extending this pipeline under the Caspian to the Kazakh port of Aktau; it was expected that formal agreements would be concluded by the end of the year.[5]

Meanwhile, Kazakhstan was also increasing oil swaps with Iran. These had been inaugurated in 1996, when the two countries signed an agreement under which Kazakhstan was to deliver 15 million barrels of crude to northern Iran, while Tehran would credit Kazakhstan with a corresponding share of Iranian oil on the world market. The deal was suspended the following year because Iran's refineries refused to accept Kazakh oil owing to the high sulphur content. However, Iran subsequently upgraded its refineries and the swaps agreement was reinstated in 2002. By early 2003 Iran was importing about 50,000 b/d from Kazakhstan. The upgraded pipeline linking the port of Neka on the Caspian to the Rey and Tabriz refineries was completed in September 2003, giving a capacity of 120,000 b/d; a further upgrade, scheduled for 2004, will raise capacity to 200,000 b/d. A second, larger pipeline from Neka to the northern refineries is also due for completion. Moreover, Iran, Kazakhstan and Turkmenistan were examining the feasibility of constructing a pipeline to run from western Kazakhstan via Turkmenistan to Tehran, and thence to the Persian Gulf; the engineering study of the route had already been carried out by TotalFinaElf.[6] Prospects for Kazakh–Iranian oil swaps were further boosted by the announcement that, from late 2003, the Canadian company PetroKazakhstan,[7] which operates the Kumkol field in southern Kazakhstan, was to start sending around 1 million tonnes of crude per year by rail through Uzbekistan and Turkmenistan to the Tehran refinery. Iran would supply the company with an equal amount of crude at Kharg Island in the Persian Gulf. A quality bank was established to compensate PetroKazakhstan for the difference in the quality of crudes.[8]

On the natural gas side, the picture was more problematic. Gas cannot be stored or transported easily, except by pipeline, and Kazakhstan's gas fields, unlike the oil, are not connected to the Russian pipeline network. The problem of exporting the gas is not helped by the fact that Kazakhstan's neighbours – Russia, Uzbekistan and Iran – have some of the largest gas reserves in the world – and are all chasing the same limited local markets. Also, finding markets for its gas will be vital for Kazakhstan's development of some of its oilfields – most notably Kashagan, Karachaganak and Tengiz – since much of its gas is 'associated', meaning that the oil cannot be produced in isolation. In response to this, in August 2001 the ministry of energy and mineral resources approved a 15-year strategy for developing the gas sector and increasing production to 1.2 trillion cubic feet per year by 2005.

Another serious challenge facing Kazakhstan's development of its hydrocarbon reserves is a legal one; it concerns the ownership and developmental rights in the Caspian Sea itself. This question is discussed elsewhere in this volume (see **Gizzatov**, **Granmayeh**), hence here only the main developments relating to Kazakhstan will be noted. Initially, Kazakhstan, like Turkmenistan and Azerbaijan – the three nations with oil reserves near their coastlines – wanted the Caspian Sea to be divided into national sectors, while Iran and Russia (arguably the more influential grouping), with little or no identified oil or gas near their coasts, wanted the sea's resources to be shared by all five nations. In 1997, Kazakhstan and Azerbaijan agreed to adhere to the borders of the sectors along the median line until a comprehensive convention on the legal status of the Caspian was signed. In the same year, Kazakhstan signed a communiqué with Turkmenistan pledging to divide their sections of the Caspian along median lines, based upon Soviet-era divisions, and again pending a final treaty. In June 2003 the two countries seemed close to signing an agreement on this issue.[9] The most significant treaty, however, was the one signed between Kazakhstan and Russia in July of 1998 which agreed to divide only the seabed along median lines between the two countries, leaving the waters (including shipping, fishing and the environment) to be shared under joint ownership. The major breakthrough in this accord was once again the agreement to jointly develop oil or gas deposits along the median line.

The fragility of the situation in the absence of a full agreement on the legal regime for the Caspian Sea was made clear in July of 2001 when an Iranian gunship forced a BP exploration vessel out of waters claimed by Iran but licensed to BP by Azerbaijan (itself a party to bilateral treaties with Russia and Kazakhstan). This event heightened tensions in the region and highlighted the need for an overall agreement addressing all the issues (see **Katik**). In April 2002, at the Ashgabat summit on the Caspian, the heads of state of the five littoral countries failed to produce such an agreement. However, a session of the Special Working Group on the Caspian, attended by deputy foreign ministers and senior officials of the littoral states, met in Baku in February 2003 and on this occasion the results were more promising. A draft convention on the proposed legal regime of the Caspian was discussed. Although it was evident that several points of disagreement remained, nevertheless some common positions were identified. It was generally accepted that the document could serve as a basis on which to move towards a more comprehensive settlement.[10] Further multilateral and bilateral meetings during 2003 and 2004 slowly moved the process forward.

The oil curse: socio-political consequences

In 1997, in his vision for Kazakhstan to the year 2030, President Nazarbaev wrote: 'I am convinced that by 2030 Kazakhstan will become a Central Asian snow leopard and will serve as an example to other developing states.'[11] The country's energy wealth was seen as the cure to all its ills, with petro-dollars viewed as a vital means of achieving higher and higher levels of growth and prosperity. As a result, the country's political leaders continuously encouraged popular expectations of imminent wealth. There was no hint of the obstacles that Kazakhstan would have to overcome in order to achieve the much publicised oil and gas production and revenue targets, especially in a world of declining oil prices. Moreover, whereas headline economic figures certainly indicated a positive trend, there were several negative consequences that became apparent. These are common to other new 'petro-states'; they include corruption – bribe taking, misappropriation of public funds, nepotism, abuse of power – at every level of society, a tendency to overspend and borrow, neglect of other sectors of the economy, and the failure to develop a reliable tax system. Kazakhstan's approach towards its energy sector is aimed at promoting political acquiescence and providing social and economic relief in the short term, yet it is actually increasing the likelihood for political instability and socio-economic decay over the long term.[12]

At first glance, all seems well with Kazakhstan's pace of development. Double digit economic growth in recent years, combined with a sharp reduction of inflation, a budget surplus, a stable currency, falling unemployment and a relatively small population, all bode well for the future. In addition,

Kazakhstan's official policy of rapid privatisation in the energy sector has led to an unprecedented level of foreign investment – higher than experienced by any other former Soviet country.

This policy of privatisation helped Kazakhstan secure aid from the US Agency for International Development and the European Union's TACIS programme, as well as keeping it in the good books of the key international lending institutions – the World Bank, the IMF and the European Bank of Reconstruction and Development (EBRD). To some extent, however, the rate of the privatisation surprised many sections of the international community who had been in favour of the policy. It was driven more by the government's pressing need for revenues after the Soviet collapse and the drying up of funds from Moscow, rather than any long-term macroeconomic strategy. Though it has to some extent been successful and led to significant short-term gains, these masked many short-term socio-political costs, and even long-term economic costs.

The fervent optimism regarding oil and gas potential shown by government officials and international energy corporations has had several negative social, political and even economic effects. Many of these are similar to those observed in other petro-states – both in the Caspian region and elsewhere in the world. Firstly, it has promoted a strong tendency towards excessive borrowing, and indeed overspending. By 1997, Kazakhstan was already the third largest borrower among the former Soviet Republics (after Russia and Ukraine), having accepted 13 loans from the World Bank since independence, totalling almost US$1 billion.[13] It did subsequently reduce its debt exposure and in the second half of the 1990s pursued economic policies that were generally regarded by international financial institutions as sound. The rate of inflation fell steadily and there was a gradual appreciation of the *tenge* (national currency) against the US dollar. Full current account convertibility was introduced in July 1996. The population at large, however, saw little improvement in their standard of living. The government frequently pre-assigned large amounts of petro-dollars to discretionary expenditures, such as the shifting of the capital from Almaty to Astana. Yet at the same time, funding for social programmes was being slashed. Health and education services were particularly badly affected. In 2002 state expenditure in these sectors stood at 5.3 per cent of GDP (EBRD 2003, p. 158). This in turn gave impetus to social discontent. As noted elsewhere, 'the failure of oil and gas revenues to benefit the vast majority of the population has already contributed to growing popular discontent about the state of Kazakhstan's economy, and consequently to the erosion of support for market reform'.[14]

A second and perhaps more serious problem, and one prevalent in many oil-rich countries, was the neglect of other important sectors of the economy – most notably manufacturing and agriculture. The focus in the first post-Soviet decade was very definitely on the oil sector. According to an IMF report published in 1998, from 1990 to 1995, the oil industry accounted for 40 per cent of all investment, and the energy sector overall (which includes power generation and coal) 60 per cent. The same report noted that 'capital investments in the national economy have shrunk by 89 per cent compared to 1991, nine out of ten industrial enterprises have stopped work, and livestock numbers are half what they used to be in 1991'.[15] This led to high levels of structural unemployment in the industrial sectors of the economy – and the virtual collapse of the food, petrochemical, machine-building and other sectors that had traditionally been strong during the Soviet era. By the end of the decade, this trend was leading to the unexpected phenomenon of mass-migration of skilled workers in search of jobs. In addition, the strong culture of labour unions that was a leftover from the Soviet era led to a growing number of organised strikes and demonstration activity.

Another result of this overdependence on the oil industry was the failure by the government to develop and enforce a reliable system of tax collection. Despite the creation of a state revenues ministry in October 1997, responsible for fiscal policy and tax regulation, tax revenues as a percentage of GDP continued their decline. The absence of a reliable tax system has wider implications than a decreased public revenue stream. Taxation is viewed by many as a vital building block towards a democratic system – essential for the developing of a direct and reciprocal relationship between government and governed, and the creating of accountability. This may in fact be why it has received insufficient attention by the government – by courting and relying upon foreign investment rather than domestic revenues, Kazakhstan's leaders could afford to centralise power and control in a shift towards further autocracy.

Kazakhstan's energy sector development policy was focused on attracting maximum foreign investment in the shortest time possible (an objective expressed clearly by former Prime Minister Akezhan Kazhegeldin back in 1996). As a result, the state sold off the bulk of its shares in the oil and gas enterprises to foreign oil companies between July 1996 and July 1997, raising almost US$15 billion. Many industry analysts, however, believed that several of the assets were severely undervalued, due to the inefficient process produced by the speed of the sales. In addition, the pace of reform and massive inflow of investment in such a short space of time led to some unsavoury consequences.

Whereas it is common for multinational oil companies investing in new countries to make socially responsible additional investments in infrastructure and education, in Kazakhstan whole areas of government responsibility were delegated to the foreign investors. As a consequence, foreign companies were often blamed for poor performance in certain sectors and worker dissatisfaction, whereas the causes of discontent in fact preceded the investment. This policy was pursued by the government with the two-fold aim of relieving itself of its fiscal burdens and winning local public support for its reforms. Apart from alienating the investor, this approach has had the additional dangerous consequence of weakening government institution building, and in the long run weakening the state itself.

Another major effect was the increased levels of corruption at all levels of officialdom and a growing distrust of government officials by the populace. Kick-backs and side payments to officials for lubricating the deal-making process were widespread, and flourished at the highest levels in government.[16] Once again, this had the dual effect of alienating both the foreign investor (with many pulling out of Kazakhstan by the end of the decade), as well as members of the public, who saw widening income disparities. In some senses, they had less economic freedom, and certainly less social protection, than in Soviet times.

In 2001, US Secretary of Commerce Donald Evans commissioned a report about Kazakhstan after the expatriate business community in the country demanded that it be given official status as a market economy. The report concluded that it did not qualify for several reasons, especially the high levels of corruption, the grip of the president and his family on all areas of business, and the lack of appropriate investment legislation to impose price controls or tariffs. The report went on to add:

> The same problems that deprive Kazakh citizens of any meaningful protection of their human rights – authoritarian government with no separation of powers, political control of the judiciary, total lack of accountability for state agencies – also leave foreign investors without any means of enforcing contracts or protecting themselves from arbitrary confiscation.[17]

The vast scale of this corruption led to competition and inefficiency between government officials and departments (particularly between those who worked within the popular oil and gas sector and those who worked outside it), further alienating them from the people they purported to serve. This system of centralisation and concentration of power in the hands of a small elite was acquiring, within the system, a permanency that further dampened aspirations for the establishment of democracy.[18]

In addition, there was growing exacerbation of regional socio-economic differences, with striking differences in poverty rates. Thus, in the south of the country the poverty rate was estimated to stand at 69 per cent (twice the national average) and in the north, only 9 per cent. Overall at least half of the population was believed to be subsisting below the poverty line, with a small political clique getting richer and richer. This had negative implications for future political and social stability in the country. All of this has highlighted the inescapable causal links between oil resources, foreign interest and domestic political stability.

Political stability and nation building

Independence for Kazakhstan came unexpectedly with the collapse of the Soviet Union in 1991. It is questionable whether it was even desired. Despite occasional outbursts of nationalist sentiment (such as in 1986, when the long-standing Kazakh First Secretary of the Communist Party was replaced by an ethnic Russian) there had never been any serious movements for independence.

In many ways the political stability of Kazakhstan – a republic whose boundaries were never intended as those of an independent state – was dependent upon its being part of the larger multinational state. Thus, not surprisingly, President Nazarbaev remained a staunch supporter of some form of revamped Soviet Union even after the failed Moscow coup in 1991 to replace Mikhail Gorbachev. It is noteworthy that Kazakhstan was the last of the former Soviet republics to declare independence – on 16 December 1991. By this time the three Slav republics – Belarus, Russia and Ukraine – had already announced their withdrawal from the Union, thereby in effect destroying it.

This reluctance to seek independence can be partially explained by Kazakhstan's demography. Kazakhstan was the only republic of the USSR in which the people for whom the nation was named, i.e. the Kazakhs, were a numerical minority.[19] This demographic imbalance, combined with Kazakhstan's strong economic ties to Russia, made it difficult for the new state to consolidate its independence. It was mainly for this reason that, within a week of Kazakhstan's declaration of independence, President Nazarbaev spearheaded the formation of the Commonwealth of Independent States (CIS), which was established in Alma-Ata (Almaty) on 21 December 1991.

The transition to independence was conspicuously devoid of violence or great social upheaval, unlike the experience of many of the other former Soviet republics. The functions of the state continued to be performed as previously, under the same leadership. Over time, however, the promotion of a national elite became a priority and this created tensions between Kazakhs and non-Kazakhs, particularly the Russian-speaking population. Despite concessions to the latter (for example, in the 1995 Constitution, Russian was included as an 'official' language and the expression 'Kazakh nation' was replaced by 'the people of Kazakhstan'), ethnicity increasingly became a focal issue in the domestic politics of the country. A covert policy of 'Kazakhisation' was introduced in both the private and public sectors.

Concurrently, the political elite became the economic elite – a narrow group that was growing ever more distant from the general population. This phenomenon had its roots in the first years of independence, when Soviet-era administrators and political authorities enjoyed enormous economic advantages because of the opportunities for 'spontaneous privatisation' (in effect, theft of public wealth). This group revolved around the president. Relatives and close associates became increasingly prominent in the political and economic shaping of the nation. They acquired extensive business interests, amounting to virtual monopolies in major commodities, including oil. Moreover, the 'family' gained control of almost all the newspapers and television channels, thereby effectively stifling any public criticism of the regime. Such behaviour was justified by reference to 'Asian values', and claims that the Kazakhs were not disposed by history or culture to be democratic and that popular rule could empower nationalist demagogues, secessionists, communists or Islamic radicals, and put the future of the nation, not to mention economic reform (and by implication oil and gas supplies), at risk. Ironically, it was the tacit approval of the democratic countries of the West, motivated by economic objectives in Kazakhstan's energy sector that enabled this system to flourish and to stifle the development of democratic institutions.

International relations and the new 'Great Game'

In addition to its significant potential energy reserves, Kazakhstan is of interest to regional and world powers because of its geographical location. The country shares long borders with Russia and China, and borders three of the other Central Asian republics, as well as having a long coast on the Caspian. It finds itself at the 'heart' of Eurasia, as well as at the heart of many of the key issues that have confronted the international community in the last decade – nuclear disarmament, Islamism, nation building, energy supplies and immigration. This has often led to talk of a new 'Great Game' in the region – with the world powers once again vying for control of this strategically important area.

An analogy is frequently made between the scramble for energy riches in the Caspian region in the present day, and the imperial rivalry in the nineteenth century between Russia, coming from the north-west as part of the expansion of the Tsarist empire, and Great Britain. The parallels are indeed striking. It is the same geographical region that is being fought over, and in both cases high stakes have been involved – in the nineteenth century it was the territory and security of the two mighty empires, while today it is the flow of vital energy supplies to the world. Yet there are also key differences.

The first 'Great Game' was played largely by individuals on both sides – often soldiers or diplomats. Today powerful lobbies and vast organisations in both the private and public sectors are at work – with business executives taking just as much of a role as politicians. Also, the nineteenth-century rivalry was between two clearly defined powers, balanced in some senses, and both physically present in the region. Today, many more countries are involved – Russia, China, Turkey, Iran, the US and the other Central Asian Republics to name a few. In addition, as is common to a 'globalising' world, there are many non-state actors with both a stake and a say, such as multinational corporations, non-governmental organisations (NGOs), intergovernmental organisations and lending organisations. These factors have created a complex challenge for Kazakhstan. It has attempted to address this situation by adopting a balanced approach in its foreign policy, underpinned by the overall objective of 'integration' at the regional and international level, economically and militarily.

Russia

The historical, geographical and economic ties to what is now the Russian Federation will no doubt continue to make this relationship the key one in Kazakhstan's foreign policy. Kazakhstan's large ethnic Russian population is a factor that potentially calls into question the viability and stability of the Kazakh state. Also, Kazakhstan's industry and oil pipelines, even after a decade of independence, remain highly dependent on Russia. At the same time as maintaining close ties to its former coloniser, Kazakhstan's identity as an independent state must to some extent rest upon its ability to delink itself from Russian influence.

Part of the complexity of developing a consistent policy towards Russia arises from the fact that Russia itself has been anything but consistent in its policy towards Kazakhstan. In the early days after the break-up of the Soviet Union, Russia attempted to cut the umbilical cord with the other Soviet republics and concentrate on a Western-orientated path to national economic development. This was despite attempts by Kazakhstan (and other former Soviet republics) to keep some form of security and economic arrangements in place. Since then, however, there have been several fluctuations in Russian policy, though the overall trend has been towards more of a focus on the former Soviet states, realism and consolidating Russia's status as a political and military power, while at the same time developing solid working relationships within the CIS. Within the Caspian region, Russia has often revealed conflicting objectives and interests. On the one hand, it is a competitor for energy supplies; on the other hand, it sees potential gain from co-operation on export routes.

Kazakhstan's response has, in contrast, been fairly consistent, with President Nazarbaev recognising the importance of Russia in Kazakhstan's development. An important stage in the development of the Russo-Kazakh relationship was the formation of a customs alliance between Russia, Belarus and Kazakhstan in January of 1995, and the subsequent protocol in August of the same year, which declared the possibility of opening the frontier between Russia and Kazakhstan. Following the example of Belarus, Kazakhstan adjusted its foreign economic and customs legislation to that of Russia.

United States

The balance of power in the bipolar era of the Cold War came to an abrupt end after the collapse of the Soviet Union, leaving the United States as the dominant global power – politically, economically and militarily. The objectives of the US in Central Asia have been fairly consistent through this period – political stability, nuclear non-proliferation, the containment of Islamic fundamentalism, access to reasonably priced oil, promotion of democracy, and protection of key allies while isolating its enemies. Yet there is an inherent incompatibility in many of these policies. For example, in the short run, political stability and the securing of oil supplies is probably best achieved by supporting the political status quo. However, as discussed above, this stifles democratic progress. Worse, it could eventually encourage Islamic fundamentalism as a political opposition movement, and possibly lead to political instability. Likewise, isolating its enemies in the region (notably the sanctions against Iran) to some extent hampers the development of feasible export routes for oil supplies.

Until late 2001 the US had no military presence in the region. It pursued its policies through diplomatic and commercial channels, placing economic interests and good relations with Russia as its priorities. The attacks of 11 September altered the strategic landscape significantly. The US now maintains a sizeable military presence in Afghanistan, Uzbekistan and Kyrgyzstan. It will not allow anything to stand in the way of the eradication of any perceived threat to its national security. At the time of writing, the long-term direction of the declared 'War on Terror' remains unclear. Suffice it to say that there is likely to be a much stronger and more direct US involvement in the region in years to come.

Kazakhstan's approach to the US has been to play to US interests in order to maximise its own economic return, while creating a balancing factor against Russian dominance in the region. A good example of this was the early issue of nuclear weapons. After independence, Kazakhstan found itself with hundreds of Soviet nuclear missiles. Despite relief when Kazakhstan ratified the Nuclear Non-proliferation Treaty, Russia was envious of the US–Kazakh agreement on the dismantling of warheads, signed on 13 December 1993. Washington offered to compensate Almaty financially, and buy the remaining uranium. This put paid to any notion Russia might have had of coming to an understanding with Kazakhstan on dismantling the warheads on its own.

China

Since the break-up of the Soviet Union in 1991, China has become an important counterweight to Russia. Calling for a new interregional 'Silk Route', particularly in the area of energy supplies, China began constructing such a link with roads and railways; pipelines are also planned. Chinese interests in the region are focused upon two issues: the security of oil and gas supplies for its rapidly growing economy, and the suppression of secessionist movements by its own ethnic minorities, especially the Uighurs of the western province of Xinjiang. Kazakhstan is probably the most important focus for China in Central Asia, due to their long common border, its potential for energy supplies, and the close ethnic and economic ties it has with the Uighurs of Xinjiang.

In June and July 1997, the Chinese National Petroleum Company invested billions of dollars in Kazakh oil ventures, including 30 per cent over estimated value for the Uzen oilfields. This was in addition to an initial pledge of US$12.5 billion for the laying of four oil and gas pipelines (total length 13,500 km) from Central Asia and Russia to China (though some of these investments were later scaled back due to a lack of international investment). In March 2003, CNOOC and the Sinopec Group, two of China's largest oil companies, were each set to acquire half of BG's one-sixteenth share in the North Caspian Sea PSA. This project, which contains not only the massive Kashagan field, but also several other important exploration prospects, was expected to make a significant contribution to covering

China's energy needs in the future. However, in May 2003, the deals were unexpectedly blocked by the other partners in the consortium.

China's interest in enhancing its energy security is also leading to increased trade with Central Asia (partly to compensate for the import of energy), highlighted by trade levels between Xinjiang and the Central Asian republics; in 1998, this reached almost US$1 billion, while the number of Chinese–Kazakh joint ventures exceeded 200. From 1990 to 1992, Kazakhstan's imports from China rose from 4 per cent to over 44 per cent. By 1995, China was Kazakhstan's fifth largest trading partner (though about half of this trade was on a barter basis) and by 1999, it was in fourth position after Russia, the US and the UK.[20]

Cross-border interethnic relations also continue to have tremendous consequences on international relations in the region. Muslims, mostly Uighurs, comprise nearly 60 per cent of Xinjiang province's population, and are the last Muslims under communist rule. Being Turkic, they share more of a cultural, religious and linguistic heritage with their Central Asian neighbours than with the Han Chinese. Moreover, there have long been calls for Uighur independence, sometimes encouraged by Russia (and, before that, the Soviet Union). China's suppression of the Uighur separatists has been given new impetus since 11 September 2001 by the US 'War on Terror', with China using this as a pretext for declaring war on its own 'Islamic fundamentalists' (much as Russia has done with Chechnya). This highlights the complex and interdependent web of relations and influences in the new 'Great Game'.

Regional neighbours

In addition to Kazakhstan's role and relevance in the great power politics of today, it also has a strong interdependence with its neighbours in Central Asia, as well as with Turkey, Iran and the rest of the Middle East. These relationships have often been viewed through the sometimes misleading lenses of 'pan-Turkism' and 'pan-Islamism'. Kazakhstan clearly shares a common heritage with the other Central Asian republics (Uzbekistan, Turkmenistan, Tajikistan and Kyrgyzstan), based on shared histories and cultural legacies. Several multilateral agreements of integration have been signed between these countries, including the Joint Declaration of the Central Asian States and Russia (resulting in the Treaty on Collective Security), and the Treaty on Unified Economic Environment.

Turkey has clear economic interests in oil and gas supplies from Central Asia, and particularly the choice of export routes. There are also religious, cultural and educational interests. These must not, however, be overstated: the Ottoman Empire never extended to Central Asia, and pan-Turkism has never really materialised as the unifying factor some expected it to be, although Turkey continues to try to assert its economic and strategic presence so as to play a role in the area of energy development.

Iran is another country that has actively pursued ties and influence in the region. Several bilateral economic initiatives have been agreed between

Kazakhstan and Iran. These, however, are more related to common economic issues such as energy exports and the Caspian developments, rather than any sense of 'pan-Islamism' as is sometimes suggested. (Islam, though the religion of ethnic Kazakhs, is not a strong political or cultural influence in Kazakhstan; moreover, the Kazakhs are Sunni Muslims, not Shia Muslims like the Iranians.)

Elsewhere in the Middle East, the Gulf states and Saudi Arabia have pursued significant private sector involvement and investment in Central Asia and in Kazakhstan. In addition Saudi Arabia has sought religious influence through the sponsoring of *madrassas* (religious schools) and mosques, though whether this trend will continue under the close scrutiny of a post-11 September world remains to be seen. Israel has also sought close ties and investment opportunities in Central Asia, and in Kazakhstan in particular. These have been pursued with the economic objective of creating new markets for its exports, and the political objective of countering any anti-Israeli influence from the Arab states or Iran.

The above developments indicate that a strong pattern is emerging, whereby Kazakhstan (like its fellow Central Asian republics) comes to be overly defined by its energy reserves and, to a lesser extent, by its geo-strategic position. Lying at the cross-roads between East and West, Kazakhstan finds itself torn in different directions by the competing and often incompatible interests of regional and world powers, with the overall effect being a strengthening of the political status quo and an exacerbation of its developmental problems.

Conclusions

At the time of writing, Kazakhstan is just over a decade old and still something of an international novelty. Forecasts and predictions about the country's future abound, and range from the very positive, emphasising the huge oil and gas potential and resultant economic growth, to the very negative, focusing on the multi-ethnic rivalries and the weak political system.

Depending on the criteria one adopts, the nation building process in Kazakhstan to date can either be considered a failure or a success. Despite all its problems, the country still exists, and does not appear likely to disintegrate in the near term. Kazakhstan does possess significant energy reserves which, if their development is well managed, could act as a catalyst for further economic growth, as well as strengthening regional and international ties. There are a number of technical challenges standing in the way of this development of oil and gas, key among them the costs of production and transportation, and the legal status of the Caspian Sea. As discussed above, there are also major negative consequences implied by over-optimistic expectations of oil wealth and overdependence on the resulting revenues. In the long run, these could threaten not only Kazakhstan's potential economic growth, but, in the worst case scenario, the viability and stability of the state itself.

The early trend towards democratic freedoms and an elected parliament in Kazakhstan has, as in other Central Asian states, been sidelined in favour of a system somewhere between autocracy and oligarchy, with President Nazarbaev and his family ruling undisputed through a mutually dependent and self-perpetuating political and economic elite. The lack of a viable political opposition has led to waste, corruption and ultimately widening economic disparities between segments of the population. A range of political and economic, national and non-state players in the new 'Great Game' epitomise the struggle for influence in Kazakhstan and the region as a whole, and the diplomatic tightrope that the country has had to manoeuvre in order to balance these sometimes opposing forces and conflicting interests. Yet the country has pursued a broad policy of integration initiatives – political, military and economic – at both the regional and international level.

The key lesson for Kazakhstan from this first post-Soviet decade is the inherent (though often ignored) interdependence between oil wealth, domestic political system and stability, and relations with the rest of the world. Current oil revenues and, more importantly, the expectation of even greater future revenues, can stifle democratic progress by creating and reinforcing a corrupt and autocratic regime – a phenomenon observed in many other oil-rich states, including several OPEC member countries. In addition, a preference for the perceived political stability of the status quo by Western powers eager for the advancement of their own economic and strategic interests reinforces the current situation and postpones a solution to the problem.

The situation is not beyond repair. Kazakhstan, and indeed other nations in a similar situation, should be encouraged to adopt a longer-term view to economic development. Before a viable and sustainable economy can be built, the rule of law and a system of enforceable property rights need to be established. Oil revenues should be used to enhance Kazakhstan's existing industrial and agricultural sectors, not merely to replace them. Also, some level of responsible macroeconomic planning needs to be undertaken to ensure an equitable distribution of revenues among the populace. The establishment of a National Oil Fund in January 2001, to guard against the shock of sudden falls in the oil price, and to husband the country's wealth for the benefit of future generations, was a positive development. By 2003, the Fund had accumulated US$3.7 billion (though there were widespread concerns about the probity of the management of these monies). On the political side, before a democratic system can be adopted, the institutions that must underpin the system, and which have been largely absent, must be developed. These include an independent judiciary, a free press, a professional and apolitical civil service, and some level of empowerment at a local government level. With better policies and the support of the international community, Kazakhstan could take its rightful place among world nations, as a role model for a newly independent state. Despite considerable challenges, with the foreign investment in its oil and gas potential, and a strategic location between Europe and Asia, there is no reason why this should not be the case.

Notes

1 Energy Information Administration (EIA), United States Department of Energy, *Country Profiles: Kazakhstan*, 2003, www.eia.doe.gov. *BP Statistical Review of World Energy*, June 2003, concurred with EIA's lower estimates. Note that EIA estimates made in July 2002 were significantly lower than either BP or EIA in 2003.

2 *Ibid.*

3 In 2001, Kazakhstan's oil production was 800,000 barrels per day, thus on a par with Qatar. By comparison Saudi Arabia produced 8.5 mb/d. Total global production was 75.8 mb/d (*World Energy Outlook 2002*, OECD/International Energy Agency, Paris, 2002, p. 97).

4 Energy Information Administration, United States Department of Energy, *Country Profiles: Kazakhstan*, 2002, www.eia.doe.gov.

5 'Aktau – BTC Governmental Agreements to be in Place this Year', *Energy Line*, 3 April 2003.

6 *Dow Jones Newswires*, 6 February 2003.

7 PetroKazakhstan, formerly known as Hurricane Hydrocarbons, began operating under the new name on 2 June 2003. For over five years the company has been active in Kazakhstan, engaged in the acquisition, exploration, development and production of oil and gas, refining of oil and the sale of oil and refined products (see www.petrokazakhstan.com).

8 World Markets Research Centre, *Daily Analysis*, 1 August 2003. However, as of mid-2004 no final agreement had been signed, though negotiations were continuing.

9 'Caspian States Closing in on Deal to Divide Sea', AFP, 27 June 2003. However, as of mid-2004 no final agreement had been signed, though negotiations were continuing.

10 H. Peimani, 'Baku Caspian Meeting Created Hopes but not Concrete Results', *Central Asia–Caucasus Analyst*, 12 March 2003.

11 N. A. Nazarbaev, 'Kazakhstan – 2030. Protsvetanie, bezopasnost' i uluchshenie blagsostoianiia vsekh kazakhstantsev', *Kazakhstanskaya pravda*, 11 October 1997, p. 15.

12 P. Luong, in R. Ebel and R. Menon (eds), *Energy and Conflict in Central Asia and the Caucasus*, Rowman & Littlefield, MD, 2000, p. 80.

13 'A Central Asian Corporate Culture', *Business Week*, 27 October 1997.

14 Luong, 2000, *op. cit.*

15 M. De Broeck and K. Kosital, 'Output Decline in Transition: The Case of Kazakhstan', *IMF Working Paper 69* (April 1998).

16 However, it should not be forgotten that corruption is a two-way process. When James Giffen, an American businessman and a long-time consultant to the Kazakh president, was arrested by the US authorities on 30 March 2003 and charged under the Foreign Corrupt Practices Act, the federal indictment implicated representatives of major foreign oil corporations. It was alleged that during 1995–2000 they used Giffen's investment bank Mercator as a conduit for channelling bribes of over $78 million to two senior Kazakh officials (presumed to be President Nazarbaev and Nurlan Balgimbayev, a former prime minister and head of the Kazakh State Oil Company). Charges were also filed against Bryan Williams, a former Mobil executive (C. Pala, 'Bribery Scandal Old Hat in Almaty', *Moscow Times*, 30 April 2003, via AMBO electronic news service; *Financial Times*, 26 June 2003).

17 *The Times*, London, 1 April 2002.

18 See S. N. Cummings, 'Kazakhstan: An Uneasy Relationship – Power and Authority in the Nazarbaev Regime', in S. N. Cummings (ed.), *Power and Change in Central Asia*, Routledge, London/New York, 2002, pp. 59–73.

19 In 1991 there were almost equal numbers of Russians and Kazakhs within its
    borders (about 40 per cent each), not to mention significant numbers of
    Ukrainians, Uzbeks, Germans, Koreans, Uighurs and others.
20 *EBRD Kazakhstan Investment Profile 2001*, EBRD, London, 2001, p. 12.

Selected bibliography

BP Statistical Review of World Energy, June 2003 (online).

Bertsch G. *et al.* (eds), *Crossroads and Conflict – Security and Foreign Policy in The Caucasus
and Central Asia*, Routledge Inc., New York, 2000.

Capisani, G. R., *The Handbook of Central Asia*, I. B. Tauris, London, 2000.

Chufrin, G., *Russia and Asia – the Emerging Security Agenda*, Oxford University Press,
New York, 1999.

Cummings, S. N., *Kazakhstan – Centre–Periphery Relations*, Royal Institute of International Affairs, London, 2000.

Dawisha, K. and Parrott, B. (eds), *Russia and the New States of Eurasia – the Politics of
Upheaval*, Cambridge University Press, Cambridge, 1994.

Dawisha, K. and Parrott, B. (eds), *Conflict, Cleavage and Change in Central Asia and the
Caucasus*, Cambridge University Press, Cambridge, 1997.

Ebel, R. and Menon, R. (eds), *Energy and Conflict in Central Asia and the Caucasus*,
Rowman & Littlefield, MD, 2000.

European Bank of Reconstruction and Development (EBRD), *Transition Report 2003:
Integration and Regional Co-operation*, EBRD, London, 2003.

Malik, H. (ed.), *Central Asia – Its Strategic Importance and Future Prospects*, St Martin's
Press, New York, 1994.

Mesbahi, M., *Central Asia and the Caucasus – Domestic and International Dynamics*,
University Press of Florida, Florida, 1994.

Mitchell, J. *et al.* (eds), *The New Economy of Oil – Impacts on Business*, Royal Institute
of International Affairs, London, 2001.

Olcott, M. Brill, *Kazakhstan – Unfulfilled Promise*, Carnegie Endowment for International Peace, Washington, DC, 2002.

Roy, O., *The New Central Asia – The Creation of Nations*, I. B. Tauris, London/NewYork,
2000.

Svanberg, I. (ed.), *Contemporary Kazakhs – Cultural and Social Perspectives*, Curzon Press,
London, 1999.

United States Energy Information Administration (EIA), Department of Energy,
Country Profiles: www.eia.doe.gov.

Vassiliev, A., *Central Asia – Political and Economic Challenges in the Post-Soviet Era*, Saqi
Books, London, 2001.

13 Jockeying for power in the Caspian basin: Turkey versus Iran and Russia

Suha Bolukbaşi

The region surrounding the Caspian Sea has experienced in the post-Soviet era what many call the recurrence of the so-called 'Great Game' of the eighteenth and nineteenth centuries, played out among the Tsarist, Ottoman and the Persian empires. This time around, observers suggest, there are a number of differences from the earlier Great Game: the United States is also involved as a major player, and the smaller regional actors try to play larger roles than before. In an effort to solidify their niche as viable independent states, the latter try to involve apparently more benevolent actors, such as the US, the multinational oil companies, and other extra-regional actors in regional politics.

Turkey considers itself one of the actors supportive of the independence of the smaller Caspian states, thus having a stake in their socio-economic viability. For its part, Ankara perceives its rivalry with Iran and Russia over the location of the routes of the Caspian oil and gas pipelines as a struggle between the forces of the good (i.e. Turkey) and the evil (i.e. Russia and Iran), trying to destroy the nascent new states.[1] The Turks are convinced that neither Russia's nor Iran's policy towards these states is conducive to furthering Turkey's national interests or the interests of the smaller Caspian states. Ankara believes that Russia is interested in recapturing its former privileged and dominant status in the region, whereas Iran is perceived as a country bent on preventing the regional countries from becoming hostile collaborators with the West and with Turkey.

Russia is also perceived as being unhappy about the involvement of extra-regional actors. Although various government agencies have different views on how to deal with the 'outsiders', a general tendency in Moscow has been to restrict the involvement of Turkey and the US in this part of Russia's 'near abroad'. Towards this end Russia has pursued various policies including the promotion of Russian pipelines as the only feasible means to export the region's oil resources, and disputing the legality of contracts the Caspian states signed with Western consortia.

In order to pre-empt a substantial Turkish and Western presence in the Caspian, Iran initially pursued a policy of currying favour with the Turkic Caspian states. Tehran offered various co-operation schemes to Kazakhstan, Turkmenistan and Azerbaijan jointly to extract and export their oil and gas resources. This policy meant that Tehran was prepared to risk deterioration in its relations with Moscow in order to achieve its goal of substantial influence in the region. Yet US opposition to most of the projects Iran had promoted eventually led Tehran to side increasingly with Moscow and to adopt a policy which in practice could be described as: 'the Caspian for the Caspians'. In the first decade after the collapse of the Soviet Union, the complex relationship between these three states was reflected in their respective positions on the legal status of the Caspian Sea, also in their initial rivalry over pipeline routes to carry Caspian oil and gas to export terminals.

The Caspian's hydrocarbon potential

Azerbaijan began to negotiate with Western oil companies to develop its offshore hydrocarbon resources as early as 1990, before the dissolution of the Soviet Union. In 1993, the State Oil Company of the Azerbaijan Republic (SOCAR) seemed on the point of signing a contract with an international consortium. In September 1993, however, the then president of Azerbaijan, the pro-Turkish Abulfaz Elchibey, was overthrown in a *coup d'état*. It is widely believed that his anti-Russian policies brought about his downfall. Heidar Aliev, who succeeded Elchibey, renegotiated the contract with the Azerbaijan International Operating Company (AIOC) and allocated the Russian oil company LUKoil (excluded from the original deal) a 10 per cent stake. The implication was that this would make Moscow more favourably disposed to the idea of Azerbaijan independently exploiting its Caspian Sea oil resources and marketing them.[2] On 20 September 1994, a consortium of Western oil companies, led by British Petroleum (BP), finally signed a US$8 billion Production Sharing Agreement with SOCAR. The contract, known as the 'Contract of the Century', provided for the development of the huge Azeri, Chirag and Guneshli (ACG) offshore oilfield in the Caspian Sea (see **Adams, Nassibli** and **Olsen**).

The Russian government's negative reaction to the Azerbaijani oil deal was not only influenced by uneasiness regarding the involvement of 'outsiders' in its geopolitical and economic backyard, but also by the belief that none of the Caspian states had a right individually to utilise the Caspian Sea's hydrocarbon resources, even if these resources were located close to their respective coast. Representatives of the Russian oil industry, by contrast, believed that the involvement of Western oil and gas consortia in the region was inevitable and might even be advantageous. The latter view prevailed and, consequently, Russian companies sought to acquire shares in several multinational projects in the Caspian basin (see **Antonenko**).

Iran initially pursued a policy that could best be characterised as ambiguous. Tehran had adopted a hostile stance towards Azerbaijan's pro-Turkish President Elchibey, but it was more accommodating towards his successor, Heidar Aliev. Interested in currying favour with Tehran, Aliev repeatedly stated that Baku intended to have mutually beneficial relations with Tehran, based on co-operation in the fields of oil production and marketing. True to his word, on 12 November 1994, Aliev tried to transfer 5 per cent of SOCAR's total 20 per cent stake in AIOC to Iran (which, like Russia, had been excluded from the original agreement).[3] However, faced with objections from the US administration, the AIOC blocked this move. Foreign Minister Ali Akbar Velayeti reacted harshly, stating that 'this would not be in the interest of Azerbaijan'. He also disputed the legality of the project, stressing that 'the agreement [with AIOC] is not valid until such time as the legal status of the region has been defined'.[4]

Recrimination and retaliation in Turco-Russian relations

Turkey played no part in the Caspian Sea legal status controversy, although technically it could be considered to be on the side of Azerbaijan because of the participation of TPAO (Turkish State Petroleum Company) in AIOC. There was, however, competition between the two countries over the routing of Azerbaijan's oil export pipelines. Moscow saw Turkey's assertiveness in this issue as a threat to its own interests.

There were also other causes of friction. Turkey resented Moscow's perceived tolerance of the activities of the Kurdish Workers' Party (PKK). This Marxist-Leninist movement aimed to establish an independent Kurdish state. Since 1984 it had been engaged in a violent guerrilla war against Turkey. It seems to have received at least tacit support from Moscow, since it was able to convene conferences in Russia.[5] Moscow, meanwhile, suspected Ankara of complicity in the Chechen revolt against Russian rule. The unhindered propaganda activities of the quasi-diplomatic Chechen representation in Istanbul often elicited angry Russian protests.[6] Moscow also criticised Turkey for not taking adequate steps to prevent the activities of Chechen émigré groups who recruited volunteers on Turkish soil and sent logistical supplies to the Caucasus through Azerbaijan or Georgia.[7]

Ankara's suspicions of Moscow's motives had been strengthened when Russian troops returned to Georgia and Armenia under various guises. Thus, for example, a predominantly Russian CIS (Commonwealth of Independent States) force was stationed in South Ossetia as part of the cease-fire agreement in June 1992. In June 1994, an additional 1,500–2,000 Russian troops were stationed in Abkhazia when the UN, the OSCE (Organisation for Security and Co-operation in Europe) and Russia managed to impose a cease-fire agreement. In February 1993 Armenia recognised the presence of Russian troops on its territory as legitimate and entrusted them with the defence of its borders, including the border with Turkey.[8] In June 1994 Armenia signed an agreement that formally recognised the Russian military bases at Yerevan and Gyumri;[9] the following year it was agreed that these bases were to be leased to Russia for a period of 25 years.[10]

Early oil eludes Ceyhan

Turkey hoped to become the main transit route for hydrocarbons from the Caspian region. The first issue to be decided was the route for the export of early oil from the ACG field. There were already two Soviet-era pipelines in place that could be used for this purpose. One followed a southern route via Georgia; the other, slightly longer, followed a northern route via Russia. Neither pipeline presented a real advantage over the other. However, Moscow may have counted on its increasingly high-profile role as one of the three co-chairs of the OSCE Minsk Group mediating the Karabagh dispute in order to win approval for the northern Baku–Novorossiysk route.[11] Yet, as Ilham Aliev, vice-president of SOCAR, pointed out, 'the question of selecting an oil transportation route was a political and not an economic decision for Azerbaijan'.[12] In the end, in October 1995, a compromise solution was reached: both routes were selected – the southern route via Georgia and the northern route via Russia.[13] Just prior to the announcement of this decision, President Clinton had held a 25-minute telephone conversation with President Aliev to assure him that the US believed that the two-pipeline option was best for Azerbaijan.[14] By 2001, on average, 50,000 barrels per day (b/d) were being exported through the northern route, and 115,000 b/d through the southern route. However, Russia continued to hinder the export of ACG oil across its territory. Moreover, it was accused of mixing low-grade Siberian crude with higher quality Azerbaijani oil, which reduced the price of the latter. AIOC decided to increase the capacity of the southern Supsa pipeline in order to lessen dependency on the northern route and also to meet the expanding export needs of the Chirag field. In 2002, after this upgrade, the southern route had a capacity of 145,000 b/d.[15] Further upgrades gave it a capacity of some 250,000 b/d by 2004 (see Map 4).

AIOC opts for the Baku–Tbilisi–Ceyhan route

The major prize, however, was the Main Export Pipeline (MEP). Ankara was eager to ensure that it would run across Turkish territory, from Baku to Ceyhan, as this would have economic as well as political advantages (see Map 7). There were also environmental considerations. There was genuine apprehension that, if the Russian option from Baku to Novorossiysk were chosen, it would increase heavy oil tanker traffic through the Turkish Straits, thus heightening Istanbul's vulnerability to tanker collisions and fire hazards (see **Adams**, p. 98). In July 1994, Turkey adopted new regulations (revised in 1998) restricting the access of oil tankers to the Turkish Straits.[16] This decision had been under consideration for some time. However, Russia claimed that the new rules violated the 1936 Montreux Convention's principle of freedom of navigation in peace time and viewed this move as a deliberate attempt to block plans to adopt the Baku–Novorossiysk route for the MEP. This interpretation was given some credibility when in October 1998, in a not-so-subtle warning to AIOC, Foreign Minister Ismail Cem stated: 'Let everyone know this and make their [pipeline] decision accordingly', thus hinting at the consequences of not choosing Baku–Ceyhan as the MEP.[17]

Yet Turkey's insistence on the environmental dangers of increased tanker traffic was not prompted solely by political opportunism. When the Montreux

Convention determining the rules of navigation in the Straits was signed in 1936, only a few hundred ships passed through the Straits. Now an estimated 40,000 ships use it annually; the average tonnage of ships is 19 times greater than it was then. Super-tankers up to 300 metres in length are no longer a rarity. The zig-zag waterways of the Straits are treacherous, full of blind turns and strong currents, and often subject to fog and bad weather. Such conditions have often led to accidents in which many people have died and tonnes of oil have poured into the Bosporus; this has caused raging fires and resulted in the closure of the Straits to traffic for days on end.[18] The International Maritime Organisation (IMO) refused Ankara's demands for more stringent curbs – such as a ban on larger vessels – but nevertheless permitted it to restrict access to the Straits.

However, AIOC refused to be pushed into taking a decision on the route of the MEP before it had considered all options thoroughly. In late November 1998, Ankara ordered its refineries to stop buying oil from BP and Amoco because these two companies – together holding 34 per cent of the shares of AIOC – actively opposed the Baku–Ceyhan route.[19] In explaining the BP–Amoco group's opposition to the MEP route, Ralph Alexander, vice-president responsible for exploration and production, said that the MEP would be feasible only if 6 billion barrels were committed by AIOC and SOCAR. At that time there were only 4 billion barrels waiting for an export solution, one-third short of the volumes required for the pipeline to work. While Alexander's statement sounded logical, it was also a fact that AIOC had had to delay implementation of the next phase of ACG by six months due to lack of pipeline capacity.[20]

Tipping the balance: the US sides with Turkey

The appointment of ambassador Richard L. Morningstar as Special Advisor to US President Bill Clinton and to the Secretary of State on Caspian Basin Energy Development in 1998 signalled growing American interest in Caspian affairs. In various speeches, Morningstar made the following points regarding US policy: (1) The United States was strongly in favour of a route from Baku via Tbilisi to Ceyhan for the MEP; (2) it would endeavour to make the Caspian (i.e. Turkish) pipelines commercially viable; (3) it would encourage other suppliers to utilise the Baku–Tbilisi–Ceyhan (BTC) pipeline in the future; (4) it believed that Russia could take part in the BTC and other Caspian projects; (5) it was against Iran's participation in the export of the Caspian hydrocarbon resources because it was dangerous to concentrate such a significant portion of the region's oil and gas in one location; moreover, Iran itself was a competitor in oil and gas sales.[21]

Ambassador John Wolf, who followed Morningstar as Special Advisor, stated in September 1999 that AIOC was not negotiating fast enough on the BTC pipeline. He expressed frustration over the pace of the talks, making it very clear that Washington would do its best to support the Turkish pipeline.[22] It was at this time that BP, the operator of AIOC, revised its view on the

Baku–Ceyhan project. It now accepted that the route to the Mediterranean was economically viable. This change of heart was partly owing to pressure from the US administration, but also because of real concerns over the environmental hazards associated with the route via Novorossiysk and the Bosporus. Consequently, on 17 October 2000, AIOC signed a framework agreement to cover the financing and preliminary design of a trunkline from Baku via Tbilisi to Ceyhan on the Mediterranean coast of Turkey – a distance of some 1,700 km.[23] This news was greeted with scepticism by many commentators, since the project did not appear to be commercially sound. However, the governments of the three states across which the pipeline was to run – Azerbaijan, Georgia and Turkey – welcomed the decision, convinced that the project would bring substantial economic and social benefits to the region.

Yet, there were still many obstacles to be overcome. It was difficult to reach agreement on the precise routing of the pipeline. Not only was the terrain difficult, but there were several environmentally sensitive areas along the way. Also, there were numerous 'hot spots' in the region (see **Gerber**) which represented potential threats to the security of the proposed pipeline. The social impact of construction, too, had to be assessed and local concerns taken into account. These included questions over land acquisition and compensation rights. Financing was another issue that had to be resolved. During this period the project was often dismissed as mere fantasy. Nevertheless, by 2002, most of these problems had been overcome. In September that year, the presidents of Azerbaijan, Georgia and Turkey attended the groundbreaking ceremony that was held in Azerbaijan, at the northern terminal of the pipeline. Also present was the US Energy Secretary Spencer Abraham, marking the strong support of the US for this project.[24]

Nazarbaev opts for Novorossiysk

Turkey and Russia were also in strenuous competition over the routes of export pipelines from Kazakhstan's giant Tengiz oilfield. Eventually, the route to Novorossiysk, Russia's Black Sea export terminal, was chosen. Turkey believed that this pipeline might be used to carry crude not only from Kazakhstan, but also from Azerbaijan. This would consolidate Moscow's stranglehold over the region. Consequently, Ankara campaigned actively against it. The idea that a Turkish pipeline would earn Turkey hard currency in royalties was perhaps secondary to the geopolitical calculation that, if Azerbaijan and Kazakhstan had to rely solely on the Russian pipeline, Ankara's hopes for improved ties with the newly independent Turkic states in the region would be frustrated. In August 1995, Turkish Prime Minister Tansu Ciller engaged in a last-ditch effort to sway Almaty to opt for a Turkish pipeline. The talks ended in failure as Kazakh President Nursultan Nazarbaev insisted that Kazakh oil should be transported to Russia's Black Sea terminals.[25] In April 1996 the Caspian Pipeline Consortium (CPC) was formed, with the aim of constructing the 1,500-km pipeline from Tengiz to Novorossiysk. Work progressed slowly but, in the autumn of 2001, it finally became operational.

Iran fared better than Turkey in securing flows of Kazakh oil. In late October 1996 Tehran and Almaty agreed to swap oil. Initially the Kazakhs were to ship 40,000 b/d of crude by marine tankers from the port of Aktau via the Caspian to the Iranian harbours of Bandar-e Anzali and Neka, to be delivered through the existing Iranian pipeline network to the Tabriz and Tehran refineries for refining. In return, Tehran would export the same amount from its own production through its Persian Gulf terminals.[26] However, the swaps were soon suspended because of disagreements on price and the inability of Iranian refineries to process the Kazakh oil, which contained high levels of sulphur, mercaptans and salt. Iran thereupon initiated the process of upgrading the Rey and Tabriz refineries to handle the Kazakh oil. Swaps were restarted and, in March 2000, Iran began construction of a pipeline between Neka, the port on the Caspian, and the Rey refinery near Tehran. By August 2003 this was near completion.[27] It became operational before the end of the year (see Map 4). A further upgrade was scheduled for 2004. Swaps in mid-2003 averaged around 50,000 b/d, but were expected to increase with the promise of substantial additional volumes from Kazakhstan. A second pipeline from Neka to the northern refineries was also under construction and scheduled for completion in 2004. These new pipelines, if filled to capacity, would enable the two countries to swap up to 500,000 b/d (see **Ehteshami**, p. 68). The swap agreements with Iran involved the direct purchase of oil at Caspian Sea ports, thus avoiding the restrictions imposed by the US Iran and Libya Sanctions Act (ILSA), which targets foreign companies with mandatory and discretionary sanctions if investments exceed US$20 million annually.

Turkmen gas: no clear winner yet

Turkmenistan was not as successful as either Kazakhstan or Azerbaijan in acquiring a major pipeline of its own through which to export its hydrocarbons to the Western world. Things did not seem bleak, however, when in 1994 former US Secretary of State Alexander Haig was able to bring his own US–CIS Ventures and Wavemeg companies together with Turkey, Iran, Turkmenistan, Kazakhstan and Russia in an international council.[28] The council was established to assess route feasibility studies, financing and other technicalities. The project foresaw a 3,500-km export pipeline for Turkmen gas through Iran and Turkey with the eventual aim of reaching European markets. The project was, however, plagued by the thorny issue of Iran's participation. The US administration's opposition to any enterprise involving Tehran led to a lack of financing for the pipeline's construction. The US could have accepted the project if Tehran had permitted foreign ownership of the 1,450-km Iranian section of the line, but Tehran was not enthusiastic about this.[29]

Faced with the US veto on Iran's participation in the pipeline, Ashgabat turned to Russia, to make use of its already existing pipeline network to sell its natural gas. This was a risky strategy because, in 1994, Moscow had simply cut off Turkmen sales through its pipeline to put pressure on the

Turkmen president. In February 1996 the Russian Gazprom joint stock company and the Turkmenistan Ministry of Oil and Gas established Turkmenrosgaz, which not only obtained the sole right to prospect for and extract hydrocarbon deposits, but also acquired the right to make agreements with CIS countries for the delivery of Turkmen natural gas.[30] Ashgabat cancelled the deal in March 1997, complaining that Russia had allowed only a fraction of the existing pipeline capacity to be used. However, by the late 1990s Turkmen–Russian relations had again improved. In 1999 Ashgabat agreed to sell Moscow 20 billion cubic metres of natural gas. In 2003, the two countries signed a 25-year agreement on co-operation in the gas sector (see **Canzi**, p. 193).

In August 1996, Turkmenistan also concluded with Iran a natural gas swap agreement; construction of a pipeline linking the onshore Turkmen gas field of Korpeje to northern Iran was completed in 1997 (see **Roberts**, p. 86). In the long run, Iran could export equal amounts of natural gas to Turkey, or Pakistan, and hence could serve as the transit country for Turkmen gas exports to world markets.[31] Tehran scored another victory in early May 1996 when the Mashhad (Iran)–Saraks–Tejen (Turkmenistan) railway was opened. 'The Silk Road Railway', as Iran's President Hashemi Rafsanjani termed it, linked Iran not only with Turkmenistan, but with all the Central Asian states.[32] The railway had an initial annual transport capacity of 500,000 passengers and 2 million tonnes of freight.

In 2000, Turkey was able to take advantage of the opportunity of this overland link with Central Asia to join its domestic network to that of Iran by the construction of some 100 kilometres of railway around Lake Van in eastern Turkey. Although Tehran might have had misgivings about this Turkish link, it nevertheless accepted the need to relinquish its newly acquired role as the sole non-CIS terrestrial route between Central Asia and the wider world.[33]

The US, Turkey and the Trans-Caspian Pipeline

The Turkish and the Turkmen governments signed an accord on gas sales in March 1999, and a final gas sales purchase agreement was concluded between the Turkmen government and the Turkish state gas firm Botaş in the summer of 1999. These agreements were signed after the Trans-Caspian Gas Pipeline project began to be promoted by the US administration. This pipeline, which was to run from Turkmenistan across the Caspian, through Azerbaijan and Georgia to Turkey, was intended to deliver 16 bcm/year of Turkmen gas to Turkey, starting in 2002. However, while negotiations were still in progress, Turkmenistan signed a separate deal with Russia in March 2000. This raised doubts as to the feasibility of the Trans-Caspian pipeline, because it seemed unlikely that volumes would be sufficient to meet both commitments in the near future.[34] Doubts over Ashgabat's commitment to the project coincided with the discovery of a huge deposit of gas at Shah Deniz, off the coast of Azerbaijan. That bonanza turned Azerbaijan potentially into a major exporter of gas as well as oil to the Mediterranean and Black Sea countries. Today, Turkmenistan and Azerbaijan, as well as Russia and Iran, are competing for the same Turkish market. If Turkey were to opt for the Turkic states as suppliers, Azerbaijan and Turkmenistan would have a more advantageous position. Furthermore, Azerbaijan could profit from its proximity to Turkey by being able to charge substantially lower prices than Ashgabat. Thus, the Shah Deniz discovery meant that construction of the Trans-Caspian pipeline, which would primarily benefit Turkmenistan, was no longer a priority for Azerbaijan. By 2003, the project had been put on hold indefinitely (see **Canzi**, p. 187).

Russia revises its Caspian thesis

The Russian Foreign Ministry had initially asserted that the Caspian is 'an enclosed water reservoir with a single eco-system and that it represents an object of joint use within whose boundaries, so all issues or activities including resource development would have to be resolved with the participation of all the Caspian countries.[35] By 1996, however, Russia was ready to recognise a 45-mile offshore economic zone for each littoral country. On 28 April 1998, when Russia and Kazakhstan jointly delimited their Caspian Sea zones, Russia effectively abandoned its argument in favour of joint utilisation. One of the reasons for Russia's change of view might have been that its Caspian Sea thesis was not tenable legally, and insisting on it would cause more harm than good in Russia's relations with the regional countries (see **Antonenko**). Nevertheless, the Russians argued that the division of the Caspian Sea seabed into national sectors was an interim solution, and that Russia desired a formal agreement by all Caspian Sea littoral states on the sea's legal status.

Iran continued to insist that the Caspian Sea resources should be shared in an equitable manner.[36] Yet the Iranian parliament approved a bill in May 2000 to authorise the national oil company to enter into contracts with foreign firms to explore and develop the offshore resources of Iran's Caspian Sea shelf.[37] This move on the part of the Iranian parliament indicated that Tehran, too, might be having second thoughts about its Caspian policy (see **Granmayeh, Namazi and Farzin**). Nevertheless, as of 2004, it was still calling for a 20 per cent share of the surface waters and the seabed.[38]

Prospects

By the beginning of the second post-Soviet decade, the competition between Russia, Iran and Turkey to secure a share in the hydrocarbon wealth of the Caspian was largely over. All three had acquired a slice of the Caspian pie. The CPC pipeline was transporting Tengiz oil to the Russian port of Novorossiysk. Iran had completed the new pipeline linking its Caspian port of Neka to the refinery in Rey to accommodate the swap agreements it had concluded with Kazakhstan. Turkey had perhaps gained most. Initial fears that Ankara's involvement in Caspian hydrocarbon exports would be marginal had proved to be groundless. By late 2003, the Baku–Tbilisi–Ceyhan oil pipeline was under construction and the parallel gas pipeline from Baku via Tbilisi to Erzurum (i.e. the South Caspian pipeline) had been formally sanctioned and construction was due to commence in 2004. Thus, Turkey was well on the way to becoming a transport hub for a significant portion of Caspian oil and gas. The Turks – like the US administration – hoped that the use of Turkish routes would eliminate the dependence of the Caspian states on Russia, and would make them more viable socio-politically.

Notes

1 S. Bolukbaşi, 'Ankara's Baku-centered Transcaucasia Policy: Has It Failed?', *Middle East Journal*, vol. 51, no. 1 (Winter 1997), pp. 80–94.
2 R. Barylski, 'Russia, the West, and the Caspian Energy Hub', *Middle East Journal*, vol. 49, no. 2 (Spring 1995).
3 *Middle East Economic Digest* (hereafter *MEED*), 25 November 1994, p. 28.
4 *MEED*, 21 April 1995, p. 22; AFP, 8 April 1995 in *FBIS-CEU*, 10 April 1995, p. 67.
5 *Turkish Daily News*, 24, 25 February and 2 November 1994; *Cumhuriyet*, Istanbul, 23 October 1994 and 3 November 1994; *Turkish Probe*, 3 November 1995.
6 *Ibid.*
7 *Turkish Probe*, 26 January 1996, p. 18.
8 'Russia' TV Channel, 25 February 1993, in *BBC Summary of World Broadcasts* (hereafter *SWB*), SU/1624, 27 February 1993, p. C 2/1.
9 *Itar-Tass*, Moscow, 22 June 1994, in *FBIS-CEU*, 23 June 1994, p. 54; *RFE/RL News Briefs*, 28–31 April 1994, p. 8.
10 *Turan*, Baku, 3 April 1995 in *FBIS-CEU*, 5 April 1995, p. 73.
11 *Turan*, Baku, 6 December 1994, in *FBIS-CEU*, 7 December 1994, p. 55.
12 *Gunay*, Baku, in Russian, 3 June 1995, p. 2 in *FBIS-CEU*, 9 June 1995, p. 86.
13 Announced on 9 October 1995 (*MEED*, 20 October 1995, p. 31).
14 *Ibid.*; also *Washington Post*, 10 October 1995; *MEED*, 20 October 1995, p. 19; *Turkish Probe*, 17 May 1996, pp. 19–20.
15 US Energy Information Administration survey, *Caspian Sea: Reserves and Pipeline Tables*, July 2002.
16 According to the new rules, which took effect in November 1994, all vessels entering the Straits had to take part in the Turkish reporting system, which required that masters use a qualified pilot; also, ships over 200 metres long had to navigate the area in daylight.
17 P. Sampson, 'Lubricating the Caspian', *Transitions*, February 1999, p. 28.
18 *Turkish Probe*, 21 July 1995, p. 9.
19 'Caspian Pipeline Plans Tied to Available Oil', *Oil and Gas Journal* (hereafter *OGJ*), 17 May 1999, p. 27.
20 'Online Story: Caspian Deadlines', *OGJ*, 24 April 2000.
21 'Caspian Pipeline Plans Tied to Available Oil', *OGJ*, 17 May 1999, p. 27.
22 'US Intruding in Caspian', *OGJ*, 27 September 1999.
23 'Online Story: Baku–Ceyhan Project Noses Ahead', *OGJ*, 18 October 2000.
24 'Baku–Ceyhan Breaks Ground', AP, 18 September 2002.
25 *Turkish Probe*, 18 August 1995, p. 7; *MEED*, 25 August 1995, pp. 29–30.
26 *MEED*, 1 November 1996, p. 38.
27 World Markets Research Centre, *Daily Analysis*, 1 August 2003.
28 *MEED*, 27 January 1995, p. 14.
29 *Interfax*, Moscow, in English, 14 March 1996, pp. 59–60; *MEED*, 28 April 1996, p. 4.

30 *Finansovyye Izvestia*, Moscow, in Russian, 27 February 1996, p. 2 in *FBIS-CEU*, 4 March 1996, p. 97.
31 *OGJ*, 5 March 2001.
32 *Turkish Probe*, 17 May 1996, pp. 17–18; *MEES*, 20 May 1996, p. A7.
33 *Ibid.*
34 'Prospects for Transcaspian Gas Pipeline Wane', *OGJ*, 30 May 2000.
35 *Financial Times*, 31 May 1994; *MEED*, 28 April 1995, p. 3; S. Blank, 'Russia's Real Drive to the South', *Orbis*, 39 (Summer 1995), pp. 369–370; Barylski, *op. cit.*, p. 223.
36 'Caspian Sea Nations Closer to Territorial Accord', *OGJ*, 26 June 2000.
37 'Iran to Allow Foreign Investment in Caspian Projects via Buy-Back Scheme', *OGJ*, 25 May 2000.
38 IRNA, 20 July 2003.

14 Division of the Caspian Sea: Iranian policies and concerns

Siamak Namazi and Farshid Farzin

Introduction

The break-up of the Soviet Union in 1991 changed the realities governing the Caspian Sea. The most obvious of these changes is the fact that the number of littoral states increased from two to five, leaving these states with the challenge of agreeing on a new legal regime for the sea. But, after more than a decade, the riparian nations have thus far failed to overcome this challenge. Given the varied and often conflicting interests of the Caspian states, and the fact that outside powers have complicated an already muddled situation by engaging in a new 'Great Game', perhaps we should not be surprised that a post-Soviet legal regime for the world's greatest lake is still pending. The stakes are high, after all. Although original estimates were wildly inflated, the Caspian is nevertheless believed to rank third after the Persian Gulf and Siberia in terms of hydrocarbon reserves. Nevertheless, as time goes by, the Caspian states have been moving towards increased consensus, particularly since the littoral states are well aware of the benefits of agreement.

Iran's position, like that of the other littoral states, has evolved over the past decade. In the early 1990s the Islamic Republic insisted on a condominium approach to the Caspian, whereas today it is willing to accept a division, so long as its share is approximately 20 per cent. The conventional explanation of Iran's behaviour is well known, if rather shallow and lacking in nuance. Analysts simply point to the fact that Iran's share of the Caspian riches would not compare to that of the other states if there were a division, and hence they explain the Islamic Republic's desire to adhere to a common-use model. Iran's shift of position is also explained with the simple logic that the country had little choice in the light of the various bilateral agreements that were being signed by the other riparian states. But the concerns and interests that Iran followed in developing its policy towards the Caspian Sea run much deeper and are more complicated than the above explanation provides. Iran's economic interests are in no way limited to hydrocarbon reserves or pipeline prospects.

In order to understand the position of the Islamic Republic towards the Caspian today, a historical review is essential. Such a review serves two important purposes. Firstly, it provides an understanding of Iran's security concerns, particularly with regard to Russia. Secondly, it gives the reader an overview of the extant treaties at the time of the Soviet Union's disintegration, which in turn form the basis on which Iran is negotiating a new legal regime.[1]

Iran and the Russian Federation

Iran and Russia share a long and turbulent history. There had been extensive relations between the countries in the eighteenth century and at the time of Nader Shah Afshar's reign in Iran. But the nature of these relations changed when Peter the Great showed a desire for southward expansion. Clashes between the two nations ensued in the early nineteenth century.

Russians tried, unsuccessfully, to gain control of Iranian territory bordering the Caspian. Things changed with the rise of the Qajar dynasty. Under these rulers, the central government in Iran was weakened and this prompted Russia to try again to realise its dream of extending its borders to the warm-water coasts of the Persian Gulf. Russia fought two wars with Iran in the early nineteenth century. Following these wars the treaties of Golestan (1813) and Turkmanchai (1828) were signed between the two countries.

These treaties did not make direct reference to the Caspian Sea's legal regime. The only mention of this sort can be found in the fifth chapter of the Golestan Treaty and the eighth chapter of the Turkmanchai Treaty, which raised the issue of shipping in the Caspian.[2] According to the above-mentioned chapters, shipping for trade purposes is legal for both countries, but only Russia was privileged with the right of having warships in the Caspian.[3] It should be mentioned that no reference to the maritime border-line between the two countries was made in the treaties and there was no article in this respect. The imbalance regarding the right for warships in the Caspian Sea was understandable, due to the fact that Russia was the victor and was therefore dealing with Iran from a position of strength. This unfavourable state of affairs continued for Iran until the fall of the Russian empire.

The Treaty of 1921 and shipping rights

When the Bolsheviks came to power in 1917, a new attitude towards Iran was adopted. The imperialistic policies of Russia towards all countries, particularly Iran, witnessed a temporary transformation. The need to revise the previous treaties was apparent. The new rulers of Russia declared that their main goal was to free all nations from the twin yokes of capitalism and capitalistic governments. In a show of revolutionary zeal, the Communists abrogated all the previous agreements that their country had made with imperialistic intentions. Consequently, in 1921, the Russians signed a new treaty with Iran in order to remedy some of the undesirable elements of the treaties of Golestan and Turkmanchai. In addition to the cancellation of the capitulation regime and the rights of Russian citizens in Iran, the

Russians evacuated several Iranian islands in the Caspian, including Ashuradeh, and left them to the Iranian authorities.[4] But more important than the above-mentioned changes was Chapter 11 of the treaty in which an equal right of shipping had been given to both countries. It reads: 'both committed parties agree equally to have the right of shipping under their flags in the Caspian Sea'.[5] This treaty put an end to Russia's exclusive right to have warships in the Caspian. According to this new treaty the Iranian government could use both cargo ships and warships in the Caspian.

This agreement led to further agreements between the two countries on issues related to the Caspian. In 1931 they concluded the 'Treaty for Residence, Commerce and Sailing between Iran and the USSR'. This was the first document in which it was implied that the Caspian Sea belonged to the two countries. Article 16 of that treaty addressed the issue of shipping in the Caspian: 'Both parties agree to act according to principles mentioned in the treaty dated 26 February 1921, between Soviet Russia and Iran, and therefore except for those carrying the flags of Iran or Soviet Russia other ships are not allowed to sail in the Caspian Sea.'[6] Essentially, the two countries declared their exclusive right for shipping in all areas of the Caspian Sea without limitations.

More significant are the notes added by Iranian foreign minister and the Russian ambassador in Iran that clarified their views on the status of the Caspian Sea. In Note 7, written by the Iranian foreign minister of the time, Iran's approach to the issue of the Caspian Sea was indicated by the following comment: 'With regard to the Caspian Sea, which is considered an Iranian–Russian sea by both governments. . . .'[7] Therefore, from early times, Iran held the opinion that the Caspian belongs to the littoral countries, exclusively. The Russian ambassador in Iran replied in similar terms. These points were repeated again in a treaty signed between the two countries in 1935. In Article 14 of this treaty it was stressed once again that only ships belonging to Iran and Russia had the right to sail in the Caspian. In the letters exchanged between the Iranian foreign minister and the Russian ambassador the fact that the Caspian Sea belonged to both countries was reiterated (but see **Gizzatov**, p. 51).

The Treaty of 1940

The last treaty between the two countries on the issue of the Caspian Sea was concluded in 1940; it addressed the issues of shipping and commerce. Once again the equal right of navigation for Iranian and Russian ships in the Caspian was stressed and the sea was referred to as an Iranian–Russian sea. It should be noted that an exclusive right of fishing in the coastal zone of both countries was specified. Thus, Note 4 of Article 15 of the 1935 Treaty, Note 4 of Article 17 of the 1931 Treaty and Note 4 of Article 12 of the 1940 Treaty, state that fishing is the exclusive right of each of the two countries for the distance of 10 nautical miles from their coasts. In other words, both countries shared the right of fishing in the Caspian except for the domain of 10 miles from their coasts, which was considered the exclusive property of that country.

It should be stressed that in all these treaties the issues of the legal status of the Caspian Sea and the territorial share of the two countries were never directly specified. The matter was only addressed, and then indirectly, in relation to two points:

1   The right of sailing cargo ships and warships was reserved for both countries in all areas of the Caspian Sea.
2   The right of exploiting the marine life also extended to both countries, except for the area of 10 nautical miles from their coasts, which was demarcated as an exclusive area for each state.

In other words, the rights of shipping and exploiting the marine life applied to both countries, and applied all over the Caspian. Moreover, only the two littoral states possessed these rights. Other states were excluded. It is for this reason that the phrase the 'Iranian–Russian sea' was often used in the letters exchanged between the authorities of these two countries.

At the time the treaties were signed the issue of exploitation of the seabed and subsoil resources did not yet exist. Consequently, there is no article in the treaties regarding this issue. In the mid-twentieth century, when oil resources were discovered and exploited off the coast of Azerbaijan, no attempt was made by the Soviet government of the day to find a legal solution to this matter.

Implications of the Soviet break-up

Following the disintegration of the Soviet Union, Iran was faced with a new set of dynamics regarding its northern borders. Iran now shared frontiers with five northern neighbours, instead of one: Russia, Kazakhstan, Turkmenistan, Azerbaijan and Armenia. With the exception of Armenia, the four other states had shores on the Caspian Sea.

This break-up presented both opportunities and threats for Iran. Previously all these countries had to a great extent been dependent on the central government of Russia. Now, they would seek venues to enhance and reinforce their independence from that country. Iran's potential role in this respect was undeniable. From a cultural perspective, the newly independent states shared a long and close history with Iran as well as a common religion. From a geo-strategic point of view, Iran served as the nexus between the Caspian Sea and the Persian Gulf. This meant that Iran was the most obvious route to link the untouched markets in Central Asia and the Caucasus to the outside world.

On the downside, new concerns arose as well. The break-up of the Soviet Union heralded a new 'Great Game' in the Caspian at a time when Iran's position in the international community was far from favourable. The best known consequence of this state of affairs was the US policy to sideline Iran in the development and transport of the hydrocarbon resources of the Caspian basin. Other issues that concerned Iran at this time included initial worries about the emergence of an independent Republic of Azerbaijan. Some academics and policy analysts predicted that the Iranian Azerbaijanis, who compose roughly a quarter of the Iranian population, would be tempted to join the new Republic of Azerbaijan. Such predictions, however, soon proved to be very far fetched. Meanwhile, the forces that wanted to limit the influence of Iran in the Caspian region began a campaign to present the Islamic Republic as having expansionist and disruptive ambitions, warning the new states that Iran would try to export its revolution to their borders. Again, history would prove that Iran did not harbour such intentions. However, antagonistic propaganda of this sort presented an immediate challenge to Iran in its attempts to win the trust of the littoral states (see **Nassibli**, p. 163).

In the background, further complicating most of the above concerns, loomed the issue of the legal regime of the Caspian Sea. As explained earlier, while there were several bilateral treaties between Iran and Russia/USSR in regards to the use of the sea, the legal status of the Caspian Sea was not entirely clear in any of them. Iran was worried – with good reason – that in the absence of an agreed legal regime the newly independent, cash-strapped littoral states of Azerbaijan, Kazakhstan and Turkmenistan would immediately embark on the exploitation of the Caspian's hydrocarbon and marine potentials without proper consideration for the environment. There was also the disturbing prospect of the militarisation of the Caspian Sea, particularly since the Republic of Azerbaijan had expressed interest in closer co-operation with NATO (see **Katik**).

In evaluating Tehran's efforts to define the Caspian Sea as a lake and, initially, to argue for the adoption of a legal regime based on common use, some commentators have suggested that Iran was impelled to take such a stance because it has a shorter coastline along the Caspian than any of the other littoral states. Also, the proven offshore reserves of oil and gas in immediate proximity to Iran are relatively small. So, the story went, Iran would naturally prefer that the entire Caspian be treated as a condominium. This analysis is not entirely baseless. However, it fails to express the logic that was driving the key debates back in Tehran. Moreover, it does not explain why Iran later agreed to a division based on national sectors, thereby shifting the dispute to the issue of percentage shares, rather than that of condominium versus division.

Emphasis on economic co-operation

Faced with the new, post-Soviet challenges and opportunities, Iran's initial reaction, favoured during the presidency of Akbar Hashemi Rafsanjani, was to concentrate on the potential for co-operation with its neighbours.[8] In pursuit of this goal, Tehran tried to develop economic and social relations with the littoral states and to help enhance their links with the outside world and international community. Tehran also did all that it could to facilitate the entrance of these newly independent states into international organisations such as the United Nations, the Organisation of Islamic Conference and the Non-Aligned Movement, as well as the Economic Co-operation Organisation (ECO).

In fact, it was during the first summit conference of the expanded ECO that Iran took the initiative to urge the governments of the littoral states to concentrate on Caspian issues. In this conference, held in February 1992, a proposal was presented to form a Co-operative Organisation of the Littoral States. Subsequently, in October 1992, the littoral states agreed to establish five committees. They were the following:[9]

- committee for surveying causes of, and means to control, water fluctuations;
- committee for ecology protection;
- committee for the protection and exploitation of biological resources;
- committee for defining the legal status of the sea;
- committee for defining shipping rights and use of ports.

It is evident that there is a seemingly counter-intuitive feature to this approach. Namely, Iran was helping its future competitors in the oil and gas game. This was certainly the way in which it was interpreted in certain camps in Iran that did not agree with Rafsanjani's approach.

The truth was more complex. Discussions concerning the economic benefits of the Caspian Sea for Iran usually focused on the potential income that might be derived from the transport of hydrocarbons across Iranian territory. Possible pipeline projects were undoubtedly an important consideration. Yet the transfer of Caspian oil and gas through Iran was not all that the country was seeking by way of economic benefit. Rafsanjani's approach was far more concerned with exploiting the post-Soviet geo-strategic realities in such a way as to become the regional hub. This policy was based on the assumption that Iran could serve as the nexus between the Caspian region and the Persian Gulf. This would enable Iran to use its Persian Gulf ports as a gateway to Central Asia and the Caucasus. Iran would also gain by providing a more direct route to Europe for the rich Sheikdoms in the south, since the journey would be cut by several days if a shipping route were developed from Bandar-e Anzali to Astrakhan. As for Russia, here, too, Rafsanjani focused more on the opportunities that the new situation offered, rather than emphasising potential threats. And there was much that Russia could offer Iran – not only could it become a superb market for Iranian goods, but it could also provide Iran with a plethora of military, industrial and scientific technology.

Thus, for Iran, the primary issue was common economic benefit. Such a strategy requires that the interests of the players be as closely intertwined as possible. Within this framework, it was no surprise that Iran insisted on a condominium or common use of the Caspian Sea. Needless to say, some of the littoral states (particularly Azerbaijan) were not at all in accord with the Islamic Republic's approach towards the legal regime and fought hard for a division into national sectors. Thus, Iran resolved to follow a short-term and long-term policy:

- The short-term policy of Iran was to persuade the littoral states to avoid exploitation of the seabed either by themselves or by foreign companies until a solution was found to the problem of the legal regime of the Caspian Sea. The Russians initially supported this policy, due to similar concerns. Consequently, when foreign companies began to develop near-shore Azerbaijani oil resources, the governments of Iran and Russia criticised these projects.[10]
- The long-term policy of Iran was to encourage the littoral states to find the most favourable solution for the legal regime of the Caspian Sea, and to make decisions based on consensus.

Iran based its arguments for the legal regime of the Caspian on two facts:

- The treaties between Iran and Russia/USSR are still valid; the newly independent states are the successors of the former USSR and should therefore observe them.
- The Caspian is not a 'sea', but the largest lake in the world.

Below the implications of these arguments are further clarified.

Newly independent states or the successor countries?

After the break-up of the Soviet Union, the main question that ensued was whether or not these newly independent states were to be considered successors of the USSR. The key implication, needless to say, was whether or not these independent states were legally bound by the treaties inked between Iran and Russia/USSR before their nascence.

There have been different theories on the issue as far as international rights are concerned. Some lawyers, giving prime importance to will-power, believed that the new countries were not obliged to pursue the commitments of the predecessor country. They argued that, because the new countries had not been involved in the decision-making process regarding the said treaties, they could not be forced to fulfil commitments made by another country. This theory is known as the 'Clean Slate Doctrine'. On the other hand, there exists a contrary theory based on succession in private rights. Adherents of this view believe that, since the new governments are successors to another government, they inherit its commitments and should honour them.

The 1978 Convention of Vienna distinguished between the commitments of newly independent successor countries, and those of successor governments formed through combination or disintegration of other governments, in such a way as to exempt the newly independent governments from previous commitments. However, the Convention added some exceptions to this general principle, including commitments related to navigation and determining borders. Thus, the key question with regard to the status of the Caspian Sea is whether the new littoral states should be considered countries formed by the disintegration of the USSR, or countries that have recently gained independence.[11]

Azerbaijan, Kazakhstan and Turkmenistan, along with the other states that emerged out of the disintegration of the Soviet Union, stated in the Minsk Declaration of 8 December 1991: 'The member governments will undertake their international commitments according to the treaties and agreements signed by the USSR.' On this basis, the Islamic Republic of Iran maintained that the previous treaties between Iran and Russia were still valid. Iranian officials repeatedly stressed that, until a new treaty had been signed by all the littoral states on the legal regime of the Caspian Sea, the previous treaties continued to be valid and should be executed.

Caspian Sea or Caspian Lake?

According to existing definitions, seas are geographical units with connection(s) to oceans, while lakes are geographical units formed by the accumulation of water in certain flat spots on land and have no connection to open seas. Given its great size, the Caspian is commonly referred to as the 'Caspian Sea', but it is not naturally connected to any sea or ocean. However, although the Caspian is not naturally connected to any ocean, the Volga–Don Canal artificially connects it to the Black Sea via the Volga and Don Rivers. Historically, it was also joined to the sea of Azov, which is essentially a branch of the Black Sea.[12] Consequently, Iran argued, the Caspian could not be considered a sea even if, according to some definitions, there were doubts as to whether it could be classed as a lake.[13]

Ultimately, the Caspian Sea has its own particular condition and cannot be considered among the seas of the world. But the arguments for defining the Caspian as a sea were supported by the littoral states because they would benefit from such a classification as it would enable them to apply the 1982 Convention on the Legal Regime for Seas in delineating their national boundaries. Should the Caspian be recognised as a sea, each littoral state would have its exclusive right to the continental shelf. Iran, however, continued to insist that the Caspian is a lake, which would imply that the rules of consortium should apply. Eventually, Tehran announced that it would agree to a division of the Caspian into national sectors, so long as it was given a 20 per cent share (see below). Some may question why Iran, despite this concession, nevertheless continued to insist that the Caspian be defined as a lake. The explanation is to be found in other legal implications of the said Convention, besides that of the division into national sectors.

Once the Convention on the Legal Regime for the seas is put into practice, not only the littoral states but also all the countries of the world would have the right of shipping in the Caspian Sea. The security of its borders has always been a critical issue for Iran. We have already reviewed the historical roots of Iran's concerns with the 'Great Russian Bear' to its north. But we should not underestimate the country's concern with the possibility of turning the Caspian into another Persian Gulf, should foreign countries find their way into that lake. Needless to say, Iran is most concerned about the possibility of the presence of the US navy in this scenario, particularly as Azerbaijan has shown interest in seeing NATO's naval forces in the Caspian. Thus, Iran must continue to push for a legal regime in the Caspian that makes that body of water exclusive to the shipping of the littoral states. Russia shares Iran's vision of keeping the Americans and others out, but wants its own navy freely to roam the Caspian. Consequently, negotiations over the legal regime of the Caspian Sea are characterised by a tug-of-war between opposing blocks of interest. Iran, as of mid-2003, accepted that the sea would be divided into national sectors, but was still seeking a share of approximately 20 per cent. Thus, in July, at the tenth session of the Special Working Group on the Legal Status of the Caspian Sea (a body comprising senior officials and lawyers from the littoral states), Iranian special envoy on the Caspian Sea Mehdi Safari proposed the application of a technical formula, based on international principles and laws, that would accord Iran a share of 19.7 to 20.3 per cent of the sea.[14]

To divide or not to divide

Security, in fact, has been the top consideration in some of the highest policy-making circles in the Islamic Republic with regard to the issue of the post-Soviet legal regime of the Caspian Sea. The Supreme National Security Council is one such body. Iran has never forgotten the threat of the Great Russian Bear to its north. The historical overview presented earlier in this chapter has outlined some of the reasons why. Thus, when the Soviet Union disintegrated, security-minded policymakers saw the fact that Iran no longer shared any land borders with Russia as a complete blessing. The best scenario for Iran, they argued, was to try to eliminate any marine borders as well, by dividing the Caspian (both seabed and surface waters) into national sectors. This thinking, some have argued,[15] is exactly why, after the accession of Mohammad Khatami to the presidency in 1997, the new administration stopped insisting on a condominium approach and announced that it would be willing to accept national sectors so long as Iran's share was 20 per cent. The methods by which the Caspian could be divided are explained below.

One of the key problems is the fact that, as mentioned earlier, the agreements of 1921 and 1940 allowed full rights of navigation, including of military ships, exclusively to the littoral states. Russia, having a strong navy, continues to favour this approach, arguing for a division of the seabed, but common use of the surface waters. Iran, by contrast, believes that the whole sea, including the surface, seabed and sub-seabed, should be divided. The bilateral agreements on the division of the Caspian that were concluded between Russia and Kazakhstan in 1998, and Russia and Azerbaijan in 2001, enshrined the Russian approach, namely dividing the seabed into national sectors, while leaving the surface waters open for common use. Naturally, this was an undesirable scenario for Iran and, consequently, the Islamic Republic logged serious protests against such bilateral agreements. The other littoral states appear to have some sympathy with Iran on this point, since they, too, are not eager to have the Russian navy freely navigate near their coasts.

How to divide

Despite the challenges and the haggling process, the fact remains that currently all the littoral states, including Iran, are in favour of dividing the Caspian. The main engine behind changing Iran's position was security concerns. However, the element of realpolitik should not be discounted either. After almost a decade of arguments over this issue, Iran had to face the fact that international oil companies were collaborating with the other littoral states without being deterred by the risks of working in an area that had no internationally agreed legal regime. Meanwhile, especially after the rise of Vladimir Putin to the Russian presidency, Russia was becoming much more active and aggressive about its interests in the Caspian (see **Antonenko**). Whether or not Iran liked it, bilateral agreements were being signed, and these were limiting the room for manoeuvre for future negotiations. Thus, there was mounting pressure on all littoral states to break the deadlock and reach an agreement on how to divide the Caspian Sea.

From a strictly legal point of view, the new legal regime for that body of water would have to fall under one of three options:

- consortium
- division
- a combination of the above two.

The consortium approach is unacceptable to the other states, hence the other options must be considered. Each state is obviously pushing for its own interests to be best served. One way to settle the issue would be to divide the Caspian between the littoral states. This solution would grant each littoral state an exclusive right of ownership in its own division and that area would become a part of the soil of that country. However, although this is the approach that has been adopted in principle, two points of contention remain. Firstly, there is the issue of whether the division is to be total, or whether it should only apply to the seabed, i.e. leaving the surface water for communal use. Secondly, there is the size of the share of the Caspian that is to be allocated to each country to be agreed.

With regard to the division of closed seas and lakes, there are no definite international norms. The international rights of seas do not apply in such cases. Consequently, the littoral states normally act according to their own judgement and conclude bilateral or multilateral treaties. There are three main opinions on how the share of each littoral state is to be determined from the Caspian Sea (see Figure 14.1).

1   *Dividing the Caspian Sea into equal parts*: According to this view, the Caspian Sea should be equally shared by the littoral states, so that each of the five littoral states owns 20 per cent of the Caspian Sea. This approach is theoretically grounded in the 1921 and 1940 treaties between Iran and Russia/USSR. As indicated above, at that time the Caspian Sea was considered an Iranian–Russian sea and used equally by both countries. Consequently, it is argued, the same logic should apply to all the littoral states today, thus allocating each country an equal share of the sea. This is the argument that has been put forward by Iran. The Islamic Republic claims that it is essential to consider the historical background in order to observe principles of fair judgement and justice.

2   *Dividing the Caspian Sea based on the hypothetical line of Astara (Azerbaijan) – Gasankuli (Turkmenistan) and the interior divisions formerly used in the USSR*: Another approach, favoured by the Republic of Azerbaijan, suggests that the Caspian Sea's divisions are clear and no further division is required. It holds that, prior to the collapse of the Soviet Union, the maritime border between Iran and the USSR extended from the city of Astara on the west coast of the Caspian, to the Gasankuli Gulf on the east coast. Proponents of this view claim that the Caspian Sea had never been shared between Iran and Russia. Moreover, since the late 1940s, the Soviet Union had extracted oil from offshore deposits in its own seawaters without any objection from Iran, who in turn had always observed the line as the border between the two countries. With respect to the sea borders of the newly independent states and the former republics of Russia, it is argued that the Soviet government determined the sea border for each republic in 1970 and that the same borders should still be applicable. Following this approach, Iran's share of the Caspian Sea would be 11 per cent of the whole area, the remainder being shared between the other countries based on the length of their coastlines. Iran has made strenuous objections to this argument. It has stressed that in none of the treaties and official documents between Iran and former Russia was there any mention of a border. There was also no mention of divisions between the former Soviet republics. On the contrary, all the evidence points to the fact that the Caspian Sea was considered to belong to both countries.

3   *Dividing the Caspian Sea according to the median line*: According to this approach, the sea should be divided based on the median line of the sea, which has the same distance from both opposite shores. This method is usually applied in places where there are only two littoral states. In areas such as the Caspian Sea where there are more than two states it cannot be applied alone. Other factors must also be taken into account, such as the length of the shore and the convexity and slope

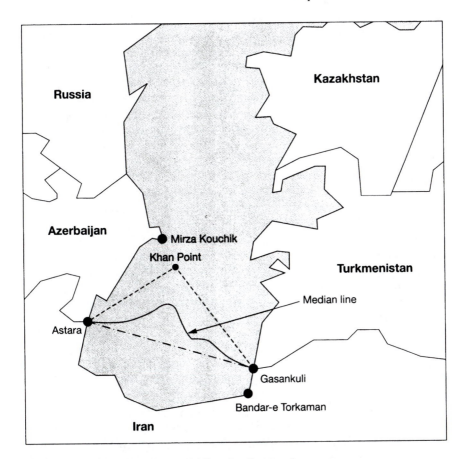

Figure 14.1 Three methods for dividing the Caspian Sea

of the seabed near the shore. Should this method be adopted, Iran's share of the Caspian Sea would be 13.6 per cent. The main winners would be Azerbaijan and Kazakhstan, with 21 per cent and 28.4 per cent respectively. Russia and Turkmenistan, meanwhile, would claim 19 per cent and 18 per cent respectively.

Conclusions

Iran's policy approach is not driven solely by the desire to receive the largest possible slice of the Caspian. On the contrary, Tehran regards the militarisation of the Caspian as a considerably more important issue. From this perspective, Iran's preferred approach for dividing the Caspian is in fact detrimental to the interests of the country itself. This is because Iran's legal premises for demanding one-fifth of the Caspian Sea are the 1921 and 1940 treaties and, according to these agreements, the navies of the littoral states were allowed to roam freely over the surface waters. This is an exclusive right, thus there is no concern in Iran that foreign navies might appear in that body of water. However, Russia is the only littoral state with credible naval capabilities in the Caspian and this provision would allow it to dominate those waters militarily (see **Katik**). Considering that there is little chance that Iran could get all that it wants – namely, 20 per cent of the Caspian as well as complete demilitarisation of the sea – the next best option is to accept a full division, based on the median-line principle, which would give each littoral state a share of both the seabed and the surface waters. Under this scenario, Iran would get a smaller portion of the Caspian, but it would enhance its security by no longer having a marine border with the Great Russian Bear. In order to achieve this, it is conceivable that Tehran might be willing to show some flexibility regarding the share of the Caspian that it hopes to acquire.

The current Russian approach, which Moscow has persuaded Kazakhstan and Azerbaijan to accept, is to divide the seabed using the median line, but leaving the surface waters for common use. Perhaps it would be better for Iran to accept this, rather than to see the Caspian turn into another Persian Gulf, with the worrying possibility of the intrusion of the American nuclear fleet into the region. Yet some security analysts suggest that it would be better to create the 'cold peace' that multiple military powers would bring about, rather than to grant the Russians a monopoly. A possible compromise might be an agreement to keep the Caspian as a nuclear-free zone, but to allow naval forces with conventional arms to roam those waters. However, Iran would prefer to keep the Russian military out altogether and is doing its utmost to achieve this. To this end, it is engaging in serious discussions with the other littoral states, all of whom share this concern.

Russia's policy has been to offer the other littoral states a range of incentives in order to 'buy' their support. For example, in the case of Azerbaijan, it is said that Moscow promised the Azerbaijanis military technology and equipment in return for Baku giving up its reluctance to allow common use of the surface waters. In the case of Iran, military technology has certainly been part of the deal sweetener. But the Russians are also appealing to Iran's desire to fulfil its vision of becoming a regional hub and the nexus of east and west. An example of this is the trilateral agreement concluded by Russia, Iran and India to create an international 'North–South Transport Corridor' to develop a shorter transit route for the transportation of goods.[16] Currently, most of the trade between Russia and India takes place through a long and expensive shipping route to Rotterdam and St Petersburg. The new deal envisions Iran as a transit country for Indian goods which could be sent via Iranian ports on the Persian Gulf to Iranian ports on the Caspian, and from there shipped on to Astrakhan and Moscow. This route would cut time and expense by an estimated 20 per cent.

Ultimately, all five littoral states would benefit from the resolution of the Caspian dispute and an agreement on a new legal regime. This would undoubtedly boost the development of their commercial interests by ensuring stability and clarity. Yet each state has issues and concerns that are of paramount importance to its national interests. Thus, Iran, like the other four states, will fight tooth and nail to have these interests assured as much as possible. The good news is that, while there are conflicting interests when it comes to the division of the Caspian, there is also tremendous potential for co-operation. This could eventually lead to a consensus formula that is acceptable and beneficial to all the players.

Notes

The authors would like to thank the International Institute for Caspian Studies, and particularly Abbas Maleki, Director-General of that Tehran-based institution, for their help and support. All shortcomings of the study, needless to say, are the sole responsibility of the authors.

1 For a more detailed survey of Russo-Iranian relations see **Granmeyah** (especially pp. 17–19). The overview presented here summarises the points relevant to the arguments made below.
2 I. Nourian, 'The Legal Regime of the Caspian Sea', in *Central Asia and the Caucusus Review* (hereafter *CACR*), vol. 5, no. 14, Summer 1996, pp. 149–150.
3 Regarding this matter Article 8 of the Turkmanchai Treaty reads: 'With regard to warships, since those with the Russian military flag have long had the right to sail in the Caspian Sea, presently also the right goes to them, meaning that except for the government of Russia no other government has the right to possess warships in the Caspian Sea.' For further discussion of this topic, see A. Khodakov, 'Legal Framework for Co-operation in the Caspian Sea', in *CACR*, vol. 4, no. 10, Summer 1995, p. 150.
4 A. A. Grantovski, *Iranian History* (Persian translation by Keshavarz, Keykhosro), Pouyesh Press, Tehran, 1980, p. 437.
5 Khodakov, *op. cit.*, p. 150.
6 'Treaties for Residence, Trade and Navigation Between Iran and the USSR' (in Persian: *gharardadhay-e eghamat va tejarat va barpeymayi beyne iran va shoravi*), in *Compendium of Laws for the Persian Year 1311*, Ruznameh Rasmi Press, p. 11.
7 *Ibid.*, p. 20.
8 Private conversation with Abbas Maleki, Director-General of the International Institute for Caspian Studies, 26 January 2001.
9 Nourian, *op. cit.*, p. 119.
10 Later Azerbaijan made partnership offers to the oil companies of the objecting countries (namely Iran and Russia) and thus gained their tacit approval.
11 M. Mir-Mohammad Sadeqi, 'The Legal Regime of the Caspian', *CACR*, vol. 4, no. 10, Summer 1995, pp. 164–165.
12 As a side note, it is worth mentioning that Iran has long cherished the visionary dream of connecting the Caspian Sea with the Persian Gulf by means of a giant navigation channel that would stretch over 1,500 kilometres. For further details on the geography of the Caspian, see S. Namazi, 'The Caspian's Environmental Woes', in *The Caspian Region at a Crossroad*, H. Amirahmadi (ed.), St Martin's Press, New York, 2000.
13 B. Budaqev, 'The Caspian: Is it a Sea or a Lake?', *CACR*, vol. 4, no. 10, Summer 1995, p. 170.
14 IRNA, 20 July 2003. However, in March 2004, the Iranian Foreign Ministry categorically dismissed the claim that Iran might be changing its position (10 March 2004, IRNA).
15 Abbas Maleki, 26 January 2001.
16 *BBC Monitoring*, 16 January 2001. See also S. Blank, 'The Indian–Iranian Connection and its Importance for Central Asia', *Pakistan Daily Times*, 14 March 2003.

15 Russia's policy in the Caspian Sea region: reconciling economic and security agendas

Oksana Antonenko

During the 1990s, the Caspian Sea region was hardly a key priority for Russian foreign and security policy. However, even with limited and often inconsistent engagement in the region, Russia has had a major influence on the transition from a post-Soviet zone of instability towards an object of a new strategic rivalry between major global powers. For the Caucasus and Central Asia, the first decade of Russia's post-Soviet transformation was characterised by the threatening uncertainty over Russia's intentions. Partially as a result of this, these newly independent states were actively engaged in the search for new strategic allies who could help them to consolidate sovereignty and independence. The reluctance of the Caspian states to accept Russia's post-Soviet influence, and their efforts to deny it economic benefits, were seen as a threat to Russia's lingering great-power ambitions. Consequently, in the 1990s, Russia's relations with the ex-Soviet Caspian states developed very slowly and painfully. This uncertainty came to an end in 2000, when, under President Putin, Russia started to re-emerge as a confident and increasingly powerful economic player in the region. However, even today, Russia's regional policy is weakened by its inability to reconcile economic and security interests into a regional strategy which could guarantee stability and prosperity for both Russia and its neighbours.

Missed opportunities in the 1990s

Under President Yeltsin's leadership, Russia's policy in the Caspian was based on three sets of interests. The first was to guarantee Russia's security on what emerged as the most vulnerable 'southern flank' of Russia's new frontiers – namely the Caucasus and Central Asia. The second was to promote Russia's economic objectives in the Caspian region. The Russian government and Russia's newly emerged private sector were unsuccessful in winning the economic competition with major Western multinational companies over contracts for developing Caspian hydrocarbon deposits. Furthermore, the Russian government achieved limited results in attempting to employ political instruments to preserve Soviet-era economic monopolies, including a monopoly on oil transit routes for Caspian energy resources. The third set of interests was to preserve influence in an ever more diversified geopolitical environment, characterised by such powerful regional players as the US, several European countries, Turkey, China and increasingly the South Asian states.

In the 1990s the Russian government was not able to incorporate these interests into a coherent regional policy in the Caspian region, let alone in the Caucasus and Central Asia as a whole. There were a number of reasons for this failure (which was not unique to the Caspian region). They included the lack of consensus on foreign-policy priorities among Russia's political elites; the inability of the central government to effectively oversee and co-ordinate policies pursued by different agencies or powerful individuals, particularly in the unreformed security and defence structures; and the growing power of economic lobbies who increasingly wielded strong influence over the government. These problems were compounded by poorly developed expertise among Russia's foreign policy, economic and other elites on contemporary regional issues in the Commonwealth of Independent States (CIS) as a whole and in the Caucasus and Central Asia in particular (for example, there was no think-tank that specialised in research on the South Caucasus and only a handful of experts knew regional languages). Post-Soviet geopolitical thinking among powerful members of the Russian foreign and security policy establishment was marked by a desire to maintain the independent states of the Soviet Union as Russia's exclusive sphere of influence; they resented any external engagement into the region. Finally, Russia lacked sufficient economic resources to underwrite its geopolitical ambitions in the region. Instead, these relied upon remaining military assets and informal post-Soviet networks.

As a result, in the first decade after the collapse of the Soviet Union, Russia did not take full advantage of the economic opportunities in the Caspian region. Notably, it did not secure a stake in the development and transportation of Caspian hydrocarbons. These failures, however, resulted not so much from wrong policy choices on the part of the Russian government, but from a range of other factors. These included domestic battles for privatisation of Russia's energy sector and poor international standing. This limited the ability of major Russian commodities companies to raise capital, domestic or international, for investment in major projects (particularly if they were located outside Russia itself). Another inhibiting factor was the lack of economic focus and expertise in the Russian Foreign Ministry. Moreover, Russian oil and gas sector experts took a sceptical view of the supposed wealth of hydrocarbon resources in the Caspian Sea. Finally, strong external pressures curbed Russia's active involvement in Caspian energy projects. On the one hand, the Caspian states themselves were eager to diversify their export routes, hence strongly opposed Russian involvement; on the other hand, international energy companies had little trust in the viability of commercial partnerships with Russian companies. Nevertheless, even in this difficult environment, Russian companies and the Russian government did achieve some of their economic objectives. For example, they succeeded in winning a stake in international consortiums for the

Azerbaijani oilfields. They also secured a role in the construction of the CPC (Caspian Pipeline Consortium) pipeline by preserving and partly modernising the northern transportation route (Baku–Novorossiysk), despite the ongoing military conflict in Chechnya. They signed contracts for the development of Iranian gas fields and initiated the construction of the Blue Stream gas pipeline to Turkey. Not least, they negotiated favourable terms for the transit of Turkmen gas to Europe across Russian territory. Other opportunities, however, were missed. Thus, they were slow to embark on the exploration of hydrocarbon deposits in the Russian sector of the Caspian Sea (this development gained momentum only after Russia and Kazakhstan signed a bilateral agreement on the legal division of North Caspian oilfields). Also, Russian companies missed out on such projects as the development of the Baku–Tbilisi–Ceyhan (BTC) oil pipeline, dismissed outright by the Russian government on geopolitical grounds.

From the point of view of security interests, Russia's policy in the Caspian region in the 1990s was even less proactive than its energy policy. There was no major military conflict (internal or interstate) in the Caspian region during this period, but this cannot be viewed as a result of Russian policy. In fact, Russia did very little to strengthen security in the region. Yet the war in Chechnya (which was going on almost continually throughout the 1990s) had a profoundly negative impact on the Caspian region (see **Blandy**). It did not prevent foreign investment in the development of Caspian hydrocarbons and southern transportation routes, but this, like the unresolved conflicts in Abkhazia and Karabagh, challenged domestic stability in all the Caucasus states and hampered political and economic reforms. The conflict in Afghanistan, and linked to this the drug traffic and illegal weapons trade, also had a negative impact on the stability and security of the entire region, including that of Russia itself. Russia's military co-operation with Iran and Russian sales of advanced weaponry exacerbated the threat of the potential escalation of disputes over the Caspian Sea (such as indeed occurred in 2001, in the military stand-off between Iran and Azerbaijan). Finally, the presence of Russian military bases in Georgia, despite opposition from the Georgian government and contrary to Russia's commitments undertaken at the Istanbul summit in 1999, further legitimised regional perceptions that Russia was determined to use military pressure as its main strategy for securing influence in the region.

By the end of President Yeltsin's term in office, Russia's position in the Caspian region was extremely weak. Its policy in the region was for the most part not merely reactive, but characterised by contradictions and inconsistencies. Most of the neighbouring states had a negative perception of Russia, regarding it as a source of instability. This was not only because of the unresolved conflict in Chechnya, but also because of Moscow's reluctance to promote a settlement of regional conflicts. In some cases, Russia was even accused of using such conflicts to reassert its power in the region. To the east, in Kazakhstan and Turkmenistan, Russia was seen as a declining power, unwilling to invest political capital and resources in regional integration, yet eager to reap unjustifiably high economic benefits by exploiting its transit monopoly for Central Asian oil and gas exports. Finally, to the south, in Iran, Russia was perceived as an important, but unreliable, partner.

Putin's pragmatic strategy for the Caspian

There was a dramatic change in Russian policy at the turn of the century, triggered by the change of leadership in the Kremlin. On 21 April 2000, Vladimir Putin, then still acting president, authorised and chaired a special meeting of the Security Council, with the object of reassessing Russia's policy in the Caspian Sea region. This was a pivotal event, attended by all the key government ministers and some business representatives. The main task that confronted the new leader was to reconcile national economic and security interests in the Caspian zone. This entailed re-establishing the credibility of Russia's regional policy. The outcome of the Security Council meeting was a new impetus for Russia's policy towards the region. Specific objectives were identified, as were strategies to achieve them. The emphasis now shifted to exploiting Russia's economic influence to gain benefits for Russia's domestic economy.[1] Thus, whereas in the early and mid-1990s Russian policy in the Caspian had been motivated primarily by political and security considerations,[2] after April 2000 economic interests became paramount. Concomitantly, President Yeltsin's policy, albeit undeclared, of winning influence through regaining territorial control by political and military means, was abandoned.[3]

The April Security Council meeting signalled that the new president attached great importance to the Caspian region. Later, in October 2000, this vision was reconfirmed at the first meeting of the interdepartmental commission on the problems of the CIS within Russia's Security Council. The document released from that meeting put the Caspian region as the second priority for Russia's policies in the CIS after Russia's union with Belarus.[4]

The official statement which was released after the Security Council meeting emphasised that 'the scale of Russia's interests in the Caspian region determines the necessity of its [Russia's] comprehensive presence in the region and the need to pursue a more vigorous policy there'.[5] The same document stressed that Russia did not aspire to a dominant role in the region, nor did it seek any confrontation; on the contrary, it supported constructive interaction with foreign partners and was ready for honest, civilised competition. Further, it asserted that Russia was interested in the development of extensive ties with the Caspian countries, in strengthening their independence and sovereignty and in the development of the large deposits of hydrocarbons discovered in the region.

In addition to policy guidelines this meeting also took a number of decisions which sought to overcome the major pitfalls in Russia's Caspian policy over the past decade. Notably, it aimed to improve co-ordination between the key players in government, military and business. A list of specific policy objectives was drawn up and a special presidential envoy for the Caspian region (with the rank of deputy foreign minister) was appointed to oversee implementation. Viktor Kalyuzhny, former fuel and energy minister, was nominated for the post. Such a co-ordinated approach was in stark contrast to Russia's policy and policy-making process during the ten years of Yeltsin's administration, which was notorious for each ministry implementing its own foreign-policy strategy.

Many analysts were sceptical about Russia's new Caspian policy. Yet Putin's administration soon revealed a real commitment to this non-confrontational, economy-driven approach. Active diplomatic efforts have since been undertaken to tackle regional issues, evidenced by high level summits with leaders of all the Caspian states, as well as active shuttle diplomacy by the Russian presidential envoy. Moreover, the US–Russian dialogue on Caspian issues has been upgraded. Important developments have included two meetings between President Putin and his US counterpart George W. Bush. Renewed activities by Russian companies and increased government backing for commercial projects involving Russia's participation have also yielded mutually beneficial results.

On a bilateral level, Russia managed to normalise relations with Azerbaijan and signed a number of important economic and security agreements with President Aliev. Relations with Kazakhstan focused on creating favourable conditions for the development of North Caspian oil resources. The strategic partnership with Iran has been expanded. At the same time, Russia has continued to apply pressure to promote the peaceful settlement of disputes between Iran and Azerbaijan over disputed Caspian oilfields. Russia emerged as a mediator in disputes between Azerbaijan, Turkmenistan and Iran, while remaining a party in negotiations on the overall legal status of the Caspian Sea. Another significant breakthrough was the Russian government's decision to drop its previous attempts at a transportation monopoly and instead to endorse the concept of multiple pipelines. This made possible participation of Russian companies in multilateral projects such as the BTC pipeline. (They did not, in fact, join the BTC Company that was to build the pipeline, but this appears to have been owing to cost/benefit concerns rather than political considerations.) Russia not only continued to emphasise the importance of regional co-operation, particularly on environmental issues, but also actively advocated the establishment of a 'Caspian Five' sub-regional organisation, modelled on the Black Sea, Baltic Sea and Barents Sea co-operation organisations. It also supported the development of a north–south transportation corridor, to run from Europe through Russia, the Caspian region, Iran and India, regarding this as a means of strengthening regional co-operation as well as diversifying regional economies.

Managing disputes over division of Caspian resources

One of the main policy objectives that emerged from the Security Council meeting that was held on Putin's initiative in April 2000 was to progress negotiations over the settlement of the legal division of the Caspian Sea. In

June 2000 the new Russian Foreign Policy Concept put the resolution of the legal status of the Caspian at the core of Russia's foreign policy priorities on the regional level: 'Russia will work for the elaboration of such a status of the Caspian Sea as would enable the littoral states to launch mutually advantageous co-operation in using the region's resources on a fair basis and taking into account the legitimate interests of each other'.[6]

From April 2000 onwards the negotiations over the legal status of the Caspian became the focus of intense diplomatic efforts by the Russian presidential envoy and the president himself. Russia's strategy included three main components:

- clearly defining Russia's position on the Caspian legal status and developing new proposals for settling outstanding territorial disputes among littoral states;
- working bilaterally with each of the littoral states through active 'shuttle' diplomacy by the presidential envoy on Caspian affairs to promote compromise on areas of disagreement;
- applying a step-by-step approach through bilateral agreements to achieve the final five-party consensus.

Russia's position in regard to the status of the Caspian Sea has undergone significant changes over the past decade. In the early 1990s, Russia's policy in the Caspian viewed the oil resources not as the end, but rather as the means for achieving its geopolitical goal of keeping the region under Russia's influence. Therefore, Russia promoted the condominium principle for defining the legal status of the Caspian Sea under which all littoral states should exploit all Caspian resources jointly. Russia argued that the principles which were stipulated in the Soviet–Iranian treaties of 1921 and 1940, on common use of the sea, should be extended to resource use.[7] This common use principle in theory granted all littoral states, including Russia, a veto power over the development of Caspian deposits. Some analysts speculated that Russia adopted such a position deliberately in order to delay the conclusion of the five-party agreement and thus to create a legal vacuum in which foreign oil companies could not proceed with their investment. Even if such a rationale was ever contemplated, it produced precisely the opposite outcome.

Azerbaijan and Kazakhstan favoured a sectoral division of the Caspian. This envisaged the division of both seabed and water resources, also the delimitation of state borders along each of the national sectors, with exclusive fishing rights and the right for increasing their border guards and naval forces. Russia, like Iran, had strongly opposed the division of the Caspian Sea surface by state frontiers, fearing that under such a scenario some disputed fields could become a source of conflict between littoral states. Moreover, such a sectoral division could jeopardise the implementation of common environmental standards. However, despite active opposition from Russia and Iran, Azerbaijan and Kazakhstan started to implement a de facto division of Caspian Sea resources. Exploiting the legal vacuum, they concluded numerous agreements with international oil companies on the exploration of their offshore hydrocarbon deposits. Therefore, in July 1998 Russia decided to change its position and abandon the condominium principle in favour of the 'sectoral division of seabed – common water use' principle. Under this new principle Russia agreed that littoral states could have ownership of resources which are extracted from their sector of the Caspian seabed, while the principle of free navigation and common ecological standards could be preserved. Russia continued to view the five-party consensus as the only legally acceptable mechanism for defining the final status of the Caspian Sea; bilateral agreements were viewed more as a tool for settling disputes over offshore oilfields between Russia's own part of the Caspian and those of its immediate neighbours, thus providing an opening for the development of its own resources in the North Caspian.

Bilateral agreements for North Caspian

This bilateral approach was reaffirmed by the Russian–Kazakhstani declaration on 'Co-operation in the Caspian Sea' which was signed by Presidents Putin and Nazarbaev in October 2000. In June 2002, Russia and Kazakhstan signed the agreement dividing responsibility over the development of oilfields located on their border in the North Caspian region. This agreement determined the exact co-ordinates of the modified median line on the bottom of the Caspian Sea dividing the Russian and Kazakhstani sectors of the North Caspian; the agreement was ratified by the Russian State Duma on 19 March 2003. Russia and Kazakhstan agreed that each side would have sovereign rights to explore oilfields in their respective geographical sectors. Moreover, they agreed that three hydrocarbon deposits located on the modified median line – Kurmangazy, Tsentralnoe and Khvalynskoe – would be developed by Russia and Kazakhstan under the 50:50 principle of joint development.

Following a similar principle, Russia subsequently concluded a bilateral agreement with Azerbaijan, thus gaining full freedom for its companies to begin exploration of Russia's own sector of the North Caspian Sea. In January 2001, when Putin visited Baku, Russia and Azerbaijan signed a declaration on co-operation in the Caspian Sea region. This reaffirmed the principle of the division of the sea shelf and the common use of water resources. Later, in April 2002, Russia and Azerbaijan signed a protocol which determined the points of demarcation of the Caspian Sea shelf along the Russian–Azerbaijani border. This followed the principle of 'sectoral division of seabed – common water use', as agreed in the declaration of January 2001. The two presidents signed a final agreement on the demarcation of the Caspian Sea shelf and its resources along their joint border in September 2002, using the method of a modified median line. Following the conclusion of these agreements between Russia and Kazakhstan, and between Russia and Azerbaijan, the sectoral division of the northern part of the Caspian was thus accomplished on the basis of bilateral agreements. This created pressure on Iran and Turkmenistan to reach a similar resolution.

Russia's bilateral agreements on the division of the seabed and its resources contradicted its official position, which called for the resolution of the legal status of the Caspian Sea by consensus among all the littoral states. The failure of the littoral states to reach accord at the summit in Ashgabat in April 2002 lent legitimacy to Russia's pragmatic policy. Yet the bilateral approach has potential negative costs for the region. In addition to splitting the Caspian region into opposing camps, comprising the winners and losers of the de facto division, Russia began to lose its leverage with Iran and Turkmenistan. No longer regarded as a fair mediator, it had to compensate with concessions on other important strategic issues. These included an increase in arms sales to Iran and support for Turkmenistan's regional ambitions in Central Asia. Both of these policies seemed likely to present Russia with long-term risks and challenges, in the Caspian and beyond.

Managing relations with Iran and Turkmenistan

By abandoning the condominium principle, Russia had to make another choice, namely as to which sectoral division principle it should support: the principle of an equal 20 per cent share for all, or a division based on the principle of the modified median line, which would result in each party receiving a very different share of Caspian resources. Against strong opposition from Iran, and compromising its own share of resources, Russia chose to support the modified median line principle. Under this scheme, Russia would have only 18.5 per cent of the Caspian Sea, while Kazakhstan would have 29 per cent, Azerbaijan and Turkmenistan over 19 per cent, and Iran only 14 per cent. The modified median line proposal made Iran the greatest loser, as it would receive the smallest share of resources. Understandably, therefore, Iran opposed this new proposal, despite the fact that it was endorsed by Kazakhstan and Azerbaijan. Iran continued to propose either the condominium principle, or a division of the seabed on the basis of an equal 20 per cent share for each of the littoral states. Russia stood to gain more seabed territory under the Iranian proposal for equal 20 per cent shares, but was concerned that a redivision of fields already under development could lead to major conflicts between the littoral states, with devastating consequences for the Caspian region as a whole (see **Granmayeh**, also **Namazi** and **Farzin**). Consequently, it opposed this approach.

In 2001, in order to reach a compromise with Iran and Turkmenistan (the latter sided with Iran), Russia proposed a new principle of 'resource sharing' which provided for a 50:50 principle for dividing the exploration of disputed fields among the two parties.[8] This principle would give Iran and Turkmenistan rights for the development of parts of fields which were currently the subject of disputes with Azerbaijan. Moreover, the Russian proposal was prepared to take account of the fact that some of these fields were already under development by Azerbaijani and international oil companies. Therefore, in addition to the 50:50 principle, Russia proposed the principle of 'compensating historic costs' for disputed deposits. This meant that the party which, through the 50:50 agreement, received rights to develop parts of the disputed fields, should compensate the other party for historic costs incurred in exploration of the field. At the same time, Russia insisted that this compensation should not draw on financial resources obtained from a third party. Thus, if the country claiming 50 per cent of the disputed fields could not compensate the other side for 'historic costs', it would automatically waive its right to its share.

Russia energetically promoted the 50:50 resource-sharing principle in order to prompt Iran and Turkmenistan to endorse the final agreement on the Caspian Sea status as drafted by Russia and Kazakhstan. This policy had unintended consequences. Instead of producing a compromise, it pushed both Iran and Turkmenistan to undertake desperate measures to secure their interests. The most dangerous incident occurred in July 2001, when Iran used its military force to stop BP- operated ships from conducting exploratory work on a disputed field in the Caspian (see **Katik**). The signing of the Russian–Azerbaijani declaration the previous January may have increased Iranian fears of a de facto division of the sea at the expense of Iranian interests and could have prompted this action in July. Nevertheless, some progress was made in finding common ground. As Kalyuzhny pointed out in early 2003, Russia still upheld 'the principle of division which is dictated by nature', but regarded a division based on the principle of resource sharing as an acceptable compromise. Thus, it tried to tempt Iran by offering participation in a Russo-Turkmen joint venture to develop hydrocarbon structures in the Turkmen sector.[9] Principles for the division of the sea were discussed further at meetings of the Special Working Group on the Legal Status of the Caspian, held in 2003 in Baku in February, in Almaty in May and in Moscow in July. These events did not produce immediate results, but both Russian and Iranian representatives indicated that some common understandings had been reached. Negotiations were still in progress in 2004.

Pipeline diplomacy: from rivalry to competition

During President Yeltsin's term, the choice of transportation routes for Caspian oil was regarded as part of a new 'Great Game', reflecting the strategic rivalry between Russia and the US. Thus, from the Russian perspective, this was not so much an issue of economic benefits, as an issue of reasserting its control over ex-Soviet states in the Caspian region. For the US (with the support of Turkey and some European allies), the choice of pipelines had two major objectives: to demolish Russia's post-imperial claims over Caspian resources, and to prevent these resources from being exported via Iranian transport routes. Therefore, the economic rationale played a secondary role in the motivations of both 'great powers'.

President Putin recognised that a zero-sum competition with the West in the Caspian was both dangerous and ineffective for securing Russia's real interests in the area. As he stated during the April 2000 Security Council meeting: 'We must not turn the Caspian into yet another area of confrontation, no way ... This is a matter of competition and we must be competitive.'[10] In December 2001, Viktor Kalyuzhny, the special presidential envoy for Caspian affairs, insisted that 'Russia is not aiming at a transport monopoly in the Caspian region, and has nothing against the idea of there being a variety of pipelines. It understands that in the course of time demand for new pipeline infrastructure will rise in tandem with increase in oil-yield.'[11] By acquiescing in the expansion of foreign economic interests in the Caspian, Russia did in fact succeed in strengthening its position in the pipeline competition. The role of the Russian government in the pipeline politics at this period was characterised by three strategies:

- promoting the interests of Russian companies in all major Caspian projects;
- giving the 'green light' to foreign investment in Caspian projects undertaken on Russian territory (e.g. the CPC project);
- using high-level political contacts to reassure Azerbaijan and Kazakhstan that Russia would not use transportation routes through its territory as a means of exerting political pressure on these countries and undermining their economic interests.

The change in Russia's policy, which downplayed geopolitical zero-sum vision in relation to pipeline routes, prompted greater US–Russian co-operation on the development of Caspian oil and gas transportation routes. This spirit of conciliation was reflected in the personal relations between Vladimir Putin and George W. Bush. In November 2001, following the Russian president's visit to the US, Viktor Kalyuzhny said in an interview that Moscow was happy with signs that the US policy was no longer oriented towards pushing Russia out of the region. He emphasised that US policy had shifted from a position of exclusion of Russian interests in the Caspian region to that of co-operation.[12]

With improvement of EU–Russian relations, the Europeans also began to look at Russia as an alternative to the Middle East and OPEC as a source of oil and gas. In this regard transportation of Caspian oil resources through the Russian pipeline network was increasingly seen as an important short- and medium-term solution for global economic problems. This was further reinforced by Russia's own investment in pipeline projects to link up with Europe, including the construction of a modern oil terminal on the Russian Baltic Sea coast. Thus, from 2000 onwards, US and European oil companies began increasing their investment in Russia, which in turn contributed to a more stable economic and political environment. An example of this greater confidence was ExxonMobil's decision to move forward with its long-planned investment of several billion dollars in the development of the Sakhalin-1 project in Russia's Far East. Confidence was further strengthened in 2002, when the Russian president acquiesced in the stationing of US troops in Central Asia.

However, there was deterioration in the security environment in the South Caucasus. It seemed likely that the coming years would present numerous challenges for the region – including potential economic and political crises in Georgia and Azerbaijan, as well as the ongoing Karabagh and Georgian-

Abkhaz conflicts. Russia did not hold the key to these problems but, never-theless, it had paid little attention to addressing them. Worse, some Russian actions had exacerbated instability. In particular, there had been a marked worsening in Russian–Georgian relations. Contentious issues included the Russian government's introduction of a visa regime for Georgians, alleged military incidents with participation of Russian troops in the Kadori and the Pankisi regions, delays over the withdrawal of Russian military bases, and unresolved bilateral economic issues.

The resolution of regional conflicts and the creation of conditions for political stability and economic reform in the entire Caucasus region were surely essential factors for the development of major infrastructure projects. Whereas in the past it might have been argued that Russia viewed regional conflicts as a tool for preventing the implementation of projects such as the BTC pipeline, this was certainly no longer the case when Russian compa-nies became involved. Yet Russia's ability to influence the situation in a positive way is limited by two considerations. First, it is too weak to play a decisive role in Abkhazia and Karabagh. Secondly, it is possible that some elements in the Russian government believe that the main focus of attention must remain the conflict in Chechnya, since any distraction from this goal would place an impossible strain on Russia's crisis-management resources. However, until Russia, through co-operation with regional states and external institutions, demonstrates a credible commitment to addressing fundamental regional security challenges, its political–military actions in the region will continue to be interpreted in a highly negative light as an attempt to block any progress for alternative pipelines.

The role of Russian companies

In March 2000 Russian Foreign Minister Ivanov stated that

> 'the international aspect of the oil and gas business will gain an increas-ingly prominent place in Russia's foreign policy strategy. This is not only one of the most considerable means of defending our foreign policy and foreign economic interests, but also an effective geopolitical factor and a tool for strengthening national security in all of its dimensions.'[13]

This policy statement formed the core of Putin's Caspian policy. Previously, the interests of Russian oil companies had regularly clashed with those of the Foreign Ministry, which did not regard the development of the oil sector as a top priority.[14] In 1997, for example, this lack of regard for economic interests prompted President Boris Yeltsin to call for the cancellation of a deal that had been signed by the Russian oil companies Rosneft and LUKoil for the development of the Kyapaz–Serdar oilfield, because Azerbaijan and Turkmenistan were in dispute over this field and the Russian foreign-policy establishment did not want to offend the Turkmen leader (see **Canzi**, p. 195).

The first signs of policy change came in 1998 after Russia and Kazakhstan signed the seabed delimitation agreement. This was followed by the conclusion of a multilateral agreement on the construction of CPC pipeline. The Russian government acquired a 24 per cent stake in the CPC project and Russian companies LukArco and Rosneft–Shell Caspian Ltd another 12.5 per cent and 7.5 per cent respectively. Construction of the CPC pipeline started in 1999 and was completed in 2001. It has a current capacity of 28 million tonnes of oil a year, with future potential to increase capacity to 67 million tonnes a year. It is expected to bring over US$300 million annual revenue to the Russian state budget by 2008.

In addition to financial benefits, the CPC project brought Russia important political dividends. On one hand, it secured the transportation of large proven Caspian oil reserves via its territory. On the other hand, it gave Western companies a stake in what has become the largest US investment in Russia. Moreover, it signalled Russia's readiness to develop Caspian resources in co-operation with the US. This fact was emphasised by President Putin during both his summit meetings with President Bush. The US responded by sending the US energy secretary to Russia for the official opening of the CPC pipeline in November 2001. Such an exchange of gestures would have been hard to imagine just a few years ago at the height of US–Russia rhetorical clashes over Caspian pipeline routes.

With Azerbaijan, too, relations improved. In January 2002, during the visit of President Heidar Aliev to Moscow, an extension of a transportation agreement for Azerbaijani oil via the Baku–Novorossiysk transport corridor was signed. This deal, which covers 5 million tonnes of oil a year, was feasible because the Russian authorities had succeeded in maintaining the northern route in operation, despite instability in the North Caucasus. On this occasion Russians did not raise concerns over the fact that in the past two years the State Oil Company of the Azerbaijani Republic (SOCAR) had transported much lower volumes of oil via this route than foreseen by the previous Azerbaijani–Russian agreement. According to Russian experts, Putin decided to avoid political controversy by downplaying the issue of the under-utilisation of the Baku–Novorossiysk pipeline. Instead, he proposed an economic solution to Baku under which Moscow would supply natural gas for the domestic market in Azerbaijan, which in turn would make additional oil available for export via Russia's northern route.[15]

With the advent of President Putin in the Kremlin, Russian oil companies were strongly encouraged to follow government policy, in exchange for government efforts to lobby their interests more actively. This approach met with some success, enabling Foreign Minister Igor Ivanov to claim, 'of all economic fields, the fuel and energy sector [private companies] have perhaps achieved the closest and most efficient co-ordination with the ministry of foreign affairs. This includes joint work on the problems of the Caspian.'[16] It was this type of co-ordination that helped to underpin the change in Russia's position on the BTC pipeline. For a while, however, the Russian government continued to maintain that the venture was not economically viable and, in November 2001, Russian Deputy Prime Minister Viktor Khristenko announced that 'the Russian side does not have any economic interest in this project'.[17] The first indication of Moscow's policy change came when two major Russian oil companies – LUKoil and Yukos – declared their interest in purchasing shares in the BP-led international consortium for the construction of the BTC pipeline. A few weeks later, in January 2002, during Heidar Aliev's visit to Moscow, President Putin gave official confirmation of this move.[18] Thereafter, however, the initiative stalled and neither company joined the BTC consortium. Moreover, in November 2002, LUKoil, which since 1994 had been a member of the Azerbaijan International Oil Consortium that was developing the Azeri–Chirag–Guneshli (ACG) complex, unexpectedly sold its shares to Japanese Inpex (see **Olsen**, p. 130). There was speculation as to whether this move was the result of pressure exerted on LUKoil by the Russian government; however a more likely explanation was that the company did not regard this project as a priority area for investment. LUKoil remained a member (first singly, then in co-partnership with Agip) of the Shah Deniz consortium, which it had joined when it was created in 1996; it also continued to participate (as LukAgip) in the consortium for the construction of the South Caucasus gas pipeline.

LUKoil continues to be one of the main players in the Caspian. In 2001, it extracted over 78 million tonnes of oil, of which only 2.2 million was extracted outside of Russia. It achieved an increase of 44 per cent in its hydrocarbon reserves, mainly through the exploitation of fields in the North Caspian Sea (in the Russian sector) and in the Timano–Pechera region of Siberia.[19] LUKoil worked closely with the Russian government in negotiations with Kazakhstan on the exploitation of the three hydrocarbon deposits located on the modified median line (i.e. Kurmangazy, Tsentralnoe and Khvalynskoe).[20] This company also played an important role in promoting the improvement of Azerbaijani–Russian relations, as acknowledged in March 2001 by Azerbaijani President Heidar Aliev.[21] LUKoil has also been participating in developing the Alov–Araz–Sharq offshore oilfield in the sector of the Caspian claimed by Azerbaijan.

However, relations between the Russian government and some of the Russian oil companies have not always proceeded so smoothly. For example, the Transneft oil company proposed the construction of a pipeline for Caspian oil to run from Russia via Kazakhstan to Iran. Victor Kalyuzhny, the presidential envoy, expressed strong opposition to this project, dubbing it 'anti-state'.[22] His objections were no doubt influenced by concern for the harm that such a project would inflict on Russia's strategic partnership with the US. Given that under Putin's administration private firms are expected to support Russia's stated national interests, it is highly unlikely that maverick schemes such as this would be allowed to proceed.

Addressing regional security concerns

In May 2002 President Putin chaired a special session of the Russian State Council, a powerful consultative body that brings together regional leaders of the Russian Federation. At this meeting, Alexander Dzasokhov, president of the North Ossetian Republic, presented a report outlining the major threats to the Russian Federation. They included 'the proliferation of extremist Islamic terrorism inside Russia, the potential for new escalation of the Chechen conflict, the threat of destabilisation in the predominantly Islamic regions of Russia, potential instability in Central Asia and refugees and migration problems'.[23] All these threats are clearly present in the Caspian region, which not only borders Chechnya and Central Asia, but also other Islamic regions of Russia such as Daghestan. Thus, the Caspian region is viewed as a focus of Russia's security policy. Moreover, the fact that Moscow is developing new pragmatic relations with NATO enables it to shift its security and defence priorities from the west to the south. This has significant implications for defence planning, modernisation and procurement.

The main objectives for Russia's security policy in the Caspian region include:

- to prevent the region from becoming a transit route for military, financial and human support for Chechen rebels operating in Chechnya;
- to contain the escalation of regional conflicts from reaching a point where they could destabilise security and stability in Russia's North Caucasus;
- to preserve former Soviet military infrastructure in the region, including key air defence, space and early warning facilities, as well as to maintain a Russian military presence at bases in Georgia and Armenia;
- to maintain an effective military force to protect Russia's oil reserves and transportation routes from external intervention;
- to address soft security threats emanating from the region such as illegal migration, drug trafficking and smuggling of contraband goods to Russia.

At different periods throughout the 1990s Russia's policy focused on different components of this list of security threats. However, the first priority for Russia has remained the need to resolve the situation in Chechnya. This has figured strongly in Moscow's considerations vis-à-vis its relations with the Caspian states. For example, Russia's political support for Iran and its readiness to supply Iran with technology and military equipment, despite US disapproval, is largely driven by Moscow's gratitude for Iran's restraint in Chechnya. Thus, although the Chechen rebels champion the Islamic cause in their fight against Russian forces, Iran has not provided them with political or military support.

The military campaigns in Chechnya in 1994–1996 and from 1999 onwards have caused huge disruption throughout the entire region, triggering a mass movement of refugees, a proliferation of arms trafficking and other criminal activities, as well as attracting militant extremists from Islamic organisations all over the world. Links between Chechen rebels and al-Qaeda were not as substantial as those between al-Qaeda and the Taleban regime in Afghanistan. Yet there is little doubt that many militants trained by al-Qaeda were involved in the Chechen conflict, either directly or by supplying weapons and funds. Inevitably, neighbouring states in the South Caucasus, have suffered as a result of this conflict. Georgia in particular has been badly affected. Already weakened by chronic domestic problems, it could not exert effective military control over the whole of its territory. Consequently, it was unable to prevent Chechen rebels from entering Georgia and becoming entrenched in the Pankisi gorge. This provoked a crisis in bilateral Russian–Georgian relations, culminating in President Putin's ultimatum to the Georgian leadership to crack down on the militants in Pankisi, or face Russian military strikes against them on Georgian territory. Russia also introduced a visa regime for Georgian citizens. By contrast, Azerbaijan has adopted a stronger and more constructive (from Moscow's perspective) policy towards Chechen rebels. Thus, for example, during Putin's visit to Baku in January 2002, the Azerbaijani leadership agreed to prosecute Chechen fighters who seek refuge on its territory and to extradite them to Russia. Azerbaijan also helped to crack down on some financing networks and drug-trafficking activities run by Chechen rebels. As a result of these actions, Russia agreed not to introduce a visa regime for Azerbaijan. Rather, it has promoted the normalisation of bilateral relations underpinned by regular political dialogue. Moscow has also concluded a number of agreements with Baku, including one on military–technical co-operation.

A second priority for Moscow's security policy in the Caspian region has been the consolidation and improvement of its own military capabilities in the Caspian region. The Russian military presence in the adjacent North Caucasus region had already been expanded due to the campaign in Chechnya. In addition, Russia started to modernise its forces in the Caspian region, including the Caspian flotilla, which until 2002 had been neglected. In August 2002, the Caspian flotilla embarked on major military exercises; these were the largest since the demise of the Soviet Union, involving 60 vessels, 10,000 personnel and 30 aircraft.[24] According to the Commander-in-Chief of the Russian Navy, Admiral Kuroedov, these exercises did not have a traditional military nature, but were designed to assist in the fight against terrorism in all its forms, the prevention of drug-trafficking activities, search and rescue at sea operations, and the creation of conditions for better exploitation of Caspian resources.[25] However, many states in the region viewed these exercises as a vehicle to exert pressure on Russia's Caspian neighbours after the failure of the Ashgabat summit in April that year. Some officials and analysts in Iran speculated that the exercises were specifically designed to force Iran to moderate its position.[26] However, this interpretation was not borne out by official reactions. Tehran sent observers to monitor the exercises. Moreover, Moscow agreed to further increase arms exports to Iran, thus placing it among the top five nations receiving Russian arms exports.[27] Moreover, in August 2002 Moscow announced that it was planning to expand its co-operation with Iran in the military–technical and nuclear fields.

A third priority has been to maintain access to military facilities and infrastructure in the region. These include the military bases which Russia currently has in Georgia and in Armenia, access to an early warning Radio-Location Station in Gabala, Azerbaijan, and use of the Baikonur space-launching centre in Kazakhstan. With the exception of Georgia, Russia's military presence in the region and its military technical co-operation with the regional states do not provide any source of friction for relations between different Caspian states. In most cases Russia and each host country have found a mutually beneficial economic (as in the case of Gabala[28] and

Baikonur) or strategic (in the case of Armenia) basis for agreement on Russia's use of the facilities.

In the case of Georgia, however, the presence of Russian military bases has been a major source of tension in bilateral relations. On 17 November 1999, Russia and Georgia signed a joint declaration at the OSCE summit in Istanbul, according to which the Russian side committed itself to close two (Vaziani and Gudauta) of the four military bases (Vaziani, Gudauta, Batumi, Akhalkalaki) by 1 July 2001. The Vasiani base was closed down according to schedule. According to Russian sources, the closure of the Gudauta base was completed by the end of 2001. The Georgian side, however, asserts that Russia is continuing to use the facility. The Istanbul declaration also stipulated that, in the course of the year 2000, Russia and Georgia would agree on the timing for the withdrawal of the two remaining bases, in Batumi and Akhalkalaki respectively.

By the beginning of 2003 negotiations on the withdrawal of these two bases had still not yielded concrete results. Russia was requesting an extension of 15 years, on the grounds that the closure of these bases would further desta-bilise the situation in Georgia. Moreover, it was claimed, the local popula-tions wanted these bases to remain open because of the economic benefits that they brought. Tbilisi, however, insisted on a three-year deadline, since it regarded the bases as a source of pressure to keep Georgia within the Russian orbit. The legitimacy of these bases has been repeatedly called into question by the Georgian parliament, which in September 2002 adopted a resolution calling on President Eduard Shevardnadze to begin unilateral closure. Some Georgian analysts see Russia's insistence on keeping its military bases as a means to prevent the construction of oil and gas pipelines which would transit Georgian territory in proximity to the volatile regions where the Russian bases are located. However, the Russian side has never declared any intention to use its forces to threaten the security of the new pipelines.

The real threat to projects such as the BTC pipeline comes from the potential escalation of the unresolved, albeit latent since the mid-1990s, conflicts in the South Caucasus – in Abkhazia and in Karabagh (see **Gerber**). Under President Putin, Russia has pursued a more consistent and balanced policy in regard to these conflicts. Deputy Foreign Minister Valery Loschinin was appointed to the post of special presidential representative on the reso-lution of the conflict in Abkhazia. Similarly, Russia undertook active discussions with the leaders of Armenia and Azerbaijan, both bilaterally and under the auspices of the OSCE Minsk Group.

Since 1994 Russia has deployed 1,500 peace-keepers in Abkhazia, acting under a CIS peace-keeping mandate. This does not actively promote the return of Georgian refugees. Georgia has repeatedly sought to extend this mandate to cover the entire Gali region and to protect Georgian refugees who are expected to begin returning there. However, neither Russia nor the CIS heads of state have reacted favourably to this request. In response, on several occasions the Georgian parliament has threatened to authorise the withdrawal of the Russian peace-keepers. However, there has been no credible offer from other states to replace Russia's 'blue helmets'. Moreover, the UN and

OSCE have been reluctant to take this mission under their own mandate. Consequently, the Georgian authorities have had to recognise that Russia's presence in Abkhazia, even under a limited mandate, represents a stabilising factor. Yet some actions on the part of the Russian government have had the opposite effect. In June 2002, for example, Russia granted citizenship to over 50,000 Abkhaz residents, thus ensuring greater political protection from Moscow. Georgian authorities regarded this as little short of the annexation of Abkhazia by Russia and claimed that it further undermined the legitimacy of Russia's mediation between the two sides in the Abkhaz conflict.[29]

In the case of Karabagh, Moscow's official position is that only two sides – Armenia and Azerbaijan – can find a compromise solution. Russia will then support their decision.[30] This position is different from strict adherence to the principle of territorial integrity. As in the Abkhaz conflict, however, Moscow has not so far invested huge resources in promoting a final political resolution to this conflict. Yet it has gradually accepted the need for greater international engagement in guaranteeing peace and security under future settlements. However, the international community, including the UN and OSCE, have not yet been prepared to commit forces to perform peace-keeping duties in the Caucasus. Therefore, willingly or not, Russia remains involved in the resolution of these conflicts.

Finally, Russia increasingly views the Caspian region as a source of new 'soft security' threats to its own national interest. Kazakhstan and Georgia represent major routes for drug trafficking into Russia. Similarly, Central Asia and the Caucasus have become major exporters of illegal economic immigrants to Russia. According to various estimates, more than half a million citizens from each of the three South Caucasus states – Georgia, Azerbaijan and Armenia – are currently working illegally in Russia. The Kazakh–Russian border, 7,000 km in length, is the main entry point for these illegal immigrants, but it is still not fully operationally equipped. Moreover, in addition to drugs and illegal migration, these borders are used for transporting economic contraband into Russia. This costs the Russian budget millions of dollars every year. Yet Russia itself lacks the resources to control effectively its southern borders. Therefore it has started to work with law-enforcement and other services from states in the region to address these issues both on a bilateral basis and under the auspices of regional organisations such as the CIS and the Shanghai Co-operation Organisation, as well as the UN and OSCE. An example of this bilateral approach is the agreement between Russia and Azerbaijan, signed in January 2002, which defines the status of their citizens residing and working in the other country.

Conclusions

The shift from a geopolitical to a pragmatic orientation in Russian policy in the Caspian region was initiated by President Putin. Recognising that the attempts of the previous administration to exert geopolitical pressure on Caspian neighbours had resulted in a decline in Russia's influence in the region and, moreover, had seriously undermined the competitiveness of

Russian companies, he adopted a policy that put Russia's oil interests at the forefront of its Caspian strategy. This entailed the use of foreign policy to promote Russia's economic interests. Russian companies eagerly embraced this change. At the same time, the new policy orientation helped to overcome the long-standing mistrust towards Russia.

Under the Putin administration, Russia took significant steps to reinforce its military presence in the region, both on its own territory and in the neighbouring states, while taking a more proactive position on addressing 'soft security' threats emanating from its southern border. However, the continuing war in Chechnya, as well as the deterioration of Russian–Georgian relations and slow progress on resolving other regional conflicts, made the South Caucasus region not more, but less secure. This insecurity has so far not presented any immediate threat to the development of Caspian oil resources or the construction of its transportation routes. Yet regional instabilities and unsettled conflicts could pose major challenges to the medium- and long-term economic development and political stabilisation of the Caspian region. In the next decade this may be further aggravated by the political leadership transition in several Caspian and Central Asian states, including Russia's immediate neighbours.

All this indicates that, despite Russia's growing economic power and political leverage in relations with the other Caspian Sea states, it is still too weak to assume the regional leadership role to which it aspires. At the same time, the US and other Western states may be losing interest in the Caspian region, which no longer offers a playground for a grand geopolitical game vis-à-vis 'Russia's post imperial ambitions'. Even Turkey, which remains an important regional power, is increasingly preoccupied by other problems such as its domestic economic crisis, its negotiations with the EU and its alliances in the Middle East. Based on this situation, the Caspian region is entering an increasingly uncertain future. It is possible that the decade of the oil boom may be replaced by a period when unresolved security problems may once again move to the forefront of regional concerns.

Notes

1 See also 'New Directions in Caspian Politics', T. Makarenko, *Jane's Intelligence Review*, 1 May 2001.
2 For a detailed account on this see 'Russian Interference in the Caspian Sea Region: Diplomacy Adrift', J.-C. Peuch in David Lane (ed.), *The Political Economy of Russian Oil*, Lanham MD, pp. 189–212.
3 See 'New Directions in Caspian Politics', Tamara Makarenko, *Jane's Intelligence Review*, 1 May 2001.
4 Ministry of Foreign Affairs, *Daily News Bulletin*, 5 October 2000 (www.In.mid.ru).
5 Factsheet on Russia's policy in the Caspian region, Russian Foreign Ministry website (www.In.mid.ru), document 396-11-5-200.
6 Foreign Policy Concept of the Russian Federation, approved by President Putin on 28 June 2000, Russian Foreign Ministry website (www.In.mid.ru).
7 For details on evolution of Russia's policy on Caspian Sea legal status see speech by Victor Kalyuzhny, special presidential envoy for Caspian affairs, at the conference on 'Managing the Development of Caspian Oil', Baku, 9 November 2000, Foreign Ministry of the Russian Federation daily news bulletin (www.In.mid.ru).

8 Lloyd's list, *International News*, 20 November 2001, p. 6; also interview with Victor Kalyuzhny in *Nezavisimaya Gazeta*, published in *Diplomatic Courier* on 28 September 2000 (Foreign Ministry, *Daily News Bulletin*, www.In.mid.ru).
9 Gazeta.kz website, reported by BBC Monitoring, 30 January 2003.
10 See C. Saivetz, *Putin's Caspian Policy*, Caspian Studies Program, Harvard University, October 2000.
11 'Russian Envoy Says Moscow Not After Caspian Transport Monopoly', *BBC Monitoring Former Soviet Union – Economic*, 22 December 2001.
12 Lloyd's list, *International News*, 23 November 2001.
13 Speech by Foreign Minister Ivanov 'Russia's foreign policy and oil and gas strategy in 21st century', delivered at the presentation of a special issue of *International Affairs* journal, Foreign Ministry of the Russian Federation website (document 194-23-3-200), 20 March 2000.
14 'Russian Interference in the Caspian Sea region: Diplomacy Adrift', Peuch, *op. cit.*, p. 212.
15 'Russia's National Interests in the Caspian Region', M. Margelov in Yelena Kalyuzhnova *et al.* (eds), *Energy in the Caspian Region*, Palgrave, Basingstoke (UK), p. 198.
16 Speech by Foreign Minister Ivanov 'Russia's foreign policy and oil and gas strategy in 21st century', delivered at the presentation of a special issue of *International Affairs* journal, Foreign Ministry of the Russian Federation website (document 194-23-3-200), 20 March 2000.
17 'Russian Deputy Prime Minister Reiterates Moscow's Indifference Towards Baku–Tbilisi–Ceyhan', *Turan News Agency*, 14 November 2001, reported by *BBC Monitoring TransCaucasus Unit*.
18 'Top Manager Welcomes Russian Oil Companies to Baku–Tbilisi–Ceyhan Project', *BBC Monitoring Global Newsline*, Former Soviet Union Economic File, 18 January 2002.
19 Caspian Information Channel CAN report, 16 January 2002.
20 Specifically, LUKoil lobbied the Russian government to claim the Kurmangazy oilfield which Kazakhoil was planning to put up for sale (Kazakh Commercial TV, 2 November 2001). Rosneft, another Russian oil company, also bid for joint exploration of the Kurmangazy oilfield.
21 'Azeri President, Head of Russia's LUKoil Discuss Co-operation in the Caspian', report by Azerbaijani TV, *BBC Monitoring Former Soviet Union – Economic*, 28 March 2001.
22 'Russia Urges Caspian States to Work Out Joint Oil Balance', March 2001, *BBC Monitoring Former Soviet Union – Economic*.
23 The State Council outlined five main threats to Russia (http://lenta.ru/russia/2002/05/22/gossovet/).
24 S. Bladov 'Russia Makes Waves in the Caspian', *Asia Times*, 15 August 2002 (see *CDI-Russia Weekly*, electronic publication).
25 V. Kuroedov, 'Military Exercises in the Caspian Sea Do Not Have a Traditional Military Nature' (http://www.strana.ru/print/154794.htlm/).
26 'Iran Largely Silent on Russian-led Caspian Sea Military Exercises', A. Moaveni, *Eurasianet*, 8 August 2002 (http://www.eurasianet.org/).
27 See *Military Balance 2001–2002*.
28 Agreement on the use of the Gabala station was reached during President Aliev's visit to Moscow in January 2002. For US$7 million a year Russia will have a right to operate the facility for ten years and will share data with the Azeri side. Russia will also compensate the Azeri side for the use of the facility from mid-1997 to 2002. Furthermore, Russia will help Azerbaijan to modernise the air defence forces which will be carrying overflight protection for the station.
29 Shevardnadze compared the process of granting Russian citizenship to Abkhaz residents with annexation (http://www.strana.ru/news/151995.htm).
30 'Russia's National Interests in the Caspian Region', Margelov, *op. cit.*, p. 202.

16 US involvement in the business and politics of the Caspian Sea region

Carter Page

The two main groups involved in the American effort to affect the political, economic and security situation in the Caspian Sea region are the major US energy companies that have made investments in the former Soviet nations and the US government. The conflicts, accomplishments and decisions in this area of US international affairs can largely be viewed through the relationships between these two groups and the respective efforts they have made in the region. While each party has staked out its own series of negotiating positions, both the oil companies and the US government have generally displayed the realisation that political and economic interests must be carefully balanced.[1] The history of the involvement by each of these two parties in the Caspian region during the first decade after the fall of the Soviet Union shows significant consistency in terms of stated goals, even in the wake of major political change in the surrounding regions and throughout the world.

During the Cold War, the Soviet republics and independent nations of the Caspian Sea region were not focal points of US–Soviet relations. Held under tight control by Moscow, the individual Soviet republics along the Caspian (i.e. Azerbaijan, Kazakhstan and Turkmenistan) were largely unable to play a significant role in their own right in the conflicts between the world's superpowers. This lack of experience in dealing with such negotiations and the types of decisions inherent in them represented an important handicap that the leaders of these new nations would be forced to overcome. Following the end of the Soviet empire, the learning curve for regional leaders was short and steep.

In the early years of the post-Cold War era, the Caspian region came into sharp focus for Washington. This new attention was based less on a direct interest in the individual former Soviet republics and more on the execution of overarching goals, such as those inherent in the Clinton administration's engagement policy.[2] In addition to the implementation of strategic doctrine, the US was also largely focused on implementing changes in its relationship with major regional actors such as Russia, Turkey and Iran. While some experts have maintained that oil was a prime factor in the strategic calculations of the US during this era, others have argued that energy resources were of secondary importance to the geopolitical agenda of supporting Turkey and containing Iran and, to a lesser extent, Russia. The thesis that oil-specific concerns were secondary is supported by the fact that interest in the region remained consistently high throughout the duration of the Clinton administration, even though estimates of cumulative Caspian resources were significantly decreased as time progressed.

If the euphoria of the early 1990s marked the beginning of US interest and involvement in the Caspian area, then the second major phase of post-Cold War US relations with the Central Asian nations began with the advent of new obstacles in the mid- to late 1990s. In these years, it became clear that large energy profits would not quickly materialise and the magnitude of future gains would be limited by various adverse conditions. The most important unexpected roadblocks included the lack of significant oil discoveries (i.e. dry holes), a drop in oil prices and unfavourable political developments. These problems were perhaps most vividly and dramatically chronicled in the ongoing saga surrounding the Baku–Tbilisi–Ceyhan pipeline which is discussed later in this chapter.[3]

The steep decrease in oil prices in 1998 was a phenomenon that caught almost all energy analysts, politicians and investors by surprise. The key problem from a practical perspective was that individual oil projects would no longer be profitable based on the return on investment required for these ventures to break even. Energy companies take a long-term view when choosing investments and do not overestimate the significance of short-term price spikes in either direction when deciding on multiyear projects. However, there was a deep-rooted concern in the late 1990s that market fundamentals had permanently changed and that the low price environment might remain the norm for a significant period of time, if not indefinitely. While oil prices have since reverted closer to their mean and have remained well above the US$20 a barrel level, the probability of continued volatility in global energy markets remains high. Predictions therefore vary widely.

Another factor that stymied Western interest in the Caspian was the discovery that original estimates regarding cumulative energy reserves were incorrect. While oil companies were not taken by surprise, the quantities did not meet the hype originally built up by many political analysts and by popular perception in general. This discovery was unwelcome news to oil industry decision makers who had by then come to understand more fully the implications of the transportation and political obstacles inherent to this region. Although subsequent finds at major new fields such as Kashagan would create new momentum in terms of potential estimates, proven resources are significantly smaller than previously anticipated by some. Triumphant banners such as the 'next Persian Gulf' have since been replaced by the 'next North Sea'.

On the diplomatic front, the once comfortable relationships between Washington and the leaders of the former Soviet republics of the Caspian basin came under increasing strain as the specificity of their negotiations deepened. Although indistinct pronouncements concerning the desire for friendship were easy to achieve in the early days, the more defined goals relating to individual projects often proved far more illusive, once the honeymoon period was over. Almost concurrent to the arrival of these diplomatic stalemates, new macroeconomic conditions led to several unforeseen problems. The devaluation of the Russian rouble in August of 1998 placed most emerging market investments worldwide under serious pressure. The proximity to the epicentre in Moscow had an undeniable psychological effect on those investors who were involved in the Caspian. In the years that followed, investors gradually began to regain confidence in the region but the turbulence had left a residual feeling of anxiety; this would take a considerable period to subside.

A classic example of temporary challenges faced by those involved in the development of the Caspian Sea was the US-supported Baku–Tbilisi–Ceyhan (BTC) pipeline. While officials in both the Clinton and George W. Bush administrations expressed continued confidence that the BTC pipeline would eventually come to fruition, these goals were not achieved without continued delays and numerous false starts throughout the late 1990s. Even in 2003, after construction had begun, significant scepticism remained that the project would be seen through to completion.[4]

While many of the political battles that the US has waged in the Caspian have been held in the energy and security arenas, Washington has also given some limited attention to the social condition of the people of these regions. This has consisted of a fairly low-profile attempt at improving the social situation. However, perhaps the element of US policy that has been most challenging has been seen in the shortfall in attempts to bolster observance of human rights and, more broadly, the 'democratisation' process in the former Soviet republics. In most instances, these objectives have lagged behind the broader geopolitical goals of increasing oil reserves and enhancing security in Central Asia.

In summary, the temporary decrease in interest in Caspian energy development during the late 1990s was concurrent with and in large part due to the advent of exceedingly low oil prices, economic instability in emerging markets and the reopening of competing energy markets. As interest in the Caspian among the US foreign policy and energy industry communities waned, it became the conventional wisdom that opportunities for substantial profit in the region were decidedly less than those envisioned by some at the outset of the post-Cold War era.

Some suggested that a Bush presidency might be inclined to change policies in the region through pro-energy policy shifts such as increased support for a warming of relations with Iran, but this speculation has so far proven unfounded. Despite the great fanfare surrounding the Bush administration's strategic energy policy review in the spring of 2001, no major alterations to the Clinton path were put into place with respect to the Caspian's energy development.[5] More significant changes would instead be seen on the security front.

From the perspective of the George W. Bush administration, which came into office in 2001, an increasingly important area of uncertainty and a defining factor in the post-euphoria era of US–Caspian relations is the unique influence of Russia. In his first years in office, President Putin asserted greater influence on the nations of the Caspian with the overt intent of rebuilding Moscow's influence in this region.[6] Though some of his comments hinted at an increased interest in old Soviet territory, the extent to which he would eventually follow through on this objective was not as onerous as some might have originally assumed. The definition of policy by high-ranking US political figures vis à vis Russia's role in the Caspian lacked clarity during the early years of the Russian presidency, while policy makers hedged their bets as to the extent of Putin's influence and power. More recently, George W. Bush's positive relationship with President Putin indicates an opportunity for long-term partnership in the region if these links are successfully managed. As of yet, the specific issue of the Caspian's development has not been high on the agenda of ongoing bilateral discussions at the highest levels. However, the sides have laid the groundwork for such co-operation by introducing various avenues for dialogue. Various intergovernmental working groups have been established and various funding efforts by the Export–Import Bank of the United States and Overseas Private Investment Corporation have been initiated.[7] In addition, several more general obstacles have been cleared and the political landscape has changed to such an extent that a co-operative dialogue is now more feasible. One example of this is that the US has quieted its complaints about Russia's activities in Chechnya (in part as an implicit concession for other US foreign-policy initiatives and concerns such as Iraq and Afghanistan). While some may criticise the motives, such understood quid pro quo arrangements stand as proof of the potential for the convergence of US and Russian policy in the region.

In addition to political changes in Russia, another country-specific development which originated at the end of the 1990s related to the limited and gradual changes in the political relationship between the US and the Islamic Republic of Iran.[8] Despite countless setbacks, the possibility of future positive trends could eventually alter the geopolitical structure of the region in a way that would lead to commercial benefits for the US and Iran and would support the developing nations of Central Asia and the Caucasus. Attempts by the US government to limit the investment of foreign oil companies in Iran have achieved limited success.[9] At times, these policies have had the unintended effect of giving increased confidence to this unique and critical Caspian state as it has attempted to gain greater prominence in the region.

In grappling with each of the individual issues outlined above, Western businesses and the US government have often held divergent views about the future shape of Caspian energy development. The treasury department's rejection of requests to allow swaps with Iran, as well as the broader squabbles over the BTC oil pipeline, are indicative examples of a string of disagreements between the public and private sectors.[10] Future disagreements seem all but inevitable, yet it is increasingly clear that a number of economic and geopolitical factors could lead to major changes in the US government position. Several of these changing dynamics are largely related to the potential for further political changes in the Middle East and the continued economic development of Russia. In practice, the negotiating stance of leading US energy corporations will require parallel reactive changes as well.

Main drivers in the US government position

A perennial subtext of the overall US policy in the Caspian and a consistent justification for the construction of an east–west pipeline route through Turkey relates to the long-standing dependence of the US on Middle Eastern crude oil supplies. Increasing security challenges in the Persian Gulf have left US government policy makers reluctant to add to the total oil output that transits through the narrow maritime bottleneck at the Straits of Hormuz. This position received renewed attention following the terrorist attacks of 11 September 2001 and continued tensions surrounding Iraq, Saudi Arabia, Iran and other littoral states of the Gulf region. Owing to these and related events, longstanding relationships with traditional Gulf state friends have come under increased pressure. In addition to more specific problems in present US–Iran relations, this general energy security concern is a consistent underlying principle that represents the source of perennial objections by the American government regarding the development of Caspian pipeline routes through Iran.

Since US policy towards Iran has at times been a main driver in Caspian affairs,[11] it is useful to review the development of positions taken by influential US policy makers in this area. Late in his administration, President Clinton began to hint at an American policy shift. In a statement before a White House audience, he remarked that, 'Iran . . . has been the subject of quite a lot of abuse from various Western nations'. After describing ways by which the US might help ease the relationship forward in a mutually respectful manner, he remarked that, 'We have to find some way to get dialogue'.[12] The comments were significant in that the language marked an important change in tone and was interpreted as aiming at a degree of reconciliation.

In April 1999, US Assistant Secretary of State Martin Indyk spoke before the Council on Foreign Relations in New York and outlined several of the concerns that, fairly consistently, have driven US policy towards Iran in recent years. These included Iran's proliferation of weapons of mass destruction, support for terrorist groups, and opposition to the Middle East peace process. While these statements echoed past positions, other points in his speech offered signals that change was indeed possible: 'President Khatami's election in Iran and the recent local elections there have made clear that a significant majority of the people of this great nation support political liberalisation, respect for the rule of law, and a constructive role for Iran in regional and international affairs.'[13] The reference to Iran as a 'great nation' left some observers with a sense that US policy was also in transition. In March 2000, Secretary of State Madeleine Albright made similar statements that reaffirmed US optimism and continued to nudge this normalisation process forward.[14]

In the early days of President George W. Bush's administration, Iran did not receive significant attention. For example, the US position towards Iran was not covered in the National Energy Policy review conducted by Vice-President Cheney while several similar emerging sources were discussed in some detail. Immediately after the attacks of 11 September 2001, a further renewed optimism arose as positive statements by President Khatami again hinted at new room for improved relations. In early 2002, however, an intercepted Iranian arms shipment to the Palestinians[15] and US–Iran disagreements over the future shape of Afghanistan[16] seemed to dash hopes for further rapprochement at least for the near term. In that same period, the president's famous reference to Iran as a member of the 'Axis of Evil' seemed to further deflate remaining hopes for a near-term rapprochement.[17]

Compared to US relations with Iran, the relationship with Russia offers a more encouraging model for co-operation between the US and Caspian nations. In December 1998, ambassador Richard Morningstar explained the value of US–Russian co-operation in the development of the Caspian Pipeline Consortium (CPC) line from the Tengiz oilfield in Kazakhstan to the Russian Black Sea port Novorossiysk. He stated, 'Our goal is to build win-win situations for US and Russian companies and to get away from any tendency towards zero-sum thinking when looking at the region'.[18] This concept of co-operative solutions has continued to grow, especially as the overall relationship between the two nations has improved. Despite disagreements which emerged in late 2002 related to the US policy in Iraq, Presidents George W. Bush and Vladimir Putin have generally shown tremendous co-operation which could hold positive implications for the Caspian.[19] Despite bumps in the road, the importance of making Russia a strategic partner in the development of the Caspian states has generally increased over time. By building on mutually achieved accomplishments, the US should successfully avoid possibilities for counterproductive rivalry. Any historical review of Soviet policy in the Caspian shows many areas where criticism of Russia is certainly warranted. However, as a historic source of stability in the region, Russia's involvement should be viewed as an asset and not a threat. The recent arrival of a significant US military force in former Soviet Central Asia has not been uniformly well received in Russia. Nevertheless, if parallel goals between the two sides are emphasised, policy makers can overcome potential tensions. An example of new opportunities for co-operation may be seen in the proposal to build a pipeline through Siberia to Murmansk, which is gaining attention and is said to have found some support in the US government.[20] Such a pipeline could potentially help Kazakh resources to reach world markets and carry positive political ramifications for US–Russian relations by offering the two countries an additional opportunity by which they can partner for mutual gains in the Caspian (as was the case with the construction of the CPC pipeline).

Although the United States government has often played a mediating role in the discussions surrounding the demarcation of the Caspian seabed and the distribution of the undersea portion of the hydrocarbon riches of the region, the US involvement on this front has been, and rightly should remain, fairly limited. Since the end of the 1990s, the American involvement in these discussions has become significantly less active and visible. The American participants in these discussions have often offered technical assistance in an effort to help clarify some of the specific details involved in certain discussions. Overall, the issue remains one of national sovereignty and will be determined by the individual governments of the region. The proactive exertion of any external pressure would run the risk of being construed as undue meddling into internal state affairs. To a large extent, it is in the best interest of the US to stay away from these discussions to avoid potential culpability for any future controversies – and there is a high probability that such controversies will arise. It is all but inevitable that no solution will provide a framework that is acceptable to all. Hence the involvement of Western experts will only serve to provide a scapegoat for any shortcomings that might in the future become a cause of friction (this despite the fact that their influence on the matter will be limited).

At the turn of the century, political inertia as well as the rise of other foreign and domestic policy priorities began to divert Washington's attention and horsepower away from the Caspian. Towards the end of the Clinton administration, although the Department of Energy and the Department of Commerce continued to lobby actively for preferred pipeline routes,[21] the focus at the most senior levels of government shifted towards other issues, in particular to US–China relations, Kosovo and the Middle East. There was significant hope that Bill Clinton would use the final days of his presidency as a catalyst for making a final attempt towards gaining some closure on several of the Caspian-related initiatives pursued in the previous several years. However, this diplomacy initiative was stalled by more pressing and visible foreign-policy priorities, notably his personal efforts to achieve progress in the Middle East.

Renewed interest in Central Asia during George W. Bush's administration has focused on the increasing imperative of finding alternative energy supplies. In preparation for the war in Afghanistan, the use of bases in Kyrgyzstan and Uzbekistan also became a new central pillar of the administration's policy towards Central Asia and the Caucasus.

Main interests for US businesses

The website of the State Oil Company of the Azerbaijan Republic (SOCAR) Coordinating Council displays the following statement:

> The combination of AIOC's [Azerbaijan International Operating Company] minimum obligatory work program (MOWP) and the early oil implementation program is fondly known as . . . [the] 'Million Dollar Experiment' within the consortium. In actuality, the cost of achieving the two programs will total approximately 1.5 billion USD . . .

The above passage, describing one of the numerous energy projects currently under way in the Caspian Sea region, exhibits (perhaps inadvertently) an important disparity in opinion and analysis between major energy companies and their local state counterparties. The governments of the former Soviet nations in this oil-rich region optimistically see the current development of energy resources as a path towards a definitive future outcome. The international energy companies involved in exploration ventures take a different view: they see their involvement as an 'experiment'. From a strictly economic perspective, the early activities by the oil companies implied a significantly lower level of definitive commitment than the individual governments assumed.

With reference to the development of regional infrastructure in general and the construction of the BTC pipeline in particular, the government leaders in the region have placed significant pressure on the potential developers to pursue aggressive investment paths and to make firm commitments sooner rather than later. The companies played an effective waiting game by making minor investments and avoiding undertaking substantial firm commitments during the early periods of study and exploration. In doing so, they purchased what is known in contemporary corporate finance as a 'real option'. As the name implies, real options apply the theory of option pricing in the financial markets to real-world situations.

A high likelihood of receiving new information is the first prerequisite for the application of real options.[22] The precise level of oil reserves currently in the region is unknown and feasibility studies currently under way will help determine this level with greater accuracy. Also, there are high political risks associated with the region. The companies are focused on the reality that, in the short time since the break-up of the Soviet Union, these countries have been plagued with ethnic wars and territorial conflict, leaving many to believe that a new pipeline across this region would be a prime target for attack.

The second prerequisite for a 'real option' is the ability to respond to the new information. A multinational consortium, the Baku–Tbilisi–Ceyhan Pipeline Company, has been formed to implement the BTC project. However, carefully worded agreements between the consortium and the host governments have thus far maintained maximum flexibility for the corporate developers. In other words, the consortium partners have structured their relationships and agreements in a way that would allow them either to abandon the project or reroute the oil along a different path if future information were to make this choice preferable. At the same time, the companies remain in a position to act decisively if positive indicators point towards favourable economic conditions and the potential for profit. While several Western companies have already invested substantial sums in the form of firm commitments, they continue to have significant flexibility in the level of further investment they undertake.

By posting a minimum upfront investment and taking a wait-and-learn approach, the consortium has effectively created a real option. The underlying asset is a fully developed pipeline – the value of which may be alternatively viewed as the present value of the operating profits. However, this value may rise or fall over time based on the actual outcome of key variables that the companies must constantly reassess. For purposes of analysis, the uncertain variables that will drive this changing value over time may be categorised into two main groups: oil prices and regional risk.

The first variable set is oil prices. The business feasibility of a pipeline of this type would be closely related to the value of the commodity that the line will ship. From the macro-perspective of the companies involved, the price of the commodity is a central driving force in the profitability of their entire upstream oil business across all projects. This key variable has shifted radically over the past 15 years as can be seen in Figure 16.1, which shows the movement of the daily current market price of West Texas Intermediary crude (WTI) since 1996. In the period of 1998 to the first half of 2003 alone, the price ranged from just under $11 to nearly $38.

Although there is usually sharp disagreement among energy experts about the future potential outcomes for this and other similar industry benchmarks, most analysts agree that volatility will remain high in the years to come and thus these prices will probably continue to follow an equally uneven path in the future.

The second variable set that is assessed by the companies is what we may refer to as 'regional risk'. This can be defined as the combination of political risk and the risk of oil reserves not meeting high expectations:

$$\text{Regional Risk} = \sum \text{Political Risk} + \text{Risk of Low Resource Reserves}$$

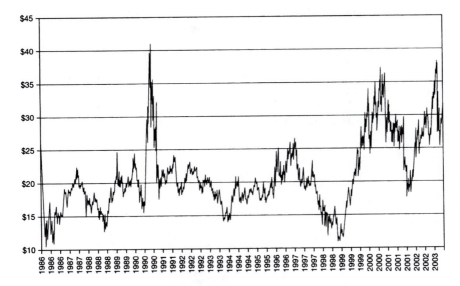

Figure 16.1 WTI spot price (June 1986–June 2003)

Source: US Department of Energy website.

Great uncertainty surrounds the size of the resource base in the Caspian region. The Soviet-era geological studies are of questionable accuracy and thoroughness. Today, state-of-the-art technology is allowing for a more rigorous assessment by the major global oil companies. The bottom line is that this will remain a major point of uncertainty until further feasibility studies have been performed. Significant information on this point will be gained during the duration of the real option's life and the scheduled period for the relevant studies.

Unlike the price of crude, the nature of political risk offers less of a continuous range of potential outcomes. Here, the analysis often consists of a binary (or 'all-or-nothing') set of outcomes. In other words, oil companies must try to assess the probability that certain outcomes within this category will occur in which members of the various consortia would choose to abandon a project entirely. Scenarios could arise which would have a partial negative effect on a project (e.g. a large increase in tariffs imposed if an anti-Western government comes to power). However, the principal concern is that of project failure and this type of 'stress testing' must thus be a major focus of any thorough analysis. Factors that could lead to a complete shutdown of a project include expropriation, litigation of issues related to property rights and contract enforcement, a terrorist attack (e.g. related to the conflict in Karabagh), conflict between two or more of the countries in the region, and failure in negotiations.[23] It must be emphasised that each of these potential and dramatic outcomes appears unlikely given the current level of stability in the region. Nevertheless, political risk is and will remain a major concern for investing companies (see Figure 16.2).

Most of the public discussion surrounding the commercial development of the Caspian region has centred around whether a project will be completed – the prime example of this is the debate over the BTC pipeline. A more appropriate question and focus of discussion might be 'when'. By delaying a firm commitment to this project, oil companies in essence capitalised upon the value inherent in their real option. Given the high levels of uncertainty that surround the region and the case-specific economics of these proposed projects, it is advantageous to delay major decisions and related expenditure until a point further into the future while still maintaining the option in the interim.

| High oil prices, Low 'regional risk' | Low oil prices, Low 'regional risk' |
| High oil prices High 'regional risk' | Low oil prices High 'regional risk' |

Figure 16.2 Summary of potential outcomes

From the perspective of the individual Caspian governments, the main political and economic focus is on long-term development and therefore they have generally remained satisfied with the progress made during the life of the option. This is the case even when a limited amount of money is committed in an irreversible manner, in the form of relatively low-priced studies and rudimentary infrastructure projects.

Finally, although most multinational oil companies are accustomed to dealing in countries where democracy, political stability and human rights are distant goals, it is worthwhile mentioning the reputational risk involved in doing business in the Caspian Sea region. Either direct or indirect association with corrupt political entities in the region has already been shown to have a negative impact on the public's perception of those companies choosing to do business in the region.[24]

Conflict between business and political interests

The disagreement and political manoeuvring between the US government and American businesses regarding the Caspian region have at times become intense over the course of the first decade of the post-Cold War era. Nonetheless, there is a realisation on each side that significant progress cannot be made without the co-operation of the other. Thus, this factor has limited the aggressiveness with which these parties have confronted each other. Based on the financial realities described previously, the tentativeness of the energy companies has allowed these firms to temper their response to 'lobbying' by the US government towards the companies themselves (i.e. policy makers exerting influence on businesses).

The main battleground between US energy companies and the government has been the choice of the appropriate route for pipelines to carry Caspian energy resources to world markets. The cross-border nature of these projects, as well as the need for mediation with Caspian state leaders, made it an area ripe for government involvement. This presented Washington with an open opportunity to wield its influence. Thus, although Washington and US energy companies have worked together on a range of projects and initiatives in the Caspian, the issue of pipelines is one where their mutual involvement has been most prominent.

An important difference between the perspective of the US government and the companies is the definition of a completed 'deal'. For the US energy firms who must undertake the hard physical tasks and accept the financial risks involved in bringing Caspian oil resources to market, the definition of completion is far more stringent and demanding than the subjective political benchmarks held by the US government. Over the course of the past several years, there have been a number of generalised agreements on various pipeline routes, often signed by the relevant heads of state with great fanfare. In many cases, these agreements reflect little more than subjective proclamations and do not reflect final resolution of all the issues involved. On this front, the energy companies have been more cautious and diligent in claiming success and assuming the completion of various achievements. This is partially related to the nature of politics and the realities of business respectively, but the distinction has helped define the direction of each party's statements and actions.

Some non-US energy firms have achieved significant competitive advantage in the region while US parties have been stalled in political arguments. TotalFinaElf of France and BP of the UK are prime examples. The momentum towards achieving a final decision among US participants has been somewhat catalysed by the realisation that the American energy firms must keep pace with non-US companies that are in the race towards similar goals. For many executives in the US energy industry, the handicap introduced by government sanctions and perceived heavy-handedness is highly frustrating.

Potential areas for change

Current US government policy towards the Caspian region could come under increased pressure in the years to come, given the divergence of opinions, drivers and priorities between US energy companies and Washington. This could occur if the economic pressure of expensive oil pushes energy issues towards the forefront of the government–business dialogue, perhaps due to the heightened interest of the American public. A similar state of affairs occurred in the 1970s, during which the Middle East reached its first high level of interest within the American political arena. While the relatively small proven quantities in the Caspian make such an intense domestic dialogue fairly unlikely, the proximity to the conflict in Afghanistan and Iraq as well as the possibility of sustained high energy prices could potentially sharpen the US public's attention on this region at some stage.

Future energy prices clearly offer one of the most critical drivers for change. Oil prices have continued to remain well above their 1998 lows. They levelled out to around $20 per barrel for the benchmark WTI until the crisis in Iraq and the disruptions in Venezuela sent prices above the US$30 level in 2003. The continued uncertainty in the Middle East, along with fundamental pressure placed on prices by OPEC countries acting to mitigate their own national budgetary constraints, would keep prices high well past the end of the initial phases of the war in Iraq. If prices were to remain high, the probability of aggressive oil investment in the Caspian region, including the full completion of the BTC line, could increase. If prices fall, these options would become less attractive. Finally, the amount by which the US government would subsidise various projects remains unclear – another important factor which could shift the balance of the economic considerations that underlie the decision-making process. If funding is postponed or indefinitely held in abeyance, the likelihood of an early development of the pipelines and fields will decrease significantly.

From the perspective of Iran–United States relations, the inherently slow pace of Caspian decision making may be advantageous if it is managed properly – it could allow the turbulent political landscape to settle and the relationship between the two parties to mature. The disparity between the position of the US government and that of Western businesses encourages a level of secrecy regarding reserve estimates and the negotiating stances on pipelines. What is certain, however, is that all options remain open until final agreements and the related financing structures are complete.

Major players in the West have an interest in seeing that decisions regarding the development of the Caspian region are not driven by parties on the political extremes. Groups opposed to reform and progress in each country may be inclined to use the issue to their own political gain. For example, groups that are generally against engagement between the Caspian region and the West will emphasise the obstacles that are all but inevitable to such a substantial endeavour. Unfortunately, the entities most hurt by such an approach would be the newly independent Caspian states themselves. Indeed, they have the most to lose from any politically induced standoff that hinders their development. As responsible world leaders, the governments of Iran, Russia and the US should take proactive steps such as the construction of multiple pipelines to ensure balanced approaches that take into account the interests of all parties.

An improvement in the relationship between Iran and the US could potentially lead to a fundamental change of plans for the Caspian region. If the US government eases back from the former enthusiasm with which it promoted east–west routes in the Caspian, the likelihood of southern routes through Iran could grow. Any further changes in the relationship between the US and Iran will occur gradually and may appear particularly far off in light of the most recent comments. However, long-term planning for Caspian resources should be viewed within the context of this potential political process and the resultant set of possible structural outcomes.

In the years immediately following the events of 11 September 2001, the US focus on Afghanistan, Iraq and the broader war on terrorism led to a lull in the pace of the Caspian Sea-specific decision-making process. This period of turbulent change has offered a good opportunity to step back and reconsider the assumptions upon which our outlooks and priorities are based. The worst potential resolution for the future of Caspian energy development would be one that keeps the resources bottled up within the region indefinitely. Such a scenario would in tandem imply a tense political standoff and thereby could carry its own negative security ramifications. Experience in the region has shown that this negative outcome is most successfully avoided through negotiation, understanding and co-operation.

Notes

1 The defining construct of the two-party conflict between government and business in the US efforts towards the development of the Caspian Sea region is one originally developed with Mathew Burrows of the Council on Foreign Relations. See Mathew Burrows and Carter Page, 'Waiting for the Flow: The Value of Patience in the Caspian', *Georgetown's National Security Studies Quarterly*, Autumn 1999.

2 For the underlying philosophy behind this foundation of the Clinton administration foreign policy, see Anthony Lake, 'From Containment to Enlargement', Address at the School of Advanced International Studies, Johns Hopkins University, Washington DC, 21 September 1993. Also *A National Security Strategy of Engagement and Enlargement*, The White House, February 1996, and Bill Clinton, *Between Hope and History: Meeting America's Challenges for the 21st Century*, Times Books, New York, 1996.

3 Pessimistic outlooks for the future of Caspian energy development include Amy Jaffe and Robert Manning, 'The Myth of the Caspian "Great Game": The Real Geopolitics of Energy', *Survival*, Winter 1998–1999. For a more recent description of the challenges, see 'Caspian Oil Development', *Strategic Comments*, vol. 5, issue 4, International Institute for Strategic Studies, London, May 1999.

4 A. Cohen, 'Istanbul Conference: Quiet Concern Over Baku–Tbilisi–Ceyhan Pipeline's Fate', 2 June 2003 (http://www.eurasianet.org/departments/business/articles/eav060203_pr.shtml).

5 Dick Cheney *et al.*, 'National Energy Policy: Report of the National Energy Policy Development Group', May 2001.

6 For a more thorough review of the changes implemented by President Putin, see chapter by Oksana **Antonenko** in this volume. See also B. Azira, 'US Caspian Pipeline Policy: Substance or Spin?', Center for Strategic and International Studies, Washington DC, 24 August 2000 (http://www.csis.org/turkey/ceu000824.pdf).

7 See 'Joint Statement by President George W. Bush and President Vladimir Putin on Development of the US–Russian Energy Dialogue', Washington DC, 22 November 2002 (http://www.whitehouse.gov/news/releases/2002/11/20021122.html).

8 While the implications of these changes remain unclear, it has led to a great deal of speculation in the American press. See Douglas Jehl, 'New US–Iran Dialogue: Psst. Mumble. Huh?', *New York Times on the Web*, 6 June 1999.

9 For a summary of non-US activity and official US government reaction, see K. Katzman, 'Iran: Current Developments and US Policy', *CRS Issue Brief for Congress*, Congressional Research Service/The Library of Congress, 3 June 2003.

10 One example was Mobil's swap request in April 1999. This swap denial was handed down on the same day that the US administration announced the lifting of a ban on food and medicine sales to Iran. Mobil simultaneously applauded the lifting of the ban and criticised the swap decision. For industry reaction, see *Mobil Editorial*, 'Mixed Signals, Mixed Feelings', 6 May 1999.

11 This was especially the case in 1998–1999, when a potential rapprochement was seriously considered. As civil unrest increases in Tehran and other parts of the country since 2003, the relative importance of Iran policy may again grow.

12 William J. Clinton, 'Remarks at Millennium Evening – The Perils of Indifference: Lessons Learned from a Violent Century', Washington DC, 12 April 1999.

13 M. S. Indyk, 'Remarks at the Council on Foreign Relations', New York, 22 April 1999.

14 Madeleine K. Albright, 'American–Iranian Relations: Remarks to the American–Iranian Council', 17 March 2000, Washington DC, US Department of State.

15 'Iran–Palestinian weapons link likely', BBC News, 5 February 2002 (http://news.bbc.co.uk/1/hi/world/middle_east/1803148.stm).

16 R. Ratnesar, 'Tehran's game: Iranian meddling in neighboring Afghanistan raises new concerns about an old troublemaker', *Time*, 4 February 2002.

17 George W. Bush, 'The President's State of the Union Address', Washington DC, 29 January 2002.

18 Richard Morningstar, 'Address to CERA Conference', Washington DC, 7 December 1998.

19 For a discussion of oil as the basis for Russia and US relations, see D. G. Victor and N. M. Victor, 'Axis of Oil?' *Foreign Affairs*, vol. 82, no. 2, March/April 2003, pp. 47–61.

20 J. Nanay, 'US Energy Security Issues: Russia and the Caspian', testimony before the US Senate Committee on Foreign Relations Subcommittee on International Economic Policy, Export and Trade Promotion, 30 April 2003.

21 See J. Kalicki, 'Transcript: Importance of Baku–Ceyhan', *USIS Washington File*, 21 October 1998. Also, 'Remarks by Secretary of Energy Bill Richardson', London, 19th Annual Oil And Money Conference, 17 November 1998.

22 Based on the two prerequisites as defined in T. Copeland and V. Antikarov, *Real Options: A Practitioners' Guide*, New York, Texere Press, 2001, pp. 14–15.

23 E. D. Porter, 'International Upstream Activity by US Firms: Trends, Prospects and Policy Issues', Research Study no. 091, American Petroleum Institute, February 1998, p. 37.

24 For details of the closely watched James Giffen case, see J. Chaffin, 'US businessman charged over Mobil oil deal', *Financial Times*, 1 April 2003. For the strategic implications of such scandals see 'Corporate ethics: Big oil's dirty secrets', *The Economist*, 10 May 2003, pp. 61–62.

17 Japan's Eurasian diplomacy: power politics, resource diplomacy or romanticism?

Reinhard Drifte

Introduction

The global changes since the end of the Cold War in 1989, in particular the end of the Soviet Union in 1991, faced Japan with the need, but also the opportunity, to adjust and broaden the diplomatic as well as geographic scope of its relations with the states on the Eurasian continent. The succession of the Soviet Union by the Russian Federation and a considerable number of new states, as well as the heavy Western support for their political and economic transition, recast the environment in which Japan had been pursuing its revisionist goal of regaining the so-called Northern Territories to the north of its most northern island, Hokkaido. Moreover, the rise of the 'Silk Road states'[1] – the five Central Asian republics (Kazakhstan, Uzbekistan, Turkmenistan, Kyrgyzstan and Tajikistan) – as well as the three South Caucasian republics (Georgia, Armenia and Azerbaijan) from the ashes of the Soviet Union demanded an adjustment of Japan's diplomacy to Russia, China, Central Asia and Europe while providing it with an opportunity to use its economic might and strengthen its standing as an Asian power. This recasting of the Eurasian political–strategic map is also influencing Japan's options in the Middle East, the source of most of its crude oil supply.

Japan's response to these challenges and opportunities was rather slow. It was only in July 1997, when Prime Minister Hashimoto declared his so-called 'Eurasian Diplomacy', that the Japanese government seems to have awakened to the new situation. The Eurasian Diplomacy was mainly aimed at reshaping its approach to Russia, but it also involved strengthening political and economic relations with the new republics in Central Asia and the South Caucasus, a policy referred to as 'Silk Road Diplomacy'.[2]

Facing a new strategic environment

Most of the changes in the strategic environment that followed the end of the Cold War occurred in the Euro-Atlantic region. They were much less spectacular in Asia. Thus, the impact created by the fall of the Berlin Wall cannot be compared to secondary phenomena such as the recognition of South Korea by Russia and China. However, the emerging security architecture in Europe and the growing political and economic relationship between Western Europe and Russia and the other successor states of the Soviet Union gave Japan a feeling of being left out. This raised the fear of losing diplomatic as well as economic opportunities and leverage.

The eastward expansion of NATO post-1990 had a major impact on Japan's strategic environment, notably in its relationship with Russia and China. Yet initially Japan was unable to exert influence on this emerging Eurasian security structure. In addition to membership expansion, in December 1991 NATO established a North Atlantic Co-operation Council (NACC), which in 1997 became the Euro-Atlantic Partnership Council (EAPC), for regular meetings with the former Warsaw Pact members. One strategist observed that in 1991–1992 'NATO found itself with closer institutional ties to its former adversaries than its indirect allies (such as Japan or the Republic of Korea) and Europe's neutrals'.[3] In 1994 NATO established the open Partnership for Peace (PfP) structure which is considered by some specialists as well as member states as a transitional phase for ultimate NATO membership.[4] Today, all successor states of the Soviet Union are members of the EAPC and almost all are members of the PfP. These structures have become very active in promoting political dialogue at all levels, and are now an essential part of preventive diplomacy and crisis management on the Eurasian continent.

These developments had several direct and indirect influences on Japan's diplomatic position and options. While Europe and the US – for reasons of geographic proximity and nuclear arms control concerns respectively – tried to support Russia politically and economically to guarantee a peaceful transition, Japan initially used its political and economic potential as a lever to achieve the return of the Northern Territories from a weakened Russia. But, instead of coming closer to this goal, Japan only deprived itself of diplomatic means to address the dispute more successfully, while isolating itself among its Western partners. Using discussions of the Russian debt rescheduling as a lever, Japan managed in 1992 to make the other members of the Group of Seven (G-7) summit meeting in Munich accept the position that the Russo-Japanese dispute over the Kuril islands was not merely a bilateral problem, but one of global concern.[5] Japan also blocked Russia's attempts to attend the annual summit meetings of the G-7 as a full member until 1997.[6]

Adjusting to new realities

The European and US use of such expressions as 'from Vancouver to Vladivostok' and 'Euro-Atlantic Community' impressed on Japan at the beginning of the 1990s that it had to become more active on the international scene in order to avoid isolation.[7] Japan therefore took several measures to strengthen its links with Europe, including the building of closer links with European institutions. Since 1996 Japan has held observer status in the Council of Europe; it established a Consulate-General in Strasbourg, seat of the Council of Europe and of the European Parliament. During the Helsinki meeting of the Conference for Security and Co-operation in Europe in July 1992 Japan expressed the wish to be represented in it and was granted associate member status.[8] In December 1996 Japan acquired the status of Partner for Co-operation in the now renamed Organisation for Security and Co-operation in Europe (OSCE) and thereafter participated in several of its missions.[9] With its status as the world's top Overseas Development Aid (ODA) donor, Japan was regarded as a 'soft-security provider' in the OSCE region, which by this time included all the Silk Road countries (SRCs).[10] In December 2000, Japan co-hosted with the OSCE a pioneering conference on Comprehensive Security in Central Asia, in Tokyo.

Greater emphasis on the rehabilitation of the Central Asian republics became a means for Japan's policy makers to counterbalance the European and American focus on Russia and Eastern Europe. Already in 1992 the Japanese press reported statements emanating from the Ministry of Foreign Affairs which stressed that, although aid to Russia was important, Japan as an Asian nation would prefer to support the new Asian republics. It was explained that focusing on the new Asian republics and on the East Asian part of Russia would provide a better political climate for a return of the disputed Northern Territories.

The Central Asian countries had declared independence between August and December 1991 and Japan had recognised them almost immediately. Diplomatic recognition of Azerbaijan, Georgia and Armenia occurred in December 1991, April 1992 and December 1992, respectively. Already in March 1992 the Japanese government began planning aid for these countries and in the same year Hideaki Ueda (a Russian specialist in the Ministry of Foreign Affairs) became the first to go on a mission to Uzbekistan and Kazakhstan. Japan ended the ban on untied loans by Japanese banks to republics of the former Soviet Union. In October 1992 it hosted a G-7 aid conference at which Japan pledged an additional US$100 million to the Commonwealth of Independent States (CIS). It took the lead in getting the five Central Asian countries on to the Development Assistance Committee list on 4 November 1992 (valid from January 1993), against French and US opposition, in order to legitimise Japanese ODA to these countries.[11] From 1993 onwards Japan became a leading donor to the five Central Asian republics.[12]

Japan was also a leader in getting the SRCs accepted in international development banks. Today all eight states are members of the World Bank, the International Monetary Fund and the European Bank for Reconstruction and Development (EBRD). In addition, thanks to Japan's efforts, the Central Asian states became members of the Asian Development Bank (ADB) in Manila, an institution which receives major funding from Japan and is normally headed by a Japanese citizen. Normally no country can be a member in more than one regional bank.[13]

Japan's government officials as well as private sector representatives had high expectations in these eight countries and a great number of delegations went to visit them.[14] Foreign Minister Michio Watanabe was the first

Japanese cabinet minister to visit the region (Kazakhstan and Kyrgyzstan) in May 1992. A high-level delegation from the Ministry of Finance, led by Deputy Minister Tadao Chino, went in October 1992 to Uzbekistan, Kyrgyzstan and Kazakhstan. They were surprised to discover the economic gains that had already been made by South Korea and China, as well as the political, cultural and religious involvement of Turkey and Iran in this newly opened region. This provided an additional impetus for Japan's involvement. Plans were announced for inviting 300 engineers and experts from the Central Asian states to Japan; also for opening embassies in Kazakhstan and Uzbekistan in January 1993.[15]

Personal preferences and national interests

However, despite the initial enthusiasm by government and business for the SRCs, and particularly for the Central Asian states, not many concrete measures were taken to give substance to this interest. It was to take until May 2000 before another embassy was opened in Azerbaijan. Eventually, the personal influence of individual bureaucrats galvanised various interest groups to create a consensus for what became, in 1997, Japan's Eurasian Diplomacy. Two senior officials emerged as the main promoters of Japan's relations with the Central Asian countries. One was the diplomat Ikeru Magosaki, who was Japan's ambassador to Uzbekistan from 1993 to 1996. The other was Tadao Chino, of the Ministry of Finance. Other officials from the Ministry of Finance who started to visit the region frequently were Seiji Kitamura and Naoko Ishi.[16] An important role was also played by the parliamentarian Muneo Suzuki. His overweening influence on the Foreign Ministry started in 1990, when he became parliamentary deputy foreign minister. This powerful member of parliament from Hokkaido held influential posts in the Liberal Democratic Party (LDP) of Japan (including the party's Committee on Economic Co-operation).[17] He took a particular interest in Russia and its former republics and helped to promote foreign aid to these countries. He had to resign in March 2002 when it became known that he had used his influence for personal gain (see below).

Cultural affinities

In Japan's public discourse, strategic arguments do not usually play a prominent role because of Japan's pacifist orientation. Thus we find in the discussion of Japan's evolving relationship with the SRCs a strong emphasis on Japan's cultural and racial affinity with these new states. The emotional affinity has not only become part of official speeches but is quite genuine and can be found with liberal as well as Realist thinkers and policy makers.[18] The 1990s saw a boom in everything related to the Silk Road states. The irony is that the Central Asian SRCs today are Islamic and view the Buddhist archaeological remnants more as a means to promote their national identity building after the long years as part of the Soviet Union or to gain foreign currency through tourism.[19]

In response to this cultural attraction and to help these countries with their nation building, the Japanese government has paid particular importance to cultural diplomacy. Cultural diplomacy was initially regarded as the central aspect of Japan's diplomacy. Thus, Ikuo Hirayama, director of the Tokyo Arts Museum, was sent in September 1998 to Uzbekistan on a fact-finding mission.[20] Most of the other Japanese visitors to Uzbekistan in the early 1990s were involved in cultural and scientific spheres.[21] Japan also gave large-scale cultural grants, including the donation of musical instruments.[22] The cultural and racial affinity argument, moreover, catered for the needs of various policy constituencies, such as those looking for strengthening Japan's identity as an Asian nation, establishing Japan as a bridge between East and West, or to reinforce Japan's legitimacy as an Asian leader.

In the case of relations with Uzbekistan, the role of Magosaki as ambassador to this country and his personal relationship with Uzbek President Karimov cannot be overestimated. What was attractive to Japan was Karimov's clear desire to cut links with Russia as far as possible. Culturally, Uzbekistan is most appealing to the Japanese because it is most closely associated with the historical Silk Road and has several Buddhist sites. Uzbekistan has reciprocated by systematically training Japanese speakers and specialists, supported by the Japan Foundation. Economically, Uzbekistan was considered to have performed best among all the other countries. In Japanese eyes, this was due to strong guidance by the government and dislike for the structural adjustment policies of the World Bank and the IMF as regards foreign exchange policy, privatisation and deregulation. By the end of 1998, the GNP of all eight SRCs, with the exception of Uzbekistan, was still less than half of what it had been at the time of independence. Japan's first ODA mission was sent in 1993 to Uzbekistan. ambassador Magosaki has described very openly how he and his colleagues agreed with the Uzbek government's opposition to the IMF's insistence that transition to a free market economy had to be done at the sacrifice of social stability.[23] In June 1994 the IMF refused to continue loan negotiations with Uzbekistan; this prompted the Japanese Ministry of Finance to give a loan to Uzbekistan's most important gas/oil project. As a result, in 1995 Japan became Uzbekistan's biggest loan provider. In the spring of that year the IMF changed its attitude to Uzbekistan, but the following year the IMF suspended a Stand-by Agreement since Uzbekistan introduced trade restrictions on foreign investment and imposed severe restrictions on hard currency flows. Because of these problems, Japan at one point interrupted its supply of yen loans to the country, but resumed them in 1999.

While Japan has become Uzbekistan's most important bilateral ODA provider, it does not rank among Uzbekistan's top three trading partners. In terms of foreign direct investment Japan with a share of 9.7 per cent, ranks fifth after the UK, Malaysia, Turkey and the US. Since most of the ODA is distributed by the Ministry of Foreign Affairs and the Ministry of Finance, individuals like Magosaki and Chino could sustain Uzbekistan's high ODA ranking.

The element of personal preference is also obvious in the case of Kyrgyzstan. Thanks to Chino's personal links to Kyrgyzstan and the role of Japanese economists such as Professor Tatsuo Kaneda (he was the Kyrgyz president's adviser for four years), Kyrgyzstan has been shown much greater attention than its size, political or economic weight would warrant. In 1994 Japan overtook the US as Kyrgyzstan's biggest individual ODA donor. As a result of its economic policies, Kyrgyzstan became a pilot country for the World Bank's Comprehensive Development Framework. In 1998 it became the first CIS country to join the World Trade Organisation. In this case its much greater adherence to IMF policies did not hurt its privileged relationship with Japan. Two Japanese politicians who had direct personal links to the Tajik leadership were the aforementioned Muneo Suzuki and Keizo Takemi, parliamentary deputy foreign minister in the late 1990s. They were instrumental in maintaining a substantial flow of ODA support for Tajikistan, despite ongoing instability in that country (in 1998–1999, as discussed below, this resulted in Japanese casualties). At the urging of Muneo Suzuki, Japan established an embassy in Tajikistan in January 2002, despite the fact that the Ministry of Foreign Affairs had favoured Kyrgyzstan.[24]

The launch of the 'Eurasian Diplomacy' policy

It took until summer 1997 before these haphazard and individual efforts to come to terms with the changes on the Eurasian continent were integrated into an official policy. This happened under the administration of Ryutaro Hashimoto who had become prime minister in January 1996. In a speech on 24 July 1997 to the *Keizai Doyukai* (Japan Committee on Economic Development), he explained his new policy towards Russia and the whole Eurasian continent. This speech can be considered as the first conceptualisation of Japan's Eurasian Diplomacy and its subsidiary policy, the Silk Road Diplomacy towards the eight SRCs.[25]

An important factor in Japan's Silk Road Diplomacy was its concern over the growing weight of China on the Eurasian continent. China was expanding its relationship with Iran for economic and political reasons (e.g. Iranian energy exports to China, Chinese arms exports to Iran) which had negative implications for regional stability, the global control of weapons of mass destruction and their delivery vehicles, and also for Iran–US relations.[26] There was, moreover, a concern regarding potential Chinese involvement in ethnic strife in Central Asia, arising from China's own problems with Turkic minorities in Xinjiang.[27] Finally, China had become an active commercial actor in Central Asia, notably in Kazakhstan in the oil and gas sector. The reason for this growing involvement was China's urgent need for energy since it became a net oil importer in 1993. Faced with American control of all sea-lanes, access to Central Asian resources had acquired an important role in China's policy towards the region.[28] China's political and commercial interests were reflected in the fact that its embassies in the SRCs had the greatest number of staff after those of Russia.

In order to give substance to the Silk Road Diplomacy, the Japanese government proposed an Action Plan to promote the exchange of high-level official visits, to open new embassies in the Silk Road region and to refocus ODA to meet Japan's strategic goals. Shortly before Prime Minister Hashimoto delivered his speech on Eurasian Diplomacy, a mission headed by House of Representatives member Keizo Obuchi visited Russia, Turkmenistan, Kazakhstan, Uzbekistan and Kyrgyzstan (28 June to 9 July 1997), followed in September by a visit of Director-General Taro Aso of the Economic Planning Agency to the region. In December of the same year, a seminar on a comprehensive strategy for Central Asia was organised by the Japanese Ministry of Foreign Affairs in Tokyo, with leaders from the five Central Asian countries and countries outside the region. The first head of state to visit Tokyo after Hashimoto's speech was Azerbaijani President Heidar Aliev (February 1998), followed by President Askar Akaev of Kyrgyzstan (October 1998), Georgian President Shevardnadze (March 1999), Uzbek Prime Minister Utkir Sultanov (March 1999) and Kazakh President Nazarbaev (December 1999). Nazarbaev had previously visited Japan in April 1994, Akaev in April 1993, and Karimov in May 1994.

The role of overseas development aid

The provision of overseas development aid (ODA) has become the main pillar of Japan's Silk Road Diplomacy and, as we have seen, actually predates Hashimoto's speech in July 1997. Japan's ODA is aimed at 'support for establishing a foundation for self-reliant economic development, support for the process of democratisation and transition to market economies, and support for the alleviation of social problems'.[29] The emphasis was on food and medical help, as well as emergency relief through international organisations (UNHCR, International Red Cross). This kind of aid was initially given on a per capita ratio.[30] Thereafter Japan focused on infrastructure support for the medium term. It gave refugee help to Tajikistan and Azerbaijan.[31] Kyrgyzstan received the first Japanese yen loans to the region in 1994 (US$39.73 million) and in 1995 (US$30.45 million).[32] The first recipients for substantial grant aid were Uzbekistan and Kyrgyzstan.[33] As part of the intention to 'deal with the negative legacy of the Soviet past', Japan organised the Tokyo International Conference on Semipalatinsk in September 1999 in order to help this environmentally devastated region where the Soviet Union conducted its nuclear tests. More than US$20 million was pledged from Japan, the World Bank and several United Nations organisations and agencies. Japan announced a special contribution of US$1 million through the Japanese/UNDP funds.

In 1997, Japan's total ODA to all eight SRCs was US$157.0 million, that of the United States US$116.0 million and of the individual EU member states US$102.7 million.[34] This was a rather large increase of Japanese ODA to the SRCs from only US$2.57 million in 1993. Japan's ODA to the Central Asian countries increased from 1997 to 1998 by 56.9 per cent but to the South

Caucasian countries by only 18 per cent.[35] In 1997, 57.9 per cent of Japan's ODA to the eight countries consisted of loans, 26.4 per cent of grant aid, and 15.6 per cent of technical aid.[36] Donor meetings for Kazakhstan and Kyrgyzstan, organised by the World Bank, were held in Tokyo in November 1996 and October 1996, respectively.

A special feature of Japan's bilateral aid to Uzbekistan, Kyrgyzstan and Kazakhstan was the very high share of yen loans, which in 1998 amounted to 85.6 per cent. This compared with a global average of only 42.5 per cent in Japan's ODA. The top recipients of technical aid were Uzbekistan, Kazakhstan and Kyrgyzstan, which received about equal shares. One reason for the low amount of technical aid was Japan's focus on receiving trainees from these countries as the main part of Japan's technical aid, rather than sending experts. Grant aid to these three countries was focused on the health sector; there was also grant aid for the increase of food production and cultural activities.[37] The continuity and consistency of Japan's bilateral aid, particularly in the technical aid sector, suffered from the difficulty of gathering information. To remedy this situation, the Japan International Co-operation Agency (JICA) established its first office in Uzbekistan's capital, Tashkent, in 1999. Also, a Japan Centre was established in Kyrgyzstan in April 1995, financed by the Ministry of Foreign Affairs. Similar centres were subsequently established elsewhere in the region. An important function of these centres was to teach Japanese language and business studies as well as to distribute information on Japan.[38]

The link with Turkey

From 1992 onwards, Turkey showed great interest in expanding its political and economic influence into the SRCs because of its ethnic and linguistic links with most countries of the region. This led Japan to view Turkey as a useful partner in developing links to the SRCs. While Turkey saw in Japan a partner to compete against Iran's efforts to spread its influence in the Central Asian states, Japan saw in Turkey a moderate Islamic force to counter fundamentalist Islamic tendencies in the region. In addition, Turkey was seen as a fitting participant for the south–south approach to development aid, whereby more advanced developing countries are assisted by ODA donors such as Japan to assist less developed countries. After President Suleiman Demirel's visit to Tokyo in 1993 Japan increased its aid to Turkey and the Japanese Export–Import Bank channelled funds to the Central Asian countries through the Turkish Exim Bank.

However, the involvement of Turkey was subsequently seen as inappropriate by the SRCs, and notably by Uzbekistan, which did not want to have the Soviet/Russian 'big brother' being replaced by yet another one. Uzbekistan and other Central Asian countries became suspicious of the activities of Turkish teachers who opened schools in the region, blaming them for introducing radical Islamic ideas.[39] In the free market sector, however, Turkish managers proved highly efficient in trilateral ventures.

Japanese economic involvement

Japan's private economic sector involvement in the SRCs has been slow to take shape. However, there is no lack of business visitors to the region. Reading the list of participating companies in conferences devoted to the SRCs one discerns considerable interest in the SRCs, but this has yet to be translated into significant commercial transactions. Even tourism has not much developed despite the cultural attraction of the SRCs. There were no direct air links with Japan until 2002, when Uzbek Airways introduced bi-weekly flights from Tashkent to Osaka. In 1998 trade between Japan and the five Central Asian countries amounted to a total of US$294 million, a decrease of 11 per cent compared with the previous year. In 1998 the share of the eight countries together in Japan's total exports was 0.04 per cent, and in Japan's imports 0.06 per cent. The most important trade partner in 1999 was Kazakhstan, followed by Uzbekistan and Azerbaijan.[40] The main Japanese export items were machinery, transport equipment and steel products. Imports from Kazakhstan were non-ferrous metals (zinc, titanium) and from Uzbekistan unfinished products and cotton. In the case of Azerbaijan, the biggest export item for Japan was steel piping. Japanese project aid (e.g. for construction of a polypropylene plant in Turkmenistan, and for the upgrading of the airport in Astana, the new capital of Kazakhstan) was an important element in sustaining trade with these countries.

The low level of investment and trade between the SRCs and Japan was not only due to the difficult economic conditions of these countries, but was also related to Japanese business being much less willing to take risk, particularly at a time of an economic slump at home. The murder of a Japanese academic, Professor Yutaka Akino, a civil affairs officer of the UN Mission of Observers in Tajikistan in July 1998, and the abduction by Tajik and Uzbek bandits in a remote valley along the Kyrgyz–Tajik border in October 1999 of four Japanese engineers exploring mineral resources reinforced these concerns.[41] There was particular disappointment with the Kyrgyz government, which managed to secure the release of some hostages, but not the Japanese prisoners, who were held for more than two months. The Japanese Ministry of Foreign Affairs had to admit its diplomatic weakness in Central Asia and its lack of information about political instability in the region.[42] Technical aid to Kyrgyzstan was suspended indefinitely. Relations with Kazakhstan were also adversely affected when it became known in 1999 that high-ranking Kazakh officials (including the defence minister) had colluded in exporting MIG-21 aircraft to North Korea, the object of Japan's most immediate threat perception.[43]

Energy

The oil and gas resources in Central Asia and the South Caucasus make the region strategically and economically increasingly important for Japan. Asia imports around 60 per cent of its oil from the Middle East, and by 2010 it will be the world's largest consumer of primary energy.[44] The need to satisfy this growing demand and to reduce dependence on the volatile Middle East gives the energy-rich Silk Road region great importance, but it also highlights great-power rivalries involving Russia, China and the United States. There are considerable oil and gas deposits in Kazakhstan, Azerbaijan and Turkmenistan. Even the SRCs that do not have these resources play an important role as potential transit corridors for hydrocarbons. Japan, as the fourth biggest energy consumer in the world, has a continuing interest in diversifying its energy supply. As part of its diversification strategy it wants to have a certain percentage of its oil coming from drilling rights owned by Japanese oil companies. Its strategic aim was to secure 30 per cent of its crude oil supplies from fields developed by Japanese companies (in 1993 the target was set at 1.2 m b/d). However, this goal was abandoned in 2000 because only about half of the target was ever achieved (650,000 b/d). Thereafter, emphasis was increasingly placed on promoting reliable supplies of natural gas.[45] To prevent transboundary sea and air pollution from China, it is also important for Japan that China should use more gas, rather than continuing to rely on coal as its main energy source. The gas reserves of the region are therefore of vital interest to Japan for environmental as well as economic reasons.

Most Japanese exploration participation is in Azerbaijan. It is supported by Japan's ODA programme, which focuses on the energy-related sector.[46] The main Japanese companies currently operational in the Caspian basin are Mitsui, Inpex and Itochu, as well as the Japanese semi-national company Japan National Oil Corporation. In November 2002, Inpex[47] acquired a stake in the Azerbaijan International Oil Consortium that was developing the Azeri–Chirag–Guneshli mega-structure (see **Antonenko**, p. 256). Prior to this, by mid-2000, Japanese companies were involved in three of the other offshore drilling areas. One exploration consortium in which Itochu was involved was dissolved in 2000 because the result was disappointing. There was further disappointment in March 2003, when it was announced that the Japanese Azerbaijan Operational Consortium (50 per cent of which was divided among Japanese oil companies, while the remaining 50 per cent was held by Azerbaijan's state oil company SOCAR) had failed to find commercially viable quantities of oil in the Ateshgakh field; further geophysical studies were to be conducted before a decision was taken on whether or not to pull out of exploration.[48]

Kazakhstan, which is after Russia the biggest oil producer in the region, may become Japan's main energy partner. In May 2000 a huge deposit was discovered in the North Caspian Sea. This was the Kashagan oilfield, located close to the Kazakh coast. It is operated by an international consortium (Agip Kazakhstan North Caspian Operating Company) that includes Inpex North Caspian Sea Oil, as well as US and European majors such as Exxon-Mobil Corporation and Royal Dutch/Shell Group. Inpex's stake (including production share) is 7.14 per cent. Drilling was originally planned to begin in 2004, with production expected to peak in 2010.[49] However, technical difficulties caused the project to fall behind schedule (see **Akiner**, p. 382). In 2004 it was announced that production would not commence until 2008.[50]

There is also Japanese interest in the oil and gas industry of Uzbekistan. The country is the only CIS member with a steady increase of oil and gas production since 1985 and is the second largest gas producer in the former Soviet Union after Russia. However, most of the production is consumed domestically. Although Turkmenistan is a major oil and gas producer, its export opportunities are hampered by the bottleneck created by the reliance on the Russian pipeline network. Itochu has been involved in discussions about an oil concession but without success so far. There are no Japanese exploration or production activities in the country.

Transport routes

One of the biggest obstacles for the export of oil and gas from the SRCs is the long distance to major markets. Yet consumers in Europe and East Asia want to diversify sources of supply and are therefore interested in gaining access to the deposits in the SRCs. This brings European and Asian consumers into competition: transport links to Europe are shorter, but Asian energy needs are growing. This competition is particularly visible around the Caspian Sea oil.[51] Japanese companies Itochu and Inpex have taken shares in the BP-led consortium that is constructing the Baku–Tbilisi–Ceyhan oil pipeline (see **Roberts**, p. 83). Japan is also interested in exploring additional transit routes through Iran or Russia. The improvement of Japan–Iran relations and growing co-operation between these two states in the energy sector make an expansion of pipeline links through Iran more likely, particularly since the economics would favour such a project. Yet the Japanese government is still careful to avoid controversial political engagement, while Japanese business is not willing to share any risk, let alone lead an international pipeline consortium.[52]

Moreover, the economic crisis and deregulation efforts have reduced confidence in future consumption since pipeline plans have to be based on 20–25-year planning horizons. It is also a handicap that Japan has no integrated national pipeline grid for gas or oil. As a result of all these circumstances Japan has up to now been only involved through bank credits and the delivery of special high-pressure steel tubes to the Russian–Turkish 'Blue Stream' gas pipeline under the Black Sea. In 1993–1995 a study was made for a 7,000-km gas pipeline from Kazakhstan via Uzbekistan to China, but in 1996 the project was put on hold.[53] Moreover, Japan would prefer supply sources that are geographically closer. Japan's first preference for a gas pipeline is from Irkutsk in Russia. The second preference is Northern Sakhalin, where Japanese companies are producing natural gas. The third option is gas from the Sakha Republic (formerly Yakutia), and only in fourth place is a pipeline from Turkmenistan considered.[54]

Turkmen President Niyazov began discussions in 1992 with Beijing and Mitsubishi for a gas pipeline to China. China's interest is to have Turkmenistan contribute gas in order to make a pipeline through the Tarim Basin more viable since production from the Tarim gas fields is low.[55] In

October 1997 the international consortium CentGas was formed to construct a gas pipeline from Turkmenistan through Afghanistan to Pakistan (TAP), 31.5 per cent of which belonged to Itochu, Inpex and Hyundai. The project was suspended in August 1998 because of the war in Afghanistan.[56] However, there is still Japanese interest in this project and, if it were to be revived, they would probably play a part (see **Canzi**, p. 189). The Tokyo-based Northeast Asian Gas and Pipeline Forum (members include Japan, China, Russia, the two Koreas and Mongolia) proposes a set of two natural gas trunk lines for East Asia, of which the southern one would connect Central Asia, northwest China and Shanghai.[57] If the reduction of tensions on the Korean peninsula were to continue, there may even be a chance of a gas pipeline from Russia/China through the peninsula and on to Japan. South Korean President Kim Daejung is said to have proposed to Russia that his country would pay for a pipeline through North Korea. Japanese participation would be vital to make the project more viable.

Conclusions

The proclamation of 'Eurasian Diplomacy' in July 1997 was the conceptualisation of a policy which aimed firstly at regaining lost leverage in Japan's relations with Russia and secondly at avoiding isolation at the end of the Cold War. NATO's eastward expansion and growing US interest in Central Asia and the South Caucasus served as an additional incentive for a Russo-Chinese rapprochement and in the process negatively influenced Japan's strategic environment. The enlargement of the EU and the growing activities of the OSCE on the Eurasian continent further threatened to sideline Japan's diplomacy by emphasising the Euro-Atlantic perspective of the Eurasian continent. Japan's commitment to the relations with the eight countries in Central Asia and the South Caucasus was therefore meant to counterbalance these developments which also disadvantaged Japan in the international competition for new energy resources.

Yet a close examination of Japanese private sector involvement in the SRCs has clearly shown that, while there may be great interest in the region, this has not been followed up by any substantial trade or investment. Trade and investment is focused on countries with energy resources, supported by targeted ODA projects. In Uzbekistan, Japan is involved in a large polyethylene plant, but this is together with other foreign countries.[58] Even in Azerbaijan, Japanese involvement in exploration and development of energy sources is marginal, overshadowed by many other countries with smaller national economies. Japan's private sector is further hampered by the economic crisis at home, which reduces its already low readiness to face risks. Moreover, energy resources in the region may, after all, not be as large as has been suggested by interested governments and companies. Commercial viability will depend on high global oil and gas prices.

Japan's ODA programme for the SRCs is still buoyant, but before the terrorist attacks on New York on 11 September 2001 there were signs that the political pillar of the Silk Road Diplomacy was weakening. Japanese visits to the SRCs declined and references to the Eurasian Diplomacy and the Silk Road Diplomacy practically disappeared from official documents and statements.[59] The killing and abduction of Japanese citizens in Kyrgyzstan and Tajikistan in 1998 and 1999 further cooled Japan's enthusiasm, exposing the vulnerability of a diplomacy that was over-reliant on personal and emotional foundations. On the other hand, the role of the LDP Diet members Muneo Suzuki and Keizo Takemi helped to prevent a total collapse of interest and ODA flows. The focus of attention of the Japanese business community shifted to some extent to Azerbaijan and the Caspian Sea. But Japan's economic and political role here is still only marginal.

After the events of 11 September 2001, Japan's focus on the region, particularly on the states bordering Afghanistan, again increased. Japan sent naval vessels into the Indian Ocean to assist US and British forces in the war against the Taleban and the followers of Osama bin Laden. It increased its ODA, particularly humanitarian relief, to the war-torn region. Muneo Suzuki, through his close personal links to Tajik President Imomali Rahmonov, skilfully exploited the situation. The latter twice called for Japan to send Suzuki to Tajikistan during this period, first in October 2001, then again in January 2002. Suzuki's political demise in March 2002 did not presage a change in Japanese policy towards the region, since Tokyo fully endorsed the US government's anti-terrorist campaign. However, it did seem likely that thereafter there would be greater scrutiny of all Japanese ODA allocations in order to prevent the misappropriation of funds that, allegedly, was perpetrated by Suzuki.

The greatest challenge for Japan's Eurasian Diplomacy will remain its relationship with Russia, but China's shadow will surely increasingly loom larger. Japan is wary of hurting its relations with Russia because of its ongoing territorial dispute; also, it fears the emergence of a closer Russian–Chinese relationship. Japan will therefore only be a reluctant partner in economic projects that may be seen by Russia as inimical to its economic and political interests. However, the disclosures about Muneo Suzuki's manipulation of Japan's Russia policy, and Russia's intransigence concerning the return of even a part of the Northern Territories, has, for the time being, severely discredited any 'soft' approach vis-à-vis Moscow by the Japanese government.

Japan's self-perception is that of an Asian country with a Western political and economic system. However, Japan–EU development aid co-operation is complicated by differences in aid strategies (e.g. the role of the state, emphasis on structural adjustment), the sheer complexities of the EU aid bureaucracy and by the EU's political conditionality requirements. The EU is more involved than Japan in helping the SRCs with the establishment of political and governmental institutions, reforming legal systems, and similar governance issues.[60] By contrast, Japan has fewer inhibitions in working together with authoritarian regimes, because it considers the role of economic rehabilitation more instrumental to stability than the emphasis on human rights and democracy. As a result, some Central Asian countries make tactical political use of Japan whenever there is a negative statement by the EU on such issues as violations of human rights. Japan's role in the Silk Road region is therefore mainly that of a development aid provider. It attempts to make a contribution to the stabilisation of the SRCs, but is not a major political or economic player, still less a moderator between local and outside political interests.

Appendix

Table 17.1 SRC visitors to and from Japan (1998)

Silk Road country	SRC visitors to Japan	SRC visitors from Japan
Uzbekistan	603	1,686
Kazakhstan	731	666
Azerbaijan	176	255
Georgia	181	215
Turkmenistan	49	186
Kyrgyzstan	203	142
Armenia	118	110
Tajikistan	47	n.a.

Source: Annual Report of Statistics on Legal Migrants for 1998, Ministry of Foreign Affairs, Tokyo, April 2000.

Table 17.2 Japanese ODA disbursements to the Silk Road countries 1994–1998 (in US$ million)

Country	Loan aid (net)	Country grant aid	Technical co-operation
Kazakhstan	109.10	8.36	33.67
Kyrgyzstan	115.38	38.75	26.44
Tajikistan	–	0.22	1.40
Turkmenistan	–	4.26	2.42
Uzbekistan	154.33	49.49	27.01
Armenia	–	8.75	1.19
Azerbaijan	0.01	5.25	1.44
Georgia	–	0.04	81.20

Source: ODA Annual Report 1999, Ministry of Foreign Affairs, Tokyo, 2000.

Table 17.3 Total number of trainees from the Silk Road countries (1998)

Country	Number
Uzbekistan	188
Kazakhstan	182
Kyrgyzstan	173
Turkmenistan	122
Georgia	50
Azerbaijan	39
Tajikistan	39
Armenia	34

Source: Japan's Official Development Assistance Annual Report 1999, Ministry of Foreign Affairs, Tokyo, 2000.

Table 17.4 Japanese trade with the Silk Road countries (in US$ million)

Country	1997	1998	1999
Azerbaijan			
Exports to Japan	20.0	18.0	34.6
Imports from Japan	2.3	0.2	0.1
Armenia			
Exports	0.3	1.8	1.1
Imports	0.1	5.7	0.7
Georgia			
Exports	1.6	3.2	6.8
Imports	1.1	0.6	1.5
Uzbekistan			
Exports	55.6	66.5	83.5
Imports	36.1	41.0	33.0
Kyrgyzstan			
Exports	2.4	1.1	6.5
Imports	1.2	0.5	0.6
Tajikistan			
Exports	1.8	5.6	3.1
Imports	1.2	0.06	0.1
Turkmenistan			
Exports	3.8	7.6	14.7
Imports	3.0	0.04	0.30

Source: Japan Export Trade Organisation (JETRO), Tokyo.

Notes

The author gratefully acknowledges the receipt of a grant from the Japan Society for the Promotion of Science to conduct research at the Shizuoka Prefectural University and a grant for relief from teaching and administration from URENCO Ltd, Marlow (UK).

1 The concept of the 'Silk Roads' as a region with historical and cultural resonance for Japan has long been popular. One of the first formal manifestations of this attraction was the generous support that Japan provided for the UNESCO programme 'Integral Study of the Silk Roads: Roads of Dialogue', inaugurated in 1988 as part of the World Decade for Cultural Development.
2 See R. Kato, 'Shiroji canvas ni efude o kuwaeru toki', *Gaiko Forum*, December 1998, pp. 34–38.
3 T. Winkler, 'The New NATO: Analysis of Metamorphosis', in Laurent Goetschel (ed.), *Security in a Globalized World: Risks and Opportunities*, Nomos Verlagsgesellschaft, Baden Baden, 1999, p. 167.
4 R. Bhatty and R. Bronson, 'NATO's Mixed Signals in the Caucasus and Central Asia', *Survival*, vol. 42, no. 3, Autumn 2000, pp. 131–132.
5 *International Herald Tribune*, 8 July 1992; *The Independent*, 8 July 1992.
6 For the use of ODA in this context see R. Drifte, *Japan's Foreign Policy for the 21st Century: From Economic Superpower to What Power?*, Macmillan/St Antony's College, London/Oxford, 1998, pp. 132–133.
7 See, for example, comment by then Foreign Minister Komura in M. Komura, 'Japan's Eurasian Diplomacy: New Perspective in Foreign Policy', *Japan Quarterly*, January–March 1999, p. 4.
8 *Japan Times*, 29 June 1992; *Pacific Research*, August 1992, p. 24.

9 South Korea and Thailand are the only other Asian countries that are partners of OSCE.

10 T. Ueta, *Japan and the OSCE: OSCE Yearbook 1997*, Nomos Verlagsgesellschaft, Baden Baden, 1998, pp. 387 and 393.

11 D. T. Yasutomo, *The New Multilateralism in Japan's Foreign Policy*, Macmillan, Houndsmill, 1995, p. 90.

12 'Waga kuni no seifu kaihatsu enjo', *ODA Hakusho*, vol. 2, 1998, p. 222.

13 'With Oil and West's Appeals in Mind, Tokyo Plans for Central Asia', *International Herald Tribune*, 16 December 1992.

14 K. Muto, 'Ima hatasu beki Nihon no keizaiteki yakuwari', *Gaiko Forum*, August 1995, p. 54.

15 Yasutomo, *op. cit.*, p. 157.

16 Interview with Y. Nagatomi, 28 April 2000. In 1991 he was chairman of the Committee for Visiting Scholar Programme of the Foundation for Advanced Information and Research (as well as chairman of its Steering Committee), a subsidiary of the Ministry of Finance.

17 The Liberal Democratic Party of Japan has been in power since 1955; it was briefly forced out in 1993, but since then has ruled in a coalition with some minor conservative parties.

18 S. Sato also mentioned the 'special cultural feelings' of the Japanese towards the SRC. Interview 7 May 1999. For an official view see Yoshida Susumu, *Gaiko Forum*, December 1998, p. 20, Round Table discussion.

19 I. Hirayama, 'Waga e no michi, unmei no michi', *Gaiko Forum*, December 1998, pp. 12–15.

20 U. Magosaki, *Gaiko Forum*, August 1995, p. 72; I. Hirayama, 'Waga e no michi, unmei no michi', *Gaiko Forum*, December 1998, pp. 12–15.

21 U. Magosaki, *Gaiko Forum*, August 1995, pp. 66–73.

22 Y. Enoki, 'Hito wa pan nomi ni ikiru ni orazu', *Gaiko Forum*, April 2000, pp. 48–53.

23 U. Magosaki, *Gaiko Forum*, August 1995, p. 68.

24 *Japan Times*, 7 April 2002. By 2003, Japan had embassies in Azerbaijan, Uzbekistan, Kazakhstan, Kyrgyzstan and Tajikistan.

25 Text provided by the Office for the Newly Independent States, Ministry of Foreign Affairs, Tokyo.

26 For further details on Iran see O. Miyata, 'Coping with the Iranian Threat', *Japan Silk Road*, vol. 1, no. 2, December 1997, pp. 35–36.

27 See further L. M. Wortzel (ed.), *The Chinese Armed Forces in the 21st Century*, Strategic Studies Institute, US Army War College, Carlisle, December 1999, pp. 20 ff.

28 M. Pillsbury, *China Debates the Future Security Environment*, Institute for National Strategic Studies, National Defense University, Washington DC, 2000, p. xlii and pp. 47–48.

29 'Waga kuni no seifu kaihatsu enjo', *ODA Hakusho*, vol. 2, 1998, p. 222.

30 'Waga kuni no seifu kaihatsu enjo', *ODA Hakusho*, vol. 1, 1998, p. 45; vol. 2, pp. 219–255.

31 For the figures, see *ODA Annual Report 1999*, Ministry of Foreign Affairs, Tokyo, 2000, p. 289.

32 K. Muto, 'Ima hatasu beki Nihon no keizaiteki yakuwari', *Gaiko Forum*, August 1995, p. 54.

33 Bhatty and Bronson, *op. cit.*, p. 134.

34 *ODA Annual Report 1999*, Ministry of Foreign Affairs, Tokyo, 2000, p. 125.

35 'Waga kuni no seifu kaihatsu enjo', *ODA Hakusho*, vol. 2, 1998, p. 223.

36 Figures provided by Japan International Co-operation Agency (JICA), 15 May 2000.

37 *Annual Report 1999*, JICA, Tokyo, 2000, p. 102.

38 *Tokyo Shimbun* (evening edition), 7 March 1998.

39 Y. Nishimura, 'Eurasia gaiko koshi suwate', *Asahi Shimbun*, 23 November 1997; B. Balci, 'Fethullah Gülen's Missionary Schools in Central Asia and their Role in the Spreading of Turkism and Islam', *The Keston Journal: Religion, State and Society*, vol. 31, no. 2, June 2003, pp. 151–177.
40 JETRO figures.
41 On the political instability in Tajikistan which led to Akino's death see M. Yamauchi, *Gaiko Forum*, December 1999, pp. 28–33. See also S. Akiner, *Tajikistan: Disintegration or Reconciliation*, Royal Institute of International Affairs, London, 2001, pp. 72–76.
42 *Asahi Shimbun*, 26 October 1999.
43 For details see 'Kazak minister fired in Arms scandal', Associated Press (Almaty), 9 August 1999, and 'Two Companies Sanctioned for Illegal Sale of MIG-21s to North Korea', *Inside the Air Force*, 25 February 2000, p. 1. See also *Nihon no Boei* (Japan White Paper on Defence), 2000, p. 37.
44 On Asian energy needs see R. A. Manning, 'The Asian Energy Predicament', *Survival*, vol. 42, no. 3, Summer 2000, pp. 73–88. Also *World Energy Outlook*, International Energy Agency, Paris, 2002, relevant sections.
45 *Financial Times*, 15 August 2000.
46 For the period 1994–1998, Japan's FDI in the energy sector in Azerbaijan, relative to other investors, ranked sixth, with a share of 3.7 per cent; the US was the largest investor (30.1 per cent), followed by Turkey (16.1 per cent), UK (15.8 per cent), Russia (6.6 per cent) and Norway (6.1 per cent). See *Country risk joho chosa. Kasupi kaihatsu kara mita Caucasus sankakoku no genjo to tenbo*, Japan Association for Trade with Russia and Central-Eastern Europe (ROTOBO), Tokyo, March 1999.
47 Inpex formerly stood for 'Indonesia Petroleum Ltd', a Japanese government-affiliated oil company; the name was changed to INPEX Corporation in September 2001, but the abbreviation 'Inpex' was retained. In 2003, the Japan National Oil Company held a 50 per cent stake in the company; the other 20 shareholders were leading Japanese companies (see INPEX Corporation official website).
48 Agence France Presse, 18 March 2003.
49 Yomiuri On-line, 4 July 2000.
50 *RFE/RL Business Watch*, 17 June 2003; *Financial Times*, 26 February 2004.
51 N. Shiokawa, 'Soren kaitaigo no Eurasia to Eurasia kukan', *Kokusai Mondai*, no. 464, November 1998, p. 16; 'Kasupi Kai mondai to kosaku suru kokusai kankei', *Kokusai Mondai*, no. 464, November 1998, pp. 23–25.
52 *Asahi Evening News*, 4 March 1999.
53 According to specialists, a gas pipeline is commercially viable up to 3,500 km, beyond that transport as LNG by ship is preferable. If there is no option other than to transport the gas overland, however, then a pipeline might still be a cost-effective solution, whatever the distance.
54 Keun-Wook Paik and Jae-Yong Choi, *Pipeline Gas in Northeast Asia: Recent Developments and Regional Perspective*, Briefing Paper no. 39, Royal Institute of International Affairs, London, January 1998, p. 5.
55 R. Forsythe, *The Politics of Oil in the Caucasus and Central Asia*, Adelphi Paper 300, International Institute of Strategic Studies, London, 1996, p. 27.
56 R. Yakemtchouk, *Les hydrocarbures de la Caspienne. La competition des puissances dans le Caucase et en Asie centrale*, Bruylant, Brussels, 1999, p. 85.
57 'A Long-term Vision of Natural Gas Trunk-line in Northeast Asia', Northeast Asian Gas and Pipeline Forum, Tokyo, 2000.
58 *Uzbekistan: 1999 Country Profile*, prepared for EBRD Business Forum, London, April 1999, p. 11.
59 Interview with Professor Masayuki Yamauchi, 10 May 2000.
60 N. McFarlane, *Central Asian and Caucasian Prospects: Western Engagement in the Caucasus and Central Asia*, Royal Institute of International Affairs, London, 1999, p. 12.

Part VI

Security Issues

18 Militarisation of the Caspian Sea

Mevlut Katik

The dispute between Azerbaijan and Iran that surfaced in July 2001 over territorial borders and offshore oil-drilling rights in the Caspian Sea revived old grievances. The incident highlighted the changing attitudes of the littoral states to the complex issues surrounding the Caspian Sea. There are a number of prisms through which this confrontation could be analysed, such as domestic pressures in the countries concerned, regional relationships and the interplay between contemporary international political and economic relations. However, there is another aspect to these events that requires attention, namely, the security setting in the Caspian basin as part of the new international relations/security environment. The current force deployment in the Caspian Sea highlights the strategic importance of the region. This chapter focuses on the naval presence and military deployment of the parties involved. It also attempts to explore areas of co-operation in a region often associated with conflict.

Confrontation in the Caspian

The confrontation erupted in July 2001, when two BP oil research ships commenced operations in an area of the Caspian Sea that would be within Iranian waters if Iran acquired a 20 per cent share of the Caspian Sea (see **Granmayeh**). Prior to July 2001, however, it had generally been accepted that this area belonged to Azerbaijan. Moreover, Iran had not objected when an oil contract was signed between Azerbaijan and an international consortium to explore the deposit in this part of the sea.[1] Thus, when Iran sent a naval vessel, supported by a fighter aircraft, to expel the BP contractors, who were working on behalf of Azerbaijan, from this area, it came as a surprise to many. BP suspended exploration work in the area until further notice. Meanwhile, Iran continued flying in Azerbaijani airspace and, as Azerbaijan claimed, even overflew Baku, the capital.[2] Meanwhile, Turkish warplanes staged an aerial display over Baku. In fact, the show had been planned long before these events,[3] a point emphasised by the Iranian deputy foreign minister, who, in an attempt to play down the Turkish show of strength, stressed that the display was part of a long-standing programme to mark Azerbaijan's national day. However, this action was interpreted as an indication of support for Azerbaijan. The Turkish and Azerbaijani media ran stories suggesting that Turkey would militarily support Azerbaijan in any Caspian conflict in which Baku might be involved.[4] The Turkish chief of staff attended the ceremonies, which added weight to this interpretation. Further Iranian violations of Azerbaijani territorial waters were reported by the Azerbaijani press in mid-April 2002, though denied by both Azerbaijani military and diplomatic officials.[5]

Naval power of the littoral states

Military expenditure of the regional countries has been on the increase in recent years. Arms transfers have also grown. In the period 1995–1999, defence spending increased by 19.2 per cent in the South Caucasus, by 36.5 per cent in Central Asia and by 23 per cent in the region as a whole.[6] Regional countries are engaged in military reforms and in upgrading defence industrial capabilities. Stocks of conventional weapons are being imported, especially by Iran, Armenia and Kazakhstan. Foreign military aid to the Caspian countries is also on the increase. US military aid is still small compared both to Washington's aid to other regions and Russian aid to the same region. Nevertheless, there has been a noticeable increase in the total amount of military aid to the region. By 2000, the US–NATO share of arms transfers to the region had increased to 4.1 per cent. Russia still accounted for 90 per cent, but China's role in military co-operation with regional countries was on the increase. By 2000, China's share in arms transfers to the region exceeded 5 per cent.[7]

The increase in volume and strength of military forces in the region indicates the perceived strategic importance of the Caspian basin. It is regarded as a gateway to Eurasia, including the internal territories of Russia and Central Asia. The maritime territory is particularly important. Since the Caspian Sea is a closed water system, there are two possibilities: either the littoral states will, jointly, achieve a fair balance of power, or one or more of them will seek to establish supremacy. The latter situation is likely to arise if one of the stronger littoral states tries to ensure that it has sufficient naval power to deter potential aggressors. However, such a development would very probably make the weaker states feel insecure, thus prompting them to search for ways to build up their own forces. Currently, there are huge disparities in naval strength, as can be seen in Table 18.1.

Iran

Iran is in the process of modernising its navy, which was hit hard during the Iran–Iraq war. Although Iran's main focus had previously been on the Straits of Hormuz, the incident of July 2001 and other developments in the Caspian have diverted Tehran's increased attention towards the Caspian. As part of its modernisation efforts, Iran first tried the C-802 anti-ship cruise missile with its Hudong class fast-attack crafts in 1997.[8] In 2001, it was

Table 18.1 Naval strength of the littoral states

Navy	Submarines	Patrol and coastal combatants	Amphibious	Support and miscellaneous
Azerbaijan	–	6	2	3
Iran	6	53	9	22
Kazakhstan	–	10	–	–
Russia	56	108	25	436
Turkmenistan	–	–	–	–

Source: Compiled from *The Military Balance 2001–2002*, IISS, 2001.

reported that it was replacing its ageing P-3F Orions with a maritime reconnaissance/anti-submarine warfare version of its own manufacture, Iran-140s, a licence-built version of Ukraine's Antonov An-140 design.[9] As emphasised by Commander Rear-Admiral Abbas Mohtaj, the Iranian navy intended to have a stronger presence in the Caspian Sea, in order to detect and deter threats.[10]

On Navy Day in 2001 (which commemorates Iran's capture of the oil platforms al-Bakr and al-Omayeh during the 1980 Iran–Iraq war), the national news agency IRNA reported that the navy would soon take delivery of heavy Mouj gunboats for patrolling its territorial waters. The agency quoted the commander of the Iranian First Navy Zone, Vice-Admiral Moharram Maequl, as saying that Iran's extensive territorial waters in the Persian Gulf, the Oman Sea and the Caspian Sea called for constant surveillance by the navy and that the Mouj gunboats would be put into operation for this purpose.[11] From time to time, Iran has held exercises in the Caspian Sea. One such manoeuvre, code-named Mirzakouchek-Khan, took place in the Bandar-e Anzali naval zone as early as 1999.[12] The navy had previously tested Iranian-made ballistic and cruise missiles in war games in the Persian Gulf.[13] In July 1998, Tehran tested the medium-range Shehab-3 missile, which reportedly has a range of 1,300 km.[14] In December that year former President Hashemi Rafsanjani commented that Iran no longer required assistance from either Russia or China, as it was now a missile-producing country and able to provide for its own needs.[15]

The Iranian Northern Command is in charge of the Caspian naval force. This consists of a few gunboats, minesweepers and naval training establishments. However, Iranian naval forces in the Gulf include Russian Kilo-class submarines, patrol boats with anti-ship cruise missiles, and various other types of missiles. Iran was the first Gulf country to acquire a submarine. In April 2002, Iran tested all its naval capacity and plans in an exercise dubbed Unity-80, which was held in the Oman Sea and the Straits of Hormuz. Operations included the use of special naval forces to disrupt oil production and transportation, likewise maritime traffic; this demonstrated Tehran's capacity to conduct amphibious operations to seize or hold offshore oil platforms.[16] This experience could potentially be of relevance to future Caspian deployments. If there were to be some redeployment of

Iranian naval forces from the Gulf to the Caspian, this would give Tehran the ability to interdict naval traffic in the Caspian and to intimidate its neighbours. Logistically, this would be difficult but, if it were accomplished, such a move would significantly alter the balance of power between the littoral states.

There are indications that, in the future, Iran might indeed accelerate its naval build-up in the Caspian. As early as 1995, Iran bought a Varshavyanka submarine from Russia, and its naval officers were trained at Russia's Baltiysk base (as part of its wider military co-operation with Moscow). In August 2000, the Azerbaijan press suggested that Iran was planning to increase its Caspian force by adding 6,000 troops, 75 armoured vehicles, eight fighter planes, 34 patrol craft, a frigate and a submarine. It was pointed out that there is a contradiction in this position: Iran bases its main arguments for joint use of the Caspian on the 1921 and 1940 agreements with the Soviet Union, yet these same agreements prohibited Iran from having a navy in the Caspian. Thus, the Azerbaijan press claimed, Iran was creating a dual application of the agreement by overlooking its military terms.

It should be emphasised that, at the time of writing, no such build-up of Iranian naval power has been confirmed. However, Iran already possesses the technology to build small diesel submarines and naval vessels that could be deployed in the Caspian. Moreover, comments in the Iranian press have indicated that Tehran is in the process of establishing tactical squadrons in the region. These squadrons would include submarines, surface vessels, marine aviation and marines.[17] Bandar-e Anzali, the largest Iranian port in the Caspian, currently houses about 50 naval craft. Other ports of possible strategic use are Now-Shahr, Bandar-e Torkaman and Babolsar.

Russia

The Soviet-era Caspian Sea flotilla was split roughly equally between the four successor states. Thus, Azerbaijan inherited 25 per cent of the total strength. Kazakhstan and Turkmenistan ceded their share to Moscow, which now operates a joint flotilla under Russian command. The present Caspian Sea flotilla consists of 36 surface combatants, of which ten are patrol and coastal combatants, five mine countermeasure, six amphibious and 15 support ships. It is based in Astrakhan, on the northern edge of the Russian sector of the Caspian Sea.

The Russian navy uses a system of layered defence, aimed to keep enemy forces as far away from home waters as possible. Apart from nuclear deterrence, it focuses on coastal defence, shore support and maritime border duties. Russian naval power has suffered a decline in recent years. However, it still possesses formidable technical capability and has acquired advanced new vessels.[18] Recent trends suggest that funding might be increased in the near future. In 2001, Admiral Vladimir Kuroedov, the commander-in-chief, called for one-quarter of the defence budget to be allocated to the navy, instead of the then 12 per cent; this would, it was suggested, enable the navy to acquire, among other things, 70 ocean-going surface combatants. He also added that construction was commencing of the new 20380 corvettes, to be used for coastal patrol, escort and anti-submarine warfare operations.[19] Despite problems of finance, personnel and other resources, President Putin charged Prime Minister Mikhail Kasyanov to form a Navy Board which would 'coordinate the work of the federal executive and government bodies . . . aimed at solving the national navy policy problems'.[20] It was announced that the Russian navy would build more facilities on the coast in Astrakhan, fund a land-based special operations unit, and provide more armoured vehicles for naval infantry. An increase in visits by the flotilla to Iranian ports was envisaged.[21]

Russia currently appears to be concentrating on the creation of rapid deployment forces to cope with instability on its southern borders. Consequently, it is likely that it will increase its efforts to strengthen the Caspian force based in Astrakhan.[22] On 23 January 2002, Russia put a new vessel into service to patrol its Caspian border. According to ITAR-TASS, a Russian news agency, the ship carries a six-barrel super-rapid-firing cannon and has a 50-knot speed capacity. The agency claimed that it would be used to protect 'biological resources', but did not elaborate how a super-rapid-firing cannon would achieve this. It was also reported that more than ten ships had been added to the fleet.[23] When President Putin visited Astrakhan in April 2002 he called for military exercises to be held by the Caspian flotilla in the summer of 2002, to give momentum to such efforts.[24]

In addition to naval power, Russia created an air command in Armenia in 1998. That same year, a headquarters was set up for a joint Ministry of Defence force in Kaspiysk, Daghestan; responsibilities included command of the 136th Motorised Rifle Brigade, ships of the Caspian flotilla, army aviation and air-borne sub-units as well as coastal units. The main naval base at Astrakhan was likewise strengthened.[25] Russia's Caspian fleet currently has 20,000 personnel, by far the largest deployment in the Caspian. The most recent Russian additions to the Caspian fleet have been some extra vessels, including four missile and artillery fast-attack craft, amphibious planes, patrol and anti-ship helicopters. It now has about 40 naval craft based in Astrakhan and Makhachkala.

One reason for this build-up of Russian forces in the Caspian region is the increasing importance of the southern policy in the Russian national security concept. Another possible reason is that Moscow is losing naval and military superiority in the Black Sea. After the disintegration of the Soviet Union, much of the Soviet-era Black Sea Fleet passed into the hands of Ukraine. This, in turn, gave Turkey a strategic advantage. By strengthening its position in the Caspian, Russia may be compensating for its weakness in the Black Sea. Finally, it is worth noting that, from a Russian perspective, the Caspian Sea–Volga Basin and the Arctic Ocean form a single, geo-strategically important system. This axis was used by the USSR in 1942 for transporting the Soviet navy to the Arctic; it is still a factor in Russian military thinking.

Azerbaijan

The Azerbaijan navy was formed soon after independence. It is based in Baku, formerly home to the Soviet navy. When the Soviet-era Caspian flotilla was split up, Azerbaijan inherited waterborne ships and infrastructural facilities. According to some estimates, the fledgling navy has about 3,000 personnel in 16 units; also one frigate, two amphibious ships, three support vessels and six patrol boats. However, in December 2000, Azerbaijani Defence Minister Safar Abiev stated that the navy consisted of 80 vessels of various profiles.[26] The defence priority for this force is to protect the Caspian Sea coast and to guard the oil refinery installations. So far, Baku has been able to achieve this goal with its current operational strength, but will need to boost it if it is to keep pace with other naval forces in the Caspian. Two patrol boats were given to Azerbaijan by the US in June 2001. However, it was stressed that the boats were given under an export control and border security programme.[27]

The Azerbaijan government recognises the need to modernise naval troops along with other branches of the armed forces. The Baku Higher Military Command School and Baku Higher Naval School have been set up to train officers and raise standards. The military agreement signed between Baku and Washington at the end of March 2002 was expected to assist the process of modernisation. Under this agreement, the US would provide military assistance to Baku worth US$4.4 million, a relatively small sum that could be increased, depending on the country's needs.[28] According to the deal, which was signed after a US defence delegation visited Baku in late March 2002, the two sides would co-operate in three main areas: peacekeeping, coastal security and the upgrading and management of Azerbaijani airfields to NATO standards. US military experts would visit the country to determine areas in need of modernising. US Deputy Assistant Secretary of Defense for Eurasia Policy Mira Ricardel said in a press conference after the signing ceremony that the objective of the security co-operation was to counter threats such as terrorism; to promote peace and stability in the Caucasus; and to develop trade and transport corridors.[29] The border protection efforts were aimed at preventing drugs and weapons from flowing through the country, she added. Ricardel underlined that the US would provide assistance aimed at 'enhancing the naval capability to secure the maritime borders of Azerbaijan'. 'What we are talking about is helping Azerbaijan in having the capability to protect its economic zone and territorial waters', she said at a press conference in Baku following her visit.[30]

In 1993, Azerbaijan (along with Armenia) was added to the US government's list of proscribed destinations for defence. In early March 2002, however, US officials made it clear that Azerbaijan might be provided with border control equipment such as radar and patrol boats, but that no US troops would be committed to the region.[31] Later that month, State Department spokesman Philip Reeker announced that, 'effective from March 29, 2002, all requests for licences or other approvals for Armenia and Azerbaijan involving items covered by the US Munitions list will no longer be presumed to be denied', adding that this would increase military co-operation between the US and the said countries.[32] On 19 April 2002, President Bush cleared the way by signing the memoranda to authorise arms sales to the Caucasus states, including Azerbaijan. Earlier, in January 2002, the US had suspended restrictions on US aid to Azerbaijan, rewarding the government for its co-operation in the US war on terrorism. US officials said the decision was in its foreign-policy and national-security interests.[33] Azerbaijani Foreign Minister Vilayet Quliev said that there would be quotas on arms sales, but stressed that nevertheless this was an important step forward as Azerbaijan attached great importance to military development.[34] Former presidential adviser Vafa Qulizade likewise hailed the decision. He commented that he interpreted it to mean that the US would come to the South Caucasus countries soon and that lifting the ban on arms supplies was linked to this.[35] He added that Baku had no funds to buy arms and that the fact of US involvement would relax Russia's grip on the Caucasus.

Azerbaijan also established close links with Turkey and the Turkish army. Turkish army officers are training Azerbaijani officers, and Azerbaijani military students train at Turkish army schools and academies.[36]

Azerbaijani President Heidar Aliev signed a decree in April 2002 'on ensuring the security of export pipelines'.[37] The decree stipulated that the security of the pipelines should be guaranteed in order to ensure the uninterrupted and reliable transportation of hydrocarbons. The pipelines in question were the Baku–Tbilisi–Ceyhan oil pipline and the Baku–Tbilisi–Erzurum natural gas pipeline (see **Roberts**). In a sign of the increasing importance attached to security arrangements around the Caspian, a state committee was set up, chaired by the prime minister. It was envisaged that a special body would be created to ensure the security of oil flow and installations, to be made up of a joint force drawn from the Ministries of Defence, National Security and the Services to Guard State Installations.[38] The administrative authorities of the districts through which the pipelines would be laid were assigned to take the measures necessary to protect the pipelines against sabotage, technical damage and the theft of oil. This development, which followed the signing of the American–Azerbaijani military co-operation agreement, marked the creation of another agency/force to defend Azerbaijan's Caspian oilfields and brought an added dimension to its Caspian security. Natiq Aliev, head of the State Oil Company of the Azerbaijan Republic (SOCAR), commented that the increase in oil extraction necessitated a strengthened security system.[39] Turkey, Georgia and Azerbaijan had already been co-operating closely in this field since 1998; in late April 2002 they signed a co-operation agreement on pipeline security and co-ordination in the fight against terrorism.[40]

Kazakhstan

Kazakhstan, like Azerbaijan, has been trying to set up a navy from scratch since it renounced its portion of the Caspian flotilla in Russia's favour.

However, in 2002, a decade after independence, its forces were still undergoing restructuring and modernisation. It had at this time ten patrol boats, excluding five non-operational Boston Whalers donated by the US in 1995. Its naval force included a large navy infantry component. According to press reports, a naval base was to be established near Bautino to protect the Caspian coastal zone.[41] In July 2001, Kazakh President Nazarbaev called for the creation of a modern army, underlining the need for such a force in Central Asia.[42] He declared that the western zone of the Caspian, together with southern Kazakhstan, areas rich in oil deposits, were of strategic importance for the country and a priority for the Kazakh armed forces.[43] An official decree was issued in early August 2001 (thus, soon after the July incident between Azerbaijan and Iran) on the creation of a defence institution called the Republic of Kazakhstan Defence Ministry Higher Naval School. The school, based in Astana, was designed to train 180 people.[44] This was an indication that the organisational development of the Kazakh army at sea was being accelerated.

The initial stage in the development of a Kazakh navy took place in 1998, when the Customs Committee assumed the functions of protecting the Caspian zone. The entire sea shelf within the limits of the national border was deemed a zone of action for the specially created *Bars* (Leopard) rapid reaction service. The state border protection forces (SBPF), organisationally part of the Kazakh armed forces, had been operating in the Caspian since 2000. They combined the former border troops and coastguard forces. The number of the troops in the SBPF is not known, since it is still at the formation stage. However, the personnel of the country's navy, which is situated mainly in the Caspian, amounts to an estimated 3,000; its arms comprise ten coastguard and two small hydro-graphic launches, three Mi-8 helicopters and six Mi-2 helicopters.[45] They are based at the ports of Aktau and Atyrau in the east and the north of the Caspian. In line with an agreement between the defence ministers of Russia and Kazakhstan, signed in January 1996, five boats were transferred to Kazakhstan to strengthen the coastguard forces. Russia pledged assistance for Kazakhstan to purchase vessels for surveying the coastal infrastructure and modernising it.

As part of the programme to develop its navy, Kazakhstan signed technical co-operation agreements with a number of countries, among them Russia, Turkey and Ukraine. The package of agreements with co-operation partners had included the training of cadres in naval higher educational institutions. These officers will eventually form the basis of the Kazakh navy. Meanwhile, Kazakhstan has already opened a naval academy of its own in Aktau, one of the main oil ports. During a visit by the Kazakh Chief of Staff General Alibek Kasimov to Turkey in July 2001, Turkey granted Kazakhstan a patrol boat at the Turkish navy base in Golcuk, north-west Turkey. Kazakhstan is also co-operating closely with the US to develop its military organisational structure. Between 1997 and summer 1998, Astana received more than ten ships from the US and Germany.[46] In July 1998,

Kazakhstan took delivery of a Kazakh-manufactured combat cutter built in Zenith shipyard in Uralsk in the west of the country. Another two were built later.[47]

Kazakhstan is still far from having a full army. The focus of its current military strategy (which covers the period up to 2005) is on rapid reaction forces and weapons upgrade to deal with perceived threats, such as those 'stemming from the lack of a legal status for the Caspian Sea, the appearance of new sources of oil, and hot spots around western Kazakhstan'.[48] The 2001 military budget was around US$172 million, 50 per cent higher than in 2000. It is scheduled to increase gradually, in line with the expected improvement in the economy as new oilfields and oil exports come on line. In mid-April 2002 Kazakhstan organised a large-scale military exercise in which 6,000 servicemen from all army branches took part. It was held in the Sari Shagan training ground in the west of the country, the area of the main oil reserves; it was attended by President Nazarbaev and the chief of staff.[49]

Turkmenistan

After the break-up of the Soviet Union, Turkmenistan inherited the largest aviation group in Central Asia. It also inherited a 25 per cent share of the Caspian flotilla but, like Kazakhstan, ceded this to Russia, in return for assurances that Moscow would guard its coastline. Thereafter, however, Turkmenistan, like Kazakhstan, began to create its own navy. Reports on recent acquisitions are characterised by confusion and misinformation. Some observers suggested that in 2001 Turkmenistan had five vessels.[50] Within the last couple of years, it would appear that Turkmenistan has acquired at least two small patrol boats; according to some reports, it also bought 20 boats from Ukraine, half of which were said to be 40-tonne boats equipped with heavy machine guns.[51] However, according to Ukrainian President Kuchma, Turkmenistan only received two patrol boats; these were apparently part payment for Kiev's debt for natural gas purchases from Ashgabat. The Russian arms trading company Rosobonexport disclosed that Turkmenistan was interested in gas-for-arms deals, including patrol craft. Azerbaijani sources, moreover, suggested that Turkmenistan had received patrol boats from the US, a claim denied by Washington. Yet a US official said that Ashgabat was given a boat under a military surplus programme a year ago: the US had donated such equipment under export control programmes to over 20 countries and was seeking to establish similar cooperation with Turkmenistan. Whatever the truth of the matter, such reports indicate that Ashgabat is pursuing an active policy on the navy front.

Ashgabat has repeatedly warned that it will defend its rights in the Caspian by whatever means necessary. A new decree was adopted in April 2002, outlining measures to improve the training and operational readiness of the armed forces.[52] A terminal, the largest such facility in the Caspian for any kind of seagoing vessel, was opened in 2002 at the Turkmenbashi port.[53]

BlackSeaFor: a model for a Caspian sea force?

In this environment of suspicion, mistrust, increasing militarisation and the threat of the use of force, new mechanisms must be found to ensure stability in the Caspian Sea. An appropriate model for this might be the Black Sea Naval Co-operation Task Group (BlackSeaFor). This was set up in 2001 by the Black Sea Economic Co-operation Organisation (BSEC) as an on-call navy task force 'to enhance peace and stability in the Black Sea Region and to increase regional co-operation'.[54] The idea for this force was originally mooted in 1998, during a meeting, held in Bulgaria, of the Black Sea navies. Thereafter, naval officers, legal experts and diplomats from the participating littoral states of BSEC – Bulgaria, Georgia, Rumania, Russia, Turkey and Ukraine – discussed the modalities of implementing such a project. Establishment and accession agreements were drawn up in the period 1998–2000; an annex regarding financial matters was appended. Follow-up meetings were held in various member states, during which the organisational structure and status of forces were reviewed. The Operational Control Authority and Chief of Staff were created to further institution-alise it.[55] The agreements and annexes formalising BlackSeaFor were officially signed by the founding members in Istanbul in April 2001. BlackSeaFor constitutes the first ever formation of naval co-operation among all the littoral states of the Black Sea. The establishing agreement stressed that it was not directed against any state, nor was it intended to constitute a military alliance. It is noteworthy that BlackSeaFor brings together Russia and Turkey, a NATO member state. The provisions of the founding documents made clear that membership of the new organisation would in no way affect rights and responsibilities deriving from other inter-national agreements. The organisation was also open to new members, by consensus agreement.

The force was activated in Turkey in late September 2001. After the inau-guration, naval ships from all member states held small-scale exercises at sea and visited different ports in participating countries from late September to mid-October 2001.[56] It was envisaged that the tasks of BlackSeaFor would include search and rescue operations, humanitarian assistance, mine coun-termeasures, environmental protection, goodwill visits and any other tasks agreed by all the parties. It would conduct joint exercises to increase inter-operability to execute these tasks. Units allocated to the Force would be based in their respective home territories and would come together for the above-mentioned tasks and exercises. It would be composed of naval elements only, without direct participation of army and air services, though these could support the naval force 'as and if necessary'. BlackSeaFor would be composed of a minimum of four to six ships, including one command-and-control ship. Main classes of warships that could be allocated to the Force were classified as frigate/destroyer, corvette/patrol boat, minesweeper, amphibious ships and auxiliary ships and vessels.[57]

The most interesting aspect of this organisation lies with its consultation and decision-making process. On the political front, this is carried out by foreign ministers or defence ministers, or their authorised representatives. High-level military consultations are carried out only by chiefs of general staff or their representatives. Political meetings focus on political aspects of BlackSeaFor activities. BlackSeaFor could be deployed outside the Black Sea, if the participating states were to agree by consensus. It could also be available for UN or OSCE-mandated operations. Each party has the right to withdraw its forces and/or its personnel during activation and to retain full command of any ships allocated to BlackSeaFor, which means that they may be withdrawn for national purposes at any time, provided that the other member states are informed. Tactical command of the Force rests with its commander, and the position of the commander of the Force will rotate annually among the signatory states. Any disputes arising from application of the BlackSeaFor agreement will be resolved 'through consultations without recourse to outside jurisdiction'.

The BlackSeaFor agreement could provide a useful model for co-operation and consultation between the Caspian littoral states. Interaction and communication of this nature would promote security rather than fear, thereby reducing tensions. A 'CaspianSeaFor' could help the weaker Caspian states develop their navies in a constructive manner, with the emphasis on environmental protection and other peaceful operations. It could, for example, minimise Iranian fears of Russian naval operations off Iran's Caspian coast through mechanisms of mutual checks and balances. Moreover, any such co-operation could prevent, or at least minimise, the risk of incidents such as the Iranian–Azerbaijani confrontation of July 2001. The entire model would provide a quasi-permanent politico-military consultation mechanism for the Caspian countries. The model could also be applied to an affiliated organisation that might ensure uninterrupted freedom of navigation and transportation.

Admittedly, some modification of the above model would be required if it were to be applied to the Caspian. Unlike the Black Sea, the Caspian Sea has no outlet/opening to an open sea. This naturally affects the nature of naval operations. There could also be some ambiguity regarding threat perceptions. Who or what would be the common threat? Given that some Caspian littoral states regard each other as the main threat to their security, it could be difficult to find common ground on which to launch any such initiative, let alone to achieve an adequate level of co-operation. However, an effective implementation of the above-mentioned mechanisms could overcome most of these problems. After all, the Black Sea countries used to belong to opposing military blocs and were accustomed to regarding each other as security threats. Yet the model of co-operation that they are now promoting is transforming interstate relations and adding new dimensions to regional interaction. There is a lesson here for the Caspian basin, a region which urgently needs joint solutions to a wide variety of problems, ranging from environmental protection to pipeline security.

Conclusions

The unresolved legal status of the Caspian Sea is a threat to regional security. The Iran–Azerbaijan confrontation of July 2001 is an illustration of the way in which the ambiguities of the present situation could be manipulated as a tool of extended diplomacy to further territorial demands. This is a precarious state of affairs. It could well lead to the further militarisation of the Caspian Sea, which would benefit no one in the long run. It is difficult to halt arms transfers. Nevertheless, every effort must be made to channel co-operation into peaceful projects and to prevent further militarisation. Otherwise, third parties such as Turkey, Armenia and the Western powers risk being drawn, directly or indirectly, into a protracted regional conflict.

The strengthening of naval forces and border troops would serve only to increase the insecurity of each of the littoral states at this stage. Worst affected would be those that have limited resources to allocate to defence spending (or, as in the case of Azerbaijan, are already engaged in a frozen conflict in Karabagh). The economic costs of any further militarisation and/or conflict could prove to be counterproductive for the already precarious economies of the region. Therefore, there is an urgent need to engage the littoral states and other parties in a more constructive process. The creation of an organisation such as CaspianSeaFor offers a potential outlet. A joint Caspian Security Conference could be created to identify problem areas and address issues of common interest. This would provide a mechanism through which the five littoral countries could establish a framework agreement on the creation of confidence-building measures. Undoubtedly, each littoral state has more to gain from co-operation than conflict. It is now time to create a new Caspian paradigm.

Notes

1 A Production Sharing Agreement was signed in July 1998 between Azerbaijan and an international consortium comprising SOCAR, BP, Statoil, ExxonMobil, TPAO and Alberta Energy to explore and extract oil in the Alov–Araz–Sharq offshore oilfield in the Caspian.
2 'Azerbaijan Protests over Iranian Ship Interception', *BBC Online*, 24 July 2001.
3 'Turkish Planes Back Up Azeri Position', *BBC Online*, 23 August 2001.
4 'Turkish Chief of Staff in Baku', *Daily Hurriyet*, 25 August 2001; 'This Message is Understood', *Milliyet*, 26 August 2001.
5 Azerbaijan News Agency (ANS), quoted in *BBC Monitoring*, 19 April 2002.
6 *The Military Balance: 2000–2001*, International Institute of Strategic Studies, London, 2001.
7 *Ibid.*
8 *Jane's Defence Weekly*, 8 January 1997.
9 *Jane's Defence Weekly*, 11 April 2001.
10 www.Iran-e-azad.org.
11 IRNA, *Iran Business Review*, December 2001.
12 IRNA, *Tehran Times*, 3 February 1999.
13 'Iran Says US Can't Curb its Missile Capacity', Reuters, 11 December 1998.
14 Brief on Iran, Representative Office of National Council of Resistance of Iran, 14 December 1998.

15 Reuters, 11 December 1998.
16 M. Eisenstadt, 'Iranian Military Power – The Executive Summary' (www.washingtoninstitute.org/pubs/mikeexec.htm).
17 'Could there be War in the Caspian Sea?', *Russia Journal*, no. 32 (125), 17 August 2001.
18 *Jane's Sentinel*, 15 August 2000.
19 *Jane's Defence Weekly*, 12 April 2001.
20 *Pravda*, 1 August 2001.
21 J. M. Walker at www.afpc.org, quoting *Jamestown Monitor*.
22 A. Jack quoting military expert Colonel Christopher Langton, 'A Need to March with the Times', *Financial Times*, 15 April 2002.
23 M. Lelyveld, 'Caspian Meeting Ends with Few Clues on Progress', *RFE/RL*, 25 January 2002.
24 'Russia Moots New Caspian Share-out', *BBC Online*, 26 April 2002.
25 T. L. Thomas, 'Russian National Interests and the Caspian Sea', Foreign Military Studies Office, *Perceptions*, vol. IV/4.
26 'Azeri Army Capable of Liberating: Interview with Defence Minister', *Financial Times*, quoted in *Azernews*, no. 49, 6 December 2000.
27 M. Lelyveld, 'US Says Patrol Boats are Gifts to Promote Regional Security', *RFE/RL*, 26 June 2001.
28 A. Sultanova, 'US, Azerbaijan Forge Military Ties', Associated Press (AP), Baku, 28 March 2002.
29 *Ibid.*
30 'US to Help Oil-rich Azerbaijan Defend Caspian Boundary', Agence France Presse (AFP), Baku, 28 March 2002.
31 M. Lelyveld, 'US Rejects Military Involvement in Caspian Dispute', *RFE/RL*, 15 March 2002.
32 'US Lifts Ban on Arms for Armenia, Azerbaijan', Reuters, Washington, 29 March 2002.
33 *Ibid.*
34 'Azeri Foreign Minister Expects Arms Quotas Following the Lifting of US Arms Embargo', Turan News Agency, Baku, 30 March 2002.
35 'Azeri Analyst Hails Lifting US Embargo', Turan News Agency, Baku, 30 March 2002.
36 *Hurriyet*, 25 August 2001.
37 'Azeri President Signs Decree on Ensuring Security of Export Pipelines', Turan News Agency in *BBC Monitoring*, Baku, 15 April 2002.
38 *Ibid.*
39 *Ibid.*
40 M. Katik, 'Caucasus Summit Cements Co-operation Among Turkey, Azerbaijan and Georgia', www.eurasianet.org/departments/insight/articles/eav050302a.shtml, 5 May 2002.
41 *Izvestiya*, quoted in *Russia/CIS Intelligence Report*, 28 January 1994.
42 K. Weisbrode, 'Patrol Boat Procurement Makes Waves on the Caspian', www.eurasianet.org/departments/insight/articles/eav071701.shtml, 17 July 2001.
43 *Nezavisimaya Gazeta*, quoted in *BBC Monitoring*, 7 August 2001.
44 *Ibid.*
45 *Ibid.*
46 'Caspian Flotilla', www.fas.org/nuke.
47 *Ibid.*
48 Y. Razumov, *Panorama*, quoted in WPS Agency, Almaty, 19 January 2001.
49 'Kazakh Army to Stage Large-scale Exercises in April', RIA News Agency, Almaty, 29 March 2002; and 'Kazakh President Attends Major Military Exercises', Interfax-Kazakhstan, 16 April 2002.
50 K. Weisbrode, *op. cit.*

51 'Conflict in the Caspian Grows', *Russian Military Analysis*, WPS Russian Media Monitoring Agency, no. 89, 3 August 2001.
52 'New Training Course Set to Improve Calibre of Turkmen Officer Corps', *Financial Times*, quoted in *BBC Monitoring*, 9 April 2002.
53 'West Turkmen Seaport Made Accessible to Larger Ships', Turkmen State News Agency, quoted in *BBC Monitoring*, 5 April 2002.
54 Black Sea Economic Co-operation Organisation (BSEC) was established in 1992 by 11 countries in and around the Black Sea. It aimed to achieve and foster multilateral economic co-operation between the member states; its headquarters were based in Istanbul. See further websites: www.bsec.gov.tr; www.blackseafor.org.
55 Ten meetings were held during that period: four in Turkey, two in Romania, one in Bulgaria, Georgia, Russia and Ukraine.
56 H. Ulusoy, 'A New Formation in the Black Sea: Blackseafor', *Perceptions*, vol. VI/4, December 2001–February 2002.
57 'Agreement on the Establishment of the Black Sea Naval Co-operation Task Group', www.blackseafor.org.

19 Chechnya: post-referendum prospects for normalisation

Charles Blandy

Introduction

Since the disintegration of the Soviet Union, the Chechens have intensified their struggle for independence from the Russian Federation. During this period two wars have been fought in Chechnya, the first lasting from 1994 to 1996, and the second from 1999 to the present. Not only have these conflicts claimed the lives of an estimated 100,000 Chechen civilians and some 8,000 Chechen fighters, but also, according to Russian Defence Ministry reports, 4,379 servicemen were killed in the first conflict,[1] and the extent of losses in the second conflict, 'from September 1999 to December 2002 currently stands at 4,572 servicemen killed and 15,549 wounded – a total of 20,121 servicemen – enough to man two motor rifle divisions',[2] let alone those missing in action. Unofficial estimates suggested that losses were far higher. The prospects for a peaceful resolution of the situation seemed remote.

However, the terrorist attacks in New York and Washington on 11 September 2001, followed by the formation of a coalition for the eradication of global terrorism, served as a catalyst for the Russian government to begin to seek the termination of the second Russo-Chechen conflict, then well into its second year. With the realisation that Russia could face a dangerous escalation of conflict in Central Asia with the potential for spill-over into Russia's southern border lands through Uzbekistan and Tajikistan, or at least the need for an increased military presence there for the foreseeable future, it is not surprising that President Putin should turn his attention to fresh efforts to stop the fighting in Chechnya, to enable a partial withdrawal of federal forces from there.

Putin's first attempt to terminate the conflict was by an ultimatum on 24 September 2001 for the *boyeviki* (Chechen combatants) to lay down their arms within 72 hours. It met with little response. Military operations continued during 2002, with well-publicised incidents and a threatened spill-over into Georgia. A poll held in June 2002 had shown 62 per cent of Russians in favour of negotiations with the Chechen resistance movement. The average poll results over the previous two years had shown only 22 per cent in favour of negotiation, with 72 per cent voting for the continuation of the war.[3] These developments convinced the Russian president that it was imperative to seek a 'normalisation' of the situation. There can be little doubt that the terrorist attack by Movsar Baraev and his group on the Dubrovka theatre in Moscow on 23 October 2002 provided a spur for the Kremlin to announce publicly its plans for Chechnya. President Putin signed a decree on 12 December 2002 authorising a referendum on the Chechen Constitution. This was to be followed by presidential and parliamentary elections in Chechnya, to be held some eight months later in November or December, to coincide with those of the Russian Duma. On 6 June 2003, the Russian Duma agreed to an amnesty to cover potentially criminal acts and the handing-in of weapons within Chechnya between 12 December 1993 and 1 September 2003.

Present situation

It is important to understand how President Putin and those around him perceive the normalisation of the situation in Chechnya.[4] His approach is fundamentally different to that advocated by the West, in particular to the tenacious advocacy on human rights issues by rapporteur Lord Judd of the Parliamentary Assembly of the Council of Europe. In part the difference is explained by the Russian conviction that the recurring Chechen military conflict is part of a much wider struggle in which Russia is the protective glacis and bastion, the front line of the civilised world against the evil, disruptive forces operating under the banner of Islamic fundamentalism. The Kremlin policy in Chechnya has been vindicated in its own eyes by its struggle against the brand of global terrorism which began lapping its southern extremities some way ahead of the US's war against terrorism.

Moreover it became clear that federal normalisation methodology would not include negotiation with separatist leaders or their representatives as people in the West believed it should. Nor would Moscow welcome international monitoring or mediation. It is important to remember that it is firmly believed in Russia that Chechnya is part of the Russian Federation, and thus remains an internal matter for Moscow to deal with as it thinks fit.

The introduction and implementation of political initiatives to bring normality back to Chechnya also necessitated the demonstration of firm political control over senior members of the military establishment, whose oft-expressed opinions have been indicative of a determination for complete and unassailable victory. Many senior Russian officers had lost sons in Chechnya, Generals Pulikovsky and Shpak to name but two.

Chechnya has become a catalyst at least for acknowledging the need to rethink military security strategy for the Russian Federation as a whole, to re-evaluate the tasks and structures of Ministry of Defence troops and those of the Internal Troops (MVD). These are urgent projects in their own right, together with the need for a professional army which is capable of producing well-trained, combat ready, rapid reaction forces, as opposed to the conscript one designed to fight NATO over 20 years ago. Lack of funds has partly been caused by the continuous drain on resources due to the two

Russo-Chechen wars, amounting to some US$100,000 million, according to Ruslan Khasbulatov and Ivan Rybkin.[5] The federal casualty lists show no sign of diminishing.

One is left with the overriding impression that this is 'an amnesty of the victors ... And victors are not judged'.[6] Those who have participated in actions against federal forces simply do not come within its terms. Should someone be killed or injured as a result of a mine, any member of a separatist group which allegedly laid the mine could be accused of murder or attempted murder and is therefore ineligible for the amnesty. With such a universal 'hook' it will be possible to apprehend and hold a former separatist fighter at any time in the future.

The new Constitution

The All-Chechen Peoples' Congress held in Gudermes on 11 December 2002 had the opportunity to read the draft Constitution in the full knowledge that the 'Constitutional Commission will not ignore a single remark'.[7] However, there is no indication that their views were reflected by changes to its provisions. Yet almost every article of this document raises controversial issues. Thus, for example, Article 1, Clause 18 refers to the 'Chechen Republic (Nokhchiyn Republic)' as a 'democratic, social, law-governed state, republican in administration'.[8] The inclusion of the Chechens' own name for the country may be intended to make the Constitution more acceptable to them. Directly reflecting the Kremlin's absolute opposition to Chechen independence, however, Clause 2 states: 'The territory of the Chechen Republic is united and indivisible and is an inalienable part of the territory of the Russian Federation.' After experiencing de facto independence from 1991 to October 1999, for the Chechen this wording seems to ignore the crux of the matter. The earlier Constitution of 2 March 1992, as amended, reflected the gain and freedom which independence bestowed on the Chechen people:

> The Chechen Republic is a sovereign and independent, democratic, legal state, formed as a result of the self-determination of the Chechen nation. It possesses the supreme right in relation to its territory and national riches; independently determining its external and internal policy; adopting the Constitution and Laws, which possess supremacy on its territory. State sovereignty and independence of the Chechen Republic are indivisible, unshakeable ...[9]

Having failed to win recognition for their self-determination, the Chechens are now faced with the cold, stark realities of the latest version of the Constitution: a bitter blow for those who strove to achieve independence from Moscow. No wonder the Kremlin is hinting at wide powers of autonomy. However, a person could be forgiven for wondering where and how the promised powers will be implemented. How will they be interpreted when changes in the leadership of the Russian Federation occur?

On the question of jurisdiction, Article 6, Clause 1, paragraph 2 states:

> In matters of exclusive jurisdiction of the Russian Federation as well as joint jurisdiction of the Russian Federation and Chechen Republic, federal Constitutional laws and federal laws shall have a direct legal effect over the whole territory of the Chechen Republic. In the event of contradiction between a federal law and a regulatory act of the Chechen Republic, the federal law will prevail.

Clause 2 goes somewhat further: 'Laws and other regulatory legal acts adopted under the competence of the Chechen Republic must not contradict federal laws and the Constitution of the Chechen Republic.' This is in line with Putin's policy since he became president; his government has spent considerable efforts to ensure this kind of conformity and subordination in other constituent parts of the Federation.

Elsewhere in the Constitution it is indicated that, even when matters are within the jurisdiction and competence of the Chechen authorities, federal authorities can interfere. This could well result in friction between federal law and customary law (*Adat*), particularly over polygamy and the ramifications of blood feuds. Thus, for example, Article 7 states:

> In the Chechen Republic local government is acknowledged and guaranteed. Local government is independent within the limits of its own authority. Organs of local government are not included within the organs of state government.

But what precisely are the institutions that are to be recognised as having a legitimate part to play in local government? Will informal organisations based on traditional Chechen social structures be accorded some standing? Or is the creation of new civic institutions envisaged? Without further clarification this is a meaningless statement.

Elsewhere (Article 8, Clause 1) it is stated that 'an ideological, political, diverse and multiparty state is declared in the Chechen Republic'. Yet in subsequent clauses this is modified in various ways. Clause 4, for example, specifically forbids

> the creation and activity of public associations the aims or actions of which are directed towards a forced change of the foundations of the Constitutional structure and violation of the unity of the Chechen Republic and Russian Federation, inflaming social, racial, national and religious dissension, the creation on the territory of the Chechen Republic of any armed or militarised formation not envisaged by the Constitution of the Russian Federation and by federal Law.

Undoubtedly, this is not only directed towards Chechen separatism but also such organisations as the Sufi Brotherhoods. These bodies were, and continue to be, semi-secret societies, albeit religious ones.[10] Historically, they have been distinguished by 'their underground, clandestine, actively militant anti-Soviet (anti-Russian and anti-Communist) character'.[11] These Brotherhoods could now be classified as being undesirable under the terms of Clause 4.

Several other concerns are raised by the Constitution, including the question of the exploitation of natural resources such as oil, other minerals and forestry. It is by no means clear how much benefit, or what percentage share, the Chechen Republic will receive, since the 'ownership, usage and disposal' of such resources is to be regulated by the Constitution of the Russian Federation and the Federal Law.[12]

Another sensitive issue is that of language. Chechen and Russian are the state languages within the Chechen Republic (Article 10), but it is specified that Russian is the language for inter-ethnic communication and official clerical work in the Chechen Republic. This is interpreted by some as linguistic discrimination.[13]

The Constitution gives the citizens of the Chechen Republic the right to elect their president in a secret ballot. The holder of this office is to be the leader of the executive authority in Chechnya and to be granted the exercise of considerable powers, including the appointment of ministers, judges and the chairman of the national bank. However, there is a clause which enables the president of the Russian Federation to dismiss a Chechen president should the need arise (Article 72, sub-clause 'g'). It would seem somewhat invidious, indeed undemocratic, for the people of Chechnya having elected their president to be faced with the fact that he could be removed by the Russian president at any time. Moreover, Moscow could be in a position to manipulate strictly Chechen affairs, for example, by allowing members of federal forces stationed temporarily in Chechnya to participate in elections in the same way that members of the permanently deployed units and subunits of the Ministry of Defence and MVD are allowed to vote there.

As these comments show, each article of the new Constitution of the Chechen Republic contains ambiguities and covert restrictions such as those mentioned above. Lack of space here precludes a detailed analysis of this document.[14] In brief, however, it ignores the basic reason for desiring independence in the first place. It does not resolve the issue of the return of Chechnya to becoming a full, valued and willing subject of the Russian Federation. Moreover, it also appears to ignore the fact that Chechens throughout their history have had a system of discussion and consultation with decisions being made on a collective basis through elders and *teip* (clan) councils. The provisions for local government to operate independently, as set out in this Constitution, do not indicate clearly whether or not villages will be allowed to run their own affairs without undue interference from Grozny or Moscow. And yet, the Chechens have endorsed the document.

Referendum proceedings

From the Kremlin's point of view, the quicker the referendum on the Chechen Constitution could be organised and carried out, the more rapid would be the divestiture of legitimacy of President Aslan Maskhadov and his government, and the transfer of power in accordance with the transitional arrangements embedded in the Constitution. This removed a major, if symbolic, obstacle to Chechnya's reincorporation not only as a *de jure* subject but also a de facto one, within the Russian Federation.

The right to vote in the referendum included all residents of Chechnya. This right had been extended to servicemen who were part of units and subunits permanently stationed in Chechnya, such as servicemen in the 46th Brigade of Internal Troops and 42nd Motor Rifle Division. These numbered approximately 35,000 to 37,000, and would comprise some 7 per cent of voters in Chechnya. The overall contingent of Federal servicemen in Chechnya at the time was around 80,000.

Despite earlier promises that provision would be made for displaced persons to participate in the referendum, refugees could only take part in the referendum if they did so on Chechen territory. Polling stations outside Chechnya had been organised only in Ingushetia, where some 66,000 were temporarily living. Chechen refugees in Daghestan and the Volgograd *oblast'* (province) of Russia had to make arrangements to travel back into Chechnya. Not everyone who wanted to participate was able to make the journey. Thus, an editorial commented, when there was a Russian general election, it was possible to vote on a ship at sea, or at an embassy when abroad: 'But here when the problem of Chechnya is being decided, refugees from Chechnya could not vote, but here are soldiers called-up into the army for 1.5 years and stationed in Chechnya, who have the right to decide the fate of a region which lies thousands of kilometres from their permanent place of residence.'[15] There were many instances of intimidation. As one commentator noted: 'Various cameras established in Chechnya were recording separate groups of citizens going to participate in the referendum . . . huge resources were mobilised for the victory over history.'[16]

In the event the results of the referendum, which was observed by 'around 150 Russian and more than 20 foreign journalists exceeded all expectations' of the Kremlin and local authorities.[17] The electorate was required to vote on the following questions: the new Constitution, the law on presidential elections and the law on parliamentary elections. There was a turnout of 80 per cent of those eligible to vote. On all three issues, a landslide majority gave their assent to the new proposals.[18] The conduct of the referendum apparently proceeded without untoward incident or observed irregularity. The prosecutor's office did not report any violations of procedure, nor did CIS observers. However, several accounts disputed the size of the turnout, claiming that it was far lower than the official estimate.

Reasons for voting

It would appear that the majority of the voters had not read the text of the Constitution nor the laws on the elections, but had voted simply 'for' the referendum.[19] The success of the referendum appears to have owed much to the skill and 'spin' of political public relations specialists who succeeded in convincing the Chechens that the inevitable alternative to voting in favour of the referendum was a continuation of the war. They used the slogan 'Take the road to peace – the referendum'. The Chechens, angered by the presence of the federal troops and by the constant acts of intimidation at road-blocks, the extortion of money for the return of bodies and other provocations against the civilian population, did not vote for the Constitution as such, but rather for self-preservation.

It should not be forgotten that the federal forces, acting individually and as a group, have perpetrated countless atrocities against the Chechens. The sheer scale of destruction by artillery bombardment and air strikes, resulting in indiscriminate damage and unnecessary deaths, injuries and psychological damage amongst the civilian population, deserve international censure. These experiences have deeply scarred the Chechen people and created bitter resentment towards the aggressors. This will remain a severe obstacle for peace in the medium to long term. In order to overcome this, the authorities will need to demonstrate great determination in bringing those who have committed criminal acts to justice. However, in a system where the morale of the officer corps is at rock-bottom and where it has become apparent that officers have been incapable or unwilling to control their own men, it is unlikely that this will happen, particularly when officer and soldier alike want above all to leave Chechnya as soon as possible and return home.

The most important question stemming from the acceptance of the new Chechen Constitution will be the relationship between the federal centre and the republic. The Russian president's announcement about the intention to bestow 'a wide autonomy' on the republic surely played a role in attracting several moderate separatists to vote for the Constitution. On the other hand, perhaps it is a sign of real preparedness on the part of the federal central authorities to present Chechnya with a special status within the Russian Federation. In going for a 'wider autonomy', the Kremlin would not be strengthening separatist tendencies, for the president of the Russian Federation has the right to remove the Chechen president by decree at any time. But the Chechen of whatever hue, having gained any sort of concession from Moscow, is hardly likely to regard it as symbolic.

Chechen society

How well will the Constitution fit local customs and circumstances in Chechnya? Historically, Chechen society has been fragmented, with a high degree of group autonomy. Today, some of the traditional structures are weaker, but they nevertheless still exert an influence on contemporary life (see Table 19.1 for the main divisions).[20] The basic cell in Chechen society is the *teip* (clan) but, in the view of a leading specialist in Chechen social structure, Mayrbek Vachegayev, it is now village society which has a greater influence.[21] Each teip comprises a group of families bound together by blood ties through the line of paternal descent. Freedom, equality and brotherhood,

Table 19.1 Traditional structure of Chechen society

Chechen name	Russian	English appellation and remarks
Kam	Narod	People/nation
Tukkhum	Obshchestvo	Society
Teip	Klan	Clan – a complex, multi-stage formation
Va'r	Vyar	According to one source, this refers to 'a blood-related group of people' a word which more accurately defined the understanding of the word *teip*'[22]
Gar	Otvetvleniye	Offshoot. Sometimes the *gar* level does not exist
Nek'	Vetv'	Branch
Tsa	Familiya	Large family/extended family – grandfather, sons, grandsons
Dozal	Semy'a	Family – husband, wife and their children
Kup	Kvartal	Each village was divided into various *teip* quarters, communities or blocks of flats in towns

Source: Extracted and compiled from M. Vachagayev, 'Sovremennoe Chechenskoe Obshchestvo', *Tsentral'naya Azia i Kavkaz*, no. 2, 2003.

although not articulated formally at any time, were the basic characteristics of this formation. The absence of any historic form of statehood in Chechnya had a strong influence on teip cohesion. Over time, some teips became dispersed, moving away from their original geographical areas, particularly in the north. In the mountainous south, however, people still for the most part live in their original locations. In these areas, teip influence and power remains a prominent feature in everyday life.

Today there are some 135–150 teips in the republic; some are larger than others, 'but contrary to widespread belief none of them has a uniform political stance towards the internal struggle in the country'.[23] One of the striking factors in Chechen society prior to both the recent Russo-Chechen conflicts was an absence of parties and political movements. It has been suggested that this is because teip relationships have tended to define the political system, the foreign policy of that country and the underlying relationships within Chechen society. Moreover, since members of a teip are distributed throughout the republic, it could be claimed that 'the teip system tends not to divide the nation. On the contrary, it tends to consolidate the Chechen nation'.[24] Whether or not this last argument is accepted, it would seem that the distribution of teip members throughout the republic has tended to increase teip political and economic influence by association and dispersion.[25] Nevertheless, according to Vachagayev, teip power is considered by Chechens to belong to yesteryear. Teips are now more concerned with land disputes, marriages, funerals and blood feuds.[26]

Chechen society is patriarchal and traditional; the norms of the common law (*Adat*) coexist with the Islamic norms of the Sharia.[27] Some of the factors of Chechen life which become apparent through the Adat are the natural informality of Chechen life and the fact that every Chechen is a free man. The power and authority of the teip leader is that of a moral teacher; he does not have the means of coercion or force at his disposal. Real power resides in the hands of the teip elders and village council. All important decisions in village life are decided by these informal structures.[28] In the view of some commentators, the crisis in Chechnya arose because the unofficial leaders were suppressed, intimidated and exterminated, and the destructive elements found themselves in power. However, during the past decade, this traditional form of authority has been corroded by the suppression and intimidation of local leaders. One of the greatest problems will be the reconstruction of effective social structures and civic institutions. This is not an issue that is addressed in the new Constitution. In fact, as indicated above, some of the provisions of this document seem designed to weaken local government yet further.

Chechen youth

Chechen youth are impatient for change. Young men and women alike are becoming tired of the slow rational approach – they want action. They want federal troops removed from Chechnya and are tempted to believe that only the most outrageous terrorist methods will achieve this aim. Far more radical than was the norm amongst the field commanders of yesteryear, they are willing to use extreme violence to achieve their aims. It should also be remarked that it is becoming more common for young women volunteers to participate in such actions, even as suicide bombers. These are often educated young women who have lost family members in the conflict. Two such participated in the Znamenskoe bombing in Chechnya on 12 May 2003.

It should come as no surprise that the youth of Chechnya are impatient and despairing. The devastating report of the situation in the republic by Ruslan Khasbulatov in November 2000 speaks for itself:

> The Chechen Republic as a unified social-economic organism does not exist any more. Industrial, commercial, social and any other form of connection between populated points which operated over centuries have either disappeared completely, or exist in a rudimentary form, occasionally breaking through the powerful 'blockers'. The population of the republic is in a state of god-forsaken isolation from the outside world. Isolation is the most successful part of the counter-terrorist operation being carried out, which in fact has been transformed into a war against all the peaceful population of the republic.[29]

Regrettably, Khasbulatov's words continue to have resonance in 2003. The radicalisation of the younger generation has already prompted some young Chechens to attach themselves to a cause far wider than the limited aims of separatism of Chechnya from Russia, as was illustrated by the number of Chechens who went to Afghanistan to fight on the side of the Taleban. This trend towards extremism is detrimental for perceptions of Islam and fuels suspicion and animosity towards all Muslims. This augurs ill for the genuine separatist who wants to win independence by peaceful means.

The interim administration

Undoubtedly one of the most significant outcomes of the referendum was that it strengthened the position of Ahmad-Haji Kadyrov, the head of the Chechen administration; that gave him a clear advantage in the run-up to the October presidential elections.[30] Kadyrov considered himself to be the main claimant for the presidential chair. Yet many Chechens viewed him as a traitor. He lived in a palace, while half the population of Chechnya were without a roof over their heads. It is reported that he had his own illegal bandit formation, which earned its living by the abduction of people. The headquarters of this group were located in Kadyrov's home village, where they also maintained a private prison.[31]

The Kremlin was 'grateful' to Kadyrov for the success of the referendum held under his auspices. However, not everyone in Putin's circle supported him. Kadyrov did not have authority as a leader in the republic and did not possess the ability to consolidate Chechen society around him. He may have had considerable administrative and economic resources for his presidential election campaign, but the Kremlin could always have blocked his candidacy for the post. Yet, in the last few weeks before the presidential elections all the major presidential candidates for some reason or other either declined to stand or were disqualified from running. In the event, on 5 October 2003, with a turnout of 86 per cent, Kadyrov secured over 80 per cent of the vote. He did not survive in office long: on 9 May 2004 he was assassinated. This was a major setback for Moscow's policy in Chechnya. Once again, the region was teetering on the brink of crisis.

Conclusions

There is much remaining from the legacy of past turmoil and the present changing balance of power not just in Chechnya but in the whole Caucasus–Caspian region. This does nothing to resolve current disputes and might well foster further instability and conflict in this troubled and volatile region -- hindering, or even preventing, the creation of the stable political environment which is essential for the security, welfare and development of civil society and the full realisation of the region's economic potential. The initial euphoria over the 'grandiose success' of the referendum soon gave way to disappointment and renewed despair.[32]

The wording of the amnesty scheduled for 6 June 2003 did not improve matters. It was not to apply to serious crimes. Worse, it indicated that federal employees rather than Chechens would be the main beneficiaries: 'I never expected anything from this amnesty – in the last amnesty in 1997 in all 39 people were amnestied and now only 10 will be, no more', Aslambek Aslakhanov, a member of the Russian Duma, commented bitterly.[33] Others noted that the amnesty would only be another opportunity for corrupt officials to seek bribes, and that whilst purges and visits at night continue no one will hand in weapons.

History does colour the minds of people, their perceptions and attitudes which in some cases are indelibly printed in a nation or people's psyche for generations. I believe that this point must be understood by people from the West, where perhaps the emphasis on history is not so marked. One of the challenges for the West is to try to understand the importance of history and family in the lives of the people who live in the Caucasus region, to offer help only if it is needed, and to remember that many of the countries there have much older civilisations than those enjoyed in the West.

It must not be forgotten that the North Caucasus, marking the southern boundary of the Russian Federation, and the former Trans-Caucasus buffer zone, today more aptly known as South or Southern Caucasus, remain areas of direct and vital concern to Moscow – in particular to the military mind, whose perceptions both in the historical past and now remain ever sensitive to penetration by influence, be it Islamic extremism or by the possibility of actual threats to the territorial integrity of Russia: not only those posed by the other two regional powers, Turkey and Iran, but also from any form of interference by the West. Specifically, NATO expansion, increased Western activity in Georgia, Azerbaijan, and the Caspian littoral states have in turn been perceived by Russia to run counter to its own vital interests, such as the choice of oil pipeline routes.

Events in the North Caucasus will have an impact on life in the South Caucasus and the Caspian basin. It goes without saying that a problem such as Chechnya has and will continue to affect other parts of the Caucasus. This could pose a serious security threat to the exploitation and transportation of Caspian oil.

Notes

1 http://chechnya.genstab.ru/russian_kia.htm.
2 B. Sapozhnikov, 'Second Chechen Campaign Takes its Toll' (http://gazeta.ru/ 2003/02/18/SecondCheche.shtml).
3 *Novaya Gazeta*, no. 62, 26 August 2002 (http://2002.novayagazeta.ru/nomer/ 2002/62n/n62n-s39.shtml).
4 For background, see Charles Blandy, *Chechnya: The Need to Negotiate*, Conflict Studies Research Centre (CSRC) Camberley, Occasional Brief no. 88, November 2001, pp. 8–9.
5 R. I. Khasbulatov and I. P. Rybkin, 'Ekonomicheskiye aspekty voyny v Chechne', *Kavkazskiy Vestnik*, internet version, 9 April 2003.
6 *Kolokol*, 21 May 2003 (http://www.kolokol.ru/chechnya/32949.html).
7 'Draft Constitution, election bills distributed among Chechen congress delegates', *Interfax*, 11 December 2002.
8 *Vesti Respubliki*, Spetsvypusk, no. 3, 19 December 2002. A slightly different version was published on the official Chechen government website www.chechnya. gov.ru. This is the text on which the current analysis is based.
9 http://www.chechen.org/content.php?catID=4.
10 See A. Bennigsen and S. Enders Wimbush, *Muslims of the Soviet Empire: A Guide*, Hurst & Co., London, 1986, p. 184.
11 *Ibid.*, p. 189.
12 Article 9, Clauses 2 and 3.

13 See A. Politkovskaya, 'Potrebleniye Novoy Konstitutsii', *Novaya Gazeta*, no. 20, 20 March 2003 (http://2003.novayagazeta.ru/nomer/2003/20n/n20n-s17.shtml). She notes that this precise formulation is not found in any other republic of Russia.

14 See further Charles Blandy, *Chechnya: Normalisation*, CSRC, Camberley, June 2003.

15 'Novaya Konstitutsiya Chechni predpologayet vvedeniye ponyatiya Grazhdanskiy Chechenskoy Respubliki', with commentary by E. Zeynalov, Director, Human Rights Centre of Azerbaijan, *Kavkazskiy Vestnik*, 13 March 2003.

16 I. Mil'shteyn, 'Lozh', video, referendum', *Kolokol*, 24 March 2003 (http://www.kolokol.ru/chechnya/26923.html).

17 'Narod Chechni progolosoval "za" po vsem trem voprosam referenduma' (http://www.prime-tass.ru/ns/7/20030324/324007.htm).

18 Regarding the Constitution, 96.5 per cent of the electorate returned a convincing 'yes' vote; on the presidential and parliamentary elections, 95 per cent and 96 per cent respectively voted in favour (Tat'yana Stanovaya, 'Chechnya poverila v Konstitutsiyu', http://www.politcom.ru/2003/zloba2019.php, 25 March 2003).

19 *Kommersant*, no. 50, 25 March 2003.

20 M. Vachagayev, 'Sovremennoe Chechenskoe Obshchestvo', *Tsentral'naya Azia i Kavkaz*, no. 2, 2003, p. 16.

21 Vachagayev, *op. cit.*, p. 23.

22 Yu. A. Aydayev (ed.), *Chechentsy istoriya sovremennost*, Mir domu tvoyemy, 1996, p. 189 (the author is a Member of the Academy of Natural Sciences of the Russian Federation and Academy of Social Sciences).

23 M. Galaev, *The Chechen Crisis: Background and Future Implications*, p. 17, CSRC, Camberley, June 1995, p. 3.

24 Y. Krutikov, 23 December 1997, *BBC Summary of World Broadcasts*, SWB SU/311/B/19 [32]. See also Charles Blandy, *Chechnya: A Beleaguered President*, Occasional Brief no. 61, CSRC, Camberley, July 1998.

25 It should be noted that Chechen society today is not exclusively composed of Chechen teips; 'new' teips have been formed from immigrant neighbouring people, including a substantial number from Daghestan, which today represent 'one quarter of the teips' (Vachagayev, *op. cit.*, p. 18).

26 Vachagayev, *op. cit.*, p. 23.

27 A. Khalmukhamedov, Department Head, Russian Ministry for Federation and Nationalities Affairs, 'How to Return to Normality in Chechnya' (http://www.ca-c.org/dataeng/bk02.03.khalm.shtml).

28 Khalmukhamedov, *op. cit.*

29 R. Khasbulatov, 'Situatsiya v Chechenskoy Respublike', *Nezavisimaya Gazeta*, no. 247, 29 December 2000.

30 Ahmad-Haji Kadyrov was born in 1954 in Central Asia. In the 1980s he completed studies at the Mir-Arab Madrassa in Bukhara. In 1996 he became Mufti of Chechnya. In 1996 he participated in negotiations with Lebed' and Maskhadov at Staryye Atagi. In 1998 he began to criticise Maskhadov for encouraging 'Wahhabism'. In 1999 he condemned the 'invasion' of Basaev and Khattab into Daghestan and went into opposition against Maskhadov. On 10 October 1999 he was removed from the post of Mufti of Chechnya by Maskhadov. On 12 July 2000, with Russian backing, he was appointed head of the Administration of the Chechen Republic (see further http://www.nns.ru/Person/kadyrov).

31 A. Politkovskaya, 'Tikhie, ili grazhdanskaya voyna silami spetssluzhb', *Novaya Gazeta*, no. 68, 16 September 2002 (http://2002.novayagazeta.ru/nomer/2002/68n/n68n-s18.shtml).

32 M. Bondarenko and A. Riskin, 'Okhrana Kadyrova strashneye zachistok', *NG Regiony*, no. 5, 31 March 2003, p. 10.

33 'Gosduma prodlila Chechenskuyu amnistiyu – do 1 Sentyabrya 2003', 4 June 2003 (http://www.gzt.ru/rub.gzt?rubric=novosti&id=31550000000013366).

20 Whither South Caucasus: to prosperity or to conflict?

Urs Gerber

Introduction

Up to the mid-1990s the South Caucasus was widely perceived as Russia's geopolitical backyard. Moreover, it was regarded as a region of endemic conflicts and problems. Thus, thinking in the West was mainly driven by a 'Hands Off' policy. However, significant Western interest and involvement in the region started soon after a deal between Azerbaijan and Western consortia had been signed in September 1994[1] on the future exploitation of offshore oil resources in the Caspian Sea. This resulted in a re-evaluation of strategic priorities.

Since then, there has been an ongoing discussion whether 'geopolitical' objectives or 'geo-economic'[2] interests are driving factors on the agenda of major players in terms of their interests in that part of the world. There is little doubt that geopolitical aspects are still largely driving the interest of regional powers such as Russia and Iran. However, there are other players for whom geo-economic interests are of paramount importance, including multinational oil companies (US and European-led). Yet the situation is not static. Geopolitical perceptions, even of superpower governments, can rapidly be influenced by economic arguments.

There is little doubt that today the key players in the Caspian region are Russia, Turkey, Iran and the US; moreover, they are likely to remain in this position for the foreseeable future. Their individual agendas and perceptions differ considerably (see **Antonenko, Bolukbaşi, Namazi and Farzin** and **Page**). Yet it seems clear that their assessments and policies are basically driven by a geopolitical framework, though economic considerations undoubtedly do have a significant impact. Estimates of the proven, or the possible, oil and gas resources of the Caspian basin have considerable implications for political as well as economic decision-making processes. Thus, 'geo-economists'[3] bolster their position with high resource expectations, while 'geopoliticians' emphasise such factors as the high transportation costs of Caspian oil.[4]

There is a further consideration that must be taken into account when assessing the prospects for exploiting the hydrocarbon resources of the Caspian: the necessary investments will only flow if investors can be assured of adequate profits. This will require stability, the rule of law, a basic perception of prosperity, and some degree of democracy in the region. Hence, the future prosperity of the region will depend in large measure on issues of stability and security. The South Caucasus unfortunately does not yet provide a positive balance sheet in this respect, even if one can argue that some level of democracy has been reached. Thus, there are two major questions to be considered. Firstly, will security and stability be achieved, or will chaos and conflict be an obstacle to development? Secondly, what recommendations might foster stability and prevent chaos in a framework of twenty-first-century *realpolitik*?

Major sources of conflict

The South Caucasus region is often compared with the Balkans. If one adds the challenges of energy resources, then we might argue that the situation is potentially even more complex. Possible sources of conflict are summarised below.

Intra-state ethnic strife

The Caucasus region is characterised by immense ethnic and linguistic diversity. The region has a centuries-old history of open and latent conflicts between the different groups. Under Soviet rule, members of the titular nation (e.g. Kazakhs in Kazakhstan) were heavily favoured for higher posts in the administration and economy.[5] This led subsequently to a quantitative increase of the titular nation within minority areas. Thus, for example, there was a heavy influx of Azerbaijanis into Nakhichevan and Karabagh (both on Azeri territory), and likewise of Georgians into Abkhazia (part of Georgia).[6] This was much resented by the local peoples, who felt that they were not only being politically and economically dominated by 'outsiders', but that their culture was being marginalised. Once Soviet rule collapsed, the volatile ethnic tensions emerged into the open. In the early 1990s there were violent clashes in Georgia, also a major war in the Karabagh province of Azerbaijan (see **Nassibli**, p. 161). Only Armenia, to date, has escaped serious civil strife. The Azerbaijani minority there (which formerly constituted over 5 per cent of the total population) has been forced out, largely due to the war in Karabagh; as a result, the population in Armenia is exceptionally homogeneous.

External and domestic migration

The regional conflicts resulted in massive forced migration of ethnic minorities to the territory of their respective titular nation.[7] These refugees, often forced to live under very difficult and humiliating conditions, have put continued pressure on the national leadership to restore the *status quo ante*, particularly in Georgia and Azerbaijan. This creates the potential for serious internal friction – a dynamic that could well be utilised by opportunistic political entrepreneurs.

Interstate conflict

After the break-up of the Soviet Union, the borders drawn in the 1920s have been the subject of disputes. On the one hand, the titular nations in the region and the international community have favoured the principle of the 'inviolability of existing borders'; on the other hand, however, ethnic diasporas have claimed the right of 'self-determination of nations'. Throughout the Caucasus border areas and minority enclaves are flashpoints for conflict. In terms of human and material damage, the war in Karabagh has had the most devastating consequences, because it is being waged not just by local communities but also by sovereign states. It is not inconceivable that this pattern could be repeated in other border areas, thus leading to yet more interstate conflict.

Weak state power

As a consequence of the above-mentioned conflicts and problems, all three states in the South Caucasus are weak in terms of state power, leadership and, most significantly, in terms of 'power instruments' such as armed forces and police. This is especially true of Azerbaijan and Georgia. Although they are member states of such bodies as the OSCE, the NATO Partnership for Peace programme, and the Council of Europe, state structures, political parties, the rule of law, human rights and other major assets of a modern state are far from being fully implemented.[8] Economic development is also lagging, despite dubious statistical claims to the contrary.

Leadership and succession

Armenia is in a much stronger position with regard to leadership and succession as its political establishment and culture is already comparatively well developed. In Georgia and Azerbaijan, there has been very little progress in this respect. Until late 2003, the presidents in both states – in Georgia, Eduard Shevardnadze (b. 1928) and in Azerbaijan Heidar Aliev (b. 1923) – were shrewd former Communist Party and KGB bosses – who had been brought back to power in the post-Soviet era by semi-democratic processes.[9] Both were successful in establishing a degree of stability, also in gaining international recognition. Very importantly, they also provided strong leadership. However, it was clear that if only because of their advanced age, these men would soon have to relinquish power. Given the lack of democratic experiences, culture and structures in these states, many analysts feared that there would be succession problems, possibly accompanied by significant internal turbulence.[10] In fact that did not happen.

In Azerbaijan the change of leadership was triggered by Heidar Aliev's failing health. By mid-2003 he was seriously ill. He had hoped to stand in the presidential elections in October, but withdrew from the race shortly before the ballot. It came as no surprise that his son Ilham was elected as his successor. Foreign observers noted many irregularities in the proceedings and were concerned by the violence and mass arrests that accompanied the elections. However, within a few weeks the situation was stable again and most people seemed prepared to give the new leader time to establish himself (see **Nassibli**, p. 177). Heidar Aliev died on 12 December. In Georgia there was also a transfer of power, but it followed a different pattern. There it was the rigging of the parliamentary elections in November 2003 that set the process in motion. Few believed the official results, which favoured the main pro-presidential party. Thousands of people joined public protests about the electoral fraud, as well as about social grievances such as poverty, corruption and lack of economic opportunity. Shevardnadze was forced to resign. The leader of the so-called 'Rose Revolution' was Mikhail Saakashvili, a 36-year-old US-educated lawyer. On 4 January 2004 an overwhelming majority elected him president. In a short while he and his allies began to consolidate their power by taking control of all the major government portfolios. In March, new parliamentary elections were held. Opposition leaders claimed that again there was widespread electoral fraud. Thus, in both Azerbaijan and Georgia, despite the fact that the change of leadership had proceeded more smoothly than anticipated, there were nevertheless worrying signs that the problems of the past were re-emerging.

Disappointed expectations and hopes of the electorate

In Georgia, and even more so in Azerbaijan, the respective governments have raised popular expectations to great heights. They have promised the settlement of conflicts and the safe return of hundreds of thousands of internally displaced persons and refugees. They have also held out the prospect of imminent prosperity from an 'oil and gas boom'. Yet to date, little has happened to sustain those promises. On the contrary, many have seen their standard of living fall drastically. This has created an atmosphere of simmering frustration and alienation. The situation could easily be destabilised. Thus, if either country (Georgia and/or Azerbaijan) were affected by internal turmoil due to unsettled succession problems, popular discontent might well be directed against the political establishment. This in turn would trigger the flight of international investment.

Energy resources and transportation routes

The importance of energy resources in the Caspian basin acquired global strategic importance in the mid-1990s, when, following the collapse of the Soviet Union, the region opened up to Western investment. It has been aptly commented:

> If the initial stage of the Caucasian conflicts was characterized by clashes initiated by various nationalist movements from 'below', at a later stage they became wars controlled by political decisions from 'above' . . . In this context, the oil contracts bounded onto the political stage. They became a major issue in political calculations, competitions, and alliance formations. Caspian oil became the reason for struggles that led to military operations, the formation of alliances, and the overthrowing of governments. The oil contracts have transformed the Caucasian political and military landscape.[11]

In September 1994 Azerbaijan concluded a Production Sharing Agreement with major Western oil conglomerates to develop the Azeri, Chirag and Guneshli (ACG) offshore oilfield. This deal, known as the 'Contract of the Century', marked the beginning of the engagement of Western powers in the development of Azerbaijan's region oil and gas resources (see **Olsen**, p. 130).

Geopolitical stalemate

The various conflicts and wars in the South Caucasus were frozen in early 1994, mainly due to substantial Russian involvement.[12] Following the signing of the Contract of the Century, there was some hope that Western pressure would accelerate the process of conflict resolution. However, so far no significant steps have been taken in this direction. But, at least for the present, the South Caucasus is regarded as a zone with an 'accepted level of violence', and a modicum degree of stability.

Yet there is the potential for a rapid escalation of local conflicts. If this were to happen, although it might not impede the exploitation of the oil, it would certainly have serious implications for the transport of hydrocarbons through the region. Pipelines are vulnerable to attacks of all sorts and are difficult to protect in unstable and insecure environments.[13] Hence, large-scale and profitable oil production is only feasible if both the exploitation area and the transport corridor are safe. Most of the conflicts listed in Table 20.1 have a direct impact on this framework. If a safe environment is to be created, they should be settled before large-scale oil projects are implemented. Table 20.1 assesses the five major conflict areas and prospects for settlement.[14]

Chechnya and other North Caucasian conflicts

The two wars in Chechnya as well as other crises in the North Caucasus (e.g. in Daghestan) have direct and indirect implications for stability in the South Caucasus (see **Blandy**). Prior to and during the Chechen conflict, Russia put considerable pressure on Azerbaijan and Georgia to prevent any influx of Chechen fighters from the south into Chechnya and into Daghestan. Georgia was accused by Russia of granting Chechen fighters 'safe havens' and indeed, it is generally accepted that villages in northern Georgia were used by Chechen fighters for 'rest and recuperation'. In retaliation, in late 2000 Russia reintroduced a visa regime for border crossings with Georgia.[18]

Geo-economic incentives

There is little doubt that a Caspian region without major hydrocarbon resources would be of relatively little interest to the outside world. The characteristics of Caspian oil can be summarised as follows:

- Proven and estimated reserves of the hitherto exploited fields account for between 16 and 60 billion barrels. European estimates tend to be more conservative than local and US estimates.[19]

Table 20.1 Major conflicts in the South Caucasus

	Current state	Options for a foreseeable future
Karabagh	The conflict is frozen basically along the lines of the Armenian and Karabagh successes of 1994. All Karabagh efforts focused on creating 'facts on the ground' to prevent resubordination to Azerbaijani rule. In late 1997 Armenian president opting for a rapprochement ousted and replaced by the 'President of Nagorno Karabagh Republic (NKR)', Robert Kocherian. In Azerbaijan, any conciliatory stance on Karabagh going beyond 'some sort of autonomy' is politically suicidal. In early 2001 the Azerbaijani stance hardened again.[15] Neither of the parties is capable (Azerbaijan) or willing (Armenia, NKR) to go for a military solution in the near future.	Renewal of significant military operation is unlikely, but cannot be excluded; a major breakthrough is unlikely; a continuation of a 'no war no peace scenario' likely;[16] significantly increased foreign efforts for a conflict resolution unlikely.
South Ossetia	Basically unchanged situation since July 1992. Several negotiation efforts since 1995 with little progress. Both sides continue to insist on their basic objectives (i.e. Georgia – integration of South Ossetia into Georgia; South Ossetia – autonomy and reunification with North Ossetia).	Renewal of widespread violence fairly unlikely; a major political breakthrough rather unlikely; no outside effort to solve the conflict to be expected; a 'Cyprus-type' scenario most likely.
Abkhazia	Basically unchanged situation since November 1993. Several rounds of negotiation but little progress. Both sides insist on their basic objectives (i.e. Georgia – Abkhazian integration into Georgia; Abkhazia – full independence). Georgia domestically under pressure from the 250,000 ethnic Georgian refugees forced out of Abkhazia. Neither party capable (Georgia) or willing (Abkhazia) to go for a military solution in the near future.	Local hostilities of extremist elements in form of terrorist acts likely at any time; renewal of combat operations fairly unlikely; a major political breakthrough is unlikely; no outside effort to solve the conflict to be expected; Russia's position likely to remain ambivalent.
Ajaria	Populated overwhelmingly by a Muslim population of Kartvelian (Georgian) origin; Ajaria plays an important role not only for the stability of a Black Sea access (port of Batumi), but equally as pivotal state for all lines of communications in the South Caucasus. So far long-standing tensions between Batumi and Tbilisi have been kept in check.[17]	Any Georgian effort to re-establish full sovereignty over the area by violence would have serious consequences.

- On a global scale most analysts agree that in any case the Caspian share of global oil reserves accounts for roughly 5 per cent,[20] which is slightly above the size of the North Sea deposits.
- Some Caspian oil is of a good quality with a low degree of sulphur and thus comparable to the Gulf oil; however, many fields have high levels of sulphur, which corrodes pipelines and requires special refining facilities (see **Ehteshami**, p. 68, **Adams**, p. 97).
- Pure extraction costs are assessed to be in the vicinity of US$5–6 a barrel, which is more than in the Persian Gulf (US$3) and less than in the North Sea (US$7–8).
- In a global perspective, the overall importance of Caspian oil is likely to be somewhat less than that of major oil deposits elsewhere in the world, owing to higher extraction and transportation costs (the proposed export routes not only stretch over long distances, but in many cases traverse unstable regions).
- As far as the three states of the South Caucasus are concerned, Azerbaijan, the only state with its own oil resources, will benefit the most. Georgia will profit from transit fees charged for pipelines crossing its territory; it will also receive some revenue from port fees for the use of its Black Sea port Supsa.[21] Armenia is unlikely to benefit directly from any oil boom, as at present no pipeline project is planned across its territory.

The Caspian basin also holds significant natural gas reserves. In terms of a global comparison, similar figures and assessment are valid for gas as for oil. Present estimates suggest that Caspian gas accounts for less than 5 per cent of global reserves. (It should be noted, however, that the region has not as yet been fully explored.) In terms of Caspian gas consumption, domestic markets currently predominate. Export markets are primarily other states of the former Soviet Union.

Pipelines

From an economic point of view, the construction of commercially viable oil and gas pipelines is one of the greatest problems for the Caspian region. Most of the existing infrastructure is of poor quality and is politically highly vulnerable. Two routes, both utilising upgraded and extended Soviet-era pipelines, were selected to carry 'early oil' from the ACG field to the Black Sea (see Map 4). The northern route crosses Lezghin territory in Azerbaijan,[22] then runs via Daghestan to the Russian port of Novorossiysk. There are several areas of high instability along this route. Originally the line ran through Chechnya, but Russia built a bypass, completed in April 2000, to avoid crossing the zone of conflict. This reduces the level of threat, but the danger that Chechen fighters or others might attack the pipeline remains real. Daghestan, too, is a 'hot spot', currently almost as volatile as Chechnya, yet there is no practical way of reaching Novorossiysk without going through it. The southern route runs through Georgia and Ajaria (which has a significant Armenian minority) to the oil port of Supsa. The security of this line depends largely on the degree of stability in Georgia – which is at best variable.

From the time that the 1994 contract was signed it was clear that, in addition to the 'early oil' export pipelines, a new Main Export Pipeline (MEP) would have to be built to meet the needs of the Azerbaijani oilfields when they reached peak production levels. Iran, Russia and Turkey all lobbied energetically for the MEP to be routed across their territory. All the proposed options had major geopolitical and/or geo-economic draw-backs. Many experts, even in the US, admitted that the most feasible option,[23] which would meet important requirements (market access, blue water port, land transportation distance, terrain, even stability), would be a pipeline through Iran into the Persian Gulf. However, given the state of US–Iranian relations this is not likely to be an option for some time to come. A pipeline through Iran to the Persian Gulf would be the shortest and arguably the most economic way to reach a blue port with large tanker capacity. However, US objections to Iranian involvement in the exploitation and transport of Caspian hydrocarbons ruled this out. The Russian option, via Novorossiysk with on-shipment across the Black Sea, raised concerns about perpetuating Moscow's hold over Azerbaijan. Moreover, there were environmental concerns about increasing tanker traffic through the Bosporus.[24] The route through Turkey, from Baku via Tbilisi to the Mediterranean port of Ceyhan, was at first regarded as economically unsustainable. It also carried consid-erable security risks, since the pipeline would pass through highly unstable areas, including the Armenian-populated area around Akhaltsikhe, as well as running for over a thousand kilometres through mainly Kurdish-populated parts of eastern Anatolia.[25] Yet, this option received strong US backing and BP, the operator of ACG, and other international oil compa-nies eventually became convinced that, taking all factors into consideration, this was the best solution.

The groundbreaking ceremony for the Baku–Tbilisi–Ceyhan (BTC) pipeline was held in Azerbaijan in September 2002. However, objections to this route were gaining momentum and a massive campaign was mounted to draw the attention of international financial institutions to the problems that were associated with this project.[26] Among the issues of concern there was the possible damage to the fragile ecology of some sections of the route, also the inadequacy of measures to safeguard the rights of local people across whose land the pipeline would be built (see **Akiner**, p. 385). As a result of these protests, the European Bank for Reconstruction and Development, the World Bank and other lending agencies that were to provide some 70 per cent of the funding postponed taking a decision on the financing for this project. The Baku–Tbilisi–Ceyhan Pipeline Company, led by BP, remained committed to the project, but by June 2003 there was a wide-spread perception that it had fallen behind schedule.[27] Financing was finally agreed in late 2003, thus ensuring that at least the first phases of the project would be completed as planned.

Regional players

Russia

There is little doubt that, after the collapse of the Soviet Union, Russia has continued to perceive the South Caucasus as one of its vital areas of interest, possibly the most important outside the Russian Federation. On 20 August 1997, at a meeting of the National Security Council, President Yeltsin issued a strong warning towards the West not to interfere in this region (see **Antonenko**). The Russian policy to limit or even diminish US power was known as the 'Primakov Doctrine'. Its most significant tenets were that

> Russia must be a superpower; ... America or American surrogates, like Turkey, must be prevented from exercising influence anywhere in the Former Soviet Union; [Russia must] ... undermine the ability of the US power projection and conflict resolution in Kosovo, the Gulf, and in the Straits of Taiwan by diplomatically supporting Serbia, Iraq, Iran, and China . . . .[28]

Nevertheless, by this time Russian influence in the region was lower than at any time in the past 200 years.[29] From a geopolitical point of view:

> one can say that in defending its interest in Transcaucasia [i.e. South Caucasus] and Central Asia, Russia is above all preoccupied with its security, giving present priority to the military–political means of ensuring its position. This is mainly the triad: 'bases–borders–peace-keeping . . .'[30]

In its geo-economic thinking, Russia fears the emergence of an anti-Russian axis created on the basis of foreign investment into the Central Asian and Caucasian states.[31] This perception has not fundamentally changed during the Putin presidency, which mostly represents the security and military establishment. Hence, it is most likely that the geopolitical view will strengthen in the foreseeable future, as is cogently summed up by a leading Russian analyst:

> Unless Russia is involved as a partner the region is unlikely to enjoy even minimal stability or benefit from the mineral wealth of the Caspian. Should its position be undermined, it may lose interest in co-operating and attempt to protect its interest by interfering in domestic politics, manipulating the existing conflicts, and acting as spoiler in oil issues.[32]

Though Russia's options have been significantly reduced over the last decade, it keeps its foot firmly in the 'South Caucasian door'.

There is a widespread consensus within the South Caucasus that the Russian military presence is detrimental to conflict resolution. Even Armenia, the only remaining Russian ally in the region, is far from happy with this situation. Its alliance with, and dependence on, Russia is more driven by a perceived strategic and economic necessity than a voluntary long-term partnership. A full withdrawal of the Russian contingent deployed in Georgia was agreed at the OSCE Summit in 1999, whereby two of the four Russian-run garrisons should have been vacated by mid-2001.[33] Yet it seems unlikely that the Russian military presence in Georgia will end soon as this provides Russia with significant leverage to put pressure on a country that is widely perceived in Moscow as supporting Chechen terrorists. From a Russian perspective, its military presence has considerably added to stability in the region and to conflict containment. In that respect a moderate military presence is perceived as fair and justifiable. It is, however, undeniable that Russia, through a policy of *divide et impera*, is quite successfully using its position to exploit its influence over the region as much as possible. Even though the military presence is indeed moderate, it matters greatly as the countries are militarily weak and Russia may increase its potential very rapidly, if need be.[34] With a basic unwillingness to foster conflict resolution, Russia as an important direct and indirect player is able to maintain a high level of influence with relatively little effort.

Turkey

Since the demise of the Soviet Union, Turkey has been very active in projecting its influence throughout the South Caucasus as well as into Central Asia. First attempts in the early 1990s largely failed when Turkey presented itself as the 'natural and logical successor' as regional power based on political and cultural grounds. The policy of 'a lot of words, but no deeds' was not appreciated by the new states, as the last thing they were expecting was a 'new big brother'. By at least officially abandoning geopolitical and hegemonic aspirations, Turkey's main interest now is geo-economic.[35] Ankara's main objectives may be summarised thus:

- Keep the West and particularly the US in a 'good mood' by convincing them of the great importance of the mineral resources in the Caspian basin, and by encouraging them to invest in pipeline projects.
- Ensure that the BTC pipeline remains the main pipeline route for Caspian oil.[36]
- Establish and maintain acceptable working relations with Russia, since Russia is, very rightly, seen as the one factor that could most seriously hamper the oil agenda.
- Keep close and good relations with Azerbaijan as the main oil-producing country and Georgia as the main pipeline transit country.

Until the turn-of-the-century economic crisis, Turkey was quite successful in promoting those objectives. Given its rather encouraging economic performance in the late 1990s, its role as major regional player rose in importance quite significantly. However, Turkey's 'black spring of 2001', during which the country plunged into financial crisis and faced the threat of insolvency, had a negative impact on these aspirations. Ankara's options were seriously reduced, as its main focus was concentrated on domestic economic issues, likewise on re-establishing its shaken credibility with world financial institutions such as the World Bank and IMF.

Iran

Unlike Turkey, Iran's interest in the South Caucasus is not greatly influenced by geo-economic considerations. Rather, its concerns are security-oriented. Firstly, there is sensitivity over the security of its northern border. The north-western part of Iran is largely populated by Azerbaijanis and, if there were to be a spillover of Caucasian conflicts, the integrity of the multi-ethnic Iranian state, which includes a large portion of ethnically Azerbaijani territory, might well be jeopardised (see **Nassibli**, p. 163). Secondly, Iran is concerned about the prospect of a Turkish intervention in the South Caucasus (see **Namazi** and **Farzin**). Thirdly, some commentators have suggested that Iran fears the possibility of a Western-led peace support operation, as this would extend NATO's influence all the way to the Iranian border.[37]

United States

When researchers and commentators speak of the West, they usually have the US in mind.[38] There are, however, distinct differences between the US and European positions. Before September 1994 there was an obvious lack of US interest in the South Caucasus apart from a specific engagement in favour of the Georgian President Shevardnadze. Increased lobbying by oil conglomerates and financial institutes thereafter had a significant influence on Capitol Hill and subsequently on the White House. One aspect of this was a significantly higher US profile within the OSCE Minsk Group dealing with Karabagh when the US took over the co-chairmanship. After the signing of the 1994 Contract of the Century, the US became much more actively involved. Currently the US agenda is 'floating' between geopolit-ical and geo-economic considerations (see **Page**). The Bush administration, continuing the policies of the previous Clinton era, appears to have three priorities: limiting, or at least balancing, Russia's influence in the region; minimising Iran's influence and its politicised form of Islam;[39] and creating stability and peace in the region through promoting democracy and human rights. The geo-economic interest is strongly influenced by big oil conglom-erates and related think-tanks. The basic objectives are focused on assuring Western access to energy resources and safeguarding the right of the new states to enter world markets. It is obvious, however, that these objectives have direct geopolitical ramifications as well. Though the Bush administra-tion, given its close links to the hydrocarbon energy producing industry, is even more concerned on energy issues and related shortages in the US economy, it has failed so far to set the scene for a high profile in the region. There is even evidence to suggest that it has been losing ground against an assertive Russia under Putin.[40]

Europe

EU, OSCE and NATO are officially present in the region and strongly involved in promoting peace, stability and prosperity. However, albeit positive statements and impressive numbers of projects, the South Caucasus has not, and does not seem likely to acquire, the status of a 'European area of vital interest'. Europe, as a conglomerate of sovereign states, seems to have indeed much less interest in the region than the US. For most (Western) European countries, the region still seems too remote, too unstable, and too similar to the Balkans to make engagement an attractive proposition.[41] Hence, the main thrust of European interest in the region lies in promoting stability and peace through co-operation and, if possible, through future integration of these states into European institutions.[42]

Oil and gas conglomerates

Big oil and gas conglomerates have had a significant impact on the governments of major players from the mid-1990s on. The sheer size of their financial and economic promises for commitment in the region has had a direct effect, particularly on the US government.[43] It is not the aim of this chapter to examine the complex, often opaque interconnections between 'big business' and government, but certainly political involvement in the region has been closely linked to large commercial investments, as is discussed by several other contributors to this volume. Thus, these conglomerates must also be regarded as 'players' who influence political and social as well as economic outcomes.

Future challenges

Strong geopolitical legacies are conflicting with economic interests, which need huge long-term foreign investment to become profitable. However, there are few regions in the world where the potential for significant wealth is so dependent on stability. This interdependency presents major challenges for the future. Without conflict resolution there is little hope of successful long-term investment. But who holds the key to conflict resolution in the South Caucasus? Is it Moscow, or are the major actors to be found in the region itself? The latter proposition seems the more likely. For this potential to be utilised, however, there must be significant Western commitment to a peace process, which may include eventual peace support operations (PSO). At the time of writing this commitment is scarcely visible. Apart from issues of political risk, the lack of political will to undertake such operations is in no small part due to the reluctance of the US and Europe to take 'body bags' in a remote area such as the South Caucasus.

Moreover, even if an acceptable level of stability could be created, transportation costs would still make the development of Caspian resources among the most expensive of all major deposits worldwide. Estimates of those in favour of large-scale investment are based on high oil-price expectations. Since it is unlikely that the current relatively high oil price will be maintained in the long run, there is considerable time pressure to establish a viable and functioning exploitation system for the Caspian deposits. The possibility of a return to full oil production in Iraq would further depress the global oil price. In mid-2003, in the immediate aftermath of the toppling of the regime of Saddam Hussein, there were predictions (over-optimistic) that this might happen within the next two to three years. Some analysts believed that this might decrease the economic significance of the Caspian deposits.[44]

Future options

In a nutshell, the current situation can best be described as not very encouraging. In terms of conflict resolution no significant breakthrough is in the offing. There is a stalemate on the ground. The warring factions seem unable, or unwilling, to compromise, as this might negatively affect their respective leadership positions. Hence, conflict resolution from within the region is most unlikely. Sufficient external pressure is, however, also rather unlikely. Russia, and to some extent Iran, have little or no interest in bringing about change or improvement as this might diminish their influence in the region. Other outside players are generous with words of encouragement, but deliver few deeds. Turkey, as the most interested external player, has been significantly weakened by domestic financial and economic problems.

There are several future scenarios that can be envisaged. Table 20.2 gives an overview of these scenarios and the likelihood of implementation. They vary from a 'best case' to a 'worst case' scenario. The projected time horizon stretches to 2005–2010. The options are based on the assumption that there are no major political and security related disturbances in Europe (e.g. in NATO and EU relations with Russia, no new war/conflict in the Balkans).

Conclusions

The rosy future of the South Caucasus as depicted by some 'geo-economists' is far from assured. Stability remains a prerequisite for sustained prosperity.[45] Yet the political situation remains frozen, contradictory geopolitical agendas still dominate. These contradictions prevent a comprehensive solution; hence, the likelihood of a quick recovery is unlikely. A prolongation of the current stalemate is the most likely option for the foreseeable future. There is even a certain negative potential, as fragile and weak democratic processes might be destabilised in leadership struggles. If Western institutions were to undertake a more active role, regional stability could be improved. In the foreseeable future, however, it is quite unlikely that the West would be willing to take such a risk. Furthermore, resources for any type of peace support operation are decreasing, as the Balkan operations and Afghanistan and probably also Iraq, are likely to continue requiring significant Western and NATO military capability.

Factors that might help to promote prosperity and exploitation of the resources would include a major Russian economic recovery, as well as its full involvement in the geo-economic agenda of the region. Also, there would need to be a normalisation of US–Iranian relations. Time does not appear

Table 20.2 Options for the South Caucasus in the foreseeable future

	Geopolitical development and framework	Geo-economic consequences and development	Likelihood
Overall euphoria	Democratic systems, the rule of law, and stable leadership are established in all the states of the South Caucasus. Their integration into European institutions increases. Turkey becomes a full-fledged EU-member and part of the Euro-zone. Russia is well on the way to recovery and has improved relations with the West. The US–Iran relationship is significantly improved.	Significant FDI flows into the South Caucasus. The high oil price is maintained; quantitative and qualitative proven deposits turn out to at least match current estimates. There is an 'investment rush' due to high shareholder values. Russia and Iran participate in the 'pipeline business', which stimulates hydrocarbon production in the entire Caspian basin.	Most unlikely.
Confined prosperity	Major regional conflicts are at least partly resolved; stability is guaranteed through strong Western-led PSO and monitoring commitment. Turkey is domestically stable. Russia's relationship with the West is deteriorating owing to Western military presence in the region. US/NATO–Iran relations face a setback.	Thanks to substantial Western involvement (e.g. 'Caucasus Stability Pact'), the investment climate in the South Caucasus is improving considerably. The oil price remains above pre-1999 levels. Pipeline and exploitation treaties are being implemented, though with some delay and massive additional costs. Profit expectations have to be reduced. Russia and Iran are hampering implementation of pipeline projects.	Rather unlikely; depends on major Western commitment; this scenario would be detrimental to interests of Russia and Iran.
More of the same	The democratisation process in the region is continuing, but very slowly; all major conflicts remain in 'no peace, no war' status. Turkey is recovering slowly from repeated economic and political setbacks. Russia's influence in the region remains significant. US and European commitment is more vocal than real.	There is slow progress in pipeline construction and oil exploitation; negative return-on-investment assessments cause a withdrawal of some outside investors and oil companies. A continuing unstable and unpredictable situation keeps FDI on a marginal level. Direct demand for Caspian oil and gas is still limited; Turkey is the only significant customer but lacks funds for investment.	Very likely for the foreseeable future.

Table 20.2 continued

	Geopolitical development and framework	Geo-economic consequences and development	Likelihood
Locals conflict(s)	Local conflicts (re-)emerge due to political radicalisation in one or more states; this might be caused by a sudden and undemocratic change in leadership. Subsequently there is no 'Western' but some Russian/CIS involvement as 'honest broker'. Turkey suffers from a domestic political backlash.	Oil exploitation falls to a low level Large-scale drop-out of outside investors due to unstable situation; withdrawal of some oil companies. New development phases of pipelines and oil fields are cancelled.	Rather unlikely, unless stagnation continues for too long; then it might become likely.
Major conflict (with outside/ Western involvement)	Local conflict escalates into full-blown regional war; existing states fail, creating major chaos; a 'Kosovo scenario' deliberately fostered by one faction or another to achieve own ends. A subsequent NATO-led intervention creates yet another Western 'protectorate'. Relations between Russia and he West tdrop to a 'Cold War' level or worse. There is a significant deterioration of US/NATO–Iran relations.	There is large-scale cancellation of existing treaties due to unstable situation in the early phase of the conflict. However, the creation of a protectorate fosters oil and gas exploitation as means of fast economic recovery. Russia and Iran are hampering pipeline and even exploitation options.	Unlikely.

to be working for the Caspian. Yet the outlook is not entirely bleak. Ongoing conflict is not in the interests of any of the major players, whatever their geopolitical agenda for the region. Very probably, the main external players do have sufficient influence and leverage on their regional partners to prevent the worst-case scenarios from happening.

Recommendations

Having outlined the complex security environment in the South Caucasus and its implications for a wider region, there is little doubt that it cannot be in the interest of Europe and the West to see yet another part of the world plummeting into chaos and war. In order to prevent this from happening, it is important to improve conditions for economic recovery. This in turn requires a proactive agenda from the West.[46] The following policy recommendations and principles would foster a positive development process:

- Recognise Russia's security concerns. There can be no solution in the South Caucasus without Russia as a major partner. Unilateral efforts against Russia's interests are unlikely to improve long-term stability and security.
- Recognise legitimate security concerns of other regional states, such as Iran and Turkey. Though not as influential and important as Russia, both regional powers are vital and instrumental for any stability progress in the region. As a NATO member state and EU applicant candidate, Turkey is inevitably bound to be influenced by Western concerns, but it would also be well placed to promote initiatives for moderation. Thus, Turkey might play a key role by mollifying Azerbaijan, improving relations with Armenia and exploiting close links with Georgia. Iran seems likely to remain in a defensive and non-active mode as long as no major external involvement is initiated (i.e. by the US or NATO). Any such endeavour might well have negative implications, with spillover effects into other regions such as the Persian Gulf.
- Put more pressure on the states of the South Caucasus to come to a solution in the different conflicts amongst themselves. There is still a widespread tendency among elites and politicians, particularly in Georgia and Azerbaijan, to blame Russia for all their misery. Though this may be partly correct, more could and should be done to find solutions and compromises of a regional nature, on a multilateral and a bilateral basis.
- Establish clear, honest and reasonable criteria for the regional states in their efforts to get closer to 'Europe'. The approach up to now has been mostly driven by vague promises and gentle recommendations. Relations with Azerbaijan, and even more so with Georgia, have been largely influenced by 'Cold War thinking'. This has entailed praise for their efforts to withstand Russian influence and support for supposedly pro-Western stances of the leadership. Yet in both countries democracy and human rights records are far from satisfactory and corruption is endemic.
- Avoid promoting any single country's role beyond the geopolitical and historical tolerance of the region. All states in the region are likely to

continue clinging to 'protective alliances' with major outside players. These include Georgia's relationship with Germany and the US, Azerbaijan's relationship with Turkey, and Armenia's relationship with Russia and Iran. Yet it is of crucial importance that nothing be done which might further intensify these long-standing interdependencies and rivalries.

• Avoid fostering irredentist movements that could lead to a 'Kosovo Scenario'. Efforts should be made to restrain the tendencies of diaspora communities abroad to support hard-line nationalist elements. Any major one-sided official political or even economic support for separatist factions might trigger renewed crisis and conflict, which could be exploited for internationalisation purposes. If the international community adopts firm, balanced positions on national and multilateral levels, this kind of harmful development could largely be minimised.

• Engage in a more active role in peace support operations, preferably within the context of the UN or OSCE. As Russia and Iran are the most important key players, US or NATO-led operations would be less accepted than a European-led force under a UN or OSCE mandate.

• Try to improve and stabilise the US–Iranian relationship, since this has a direct impact on the security and stability of the South Caucasus.[47] The exploitation of Caspian resources should include at least Iranian consent, if not actual participation (e.g. in pipelines projects).

• Invest in new pipeline projects only after securing adequate regional stability. Until this is achieved, investments into the region are likely to be at high risk.

Notes

1 A first deal failed in July 1993 when, only some days short of the official signing, the then Azerbaijani head of state, Abulfaz Elchibey, was ousted by a military coup. The coup brought back into power former Soviet Politburo member and Azerbaijani KGB head Heidar Aliev. Aliev suspended the negotiations. For alleged involvement of British oil companies in the coup see D. Leppard *et al.*, 'BP Accused of Backing "Arms for Oil" Coup', *The Sunday Times*, 26 March 2000.

2 'Geopoliticians' in this context are defined as those who give priority to influence and/or stability, and place oil/gas production and prosperity second. 'Geoeconomists' are defined as those who are primarily concerned with furthering economic interests, and who assume that stability will follow, as a logical consequence, at a later stage.

3 For a survey of the 'geo-economists', see, for example, S. Brownback, 'US Economic and Strategic Interests in the Caspian Sea Region', *Caspian Crossroads* (US), vol. 3, no. 2, Fall 1997; B. Gökay, 'Caspian Uncertainties: Regional Rivalries and Pipelines', *Perceptions*, vol. 3, no. 1, 1998; P. M. Wihey, *The Southern Eurasian Great Game*, Institute for Advanced Strategic and Political Studies, no. 8, April 1999, and E. Kreil, *Caspian Sea Region*, Energy Information Administration, 30 June 2000.

4 The 'geopolitical camp' consists, on the Western side, largely of independent analysts, also researchers within the EU and the US Defence Establishment. See, for example, W. Rees-Mogg, 'Oil in the Flames. Nato must Beware of Repeating the Vietnam Catastrophe in Central Asia', *The Times*, 7 February 2000; A. Lieven, 'The (Not So) Great Game', *The National Interest*, Winter 1999/2000. Analysts in the Russian Federation, and to a certain extent those

in Iran, argue mainly on the basis of vital national interests. The Russian position is well represented in D. Trenin, 'Conflicts in the South Caucasus', in *Brennpunkt Südkaukasus*, Vienna, 1999; see also the interview given by former Russian Prime Minister Evgeni Primakov to the French journal *Politique Internationale* (G. Ackerman and A. Grachev, 'Moscou, ton univers impitoyable ... Entretiens avec Evgueni Primakov', *Politique Internationale*, no. 86, Winter 1999/2000). For a broader overview of these issues, see M. P. Amineh, *Globalisation, Geopolitics and Energy Security in Central Eurasia and the Caspian Region*, Clingendael International Energy Programme, The Hague, 2003, esp. pp. 11–27.

5   V. Cheterian, *Dialectics of Ethnic Conflicts and Oil Projects in the Caucasus*, Geneva, PSIS Occasional Paper, no. 1/1997, p. 16.

6   See further G. Hewitt, *The Abkhazians: A Handbook*, Curzon Press, London, 1999.

7   Georgia 'hosts' 200,000 Georgians from Abkhazia, Azerbaijan almost 1 million Azerbaijanis from Karabagh and the surrounding districts under occupation, while 300,000 Armenians left Azerbaijan. See further U. Halbach, *Migration and Refugees in the Caucasus. A European Problem*, Berichte des BIOst (Bundesinstitut für ostwissenschaftliche und internationale Studien), no. 13/1999.

8   Considerable efforts have been made to avoid widespread rigging of parliamentary and presidential elections. However, the last parliamentary elections (5 November 2000 and 7 January 2001) in Azerbaijan were, according to the election monitoring of the OSCE, still far from free and fair.

9   Shevardnadze was recalled from Moscow by the warlords Iosseliani and Kitovanis after the ousting of the elected nationalist president Gamsakhurdia. Shevardnadze was only formally elected president in 1995. Aliev took over in Baku after the elected nationalist president Elchibey had been ousted by a military coup.

10 Over the last years of his life Heidar Aliev groomed his son Ilham to succeed him. In August 2003, Ilham became prime minister, thereby ensuring that he would assume power in the event of his father being incapacitated or dying in office. As a further insurance policy both men registered to stand as presidential candidates in the October 2003 election. Just before the election Heidar Aliev withdrew, leaving the way open for his son to be elected. As anticipated, Ilham Aliev won the poll, gaining some 77 per cent of the vote. Heidar Aliev died on 12 December 2003.

11 Cheterian, *op. cit.*, p. 43.

12 Russian-dominated 'peacekeeping forces' are deployed in South Ossetia and in the Ghali region in Georgia towards Abkhazia. Both interventions were post-mandated and are monitored by the UN and OSCE respectively.

13 S. Blank, 'Pipelines: Conduits for Terrorism', *Asia Times*, 6 March 2003.

14 For details of the different conflicts in terms of development, incidents, figures and facts and major political initiatives see E. O. Balance, *Wars in the Caucasus, 1990–1995*, Macmillan, London 1997, and J. Aves, *Georgia: From Chaos to Stability?*, Royal Institute of International Affairs, London, 1996.

15 See *Caucasus Report*, 'What is Baku's Game Plan?', vol. 4, no. 10, 9 March 2001.

16 Meetings between the presidents of Armenia and Azerbaijan in 1999–2000 created some hope that a negotiated settlement might be possible (see 'Is a Settlement Possible?', *The Economist*, 24 June 2000, pp. 56–57). However, efforts at conflict resolution were derailed by violent protests in Azerbaijan and in Armenia. Border clashes continued, albeit intermittently. In mid-2003 such incidents took on a more serious character, possibly presaging an escalation of hostilities (T. de Waal, 'Karabakh Ceasefire under Strain', *IWPR Report*, no. 190, 7 August 2003).

17 The Ajarian leader Aslan Abashidze exploited the political chaos in mainland Georgia in the early 1990s so successfully that Ajaria today is de facto a fully autonomous republic within Georgia. The fact that Russia keeps one of its military bases in Batumi and that Abashidze has established close relations with this contingent is resented in Tbilisi, but little can be done to change this situation. See Aves, *op. cit.*, p. 41.

18 U. Halbach, 'Regionale Dimensionen des zweiten Tschetschenienkriegs. Teil I: Der kaukasische Kontext', *Aktuelle Analysen*, Bundesinstitut für ostwissenschaftliche und internationale Studien, no. 1/2000, p. 4.

19 Compare US Energy Information Administration (EIA), *Caspian Sea Region: Key Oil and Gas Statistics*, August 2003, oil and gas estimates with BP *Statistical Review of World Energy*, June 2003.

20 Freitag-Wirminghaus, *op. cit.*, p. 249.

21 It is estimated that Georgia will get US$52.5 million a year in transit fees. See M. Lelyveld, 'Georgia/Azerbaijan: More Questions Raised About Baku–Ceyhan Pipeline', *Radio Free Europe/Radio Liberty (RFE/RL)*, 27 March 2000.

22 The Lezghins are a Caucasian people. Some two-thirds live in Daghestan, mostly south of Derbent. One-third lives in Azerbaijan, where they form a fractious, suppressed minority.

23 Gökay, p. 65; Freitag-Wirminghaus, p. 27; J. Radvanyi, *Transports et géostratégie au sud de la Russie*, Le Monde diplomatique, juin 1998.

24 Furthermore, owing to bad weather conditions Novorossiysk is closed for several months of the year.

25 See R. Khatchadourian, *Path of a Pipeline*, parts 1, 2 and 3, February–March 2003 (http://www.villagevoice.com).

26 A. Blua, 'Rights Groups Increasingly Critical of Baku–Tbilisi–Ceyhan Pipeline', *RFE/RL*, 2 June 2003.

27 10 June 2003, *RFE/RL Business Watch*.

28 Wihey, *op. cit.*, pp. 2–3.

29 D. Trenin, 'Conflicts in the South Caucasus', in *Brennpunkt Südkaukasus*, Vienna, 1999, p. 298.

30 V. Naumkin, 'Russia and Transcaucasia', *Caucasian Regional Studies*, vol. 3, no. 1, 1998, p. 3.

31 'The oil contract – production and transportation – is in a position, using foreign investors' money, to unite most of the countries of Central Asia and Trans-caucasia on an anti-Russian basis.' This view was put forward in an anonymous report in *Nezavisimaya Gazeta* under the title 'The CIS: The Beginning of the End of History?' (Naumkin, *op. cit.*, p. 3). Traditionally the Russian elite has been split over the importance of the Caspian oil issue. The geo-economists, represented by the reformers of the early 1990s and the energy giants LUKoil and Gazprom, see economic gains through a combination of co-operation and competition.

32 Trenin, *op. cit.*, p. 298.

33 The agreement foresees a closure of the bases in Vaziani and in Abkhazian-controlled Gudauta until mid-2001. Vaziani was vacated for Gudauta due to 'ongoing demonstrations' in favour of a continuing Russian presence, there is an ongoing Russian deployment. Deadlines for the withdrawal of the other two bases have yet to be established.

34 In Georgia particularly there is great resentment of the 'Russian thorn in the flesh'; yet two of the four Russian bases are located in secessionist or autonomous regions. Gudauta is currently part of Abkhazia, Batumi is the capital of de facto autonomous Ajaria, Akhalkalazi is the main centre of the strong Armenian minority in Georgia. The fourth base, located in Vaziani, a suburb of Tbilisi, was withdrawn in early 2001.

35 Turkey has as its objective keeping the South Caucasus and Central Asia free of Russian domination and ultimately turning these regions into a belt of at least friendly states. See 'Ismail Cem, a Turkish strategist', *The Economist*, 5 February 2000, p. 48; also Amineh, *op. cit.*, pp. 89–98.

36 The BTC pipeline achieves Turkey's political goals and also offers substantial economic benefits including transportation fees and access to comparatively cheap oil. Moreover, it avoids the environmentally hazardous passage through the Bosporus and the Dardanelles. See Gökay, *op. cit.*, pp. 59–62.

37 Trenin, *op. cit.*, pp. 300–301. See also S. Chubin, 'Iran's Strategic Predicament', *Middle East Journal*, vol. 54, no. 1, Winter 2000.

38 See N. MacFarlane, *Western Engagement in the Caucasus and Central Asia*, Royal Institute of International Affairs, London, 1999.
39 MacFarlane, *op. cit.*, pp. 18–19.
40 U. Halbach, 'Zwischen "heissem Krieg" und "eingefrorenen Konflikten" – Russlands Aussenpolitik im Kaukasus', *Osteuropa*, no. 4/5, April/May 2001; 'US Losing Influence in Caucasus', *Caucasus and Caspian Sea Intelligence Report on Oil and Pipelines*, 20 January 2001.
41 Shortly after a ceasefire had been established for the Karabagh conflict in 1994, the OSCE started efforts for launching a peace support mission. Though still perceived within NATO, EU, and particularly the OSCE as a possible target for such an operation, there is little visible political will particularly among Europeans to implement this policy. In fact, while there is a strong and, in terms of sustainability, rather demanding military presence in the Balkans, a major European peace support operation in the Caucasus is hardly likely.
42 The EU and particularly the OSCE are active in the South Caucasus. Whereas the latter has been successful mainly in monitoring, the EU has launched several infrastructural projects (e.g. TRACECA and INOGATE). Georgia has also been granted membership of the Council of Europe. NATO is involved with Partnership for Peace but is rather cautious in response to regional demands (e.g. of Georgia for NATO membership, or Azerbaijan for NATO force deployment). In addition to collective efforts, some European states or institutions are involved in specific projects, such as, for example, German initiatives for Georgia (political and cultural) or France-based Armenian diaspora support for Armenia and Karabagh. See Halbach, *Migration*, p. 5.
43 By 2002, some 20 Production Sharing Agreements had been concluded. See Freitag-Wirminghaus, *op. cit.*, pp. 256–258, for details of the different contracts and participating companies. See also S. Brownback, 'US Economic and Strategic Interests in the Caspian Sea Region', *Caspian Crossroads* (US), vol. 3, no. 2, Fall 1997.
44 See, for example, comments by S. Mann and R. Wilson, 'U.S. Officials Say Iraq, Caspian to Compete for Investment', press conference in Baku, 4 June 2003 (Ambo News Service).
45 In other words, 'pipeline can follow peace, but peace cannot follow a pipeline' (R. Ebel, *Caspian Energy Update, Energy and National Security Program*, Washington, CSIS, March 2000, p. 1).
46 See S. T. Hunter, *Post Soviet Transition in the South Caucasus: Regional and International Implications*, CEPS Paper no. 61, Centre for European Policy Studies, Brussels, 1994, pp. 140–141; also S. Celac *et al.*, *A Stability Pact for the Caucasus: A Consultative Document of the CEPS Task Force on the Caucasus*, Centre for European Policy Studies, Brussels, 2000.
47 During the late 1990s, there was a lessening of tension between Iran and the US, and a willingness, at least behind the scenes, to explore ways of imitating a rapprochement. After the election of George W. Bush, however, the US administration adopted a tougher stance towards Tehran. In August 2001, the Iran and Libya Sanctions Act (ILSA), first enacted in 1996, was extended for another five years. In March 2003, the president declared that Iran continued to pose a threat to the US and that the National Emergency with respect to Iran, declared by Executive Order 12957 on 15 March 1995, and clarified and consolidated by later Executive Orders, should remain in force for another year (notice issued by the White House, Office of the Press Secretary, 13 March 2003). The renewal of the emergency meant that US citizens and companies were barred from entering into oil development contracts with Iran.

21 Environmental security in the Caspian Sea

Shirin Akiner

Over the past decade, much of the attention that has been focused on the Caspian Sea has been concerned with the political, economic and strategic aspects of extracting and transporting the region's oil and gas reserves. Less attention has been devoted to the environment. Although reports on the catastrophic decline in stocks of the caviar-producing sturgeon or the unexplained deaths of thousands of Caspian seals have occasionally been the subject of dramatic headlines, the long-term problems of managing a delicate ecological system under conditions of intensive economic exploitation are deemed less newsworthy. Indeed, environmental considerations sometimes appear to be regarded as theoretical abstractions, unlike the serious business of 'big' politics and high finance. Environmental objections to pipeline schemes, for example, are often dismissed as 'ill informed', or even as being politically motivated. Such attitudes are not necessarily true of the major energy companies, most of whom take pride in the degree of environmental protection that they provide.[1] Nevertheless, those who live outside the region and have no firsthand knowledge of local conditions often fail to appreciate the fragility and vulnerability of the Caspian ecosystems. Once harm has been inflicted, it is extremely difficult to repair. Moreover, environmental damage has consequences that impact directly on questions of national security. Severe degradation of the environment causes population movements, contaminates food supplies and hinders economic productivity. It also influences relations with neighbours, since many environmental issues in the Caspian Sea are transboundary in nature. Thus, an analysis of the political, economic and security outlook for the Caspian states must take account of these factors.

Geography and hydrography

The Caspian Sea, the largest enclosed stretch of water in the world, is located between 37° to 47° N, and 47° to 55° E. It has a coastline of some 7,000 kilometres. Around its northern and north-western rim it is bounded by the Russian Federation (including the constituent republics of Daghestan and Kalmykia), Kazakhstan along the north and north east, Turkmenistan along the south east, Iran along the south, and Azerbaijan along the south west.

The longest stretches of coastline belong to Kazakhstan, Turkmenistan and the Russian Federation (each over 1,700 kilometres). The precise length of the respective coastlines is a matter of keen debate, since calculations vary considerably depending on such factors as the maps and measuring techniques that are used, also on prevailing climatic conditions (wave surges, for example); political considerations, too, can influence the assessments. The sea has a surface area of approximately 371,000 square kilometres. It measures some 1,210 kilometres from north to south, with a maximum width from east to west of about 320 kilometres (though these measurements are subject to cyclical variation and differ considerably over time). The Caspian is a saltwater sea, but salinity levels are low, and the waters are brackish rather than salty. It is fed by some 130 rivers. In the north, the Volga accounts for nearly 80 per cent of river-water supplies.[2] Rivers in the west (mainly the Kura and the Araks) add another 7 per cent, while in the south, Iranian rivers account for approximately 5 per cent. The remainder of the water input is from direct precipitation and groundwater contributions. Most of the water loss is from evaporation; a small amount (an estimated 3 per cent) flows into the Garabogaz Gulf (Turkmenistan).

The Caspian Sea has no outlets or tides. Main currents follow the coastline and flow in a counter-clockwise direction. Average air temperatures in the north range from −10°C in the winter to 26°C in the summer, and in the south, from 10°C to 30°C respectively. The coastal waters in the north are icebound for some four months a year. In very severe winters, such as in 1968 and 1971, the ice cover can extend as far south as the Apsheron peninsula. High-velocity winds exacerbate the harsh climatic conditions. Storms – snow, wind and hail – are a frequent occurrence. The winds also create wave surges, sometimes reaching 3 metres, but occasionally 8 metres high.

The Caspian fills the deepest part of a huge depression (see Map 6). Its surface lies at about 28.5 metres below sea level. Once part of a much larger body of water, it was originally linked to the Aral Sea and Black Sea. Today, a thick layer of yellow-green clay, deposited by this ancient Eurasian ocean, covers much of the coastal area. The north western littoral (Russian Federation) is scored by a multitude of narrow lagoons (*liman*), up to 50 kilometres in length and separated by hillocks and sandbanks. In the north east (Kazakhstan), lowlands give way to a plateau that extends eastwards towards the Aral Sea. In the central-eastern section (Turkmenistan) lies the Gulf of Garabogaz. The mouth of this small basin (approximately 18,400 square kilometres) is blocked by a sandbank, naturally breached by a narrow strait. This passage connects the main body of the Caspian to the gulf, thereby allowing a significant volume of water to flow out of the sea. In the late Soviet period this strait was closed, but later reopened (see below). There are lowlands along the south-eastern littoral, but in the far south (Iran) the coastal strip is narrowed by the foothills of the Elbruz mountains. Mountain ranges dominate the south-western shore, too, and, apart from a relatively narrow plain around the mouth of the Kura river, stretch northwards to Makhachkala (Daghestan).

The Caspian Sea has a complex hydrogeology. It divides into three sections. The northern basin is the shallowest. Bordered by Kazakhstan and the Russian Federation, it has an average depth of 25 metres, although in some places the coastal waters measure less than 5 metres in depth. The middle section stretches south from a notional east–west line between the Mangyshlak peninsula (Kazakhstan) and the Chechen Island (Russian Federation) to a similar notional line between the Turkmenbashi peninsula (Turkmenistan) and the Apsheron peninsula (Azerbaijan). This section has a 'doughnut' formation, with shallow coastal waters, a middle band that averages 100 metres in depth, and a relatively small central core that sinks to 500 metres (the lowest point measuring 788 metres). The southern, deepest part of the Caspian Sea is bordered by Iran and southern Turkmenistan. Separated from the middle section by a massive submarine ridge (which links the Greater Caucasus Mountains in the west to the Kopet Dagh range in the east), it has a large central core that reaches depths of more than 500 metres (the absolute lowest point is below 1,000 metres).

Environmental hazards

The Caspian Sea has a unique ecology. Owing to its long isolation from open seas, it has a rich and diverse flora and fauna, including many species not found elsewhere in the world. The shallow wetlands and lagoons attract a great variety of birdlife; migrants such as flamingos, swans, pelicans, ducks and pheasants winter on the Caspian coastal plains. The sea itself is home to numerous aquatics, from molluscs and sponges to rare species of fish (among them four species of sturgeon, including the highly prized beluga sturgeon), as well as a mammal, the Caspian seal. The Caspian littoral has a long history of human settlement and land use. The southern coast (Iran) and south-western coast (Azerbaijan) in particular have relatively high population densities.[3]

Like all enclosed bodies of water, the Caspian is highly susceptible to environmental impacts. Some of these are caused by naturally occurring phenomena, such as flooding, storms and wave surges, which alter and erode the existing landscape. Other changes have been generated by anthropogenic activity. During the twentieth century, and particularly in the past 50-odd years, intensive economic exploitation of the Caspian Sea and adjacent coastal regions has resulted in serious environmental degradation. The wildlife habitat has been impaired, thereby damaging the bio-resources and bio-diversity of this region. The socio-economic impact has also been very considerable, lowering standards of living and jeopardising the quality of life of local communities.

In the 1990s, following the collapse of the Soviet Union, the situation deteriorated still further. This was partly owing to political factors such as the lack of consensus among the five littoral states on a legal regime for the Caspian Sea and, related to that, the lack of environmental controls in the region. Partly, too, it was a result of the economic disruption in the former Soviet republics, as a consequence of which funds for environmental monitoring and protection were drastically reduced. This coincided with heightened onshore and offshore activity in the extraction of hydrocarbons in the central and northern sections of the Caspian, also a sharp rise in the volume of marine traffic. Some of this was related to the needs of the oil industry (for example, tanker movements). There was also a rise in military activity (see **Katik**) and in smuggling and poaching.

Fluctuating water levels

One of the peculiarities of the Caspian is the fluctuating level of the water. These annual changes follow an irregular cycle that can last several decades. There are also smaller seasonal variations that raise and lower the level of the sea by up to 40 centimetres. These movements have been plotted by instrumental measurements since 1837.[4] Earlier rises and falls can be traced by palaeographic reconstruction. In modern times, there have been three cycles of rise and fall. The first, from 1840 to 1930, showed an amplitudinal variation of 40–70 centimetres. During this period, in 1882, the Caspian reached its highest point ever, measuring 26 metres below sea level. The next period, 1931–1977, showed a fall of 2.8 metres, during which it reached a low of 29 metres below sea level. In the third period, 1978–c.1998, the level rose by 2.5 metres.[5]

Many hypotheses have been advanced to explain this phenomenon. Some believe that the environmental stress generated by such factors as increased irrigation needs, growing municipal demands, hydraulic engineering projects, the construction of water reservoirs and hydroelectric stations on the Volga have triggered fluctuations in water levels. Others have mooted the possibility of a compensatory balance between the falling level of the Aral Sea and the rising level of the Caspian Sea. It has also been suggested that submarine tectonic activity or climate change might be the cause of these fluctuations.[6] As yet none of these theories has been conclusively proven and there is no generally accepted scientific explanation.

The fluctuations of level can take place suddenly and quite rapidly. In the period 1933–1941, for example, there was a fall of 1.7 metres. This caused great concern and various schemes were advanced to try to stem the decline, including the construction of a dam to close off the Garabogaz Gulf and thereby prevent further loss of water. This plan was implemented in 1980. It created major environmental problems. The Garabogaz Gulf has one of the world's largest deposits of sodium sulphate. Starved of water, the basin dried up, leaving behind a massive dust bowl. Winds scattered the salt deposits over a wide area, devastating the countryside. Local industries were destroyed and the local people were forced to move elsewhere.

Ironically, by the time the dam was constructed, the Caspian was again beginning to rise and in 1978–1994 an increase of 2.4 metres was recorded.[7] In September 1984 the authorities partially opened the dam to allow for some discharge of water into the gulf. Environmentalists, however, campaigned for the dam to be completely demolished. This was accomplished in June

1992, a move that was seen by some as a celebration of Turkmenistan's independence. Meanwhile, the waters of the Caspian were still rising. There was also an increase in strong winds and wave surges, which intensified the erosion of exposed and submerged marine slopes and drove the flood waters more forcefully on to the land. This process continued until the mid-1990s, when the level began to fall. In 1996–2001, a decrease of some 50 centimetres was recorded, but in early 2002 there were indications that this trend had again been reversed, suggesting that the level might rise by up to 4 centimetres over the next few years.[8] Some forecasts suggest that the level will continue to rise for the next decade at least, possibly reaching a height of 25 metres below sea level by 2010, a level last seen in 1882.[9]

Degradation of coastal areas: flooding and desertification

One of the major environmental problems in the Caspian region in recent years has been the degradation of coastal areas. In the late nineteenth century, there was relatively little economic exploitation of the littoral zone. Urban populations were for the most part small. There was little industrial development; agricultural land use was also quite light. This situation began to change in the early twentieth century, especially after the establishment of Soviet rule. From the 1920s onwards there was heavy migration into the coastal zones. In Azerbaijan, much of this was connected with the burgeoning oil industry. However, crop production and livestock rearing was also intensively developed in the fertile coastal lowlands. For the next 50 years, until the mid-1970s, the sea was at a low level in its cyclical fluctuation. The memory of high water levels, and likewise the experience of living with the vagaries of the sea, faded. As a result, areas that had previously been regarded as marginal began to be utilised. Around the entire perimeter of the sea, including the southern, Iranian rim, housing and recreational complexes were sited near the sea. Factories and processing plants, too, were constructed in zones that had hitherto been regarded as vulnerable.

When the sea began to rise again in the late 1970s, the effect was catastrophic. By the mid-1980s, roads, railways and ports were being inundated, as were factories and oil wells located near the shore. Soon, large areas of valuable agricultural land were swamped and irrigation systems destroyed. In inshore waters, fish farms and hatcheries were flooded and rendered useless. Many people were left homeless and without any means of earning a livelihood. There were also health hazards. The flooding caused groundwater levels to rise and spread fertilisers, toxic waste and untreated sewage over a wide area, contaminating water supplies. This led to outbreaks of cholera and plague. Mosquitoes rapidly colonised the newly formed wetlands, adding to the health problems of the local population. By the early 1990s, thousands of families from the Iranian coastal cities, as well as from Daghestan and parts of Azerbaijan, had been resettled. On the east side of the Caspian, the low-lying beaches of Turkmenistan were heavily eroded and, for a while, it seemed as though the port of Turkmenbashi, too, might be inundated. The flooding affected land as far north as Kalmykia and the Mangyshlak peninsula. In all, more than 40,000 square kilometres of land were adversely affected by the rising level of the sea.[10] In 1994, experts concluded that the cost of the flood damage inflicted on the five littoral states during this period amounted to some US$30–50 million.[11]

The rising sea level and consequent flooding of coastal zones is not the only cause of land degradation in the Caspian basin. Climatic conditions, characterised by high aridity and strong winds, as well as the regional geology, have created an environment that is prone to desertification. Over the past half century, this process has been greatly hastened by unsustainable anthropogenic activities. These have included intensive rearing of sheep, cattle and camels, resulting in overgrazing and contamination of groundwater, and large-scale cultivation of cash crops and aggressive timber logging. Inappropriate and harmful technologies have also been employed in industry (e.g. in salt mining as well as in oil and gas extraction) and in large-scale construction works. As a result of such practices, there has been serious damage to the environment. The economic potential of the region has also been adversely affected. The acreage of arable land has been reduced by the spread of sand, while soil fertility has fallen as a result of increased salinisation. Residential housing as well as infrastructural facilities such as roads, railways, pipelines and industrial plants have also suffered from silting.

The net effect of these developments has been the pauperisation of large sectors of the local population. Current monitoring and research indicates that a belt of 50–100 kilometres wide around the perimeter of the sea is now desertified. The total area so affected is about 400,000 square kilometres. Over a third of this is classified as severely or very severely desertified. Kazakhstan has suffered the greatest degree of degradation of soil and vegetation, largely the result of oil and gas exploitation in the past. There are also serious problems elsewhere. Kalmykia has experienced rampant desertification, aggravated by wind erosion, while Iran and Azerbaijan have been afflicted by deforestation and water erosion, and Turkmenistan by salinisation of low-lying parts of the coast.[12]

The rehabilitation of the coastal zones has as yet scarcely begun. If present trends of soil degradation continue, very possibly accelerated by renewed flooding if the sea level rises as expected over the next decade, there will be further land loss, as well as the disruption of transportation, the destruction of local industries and the risk of inundation to oil and gas installations. Local populations, unable to subsist in such conditions, would be forced to migrate. Thus, the economic and social costs of environmental damage could be very substantial. The implications for national budgets would undoubtedly be onerous and would have a negative effect on future development strategies.

Land-based sources of pollution

The greatest man-made threat to the ecology of the Caspian Sea is pollution. All the littoral states bear some share of responsibility for this problem.

Land-based pollution enters the sea through waste water that is discharged either into the rivers that flow into the sea, or directly into the sea itself. The most severely polluted areas are in the North Caspian, which is bordered by densely populated, industrialised regions. It is not only the sea that is contaminated, but also the air, the soil, the rivers and the groundwater. To date, there has been too little scientific research (and perhaps too much political posturing) for it to be possible to identify with certainty the main sources of pollution. The chief culprits are generally held to be the heavy industrial and military–industrial plants that are located within the catchment area of the Volga – the economic heartland of Russia – which discharge substantial quantities of hazardous pollutants such as heavy metals, oil and phenols into the environment. Since the collapse of the Soviet Union, however, production has fallen and this has somewhat reduced the pollution discharge to the river.[13] Further south, Azerbaijan, too, suffers from high levels of soil, air and water pollution, especially in and around Baku and Sumgait. The main transgressor here is the oil industry. This has been in operation for over a century and many current problems are the legacy of earlier stages of development (see **Akiner**, p. 6). Soviet-era installations used designs and technologies that were, from the outset, harmful to the environment. This infrastructure is now in a chronic state of decay and represents a considerable environmental hazard. Abandoned oil wells, some dating back to the early twentieth century, are a particular source of contamination. Since the late 1970s, when the sea began to rise again, several have been inundated. This has caused oil to seep out, creating slicks several kilometres long over the surrounding area. Similar problems, though on a lesser scale, are encountered in Turkmenistan and Kazakhstan. The cost of capping these wells and cleaning up the leaks is very considerable.[14]

Other sources of land-based pollution include manufacturing and heavy-engineering complexes in Azerbaijan, Georgia and Armenia; contaminated waste water from all three states is washed downstream via rivers that flow into the Caspian. Iran and Turkmenistan are the smallest contributors of industrial pollution, though the latter is responsible for considerable flows of toxic waste from the Turkmenbashi refinery and from the extensive mineral extraction and processing plants (particularly of salt) that are located along the low-lying northern coast. All the littoral states are responsible for discharging untreated agricultural and municipal sewage into the sea. Waste water run-off from these sources includes toxic residue from chemical fertilisers, pesticides, defoliants and detergents, also large quantities of solid waste.

Overland pipelines have not, to date, been a major source of environmental damage. There have been accidents (e.g. leakages and fires) from time to time but, compared with other causes of pollution in the region, the effects of such incidents have been local and generally of relatively short duration. The objections that have been raised regarding the proposed construction of the Baku–Tbilisi–Ceyhan (BTC) pipeline are mostly directed at the Caspian hinterland to the west. Moreover, they relate primarily to the social impact of this project and the consequent violation of human rights of communities.[15]

Concerns regarding possible radioactive pollution have been raised from time to time by environmental groups and by the media. During the Soviet period several nuclear facilities were located in the Caspian basin. These included reactors used for power generation and research, uranium mines and processing plants, and dumps for radioactive waste. Several such sites lie within the drainage area of rivers that flow into the Caspian, but most are situated at some distance from the sea and thus in all probability pose little direct threat to this region. Of more immediate relevance is the site of the former nuclear power plant (BN 350 reactor) in Aktau (formerly known as Guriev) near the Kazakh coast. This facility was closed down in April 1999. No scientific evidence has been published to indicate that it might be a cause of contamination, but there are persistent allegations that it does constitute an environmental hazard.[16]

Offshore sources of pollution

Offshore sources of pollution currently represent somewhat less of a hazard than onshore sources. This is not to say that they are insignificant. Rather, they add to the overall inventory of contaminating factors, thereby intensifying the stress on the ecosystems of the sea and its immediate environs. One of the main sources of offshore pollution is oil. Visually, this is indicated by the greasy sheen that covers the surface of the water, particularly off the coast of Azerbaijan. It is further confirmed by analyses of sediment from the seabed, which reveal significant levels of oil and oil production-related pollution. This is not a new phenomenon. As on land, it is in part a historic legacy. The extraction of oil in the Caspian Sea dates back to the inauguration of the Oil Rocks platform off the Azerbaijan coastline in 1949. This was a pioneering technological achievement, but it was also responsible for considerable damage to the environment not only through operational errors, but also through the failure to observe acceptable norms for noxious emissions. Installations from this period continue to represent an environmental hazard. In the post-Soviet era there has been a major expansion of offshore oil extraction. Modern production technologies are very much cleaner than those used in the past and there are some who consider the danger of pollution from this source to be minimal.[17] Nevertheless, by their very nature, offshore drilling and transportation carry inherent risks for the environment. Accidents do occur, sometimes with very significant consequences. Kazakh environmentalists have expressed grave concerns over offshore drilling operations, particularly in the Kashagan field.[18]

The increase in economic activity in and around the Caspian Sea has led to a corresponding increase in the volume of shipping. A network of maritime routes now links all the main littoral ports. Much of the legal traffic is related to the oil industry. In particular, the movement of crude oil by tanker from Kazakhstan (and to a lesser extent Turkmenistan) to the Iranian port of Neka has grown considerably in recent years.[19] Other commercial cargoes are also transported across the length and breadth of the sea, as are passengers. This trend is likely to increase.[20] At the same time, there has been a huge rise in illegal traffic, as smugglers and poachers seek to exploit the resources of the Caspian. In response, the littoral states have been enhancing their naval capacity in order to patrol the sea more effectively. The naval build-up is in part also motivated by a desire to protect national territorial claims in the Caspian Sea. As discussed in other chapters (see, for example, **Granmayeh**, **Katik**) there are a number of unresolved demarcation disputes. In July 2001 one such dispute resulted in a tense naval confrontation between Iran and Azerbaijan. The situation was defused relatively quickly, but it is by no means inconceivable that there will be a repetition of such an incident in the future. The likelihood is that the militarisation of the Caspian will continue, unless and until it is circumscribed by enforceable treaty constraints. Even so, the increase in shipping, commercial and military, that has already taken place over the past ten years, has greatly added to the anthropogenic load on the Caspian.

The bed of the Caspian is subject to high levels of seismic activity and to mud volcanoes. There are as yet no large underwater pipelines across the sea, but two routes have received active consideration. A Trans-Caspian gas pipeline from Turkmenistan to Azerbaijan was under discussion in the late 1990s, but the project was shelved indefinitely when in March 2003 Royal Dutch/Shell, the proposed operator, decided to reduce its activities in Turkmenistan (see **Canzi**, p. 187). Meanwhile, a project to construct an underwater oil pipeline from Aktau (Kazakhstan) to Baku gained momentum (see **Akiner**, p. 367) and intergovernmental negotiations were close to finalisation by the end of 2003.[21] Moscow, however, adamantly opposed the project and called for a ban on the construction of any pipelines along the bottom of the sea on account of the dangers that this would pose to the marine environment.[22] Given the storm of international protest over the proposed BTC pipeline, it seemed likely that any action that might further endanger the fragile Caspian ecology would face massive and highly publicised condemnation from non-governmental organisations round the world. This would make it difficult to secure funding from publicly accountable bodies and would also present reputational risks to the companies involved. These considerations would surely delay, and possibly prevent, the implementation of this project.

Invasive alien organisms

One of the results of industrial pollution has been an increase in eutrophication – a process whereby the fertilisers in agricultural run-off stimulate the rampant growth of algae. The algae form a dense blue-green carpet on the surface of the water; as they decay, they rob the water of oxygen, creating a dead zone in which all other forms of marine life suffocate and perish. Eutrophication occurs mainly in the North Caspian, in and around the Volga delta, but there is also a progressive spread of such patches in other river deltas and near large industrial centres, notably in the vicinity of the

Apsheron peninsula. The experience of enclosed bodies of water in other parts of the world indicates that, if there were to be a continuing spread of eutrophication, brought on by increased loads of nutrients in the rivers that empty into the sea, it could precipitate an ecological crisis in the Caspian.

Another deadly growth is the azolla plant. This spongy aquatic weed was brought to Iran from the Philippines in the 1980s for use as a fertiliser. Rich in nitrogen, it was intended to boost the rice harvest. At first the results were encouraging, but the plant soon began to reproduce at an uncontrollable rate, doubling its weight in a week. It infiltrated the Anzali wetlands and then spread into the sea, where it now floats over a large expanse of water. It forms a thick green blanket and, like the algal bloom of eutrophication, suffocates the area that it covers.[23] To date, no way of eliminating this aggressive intruder has been found.

A new ecological threat appeared in the Caspian Sea at the end of the 1990s: invasion by a comb jellyfish, some 5 centimetres in width, known as *Mnemiopsis leidyi*. A native of the estuaries of the east coast of America, this organism was accidentally introduced into the Black Sea in the early 1980s, probably imported in ballast water. From there it spread via the Volga–Don canal to the Caspian. In early 2000 the mnemiopsis was found in the middle and southern sections of the Caspian Sea, but within a few months it had spread to the northern section. The mnemiopsis has a voracious appetite and reproduces at an exponential rate. It can double its size in a day, and within a fortnight reaches maturity. Thereafter it produces 8,000 offspring a day. It feeds on zooplankton, which is also the mainstay of the diet of the small fish such as sprat (*kil'ka*). Sprats are in turn consumed by larger predators such as the sturgeon and the seal. Thus the entire feeding cycle of the indigenous fish population is put at risk by this invasion. Moreover, the mnemiopsis explosion has devastated the fishing industry. By mid-2001 hauls of sprat had dropped by half.[24] The problem was particularly bad in the south, where there was the highest density of the mnemiopsis. Boats had to be laid off as the catches were too small to cover the costs of fuel and wages. The mnemiopsis is able to thrive in the Caspian Sea because it has no natural enemies. The only hope of combating this deadly organism appears to be the introduction of yet another type of jellyfish, *Beroe ovata*, which feeds on the mnemiopsis. In the Black Sea, where fish stocks were devastated as a result of the mnemiopsis invasion, the beroe (also imported by accident) rapidly devoured the rival jellyfish and within a year or two had almost entirely eliminated the mnemiopsis from this area. There were apparently no ill effects on other organisms in the sea. Consequently, in September–October 2001, experiments were begun at the Fisheries Research Centre of Mazandaran (Iran) to evaluate the effects of introducing beroe into the Caspian.[25]

Threats to fish stocks and seals

The Caspian Sea is home to a varied array of fish, comprising over 100 species, some of which are unique to this habitat. Many species (including sturgeon) spend the winter in the middle or south of the sea, but migrate northwards in the summer to spawn. Around 20 types of fish are harvested commercially. Of these, by far the most valuable fisheries are sturgeon, sprat (*kil'ka*) and herring. In the first half of the twentieth century, herring fishing was the largest industry, yielding at its height catches of up to 140,000 tonnes annually. Thereafter, priority was given to the harvesting of sprats. This is now a considerably larger operation than either the herring or the sturgeon fisheries.[26] Sprats, conserved in oil and tinned, are a popular food item in the Caspian states; they are also an important export commodity. In recent years, Iran has developed an additional use for the sprat, processing it into fish protein concentrate for markets in the Far East.

Commercial sturgeon fishing and the trade in caviar (sturgeon roe) were inaugurated by Peter the Great in 1672. From 1917 to 1991, the fisheries of the Caspian were divided between the Soviet Union and Iran. Up to 1951, sturgeon was caught by net in the open sea. Thereafter, with stocks already dwindling, fishing in the northern basin, under the control of the Soviet authorities, was restricted to the lower reaches and delta of the Volga. In the southern basin Iran, too, banned fishing with nets in the open sea. The falling level of the sea was partly responsible for the decline in fish stocks, but pollution and the loss of habitat through industrial development undoubtedly contributed to the trend. During this period, both countries invested in maintaining fish stocks at a sustainable level. In the 1960s, Soviet hatcheries released 4 million juvenile sturgeon; by the late 1980s, they were releasing 80 million sturgeon annually. Iran also established extensive hatcheries along the southern coast, breeding such fish as sturgeon, bream, pike-perch and Caspian trout. In 1979, Iran abolished its trade in caviar on the grounds that it was against Islamic law. This ruling was later reversed and trade was recommenced in 1989.

Until the collapse of the Soviet Union, the Caspian Sea was the source of some 95 per cent of the world's supply of caviar.[27] Subsequent economic and social problems in the successor states had a highly detrimental impact on the sturgeon fishery and during the 1990s the Caspian lost some of its market share.[28] Hatchery releases were drastically reduced, while at the same time earlier constraints on fishing limits were ignored. The private entrepreneurs who took the place of the former state-owned companies were eager to maximise their profits and this led to massive over-harvesting. There was also an explosion of poaching, as heavily armed criminal groups established a hold on the multimillion dollar caviar trade.[29] In just two decades, from the late 1970s to the late 1990s, officially recorded sturgeon catches plummeted from 30,000 tonnes to less than one-tenth that amount.[30] Meanwhile, in the four ex-Soviet states, poachers were catching ten to 12 times higher than the permitted amount.[31] The pressure on sturgeon stocks was further heightened by increasing levels of pollution. Some reports suggested that the fish were contaminated by heavy metals that affected their vital organs and caused muscle dystrophy.[32] Other problems included the comb jellyfish invasion (see above), which threatened the sturgeon's food supply. The combination of adverse factors such as these provoked fears that the sturgeon population had fallen below a sustainable level and that it was on the way to extinction.

In response to this situation in April 1998 the Convention on International Trade in Endangered Species of Wild Fauna and Flora (CITES)[33] brought in strict controls for all species of sturgeon, requiring among other things the introduction of export permits and labelling of products. At a meeting of CITES held in Paris in June 2001, Azerbaijan, Kazakhstan and Russia agreed to a voluntary moratorium on sturgeon fishing in the Caspian for the rest of the year. Iran was not subject to these restrictions as it already had an effective management programme in place. Turkmenistan, though not represented at the meeting, was required to adhere to the agreement or face a complete ban on its caviar exports.[34] Fixed export quotas were set for all five littoral states.[35] Additionally, the former Soviet republics were required to establish a survey and management programme for the sturgeon fisheries, to regulate domestic trade, to implement a caviar labelling system and to boost efforts to combat poaching and illegal trade.

By March 2002, they were considered to have fulfilled these undertakings so successfully that CITES lifted the ban on sturgeon fishing. A senior CITES official commented that, at a conservative estimate, the number of sturgeon in the Caspian had more than doubled, from 5 million in 2000 to 11.6 million in 2002; of these, some 40 per cent were adult fish, including caviar- (roe-)bearing females, compared with a mere 5 per cent three years earlier.[36] These figures were disputed by independent environmentalists, who believed that the sturgeon population had in fact fallen and that the beluga should be placed on the endangered species list.[37] In August 2003, Kazakhstan became the first littoral state to agree to the tagging of baby beluga sturgeon, in order to monitor the survival rate.[38] The natural spawning ground of the beluga sturgeon is the Ural river, which flows across Kazakh territory to the sea. The Kazakh government hoped that this measure would enable scientists to differentiate between the fish that had originated in Kazakh waters and those that had been bred in the hatcheries of the other states. This information could then provide the basis for a claim for a larger quota of caviar exports.

The decline in fish stocks has been observed and documented over a long period. The sudden death of thousands of seals in 2000 was, however, an unexpected development. This mammal (*Phoca caspica*) is unique to the Caspian Sea, although it shares some of the characteristics of the ring-neck seal (*Phoca hispada*), a native of arctic and sub-arctic zones (possibly indicating a prehistoric connection between the Caspian and the Arctic). The seals winter mainly along the northern coast, on the exposed ice rim, though a few colonies are to be found further south. They breed in January–February, then in the spring migrate southwards, returning to the north in the autumn. They take eight years to become fully mature and can live for 50 years. Full-grown seals measure up to 1.5 metres in length and on average weigh 50–60 kg.

In the early twentieth century the seal population in the Caspian was estimated at over 1 million. The creatures were intensively hunted until the 1940s, when restrictions were introduced to limit the size of the kill. Provision for an annual cull of 40,000 seal pups was introduced in the 1980s, slightly below the estimated birth rate of 50,000 per year. Since 1991, records in the four ex-Soviet littoral states have been poorly maintained and it is impossible to know how many seals have been harvested during the past decade. It is rumoured that there is substantial poaching of young seals in the North Caspian to cater to commercial demands in Western Europe. The seal population at the end of the 1990s was variously estimated at 360,000 to 600,000.

In the spring of 1997, there was a mysterious outbreak of seal deaths along the Azerbaijani coast. Post-mortem examinations revealed high levels of DDT compounds in their tissue. In mid-2000 there was an even larger death toll. Some 4,000 seal carcasses were discovered within a few weeks. They were mostly concentrated around the northern shore of the sea, but substantial numbers of dead seals were found along the eastern and western coasts and a few even as far south as the Iranian coast. Preliminary scientific investigation indicated that they were suffering from salmonella poisoning and pasteurellosis caught from bacteria.[39] Later reports pointed to the canine distemper virus as the cause of death. Nevertheless, Kazakh environmentalists believed that the seals were poisoned by the discharge of toxic waste from drilling rigs in the Kashagan field. This accusation was strongly rejected by the oil companies, who insisted that no harmful substances had been released into the environment. Local environmental groups also claimed that air pollution, produced by the release of gas into the atmosphere at the nearby Tengiz oilfield, might have had a lethal effect on the seals.[40] Arguments over the causes of these sudden peaks of mortality continue, but what is beyond dispute is the worsening condition of the seals. Long-term exposure to pollution has weakened their resistance to disease; alien predators such as the comb jellyfish (see above) have diminished food supplies; and ruthless poaching has decimated the numbers of pups. It is the combination of malign factors such as these that has resulted in the dangerous decline of the Caspian seals. They are now recognised as a vulnerable species on the Red List of the International Union of Conservation of Nature and Natural Resources (IUCN).

Conservation, monitoring and protection

In the immediate aftermath of the collapse of the Soviet Union the systems that were in place to protect the Caspian environment were disrupted, especially in the newly independent states of Azerbaijan, Kazakhstan and Turkmenistan. However, during the 1990s the regional governments began to undertake new initiatives in environmental protection. Kazakhstan in particular was concerned to ensure that foreign energy companies comply with strict environmental standards.[41] Non-governmental organisations in the region have also been active in drawing attention to environmental problems, likewise in highlighting the abuses perpetrated by companies and by governmental bodies.[42]

Over the past decade there has been a growing awareness that the environmental problems of the Caspian require a co-ordinated approach, involving all the littoral states, since the most pressing issues are of a transboundary nature. One of the first intergovernmental initiatives was the formation of the Caspian Sea Co-operation Zone in February 1992. This Tehran-based organisation aimed to promote co-operation among the five littoral states in a variety of fields, including environmental protection. Possibly the timing was premature for a multilateral formation of this type; it did not attract sufficient support and soon withered away. Other initiatives proved to be more successful. One of these was the Co-ordination Committee for Hydrometeorology and Pollution Monitoring of the Caspian Sea (CASPCOM). Formed in 1994 in Tehran, with support from the World Meteorological Organisation, it aimed to improve co-operation and co-ordination between the national hydrometeorological services of the Caspian states. Its priorities included the restoration and modernisation of station networks and observation systems, the mutual exchange of data, and the elaboration and implementation of joint action plans.[43] In 1997, under UN auspices, it adopted a comprehensive hydrometeorological and environmental programme for the Caspian. The hydrometeorological services of all the littoral states are members of this organisation, which convenes on a rotational basis in the regional capital cities. In September 2003, at the eighth annual session, held in Ashgabat, the draft text of the Convention on the Environmental Protection of the Caspian Sea was finalised, in preparation for formal signature by the heads of state later that year. All five states formally signed it (though have yet to ratify it) at a meeting held in Tehran on 4 November that year.

A parallel development was the establishment of a large-scale integrated environmental management programme, the Caspian Environmental Programme (CEP). This is backed by multinational agencies such as the World Bank, European Commission Technical Assistance to the Commonwealth of Independent States (EU-TACIS), Global Environmental Facility, United Nations Environment Programme (UNEP) and the United Nations Development Programme (UNDP), as well as some private-sector donors. This initiative grew out of a series of regional agreements that were concluded in the period 1991–1994 (for example, the Declaration on Environmental Co-operation in the Caspian, signed in Almaty in 1994). In 1997, the organisational basis began to take shape with the establishment of a co-ordination framework and the identification of the key elements of a transboundary diagnostic analysis. Thereafter, teams of country experts produced national reports setting out the main issues and problems as seen from their perspective. In May 1998, at a meeting held in Ramsar (Iran), CEP was officially launched.

Key diagnostic themes were allocated to each littoral state, with programmes to be directed and co-ordinated by dedicated Caspian thematic centres located in the respective regional capitals. Thus, responsibility for issues such as data management and strategies to strengthen contaminant abatement and control policies were assigned to Azerbaijan; the strengthening of institutional, legal and regulatory frameworks, also strategies for sustainable management of fish resources and other commercially exploited aquatic bio-resources to Russia; the regional assessment of contaminant levels, the planning and management of regional emergency responses and strategies for transboundary coastal areas to Iran; strategies for combating coastal desertification and land degradation to Turkmenistan; and strategies for living with water-level fluctuations and the assessment of transboundary biodiversity priorities to Kazakhstan. In addition to these thematic centres, a programme co-ordination unit was established in Baku, to provide a base for overall co-ordination and management of CEP; in January 2004, this unit was re-located to Tehran. A regional steering committee was formed comprising representatives from the Caspian states at the level of deputy minister of environment, as well as senior representatives of such bodies as international organisations and regional aid and development programmes. Initial funding of US$16.6 million was committed by the World Bank and other donor agencies. Subsequently, the European Union and the Global Environmental Facility pledged some US$10–11 million additional funding for CEP. A Framework Convention has been signed and a Caspian Strategic Action Plan has been agreed by all the participants.[44]

Conclusions

It is abundantly clear that the problems of the Caspian region cannot be solved by any one of the littoral states working in isolation. A co-ordinated, integrated approach is vital if transboundary issues such as coastal degradation, unsustainable exploitation of fish stocks, industrial and agricultural pollution, invasion by alien species, degradation of biodiversity, and the damage to the health and well being of local populations are to be addressed effectively. One of the most positive developments during the past decade has been that the littoral states have accepted the need for such an approach. Several regional initiatives are now under way. Some of these are small-scale and local, whereas others, such as the joint action plans of the national hydrometeorological services, are receiving high-level official support. The signature of a Convention on the Environmental Protection of the Caspian Sea at a summit meeting in Tehran on 4–5 November 2003 – the first legal document to receive the support of all the littoral states – marks a significant stage in the institutionalisation of regional co-operation in environmental matters.

An important development during the past decade has been the recognition by the international community that the environmental problems of the Caspian are of such magnitude that they cannot be resolved solely by the efforts of the littoral states. The inauguration of CEP, under the aegis of UN agencies and supported by major international donors, was a significant event. It has provided a mechanism for re-engaging the professional expertise that exists within these states, and for combining this with relevant international experience. Much valuable research has already been carried out by constituent elements of this programme. The results have been disseminated in the public domain through conferences and workshops, as well as the publication, in print and on the Internet, of extensive expert reports.

Another indication of growing international awareness of the problems of the Caspian Sea has been the globalisation of campaigns to protect the environment. There have been several instances of NGOs in the Caspian region combining forces with counterparts abroad to combat particular instances of environmental abuse. However, the co-ordinated and highly professional campaign that was undertaken in 2003 to protest against the construction of the Baku–Tbilisi–Ceyhan pipeline was on a very different scale. Organised by a weighty coalition of NGOs from many different countries, this campaign lifted Caspian environmental issues out of the purely local context, and instead located them in a global framework, thereby internationalising the debate (see **Akiner**, p. 386).

Thus, at the beginning of the new millennium, prospects for the environmental safety of the Caspian Sea are not as bleak as they seemed ten years ago. The situation is not as catastrophic as some alarmists had predicted, but the environment is certainly highly stressed. Thus, there are still ample grounds for concern. One of the most pressing problems is the question of adequate funding. The financial support that has to date been committed (though not necessarily delivered yet) by the international community is very far from adequate to implement stated goals. The littoral states themselves have substantial professional expertise, but are not able to cover the shortfall in funding. Consequently, there is a real danger that important programmes will either not be undertaken or, if commenced, will not be completed as planned. A second problem is that of growing regional tensions, which might eventually lead to armed conflict. If this were to happen, it is very probable that, directly or indirectly, it would have a detrimental effect on the vulnerable ecosystems of the Caspian. Negotiations on the legal status of the Caspian Sea are, at the time of writing, progressing in a positive fashion. If the littoral states succeed in forging a binding consensus on this issue, this would certainly help to regulate regional relations, thereby reducing the threat of conflict. Nevertheless, given the range of unpredictable internal and external factors that are likely to impinge on the situation in the Caspian Sea for the foreseeable future, the possibility remains that any agreement that is reached could, at some later date, be abrogated.

A third problem is that, whatever precautions are taken by the oil industry to maximise environmental safety, a degree of risk will always remain. It may be marginal but, in the fragile setting of an enclosed body of water, the impact of any technical failure could be catastrophic. Moreover, there is a real possibility that popular anger over accumulating environmental problems and disasters might become a significant channel for the expression of political discontent (as happened during the late Soviet period). Environmental protests could readily serve as a rallying cause for opposition groups. Aware that such issues attract sympathetic attention in the West, they would be able to mobilise widespread international support and thereby exert pressure on their own governments as well as on Western oil companies. Finally, the possibility of terrorist attacks, by local groups or by international networks, cannot be discounted. The physical infrastructure of oil extraction and transportation presents a relatively easy target for hostile forces. It is impossible to provide full protection against such actions, but, as with accidents, the damage that would be inflicted could be huge.

Over the past century, and particularly in the recent decade, the anthropogenic load on the Caspian environment has been increasing. As a result of the rapid acceleration of 'the exploitation of the vast natural resources and economic activities . . . [the Caspian basin] has essentially now become a "hot spot" of environmental pollution and degradation'.[45] Barring cataclysmic upheavals, there are no realistic prospects of these activities being halted. Moreover, governments and populations within the region would not wish to turn the clock back. The oil industry in the Caspian Sea has, since its inception in the late nineteenth century, brought economic development. This has sometimes had harmful social and environmental impacts, yet for many people there have also been positive outcomes, including greater prosperity and a better standard of living. The challenge for the future will be to maintain a balance between, on the one hand, exploitation of the sea's natural resources and, on the other hand, the highest possible level of environmental security.

Notes

1 See, for example, the detailed Environmental and Social Impact Assessments covering the length of the BTC pipeline and associated facilities in Azerbaijan, Georgia and Turkey that were undertaken by BP.

2 In recent years its overall contribution to the Caspian may have diminished owing to extensive dam construction (Caspian Environment Programme, CEP, http://www.caspianenvironment.org/envissues.htm).

3 According to the 1999 census, almost 50 per cent of the population of Azerbaijan live in the coastal zone, mostly in the Apsheron peninsula and the Lenkoran lowland (CEP, *Coastal Profiles*: Azerbaijan, 3.1 Demography, http://www.caspianenvironment.org/itcamp/azeri3_1.htm).

4 M. Glantz and I. Zonn (eds), *Scientific, Environmental and Political Issues in the Circum-Caspian Region*, Kluwer Academic Publishers, Dordrecht/Boston/London, in co-operation with NATO Scientific Affairs Division, 1997, p. 18; G. Golitsyn, 'The Caspian Sea Level as a Problem of Diagnosis and Prognosis of the Regional Climate Change', *Atmospheric and Oceanic Physics*, vol. 31, no. 3, December 1995, American Geophysical Union (http://eos.wdcb.rssi.ru/trlansl/izva/9503/pap09.htm).

5 Glantz and Zonn, *op. cit.*, p. 107.

6 Glantz and Zonn, *op. cit.*, p. 69.

7 Golitsyn, *op. cit.* Also A. Tolkatchev, *Caspian Sea-level Rise: An Environmental Emergency*, summary report on Workshop held by International Oceanographic Commission, International Atomic Energy Agency and International Hydrological Programme of UNESCO, Paris, 1–12 May 1995.

8 Assessment made by the Russian Ministry for Emergency Situations in early 2002 (Agence France-Presse, AFP, 2 January 2002).

9 Report by Global Ecological Fund [in Caspian states this term is often used to render 'Global Environmental Facility'], Caspian Ecological Programme, Baku, 1998 (http://www.grida.no/caspian/additional_info/azerbaijan_98.pdf.), (hereafter GEF Report 1998), pp. 11–14.

10 M. Mansimov (Azerbaijan Vice-Chairman of the State Committee for Hydrometeorology) and A. Aliev (Head of Hydro-meteorological Center 'The Caspian'), *Caspian Sea Level*, Azerbaijan International, Autumn 1994 (http://www.azer.com/aiweb/categories/magazine/23_folder/23_article/23_caspiansea).

11 Workshop on the Caspian United Nations Environment Programme (UNEP), held in May 1994 in Moscow (Glantz and Zonn, *op. cit.*, p. 22).

12 CEP, *Caspian Desertification* (http://www.caspianenvironment.org/cd/menu2.htm).

13 There is some disagreement as to quite how high the concentrations of heavy metals are. Some studies suggest that, on a global scale, the levels in the Caspian are still relatively low and, moreover, that they may be decreasing; see, for example, report by G. Mueller and A. Yahya, University of Heidelberg, Institute of Environmental Geochemistry, that draws on research from the late 1990s (http://www.uni-heidelberg.de/institute/fak15/ugc/i02/muelhome/wolga.htm).

14 In March 2001, for example, two disused wells in western Kazakhstan were flooded by the rising Caspian Sea; oil seeped over 1 kilometre from the well, creating a slick up to 10 metres wide under the ice (AFP, 13 March 2001). In June 2003 a similar incident was reported, involving three mothballed oil wells, in the same area. The cost of stopping these leaks was estimated at around US$1 million per well (*RFE/RL Newsline*, 10 June 2003).

15 See, for example, the report produced by Amnesty International, *Human Rights on the Line: The Baku–Tbilisi–Ceyhan Pipeline Project*, Amnesty International UK, May 2003.

16 See, for example, B. A. Diba, 'Pollution in the Caspian Sea', *Payvand Iran News*, 30 July 2002.

17 Azerbaijani Minister for Ecology and Natural Resources Gusein Bagirov insists that oil spills represent a very small threat to the Caspian, whereas rivers, particularly the Volga, account for 85 per cent to 90 per cent of the pollution in the sea (AFP, 6 May 2002).

18 See, for example, comments by chairman of the environmental movement Caspiy-XXI ('Kazakh Greens Say Drilling in the Caspian Sea Damages the Environment', Interfax-Kazakhstan, 22 February 2001, reported by the BBC Monitoring).

19 Since the turn of the millennium, Tehran has invested heavily in modernising its refineries in northern Iran and in upgrading the pipeline from the Caspian coast. In early 2003, Iran was importing about 50,000 b/d from Kazakhstan. However, according to Iran's ambassador to Kazakhstan, Morteza Saffari, it was anticipated that by 2004 volumes could be increased to 500,000 b/d (*Dow Jones Newswires*, 6 February 2003).

20 Azerbaijan's Caspian Sea Shipping Company, for example, had 69 ships in 2003, of which 34 were tankers and 35 dry freight vessels. It planned to increase its oil transportation capacity by 67 per cent over the next two years, from 12 million tonnes to 20 million tonnes per annum (Interfax, 16 June 2003). At the same time, Iran was also boosting its Caspian tanker fleet; six 60,000-tonne-capacity oil tankers were under construction (three being built in Iran, three in Russia) for delivery in 2004 (personal communication to author by senior Iranian official in October 2003).

21 'Aktau – BTC Governmental Agreements to be in Place This Year', *Energy Line*, 3 April 2003.

22 A. Sultanova, *Moscow Times*, 27 February 2003; also reported by AP and Ambo News.

23 B. Murphy, 'Caspian Environment Struggles' (AP, 19 April 2002).

24 J. Muir, 'Monster Muncher Threatens Caspian Fishing' (BBC, 23 July 2001, via Ambo News Service).

25 A number of reports and workshops on this phenomenon have been conducted within the framework of the Caspian Environment Programme. See, for example, *Laboratory Study on Beroe Ovata and Mnemiopsis Leidyi in Caspian Water*, A. Kideys (Turkey), G. Finenko and B. Anninsky (Ukraine), T. Shiganova (Russia), A. Roohi *et al.* (Iran), http://www.caspianenvironment.org/mnemiopsis/mnemmenu6.htm.

26 In 1940, the total sprat haul amounted to 89,000 tonnes; by 1991, it had reached 3,652,000 tonnes per annum (GEF Report 1998, pp. 47–48).

27 The price of black caviar is determined by type – beluga, osetra and sevruga – also by place of origin. Iranian beluga caviar is the most expensive, on average retailing at over US$1,000 more per kilogram than Russian beluga (see price lists of reputable stockists). Red caviar is the roe of salmon; it is much cheaper than black caviar.

28 Estimates tend to be vague, often indiscriminately conflating supplies of different types and qualities of caviar. However, it is probably safe to assume that at least 10 per cent of black caviar is now produced elsewhere in the world, in fisheries in Europe and North America.

29 In 2001, the legal trade in caviar was estimated at US$100 million. The wholesale price for legally traded beluga caviar could reach US$4,000 per kilogram (J. Fowler, 'U.N. Panel Ups Caspian Caviar Quotas', AP, 5 September 2003). By contrast, black-market beluga caviar could be purchased in Russia for just US$200 per kilogram (C. Pala, 'Kazakhs Crack Open Secrets of Caviar, *Moscow Times*, 1 August 2003).

30 Estimates for recent legal catches of sturgeon vary, but there is general agreement that by 2001 it was below 3,000 tonnes. See 'Caviar Crisis Spurs Caspian Sea Summit', *National Geographic News*, 13 June 2001; also 'None Left for the General', *The Economist*, 21 June 2001.

31 An idea of the scale of this illegal trade may be gained from the fact that in 2001 alone, in the Astrakhan Region of the Russian Federation, 42 tonnes of sturgeon were seized from poachers (*BBC Monitoring International Reports*, 28 February 2002). In Daghestan in that same year 10 tonnes of sturgeon were confiscated. An area of high unemployment, thousands of people were reportedly engaged in poaching operations. Moreover, they would resort to bomb attacks, assaults on coastguard stations and kidnapping of officials to protect their activities (S. Saradzhyan, '"Caspian Mafia" Invades Caspian Guard Station', *Moscow Times*, 18 April 2001).

32 GEF Report 1998, pp. 50–51.

33 Initially proposed in 1963, the text of CITES was agreed in 1973 and entered into force on 1 July 1975. It is an international agreement to which states adhere voluntarily. It now has 160 signatories.

34 All the littoral states except Turkmenistan are members of CITES.

35 For details of permitted sturgeon catches and export quotas see CITES website (http://www.cites.org/eng/resources/quotas/index.shtml/) and follow links to relevant countries and years.

36 Fowler, *op. cit.*

37 Pala, *op. cit.*

38 Pala, *op. cit.*

39 'Oil and the seals of Kazakhstan', *The Economist*, 1 June 2000.

40 *Ibid.*

41 In May 2003 Kazakh President Nazarbaev put his signature to a state programme
    for developing the Kazakh sector of the Caspian in the period 2003–2005. In
    September, at a conference on ecological safety held in the Mangistau province,
    Vladimir Shkolnik, the Kazakh minister for energy, indicated that the
    programme would require companies working in the region to adhere to
    increased ecological requirements (C. Carlson, 'Caspian States Sign Declaration
    at Inaugural Ecology Conference', RFE/RL, 12 September 2003).
42 NGOs such as the Centre for Russian Environmental Policy in Moscow, the
    Catena Ecology Club in Ashgabat and the Kazakh environmental movement
    Caspiy-XXI, to name but a few, campaign strongly on such issues.
43 Statute of the Co-ordination Committee for Hydrometeorology and Pollution
    Monitoring of the Caspian Sea.
44 For full description of CEP reports, also information on activities, achievements
    and plans, see CEP website (http://www.caspianenvironment.org).
45 G. Obasi, General Secretary of the World Meteorological Organisation, formal
    statement delivered on the occasion of the Second Session of the Co-ordinating
    Committee on Caspian Sea Hydrometeorology and Pollution Monitoring, 11
    February 1997, Baku.

Part VII

Emerging Caspian Challenges

22 Ten years on: achievements, new concerns, future prospects

Shirin Akiner

The first post-Soviet decade: 1992–2002

In the early 1990s, there were several uncertainties regarding the development of Caspian oil and gas reserves. By the end of the decade, as discussed in previous chapters in this volume, several of these issues were progressing towards a level of greater clarity. These developments are reviewed below.

One of the questions that attracted most attention in the early 1990s was the size of the Caspian hydrocarbon deposits. By the end of the first post-Soviet decade, it was still too early to make firm predictions, but it was estimated that Azerbaijan, Kazakhstan and Turkmenistan together held in the range of 16.5 to 32 billion barrels of proven oil reserves and around 166 trillion cubic feet of natural gas.[1] The lower estimates placed it closer in scale to reserves of the North Sea rather than to those of the Persian Gulf. Expectations of large finds in the southern sector of the Caspian Sea were dampened when exploratory drilling in a number of prospective areas failed to discover commercial quantities of oil and gas. By contrast, opportunities in the North Caspian basin were highly promising, strengthening yet-to-find projections. Estimates as to possible future discoveries differed widely, with some analysts insisting that the regional total for these three countries, on and offshore, could reach 193.8 billion barrels of oil and 448.2 trillion cubic feet of gas (though admittedly, with only a 50 per cent rate of probability).[2] More conservative predictions suggested that Caspian energy supplies, even at their peak, would satisfy around 3 to 7 per cent of global needs. Nevertheless, as Terry Adams argues, they would be of strategic importance to the overall energy balance worldwide and, in particular, to consumers in Europe and the Black Sea region.

Another question that was fiercely debated in the 1990s was the construction of new export pipelines. Numerous routes were proposed, leading in all directions. It was not merely economic, or even environmental, considerations that were at stake, but political influence. There were two main geographic focuses. One was the North Caspian basin, the other the South Caspian. In the north, the idea of a pipeline to link the Tengiz field in Kazakhstan to the Black Sea port of Novorossiysk, a distance of some 1,500 km, was first mooted in 1992. Yet it was to take several more years of wrangling over such issues as finance, management structure, operational rights and political concerns before work finally commenced on the Caspian Pipeline Consortium (CPC) pipeline in 1999. It was completed in March 2001 and, by July 2002, was fully operational. In April 2003, the State Commissions of Kazakhstan and Russia formally confirmed that the safety and environmental standards were acceptable, thereby signalling the completion of the first phase of the construction and approving the commencement of commercial operations. During later phases, the aim was to increase the pipeline's throughput to 1.34 million barrels per day by 2015.[3]

Further south, in Azerbaijan, the situation was more complicated. Physically, the terrain presented many difficulties. There were also serious security concerns in the Caucasus, owing to the Chechen and Karabagh conflicts. As John Roberts points out, the initial priority was to get 'early oil' to market, to be followed at a later stage by the construction of a Main Export Pipeline (MEP). Eventually, two routes were chosen for the first phase: the existing Baku–Novorossiysk line was renovated (pumping commenced in 1997) and a new line was constructed through Georgia, running from Baku to Supsa (opened in December 1998). The route of the MEP hung in the balance for several years. The governments of Azerbaijan, Georgia and Turkey, with strong support from the US administration, favoured a line from Baku via Tbilisi to Ceyhan. The energy companies – and it was they, not the governments, who would be investing in the project – were more hesitant. Many analysts doubted the economic sense of this route, which measured some 1,760 km, much of it running across difficult and dangerous terrain.[4] Yet eventually two factors tipped the balance in its favour. One was that this route had the incalculable advantage of avoiding the Bosporus. As Terry Adams and Suha Bolukbaşi discuss, any increase of tanker traffic through this narrow waterway would involve major environmental hazards – in the case of an accident, operating companies would not only be liable for huge reparations, but would incur serious reputational damage. The second factor was that by the turn of the century it had been established that the Azeri–Chirag–Guneshli (ACG) reserves were of sufficient magnitude to ensure the commercial viability of the route through Turkey. At this point, BP, the operator of the ACG and Shah Deniz Production Sharing Agreements, took the lead in driving forward the BTC pipeline. The Baku–Tbilisi–Ceyhan (BTC) Pipeline Company, with BP as the main operator, was formally established in August 2002 and construction of the three sections (Azerbaijani, Georgian and Turkish) began some months later. Thus, the future of BTC seemed nearly assured (but see section on BTC below).

The Kazakh authorities had often expressed interest in exporting crude from Kashagan through the BTC pipeline, but had delayed making a firm commitment.[5] However, in November 2002 they began serious negotiations and by March 2003 had reached agreement in principle. It was anticipated that formal intergovernmental and host government agreements would be in place before the end of the year. Also, despite Russian objections to the construction of underwater pipelines in the Caspian, a working group was set up to study the feasibility of a Trans-Caspian extension to link the Kazakh port of Aktau to the Baku–Tbilisi–Ceyhan pipeline.[6]

These developments – the completion of the CPC pipeline, the launching of the 'early oil' pipelines and the commencement of the construction of the BTC pipeline – meant that by 2003 the short- and intermediate-term needs of Caspian oil exporters were being met (see Map 4). It was clear by this time that the Caspian resource base could support multiple pipelines. Projects for other routes were for the time being on hold, but it was widely anticipated that some of them (for example, lines from Kazakhstan to China, and from Kazakhstan to Iran) would be implemented in the future. Expanding the gas pipeline infrastructure was also important, but regarded as a less immediate priority. Proposals to build gas pipelines from Turkmenistan were still under consideration, but had not progressed beyond the initial planning stages, except for a short line to Iran. However, the gas pipeline from Baku to Erzurum (the South Caucasus pipeline) that was to run parallel to BTC received formal sanction in February 2003 and construction was expected to commence in 2004, with completion anticipated for 2006 (dependent, of course, on the progress of the BTC project).

A third area of uncertainty was the legal regime of the Caspian Sea. By the end of the first decade, the Caspian littoral states had still not reached agreement on this issue. Nevertheless, important steps had been taken. In July 1998, Presidents Nazarbaev and Yeltsin signed a crucial agreement on the demarcation of the seabed between Russia and Kazakhstan in the northern sector of the Caspian; in May 2002, the Kazakh and Russian leaders signed a protocol setting out the geographic co-ordinates of the modified median line. A demarcation agreement between Kazakhstan and Azerbaijan had already been concluded in November 2001. In September 2002, after some delay, Presidents Aliev and Putin likewise signed a bilateral demarcation agreement. On the basis of these sets of agreement, a trilateral document was drafted in February 2003; following the meeting of the Special Working Group on the legal status of the Caspian Sea, held in Almaty in May that year, the three countries formally concluded an agreement on the meeting point between their respective sectors on the floor of the sea.[7] Thus, despite the fact that a final multilateral framework had not been achieved yet, this in effect completed the division of the seabed in the North Caspian into national sectors.

In the South Caspian, no formal demarcation agreements had been concluded. Yet, as Ali Granmayeh indicates, Iran and Turkmenistan had for some time adopted a pragmatic approach to co-operation in disputed border areas; in March 2003, they began discussions on delimiting their respective sectors. Relations between Kazakhstan and Turkmenistan were amicable and there were no ongoing territorial disputes. In June 2003 experts from the two countries held a round of negotiations in Ashgabat, following which it was announced that a bilateral agreement on national sectors would be signed by Presidents Niyazov and Nazarbaev later in the year.[8] This did not happen, but in early 2004 negotiations were proceeding amicably. There were tensions between Iran and Azerbaijan, likewise between Azerbaijan and Turkmenistan but, despite some heated exchanges in 2001–2002, all parties were making constructive efforts to resolve their differences.[9] At the end of 2003, senior officials from the three states were hinting that agreement had in principle been reached on the equitable division of the South Caspian and would be announced officially in the course of 2004.

On the multilateral level, the Special Working Group (SWG) on the legal regime of the Caspian Sea, comprising senior government officials and academics from all the littoral states, had been created in 1996 and thereafter convened on a regular annual basis. Their joint efforts resulted in the preparation of a draft convention on the legal regime of the Caspian Sea, presented at the eighth session of the SWG in Baku on 26–27 February 2003. The document pinpointed issues on which there was already common agreement, such as the need for the demilitarisation of the sea, free commercial shipping for the littoral states, and protection of the environment. Inevitably, wide divergences of opinion on several vital questions remained. These continued to be discussed at subsequent sessions of the SWG, which in 2003 were held every few months rather than, as previously, once a year.[10] There was general acknowledgement that genuine progress had been made at the Baku meeting and that a process was finally under way that would result in a consensus agreement on the legal regime. If and when this was achieved, it would greatly reduce the danger of armed confrontation on the sea, such as that witnessed in mid-2001 between Azerbaijan and Iran.

A fourth issue that aroused anxiety in the early 1990s was the possibility of violent ethnic/separatist conflicts in the Caucasus. By the early 2000s, the situation was still fragile, but such clashes that occurred were localised and did not have a significant impact on the wider region. The most important, and potentially explosive, problems were still Karabagh and Chechnya. In Karabagh, on a number of occasions a peace settlement had appeared to be close, but each time the process was derailed. In May 1994, official representatives from Azerbaijan, Armenia and Karabagh (the self-proclaimed 'Nagorno-Karabakh Republic') signed a protocol on a cease-fire. Despite numerous violations by both sides, this is still in force. In 1999, under international pressure (notably from France, Russia and the US), the presidents of Azerbaijan and Armenia began direct talks and in October that year they appeared to be at the point of signing a preliminary agreement. In Azerbaijan, this triggered the resignations of several senior officials. In Armenia, reactions included a terrorist attack on the parliament, as well as a spate of assassinations (among them the murders of the parliamentary speaker and the prime minister). These responses effectively stalled the peace process. Nevertheless, apart from the large-scale military exercises in border areas held by both Armenian and Azerbaijani armed forces in 2001, and ongoing local cease-fire violations, there was no return to open hostilities.[11]

In Chechnya, there were two wars during this period, in 1994–1996 and in 1999–present. Even during the three years of 'peace', there were constant clashes between Russian troops and local combatants. The civilian population was subjected to brutal abuse and violence, while the damage to private and public property was immense. There were several issues at stake, but the overriding goal for the Chechens was to win independence. Yet, as discussed by Charles Blandy, a referendum was held in March 2003 in which a large majority voted in favour of remaining part of the Russian Federation. Chechen and foreign commentators cast doubt on the validity of the result, claiming that there was gross falsification of the ballot. There were similar concerns regarding the conduct of the presidential election, held later that year.[12] Nevertheless, there was now in place a legal framework which, however flawed, could conceivably provide a platform from which to work towards a more enduring peace settlement. The assassination of recently-elected President Kadyrov in May 2004 was a serious blow to such hopes. In the immediate aftermath of the event it was impossible to predict whether the Moscow-backed administration would succeed in consolidating the peace process or whether there would be renewed conflict.

International politics continued to impinge on Caspian affairs. However, there were some positive trends in this area. In the 1990s the major powers had been eager not only to secure their own spheres of influence, but to exclude others from playing any role in the region. Ten years later, relations between Russia and the West had improved and in some areas wary co-operation was taking the place of outright rivalry. Russian energy companies had a share in some of the large Western-led consortia that were exploring and developing Caspian resources. There was also Russian involvement in multinational transportation projects, notably the CPC pipeline. The US remained implacably opposed to Iran. In March 2001, the Bush administration extended the Iran and Libya Sanctions Act, citing concerns over 'the objectionable policies and behaviour' of these two countries.[13] European diplomatic action took a more co-operative approach.[14] A number of European companies were working in Iran and this had some bearing on their strategy in the Caspian Sea. Thus, for example, when Iran took exception to BP-led exploration in the disputed Alborz/Alov offshore field in July 2001, BP immediately suspended its operations.[15] Leaving aside the issue of the legal regime of the Caspian, relations between Iran and the other Caspian states were generally cordial. The closest ties were with Turkmenistan, but Russia and Kazakhstan also maintained good economic and diplomatic relations with Iran.[16] Even Azerbaijan, despite the hostile confrontation of July 2001, was expanding co-operation with Iran.[17]

Progress was also made in matters of environmental security. There were still major concerns over pollution, overfishing and the fluctuating level of the sea. However, the Almaty Declaration on Environmental Co-operation in the Caspian (May 1994) was an important step towards the formulation of a joint approach towards these problems. The launching of the Caspian Environment Programme in May 1998, funded by the Global Environmental Facility and the European Union, with additional support from the private sector, institutionalised a multi-sectoral plan of action to address environmental and bioresource issues. In 1998–2002, transboundary analytical studies were produced, as well as strategic action programmes. This created a framework within which to undertake projects that were regionally and thematically inter-linked. The Convention on the Environmental Protection of the Caspian Sea was signed on 4 November 2003 in Tehran. This historic document – the first post-Soviet agreement to which all the Caspian states acceded – set legally binding rules for environmental good conduct. It was envisaged as an integral part of the final treaty on the legal status of the Caspian Sea and, when this larger document was eventually ready for signature, the Convention on Environmental Protection would be incorporated into it in full.

New concerns

By the early years of the twenty-first century, risk assessments for the Caspian region were increasingly focusing on a few core issues that had previously been regarded as minor or peripheral. As several of the contributors in this volume have emphasised, poor governance was now seen as a serious threat to the stable and prosperous development of the region. Initially, at home as well as abroad, there had been a general assumption that the newly independent Caspian states had already reached such a high level of socio-economic development that they would have little difficulty in making the transition from the Soviet system to Western political and economic models. During the 1990s, it became increasingly clear that this was not happening. The situation was complicated by the fact that, when these new states began to receive substantial oil rents, they were still in the early stages of creating new civic institutions and systems of public administration, as well as defining new national identities and new foreign policies. Moreover, they were strug-gling to overcome the effects of the devastating economic dislocation that was caused by the sudden disintegration of the Soviet Union. An extraor-dinary combination of political acumen, wisdom and strategic vision would be required if these young countries were to manage their national resources in such a way as to lay the foundations for future development, yet to weather the problems of transition without sacrificing the socio-economic well-being of the population at large.

In retrospect it became clear that neither national governments and their local experts, nor foreign consultants, had realised the enormity of the challenges that lay ahead. The advice that was given by international organ-isations was not always appropriate to the reality on the ground. Reforms were often introduced haphazardly, without adequate consideration as to how they were to be implemented or what knock-on effects they were likely to have. In this chaotic environment, when the power of the old state – i.e. the Soviet state – had evaporated and the new states were still weak, the primary concern at all levels of society was personal welfare rather than any grand concept of the national good. These changes reshaped the nature of governance, economic development and societal relations.

In the economic sphere, as Richard Auty, Willy Olsen and other contrib-utors to this volume discuss at some length, these new states soon began to repeat the mistakes made by so many other resource-rich states, falling prey to the malady that has been called the 'paradox of plenty', 'Dutch disease', 'economic indigestion' and, most graphically, 'devil's excrement'.[18] It is characterised by over-reliance on revenue from the export of a single commodity. This distorts economic development, since the lion's share of investment, foreign and domestic, is channelled into one sector, with little or no attempt at diversification. Other, potentially productive areas of the economy, are neglected. Employment is largely concentrated in the one sector; this in turn influences choices in education and training. Thus, the prosperity of the state is fundamentally linked to global demand for this sole commodity. There is little protection against fluctuations in world market prices; a downturn can have a devastating effect on the entire social and economic environment. By the end of the first decade of independence, Azerbaijan and Turkmenistan were displaying these symptoms. The case of Kazakhstan was somewhat different.[19] During the Soviet era, this republic had had a more diverse economy than Azerbaijan and Turkmenistan (see p. 8). Consequently, after independence, it was in a better position to develop a balanced national economy. Like the other states, it experienced a severe crisis in the 1990s, but by the end of the decade had achieved a notable degree of macroeconomic stabilisation. Since 2000, GDP growth rates in Kazakhstan have been among the highest in the world (reaching a peak of 13.2 per cent in 2001). This impressive performance was in large measure the result of the rapid increase in oil production and high oil prices. However, it was also clear that the government was aware of the dangers of over-dependence on the hydrocarbons sector. Since 2001, it has pursued a policy of industrial innovation and diversification. Areas earmarked for development include information technology and electronics, heavy engineering, power generation and biotechnology. The revival of the agricultural sector is also a priority. Such measures have not as yet been sufficient to overcome the threat of 'Dutch disease', but they have served to contain it. Some commentators fear that these positive developments may be temporary and are therefore still cautious about the longer-term economic prognosis for Kazakhstan. However, international financial institutions have generally expressed satisfaction with progress. An indication of growing international confidence in Kazakhstan's economic performance and stable outlook was New York ratings agency Moody's grading of Kazakhstan: first rated in November 1996, marked as Ba3, then upgraded to Ba2 in June 2001, and upgraded again in September 2002 to Baa3 (regarded as investment grade). As a point of comparison, Russia was only awarded this rating in October 2003, Azerbaijan is currently rated at BB (since July 2000) and Turkmenistan at B2 (since December 1997).

In the political sphere, all three states exhibited the characteristics of rentier states and, consequently, as Richard Auty, Anoushiravan Ehteshami and Majid Jafer argue, were suffering from the same weaknesses and internal volatility. As in so many resource-rich countries, autocratic regimes had been established. Corruption was rife and social fragmentation showed signs of becoming a political liability. In so far as there was a difference between petrostates elsewhere and the Caspian states, it was that the latter still bore the imprint of the Soviet legacy, even after the outer 'packaging' had been abandoned. Yet at the same time, precisely because the Soviet framework no longer existed, there were areas in which there were no established precedents. The transfer of executive power was one such issue, hence the uncertainties and speculation regarding this matter in each of the new states. Other areas of concern included the erosion of contracts, threats to security and the impact of globalised environmental campaigns. As broad issues, these matters were not unique to the Caspian region, but the specific manifestations were rooted in local conditions. Such questions were not simply of theoretical interest, but were of direct concern to foreign investors, in that they had a strong bearing on the business climate. In the following sections, these and other issues are discussed in more detail.

Post-Soviet political order

During the 1990s, Azerbaijan, Kazakhstan and Turkmenistan, despite having emerged from a common experience, began to follow different trajectories. Azerbaijan and Kazakhstan were more open to external influences, while Turkmenistan followed a path of increasing isolation and repression. Yet in all three states, whatever institutional trappings were adopted, the underlying reality of the new political order was the concentration of power in the hands of the 'leader'. Moreover, national security came to be regarded as synonymous with regime security, which in turn was understood as maintaining the incumbent presidents in power. Thus, criticism of the leadership, no matter how legitimate, was interpreted as an attack on the state.[20]

At the time of independence, the incumbent presidents in Azerbaijan, Kazakhstan and Turkmenistan were former first party secretaries of the Communist party of their respective states. Presidents Nazarbaev and Niyazov (both born in 1940) had come to power in the 1980s, during the Gorbachev era, and had remained at the helm of state ever since. Heidar Aliev (born 1923) was appointed head of the KGB in Azerbaijan in 1967; thereafter he held several prominent posts in Baku and in Moscow, but in 1987 was marginalised by the Soviet political establishment. However, he re-emerged as a national leader in mid-1993 and was elected president later that year. Throughout the 1990s, all three men steadily consolidated their control over the state apparatus, including the security and law enforcement services.

At first, there had been some attempt to build new political institutions. Post-Soviet constitutions were adopted in Turkmenistan in 1992, Kazakhstan in 1993 and Azerbaijan in 1995. Laws on elections were passed that promised a degree of democratic participation in government. Thereafter, amendments were introduced that eroded the power of the new legislatures and either reduced the opportunity for political competition, or, in Turkmenistan, completely eliminated such a possibility.[21] As a result, although contested presidential and parliamentary elections were held at regular intervals in Azerbaijan and Kazakhstan, the outcome of such polls was a foregone conclusion. The media, largely state-owned and state-run, exhibited blatant bias in favour of the incumbent president, while the actual electoral proceedings were controlled and manipulated by government officials. When international agencies (e.g. the OSCE) sent observers to monitor such elections, they noted innumerable instances of bribery, intimidation, proxy voting, stuffing of ballot boxes and falsification of the count. In Turkmenistan, there were no contested elections. The president's term of office was first extended to 2002, and then, before the expiry of this period, he was made president for life.

There was a proliferation of political parties in Azerbaijan in the early 1990s. However, after President Heidar Aliev came to power, very few new parties were registered other than those that supported the government. In Kazakhstan, too, most of the registered parties were pro-presidential. In both countries, independent parties were mostly small, drawing on a narrow regional and social base. In Turkmenistan, only one party was granted registration, the pro-presidential Democratic Party of Turkmenistan.[22]

Civil society, in a Western sense, is weak throughout the region. The most vigorous associations are informal groupings based on traditional family and neighbourhood structures. In Azerbaijan and Kazakhstan, a number of non-governmental organisations (NGOs) appeared in the early 1990s. Many were funded by overseas sponsors and, in part at least, run by foreign staff. Such groups were often poorly integrated into local society and were regarded with suspicion by the general public. Indigenous NGOs tended to be small, poorly managed and chronically under-funded; most were incapable of implementing their stated objectives. By the late 1990s, especially in Azerbaijan, some NGOs were becoming more active and beginning to play a significant, albeit limited role, in society. Yet despite some positive developments such as these there was still very little public scrutiny of government actions.[23]

Initially, the authoritarian nature of the post-Soviet political order in these new states was tolerated and even to some extent welcomed by foreign companies (and possibly by foreign governments). It simplified the decision-making process, since presidential approval for a given project, if granted, ensured that agreements could be concluded in a relatively short period and bureaucratic hurdles rapidly removed. Also, the emphasis on maintaining stability inspired confidence in foreign investors, even though the methods that were employed to achieve this might not be wholly acceptable by international standards. Later, it became clear that, whatever the short-term benefits, there were longer-term dangers in this highly personalised form of government.

Presidential succession

The fact that these regimes were not only autocratic, but had been established prior to independence, meant that they had not experienced a transfer of power. At first, this did not appear to be a problem. Gradually, however, concerns began to surface as to how the presidential succession was to be decided. In early 2003, all three leaders seemed determined to stay in office indefinitely. The Turkmen president had a mandate for life,[24] and the other two presidential incumbents had indicated that they would stand again for election. Yet eventually, if only owing to natural causes, there would have to be a transfer of power. The constitutional provisions for such an eventuality existed on paper, but neither the local population nor the foreign community had confidence that they would be sufficient to prevent the outbreak of vicious power struggles between business and regional groupings, aided and abetted by factions within the security forces and possibly, too, by interested foreign powers.

The change of leadership occurred first in Azerbaijan. On the eve of the 2003 presidential elections, Heidar Aliev, frail and in chronically poor health, suddenly pulled out of the contest. He had long been paving the way for his son Ilham to succeed him.[25] This duly happened: Ilham was elected on 15 October 2003, securing, according to official estimates, 76.8 per cent of the poll.[26] However, the proceedings were marred by gross violations of the electoral law, public protests and police brutality. In the opinion of some local and international observers, the 'government clearly stole the election'.[27] The level of violence was shocking enough to recall to mind the instability of the early 1990s, when the country had seemed close to disintegration. It was far from certain that Ilham Aliev would be able to exercise the political skill and resolve that had enabled his father, ten years earlier, to restore order. Nevertheless, within a few weeks a degree of calm had been restored to the country and when Heidar Aliev died on 12 December, the genuine grief that was felt by many people helped, at least temporarily, to strengthen popular support for his son.

Elsewhere, the issue of succession was possibly not so imminent. Nevertheless, President Niyazov had had a serious heart condition for several years and the state of his health was a matter for speculation. There were rumours – unconfirmed and perhaps not reliable – that President Nazarbaev was suffering from chronic health problems. The danger of assassination attacks could also not be excluded. (There was an abortive attack on President Niyazov in November 2002 and reports of attempted attacks on President Nazarbaev in December 2001.)[28] In both countries, it seemed likely that, as in Azerbaijan, the incumbent presidents would try to groom an 'heir' of their own choosing. This might initially avoid a power vacuum by ensuring a relatively smooth transition. Yet if the new leader were not sufficiently experienced, and lacked a strong power base, factional rivalries would flourish and easily spin out of control. Thus, although in the short term the level of political risk seemed relatively low, the longer-term prospects in all three states were less certain.

Corruption in higher echelons

As several of the contributors to this volume indicate, one of the immediate problems that foreign investors in the Caspian states had to come to terms with was the level of corruption amongst senior officials. This was not a new experience for them – they had encountered similar problems in many other countries. However, in the Caspian states the issue was more complicated owing to specific features of the recent historical legacy. During the Soviet period a degree of corruption had been entrenched in the higher echelons of the system. It was not uncommon for Communist Party officials and administrators to embezzle state property. It was also accepted practice to give and receive 'gifts' of varying degrees of opulence, and to bestow 'favours' – for example, bending the rules to expedite some personal request. This was not an incidental phenomenon and, arguably, not even a moral issue. Rather, it was the product of two specific aspects of the Soviet system. One was the dense jungle of bureaucratic red tape that not only inhibited transparency in official dealings, but clogged up the entire system and created endless delays. The other was the distortion created by the 'economics of shortage'. This phenomenon was characterised by a chronic shortage of goods in the shops, also of the availability of non-essential 'luxury' services. In such a situation, money was relatively unimportant as there was very little on which to spend it. To cope with both these problems – to negotiate the bureaucracy and to overcome the shortages – it was necessary to be able to call upon the services of 'helpers' or facilitators. This gave rise to *blat*, a concept for which there is no exact equivalent in Western languages. It describes a social relationship based on an informal exchange of goods, services and other such needs. This interdependence was characteristic of society as a whole during the Soviet period, but, especially in the higher circles of the administration, such relationships were used as a means of cementing patronage networks and accumulating political capital.

There were, however, unspoken norms as to the extent that relationships could be manipulated and used in this way. Such norms were not usually breached, if only because of fear of the consequences of a crackdown by the central Party authorities. This prevented wholesale abuse of the system. When the Soviet Union collapsed, the inhibitions also disappeared. Those who were in positions of power very rapidly took advantage of the new freedom to 'capture the state' – to take charge of the state's resources and, at the same time, to set their own 'rules of engagement', determining how, and on what terms, access to the national wealth should be divided. Thus, there was no period of transparency and open competition but, rather, a seamless transition from one closed system to another.

Yet there was in one respect at least a qualitative difference in post-Soviet use of *blat*. It was brought about by the sudden and intensive monetisation of society. This happened very rapidly in urban centres and bought about a marked change in social relationships. The political influence – and loyalty – that had previously been secured by the exercise of patronage rendered in kind, now had to be bought for money. Consequently, money acquired a significance that it had not previously possessed, in that it became the new vehicle for informal, behind-the-scenes state management. Hence the race to accumulate instant cash, also to 'capture' ongoing flows of revenue for the future as provided by control of commodity monopolies, large enterprises, media outlets and so on. Viewed through this prism, foreign investment was expected to fulfil two functions. Firstly, it would replace

Soviet-era central government funding for capital projects and the related provision of social services. Secondly, it would create new opportunities that could be exploited for personal gain. Moreover, all of this – or so it seemed to the recipients in the early days – was to be delivered without the ideological strings and, more importantly, without the oversight and controls of the previous system. Not surprisingly, this was regarded as an open charter for corruption.

There were some differences in the way in which the three countries adapted to the new situation. In Turkmenistan, from the outset, the president projected an image of himself as the embodiment of the state. Consequently, the distinction between the private presidential purse and the public purse was reduced to little more than sophistry. At ministerial level and below, bribe taking and misappropriation of public funds was limited by the expedient of constantly shifting officials who might have access to 'informal income'; as an additional measure, individual offenders were randomly selected for exemplary punishment and public humiliation. In Azerbaijan and Kazakhstan, the system was also tightly controlled by the respective presidents. However, both had fairly large circles of relatives and associates, many of whom reaped economic benefit, openly and covertly, from their privileged socio-political position. Consequently, the spread of beneficiaries was considerably larger than in Turkmenistan. Some younger, more independent businessmen did eventually emerge in Azerbaijan and more particularly, in Kazakhstan. They were almost always the relatives or protégés of those who held political power but they did, nevertheless, succeed in opening up the system a little. In Kazakhstan, there was the additional factor of powerful provincial centres, physically far removed from the capital, and therefore able to act more independently. Patronage networks here were centred on local officials who, though linked to the central government, were nevertheless dominant players within their own areas of jurisdiction. All these players expected – and sometimes demanded – 'rewards' from foreign businessmen. Thus, the situation in Kazakhstan was more complex than in the other two states, with more internal competition among local players and stakeholders.

To put this issue of corruption into context it is important to remember that it is not unique to this part of the world, or even to the developing world as a whole. There have been spectacular cases of corporate abuse in recent years in the US, France and other Western countries, involving not only senior executives of large and respected companies, but sometimes also high-ranking government officials. Yet there is an important difference: in the West, such behaviour is viewed as wrong and, when such corruption is uncovered, the perpetrators are put on trial and punished. In the Caspian states – as in so many other resource-rich states – such behaviour is also regarded as wrong, but the nature of the political regimes is such that high-ranking individuals generally remain beyond the reach of the law. Consequently, the anti-bribery campaigns that have been launched from time to time had very little effect. There have usually been only two targets: minor officials and political opponents of the incumbent regime.[29]

Reports from organisations such as Transparency International and Freedom House indicated that, at the end of the first post-Soviet decade, the incidence of corruption in the Caspian states ranked among the highest in the world.[30] Anecdotal evidence suggested that bribery here, especially in Kazakhstan, was characterised not only by the scale and frequency of the bribes that were demanded, but by uncertainty as to whether the desired result would be achieved. Some of the energy companies that worked in the Caspian region undoubtedly maintained strict ethical codes of conduct. Others may not always have been averse to using bribery in order to further their aims. This was highlighted by the disclosures and commentary prompted by the arrest in New York on 30 March 2003 of James Giffen, a consultant and close associate of President Nazarbaev. An American citizen, Giffen was arraigned as a result of an extensive US grand jury investigation. Charges laid against him included receiving an estimated US$115 million in illegal commissions and fees from Western oil companies in 1995–2000, thereby violating the Foreign Corrupt Practices Act (the US law banning bribery of foreign officials).[31] Some $78 million of this money was channelled to the Swiss bank accounts of two high-ranking Kazakh officials.[32] Allegedly, around US$41 million came from Mobil Oil Corporation (now part of ExxonMobil), when in 1996 it successfully negotiated the acquisition of a 25 per cent stake in Kazakhstan's Tengiz oilfield.[33] In connection with this deal, the US authorities filed charges against J. Bryan Williams, a former Mobil executive in Kazakhstan. However, a company spokesman insisted that Mobil had had no 'knowledge of any illegal payments made to Kazakh officials by any current or former Mobil employees'.[34] Other US and European oil companies were also allegedly implicated in illegal transactions associated with the purchase of rights to the offshore Kashagan field in 1997.[35]

The Kazakh authorities firmly rejected any suggestion of wrongdoing in these cases. In April 2002, the then prime minister, Imangali Tasmagambetov, acknowledged the existence of a secret fund in a Swiss bank, tied to the name of the president, which had received payments from foreign companies, but claimed that it had been set up for the benefit of the nation, for such purposes as preventing inflation. He also admitted that there were other foreign bank accounts in the president's name, but did not give further details.[36] Some or all of these monies were later transferred to the National Oil Fund (see below). Giffen's trial was tentatively scheduled to begin in January 2004, but later postponed until October 2004.[37] Meanwhile, another US bribery investigation was under way that implicated the political elite in Azerbaijan. In September 2003, a Swiss banker was indicted of 'paying millions of dollars in bribes' to unnamed, but 'decision making' Azerbaijani officials at the time of the privatisation of the State Oil Company of the Azerbaijan Republic (SOCAR).[38] Yet, whatever the outcome of the proceedings in either the Kazakh or the Azerbaijani affair might be, revelations regarding the circumstances surrounding these cases had already illustrated clearly the extreme difficulty of operating in such an environment. The very fact of being present in the region could carry risks, if only by association, to a company's corporate ethical reputation.

International and local pressure on governments to use oil revenues more responsibly resulted in the creation of National Oil Funds in Azerbaijan (in December 1999) and Kazakhstan (in August 2000),[39] although not in Turkmenistan. They were intended to mitigate the problems associated with Dutch disease and to safeguard the oil revenues for 'future generations', as it was often stated, by preventing the squandering of resources on ephemeral prestige projects. The governments of the two countries received assistance on the design of their respective oil funds from the IMF and World Bank and, in Kazakhstan, also from the Norwegian State Petroleum Fund. Yet, despite efforts to establish mechanisms to ensure transparency and accountability, doubts remained as to the purpose of the funds and the way in which they would be managed. Thus, although the creation of these funds was a positive development, question marks still hung over the extent to which they might exercise a beneficial influence on the development of these states.

The major concerns related primarily to the extraordinary degree of control over the funds that was granted to the incumbent heads of state. In Azerbaijan, presidential powers included the right to establish and dissolve the National Oil Fund; issue decrees approving all the rules of the fund; appoint and dismiss the executive director of the fund, likewise members of the supervisory council; and choose or approve the fund's auditor.[40] In Kazakhstan, President Nazarbaev's powers included the exclusive right to make and to change the rules of the National Oil Fund; authorise expenditures from the fund (no guidelines existed regarding either what constituted permissible expenditure or what were the limits of such expenditure); approve the annual report of the Finance Ministry; determine the composition of the Oversight Council and serve as its chairman; and to issue binding instructions to the Oversight Council and other bodies regarding the Oil Fund.[41] In both countries, there was concern over the lack of key information in the public domain. The Azerbaijani and the Kazakh Oil Funds created impressive multilingual websites on which information and official documents were regularly posted. However, when examined in detail, there were gaps and ambiguities, particularly in the material provided by the Kazakh Oil Fund.[42] There was also popular resentment of the fact that there had been so little public discussion of the way in which the oil revenues were to be used. Opinion was sharply divided, for example, on the question of whether or not more money should be spent to alleviate immediate social needs and to promote economic growth today, rather than focusing solely on investing for the future.[43] A positive outcome was that these issues provoked lively debate and stimulated active, albeit often critical, comment from local NGOs, opposition activists and independent journalists in Kazakhstan and Azerbaijan.[44] This, in turn, together with pressure from the oil majors and other international bodies, prompted the Azerbaijani authorities to set up a National Committee on Extractive Industries Transparency Initiative, in line with the Extractive Industries Transparency Initiative

(EITI) launched by British Prime Minister Blair at the World Summit on Sustainable Development in Johannesburg, September 2002. Azerbaijan announced its intention to join EITI in June 2003, but the committee was established in November 2003, following one of President Ilham Aliev's first formal directives. In Kazakhstan, the authorities expressed interest in joining EITI, but as of early 2004 had not taken any action to implement this initiative.

Societal fragmentation

Another concern arising out of poor governance highlighted by Willy Olsen, is prompted by the growing economic inequalities in society. In Azerbaijan and Kazakhstan, small, extremely affluent elites emerged soon after the collapse of the Soviet Union. Fortunes were often amassed as the result of privileged political access to lucrative privatisation deals. In Turkmenistan, a similar process took place, but individual wealth was overshadowed by the grandiose excesses of the president himself. By contrast, in all these states large sectors of the population saw a drastic fall in their income as well as in access to resources. The concept of free education for both sexes, one of the major achievements of the Soviet regime, was undermined as state funding was cut. Children from poor families, especially girls, were often unable to complete their schooling owing to lack of funds. Health care, too, suffered as charges were introduced for medicines and basic services. As a result of these and similar downward trends in social welfare, an under-class was emerging. In effect, parallel societies were being created: physically they inhabited the same country, but in economic status, social organisation and cultural environment they belonged to different worlds.

The phenomenon of 'parallel societies' is to be found throughout the post-Soviet space. It is also a common feature of societies in many other parts of the globe, in the developing world as well as in rich Western states (witness, for example, in many European capitals the gulf in standards of living between deprived inner city areas and wealthy suburbs). Here, in these former Soviet republics, however, there are several crucial differences. One is the extent of the economic gap between the 'haves' and the 'have-nots'. Another is the large proportion of people who have been adversely affected in terms of such factors as income, education, nutrition and longevity.[45] A third is the speed with which this process of differentiation has occurred – people still remember a time when there was a high degree of equality of opportunity for all. Given the severity of the economic crisis that followed the collapse of the Soviet Union it is not surprising that the governments of the newly independent states were at first unable to maintain basic social services. However, after the initial crisis had passed and some degree of macroeconomic stabilisation had been achieved, they were still not able – or perhaps, not willing – to prioritise sufficiently the welfare of the population. Thus, people were deprived of essential state-funded public services, yet no alternative social safety net was provided.[46]

Informal systems emerged to fill the space that had been vacated by the state. 'Connections' – personal relationships – now became the prime lever for resolving problems, while bribes became the necessary 'lubricant' in any transaction. Bribes were a prerequisite to obtain medical attention, pass marks in school examinations and so on. This was not a new phenomenon: informal arrangements of this type had, as described above, flourished during the Soviet period. However, then there had been certain social restraints, as well as the formal controls exercised by the state and the Communist Party authorities. In the post-Soviet period, in the higher echelons of the state as well as at grassroots level, such mechanisms all but ceased to function. For those without power there was now no protection against extortion and abuse of office by those in authority. Consequently, the question of social injustice was something that people encountered directly, every day. For the population at large, this created a perception that they had been abandoned by the state.

Had an economic system rapidly been put in place that encouraged the development of a small and medium business sector, some of these social problems might have been alleviated. This would also have entailed creating a proper regulatory framework, underpinned by appropriate legal and financial services. While it is certainly true that in the first post-Soviet decade some progress towards achieving these goals was made in Azerbaijan and Kazakhstan, nevertheless the effects were very limited and almost entirely confined to the capital cities and main oil centres. In Turkmenistan, small private businesses had flourished in the 1990s, often supported by 'shuttle traders' who imported foodstuffs and cheap manufactured goods from China and the Middle East. However, in 2003, following the assassination attempt on President Niyazov in late 2002, there was a general tightening of controls. Cross-border trade was badly affected and there was a clampdown on the most innocuous private enterprises.[47]

By this time, in all three states there was a growing sense of disillusionment as the majority of the population began to realise that, oil wealth or no, there would be little improvement in their situation in the foreseeable future. It was this loss of trust in the political leadership that exacerbated the problems created by economic deprivation and inequality. Moreover, it created conditions in which extremist tendencies – aggressive Islamic radicalism, xenophobic nationalism and fierce anti-Western sentiments – could take hold. At the time of writing, there was little sign that this was happening to any significant extent. However, given that militant movements of this type were already entrenched in the Caucasus and in some parts of Central Asia, the possibility that they might spread to Azerbaijan, Kazakhstan and Turkmenistan appeared to be real.[48]

Stability of contracts

A serious concern for foreign companies working in Kazakhstan has been the government's ambiguous attitude to contracts, characterised by a propensity to indulge in unilateral interpretations of such documents. In the late 1990s, the Kazakh authorities began trying to alter existing major resource contracts (Joint Ventures and Production Sharing Agreements) in such a way as to extract more revenue. In some cases, additional taxes were added, in others, clauses were reinterpreted in a way that favoured the government while inflicting very considerable additional burdens on the companies. In order to understand these actions of the Kazakh government it is necessary to look back at the grievances that accumulated during the first ten years of independence. In no small measure, these were rooted in misperceptions on the part of investors as well as of the host government. The former, for example, did not understand the Soviet model of welfare provision, much of which had been channelled through state-owned enterprises. Under this system, an industrial complex would be required to deliver a wide range of social services to its employees free of charge. On the Kazakh side, there was a lack of familiarity with Western investment concepts and practice, including the significance of commercial contracts and the role of arbitration. This was to some extent remedied by the use of foreign consultants, accountants and law firms but, nevertheless, in decision-making circles, misperceptions of Western business practice persisted for several years.

Given this mutual incomprehension over key issues, it was scarcely surprising that the relationship between the Kazakh authorities and Chevron, the first major Western investor in the region, did not always run smoothly. Equally, it is perhaps not surprising that this experience coloured subsequent Kazakh attitudes to foreign companies. The first stumbling block surfaced very quickly. It concerned the scale of Chevron's investment in the social sphere. Officials in Astana claimed that the US administration had made its support for international and bilateral economic assistance for Kazakhstan contingent on the success of the Chevron bid to develop Tengiz.[49] At the time, the Kazakh authorities were happy to agree to this deal, believing that the presence of a US company would bring significant social and economic benefits to the region. Once having gained access to the project, however, Chevron adopted a tough stance on social programmes. It allocated a meagre 3 per cent of its total investment to social infrastructure – an amount that seemed reasonable by Western standards, but was far below Kazakh expectations.[50] The matter was eventually resolved, but on the Kazakh side there was a sense of grievance. Further problems arose in 1994, this time over the corporate restructuring of the Caspian Pipeline Consortium. Chevron (later to merge with Texaco), unhappy with the proffered terms, drastically cut its planned investment for the year. Again, a compromise was agreed upon, but ill feeling remained.

In 2001, relations took another turn for the worse. The Kazakh authorities changed their accounting procedures and, as a result, the Tengiz Chevroil (TCO) Joint Venture became liable for higher levels of taxation. This was prompted by TCO's attempt to exercise its contractual rights in such a way as to minimise tax payments. TCO believed that this was a legitimate course of action; however, the government sought to forestall it by a complicated stratagem involving KazMunaiGaz, the state oil company of Kazakhstan, which was the local partner in the Joint Venture.[51] The Kazakh manoeuvre was wholly unacceptable to ChevronTexaco, as it would result in exorbitant additional costs. In November 2002, TCO decided not to implement the next phase of development until the contractual dispute had been resolved. In the meantime, the Kazakhs took further action against TCO by imposing a fine for ecological damage amounting to over US$70 million for the way in which it was storing the huge quantities of sulphur (more than 6 million tonnes) that had been extracted from the oil. It was claimed, despite TCO's assurances to the contrary, that this represented an environmental hazard.[52] In January 2003, a settlement of sorts was reached and TCO announced that it would proceed with the project as planned. The ecological fine was reduced to US$7 million. However, yet further strain had been placed upon the relationship between the Kazakh authorities and ChevronTexaco.

The TCO experience was not unique. The other large energy projects in Kazakhstan suffered similar problems. For example, in the Karachaganak oil and gas field, the BG/Eni-led consortium also had a number of serious disagreements with the revenue authorities. In 2001, it came close to suspending production over the proposed imposition of double Value Added Tax (VAT) on exports of gas condensates from Kazakhstan to Russia. Even the highly promising Kashagan project did not escape such confrontations. In 2003, the Eni(Agip)-led consortium developing this giant field was stunned by the revocation of the exemption on paying VAT that it had previously enjoyed; worse, this ruling was back-dated to 1999. The consortium regarded this as a violation of the terms of the Production Sharing Agreement that had been signed in 1997. The Kazakh government claimed that its position was based on a legitimate interpretation of the relevant clause.[53] Further problems arose when the consortium indicated that the start of production would need to be rescheduled. This had originally been set for 2005 (to coincide with the run-up to the presidential elections). However, it soon became clear that there were complex technical issues to be addressed. Apart from difficult environmental conditions (the shallow waters of the North Caspian are covered by ice for several months in winter, and instead of drilling platforms, artificial islands have to be constructed), the Kashagan reservoir is highly fractured, with deep wells and high pressure. Also, the presence of highly poisonous hydrogen sulphide (H_2S) and sulphur in significant quantities requires exceptional safety standards in facilities design, construction and maintenance. Therefore the drilling programme had to be re-planned and additional data obtained from the field to adjust the development plan. The consortium anticipated a lag of one to two years. The government threatened to impose heavy penalties if there was slippage in the schedule and put off signing off the project development plan, thereby causing yet further delay. After much discussion, in February 2004 it was finally confirmed that the first commercial oil was expected to flow in 2008. The penalty for this delay was not disclosed, but was rumoured to be in the region of US$150 million.

Episodes such as these severely damaged Kazakhstan's reputation as an investor-friendly country. Attempts were made from time to time to reassure foreign companies that there would be no revision of contracts that had already been signed.[54] Since mid-2003 some persistent problems had been resolved, following governmental re-shuffles. Yet the impression remained that the Kazakh government was likely to continue trying to achieve the renegotiation of existing contracts in order to obtain a greater share of the project revenues for Kazakhstan. For investors, this was a highly detrimental trend as it eroded trust and undermined confidence in contractual arrangements. Moreover, it created an atmosphere in which relations between foreign companies and the local population were liable to be damaged. When disputes resulted in operations being suspended or cut back, sub-contractors, local businesses and the labour force suffered and inevitably blamed the project operators. Consistent with the explicit objective of achieving a greater share of the wealth for Kazakhstan was the new minerals taxation regime, effective from January 2004, the provisions of which would adversely affect the profitability for investors of ventures under new contracts. Despite these problems, the business environment in Kazakhstan was not yet so hostile that major private investors were leaving, but it was already much less attractive than had been the case in the early 1990s. It was beginning to seem likely that this might deter new private investment and possibly slow down or cap projects that were already under way.

In Azerbaijan, by contrast, the situation was more stable. The Production Sharing Agreements that governed hydrocarbon development had been drawn up with considerable skill and professionalism.[55] As Marika Karayianni discusses, they were enacted by parliament and incorporated into the prevailing legal regime. To date, there have been no attempts to renegotiate these documents, though there have been occasions on which further clarification of certain points was required. A potential weakness is that, in the future, a government of a different political orientation might seek to abrogate such agreements. For the foreseeable period this is not an issue, however, since the main opposition parties did not object to these contracts. Only the Islamists and Communists were opposed to them. In the unlikely event of their coming to power, they would still be bound by certain liabilities and would also no doubt wish to continue to receive oil revenues. Thus, this was not regarded as an area of serious concern. In Turkmenistan, there were also no direct worries regarding the stability of contracts, since so few foreign companies were still active there.

Security

By the end of the first post-Soviet decade, security threats were an emerging source of concern. An obvious area of vulnerability was the safety of pipelines. There were several types of hazard. One was oil theft, caused by local gangs hacking into the pipelines. This was a particular problem for the northern 'early oil' pipeline that ran from Baku to Novorossiysk across Chechnya.[56]

Such assaults damaged the pipelines and posed a threat to the environment through leakages, explosions and fires. Sabotage, including arson and the theft of vital equipment, was another problem. It remained an open question whether these were the acts of vandals working independently, or whether, as some suspected, they were politically motivated (i.e. masterminded by Russia).[57] Incidents such as these – theft and sabotage – imposed additional costs and caused delays but, overall, the disruption was temporary and fairly minor. However, if international terrorist groups were to target the region, attracted by the propaganda value of a dramatic attack on Western commercial interests, the damage would very likely be much more serious. In this case, not only would pipelines be vulnerable, but key installations such as terminals, offshore rigs and platforms would be open to attack.[58] Improved surveillance systems could reduce the level of risk, but it would be virtually impossible to provide protection against a determined assault, as shown by experience in other parts of the world (e.g. in Colombia). Any such attempt (or credible threat of such an attempt) would cause insurance premiums to skyrocket, as happened after the sea-borne suicide attacks · on Iraqi oil export facilities in April 2004.

Protecting the Baku–Tbilisi–Ceyhan pipeline would present greater challenges, even though the line would be buried for most of its length, because it would pass through or near areas where there were numerous secessionist/territorial disputes. Although, as discussed by Urs Gerber, in the early years of the twenty-first century most of these conflicts were quiescent or localised and relatively low level, there was always the possibility that they could be fanned into open warfare. Karabagh in particular remained susceptible to such manipulation. Under President Heidar Aliev real efforts had been made to find a peaceful solution. However, Ilham Aliev, elected in October 2003, was an unknown quantity: under his leadership (or perhaps that of a future leader), the Azerbaijani government might lose patience with the negotiating process and adopt a more bellicose policy, using oil revenues to acquire arms and prepare for combat. The Armenians would certainly retaliate, making war virtually unavoidable. This scenario is by no means inevitable, but until the Karabagh issue has been resolved it will continue to be a potential source of destabilisation. Consequently, the prospect of a serious conflict in the vicinity of the BTC project must be factored into any calculations regarding the security, and hence the operability and profitability, of this pipeline.

Another security concern, at present still latent, is the possibility of a direct threat to the personal security of company employees. This would obviously arise if there was a serious regional conflict. It might also occur if there was widespread social unrest. As discussed above, the trend towards social fragmentation, with its attendant symptoms of frustration and alienation in the disadvantaged sectors of the population, is creating an environment in which this is a possible outcome. However, currently there are no indications of imminent disruption in Kazakhstan. In Turkmenistan, the political situation is potentially more volatile, owing to the erratic policies of the incumbent regime. Yet, if there were to be a leadership challenge, it is likely that the struggle would be of fairly short duration and limited to elite factions. The impact on the foreign community, which is very small and mostly located in compact communities, would probably be negligible.

The potential for civil unrest is stronger in Azerbaijan. Here, in 1993–1995, warring factions brought anarchy and violent crime on to the streets. The country had seemed on the verge of disintegration as separatist movements took advantage of the weakness of the government to press for independence.[59] The expatriate community was not greatly affected by these upheavals, though there was anecdotal evidence to suggest that some senior oil company executives received kidnap threats. President Heidar Aliev used political skill as well as tough military action to restore law and order. Today, if President Ilham Aliev (or his successor) were to be too weak to maintain a hold on power, there could be a return to internecine in-fighting. Under such circumstances, the safety of foreign personnel – now far more numerous and dispersed than in the early 1990s – might be at risk. This would be of real and immediate concern to oil companies and would very likely result in a curtailment, or at least a temporary cessation, of some projects.

A more hypothetical danger is the possibility of increased regional instability arising out of an expanded Western presence in South Caucasus and Central Asia. If US and/or NATO bases were to be sited in Georgia and Azerbaijan – both countries joined the NATO Partnership for Peace in 1994 and have since sought to develop close ties with NATO and with the US defence establishment – this would provoke negative reactions from Russia and Iran. At the very least, this would evoke strong official protests and heightened diplomatic activity. It might also prompt covert responses in the form of attempts to foster secessionist movements and other destabilising actions.[60] At the time of writing, such a development did not seem likely but, given the uncertainties of the international situation after the war in Iraq in 2003, the possibility of this happening could not be entirely excluded.

An even more hypothetical development, but one that would pose a greater threat to regional stability, would be US-led attempts to effect 'regime change' in Iran. One approach to this issue, which for a while appeared to gain favour in some circles in Washington, was to stir up discontent among the Azeri population in Iran (variously estimated to number between 16 and 30 million) with the aim of provoking a challenge to the incumbent leadership.[61] Whether or not such a policy might have any chance of success is open to debate. What is more certain is that, if implemented, it would heighten regional animosities and suspicions, thereby making the possibility of conflict in the Caspian basin more likely.

Environmentalist objections to the Baku–Tbilisi–Ceyhan pipeline

Environmental protest movements have been active in the Caspian region for several years. During the 1990s, local NGOs frequently spoke out against the ecological damage that was caused by on and offshore oil developments.

However, these actions had had very little impact outside the affected area. The storm of protest that erupted in early 2003 over the construction of the Baku–Tbilisi–Ceyhan pipeline was of a very different order. Prior to that, objections to the BTC had been largely theoretical, based on economic and political arguments. As discussed above, by mid-2002 most of these issues had been resolved. The finance was in place and, though not finally signed and sealed, appeared to be secure. Consequently, as John Roberts points out, the project seemed unstoppable. There were still some residual concerns, for example, regarding unresolved problems over land expropriation and taxes in Turkey.[62] Also, there were some who feared that President Aliev's failing health might be used as a pretext to delay the project, since it was he who had been the main driving force behind it, placing it firmly at the top of the national agenda in Azerbaijan. However, neither of these factors seemed likely to have a serious impact on the project.

Then, in early 2003, a broad coalition of local and international environmental, anti-globalisation and human rights organisations, including Amnesty International, Campagna per la Riforma della Banca Mondiale, CEE Bankwatch, Friends of the Earth, WWF and the Kurdish Human Rights Project, launched a concerted campaign to draw attention to the abuses that they believed were associated with the BTC pipeline.[63] They published detailed studies which enumerated their concerns and energetically lobbied governments and international financial institutions that had shown support for the project.[64] In response, the BTC Pipeline Company commissioned its own hefty Environmental and Social Impact Assessment in an attempt to demonstrate the care it was taking to resolve these issues. It also somewhat modified the route of the proposed pipeline, so as to take account, where possible, of the objections raised by its critics.

The chief environmental concern was that, in Georgia, the pipeline would skirt one of the country's most famous national parks.[65] Not only is this area ecologically sensitive on account of its rich biodiversity, but also because it is part of the catchment area of the Borjomi springs, the source of a highly popular mineral water. This water is greatly prized throughout the CIS and accounts for 10 per cent of Georgian exports.[66] If there were to be a spillage from the pipeline, not only would it harm the environment, but it would destroy the reputation of Borjomi mineral water. This would be a shattering blow to the local economy and put many people out of work.

BP, the project operator, had already incorporated a number of special safety features to minimise the possibility of damage of any sort to the pipeline. Also, the pipeline was to be buried underground along its entire length; hence, when construction work was completed, the landscape would be restored to its original state. Nevertheless, there were hazards against which there could be no adequate protection. The area is one of high seismic activity and severe earthquakes (sometimes measuring over 7 on the Richter Scale) are a frequent occurrence. Massive landslides, too, are common. There is also, as discussed above, a real danger that the pipeline could become a target for terrorist attacks, since it passes through territory that is riddled with local and regional conflicts. Thus, whatever security measures are introduced, a determined band of saboteurs might still be able to blow up the line, resulting not only in losses for the company, but also, and perhaps more seriously, for the local population and environment.

Objections on the grounds of human rights focused on a number of issues. A general concern was that the agreements that had been concluded between the BTC Company and the host governments (i.e. Azerbaijan, Georgia and Turkey) did not bind the latter to observe international standards of respect for human rights. They did not even place a binding obligation on these governments to implement the terms of the agreements with regard to their own populations. Thus, for example, compensation payments for land acquisition in Turkey were set at a far lower level than elsewhere. BP went to great lengths to involve local communities in the consultation and planning process – and many were reassured by these efforts – but inevitably, there were groups who felt that their needs had not received adequate consideration. The host governments appeared to take little interest in such matters. They strongly supported the construction of the pipeline, regarding it as vital to their economic development; Azerbaijan and Georgia also saw it as a means of consolidating their political independence, since it would reduce their dependence on Russia.[67] In all three countries, those who objected to the project were dismissed as troublemakers and, in some cases, attempts were made to intimidate and threaten protestors into silence.[68] Off the record, local officials insisted that the campaign had been fabricated by hostile neighbours, namely Russia and Armenia.

By mid-2003, the movement to raise awareness of the BTC project had achieved such international coverage that it was no longer possible to ignore it. The issue became linked to other controversial projects such as the Chad–Cameroon pipeline and was thus incorporated into the global debate on whether or not large-scale infrastructural projects genuinely serve the interests of the public. Institutions such as the EBRD and IFC (an arm of the World Bank) that were to have provided a significant portion of the finance for BTC decided to reconsider their position. They deferred a final announcement on commitment to the project to the end of 2003, to allow time for further consultations to take place. However, there were other considerations that were driving the project forward. The profitability of the offshore Azeri–Chirag–Guneshli field depended on the construction of the BTC oil pipeline. Moreover, construction of this pipeline was linked to the construction of the South Caucasus gas pipeline from Baku to Erzurum, without which it would be almost impossible to 'unlock' the Shah Deniz gas field. Thus, whatever the strength – or validity – of the protest campaign, the internal economic dynamics of both these pipeline projects meant that the first phases of construction would almost certainly proceed as planned, even though funding might have to be sought elsewhere – if necessary, being provided by the consortium partners themselves. However, in November 2003 the EBRD and the IFC both agreed financing for the project, thereby not only removing this final uncertainty but also, very importantly, validating the undertaking with their seal of approval. In February 2004, US Overseas Private Investment Corporation (OPIC) announced that it would provide US$100 million in political risk insurance for commercial bank loans for this project.

Prospects: global competitiveness

The US-led war in Iraq in 2003, which resulted in the ousting of Saddam Hussein and subsequently the lifting of UN sanctions on the export of Iraqi oil, inevitably raised questions as to the impact that this might have on Caspian energy projects. Once Iraqi resources, huge in volume and very cheap to produce, became accessible to Western energy companies, arguably the lure of Caspian oil would be somewhat diminished. In mid-2003, in the immediate aftermath of the early stages of the war in Iraq, some analysts anticipated that Iraqi oil exports would soon rise dramatically, possibly to reach 6 million b/d by 2010.[69] By 2004, ongoing instability in the country made it seem unlikely that this target could be achieved so soon. Nevertheless, in the longer term Iraqi production will certainly revive. The normalisation of relations between Libya and the international community will also bring new flows of oil on to world markets (and new investment possibilities). Developments such as these would almost certainly result in a fall in the price of oil. This would cause critical economic problems for Saudi Arabia, Iran and other large, long-established petrostates of the world, let alone for new-comers such as Azerbaijan, Kazakhstan and Turkmenistan. As Terry Adams comments (p. 105), Caspian oil 'needs a sustainable oil price in excess of US$18–20 per barrel to maintain commerciality and investor confidence'. If there were to be a significant and prolonged downturn in price, it would almost certainly retard the development of Caspian hydrocarbon resources.

However, while multinational oil companies formulate their strategies in such a way as to ensure that projects are robust under unfavourable as well as favourable scenarios, the key issue is that, once phased financial commitments have been made, mega-projects will continue, regardless of cyclical price fluctuations. In the Caspian region, major investments have already been made in the infrastructure, most of which is now in place. These costs will only be recovered by producing and exporting oil. Thus, if the commercial competitiveness of Caspian oil were to be seriously jeopardised by a prolonged period of low prices, this might slow the pace of development, but it is very unlikely that it would cause projects already under way to be abandoned. Agreements governing the larger projects are due to run for 20–40 years, thus multinational energy companies will almost certainly remain active in the region for at least that period, if not for longer. The one factor that might alter this situation would be, as discussed above, an ongoing erosion of contracts. If the stability of agreements were to be undermined to such an extent that the risk to profits became incalculable, then investors might be forced to reconsider the viability of some operations in the Caspian region.

Nevertheless, despite the undoubted difficulties of working in this region, there were factors that continued to make it attractive to large energy companies. One of the most important of these was that the level of political risk (at least at the time of writing) in the Caspian states was lower than in several of the other large oil-producing countries. For example, Nigeria, a major producer of crude oil, was mired in political turmoil. In 1999, the election of President Obasanjo had brought to an end 20 years of military dictatorship. There were high hopes for a 'democracy dividend' that would set the country on the road to peace and prosperity. This did not happen. Instead, economic and social problems mounted and, by 2003, the country was teetering on the brink of civil war. In March, the threat of ethnic violence in the Niger Delta was so overwhelming that two of the oil majors, Chevron Nigeria and Royal Dutch/Shell, declared *force majeure* and briefly ceased production. In mid-April four oil rigs were attacked and nearly 100 foreign workers were held captive for over three weeks. The situation seemed likely to remain chaotic even after President Obasanjo's re-election.

Venezuela, another important oil producer, was also racked by chronic civil strife. The long stand-off between government and opposition came to a head in April 2002 when President Chavez was deposed by a military coup. A counter coup soon brought him back to power, but tensions remained high. In December, following months of unrest, the petroleum industry was hit by a strike that brought production to a near standstill. As a result, billions of dollars of revenue were lost, thus deepening the country's economic crisis. There seemed little likelihood that Venezuela would in the near future succeed in halting the downward spiral of violence and confrontation.

There were deep systemic economic and political problems in many other oil-producing states, particularly in the Middle East and North and West Africa, the largest oil provinces in the world. Against this background, the Caspian states seemed quite stable. Consequently, the level of political risk, though by no means negligible, did not appear to be unacceptably high.

Asian markets

Another reason why Caspian hydrocarbons would undoubtedly continue to be seen as important was the rapidly expanding Asian market. In order to sustain economic growth, Asian consumers – especially China, Japan and India – needed both to secure additional flows of energy and to diversify existing supply sources. Currently, Japan receives over 80 per cent of its oil imports from the Middle East and, in the near future, this dependency is set to rise still further.[70] As Reinhard Drifte points out, it is thus highly exposed to the risk of instability in this region. One of the ways in which Tokyo is addressing this problem is to seek out other suppliers.[71] In 1997, when Prime Minister Hashimoto launched the 'Eurasian Diplomacy' policy, one of its target areas was the Caspian basin. Companies such as Itochu, Marubeni, Mitsui and Komatsu had already been active in engineering and infrastructure projects in Azerbaijan, Kazakhstan and Turkmenistan for sometime but, towards the end of the decade, they began to acquire stakes in oil exploration and development projects. One of the lead corporations today is Itochu, a member of the Azerbaijan International Operating Company (the consortium that is developing the Azeri–Chirag–Guneshli field off the coast of Azerbaijan), and of the BTC Pipeline Company; Itochu has also shown support for the construction of the Turkmenistan–Afghanistan–Pakistan pipeline. The other lead corporation is Inpex.[72] In 1998, along with three other Japanese companies, it created Inpex–North Caspian Oil; this partnership joined the North Caspian Production Sharing Agreement (developing the Kashagan field in the North Caspian), now operated by the Agip Kazakhstan North Caspian Operating Company (Agip KCO). Inpex is also active in the South Caspian and bought into AIOC in April 2003 (currently holding a 10 per cent stake). It is, too, a partner in the BTC Pipeline Company.

China, a country with growing energy needs, is also looking to the Caspian region. Having failed to find substantial domestic hydrocarbon reserves, it became a net importer of oil and refined oil products in 1993, most of which came from the Middle East. By 2003, it was set to 'overtake Japan as the world's second biggest consumer of crude after the United States'.[73] By 2010, according to current estimates, imports will account for over half of China's total energy consumption. This is unsatisfactory on two counts. Firstly, there are concerns over the level of political risk in the Middle East. Secondly, oil from the Middle East is shipped through the Straits of Hormuz and Malacca, a line of supply that could, in a crisis, be vulnerable to US pressure. Such considerations prompted China to explore other options. The contiguous Caspian basin was an area of obvious interest. China's first significant bids to access Caspian energy resources were made in 1997, when, in the face of stiff competition from US oil majors, the state-owned Chinese National Petroleum Company (CNPC) won tenders for the development of two Kazakh oilfields, Aktobe (Aktyubinsk) and Uzen. Although the latter was the second largest onshore deposit in Kazakhstan after Tengiz, the Chinese did not proceed with this project.[74] Chinese companies subsequently bought into other Caspian energy projects, including three onshore fields in Azerbaijan.

A distinct upward change of gear came in March 2003, when Sinopec (China's second largest oil and gas producer) and CNOOC (China's third largest oil company) tried to acquire half each of BG's stake in the giant offshore Kashagan field in the North Caspian. The deal was thwarted when the other consortium partners exercised their pre-emptive rights to buy the shares. The Kazakh authorities reportedly favoured Chinese participation in this project and were displeased when their offer was rejected.[75] Sinopec and CNOOC, however, accepted this setback with (at least in public) good grace and signalled their intention to pursue other projects in the Caspian. In June 2003, Sinopec signed an agreement with SOCAR and became the operator of a consortium to develop the Pirsaat field (recoverable reserves estimated at 1.5 million tonnes), some 70 km south of Baku. The acquisition of stakes in properties in Azerbaijan and Kazakhstan were accompanied by ambitious plans for the construction of pipelines. The first such proposal had been made in 1992, when CNPC, together with Mitsubishi and Exxon, piloted a project for a Trans-Asia gas pipeline from Central Asia to China's Pacific coast (an estimated length of 6,130 km).[76] Projects for oil pipelines were also discussed at various times. In the 1990s it was generally assumed that the cost of these ventures made them uneconomic, but by 2003 it was beginning to seem more likely that Caspian oil and gas pipelines would flow to the east. The political backing for such pipelines, as well as for strengthening east–west energy links in general, was given priority at the highest level in China, and was similarly reciprocated in Azerbaijan and Kazakhstan.[77] The Chinese and Kazakh governments were particularly eager to press forward with the construction of a pipeline from Atyrau on the Caspian, via Keniyak, Atasu, Alashankov (on the border) and on to the refinery in Dushanzi (Xinjiang, western China). In March 2004, Chinese and Kazakh spokesmen simultaneously announced that CNPC and KazMunaiGaz were intensifying their efforts to implement this project, which would require the renovation and upgrading of existing lines, as well as the construction of new sections. Funding details were not disclosed, but it was anticipated that the respective governments would invest significant sums in the venture.[78]

India was at this time still a very minor player in the Caspian energy sector. Previous investment in the energy sector in the CIS had been directed to the Sakhalin oilfield in the Russian Far East. However, in June 2002, when Prime Minister Vajpayee attended the summit meeting of the Kazakh-sponsored Conference on Interaction and Confidence-Building Measures in Asia (CICA), he stressed the importance of Caspian basin energy supplies for India. He concluded an agreement for the acquisition of stakes in a number of oil and gas fields, to be developed by the Indian conglomerate ONGC Videsh.[79]

The energy needs of Asian consumers will certainly play a role of increasing importance in regional politics. If current rates of growth are maintained, China, Japan and India might find themselves in competition over Caspian resources. In June 1999, a Japanese analyst, Akiko Fukushima, called for the building of an energy and environmental community in northeast Asia, similar to the European Coal and Steel Community, in order to ensure 'functional co-operation' on these issues. The motivation for this proposal was not only to secure a stable energy supply, but the acknowledgement that energy is a security concern. This point was underlined with a striking reference to the Second World War:

> Fundamental to any strong security partnership – indeed, to any stable diplomatic interaction – is a mutual appreciation of one's partner's national circumstances. The lack of such mutual appreciation between the US and Japan with respect to energy was a major factor behind the Japanese attack on Pearl Harbor in 1941, which recent scholarship has linked to the Roosevelt Administration's oil sanctions following the

Japanese occupation of Indochina in 1940. Energy perception gaps are a serious, if subtle, irritant in trans-Pacific relations today, and are likely to grow far more serious over the coming fifteen years.[80]

Japanese companies have in fact been working together with American partners in international energy consortia in the Caspian region. Nevertheless, there is an underlying fear that, as implied in the above passage, US policy makers are ignoring Japan's needs. If this issue is not resolved, this could have undesirable consequences. More recently, similar concerns have surfaced with regard to an Asian neighbour. In mid-2003, Japanese government officials were reportedly speaking of 'an imminent "energy war"' with China.[81] The immediate reason for this latest tense exchange was Sino-Japanese competition over drilling rights in Iran. However, it was anticipated that the energy rivalry between these two countries would spread to other parts of the world, including Azerbaijan and Kazakhstan. India, too, would soon join the competition for oil and gas. Hence, a determined diplomatic effort would be required by Asian as well as Western nations to prevent energy rivalries from acting as 'a catalyst for regional conflict'.[82]

Tentative conclusions

At the beginning of the second decade after independence, interest in the oil and gas resources of the Caspian Sea was still high, although development prospects were generally more soberly assessed than had been the case ten years previously. Substantial progress had been made towards resolving the issues that had seemed most pressing in the early 1990s but, since then, more complex socio-economic problems had surfaced. Most of these were linked to the structure of state and society in the three newly independent Caspian countries. Although on a global scale of comparisons they were relatively stable, nevertheless, there were elements of incipient instability in each of them. Some efforts were being made to address these problems in Azerbaijan and in Kazakhstan but, in Turkmenistan, the situation was already acutely volatile. The erratic behaviour of President Niyazov, the increasingly vicious suppression of civil liberties and the ever greater reliance on the security services to maintain the regime in power, were generating tensions that could conceivably result in a sudden, spontaneous insurrection.

In all three states, immediate prospects for a more equitable distribution of the national wealth seemed remote. In the longer term, with better governance and stronger institutions, it might be possible to halt the erosion of social welfare provision, and to counteract the concomitant effects of fragmentation and alienation before a point of crisis was reached. This, however, would require greater support and determination from the political establishment in these countries than has yet been witnessed. Efforts by external actors such as the OSCE, international financial institutions and numerous human rights organisations to press for better standards of governance have not greatly improved the situation. In the aftermath of the war in Iraq, some foreign officials, including ambassador Mann, senior adviser on Caspian basin energy at the US department of state, adopted a more outspoken approach, pointing out that, unless the Caspian states were prepared to implement necessary reforms, they would lose out on future investments.[83] There might well be some truth in this assertion but, unless the international donor and investment community is prepared to take a firm and united stand on such issues, it is unlikely that this argument will yield much leverage.

Integration into the global economy has brought new opportunities for the Caspian states, but also new vulnerabilities. Political and economic developments in other parts of the world now have a direct impact on the Caspian region. National governments have no control over such factors. The war in Iraq is a case in point: the pace of development of Caspian oil and gas might well be affected by the speed with which Iraqi hydrocarbons can be brought on stream. Likewise, the strategies adopted by other countries to meet their energy needs in the coming decades will influence the demand for Caspian supplies. Current predictions suggest that the Black Sea states might, in a near-term context, be the main consumers of production from this region, but there could also be scenarios which would see Caspian oil and gas utilised to serve domestic markets in such countries as Iran and Pakistan, thereby freeing up production from these sources for export to world markets. The logical longer-term scenario, reflecting anticipated changes in global energy demand over the next decade or two, points to Asian consumers taking an increasing share of Caspian energy.

Thus, the situation in the Caspian region is fluid, marked by uncertainties in the domestic context, as well as in the regional and international contexts. With so many incalculable factors in play, the only safe assumption is that Caspian oil and gas will continue to be developed for some time to come. Whether this will take place under conditions that will be beneficial for all concerned, or whether, as many of the authors of this volume fear, the Caspian states will repeat the difficult experiences of so many other petrostates, is less certain.

Notes

1 Energy Information Administration (EIA), US Department of Energy, *Caspian Sea Region: Reserves and Pipelines*, August 2003, provided the more optimistic assessments, while *BP Statistical Review of World Energy*, June 2003 (online at www. bp.com/centres/energy) was more cautious.
2 EIA, *op. cit.*
3 EIA, *op. cit.*, July 2002.
4 M. Berniker, 'As Baku–Ceyhan Construction Date Draws Near, Debate Continues over Project's Viability', *Business and Economics: Eurasianet*, 17 June 2002.
5 On 1 March 2001, officials from Kazakhstan, countries participating in the Baku–Tbilisi–Ceyhan project and the United States met in Astana to sign a memorandum of mutual understanding for the BTC project. This did not oblige Kazakhstan to transport oil along the pipeline, but was nevertheless a firm indication of Kazakhstan's interest in the project. Various ways of transporting oil

produced in its territory (J. Burke, *Kazakhstan Daily Digest, Eurasianet*, 2 March 2001).

6 'Aktau–BTC governmental agreements to be in place this year', *Energy Line*, 3 April 2003. However, Viktor Kalyuzhny, Russian special envoy to the Caspian region, had insisted that Moscow would seek to ban pipelines along the bottom of the sea because of the danger of environmental damage (A. Sultanova, *Moscow Times*, 27 February 2003, also reported by AP and Ambo News).

7 *RFE/RL Newsline*, 15 May 2003.

8 AFP, 27 June 2003.

9 In September 2003, Azerbaijani Deputy Foreign Minister Khalaf Khalafov proposed the resumption of bilateral negotiations with Turkmenistan on the division of the Caspian Sea and called for talks to resolve the status of two disputed offshore Caspian oilfields (*RFE/RL Newsline*, 9 September 2003).

10 The eleventh session of the SWG, at which a second draft of the proposed convention was discussed, was held in Ashgabat in September 2003 (*ibid.*).

11 In March 2003, the US announced its intention to intensify efforts to broker a peace agreement, with Secretary of State Colin Powell playing a direct role in the process (AFP, 14 March 2003). There was an increase in cross-border clashes in mid-2003. However, no diplomatic action seemed likely until after the elections in Armenia and Azerbaijan, thus effectively postponing any intervention until 2004.

12 The election was held on 5 October. According to official estimates, Ahmad-Haji Kadyrov, the favoured Kremlin candidate, gained over 80 per cent of the vote.

13 See text of President Bush's statement on 3 August 2001 (press release from White House, office of the Press Secretary). See also President Bush's statement of 12 March 2003 (same source).

14 For example, in February 1998, Kees Wittebrood, head of the EU's Central Asian department, told President Niyazov that the EU supported the idea of a Turkmenistan–Iran–Turkey gas pipeline. During the same month, at the end of his visit to Brussels, Niyazov signed a memorandum of agreement with Shell for the proposed pipeline and met, among others, NATO Secretary-General Javier Solana and Belgian Prime Minister Jean-Luc Dehaene (RFE/RL, 24 February 1998, 'Turkmen President in Brussels'). In July 2001, European Union foreign ministers made a strongly worded appeal to the US not to extend the Iran Libya Sanctions Act, due to expire on 5 August, since it would harm bilateral relations. The EU has always opposed the Act, arguing that it violates international law (*Reuters*, 17 July 2001).

15 Moreover, Ali Granmayeh notes that the UK ambassador to Iran indicated that British companies would not operate in areas which were subject to Iranian objection. This, however, was a controversial statement and it is not clear that it was backed by London.

16 It was anticipated that, as part of a swap agreement, Kazakhstan would dramatically increase oil exports to Iran, from 50,000 b/d in 2003 to 500,000 b/d in 2004 (*Dow Jones Newswires*, 6 February 2003).

17 In March 2003, for example, Azerbaijan's state-owned energy company Azenergo and Iran's Tavanir signed an agreement on building a second power line from Iran to the Azerbaijani enclave of Nakhichevan (*Tehran Times*, 26 March 2003). The following month, it was announced that Iran was to provide a US$40 million credit package for a natural-gas project in Azerbaijan, also to finance some transportation projects (*RFE/RL Newsline*, 15 April 2003).

18 S. Tsalik *et al., Caspian Oil Windfalls: Who Will Benefit?*, Caspian Revenue Watch, Open Society Institute, Central Eurasia Project, New York, 2003, p. 1.

19 During the Soviet era, Kazakhstan had a more diverse economic profile than Azerbaijan and Turkmenistan. Consequently, after independence it was in a

better position to develop a balanced national economy. Certainly the government has tried to support and encourage diversification, but with debatable results. See, for example, Ye. Kalyuzhnova, *The Kazakstani Economy: Independence and Transition*, Basingstoke/New York, Macmillan/St Martin's Press, 1998; A. Peck, *Economic Development in Kazakhstan: The role of large enterprises and foreign investment*, London/New York, RoutledgeCurzon, 2004.

20 Articles were introduced into the criminal codes of all these countries making it an offence, punishable by fines or even lengthy prison sentences, to impugn 'the honour and dignity' of the president. This placed severe curbs on the freedom of the media. It also effectively muzzled any would-be political rivals. For a detailed review of the legal framework for the media in these states, see G. McCormack (ed.), *Media in the CIS: A Study of the Political, Legislative and Socioeconomic Framework*, 2nd edition, Düsseldorf, European Institute for Media, 1999.

21 *EBRD Transition Report*, European Bank of Reconstruction and Development, London, 2002, p. 9.

22 For a survey of the political parties in these states, see *Political Parties of the World*, 5th edition, John Harper Publishing, London, 2002, under respective country entries.

23 For discussion of issues relating to the development of civil society in these countries, see S. Akiner, 'Emerging Political Order in the New Caspian States: Azerbaijan, Kazakstan and Turkmenistan', in Gary K. Bertsch *et al.* (eds), *Crossroads and Conflict: Security and Foreign Policy in the Caucasus and Central Asia*, New York, Routledge, 2000, esp. pp. 101–109; also *Nations in Transit*, Freedom House (http://www.freedomhouse.org/research/nattransit.htm), under respective country entries.

24 From time to time President Niyazov indicated that he might step down on his seventieth birthday, but no formal steps were taken to prepare for this event.

25 On 9 July 2003 Heidar Aliev flew to Turkey for further medical treatment. Four days earlier, the Azerbaijan Central Electoral Commission confirmed that Ilham Aliev would stand in the October presidential elections. His nomination was submitted just 30 minutes before the list was closed.

26 *RFE/RL Newsline*, vol. 7, no. 200, 21 October 2003.

27 P. Boukaert, 'A Stolen Election and Oil Stability', *International Herald Tribune*, 20 October 2003 (via *Turkistan-Newsletter*).

28 The attack on President Niyazov on 25 November 2002 was widely reported in the media; numerous suspects, including the former foreign minister, Boris Shikhmuradov, were arrested and later put on public trial. By contrast, the attacks on President Nazarbaev were only mentioned in passing by Qasymzhomart Toqaev, the then prime minister, in a televised speech made on 20 November 2001. He stated that the Kazakh security organs had uncovered two assassination plots against Nazarbaev in the last three months alone, but gave no further details or corroboration (*RFE/RL Central Asia Report*, 22 November 2001, vol. 1, no. 18).

29 In Kazakhstan, for example, an official commission to investigate state corruption was created by presidential decree on 2 April 2002, headed by presidential adviser Sat Toqpaqbaev (*RFE/RL Newsline*, 12 April 2002). The most notable figures to be charged with corruption during that year were Mukhtar Ablyazov, a former minister of energy, trade and industry, and Ghalymzhan Zhakiyanov, former governor of Pavlodar province. Both were outspoken critics of the president. They may well have been guilty of the stated offences, but there was a widespread perception that they had been prosecuted because of their political activities.

30 See *Transparency International Corruption Perceptions Index 2002* (http://www.transparency.org). The Corruption Perception Index relates to perceptions of the degree of corruption as seen by business people, academics and risk analysts,

and ranges between 10 (highly clean) and 0 (highly corrupt). Azerbaijan and Kazakhstan scored 2 and 2.3 respectively in 2002, ranking alongside Cameroon, Haiti, Indonesia and Angola. Turkmenistan was not listed.

31 Giffen was nicknamed 'Mr 7½ cents' after allegedly securing a fee of $0.075 on every barrel produced from the Tengiz field, as a reward for helping Chevron to secure this deal in 1993 (J. Chaffin and D. Stern, 'Kazakhstan's Gatekeeper Becomes a Legal Liability', *Financial Times*, 15 April 2003 (www.ft.com)). If these and similar transactions were to be proven, the case would amount to the single largest violation of the Foreign Corrupt Practices Act.

32 Reports in the media (e.g. *The Wall Street Journal* 23 April 2003) indicated that one of these officials was former Prime Minister Nurlan Balgimbaev, later the director of the Kazakh State Oil Company, while the other was President Nazarbaev. These allegations were made explicit by US federal prosecutors in court papers in April 2004 (16 April 2004, Bloomberg.com).

33 On 12 June Bryan Williams pleaded guilty to a charge of tax evasion for taking what prosecutors characterised as 'US$7 million in kickbacks' (*Eurasianet*, 1 July 2003).

34 *Ibid.* See also 'Corporate Ethics: Big Oil's Dirty Secrets', *The Economist*, 10 May 2003, pp. 61–62.

35 *RFE/RL Organized Crime and Terrorism Watch*, vol. 3, vol. 17, 15 May 2003.

36 S. Tsalik, *Caspian Oil Windfalls: Who Will Benefit?*, R. Ebel (ed.), Caspian Revenue Watch, Open Society Institute, Central Eurasia Project, New York, 2003, p. 145; also *RFE/RL Crime and Corruption Watch*, vol. 2, no. 43, 19 December 2002.

37 It was anticipated, that pre-trial procedural moves by both the defence and prosecution would prompt a postponement of the start date (*Eurasianet*, 1 July 2003), and this indeed happened.

38 J. Chaffin, 'Bribery Case Gives Hope to Azerbaijan Opposition', *Financial Times*, via *Turkistan-Newsletter*, 15 September 2003.

39 In 1996, a secret account, linked to President Nazarbaev, was opened with a Swiss bank. Some US$1 billion was deposited here, proceeds of the sale to Mobil of a share in the Tengiz oilfield. In April 2002, Prime Minister I. Tasmagambetov disclosed the existence of this account to parliament, claiming that it had been established for the benefit of the nation and that it had been used for such purposes as preventing inflation and paying pension arrears (Tsalik, *op. cit.*). Money from this account was later transferred to the newly established National Oil Fund.

40 Tsalik, *op. cit.*, p. 183.

41 *Ibid.*, pp. 150–151.

42 Tsalik, *op. cit.*, p. 116.

43 In Azerbaijan, two current projects are being financed by SOFAZ; one is the provision of housing for the refugees, the other is the funding of SOCAR's share of the construction costs of BTC.

44 In March 2002, for example, Kazakh activists wrote a public letter to the chairman of Ernst and Young, the official auditors of the Kazakh National Oil Fund (http://forumkz.org). See also reports by N. Gulieva and R. Abbasov, 'Azeri Oil Ignites Debate', IWPR's *Caucasus Reporting Service*, no. 185, 7 July 2003; Bruno De Cordier, 'Will a "Resource Curse" Befall Azerbaijan and Kazakhstan?', *Eurasianet*, 29 June 2003.

45 Recent levels of poverty were assessed at 64.2 per cent in Azerbaijan, 30.9 per cent in Kazakhstan and 34.4 per cent in Turkmenistan (*EBRD Transition Report*, 2002, pp. 120, 164 and 208); official national estimates were much lower, but unofficial estimates from these countries were considerably higher.

46 I am grateful to Fumitaki Okubo for an enlightening discussion on some of the issues raised in this section, as well as in other parts of the chapter.

47 For example, in July 2003, a decree was issued banning chickens and cattle from the capital. Keeping domestic livestock had previously provided an important supplement to family diets and had also been a source of additional pocket money, since surplus production was sold in local markets (M. Novruzov, IWPR, RCA no. 215, 9 July 2003).

48 According to a report in an Azerbaijani newspaper (*Zerkalo*, 4 January 2002), drawing on research by Rovsan Novruzoglu, there were 'more than 1,000 Wahhabis' in Azerbaijan. Cross-border links with Wahhabi organisations in neighbouring Daghestan had apparently been established in September 1994. By 2002, numerous 'Wahhabi' cells were said to be operating in northern Azerbaijan. The term 'Wahhabi' is commonly used in the CIS to refer to radical Muslims of any orientation.

49 A good discussion of the Kazakh view is provided by R. M. Cutler, 'Kazakhstan's New Foreign Investment Law', *Central Asia–Caucasus Analyst*, 26 February 2003.

50 President Nazarbaev was reportedly so incensed that he considered cancelling the deal (*ibid*).

51 *Ibid.*

52 *Rigzone*, 3 December 2002 (http://www.rigzone.com).

53 It was, however, rumoured that the action was, in part at least, a punitive retaliatory measure against the consortium partners who blocked the sale of BG shares to two Chinese companies – see section on China below.

54 In the first half of 2002, rumours began circulating that the Kazakh government intended to revise major resource contracts. President Nazarbaev and senior ministers, however, made several statements denying that this was the case (*RFE/RL Newsline*, 24 June 2002; *ibid.*, 1 July 2003; *ibid.*, 3 September 2003).

55 The Azerbaijani legal team was led by the highly respected Valekh Aleskerov, head of the Foreign Investment Department of SOCAR.

56 In 1996, in just two weeks in August, 149 mini-refineries were discovered and closed in the Chechen section of the Baku–Novorossiysk pipeline (David Nissman, 'Azerbaijan and Japan: New Allies?', *Caspian Crossroads*, electronic version, vol. 3, no. 3, Winter 1998).

57 S. Blank, 'Pipelines: Conduits for Terrorism', *Asia Times*, 6 March 2003.

58 In autumn 2002, statements attributed to senior al-Qaeda leaders suggested that economic interests, including oil, were being considered for strikes. The terrorist bombing of a French oil tanker off Yemen and a foiled attack on a Saudi oil complex seemed to confirm this trend. It indicated a new tactic for the terrorist network, which had previously focused its attacks on US military and diplomatic representatives (AP, 17 October 2002). In September 2003, a senior official in the Azerbaijan Ministry of Defence stated that the country's oil infrastructure was a potential target for international terrorism. Preparations to combat this threat included a simulated security operation at an oil refinery, held with assistance of NATO Civil Defence experts (*RFE/RL Newsline*, 12 September 2003).

59 A short-lived Talysh–Mugan republic was declared in the south. For a succinct account of this period, see A. Altstadt, 'Azerbaijan's Struggle toward Democracy', in K. Dawisha and B. Parrot (eds), *Conflict, Cleavage, and Change in Central Asia and the Caucasus*, Cambridge University Press, Cambridge, 1997, esp. pp. 118–137.

60 To date, NATO's initiatives in the Caucasus and Central Asia have been relatively low key and lacking in focus. This may reflect the difficulties of forging a firm consensus as to appropriate regional policies, given the divergent interests and approaches of the different NATO member states. See further R. Bhatty and R. Bronson, 'NATO's Mixed Signals in the Caucasus and Central Asia', *Survival*, vol. 42, no. 3, 2000, pp. 129–145.

61 See discussion by Afshin Molavi (Iranian-born now Washington-based journalist), *EurasiaNet Commentary*, 8 April 2003 (http://www.eurasianet.org).

62 Statement by Foreign Minister Abdullah Gül, reported by Caspian News Agency, 22 April 2003.

63 The coalition of protestors included over 70 non-governmental organisations from 29 countries (Friends of the Earth, Kurdish Human Rights Project, The Corner House, *The Baku Ceyhan Campaign: Joint Press Release by NGOs*, 13 June 2003).

64 There has been extensive coverage of this issue in the press and in the publications of the various organisations. See, for example, *Human Rights on the Line: The Baku–Tbilisi–Ceyhan Pipeline Project*, Amnesty International, May 2003; also websites of Campagna per la Riforma della Banca Mondiale (www.crbm.org); CEE Bankwatch Network (www.bankwatch.org); Kurdish Human Rights Project (www.khrp.org).

65 Other routes had initially been considered but rejected on grounds of security or the difficult nature of the terrain. Objectors to the pipeline, however, did not accept that these options had been fully explored. R. Khatchadourian, 'Path of a Pipeline: The Price of Progress', 23–29 April 2003, via *Ambo News*.

66 *Ibid.*

67 See, for example, the report by C. Mortished, 'Oil Pipeline Has the Power to Change Lives', *Times Online*, 14 February 2003.

68 See, for example, incidents reported in the press release of the Baku–Ceyhan Campaign, Kurdish Human Rights Project, 18 March 2003 (khrp@khrp.demon. co.uk).

69 Estimates as to the exact extent of Iraqi oil reserves vary greatly. It is certain, however, that these reserves are very considerable and that production costs are low. In 2002, Iraq produced just over 2 million b/d (BP, *op. cit.*). Yet, given 'a stable political situation, heavy investment, and a political environment conducive to economic development', Iraq might be able to raise production to '6 million b/d by 2010 and 7–8 million b/d by 2020'. See G. Luft, *Analysis on the Iraq Crisis*, memo no. 16, 12 May 2003, Saban Center, Brookings Institution (http://www.brookings.edu/sabancenter).

70 Annual primary energy demand in Japan, Australia and New Zealand (OECD Pacific) is currently projected to grow by 1.2 per cent until 2010, then gradually to fall to 0.3 per cent in 2020–2030. Oil import dependence is expected to stabilise at 92 per cent by 2010, with Japan accounting for most of the net oil imports (International Energy Agency (IEA), *World Energy Outlook*, OECD/IEA, Paris, 2002, p. 212).

71 The Japanese government is actively seeking to reduce dependence on oil by promoting the use of nuclear power, natural gas and renewable energy (IEA, *op. cit.*, pp. 208–219). See also T. Uyama, 'Japanese Policies in Relation to Kazakshtan: Is There a "Strategy"?', in R. Legvold (ed.), *Thinking Strategically: The Major Powers, Kazakhstan, and the Central Asian Nexus*, American Academy of Arts and Science, MIT Press, Cambridge MA/London, 2003, esp. pp. 171–172.

72 According to its official website, 'The mission of INPEX CORPORATION is to secure a stable supply of oil and natural gas for Japan, a nation that is poor in energy resources'.

73 'Oil-thirsty China and Japan Battle on Drilling', *The Times*, 21 July 2003.

74 CNPC remained active in Aktobe, holding (as of July 2002) a 63 per cent stake in a Joint Venture with local partner Aktobemunaigaz.

75 It is widely believed that President Nazarbaev personally backed the Chinese bids. The announcement that the Kazakh authorities were to withdraw the Kashagan consortium's pre-production VAT exemptions, mentioned above, was made almost immediately after it was confirmed that the offer of the Chinese companies had been rejected. It is possible that the timing was mere coincidence, but some analysts linked the two events, suggesting that displeasure over the failure of the deal had influenced the Kazakh decision ('Kazakhstan Ends

Tax Break after China Cut from Project', *Ambo News*, vol. 81, no. 95, 19 May 2003; also *RFE/RL Business Watch*, 17 June 2003).

76 O. Skagen, *Caspian Gas*, Royal Institute of International Affairs, London, 1997, p. 87.

77 For example, when President Hu visited Almaty in June 2003 (his first trip abroad as Head of State) his discussions focused largely on energy related projects. President Nazarbaev welcomed this interest, describing it as 'timely' (T. Weihman, 'China Making Diplomatic Push in Central Asia', Eurasianet, via *Ambo News*, 6 July 2003). Kazakhstan's ambassador in China, Zhanibek Karibzhanov, similarly stressed the need for co-operation in the energy field, calling in particular for the early construction of the long-planned Sino-Kazakhstan pipeline (Interfax, 4 March 2003). See also comments by President Aliev and by the Azerbaijani ambassador in Beijing welcoming increased Chinese activity ('Azerbaijan Wants Chinese Investment', Xinuha News Agencies COMTEX News Network, 24 February 2003; AFP, 4 June 2003).

78 It was anticipated that blueprints for part of the pipeline would be signed during President Nazarbaev's visit to China in May 2004, giving the project interstate status. Construction of the Atasu–Alashankou stretch, a distance of some 1,300 km, was slated to commence in June of that year ('China, Kazakhstan to intensify pipeline construction', Interfax-China, Beijing, 4 March 2004); see also 'Kazakh PM orders start of China pipeline this year' (Interfax, Astana, 3 March 2004). On 17 May Presidents Hu and Nazarbaev duly signed an agreement for joint exploration and development of Caspian hydrocarbon resources (AP 18 May 2004).

79 'India to Explore Oil in the Caspian Sea', *IslamOnline*, 4 June 2002.

80 Akiko Fukushima, Senior Researcher, National Institute for Research Advancement, Tokyo, *Co-operation for Peace and Stability in the Caspian Sea/Central Asia Region*, paper presented at the Seventh Annual Seminar on Central Asians the Caucasus, Tehran, June 1999.

81 'Oil-thirsty China and Japan Battle on Drilling', *The Times*, 21 July 2003.

82 Fukushima, *op. cit.*

83 Speech of Steven Mann to annual oil conference in Baku in June 2003; a similar message was delivered by David Woodward, head of BP in Azerbaijan (D. Zhdannikov, 'Caspian States Urged to Reform in Face of Iraqi Oil', Reuters, 6 June 2003).

Index

CPSIA information can be obtained
at www.ICGtesting.com
Printed in the USA
FFOW01n1714050115
10022FF

9 780415 405744